VOICES WITHIN THE ARK

VOICES WITHIN THE ARK

The Modern Jewish Poets

EDITED BY

HOWARD SCHWARTZ & ANTHONY RUDOLF

AVON
PUBLISHERS OF BARD, CAMELOT, DISCUS AND FLARE BOOKS

AVON BOOKS
A division of
The Hearst Corporation
959 Eighth Avenue
New York, New York 10019

Cover illustration by John Swanson
Published by arrangement with the authors
Library of Congress Catalog Card Number: 80-66152
ISBN: 0-380-76109-2

First Avon Printing, October, 1980

AVON TRADEMARK REG. U.S. PAT. OFF. AND IN
OTHER COUNTRIES, MARCA REGISTRADA, HECHO EN
U.S.A.

Printed in the U.S.A.

DON 10 9 8 7 6 5 4 3 2

Acknowledgments

The editors have made every effort to trace copyright owners. Any additional information will be incorporated in future editions of this book.

I. Hebrew

Publication of the poems in the Hebrew section of this anthology was made possible by the generous assistance of the Institute for the Translation of Hebrew Literature, Ltd., Tel Aviv, and by the assistance of ACUM, Ltd., in obtaining rights to many of these poems.

NATHAN ALTERMAN: "Tammuz" from *Anthology of Modern Hebrew Poetry*, ed. by S. Y. Penueli and A. Ukhmani, Israel Universities Press, Jerusalem 1966. Translation ©by the Institute for the Translation of Hebrew Literature. "This Night," "Poem About Your Face," "To the Elephants," "The Spinning Girl" used by permission of Ruth Nevo. Translations ©1979 Ruth Nevo. All Alterman poems reprinted by kind permission of the Alterman Institute for the Ben-Gurion Inheritance, Sdeh-Boker, and the Kibbutz Hameuchad Publishing House.

Note: These acknowledgments continue on page 1173 and shall constitute an extension of this copyright page.

For Gabriel Preil

The Grand Duke of New York

We are festive weepers, etching names on every stone,
touched by hope, hostages of governments and history,
blown by wind and gathering holy dust.

Yehuda Amichai

I hear the voice
of David and Bathsheba
and the judgment
on the continual backslidings
of the Kings of Israel.
I have stumbled
on the ancient voice of honesty
and tremble
at the voice of my people.

Carl Rakosi

Howard Schwartz was born in St. Louis in 1945. He attended Washington University and presently teaches at the University of Missouri-St. Louis. He is the author of two books of poetry, Vessels *and* Gathering the Sparks, *and of four books of fiction,* A Blessing Over Ashes, Lilith's Cave, Midrashim: Collected Jewish Parables *and* The Captive Soul of the Messiah. *He has also published a volume of his selected translations from Hebrew and Yiddish,* Lyrics and Laments. *In addition to* Voices Within the Ark: The Modern Jewish Poets, *he has edited* Imperial Messages: One Hundred Modern Parables, *also available from Avon Books. He is currently editing* Gates to the New City: A Treasury of Modern Jewish Tales, *also for Avon Books, and writing his first novel,* The Four Who Entered Paradise.

Anthony Rudolf was born in London in 1942. He studied at Cambridge University and has held various positions. He is the author of three books of poetry, The Manifold Circle, The Same River Twice, *and* After the Dream: Poems 1964–1979. *He has also published individual volumes of translations of Yves Bonnefoy, Edmond Jabès, Alexander Tvardovsky, Evgeni Vinokurov, and Eugene Heimler. He is the founder and editor of The Menard Press, advisory editor to* Modern Poetry in Translation *and* The Jewish Quarterly, *and former editor of* European Judaism. *He has also guest-edited several magazines, including the French Poetry Anthology issue of* Modern Poetry in Translation, *and edited the book* Poems for Shakespeare IV.

Contents

General Introduction xxxi

I **Hebrew**

Introduction to Book I by Laya Firestone 2

Nathan Alterman 21
Tammuz ◦ *This Night* ◦ *Poem About Your Face* ◦ *To the Elephants* ◦ *The Spinning Girl*

Yehuda Amichai 27
Of Three or Four in a Room ◦ *Not Like a Cypress* ◦ *God Has Pity on Kindergarten Children* ◦ *On the Day of Atonement* ◦ *Shadow of the Old City* ◦ *Jerusalem, Port City* ◦ *Sodom's Sister City* ◦ *I Am Sitting Here* ◦ *I Think of Oblivion* ◦ *Advice* ◦ *Lament* ◦ *I Am a Leaf* ◦ *Since Then* ◦ *In the Old City* ◦ *On the Wide Stairs* ◦ *The Town I Was Born In* ◦ *Lay Your Head on My Shoulder*

Aharon Amir 37
Nothingness

Edna Aphek 38
Sarah ◦ *The Story of Abraham and Hagar*

Eli Bachar 40
Room Poems ◦ *A Dawn of Jaffa Pigeons* ◦ *Houses, Past and Present*

Yocheved Bat-Miriam 42
The Monasteries Lift Gold Domes ◦ *Distance Spills Itself*

Hayim Be'er 43
Tabernacle of Peace ◦ *The Sequence of Generations* ◦ *Love Song*

Anath Bental 47
Jerusalem in the Snow ◦ *The Angel Michael*

Avraham Ben-Yitzhak 48
I Didn't Know My Soul ◦ *Blessed Are Those Who Sow and Do Not Reap* ◦ *Psalm*

Hayim Nachman Bialik 51
When the Days Grow Long ◦ *After My Death* ◦ *Summer Night* ◦ *I Didn't Find Light by Accident* ◦ *Footsteps of Spring* ◦ *My Song* ◦ *I Scattered My Sighs to the Wind* ◦ *The Sea of Silence Exhales Secrets* ◦ *Place Me Under Your Wing*

Erez Biton 61
Beginnings ◦ *A Bird's Nest* ◦ *Buying a Shop on Dizengoff*

VOICES WITHIN THE ARK

T. Carmi 63
The Condition ◦ The Author's Apology

Abraham Chalfi 68
My Father ◦ The One Who Is Missing

Raquel Chalfi 69
Like a Field Waiting ◦ A Childless Witch ◦ A Witch Going Down to Egypt

Shlomit Cohen 72
The Same Dream ◦ An Unraveled Thought ◦ Wife of Kohelet

Moshe Dor 73
The Dwelling ◦ Small Bones Ache ◦ Among the Pine Trees ◦ Nightingales Are Not Singing

Anadad Eldan 77
Words That Speak of Death ◦ Who Will Give Cover? ◦ Samson Rends His Clothes

Jakov Fichman 78
Eve ◦ Abishag

Amir Gilboa 80
Isaac ◦ Moses ◦ Joshua's Face ◦ Saul ◦ My Brother Was Silent ◦ Samson ◦ Seeds of Lead ◦ Birth

Zerubavel Gilead 86
Absalom ◦ Pomegranate Tree in Jerusalem ◦ Flying Letters

Leah Goldberg 89
Heavenly Jerusalem, Jerusalem of the Earth ◦ A God Once Commanded Us ◦ From My Mother's Home ◦ Toward Myself ◦ Answer

Uri Zvi Greenberg 92
With My God, the Smith ◦ Like a Woman ◦ The Great Sad One ◦ How It Is ◦ The Valley of Men ◦ There Is a Box ◦ The Hour ◦ On the Pole ◦ Song at the Skirts of Heaven

Zali Gurevitch 96
Short Eulogy ◦ Not Going with It

Haim Guri 98
Isaac ◦ Anath ◦ My Samsons ◦ Nine Men Out of a Minyan ◦ And on My Return ◦ Rain ◦ A Latter Purification

Shimon Halkin 104
Do Not Accompany Me

Hedva Harkavi 106
Talk to Me, Talk to Me ◦ It Was Gentle ◦ Whenever the Snakes Come

Avraham Huss 108
A Green Refrain ◦ Time ◦ Nocturnal Thoughts ◦ A Classic Idyll

Yehuda Karni 111
The Four of Them ◦ Chambers of Jerusalem

Rav Abraham Isaac Kook 113
The First One Drew Me ◦ Radiant Is the World Soul ◦ When I Want to Speak

Abba Kovner 114
Near ◦ Observation at Dawn ◦ I Don't Know if Mount Zion

Yitzhak Lamdan 118
Massada

Jiri Mordecai Langer 119
On the Margins of a Poem ∘ Riddle of Night

Rena Lee 121
An Old Story

Hayim Lenski 122
Purity ∘ Language of Ancients ∘ Upon the Lake

Matti Megged 123
The Phoenix ∘ White Bird ∘ The Akedah

Hayim Naggid 126
A Snow in Jerusalem ∘ After the War ∘ Like a Pearl ∘ My Mother

Dan Pagis 128
The Last Ones ∘ The Tower ∘ Instructions for Crossing the Border ∘ Scrawled in Pencil in a Sealed Railway Car ∘ Draft of a Reparations Agreement ∘ Brothers ∘ Autobiography ∘ The Grand Duke of New York

Israel Pincas 134
Mediterranean

Berl Pomerantz 135
End of Summer ∘ Young Virgins Plucked Suddenly

Gabriel Preil 137
Words of Oblivion and Peace ∘ Rains on the Island ∘ From Jerusalem: A First Poem ∘ Arriving ∘ Autumn Music ∘ Like David ∘ Parting ∘ Memory of Another Climate ∘ A Summing Up ∘ Giving Up on the Shore ∘ A Late Manuscript at the Schocken Institute ∘ Fishermen ∘ A Lesson in Translation ∘ Letter Out of the Gray ∘ Biographical Note

Esther Raab 145
Folk Tune ∘ A Serenade for Two Poplars

Rachel 147
Rachel ∘ My White Book of Poems ∘ Revolt ∘ My Dead ∘ Perhaps

Yonathan Ratosh 149
Lament

Dahlia Ravikovitch 150
A Dress of Fire ∘ Surely You Remember ∘ Requiem After Seventeen Years

Abraham Regelson 153
Moses on Mount Nebo

I. Z. Rimon 155
I Am a King

David Rokeah 156
Beginning ∘ I Am Like a Book

Hemda Roth 157
A Young Deer/Dust ∘ Treason of Sand ∘ The Song

Tuvia Ruebner 160
Among Iron Fragments ∘ First Days ∘ I Left ∘ Document

Pinhas Sadeh 162
In the Forest ∘ In the Garden of the Turkish Consulate ∘ Raya Brenner ∘ Elegy

Shin Shalom 165
Splendor

VOICES WITHIN THE ARK

Aliza Shenhar 170
Trembling ◦ Expectation ◦ Resurrection of the Dead ◦ The Drunkenness of Pain ◦ Sea-Games ◦ The Akedah ◦ Song of the Closing Service

Avraham Shlonsky 173
Prayer ◦ The Stars on Shabbat ◦ Pledge ◦ A New Genesis ◦ Dress Me, Dear Mother

David Shulman 176
A Diary of the Sailors of the North

Eisig Silberschlag 178
Abraham ◦ Proust on Noah

Arye Sivan 180
Children's Song ◦ In Jerusalem Are Women ◦ Forty Years Peace ◦ To Xanadu, Which Is Beth Shaul

Jakov Steinberg 182
With a Book at Twilight ◦ The World Is Not a Fenced-Off Garden ◦ A Donkey Will Carry You

Noah Stern 184
His Mother's Love ◦ Grave at Cassino

A. L. Strauss 186
Lament for the European Exile ◦ In the Discreet Splendor ◦ On the Path ◦ Voice in the Dark

Joshua Tan Pai 188
Trees Once Walked and Stood ◦ My Soul Hovers Over Me ◦ The Life of Hard Times

Shaul Tchernichovsky 190
Man Is Nothing But ◦ The Grave ◦ Saul's Song of Love ◦ The Death of Tammuz

Mordecai Temkin 196
Seal of Fire ◦ Foul Water ◦ Hidden Bow ◦ Your Presence

Avner Treinin 198
The Cage ◦ Salmon Cycle ◦ Deserted Shrine

Shlomo Vinner 200
Jerusalem ◦ In the Cabinet ◦ Training on the Shore ◦ Midnight and Ten Minutes ◦ The Need to Love ◦ Parting ◦ Lullaby

David Vogel 206
Days Were Great as Lakes ◦ Our Childhood Spilled into Our Hearts ◦ How Can I See You, Love ◦ Black Flags Are Fluttering ◦ Plain, Humble Letters ◦ When I Was Growing Up ◦ In Fine, Transparent Words ◦ Now I Have Forgotten All

Yona Wallach 211
Cradle Song ◦ When the Angels Are Exhausted ◦ Death; She Was Always Here

Manfred Winkler 213
One Goes With Me Along the Shore ◦ If My Hands Were Mute ◦ Somewhere You Exist ◦ I Love What Is Not ◦ She

Avot Yeshurun 216
The Poem on the Jews ◦ The Poem on the Guilt ◦ The Poem on Our Mother, Our Mother Rachel

Nathan Yonathan 218
Another Poem on Absalom ∘ South Wind ∘ And the Silver Turns into Night

Natan Zach 221
When God First Said ∘ The Quiet Light of Flies ∘ To Be a Master in Your House ∘ When the Last Riders ∘ In This Deep Darkness ∘ A Short Winter Tale ∘ Perhaps It's Only Music ∘ A Peaceful Song ∘ As Sand ∘ Against Parting ∘ No ∘ Listening to Her ∘ A Foreign Country

Zelda 228
I Stood in Jerusalem ∘ The Moon Is Teaching Bible ∘ In the Dry Riverbed ∘ With My Grandfather ∘ Light a Candle

Ezra Zussman 231
At Dante's Grave ∘ The Last

II Yiddish

Introduction to Book II by Ruth Wisse 236

B. Alquit 243
The Light of the World ∘ Wandering Chorus

Asya 244
The Deer ∘ Celan ∘ Pause a Moment ∘ My True Memory ∘ My Strawlike Hair ∘ A Grain of Moonlight

Ephraim Auerbach 247
Seismograph

Rachel Boimwall 248
Diaspora Jews ∘ Lifelong ∘ Round ∘ At Night

Nahum Bomze 250
Pshytik ∘ City of Light

Celia Dropkin 252
A Circus Dancer

Lazer Eichenrand 252
The Mute City ∘ Prologue ∘ From Life

Rachel Fishman 254
In the Beginning ∘ Even If

A. Glanz-Leyeles 256
Castles ∘ White Swan ∘ Madison Square

Jacob Glatstein 258
The Poet Lives ∘ Mozart ∘ I'll Find My Self-Belief ∘ In a Ghetto ∘ Loyal Sins ∘ Like Weary Trees ∘ Memorial Poem ∘ Move On, Yiddish Poet ∘ Evening Bread ∘ Praying the Sunset Prayer

Naftali Gross 270
The Fire Goes Out ∘ Where Rests the Wind

Moishe Leib Halpern 270
Just Because ∘ Go Throw Them Out ∘ Memento Mori ∘ Zlotchev, My Home ∘ Considering the Bleakness ∘ Isaac Leybush Peretz ∘ That's Our Lot ∘ Sacco-Vanzetti

Mordechai Husid 278
On the Way ∘ The Cry of Generations ∘ Windows

VOICES WITHIN THE ARK

Rachel Korn 279
I'm Soaked Through with You ∘ Longing ∘ My Body ∘ A Letter ∘ Sometimes I Want to Go Up ∘ A New Dress ∘ The Thirty-One Camels ∘ Too Late ∘ Put Your Word to My Lips ∘ With Poems Already Begun ∘ From Here to There

Moishe Kulbak 286
I Just Walk Around, Around, Around ∘ Spring ∘ Summer ∘ Two ∘ Vilna

Leib Kwitko 291
Esau ∘ My Fiddle

Zishe Landau 292
I Have a Big Favor to Ask You, Brothers ∘ Parts ∘ Tuesday ∘ Of Course I Know ∘ The Little Pig

Mani Leib 295
The Pyre of My Indian Summer ∘ Winter ∘ In Little Hands ∘ A Plum ∘ Psalmodist ∘ From the Crag ∘ They

H. Leivick 299
How Did He Get Here? ∘ Two Times Two is Four ∘ Through the Whole Long Night ∘ I Hear a Voice

Malka Locker 301
Clocks ∘ Drunken Streets

Itzik Manger 302
Rachel Goes to the Well for Water ∘ Abishag Writes a Letter Home ∘ Alone ∘ Autumn ∘ Abraham and Sarah ∘ On the Road There Stands a Tree ∘ The Strange Guest ∘ Dying Thief ∘ Fairy Tales ∘ Evening ∘ Under the Ruins of Poland ∘ A Dark Hand

Anna Margolin 312
Ancient Murderess Night ∘ Years ∘ My Kin Talk ∘ Homecoming ∘ Mother Earth

Peretz Markish 316
In the Last Flicker of the Sinking Sun ∘ Your Burnt-Out Body

Kadya Molodovsky 317
In Life's Stable ∘ Night Visitors ∘ And Yet

Mendel Naigreshel 320
What Will Remain After Me? ∘ Nation

Leib Neidus 321
In an Alien Place ∘ I Often Want to Let My Lines Go ∘ I Love the Woods

Melech Ravitch 322
Twelve Lines About the Burning Bush ∘ A Poem—Good or Bad—a Thing—With One Attribute—Flat ∘ Twilight Thoughts in Israel ∘ Let Us Learn ∘ Verses Written on Sand ∘ Conscience

Abraham Reisen 329
The Family of Eight ∘ What Is the Case in Point? ∘ Newcomers ∘ An Endless Chain ∘ Girls from Home

Joseph Rolnik 333
In Disguise ∘ I'm Not Rich ∘ At God's Command

Leah Rudnitsky 334
Birds Are Drowsing on the Branches

Beyle Schaechter-Gottesman 335
Meditation

Jacob Isaac Segal 336
Candle ◦ Rest

Zvi Shargel 337
Pictures on the Wall ◦ I Will Go Away ◦ Let Us Laugh

Eliezer Steinbarg 339
Where Is Justice? ◦ Shatnes *or Uncleanliness ◦ The Umbrella, the Cane, and the Broom ◦ The Horse and the Whip ◦ The Bayonet and the Needle*

Moishe Steingart 344
The Last Fire ◦ Generations

A. N. Stencl 346
Ezekiel

Abo Stoltzenberg 347
In Vistas of Stone ◦ What Am I? ◦ The French Mood

Abraham Sutskever 348
On My Wandering Flute ◦ Song for a Dance ◦ Landscape ◦ Songs to a Lady Moonwalker ◦ The Banks of a River ◦ How ◦ Song of Praise for an Ox ◦ Poetry ◦ Under the Earth ◦ Yiddish ◦ Toys ◦ A Cartload of Shoes ◦ To My Child

J. L. Teller 358
Lines to a Tree ◦ Minor Key ◦ To the Divine Neighbor

Malka Heifetz Tussman 360
At the Well ◦ I Say ◦ Thou Shalt Not ◦ Water Without Sound ◦ Love the Ruins ◦ Songs of the Priestess

Miriam Ulinover 366
Havdolah Wine ◦ In the Courtyard

Moshe Yungman 367
The Sacrifice ◦ Don't Say ◦ The Messiah ◦ Encounter in Safed ◦ Melons

Aaron Zeitlin 370
A Dream About an Aged Humorist ◦ Text ◦ The Empty Apartment ◦ Ode to Freedom

Rayzel Zychlinska 374
Remembering Lutsky ◦ The Clothes ◦ My Mother's Shoes

III English

Introductions to Book III by Howard Schwartz and Anthony Rudolf 378

UNITED STATES

Paul Auster 401
Scribe ◦ Hieroglyph ◦ Song of Degrees ◦ Covenant

Willis Barnstone 405
The Good Beasts ◦ The Worm ◦ Grandfather ◦ Gas Lamp ◦ Miklos Radnoti ◦ Paradise

Anita Barrows 408
Avenue Y ◦ The Ancestors

VOICES WITHIN THE ARK

Marvin Bell 413
Getting Lost in Nazi Germany ◦ The Extermination of the Jews ◦ The Israeli Navy

Stephen Berg 415
Desnos Reading the Palms of Men on Their Way to the Gas Chambers

Suzanne Bernhardt 421
In a Dream Ship's Hold ◦ The Unveiling

Chana Bloch 423
Paradise ◦ Noah ◦ The Sacrifice ◦ Yom Kippur

Emily Borenstein 427
Life of the Letters

Alter Brody 427
Lamentations ◦ Ghetto Twilight ◦ A Family Album

Stanley Burnshaw 433
Isaac ◦ House in St. Petersburg ◦ Talmudist

Michael Castro 436
Grandfathers ◦ Percolating Highway

Eric Chaet 441
Yom Kippur ◦ A Letter Catches Up with Me

Kim Chernin 443
Eve's Birth

Elaine Dallman 443
From the Dust

Lucille Day 444
Labor ◦ Yom Kippur

Rose Drachler 446
Isaac and Esau ◦ The Dark Scent of Prayer ◦ Under the Shawl ◦ Zippora Returns to Moses at Rephidim ◦ As I Am My Father's ◦ The Letters of the Book

Larry Eigner 452
The Closed System ◦ Remember Sabbath Days

Marcia Falk 454
Shulamit in Her Dreams ◦ Modern Kabbalist ◦ Woman through the Window

Irving Feldman 456
The Pripet Marshes

Ruth Feldman 459
Lilith

Donald Finkel 460
Genealogy ◦ Lilith ◦ Cain's Song ◦ Lame Angel ◦ Finders Keepers ◦ Feeding the Fire ◦ How Things Fall

Laya Firestone 467
Listen to the Bird ◦ Thoughts for My Grandmother ◦ Crow, Straight Flier, But Dark ◦ For Gabriel

Allen Ginsberg 469
Kaddish

Joseph Glazer 473
A Visit Home

Albert Goldbarth 474
Dime Call ◦ Recipe

Lynn Gottlieb 476
Eve's Song in the Garden

Arthur Gregor 477
Spirit-like Before Light

Allen Grossman 479
Lilith

Martin Grossman 480
Into the Book ◦ The Bread of Our Affliction

Anthony Hecht 481
"More Light! More Light!"

Jack Hirschman 482
Zohara ◦ NHR

John Hollander 487
The Ziz

Barry Holtz 489
Isaac

David Ignatow 491
1905 ◦ Kaddish ◦ Dream ◦ The Heart

Dan Jaffe 493
The Owl in the Rabbi's Barn ◦ Yahrzeit

Rodger Kamenetz 495
Why I Can't Write My Autobiography ◦ Pilpul

Marc Kaminsky 497
Erev Shabbos

Jascha Kessler 498
Waiting for Lilith

Sol Lachman 499
Sukkot

Barbara F. Lefcowitz 500
Driftwood Dybbuk ◦ At the Western Wall ◦ The Mirrors of Jerusalem

Harris Lenowitz 504
The Fringes ◦ Panegyric

Molly Myerowitz Levine 506
Safed and I

Philip Levine 508
Zaydee ◦ 1933 ◦ After ◦ Now It Can Be Told ◦ Words ◦ Here and Now ◦ On a Drawing by Flavio

Stephen Levy 520
Home Alone These Last Hours of the Afternoon, Dusk Now, the Sabbath Setting In, I Sit Back, and These Words Start Welling Up in Me ◦ Friday Night After Bathing ◦ Freely, from a Song Sung by Jewish Women of Yemen ◦ A Judezmo Writer in Turkey Angry

VOICES WITHIN THE ARK

Susan Litwack 522
Inscape ◦ *Tonight Everyone in the World Is Dreaming the Same Dream* ◦ *Havdolah* ◦ *Creation of the Child*

Mordecai Marcus 526
Two Refugees

David Meltzer 527
Tell Them I'm Struggling to Sing with Angels ◦ *The Eyes, the Blood*

Susan Mernit 537
Song of the Bride ◦ *The Scholar's Wife*

Jerred Metz 539
Angels in the House ◦ *Speak Like Rain* ◦ *Her True Body* ◦ *Divination*

Bert Meyers 542
The Garlic ◦ *The Dark Birds* ◦ *When I Came to Israel*

Robert Mezey 544
New Year's Eve in Solitude ◦ *The Wandering Jew* ◦ *White Blossoms* ◦ *Theresienstadt Poem* ◦ *I Am Here*

Stephen Mitchell 554
Adam in Love ◦ *Abraham* ◦ *Jacob and the Angel*

Howard Moss 556
Elegy for My Father

Stanley Moss 557
God Poem ◦ *Two Fishermen* ◦ *Scroll* ◦ *Apocrypha*

Jack Myers 561
The Minyan ◦ *Day of Atonement*

Joachim Neugroschel 562
Eve's Advice to the Children of Israel ◦ *Doves*

Gerda Norvig 564
Desert March ◦ *The Tree of Life Is Also a Tree of Fire* ◦ *The Joining*

George Oppen 567
If It All Went Up in Smoke

Cynthia Ozick 573
The Wonder-Teacher ◦ *A Riddle*

Gary Pacernick 576
I Want to Write a Jewish Poem

Linda Pastan 577
Yom Kippur ◦ *After Reading Nelly Sachs* ◦ *At the Jewish Museum* ◦ *Pears* ◦ *Elsewhere*

Stuart Z. Perkoff 579
Aleph ◦ *Gimel* ◦ *Hai*

William Pillin 581
O, Beautiful They Move ◦ *Night Poem in an Abandoned Music Room* ◦ *A Poem for Anton Schmidt* ◦ *Farewell to Europe* ◦ *Ode on a Decision to Settle for Less* ◦ *Poem*

Hyam Plutzik 588
The King of Ai ◦ *The Begetting of Cain* ◦ *On the Photograph of a Man I Never Saw*

Carl Rakosi 590
Meditation ∘ Meditation ∘ A Lamentation ∘ Meditation

Rochelle Ratner 592
The Poor Shammes of Berditchev ∘ Davening

Charles Reznikoff 593
The Hebrew of Your Poets, Zion ∘ Jacob ∘ Luzzato ∘ Out of the Strong, Sweetness ∘ Lament of the Jewish Women for Tammuz ∘ Dew ∘ The Body Is Like Roots Stretching ∘ Raisins and Nuts ∘ Te Deum ∘ Autobiography: Hollywood ∘ The Letter

Martin Robbins 600
A Cantor's Dream Before the High Holy Days

Edouard Roditi 601
Shekhina and the Kiddushim ∘ The Paths of Prayer ∘ Kashrut ∘ A Beginning and an End ∘ Habakkuk

David Rosenberg 610
Maps to Nowhere ∘ Rain Has Fallen on the History Books

Joel Rosenberg 614
The First Wedding in the World ∘ The Violin Tree

Jerome Rothenberg 617
The Alphabet Came to Me ∘ A Letter to Paul Celan in Memory

Muriel Rukeyser 620
Akiba

Benjamin Saltman 627
The Journey with Hands and Arms ∘ The Fathers

Susan Fromberg Schaeffer 629
Yahrzeit

Delmore Schwartz 630
Abraham ∘ Sarah ∘ Jacob

Howard Schwartz 635
Our Angels ∘ Gathering the Sparks ∘ Adam's Dream ∘ Abraham in Egypt ∘ Iscah ∘ The New Year for Trees ∘ The Eve ∘ The Prayers ∘ Vessels ∘ A Song ∘ These Two ∘ Blessing of the Firstborn ∘ Shira ∘ Psalm

Harvey Shapiro 647
The Six Hundred Thousand Letters ∘ Lines for the Ancient Scribes ∘ Exodus ∘ Riding Westward ∘ For the Yiddish Singers in the Lakewood Hotels of My Childhood ∘ Like a Beach ∘ Musical Shuttle

Karl Shapiro 651
The Alphabet ∘ The 151st Psalm ∘ Jew

David Shevin 653
Shechem ∘ Dawn

Danny Siegel 655
Binni the Meshuggener ∘ Snow in the City ∘ The Crippler

Maxine Silverman 657
Hair

Myra Sklarew 658
What Is a Jewish Poem? ∘ Benediction ∘ Instructions for the Messiah

VOICES WITHIN THE ARK

Arlene Stone 661
Germination

Nathaniel Tarn 664
Where Babylon Ends

Constance Urdang 665
The Invention of Zero ◦ *Birth* ◦ *Change of Life*

Ruth Whitman 667
Translating ◦ *Dan, the Dust of Masada Is Still in My Nostrils* ◦ *Mediterranean* ◦ *Watching the Sun Rise Over Mount Zion*

Melvin Wilk 671
Blessing

J. Rutherford Willems 672
Hebrew Letters in the Trees

C. K. Williams 673
Spit

Linda Zisquit 675
Rachel's Lament ◦ *Sabbatical* ◦ *The Circumcision*

Louis Zukofsky 678
From the Head ◦ *A Voice Out of the Tabernacle* ◦ *Expounding the Torah*

ENGLAND

A. Alvarez 681
A Cemetery in New Mexico ◦ *The Fortunate Fall* ◦ *Dying* ◦ *Mourning and Melancholia*

Anthony Barnett 684
A Marriage ◦ *Celan* ◦ *Cloisters* ◦ *The Book of Mysteries* ◦ *Crossing*

Asa Benveniste 688
The Alchemical Cupboard

Richard Burns 693
Mandelstam ◦ *Angels*

Ruth Fainlight 697
Lilith ◦ *God's Language* ◦ *The Hebrew Sibyl* ◦ *Sibyl of the Waters*

Elaine Feinstein 700
Against Winter ◦ *Under Stone* ◦ *Dad* ◦ *Survivors*

Michael Hamburger 703
At Staufen ◦ *The Search*

Gad Hollander 707
Axioms ◦ *Argument Against Metaphor* ◦ *In Memoriam Paul Celan* ◦ *Fugato (Coda)*

Lotte Kramer 710
Genesis

Francis Landy 711
The Princess Who Fled to the Castle ◦ *Lament for Azazel* ◦ *Midrash on Hamlet* ◦ *Seli̲chos*

Emanuel Litvinoff 714
If I Forget Thee ◦ *To T. S. Eliot*

Tali Loewenthal 717
Hebrew Script (Eight Poems)

Edward Lowbury 719
Tree of Knowledge ◦ *In the Old Jewish Cemetery, Prague, 1970*

Tom Lowenstein 722
Noah in New England ◦ *Nausicaa with Some Attendants* ◦ *Horizon Without Landscape*

Asher Mendelssohn 724
Cordoba

Jeremy Robson 725
The Departure

Isaac Rosenberg 726
God ◦ *Break of Day in the Trenches* ◦ *Chagrin* ◦ *Dead Man's Dump* ◦ *Saul* ◦ *The Jew* ◦ *Returning, We Hear the Larks* ◦ *The Destruction of Jerusalem by the Babylonian Hordes*

Anthony Rudolf 734
Ashkelon ◦ *Hands Up* ◦ *Evening of the Rose* ◦ *Dubrovnik Poem (Emilio Tolentino)* ◦ *Prayer for Kafka and Ourselves* ◦ *Ancient of Days*

Jon Silkin 738
Death of a Son ◦ *The Coldness* ◦ *A Word About Freedom and Identity in Tel Aviv* ◦ *It Says* ◦ *Jerusalem* ◦ *Resting Place*

Daniel Weissbort 747
Anniversary ◦ *Murder of a Community* ◦ *Walking Home at Night*

CANADA

Leonard Cohen 750
Story of Isaac

Deborah Eibel 752
Hagar to Ishmael ◦ *The Kabbalist* ◦ *Freethinkers*

Phyllis Gotlieb 755
The Morning Prayers of the Hasid, Rabbi Levi Yitzhok

A. M. Klein 758
And in That Drowning Instant

Irving Layton 760
Jewish Main Street

Seymour Mayne 760
In the First Cave ◦ *Locusts of Silence* ◦ *Abraham Sutskever* ◦ *Yehuda Amichai* ◦ *Afternoon's Angel*

Sharon Nelson 765
Pedlar

Joseph Sherman 766
Sarai

Miriam Waddington 768
The Survivors ◦ *The Field of Night* ◦ *Desert Stone*

VOICES WITHIN THE ARK

ISRAEL

Henry Abramovitch 772
Psalm of the Jealous God

Ruth Beker 772
Don't Show Me

Edward Codish 774
Yetzer ha Ra ∘ *A Juggle of Myrtle Twigs*

David Eller 776
To a God Unknown

Richard Flantz 777
Shir Ma'alot/A Song of Degrees

William Freedman 778
Benediction ∘ *Formations*

Rivka Fried 779
Sabbath

Robert Friend 780
The Practice of Absence ∘ *Identity*

Shirley Kaufman 782
Wonders ∘ *Next Year, in Jerusalem* ∘ *Looking for Maimonides: Tiberias* ∘ *New Graveyard: Jerusalem* ∘ *Leah* ∘ *Starting Over* ∘ *Loving*

Gabriel Levin 787
Adam's Death ∘ *Ishmael* ∘ *Étude for Voice and Hand*

Marsha Pomerantz 789
Adam and Eve at the Garden Gate ∘ *How to Reach the Moon*

Paul Raboff 791
Jars ∘ *Reb Hanina*

Betsy Rosenberg 792
Bird Song ∘ *Unearthing*

Harold Schimmel 793
Ancestors

Myra Glazer Schotz 795
The First Love Poem ∘ *Thespian in Jerusalem* ∘ *Santa Caterina*

Mark Elliott Shapiro 798
Dying Under a Fall of Stars

Richard Sherwin 799
Jacob's Winning

Dennis Silk 800
Guide to Jerusalem ∘ *Matronita*

Avner Strauss 803
The Hollow Flute ∘ *Portrait of a Widow*

AUSTRALIA

Nancy Keesing 804
Wandering Jews

David Martin 807
I Am a Jew

Fay Zwicky 808
The Chosen—Kalgoorlie, 1894

SOUTH AFRICA

Sydney Clouts 810
Of Thomas Traherne and the Pebble Outside ∘ The Portrait of Prince Henry ∘ The Sleeper ∘ Firebowl

Mannie Hirsch 813
Cry for a Disused Synagogue in Booysens

Allan Kolski Horvitz 814
King Saul ∘ The Radiance of Extinct Stars

Jean Lipkin 815
Apocalypse

Fay Lipshitz 816
Encounter in Jerusalem ∘ Judean Summer ∘ The Aleph Bet

SCOTLAND

A. C. Jacobs 818
Poem for My Grandfather ∘ Yiddish Poet ∘ Isaac ∘ Painting

WALES

Dannie Abse 822
Song for Dov Shamir ∘ Tales of Shatz

INDIA

Nissim Ezekiel 826
Totem ∘ Lamentation ∘ How My Father Died

SRI LANKA

Anne Ranasinghe 828
Holocaust 1944 ∘ Auschwitz from Colombo

IV Other Languages

Introduction to Book IV by Edouard Roditi 832

AMHARIC

Yosef Damana ben Yeshaq 849
The Rusted Chain

ARABIC

Shalom Katav 851
Pleading Voices

Shmuel Moreh 852
The Tree of Hatred ∘ Melody ∘ The Return

VOICES WITHIN THE ARK

David Semah 856
Prostration ∘ Tomb

Anwar Shaul 857
Mother ∘ To a Cactus Seller ∘ Prayers to Liberty

CZECH

Ludvik Askenazy 861
The Wall

Otakar Fischer 862
From the Depths

Pavel Friedmann 863
The Butterfly

Jiri Gold 863
In the Cellars ∘ An Inhabited Emptiness

František Gottlieb 866
Between Life and Death ∘ Just a While

Dagmar Hilarová 867
Questions

DUTCH

Jakov de Haan 868
Unity ∘ All Is God's ∘ God's Gifts ∘ Hanukah ∘ Sabbath

Judith Herzberg 869
On the Death of Sylvia Plath ∘ Yiddish ∘ The Voice ∘ Commentaries on the Song of Songs ∘ Kinneret ∘ Nearer

Hanny Michaelis 872
We Carry Eggshells ∘ Under Restless Clouds ∘ Listening

Leo Vroman 874
Old Miniatures ∘ The River

FRENCH

Charles Dobzynski 877
Memory Air ∘ Zealot Without a Face ∘ The Never Again ∘ The Fable Merchant

Edmond Fleg 880
The Dead Cities Speak to the Living Cities

Benjamin Fondane 881
Lullaby for an Emigrant ∘ By the Waters of Babylon ∘ The Wandering Jew ∘ Hertza ∘ Plain Song

Yvan Goll 888
Lilith ∘ Raziel ∘ Clandestine Work ∘ Neïla

Edmond Jabès 892
The Condemned ∘ Song of the Last Jewish Child ∘ Song of the Trees of the Black Forest ∘ A Circular Cry ∘ Song ∘ The Pulverized Screen ∘ Water ∘ The Book Rises Out of the Fire

Gustave Kahn 901
The Temple ∘ The Word

Joseph Milbauer 902
Interior ◦ Paris by Night

Pierre Morhange 904
Lullaby in Auschwitz ◦ Jew ◦ Salomon

Shlomo Reich 905
The Golem ◦ The Windmill of Evening ◦ The Vigil ◦ A Tribe Searching

Ryvel 908
The Pilgrimage to Testour

David Scheinert 909
The Drunken Stones of Prague ◦ The Stone and the Blade of Grass in the Warsaw Ghetto

André Spire 911
Hear, O Israel! ◦ Pogroms ◦ The Ancient Law ◦ Nudities ◦ Poetics

Tristan Tzara 916
Evening ◦ Mothers

Claude Vigée 917
The Tree of Death ◦ The Struggle with the Angel ◦ House of the Living ◦ Light of Judea ◦ The Phoenix of Mozart ◦ Every Land Is Exile ◦ Destiny of the Poet ◦ Song of Occident ◦ The Wanderer ◦ Poetry

Ilarie Voronca 922
The Quick and the Dead ◦ The Seven-League Boots

Jean Wahl 924
Decayed Time ◦ A Lean Day in a Convict's Suit ◦ Prayer of Little Hope ◦ Evening in the Walls

GERMAN

Rose Ausländer 926
My Nightingale ◦ Father ◦ Jerusalem ◦ Passover ◦ Hasidic Jew from Sadagora ◦ Phoenix ◦ In Chagall's Village ◦ The Lamed-Vov

Richard Beer-Hofmann 932
Lullaby for Miriam

Ilse Blumenthal-Weiss 933
A Jewish Child Prays to Jesus

Martin Buber 933
I Consider the Tree ◦ The Fiddler

Paul Celan 935
Psalm ◦ In Prague ◦ Death Fugue ◦ Ash-Glory ◦ Cello Entry ◦ In Egypt ◦ Tenebrae ◦ Zürich, zum Storchen ◦ Corona ◦ Hut Window ◦ Just Think ◦ A Speck of Sand ◦ Turn Blind ◦ Over Three Nipple-Stones

Hilde Domin 946
Catalogue ◦ Cologne ◦ Dreamwater

Alfred Grünewald 948
The Lamp Now Flickers

Jakov van Hoddis 949
End of the World ◦ The Air Vision ◦ Tohub

VOICES WITHIN THE ARK

Alfred Kittner 951
Old Jewish Cemetery in Worms ∘ Blue Owl Song

Alma Johanna Koenig 953
Intimations

Gertrud Kolmar 954
The Woman Poet ∘ The Jewish Woman ∘ Sea-Monster

Else Lasker-Schüler 957
Abraham and Isaac ∘ Hagar and Ishmael ∘ Homesickness ∘ Abel ∘ Jacob ∘ Moses and Joshua ∘ Pharaoh and Joseph ∘ Saul ∘ Lord, Listen

Alfred Lichtenstein 962
The Journey to the Insane Asylum ∘ Repose

Conny Hannes Meyer 963
Of the Beloved Caravan ∘ The Beast That Rode the Unicorn

Alfred Mombert 966
The Chimera

Joseph Roth 967
Ahasuerus

Nelly Sachs 968
Burning Sand of Sinai ∘ Hasidim Dance ∘ O the Chimneys ∘ O Night of the Crying Children ∘ What Secret Desires of the Blood ∘ To You Building the New House ∘ One Chord ∘ Chorus of the Rescued

Hans Sahl 973
Memo ∘ Greeting from a Distance

Gershom Scholem 975
The Trial

Thomas Sessler 977
When the Day ∘ You Move Forward ∘ Burnt Debris

Hugo Sonnenschein 979
In the Open Fields ∘ In the Ghetto

Friedrich Torberg 980
Seder, 1944 ∘ Amalek

Alfred Wolfenstein 982
Exodus, 1940

Karl Wolfskehl 983
Shekhina ∘ From Mount Nebo ∘ We Go

GREEK

Joseph Eliyia 987
Rebecca ∘ Dream ∘ Slender Maid ∘ Your Passing, Fleet Passing ∘ Epilogue

HUNGARIAN

Milan Fuest 991
Moses' Account

Agnes Gergely 991
Birth of a Country ∘ Desert ∘ Conjuration

Anna Hajnal 994
Dead Girl ∘ Tree to Flute

Eugene Heimler 995
Psalm ◦ After an Eclipse of the Sun

Jozsef Kiss 998
The New Ahasuerus

Emil Makai 1000
The Comet

Otto Orban 1001
Hymn ◦ Computer ◦ Ray

Gyorgy Raba 1003
Message ◦ Conversation

Miklós Radnóti 1005
Song ◦ I Hid You ◦ Root ◦ Metaphors ◦ In Your Arms ◦ Fragment ◦ Letter to My Wife ◦ Seventh Eclogue ◦ Forced March ◦ Picture Postcards

Judit Tóth 1014
Remembering ◦ The Southeast Ramparts of the Seine ◦ Wildfire

István Vas 1016
What Is Left? ◦ Catacombs ◦ Tambour ◦ Just This

ITALIAN

Edith Bruck 1021
Childhood ◦ Let's Talk, Mother ◦ Equality, Father! ◦ Sister Zahava ◦ Go, Then ◦ Why Would I Have Survived?

Aldo Camerino 1028
Night ◦ Calm ◦ Fear ◦ For a Voice That Is Singing ◦ Mother ◦ Recluse

Franco Fortini 1032
For Our Soldiers Who Fell in Russia ◦ The Gutter ◦ In Memoriam I ◦ In Memoriam II

Primo Levi 1034
Lilith ◦ Shema ◦ For Adolf Eichmann

Rossana Ombres 1036
Bella and the Golem

Umberto Saba 1039
Sleepless on a Summer Night ◦ The Goat ◦ Three Streets

JUDEO-ROMANESQUE

Crescenzo del Monte 1043
A Roman Roman ◦ Those Zionists ◦ One Thing to Take, Another to Keep

JUDEZMO

Isaac de Botton 1045
Desire

Rachael Castelete 1045
When I Came to London

Clarisse Nicoïdski 1046
Eyes ◦ Mouth ◦ Breaking Off from Waiting ◦ Open Earth ◦ Remembering

VOICES WITHIN THE ARK

POLISH

Henryk Grynberg 1053
Anti-Nostalgia ∘ *Poplars* ∘ *The Dead Sea* ∘ *Listening to Confucius*

Mieczyslaw Jastrun 1057
The Jews

Ewa Lipska 1058
If God Exists ∘ *Wedding* ∘ *The Cock* ∘ *The Flood*

Antoni Slonimski 1061
Elegy ∘ *Conrad* ∘ *Conversation with a Countryman* ∘ *Jerusalem*

Julian Tuwim 1065
The Gypsy Bible ∘ *Mother* ∘ *Jewboy* ∘ *Lodgers*

Aleksander Wat 1069
Willows in Alma-Ata ∘ *There Is No Place*

Adam Wazyk 1071
Ars Poetica ∘ *Hotel* ∘ *Nike*

Jozef Wittlin 1073
To the Jews in Poland ∘ *St. Francis of Assisi and the Miserable Jews* ∘ *On the Jewish Day of Judgment in the Year 1942 (5703)* ∘ *A Hymn About a Spoonful of Soup*

Stanislaw Wygodski 1076
Voyage ∘ *Winter Journey* ∘ *Those Betrayed at Dawn* ∘ *Going to the North*

ROMANIAN

Maria Banus 1079
Eighteen ∘ *Gift Hour*

Nina Cassian 1080
Blood ∘ *Cripples* ∘ *Self-Portrait* ∘ *All Night Long* ∘ *Like Gulliver*

Veronica Porumbacu 1082
Of Autumn

RUSSIAN

Margarita Aliger 1084
To a Portrait of Lermontov ∘ *Two* ∘ *House in Meudon*

Joseph Brodsky 1087
A Jewish Cemetery Near Leningrad ∘ *Pilgrims* ∘ *Verses on Accepting the World* ∘ *Étude* ∘ *Monument to Pushkin* ∘ *To a Tyrant* ∘ *Soho*

Eva Brudne 1093
Memento Vivendi ∘ *A Farewell Ballad of Poppies*

Sasha Chorny 1096
A Vilna Puzzle

Dovid Knut 1096
Walking Along the Sea of Galilee ∘ *A Woman from the Book of Genesis* ∘ *Haifa* ∘ *Safed* ∘ *Rosh Pina*

Naum Korzhavin 1102
Children of Auschwitz

Aleksandr Kushner 1103
To Boris Pasternak

Lev Mak 1105
Eden ◦ The Flood ◦ Prayer

Osip Mandelstam 1107
This Night ◦ Like a Young Levite ◦ Concert at the Station ◦ Twilight of Freedom ◦ Bitter Bread ◦ A Reed

Samuel Marshak 1111
The Little House in Lithuania

Yunna Moritz 1113
In Memory of François Rabelais ◦ Whiteness ◦ Snow-Girl

Lev Ozerov 1116
Babi Yar

Ilya Rubin 1121
Poem from "The Revolution" ◦ No Sense Grieving ◦ Escape ◦ Slow Oxen ◦ Handful of Ashes

Boris Slutsky 1124
God ◦ How They Killed My Grandmother ◦ Dreams of Auschwitz ◦ Burnt

Anatoly Steiger 1127
An Ancient Custom ◦ Words from the Window of a Railway Car

SERBO-CROAT

Monny de Boully 1129
Beyond Memory

Stanislav Vinaver 1130
The European Night ◦ An Inscription ◦ A Cathedral

SLOVAK

Susannah Fried 1134
Winter Day ◦ To My Father ◦ Scraps

SLOVENE

Tomaž Salamun 1137
Air ◦ Eclipse

SPANISH

Juan Gelman 1140
Customs ◦ The Knife ◦ The Stranger

Isaac Goldemberg 1141
Bar Mitzvah ◦ The Jews in Hell

José Isaacson 1143
Pre-positions

Noé Jitrik 1144
Addio a la Mamma

Ruben Kanalenstein 1146
Jerusalem

VOICES WITHIN THE ARK

José Kozer 1149
Cleaning Day ◦ The Store in Havana ◦ My Father, Who's Still Alive

Alejandra Pizarnik 1151
The Mask and the Poem ◦ Dawn ◦ Who Will Stop His Hand from Giving Warmth ◦ The Tree of Diana ◦ Privilege ◦ Apart from Oneself ◦ Vertigos or Contemplation of Something That Is Over

Jorge Plescoff 1156
The Ladder Has No Steps ◦ Tongues of Fire ◦ Violins in Repose ◦ Ourobouros

David Rosenmann-Taub 1158
Sabbath ◦ To a Young Girl ◦ Prelude ◦ Reconciliation ◦ Elegy and Kaddish ◦ Moral Ode

Mario Satz 1162
Fish ◦ Coconut ◦ Lemon

Cesar Tiempo 1165
The Jewish Cemetery

SWEDISH

Oscar Levertin 1166
At the Jewish Cemetery in Prague ◦ Solomon and Morolph, Their Last Encounter

TURKISH

Musa Moris Farhi 1168
Smile at Me ◦ Paths to God ◦ Who Says ◦ God and Nature ◦ Thirst

Jozef Habib Gerez 1170
We Are Acrobats ◦ We Fooled Ourselves ◦ Call from the Afterworld

Acknowledgments 1173

Index of Poets 1199

Index of Translators 1205

General Introduction

The primary intention of the editors of this anthology has been to gather together in one volume representative selections of the finest poetry written by Jewish poets since the turn of the century. As the size and scope of this book suggests, there has been an abundance of poetry written by Jewish poets in this period. And while the work of Jewish poets resembles, in many respects, that of other poets writing in the same country or language, it should quickly become apparent that the Jewish heritage of these poets has left its distinctive and profound mark on virtually all of them. Sometimes Jewish themes are treated directly, but more often modern Jewish poets, especially those writing in Hebrew and Yiddish, prefer secular poetry with religious overtones, which often derive from the resonance of the languages they write in.

The genesis of this collection came about as a result of the editors' mutual interest in the modern Jewish literary tradition. We were first drawn to the work of a handful of poets, among them: Yehuda Amichai of Israel, writing in Hebrew; Paul Celan of Romania, writing in German; the Yiddish poet Jacob Glatstein; the French poet Edmond Jabès; and the American poet Charles Reznikoff. Each of these poets stood out as an individual voice in the world of modern poetry. They were among the very seminal poets who played an increasingly influential role in the ever-broadening horizon of world poetry. Among young American poets, in particular, there has been a search in recent years for models of form and style that has extended far beyond the small circle of established American poets. Poets such as Pablo Neruda of Chile, Zbigniew Herbert of Poland, and Yehuda Amichai have become models for a great many young poets, supplanting such poets as Robert Lowell, John Berryman, Sylvia Plath, and Anne Sexton. In addition, major American poets such as W. S. Merwin, James Wright, and Robert Bly opened their own poetry to the influences of modern European poets. In good part due to the high regard both for their own poetry and their fine translations, much attention came to be paid to their European sources.

It was this exploration of European poets that led us, independently of each other, to discover the aforementioned poets. These poets, in turn, led us to Hebrew poets such as Amir Gilboa, Dan Pagis, and Gabriel Preil; to German poets such as Nelly Sachs, Else Lasker-Schüler, and Gertrud Kolmar; to French poets such as Yvan Goll and Claude Vigée; and to Yiddish poets such as Itzik Manger, Rachel Korn, Moishe Leib Halpern, and Abraham Sutskever. Feeling a strong link to our own Jewish heritage, we became aware that while many Jewish poets worked within a poetic tradition in their own languages, a common tradition was being shared and also being created.

This tradition was the Jewish literary tradition, which reaches back thirty-five hundred years and has remained unbroken. It includes the books of the Bible, the Apocrypha, the Talmud, the Midrash, the Kabbalah, medieval folklore (the first secular Jewish literature), the medieval Jewish poets and the more recent Hasidic tales. Some of the poets we discovered for ourselves were conscious of working in that tradition. Hebrew poets such as Hayim Nachman Bialik and Shaul Tchernichovsky saw themselves as a part of a continuing literary tradition that included the poets of the Golden Age in Spain, such as Judah Halevi, Shmuel Hanagid, and Abraham Ibn Ezra, as well as the Bible and the subsequent sacred books. And in fact the poetry of these medieval poets, who wrote in the thirteenth century, has two fully developed genres, one sacred, one secular. The secular poems are quite down-to-earth and often erotic. More recently, Yehuda Amichai has chosen for his primary model another one of these medieval Spanish poets, Solomon Ibn Gabirol. And the younger Hebrew poets, for whom Amichai has long been the primary model, are in this way influenced by Solomon Ibn Gabirol, whose poetry is mirrored in Amichai's.

So too does the Egyptian-born French poet Edmond Jabès obviously consider himself to be writing in a direct line with Talmudic literature, creating a style that owes much to the terse, aphoristic original. Paul Celan, on the other hand, appears to have regarded his hermetic poetry as part of the general European experiment. Yet it is not at all difficult to see that his model for his most famous poem, "Death Fugue," a poem of great power which reflects his experiences as an inmate at a Nazi labor camp, was the poetry of the Psalms, which is echoed in Celan's unique voice. And although the Yiddish poet Jacob Glatstein appears at first to be a unique phenomenon (as does I. B. Singer among Yiddish writers of fiction), it is also gratifying to discover the Yiddish tradition that lies behind Glatstein's poetry (and Singer's prose), which he was supremely conscious of being a part of.

Somewhere along the line the notion of compiling this anthology evolved. Af first we imagined that there might be as many as fifty, or at most a hundred, such Jewish poets. But our research amazed us by revealing the existence of a great many respectable poets, most of them with books of their own to their credit, writing in various countries and in various languages—we have representatives of twenty-three languages—in this century. This discovery also dismayed us to some extent, since it would be impossible to offer substantial selections of each and every one. At that point we became very conscious of the necessity of establishing criteria in order to select from this multitude of poets the primary representatives. *Voices Within the Ark* (the title is from a line of one of Paul Celan's poems) is the result of this effort. In it is included a total of four hundred modern Jewish poets from more than forty nations. Of these, there are three primary languages: Hebrew and Yiddish, as would be expected, and English, as a great many Jews and therefore a great many Jewish poets live in the United States, Great Britain, Canada, Israel, and other countries where English is either the primary language or an important secondary one. Each of these languages has been given a separate section in the book. In the fourth section we have collected the poets writing in the remaining twenty languages—Amharic, Arabic, Czech, Dutch, French, German, Greek, Hungarian, Italian, Judeo-Romanesque, Judezmo, Polish, Romanian, Russian, Serbo-Croat, Slovak, Slovene, Spanish, Swedish, and Turkish. In addition, each section of *Voices Within the Ark* has an Introduction which describes the historical and literary background appropriate to the material. The Hebrew section is introduced by Laya Firestone, the Yiddish section by Ruth Wisse, the Other Languages section by Edouard Roditi, and the English section, in two parts, by the editors.

The English-language section is structured by country. This would not have been possible for the Yiddish section because of boundary changes, migration by the poets, etc. and it is, therefore, alphabetical. The Hebrew section follows the same principle for similar reasons, though most of the poets live in Israel. The "other languages" section is what it says. Thus, for example, the French section contains poets from seven countries.

These four sections, of about equal length, are in fact four separate anthologies, representing separate and highly developed literary traditions. But at the same time they are bound together by their common Jewish heritage. In editing each of these sections we have attempted to present a selection that is balanced and representative and that gives equal weight to the now-established canon of the poets writing in the first four decades of this century and to the new and as yet lesser known work of contemporaries writing since 1950. We have also been open to the work of young poets, many of whom are represented in an anthology for the first time.

VOICES WITHIN THE ARK

As readers of Dante, Milton or S. Y. Agnon are well aware, a writer who can make convincing use of a religious tradition is blessed indeed. In our time it is increasingly difficult for writers to have the sense that they belong to a tradition. Consequently they are unable to commit themselves to a symbolic system which can serve their writing as a continual spring of inspiration. While all of the poets included in this anthology are a product of our fragmented age, most of them have found, in varying degrees, a sense of attachment to the ancient Jewish tradition that is their own heritage. Making use of the tradition in this fashion is exactly what it was intended for. The existence of this book should serve as proof in itself that for a great many poets worldwide, who are located in very different cultures, it is possible to find much in the Jewish religious tradition that they can make good use of.

One example may demonstrate the highly original techniques that have been used to approach this ancient material, in order to make it alive for the poet and his generation. Consider the biblical story of the binding of Isaac, known as the *Akedah,* in which Abraham is prepared to obey the command of the Lord that he take his son Isaac and sacrifice him on Mount Moriah. A great many interpretations have been given to explain this episode, and this variety is reflected in the different approaches of the nine poets in this anthology who have chosen to reconsider this story.

Stanley Burnshaw's poem "Isaac" is unique because of the distance Burnshaw permits himself from the biblical tale. He begins as if he were an anthropologist describing "this tribe." Then he both observes and at the same time becomes drawn into the fascination when "Even my own father" is caught up in "the blind obsessive tale." It is instructive to compare this Isaac with the version of other poets. Three were written by Israeli poets, Amir Gilboa, Haim Guri and Matti Megged, and three by young American poets, Chana Bloch, Barry Holtz and Henry Abramovitch, one by the Scottish poet A. C. Jacobs, and one by the Canadian poet Leonard Cohen. Each version casts light on a new aspect of this key biblical tale. Gilboa relates the story to the Holocaust, while Megged ties it to the Israeli wars, and Guri sees in it a curse that has lasted throughout the generations because "That hour/He bequeathed to his descendants/Still to be born/A knife/In the heart."

A. C. Jacobs' "Isaac" reminds us that Abraham was the father of Ishmael as well as of Isaac.* This way Jacobs manages to achieve a voice that has ancient and modern echoes at the same time, and thus reflects the present conflict in Israel in the biblical mirror. This is similar to the

*It is interesting to note that in the Koran it is Ishmael, not Isaac, who accompanies Abraham to Mount Moriah.

objective of Leonard Cohen in his striking poem that also succeeds equally well as a song, "Story of Isaac." In introducing this song Cohen has said: "This song ... is about those who would sacrifice one generation on behalf of another one."

Chana Bloch, on the other hand, sees in Abraham's role in the *Akedah* a metaphoric rehearsal of "the Death of an Only Son," while Isaac "waits as women wait." In this way the original tale is both abstracted and yet made more immediate at the same time. For his part, Barry Holtz seeks to link the binding of Isaac to the birthright stolen by Isaac's son, Jacob, and in the poem "Psalm of the Jealous God" Henry Abramovitch sees evidence that the promise of God to Abraham was never fulfilled and asks "Are not his sons/still slaughtered/under the psalm/of the jealous god?"

All of these poems operate in the midrashic tradition, freely interpreting the biblical tale according to their own views of it. And Gilboa's "Isaac" even demonstrates use of the Kabbalistic interpretations of the story of Isaac, in which he describes Isaac's hand in Abraham's as they climb up Mount Moriah, "my right hand in his left." In the Kabbalah, the body of Jewish mystical texts, the right symbolizes the attribute of God's Mercy, while the left symbolizes the attribute of Justice. In bringing Isaac to be sacrificed Abraham thus demonstrates the attribute of Justice, which is often required to be harsh, and Isaac, of course, represents the attribute of Mercy. In Gilboa's image these two attributes are bound together, "my right hand in his left." It is in this symbolic shorthand that many of the poets included in this anthology write, able to condense meaning into the resonant symbols they make use of.

By the very nature of this collection it became necessary for the editors to establish a working criteria for the purpose of distinguishing who is a Jewish poet. We did not relish the position of having to operate like a *Beit Din,* a rabbinic court of justice, in order to make such a determination. By and large there was no difficulty—almost all of the poets included were born Jewish according to the *Halakah,* the traditional Law. But a few difficult cases did arise. There were, for example, some poets whose sole Jewish parent was their father rather than their mother, as called for by Jewish law. Obviously such poets deserve inclusion.

On the other hand, we were faced with the difficult issue of conversion away from Judaism by a number of important poets who had been born as Jews. In these cases our first impulse was to exclude these poets altogether, for they conflicted with what had become our elementary rule of thumb: that we include poets who identify themselves as Jews. Ironically, the rabbinical court would have judged them still to be Jewish—for once born a Jew, one always remains a Jew, according to the traditional Law. On closer inspection of individual cases, however, it became apparent that a rigid position on our part could well be in error. Instead we decided to work on a case-by-case basis. A very fine poet such as Joseph Brodsky, who converted to Christianity, had already demonstrated his identification with the Jewish people in the poem "A Jewish Cemetery near Leningrad." We were able to contact Mr. Brodsky directly and he was quite clear about his desire to be included in this book. On the other hand, Boris Pasternak, certainly one of this century's most important poets, also became a convert to Christianity, but did not demonstrate in his poetry any attraction to Jewish themes, and we felt for this reason that it would not be appropriate to include his work in this particular collection. Nor did we seek out poets known to have a remote Jewish ancestry. Once again the rule of thumb was the poet's self-identity.

It may also be useful to address the issue of the Jewish content of the selections in this book. Even a casual reader will soon perceive that this ranges from a total preoccupation with Jewish themes on the part of some poets, such as Edmond Jabès, Rose Ausländer, and Nelly Sachs, to none whatsoever on the part of others, such as Miklós Radnóti (despite the fact that his last poems were recovered from the mass grave he was killed in by the Nazis), Tristan Tzara, and Alejandra Pizarnik. More often it is a question of emphasis: perhaps half of Paul Celan's hermetic poems make use of Jewish imagery; more than half of those of Yehuda Amichai are concerned with Jewish issues and imagery; and it is the dominant theme in the poetry of Else Lasker-Schüler.

In fact, it may appear that the poets most deeply involved in a Jewish cultural context, i.e. those writing in Hebrew and Yiddish (and in such singularly Jewish dialects as Judezmo and Judeo-Romanesque), are the least committed to their Jewish heritage, and of course that would be a false impression. To an Israeli reader any poet who expresses himself in Hebrew, even on a theme that might not be at all specifically Jewish, may, by the use of the Hebrew language with its perpetual link to the language of the Bible, affirm his link to a tradition that does not overtly appear in his writings. In addition these poets usually live in a cultural context that is predominantly Jewish. They do not need to constantly reaffirm their Jewish ties, and in such cases it became obvious that language (and, of course, quality) be the determinant rather than theme.

On the other hand, in the cases of those poets writing in the languages of the Diaspora, who must reaffirm their ties to the Jewish tradition in order for such a tie to exist, theme became the central determinant. Of course this matter of theme can be widely interpreted. Not only themes based on the laws and legends of the Bible and the subsequent sacred books were appropriate, but also those secular themes based on superstitions and customs of various Jewish communities. And of course no anthology of Jewish poetry published in the last quarter of the twentieth century can fail to reflect the Nazi Holocaust and the creation of the state of Israel, the two matrix events of Jewish history since the Dispersion. Considering these events, it is no wonder that there has been a poetic resurgence in the last thirty years—the People of the Book continuing to obey the injunction of the Psalmist: "Sing unto the Lord a new song."

It should be apparent that with the exception of the poems in the English-language section of this book, all of the remaining poems included are translations. While a substantial loss inevitably occurs whenever a poem is translated from its original language, we believe that this considerable body of translations affirms the profound service translation performs in making available literatures that would otherwise be completely lost to those unfamiliar with the original languages. One gratifying modern development is the large number of poets who are also translators, as is the case with a great many of the translations in this anthology. The primary goal of these translators, by and large, has been to create an authentic poem in English that is as close as possible to the original without sacrificing the poetic necessities of the new language. And our intention as editors has been to limit our choices only to those poems that we feel have succeeded in carrying into English the essential sense and voice of the original poet as well as existing as authentic and independent poems in their own right.

At this point it should be apparent that the editors were compelled, of necessity, to be flexible in the criteria used to determine both the poets to be included and the nature of their selections in this book. The one standard, however, which we hope we have rigidly adhered to is that of the quality of the original poems and translations which we have selected. As much as possible we have attempted to choose poems which are both representative of their author's expression of his or her Jewish heritage, whatever the relative commitment to this heritage, and at the same time are representative of the finest work of each particular poet.

Readers familiar with current trends in modern poetry around the world are aware that modern poets have evolved something of a universal language whose primary symbols are images. These images lend themselves to translation and also make it possible for a poet such as Yehuda Amichai to preserve his voice in translation even though it is being conveyed by several different translators. All in all, we feel quite fortunate in having been able to utilize the talents and dedication of the many translators who have contributed to this anthology, and we wish to acknowledge their efforts, without which this book could not exist.

In addition to the superb efforts of the translators, our work has been assisted immeasurably by the support and advice of a large number of specialists more familiar with the poets and poetry of some of the individual languages and countries from which they derive than any pair of editors ever could be. We would like to acknowledge their assistance in the list that follows.

We are especially grateful to Walter Meade of Avon Books, for the unfailing support he has given this project from its inception. We would also like to give special thanks to Laya Firestone, Ruth Wisse, and Edouard Roditi, the authors of the lucid Introductions to the Hebrew, Yiddish, and Other Languages sections, respectively. Special thanks are also due to Shirley Kaufman, Gabriel Preil, Shlomo Vinner, and Ruth Whitman for their invaluable contributions to the Hebrew and/or Yiddish sections of this book; and to Shmuel Moreh, Edouard Roditi, and Daniel Weissbort for their considerable assistance in the Other Languages section.

In addition, we would like to give our grateful thanks to the following people, who generously assisted us in this project: M. Avidom of ACUM, Ltd., Yehuda Amichai, Willis Barnstone, Keith Bosley, Nilli Cohen of the Institute for the Translation of Hebrew Literature, Barbara Cort, Moshe Dor, Marcia Falk, Nina and Musa Farhi, Robert Friend, Karl Gay, Jeremy Garber, Emery George, George Gomöri, Yitzhak Greenfield, Michael Hamburger, James Hogan, A. C. Jacobs, Edward Johnson, Ruben Kanalenstein, the Khanem family, Isaac Komem, Francis Landy, Gabriel Levin, Stephen Levy, Yael Lotan, David Meltzer, Robert Mezey, Dan Miron, Stephen Mitchell, Aleksander Nejgebauer, Joachim Neugroschel, Ruth Nevo, Naomi Nir, Dov Noy, Ewald Osers, Poets and Writers, Inc., Jennifer Rankin, Nessa Rapoport, Mira Reich, Rabbi Jack Reimer, Brenda Rudolf, H. C. and E. Rudolf, Nelly Sabin, Tsila Schwartz, Myra Glazer Schotz, Richard Siegel, Michael Strassfeld, Mary Ann Steiner, John Swanson, Yishai Tobin, Hava Vinner, Manfred Winkler, Mary Zilzer, Linda Zisquit, and Harry Zohn.

Thanks are also due to the University of Missouri-St. Louis for a Summer Research Fellowship that assisted in the editing of this book.

Howard Schwartz
Anthony Rudolf

I *Hebrew*

Introduction to Book I
by Laya Firestone

In the last century, modern Hebrew poetry has undergone dramatic change and development, reflecting the profound physical and spiritual upheaval experienced by the Jewish people. The revival of the Hebrew language as a *spoken* tongue after more than two thousand years represents the most striking development affecting Hebrew literature. Building on the wealth of a literary tradition developed over centuries, the modern literature draws from biblical, mishnaic, rabbinic, and liturgical Hebrew, as well as from religious and secular poetry and prose of the Middle Ages. Yet the transition from a sacred language to one that could be used in the marketplace required an expanded vocabulary and a deep commitment to the rebirth of the language.

Eliezer Ben Yehuda, settling in Palestine in 1881, made Hebrew speech a national goal, convinced that a living Hebrew was essential for the political and cultural rebirth of the Jewish nation. The struggle to expand the limited Hebrew vocabulary and to establish Hebrew as the primary spoken language took place as Zionist leaders sought to rebuild the Jewish national homeland. The dual commitment to the Hebrew language and to the homeland reflected the urgent need to build a revised Jewish identity during a period of chaos beginning with the Eastern European pogroms and ending with Hitler's Final Solution—the destruction of European Jewry. The historical events of this critical period have contributed significantly to Hebrew literature, both in language and content, creating a new body of Hebrew prose and poetry.

The beginnings of modern Hebrew literature date back to the Haskalah (Enlightenment), the period from 1780 to 1880 in which a fierce campaign was waged to modernize the traditional Jew, to divest him of his seemingly outdated garb of piety and provincialism and clothe him instead in modern European culture. Early Haskalah writers willingly abandoned the constrictions of rabbinical culture for a secular culture they considered to be far more humane and rational. Leading poets during this period were Naftali Herz Wessely, Efraim Luzzato, Shalom Cohen, Shlomo Levinson, Adam HaCohen, Meir Letteris, Adam H. Lebenson, Micha J. Lebenson, and Judah Leib Gordon, the outstanding literary figure of the Russian Haskalah.

As with the prose, the poetry of the Haskalah is generally marred by excessive rhetoric, a pseudo-biblical style, overintellectualization and the driving impulse to preach the new gospel of secularism. With the exception of some genuinely lyrical poetry by Efraim Luzzato of Italy or Micha J. Lebenson of Russia, the poetry has little aesthetic value on its own and is judged more for its historical significance than its literary merit.

Beginning with Hayim Nachman Bialik and Shaul Tchernichovsky, a genuine modern Hebrew poetry emerges, poetry capable of withstanding the test of generations. Since the twentieth century, the period which the anthology at hand covers, a series of trends and countertrends in poetic expression can be traced, often with one or two outstanding names dominating the latest developments in poetry.

Such was the case with Bialik and Tchnernichovsky, who broke from the Haskalah tendency to use literature for expounding social doctrine and treated the poem itself as an aesthetic whole. Both Bialik and Tchernichovsky were hailed in their time as national poets singing the soul of the Jewish people, expressing the social unrest and unstable situation of Jews in Europe at the turn of the century. Yet, as contemporary Hebrew critics beginning with Baruch Kurzweil have pointed out, and as the poems of this anthology clearly demonstrate, their poetry in its pure lyricism transcends the boundary of nationalism.

Bialik's poetry, mostly written in Russia before his emigration to Palestine, and all in the European Ashkenazic pronunciation,* portrays a solitary man pained by spiritual loss and filled with longing. His early background in traditional Judaism, and his familiarity with the extensive Hebrew literary tradition, enabled Bialik to create a poem in a biblical tone or rhythm while preserving his singular voice. Thus, for example, his poem "When the Days Grow Long" echoes the style of ancient prophetic

*The Hebrew Committee, founded in Jerusalem in 1890 to supervise the development of the Hebrew Language, attempted to preserve the Oriental qualities of the language, establishing Sephardic as the standard pronunciation for spoken Hebrew. Bialik, like many other European-born Hebrew writers, found this a difficult transition, and the poetry that had been written in the old country often lost some of its musical rhythm when rendered in the Sephardic pronunciation.

judgment, even as it captures a modern tone of ennui and restless discontent:

When the days grow long, each one an eternity,
Each one as alike as yesterday and the day before it,
Just days, without much pleasure and filled with dullness,
And men and animals are seized by boredom,
A man will go out at sunset to walk on the seashore,
And see that the sea has not fled,
And he will yawn,
And go to the Jordan, and it will not flow back,
And he will yawn,
And see the Pleiades and Orion, not budging from their places,
And he will yawn;
And men and animals will sit, bored, together,
With their lives weighing heavily upon them,
And men will pluck the hairs of their head in distraction,
And cats will lose their whiskers.

For Bialik, the reality of emigrating to Palestine did not act as a vital source of poetic inspiration. After his earlier poetry calling for a national rebirth, Bialik observed the development of poetry in Palestine without making a major new contribution to it, as if leading the people to the promised land without himself being able to taste of its fruit. Following several years of elegiac poetry of deep despair, Bialik's poetry terminated in a silence that lasted for the rest of his life, with the exception of a handful of poems. Bialik explained his long poetic silence by saying that he had passed his "Song of Songs period" and had "entered upon that of Proverbs and Ecclesiastes—that is to say, the period of scientific matters and practical affairs."*

Although Bialik was still regarded as the national poet and on occasion functioned as cultural ambassador for Palestinian Jewry, his later poetry reflects a need for personal expression divorced from national interest. In the poem "After my Death," Bialik conveys the sense of his unfulfilled expressive powers, as though the best had been left unsaid:

After I am dead
Say this at my funeral:

There was a man who exists no more.

That man died before his time
And his life's song was broken off halfway.
O, he had one more poem
And that poem has been lost
For ever.

*Ovadyahu, Mordecai, *Bialik Speaks: Words from the Poet's Lips, Clues to the Man,* p. 87. New York, Herzl Press, 1969.

Shaul Tchernichovsky, less familiar with the overall Hebrew literary past than Bialik, adapted many elements from Western literature to Hebrew poetry, both in form (sonnets, ballads, idylls, and epics) and content. His fascination for Canaanite ritual and customs manifested itself in many poems in which he praised the primitive energy underlying this and other ancient cultures. This predilection, reminiscent of the Haskalah's irreverence and even repudiation of Jewish rabbinic tradition, earned him the title of "Pagan" among some, and the reputation as an influential predecessor of the "Canaanites."*

Tchernichovsky's exploration of pagan roots, however, in no way severed his relation to the Jewish tradition in literature as did the Canaanites. His commitment to the total Jewish historical experience, both in the Diaspora and Palestine, is indicated repeatedly, especially in his later works. Tchernichovsky's immigration to Israel for the last ten years of his life, unlike that of Bialik, contributed greatly to his body of poetry—by innovation in speech and rhythm and adaptability to the Sephardic pronunciation, as well as by his spirited representations of the communal efforts during the early pioneering experience of the country.

Along with Bialik and Tchernichovsky, there were other less well known poets who made the transition from the Eastern European culture to the one then developing in Palestine. Among them were Jakov Fichman, who wrote subdued lyrical verses on love, the Palestinian landscape, and various biblical subjects, of which two poems, "Eve" and "Abishag," are represented in this volume. Both, interestingly, are written from a female perspective. The poem "Abishag" elaborates on the brief reference in Kings I:2-4 to the beautiful virgin brought to warm King David in his old age. In short couplets, Fichman empathetically conveys the bittersweet passion of the young girl for the king.

Another poet of this generation was Yehuda Karni, whose popularity has increased with time, no doubt due to his early Expressionist leanings. Karni wrote of the profound effect of the landscape upon him, particularly of Jerusalem:

The hills of Zion
poured loftiness into me,
and her valleys—
depth.

*This group of poets, which formed in Israel after the Second World War, was preoccupied with ancient Canaanite and Near Eastern myth and an ideology that viewed Israel as a nation that must relinquish its Jewishness in order to reintegrate itself into the Middle Eastern culture from which it arose. Among the poets were Yonathan Ratosh, the outstanding spokesman for this controversial group, Aharon Amir, and Haim Guri at the start of his poetic career.

From an eagle
flying in the sky
like an orphan
I learned
loneliness.

I. Z. Rimon was also a contemporary of Bialik and his generation and is known primarily for his mystical and often ecstatic poetry. The lyrical poetry of Jakov Steinberg, a younger contemporary of Bialik, is deeply personal, pessimistic—especially in his earlier work—and frequently veiled in paradox. Other poets of this period whom it was not possible to represent are Zalman Shneur, Yakov Cahan, David Shimoni, and Avigdor Hameiri.

The poetry of Rav Abraham Isaac Kook, the first Chief Rabbi of Palestine, represents a category of liturgical poetry set apart from the developing Palestinian poetry of the day. Writing in a medieval style reminiscent of Yehuda Halevi's religious poetry, Rav Kook expressed his longing for God and mystical perception of the universe:

The first one drew me with his rope
Into his palatial abode,
And I listened to his song
From the strings of his violin.

The sea of knowledge rages,
Its waves beat in me,
Thought mounts upon thought, like a wall,
And God stands above it.

In all cases, the Hebrew poets mentioned immigrated to Palestine, and others yet to be mentioned either immigrated to or were born there. However, one should note the important few who continued to write Hebrew poetry while living in the Diaspora. Poets such as David Vogel, Hayim Lenski, and Berl Pomerantz in Europe, and Hillel Bavli, Ephraim Lissitsky, M. Feinstein, N. B. Silkiner, and Eisig Silberschlag in the United States, maintained strong bonds with Hebrew, despite their distance from the spoken language in Palestine and subsequently Israel. Lenski's poem "Language of Ancients" exudes love and awe for the Hebrew language:

Language of ancients, of Hayman, Halevi,
Some miracle made you mine, gentle-voiced Queen.
Your cadences kindled my soul, and your words
Burnt my lips like the kisses of passionate lovers.

Virtually all of the major American Hebrew poets, except Gabriel Preil, immigrated to Israel. Among these poets were Shimon Halkin, Israel Efros, Noah Stern, and Abraham Regelson.

Once in Palestine many of the early immigrants responded to the new conditions with the idealism necessary to cope with the hardships of a strange environment. Yet even with a commitment to pioneering goals and a romanticization of the stark landscape, there remained an inevitable nostalgia for the families, experiences and traditions that were forever left behind. The ideal of the pioneer was essential for survival, yet it presented small consolation when measured against the intensity of the longing of a people severed from the culture that had evolved over centuries in exile.

The poetry of this early settlement period is varied, fluctuating between memories of the past, realities of the present, and dreams of the future. There remains also, as we have seen with Bialik, a continued tension in the poetry between the personal voice of the poet and the national voice of the poet speaking as prophet. Each poet is forced to take a stand on this significant and continuing issue in modern Hebrew poetry. The varying responses to this question in the twentieth century profoundly affected the direction in which poetry developed.

The poetry of David Vogel poignantly expresses the tragic dilemma of the transitional Jew. Vogel himself spent only two years in Palestine, traveling from there to Berlin and Paris and finally to his death in a concentration camp. Grief over an irretrievable past is expressed succinctly by Vogel in a modern idiom which was influenced by current trends in Russian and German poetry. In the free-verse poem "Our Childhood Spilled into Our Hearts," for example, Vogel uses only a few brushstrokes to convey his personal anguish. His use of the first person plural rather than singular in this and other poems should be noted, as he clearly spoke for many others besides himself:

The Talmud chant,
Heavy with dreams and longing,
Still rises at times,
Unsought, to our lips.

We wander through life
Weeping,
With empty palms
Held out shaking
To every passer-by.

Again, in "Plain Humble Letters," Vogel is alone, dwelling on the past:

And now I speak strange words
Every night
To the surprised city,
Which doesn't know I am talking inwardly to you,
My sister, hidden
In Bessarabian evenings.

Another poet of the early settlement, Rachel Bluwstein, who came to be known simply as "Rachel," embodied the ideals of the early pioneer woman while her poetry served as lyrics for many popular folksongs. Giving up her study of art in Russia, Rachel immigrated to Palestine and committed herself to a pioneering life, making a deep and vital connection to the historic past of the biblical culture. This bond is clearly expressed in her poem "Rachel," in which the ancestor Rachel and the poetess merge in identification:

> For her blood runs in my blood
> and her voice sings in me.
> Rachel, who pastured the flocks of Laban;
> Rachel, the mother of the mother.
>
> And that is why the house is narrow for me,
> and the city foreign,
> for her veil used to flutter
> in the desert wind.

Most of Rachel's poetry was written in the last few years of her life, when, suffering from consumption, she was forced to abandon the rural life she loved. In "My White Book of Poems," Rachel reveals her sense of isolation and grief, while realizing that her despair was a major source of her inspiration:

> Hidden things not revealed to a friend
> have been revealed,
> that which was sealed in me with fire
> has been laid bare,
>
> and the grief of a heart
> going under
> everyone can now
> calmly finger.

During the same period, Yitzhak Lamdan adopted the mission of expressing the national consciousness, feeling Jewish survival itself to be at stake. Lamdan, who had witnessed pogroms before immigrating, is best known for the long poem "Massada," a selection from which appears in this anthology. In this poem he links the symbol of the mountain fortress, where Jews gave their lives in the struggle against the Romans, with contemporary Jewish experience, which once again demanded a fight for survival. This Expressionist poem became a classic for the Chalutz (pioneer) movement, arming a generation of Zionists with moral fervor.

Also at this time, Avraham Ben-Yitzhak introduced the modernist influences of Rilke, Valéry, and others, in a poetry with no apparent national message or expressions concerning the developing pioneer culture. Ben-Yitzhak's work, which was limited to eleven poems published during his lifetime and only a few discovered and published after his death, reveal him to be a master of style and imagery, conveying a heightened sense of awareness in which moments and perceptions become so crystallized that expression itself appears to be superfluous. His final poem "Blessed Are Those Who Sow and Do Not Reap," published in 1928 after a twelve-year silence, evokes passages from the Psalms ("They who sow in tears, shall reap in joy," Psalm 22) but skilfully manipulates them into paradoxes to suggest that the joyful shall be those who do *not* reap, those whose "hearts cry out in deserts and on whose lips silence blossoms." "Blessed are they," he says with resolve, undoubtedly including himself among them, "for they will be taken into the heart of the world/Wrapped in a cloak of unremembrance/Forever remaining without speech."

Another poet of this pioneering period was Shin Shalom, from a distinguished line of Hasidic rabbis, who brought mystical imagery into his poetry, which is both national and personal. The poem "Zohar," translated here as "Splendor," itself conjures up the heritage contained in the Kabbalistic work of that name. Yocheved Bat-Miriam, also of a Hasidic background, evoked nostalgia for the past in her poetry, which was influenced by Russian versification; Esther Raab is noted for her landscape imagery, while Mordecai Temkin's poetry resonates with a devotional, psalmlike quality and Ezra Zussman, who was first noted for his Russian poetry, later gained a reputation as a sensitive Hebrew poet and critic.

Most influential during this Palestinian period were Avraham Shlonsky, a leader of the new literary left, and Nathan Alterman and Leah Goldberg. Introducing a distinctively modern idiom, Shlonsky often brought neologisms, innovative grammatical forms, and even slang into poetic diction in an attempt to break away from the literary classicism of Bialik and his generation. A prolific writer and translator, Shlonsky developed sophisticated techniques, experimenting with rhythm and rhyme as the themes of his poetry also moved between expressions of the creative pioneer roadbuilder (as in the poem "Toil") and that of the secularized, urban dweller, between the comfort of childhood and the realities and horrors of modern life.

As with Shlonsky, Alterman's innovations in style, rhythm, and idiom greatly expanded the poetic flexibility of the Hebrew language, bringing the modern "spoken" tongue into the literary realm. The abundant use of imagery and symbolism and manipulation of meter and rhythm to achieve desired effects characterize Alterman's poetry. Like Bialik, Alterman's influence and popularity persisted despite attacks launched against him by younger, rebellious poets, particularly by Natan

Zach. Many of Alterman's poems have been set to music and are now contemporary favorites sung by popular singers such as Hava Alberstein. The balladlike quality of many of Alterman's poems lend themselves to such musical adaptation.*

The poetry of Leah Goldberg, modern in its understated tone, rejects any rhetorical flourishes or stylistic embellishments. Expressed simply, even starkly, her poetry captures a tone of controlled despair and disillusionment which represents a universal loss of faith as much as her own personal vision. In "Heavenly Jerusalem, Jerusalem of the Earth," the city that had been referred to from biblical times as the "city of the faithful" becomes a means for Goldberg to express the modern condition:

People are walking in the counterfeit city
whose heavens passed like shadows,
and no one trembles.
Sloping lanes conceal
the greatness of her past.

The children of the poor
sing with indifferent voices:
"David, King of Israel, lives and is."

Goldberg's later poems are meditations on silence, and like the poet she admired, Avraham Ben-Yitzhak, she also virtually stopped writing poetry toward the end of her life.

Uri Zvi Greenberg was also a leading poet of the Palestinian period, and he is still writing today in his own unique style. Faced with the everpresent Jewish conflict of speaking in a personal voice or a national one, Greenberg opted for the latter, abandoning the restrained and often beautiful lyrical poetry of his early period to raise the banner of ultranationalist-messianic redemption. Most Hebrew critics agree that the later work usually gives way to a rhetorical style, arguing political dogma and ideology, while the early work is superior in literary quality. The poems represented in this anthology are thus largely drawn from the early period, in which the poet-prophet contemplates his own dilemmas.

The center of Hebrew literary activity had already been transplanted to Palestine for several decades as World War I was succeeded by World War II and the situation of European Jews degenerated from sporadic pogroms to the Holocaust itself. During this time, poets in Palestine were reacting to the destruction of European Jewry, while they fought, literally, for the establishment and survival of their own state.

The poems dealing with the Holocaust were varied, expressing mixed emotions of despair, helplessness, guilt, and rage. U. Z. Greenberg,

*Among contemporary Israeli poets, the poems of Yehuda Amichai and Nathan Yonathan, like those of Rachel and Alterman, have frequently been used as lyrics for popular songs.

A. L. Strauss, Abba Kovner, Amir Gilboa, and Dan Pagis are noted for their poetry on the Holocaust. Others also have attempted to approach this catastrophe, either explicitly or by allusion.

In Greenberg's poem "Homesong," we see a very personal response, although certainly it is not his only style of poetic expression concerning the Holocaust. In the poem, Greenberg returns to his original home, as so many other Israeli writers have done in their imaginative works—it being impossible to do so in reality. The sweetness of the initial dreamlike encounter gives way to the powerful suggestion of a brutal present:

She is silent, my martyred mother,
Her eyes rise against my face, not looking at me, but beyond.
I look behind her, behind my back, at the wall,
The hanging mirror is shrouded in a sheet
And below, a barrel of darkest water,
My father's prayer shawl floating in it
Its silver neckpiece gone.

A. L. Strauss's "Lament for the European Exile" expresses the pain of those who survived the slaughter:

Can I mourn?
I am an elegy.
Lament?
My mind is lamentation.
Can I rise
With death heavy on my limbs,
Or see
When Nothing hangs at my eyelash?
I will mourn and rise.
Your look will ask in my eyes
Atonement for your blood
At the hands of the world
That shed it.

Amir Gilboa, a representative of the new "Israeli" (post-1948) poets, came to Palestine as an illegal immigrant in 1937 after having witnessed the early effects of the Holocaust, in which his family ultimately perished. In the poem "Isaac," Gilboa speaks in the first person, identifying himself with the biblical character Isaac and the motif of the sacrifice. Beginning first as a child's account of a walk with his father, we are then presented with the suggestion of violence:

A knife flashed between the trees like lightning
and I was afraid, for my eyes
saw the blood on the leaves.

Isaac calls to his father, mixing the urgent and the mundane:

Father, Father, hurry to save Isaac
so that no one will be missing
at the next meal.

But, in an ironic twist, the father answers, "I am the one who is slain, my son." This poem can be read simultaneously on several levels and has generally been regarded as an allegory of the Holocaust, with the father representing the destroyed European Jewry, and the son the helpless Jews watching from the outside. Gilboa's strength in this and the other biblical poems represented here derives from the sense of immediacy and identification with the experience. At the same time, there is the slight distance of a narrator relating a dream nightmare—" And I woke up./ And there was no blood left/in my right hand."

Abba Kovner, a leader of the Jewish resistance in the forests surrounding Vilna who settled in Israel in 1946, rechannels his experience and loss in his poetry. Even in the love poem selected for this anthology, one can read underlying horror in the poet's background:

Rain
it's just rain! like an oath I repeat
for the third time. Not your blood.

Dan Pagis, also a Holocaust survivor, equates the destruction of European Jewry with the archetypal murder of Cain's slaying of Abel:

here in this transport
i eve
and abel my son
if you should see my older son
cain son of man
tell him that i

Haim Guri, a native Israeli, along with Tuvia Ruebner, Avner Treinin, Avraham Huss, Anadad Eldan, Yehuda Amichai, and many others fought in the War of Independence. He is often cited as a representative voice for the Palmach generation.* Guri's commitment to Socialist Zionist ideology and his dedication to the national cause are expressed in his early work. In "My Samsons," for example, Guri uses the biblical hero Samson to represent the contemporary Israeli soldiers returning from war:

Behold, my Samsons are returning, no harshness in their glance;
They are returning to me from Gath,
Now that the firing has ended.

*The Palmach was the permanently mobilized striking force of the illegal pre-State army (Haganah) and later, until its dissolution, part of the Israel Defense Forces.

Guri's poetry, which has maintained a consistently high level, moves from the collective plural in his early work to a more personal voice, symbolizing the change experienced by many Israelis as the postwar disillusionment set in.

The reaction in the literature of the late '50s and the '60s against the confidence in ideological values that existed in the previous period has been described by the contemporary Hebrew critic Shimon Sandbank as "the withdrawal from certainty."* The trend against the versification of poets such as Shlonsky and Alterman was inseparable from the ambivalence and alienation that affected the succeeding generation. This general movement from a collective voice to a purely personal one began in the 1950s with the vehement rejection of these influential poets, whose style was criticized as being overly mechanical and regularized, even "inauthentic." Yehuda Amichai and Natan Zach were at the forefront of this avant-garde movement, articulating a position held by a generation of younger poets who were experiencing the existential anxiety that had rocked European literature two decades before. Among the participants in this "New Wave" were Tuvia Ruebner, Dan Pagis, Dahlia Ravikovitch, and David Rokeah. These new poets replaced the national literary figures of the previous periods, Bialik, Shlonsky, and Alterman, with less familiar models from the same period, such as David Vogel, Yehuda Karni, and Hayim Lenski, admiring them for their qualities of understatement, irony, prosaic diction, and use of free verse.

It was in the same spirit of Shlonsky and Alterman's rebellion against Bialik that Amichai and Zach broke from the leading Palestinian poets—ironically, Shlonsky and Alterman themselves. Even more radical than the first break, the avant-garde movement of the '50s was the beginning of a total turning away from ideological content. The poet as an individual, perceiving the world from very human, everyday dimensions, replaced the socially minded national poet.

In an interview in *The Jerusalem Post,* the poet considered by many to be not only the outstanding living poet in Israel today but one of international stature, Yehuda Amichai, expressed his ideas about the purpose of poetry and its relationship to the world:

> I believe the purpose of poetry is to help you live with your own reality, and that means that nothing must be excluded. Poetry to me is a kind of remedy. It's never a poison, it's not escapist, it's not a drug. It's more like an antidote. A horse is used to produce antitetanus vaccine. It goes through tetanus and recovers and

*Shimon Sandbank, "Contemporary Israeli Literature: The Withdrawal from Certainty," *Contemporary Israeli Literature: An Anthology,* E. Anderson, ed. (Philadelphia, Jewish Publication Society, 1977).

> becomes immune. And from the blood of the horse the serum is made. In the same way the poet uses the matter of his life to cure himself of the bad things in life, and this means that poetry has concentrated doses of disease, but also of its cure.*

Indeed, in Amichai's poetry, nothing is excluded. Biblical allusions and religious imagery drawn from his traditional Orthodox background are juxtaposed against the secular and commonplace. In the tradition of the Jewish medieval Spanish poets such as Yehuda Halevi, Ibn Ezra, Ibn Gabirol, and especially Shmuel Hanagid, whom he acknowledges as primary influences on his work, Amichai uses biblical phrases and liturgical rhythm, although often in a modern, antitraditional context.

Ancient and modern are united in Amichai's poetry as the realities of Israeli life blend with the underlying Jewish tradition in consistently original imagery. The resulting effect is a deep irony filled with humor and pathos. Yet, despite the irony, Amichai remains within a spiritual tradition that argues with God for justice. In the poem "Lament," for example, Amichai conveys a greater sense of God's betrayal of mankind than of his own loss of faith in God:

> And I won't speak
> of the cry of the orphans
> that reaches God's chair and from there
> makes the circle endless
> and godless.

A similar ironic tone is evident in the poetry of Natan Zach. Although Zach's colloquial tone is guarded against the display of any emotion, the emotion emerges—as if by default. His impulse to hold back from expressing pain, despair, or sentimentality creates an effective tension in his poetry that transmits intensity despite the simple phrasing and forthright rhymes. In the poem "In This Deep Darkness," Zach speaks in an untraditional yet religious vein to a God who, although He is never mentioned explicitly, nevertheless is the focus of attention. Even as Zach beseeches that God remember him, he himself does not forget the realities that make it almost impossible to establish such a relationship. Thus Zach's acute awareness negates that which he wants the most:

> Remember me among your flocks;
> remember me more than you remember all your orphans
> in this deep heavy darkness

*"A Way to Reality: An Interview with Yehuda Amichai Conducted by Howard Schwartz," *The Jerusalem Post Magazine,* February 17, 1978.

where I am lost more than an orphan,
more than a lamb, for my eyes are open
and I see how the blue darkens, I am not deceived:
I see how blood thickens, the voice stumbles. . . .

In some of his poetry, Zach appears to be directly continuing the Jewish tradition of analyzing biblical sentences, questioning and interpreting them, although he does so in a modern tone that is bewildered or disenchanted. The poem "As Sand," for example, reads as a modern poetic form of exegesis:

And yet it's explicitly said
as sand, which implies, of course,
the capacity for suffering.
Or maybe it's possible to imagine that
all was then permitted: and no words made
a difference any more.

It is ironic that the modern poets of the '50s and '60s used biblical themes in poetry, even when the philosophy they espoused was antitraditional, sometimes verging on the satirical. But by putting God and the Bible directly back into the frame of poetic reference, they reconnected modern poetry with its ancient roots—adding a new twist.

In contrast, the poet Zelda, who began publishing poetry late in life, deals directly with traditional material without injecting irony. Instead, she gives the ancient religious aspirations a pure and sensitive expression. In the poem "With My Grandfather," for example, Zelda directly and unaffectedly relates the biblical character of Abraham to her own grandfather:

Like our father Abraham
who counted stars at night,
who called out to his Creator
from the furnace,
who bound his own son
on the altar—
so was my grandfather.

During this period of the late 1950s and early 1960s, along with varied expressions ranging from the devotional to the nontraditional, external influences also became more prevalent. American and English poetry in particular, including poets such as Wallace Stevens, W. H. Auden, and T. S. Eliot, exerted considerable impact on the sensibility of the younger generation.

Writing both in Hebrew and Yiddish while living in New York, Gabriel Preil achieved a significant position in the Israeli literary world at this time. Recognized as an important innovator in theme, tone, image, and style, Preil used varied techniques with no fixed meter or form. The American landscape and history are a deeply rooted element in his work, and American poets such as Walt Whitman, Carl Sandburg, and Wallace Stevens have influenced him, as have the Yiddish poet Jacob Glatstein and Hebrew poets such as David Vogel. In turn, Preil's poetry injected these influences into the modern idiom of Hebrew poetry, even as he moved beyond them in his own direction. His style and range of subject is broad, yet distinctly personal, and he is bound neither to Jewish subject matter nor to the rejection of it. Preil responds lyrically and imagistically to fleeting moments, memories, and landscapes. In the poem "Autumn Music," for example, Preil demonstrates his openness to varied stimuli—the quality of an autumn in Jerusalem, as well as the music of Debussy and Chopin:

> Jerusalem's autumn has prepared a text
> clear and unclear, detailed and vague.
> I survey passages and discover its music
> that captures you with nets
> and frees you with the waters.
> This austere, seductive season
>
> is like you. It prepares me to receive you
> like a flickering prelude by Debussy,
> like the wandering fire of Chopin.

American-born T. Carmi also brought refinement to Hebrew poetry by combining American-English poetic influences with sensitivity to and scholarship in the Hebrew literary tradition. During the '60s other poets continued writing in the freer style prompted by non-Jewish influences. The quality of the subject and inner feeling of the poet determined the rhythm and structure of each poem.

Dahlia Ravikovitch's intensely personal poetry expressed the condition of anxiety produced in a fragmented world. In the poem "Hard Winter," for example, she touches the core of the modern situation while revealing her inner suffering:

> The little berry crackled in the blaze,
> and before its splendor vanished it wrapped itself in sadness.
> Rain and sun triumphed by turns, and we, in the house,
> Were afraid to think of what would happen to us.
> The bushes reddened from within, and the pool in hiding:
> Everyone set his mind on his own being.
> Yet in a moment when my own mind was scattered
> I saw how men are uprooted from the world.

Shimon Halkin, long recognized as a leading critic of Hebrew poetry, also began to gain recognition as a poet during this period. In many of his poems, he contemplates the passage into old age and ultimately death, a good example of which is represented in the poem "Do Not Accompany Me."

The highly intellectual poetry of Dan Pagis, which also emerged at this time, treats a variety of subjects in whatever style seemed most appropriate. In the majority of the selections represented in this anthology, Pagis develops various biblical references in a unique and compelling fashion, as for example "The Tower," referring to the legendary Tower of Babel, or "Brothers" and "Autobiography," both referring once again to Cain and Abel, using biblical archetypes in a poetical midrashic approach to convey his personal understanding of the world. In Pagis' poetry, the transition from the collective voice of the nation to the subjective voice of an individual seems to be complete. Along with the occasional use of biblical subject matter, the quality of the subjectively universal dominates Pagis' poetry.

Inevitably, the trend toward a personal idiom and colloquial expression which occurred in the '50s and '60s succumbed to the criticism of the younger generation. Traditional biblical references, used in an ironic sense by the previous generation, were often abandoned by the younger poets entirely. The use of central unifying metaphors and devices such as parallelism became less significant in the new fragmented, often surrealistic and nonlyrical poetry.

Avot Yeshurun, a poet of the 1940s and 1950s, who had contributed greatly to Hebrew poetry by coining new words and borrowing words from Yiddish, Arabic, and contemporary street language, became a poetic model for the younger generation. As with the preceding literary movement, the younger poets criticized their contemporary predecessors and expressed their new direction by means of literary magazines such as *Siman Kriah* and *Achshav.* Poets such as Moshe Dor, Anadad Eldan, Avner Treinin, Pinhas Sadeh, and Yona Wallach emphasized style and experimented lexically, as well as stylistically, to expand the poetic limits of the language.

Avner Treinin, a chemist by profession, has introduced the use of a scientific subject matter, language, and even a scientific sense of objectivity in some of his poems. The poem "Salmon Cycle," for example, takes place in "the boundary between the bitter water" and "the water of the river, o sweetness of beginning/ in whose existence I had already stopped believing." The poet Pinhas Sadeh, on the other hand, utilizes material derived from dreams, presenting it with surrealistic vividness:

> While walking at dusk in a strange city,
> he says to the girl, "Walk in front of me,
> bring me to the strange streets of evening,

among shadows and stone houses."
Vagrant lights, colors, names,
I don't know your name.

While some Israeli poets, of all ages, have been preoccupied with literary experimentation, other Israeli poets have been independently expressing their responses to a multifarious environment, without apparent concern for its impact on the literary development of Hebrew poetry. Although each of these poets represents an individual voice, together they illuminate the dynamics and tensions of Israeli life and culture. Falling into this broad and unclassifiable group of poets are Shlomo Vinner, Zerubavel Gilead, Hedva Harkavi, Aliza Shenhar, Matti Megged, Hayim Be'er, Manfred Winkler, and Hayim Naggid.

Among these poets, there appears to be a renewed sensitivity to the echoes of biblical and post-biblical themes, creating an awareness of the parallels between the past and present in all aspects of Israeli life. In the poem "Training on the Shore," for example, Shlomo Vinner juxtaposes God's promise to Abraham against the cruel realities of a nation fighting for survival:

Children
They teach to walk,
Soldiers
To crawl.
And between one lesson and another
They are shown the sand
God showed to Abraham
The hour He made him a nation
Wandering like sand.

The Israeli landscape—an object of longing for centuries—frequently provides the backdrop for Vinner's emotionally charged expressions of resignation to the inevitable facts of war, love ("the need to love is the need to leave and move on"), death, and unfulfilled dreams:

The hearts of old trees are heavy as stone
And longings that last too long
Turn into thorns in the valley
While dreams are exchanged
For piles of rusted scrap.

Matti Megged also draws parallels between the past and present, as in his poem "The Akedah,"* describing a soldier going off to war in a tank:

When I was led again to the Akedah
(Not on foot, not on donkey,
Imprisoned in an iron womb)

*The Akedah was the near-sacrifice of Isaac by Abraham, a subject frequently returned to by Israeli poets. Note, in addition to the poems of Amir Gilboa and Matti Megged, the poem "Isaac" by Haim Guri.

My father's hand
Did not hold my own.
Nor did the angel come
To hold back the knife.

Another young poet, Aliza Shenhar, who has devoted herself to the collection of Jewish folklore, makes use of her extensive knowledge of the Jewish legendary tradition. In the poem "The Drunkenness of Pain," for example, she reinterprets the ladder image of Jacob's dream, shedding further light on the original story while she imbues it with a highly personal quality:

A ladder ascends and descends
making itself holy
and self-afflicting.
The angels of God
whistle as they climb
its splintered rung.

Manfred Winkler, who came to Israel less than two decades ago, rapidly mastered the Hebrew language and now writes exclusively in it, despite the fact that his first two books were written and published in German. Primarily a lyrical poet, Winkler's work reflects the influence of the German poet Paul Celan, whom he has translated into Hebrew. In the poem "If My Hands Were Mute," Winkler's lyrical voice is apparent:

If my hands were mute
they would cover us with tents
and we would again
be born under the tree,
would taste of the sweet and bitter fruit and
lick the sweat of our soul,
would spit out our death
from the sweet and bitter fruit. . . .

Another highly lyrical poet is Hayim Naggid, whose poem "Like a Pearl" resonates musically:

One day the tired sea will open to the sun
Like the petals of the white rose,
And I'll lie in the hollow of the light
Like a snail in its shell .

Erez Biton, of Moroccan origin, represents the Sephardic branch of Israeli poetry, which as yet is still largely undeveloped. In expressing isolation from the mainstream of Israeli life, his poetry reflects the condition of the Sephardic Jew in Israel today.

In surveying twentieth-century Hebrew poetry, it becomes clear that the distinctive elements of Hebrew poetry remain constant. The inherently poetic nature of the Hebrew language, which can evoke multiple associations, continues to have a profound effect, as contemporary poets still tap the ancient literary wealth of the language for its resonant echoes. At the same time, there is a movement among Israeli poets to create a poetry that can transcend the boundaries of their small country and have a universal dimension.

As to what direction Hebrew poetry will take, it is difficult to predict, but exciting to imagine. Whether the course of contemporary poets will ultimately lead to a unified pattern or whether their diverse energy will scatter them remains for the interested reader to follow. Outside of the literary trend indicated in current magazines, the poets of the post-Amichai/Zach generation seem to be pursuing independent paths, open to multiple influences, and determined to find voices and perspectives that will illuminate not only the Jewish, but the human, condition.

Laya Firestone (Seghi) was born in Missouri, in 1947. Since then she has lived in Israel, Wisconsin, Illinois, and Canada before returning to live in Missouri. She has worked as a Hebrew teacher and translator. Her translations from the Hebrew have included poets such as Yehuda Amichai, Gabriel Preil, Shlomo Vinner, and Natan Zach.

Nathan Alterman

Nathan Alterman was born in 1910 in Warsaw and came to Palestine in 1925. Alterman wrote children's poems, translated the works of Racine, Shakespeare, and Moliere into Hebrew, and published a weekly column of responses to political and social events. His collected works were published in 1965, and an English-language selection in 1978. He died in 1970.

Tammuz

I go
towards the trumpets of light,
towards the sun on its summit of rock.
Bright guardian, watch over your flock
lost in the countries of drought.

Boulevards leap in a mane-like blaze.
How shall I raise
my eyes of drunkenness?
The girl of the skies
laughs in her nakedness.
Kiss her. Full on the mouth!

Because of her
the stars at night confound the astronomer.
Because of her
he weeps into his telescope.
I ask for nothing—nothing is my hope.
Therefore is the cyclamen so red
upon the path I tread.

As I step out
upon the empty platform, it is whirled
in glaring, tearing flight,
and I am hurled
heavily to my knees, commanded to cry out
in the multitudinous, deaf-as-thunder light.

Kneel and behold the tints
that set the days aflame,
its dazzling brothers ruling everywhere
when they climb the battlements
with their green braids
and open, like a city, our new day.

My land, the eye must look away
that dares to stare at you.
Like lightning, you reveal
name and place and thing.
No flattering
of voice or shade
has pampered you. The blue
giant has given you all his heart;
the teeth of the gold one hold—
the slaughtering blade.

The silence you have praised, stripped bare,
pierces, like a shriek, the air.
Only when you see your soul a sheep, storm-lost,
do you acknowledge it as yours.

The battles glitter on the distant plain.
The sun will not go out, sky crumbles in the dust.
In the far day, a dumbfounded pine
(my emerald soldier!) still runs, attacks, and thrusts.

Translated by Robert Friend

This Night

This night.
These alien walls.
Confrontation with silence.
The cautious life
of a tallow candle.

Only a rumor of unease like a chill wind
slides along broken-down fences
fondles unconscious quays
rocks bridges like a row of cradles.

In the empty square a shadow passes, disappears.
The tapping of its steps goes on alone.
Do not forget, do not forget, dust of the world
that human feet walk over you.

This night.
The tension of these walls.
A voice awakes and asks. A voice replies, falls silent.
Strange embrace. Light of an assumed smile.
The life and death
of a tallow candle.

Then the moon puts masks of wax
on windows, cold eyes, landscapes,
the market, turned to stone
in the monstrous outstretched arms
of cranes and wagons.

Poem About Your Face

If no one sees you, friend,
your face begins to die.
There's no way to stop it,
no way to save it.
Its chin pointed like a Polar bear's,
it dies.
You put in on a pillow,
you float with it along a wall,
you display it in a window
high against the starry air.

June nights are more fragile than glass and silence.
Streets stare like blue binoculars.
A fossil moon hangs above the town
world without wind or sound.

Midnight silence stands guard in the square
hushed in the vertigo of towers.
Prepare to give in to its cold touch.
There is no tumult, friend, that does not die in silence.

Your face twitched and died in the window
like a country gradually forgotten
masked by the dream of distance
along lonely moonlit roads.

While your eye still stared amazement
and awe ached at the corners of your mouth
you were lit to terror by God's image
reflected in his worlds of pallid stone.

To the Elephants

1

There's no end to wisdom, no mask for folly—
even your white hand is at fault.
I shall therefore get dressed in a plain summer suit
and go for a stroll
with the elephants of heaven.

For the day that is past and the storm at sea
and the lights cut down like a cedar
are floating towards them
the blue-haired, floating
towards them
soft-bellied.

They stand splay-eared, hearing the ram's horn
while the thunder pleads for repose.
They sink in the pink clay of the sunset
terrible and touching in their great strength.

So I'll sing them a song of whitening nights
a song of wide eyes without laughter or doves.
They will bend heavy heads, they will understand.
They are wise beasts,
the elephants.

And as they follow me—royal kings!
The virgin will fall on her face and cry:
The heavens are marching,
the heavens are marching,
and a little child shall lead them.

2
Beautiful,
oh, beautiful!
With a great roar they come out
with a beat of feet, a clapping of eyelashes.
We heard
we heard their huge body
rubbing against the wall.

We heard!
Look, from our sick beds this storm will snatch us.
Look
like a siege
heavy with murmur
they rise, place their hooves on our shoulder.

It's good to fall! To the beat of the storm.
They are dragging the street by its hair!
Good to open a hundred eyes
that were closed and enclosed in the body.

And to cry: Turn and strike!
Speak from the thunder!
Tear down the roofs of the years
raise a festival floor!
The meanest and lowest of all our sadnesses
shall sit in honor at the feast of revenge.

For our wild body, the blood groom,
still burns under cover of smiles.
His sorrow's tricked out with rings and bangles
but the forest rage glints in his eyes.

Ah, my prisoned king, humbled to dust,
led, silent, to slavery and slaughter.
How shall we bring him songs of praise
when his dark weeping gapes in our heart?

In his dream's lightning our sleep is shattered;
we fall, we are torn—like Sodom.
He bursts from within us as out of a prison
with a cry of wild love, with an axe.

3
Evening.
Evening calm in the world.
And sunset upon
Cows in the field.
There's no end to that winding path.
Paths end in longing only.

Merciful world,
merciful uddering world
I come to you
from a fasting land
lost in your milk's warm steam.

Tell me, am I not as lovely as your rivers?
Your sunsets rejoice for me.
Make good your harms
beg forgiveness for each poisoned well.

For see, my soul is virgin
fragrant with fields and myrrh,
naked, it goes in search of you
to fall on the lap of light.

The Spinning Girl

The silent girl at the spindle
Spun a thread pomegranate red.
Said a king as he sat in his chamber:
She has spun me a royal cloak.

The silent girl at the spindle
Spun a thread that darkened the day.
Said a thief as he lay in the dungeon:
She has spun me a shift for the block.

The silent girl at the spindle
Spun a thread gold as lightning flashed,
Said a jester loitering by the wayside:
She has spun me a motley cape.

The silent girl at the spindle
Spun a thread gray as age-old cloth.
Said a beggar to his cowering mongrel:
She has spun me a mourning coat.

She took all the threads from the spindle
And set them upon her loom.
Then down she went to the river
And washed her pure white skin.

Then she put on the woven garment,
A timeless garment of grace.
And since then she is thief and beggar,
And sovereign queen and buffoon.

Translated by Ruth Nevo

Yehuda Amichai

Yehuda Amichai was born in 1924 in Würzburg, Germany, and travelled to Palestine in 1935. He has published six volumes of poetry, a collection of short stories, and two novels. He has been translated into many languages and has read his poetry at international poetry festivals. Amichai lives in Jerusalem with his family. To date five books of his poetry have been translated into English: Poems, Songs of Jerusalem and Myself, Amen, Travels of a Latter-day Benjamin of Tudela, *and* Time. *His novel* Not of This Time, Not of This Place *has also appeared in English translation.*

Of Three or Four in a Room

Of three or four in a room
there is always one who stands beside the window.
He must see evil sprouting among the thorns
and fires on the hill.
And how men who went out of their houses whole
are given back in the evening like small change.

Of three or four in a room
there is always one who stands beside the window.
His dark hair over his thoughts.
Behind him, words.
And in front of him voices wandering without a knapsack,
hearts without supplies, prophecies without water,
and large stones which have been returned
and remain sealed, like letters which have no
address and no one to receive them.

Not Like a Cypress

Not like a cypress,
not at once, not all of me,
but like the grass, in thousands of slow green exits,
to be hidden like many children at play
while one seeks.

And not like the single man,
like Saul, whom many men found
and made king.
But like the rain in many places
from many clouds, to be absorbed, to be drunk
by many mouths, to be breathed in
like the air all year and scattered like blossoming in spring.

Not the sharp ring which wakes up
the doctor on call,
but with tapping, on many windows
at side entrances, with many beats of the heart.

And afterwards the quiet exit, like smoke
without blasts of the trumpet, a statesman retiring,
children tired from play,
a stone in its last revolutions
after the steep decline, in the place
where the plain of great renunciation begins, from which,
like prayers that are granted,
dust rises in many myriads of grains.

God Has Pity on Kindergarten Children

God has pity on kindergarten children.
He has less pity on school children.
And on grownups he has no pity at all,
he leaves them alone,
and sometimes they must crawl on all fours
in the burning sand
to reach the first-aid station
covered with blood.

But perhaps he will watch over true lovers
and have mercy on them and shelter them
like a tree over the old man
sleeping on a public bench.

Perhaps we too will give them
the last rare coins of charity
that Mother handed down to us,
so that their happiness may protect us
now and on other days.

Translated by Stephen Mitchell

On the Day of Atonement

On the Day of Atonement in the year 5728,* I put on
dark holiday clothes and went to the Old City in Jerusalem.
For a long time I stood in the niche of an Arab's shop,
not far from the Nablus Gate, a store
for buttons and zippers and spools of thread
in every shade and snaps and buckles.
A rare light and many colors, like a Holy Ark opened.

I said without speaking that my father
had a store like this for buttons and thread.
I told him without words about the decades,
the causes, events, that now I am here,
and my father's store was burned there and he's buried here.

When I finished it was time for the closing prayer.
He too lowered the shutter and locked the door,
and with all those who prayed, I went home.

*1967 according to the Jewish calendar.

Shadow of the Old City

In the morning the shadow of the Old City falls
on the new. After noon—the reverse.
Nobody profits. The muezzin's prayer
wastes itself on new houses. A ringing
of bells, rolling like balls, and bouncing.
From synagogues the cry of Holy, Holy will fade like gray smoke.

At the end of summer I breathe this air,
burned and hurting. Thoughts
are silent as closed books
all crowded together, most of the pages
stuck like eyelids in the morning.

Jerusalem, Port City

Jerusalem, Port City on the shore of forever.
The Temple Mount a great ship, a splendid pleasure
boat. From the portholes of her Western Wall smiling saints
look out. They are travelers. Hasidim wave greetings
from the pier, shouting *hurrah, au revoir.* She's
always arriving, always leaving. And walls and wharfs
and guards and flags and tall masts of churches
and mosques and chimneys of synagogues and boats
of praise and mountain waves. The sound of the *shofar:* one
more has set out. *Yom Kippur* sailors in white uniforms
climb on ladders and ropes of tested prayers.

And trade and gates and golden domes.
Jerusalem is the Venice of God.

Sodom's Sister City

Jerusalem is Sodom's sister city,
but the merciful salt had no pity on her,
didn't cover her with quiet whiteness.
Jerusalem is Pompeii refusing.
History books thrown into fire,
their pages unroll, harden to redness.

An eye too bright, blind,
always shattered in a sieve of veins.
Many births gape wide below,
a womb with numberless teeth,
she of the double-edged mouths and the heavenly breasts.

The sun thought Jerusalem was a sea
and set in her, a terrible mistake.
The fish of heaven were caught in a net of alleys,
tearing each other apart like fish.

Jerusalem. An incision left open.
The surgeons went to sleep in distant skies
while the dead arranged themselves
slowly, slowly, round and round
the calm petals around the stem:
God!

Translated by Shirley Kaufman

I Am Sitting Here

I am sitting here now with my father's eyes,
and with my mother's graying hair on my head,
in a house that belonged to an Arab
who bought it from an Englishman
who took it from a German
who hewed it from the stones
of Jerusalem, my city.
I look upon God's world of others
who received it from others.
I am composed of many things.
I have been collected many times.
I am constructed of spare parts
of decomposing materials
of disintegrating words. And already
in the middle of my life, I begin,
gradually, to return them,
for I wish to be a decent and orderly person
when I'm asked at the border, "Have you anything to declare?"
So that there won't be too much pressure at the end,
so that I won't arrive sweating and breathless and confused,
so that I shan't have anything left to declare.
The red stars are my heart, the Milky Way
its blood, my blood. The hot khamsin
breathes in huge lungs, my life
pulses close to a huge heart, always within.

HEBREW

I Think of Oblivion

I think of oblivion as a ripening fruit
which will not be eaten when ripe
because it will not be, and will not be recalled:
its ripeness is its forgetting. When I lie
on my back, my bones fill with the sweetness
of my small son's breath.
He breathes the same air as I,
sees the same things,
but my breath is bitter and his is sweet
as rest to tired bones.
Blessed is the memory of my childhood. His childhood.

Advice

Advice for good love: Don't love
the far away, take the one who's near.
As a properly built house gets itself built
of local stone
that has suffered cold and been baked in the sun.
Take the one with a golden circle
round the dark pupil, who has a certain knowledge
of your death. Make love
even within destruction, like honey
in the dead lion of Samson.

Advice for bad love: with the love left over from the one before
make yourself a new woman, and with what remains
of her make yourself
new love,
until nothing's left.

Translated by Ruth Nevo

Lament

The diameter of the bomb was thirty centimeters,
and the diameter of its destruction—
about seven meters,
and in it four killed and eleven wounded.
And around these, in a larger circle
of pain and time, are scattered
two hospitals and one cemetery.

But the young woman
who was buried in the place
from where she came, at a distance
of more than one hundred kilometers,
enlarges the circle considerably.
And the lonely man
who is mourning her death in a distant country
incorporates into the circle
the whole world. And I won't speak
of the cry of the orphans
that reaches God's chair and from there
makes the circle endless
and godless.

I Am a Leaf

I am a leaf that knows its boundaries
and doesn't want to expand any more than this.
Neither to fuse with nature
nor to flow into the universe.
I am so quiet now
that I can't imagine
that I ever screamed, even as an infant.

And my face is what has been left
after they hewed the love from it
as from a quarry
already abandoned.

Since Then

I fell in the battle of Ashdod,
in the War of Liberation.
My mother said, then, he is twenty-four.
And now she says, he is fifty-four.
And she lights a *Yahrtzeit* candle
like birthday candles on a cake
to be blown out.

And since then my father died of too much pain and sorrow.
And since then my sisters got married
and named their sons after me,
and since then my home is my grave,
and my grave, my home.
Because I fell in the pale sands
of Ashdod.

And since then all the cypresses
and all the trees of the orchards
between Negbah and Yad Mordechai
move in a slow march,
and since then all my children and all my ancestors
are orphans and bereaved parents,
and since then all my children and all my ancestors
go together arm in arm
in a protest against death.
Because I fell in the war
in the soft sands of Ashdod.

I carried my friend on my back
and since then I always feel his body
like a heavy sky above me,
and since then he feels my back bent beneath him
like peace around the earth.
Because I fell in the terrible sands
of Ashdod,
not only him.

And since then I appease myself for my death
with loves and with dark feasts.
And since then I am of blessed memory.
And since then I don't want God to revenge my blood.
And since then I don't want my mother to weep over me
with her beautiful and precise features,
and since then I fight against pain,
and since then I march against my memories
like a man against the wind,
and since then I grieve over my memories
like a man does over his dead,
and since then I extinguished my memories
like a man does a fire,
and since then I am quiet.
Because I fell in the soft and pale sands
of Ashdod
in the War of Liberation.

Translated by Shlomo Vinner and Howard Schwartz

In the Old City

We are festive weepers, etching names on every stone,
touched by hope, hostages of governments and history,
blown by wind and gathering holy dust.
Our king, a beautiful boy, is crying;
his portrait hangs in every place.
And the stairs always force us to leap
as in a happy dance, even he who is sad
and with a heavy heart.

But the divine couple sits on the balcony
of the coffeehouse: he with a strong hand and outstretched arm,
she with long hair. Both wear nothing
but long transparent gowns. They are calm now,
after the *halvah* sacrifice and offering of hashish.

When they rise from their rest
against the sinking sun at the Jaffa Gate,
everyone stands
and stares at them:
two light auras surround their dark bodies.

On the Wide Stairs

On the wide stairs that descend to the Western Wall
a beautiful woman came up to me and said:
"You don't remember me. I am Shoshana in Hebrew.
Others in other languages. All is vanity."

So she spoke at twilight between destruction
and restoration, between light and darkness.
Black birds and white birds succeeded each other,
this with that in the rhythm of a deep breath.
The flash of a camera also lit up my memory:
"What are you doing here
between the promised and the forgotten,
between what is hoped for and what imagined?
What are you doing here
lying in ambush for happiness
with your beautiful face
and your soul as rent and torn as mine?"

She answered me: "My soul is rent and torn,
like yours, but it is also beautiful,
like lace."

Translated by Laya Firestone and Howard Schwartz

HEBREW

The Town I Was Born In

The town I was born in was wiped out by guns,
The ship I immigrated on was later sunk in war,
The barn in Hamadiya where I made love burned down.
The kiosk at Ein Gedi was blown up by the enemy,
The bridge at Ismailia I used to cross
Back and forth on the eve of my loves
Got smashed to pieces.

My life's erased behind me like on a precise map.
How long will my memories hold on?
They killed the girl who shared my childhood,
And my father's dead.

So don't pick me for a lover or son,
A crosser of bridges, a tenant or a citizen.

Translated by A. C. Jacobs

Lay Your Head on My Shoulder

Lay your head on my shoulder
because my shoulder
knows things
your head dare not dream
and your mouth cannot say.

The fates say
one of us must be the wind,
the other a tree in the wind,
or a tree on a windless day.

The fates say
your being born in the war
augurs my end.
My end will be yours that day.

How long will they lay
upon us pacts of grief,
treaties of despair?

Let me put it this way:
time does not suffice
to be
two together twice
through all one lifetime.

Let me put it this way:
even this tender, even this
  finite heart
is nothing but a shoulder.

Rest, rest your head, therefore.

Translated by Robert Friend

Aharon Amir

Aharon Amir was born in 1923 in Kovno and immigrated to Palestine in 1935. He was a co-founder, with Yonathan Ratosh, of Aleph, *the periodical of the Canaanite literary movement, and later founded* Keshet, *a literary and political quarterly. He has translated many books into Hebrew from English and French, and also edited several books and anthologies. His books of poetry include* Sirocco *and* Fiery Angel.

Nothingness

I woke up at night and my language was gone
no sign of language no writing no alphabet
nor symbol nor word in any tongue
and raw was my fear—like the terror perhaps
of a man flung from a treetop far above the ground
a shipwrecked person on a tide-engulfed sandbank
a pilot whose parachute would not open
or the fear of a stone in a bottomless pit
and the fright was unvoiced unlettered unuttered
and inarticulate O how inarticulate
and I was alone in the dark
a non-I in the all-pervading gloom
with no grasp no leaning point
everything stripped of everything
and the sound was speechless and voiceless
and I was naught and nothing
without even a gibbet to hang onto
without a single peg to hang onto
and I no longer knew who or what I was
and I was no more

Translator unknown

HEBREW

Edna Aphek

Edna Aphek, born in Haifa in 1943, is an artist, poet, and university lecturer. She has done stylistic analysis of Agnon's short stories and exhibited her paintings in Jerusalem and New York. Ms. Aphek received her doctorate in Hebrew literature from the Jewish Theological Seminary.

Sarah

1
Sarah
was a woman
soft and pliant
like a furrowed field
and he with
Hagar.

2
Sarah was
soft and pliant
quiet and kind
a woman
and he with
Hagar.

3
Sarah was
a woman
quiet and kind
crushed and cruel
and he with
Hagar.

4
Sarah was
crushed and cruel
a woman
when her womb
was soft with son
call her the
laughing one.

The Story of Abraham and Hagar

1
Abraham and Hagar
a marriage torn asunder
she to the wilderness afar
with bread was sent to wander.

2
Abraham and Hagar
she to the wilderness afar
by the law of Israel
in her hand he placed
his son
the wild Ishmael.

3
Abraham and Hagar
she to the wilderness afar
with charity grace and mercy
on her shoulder
the bowl he placed
and sent her to
the wilderness.

4
Abraham and Hagar
an old story of divorce
and Sarah the jealous wife
put Hagar on her course.

5
He didn't see how Ishmael
withered in his thirst
for at that very hour
he knew his wife first
(or so the legend says).

6
Abraham and Hagar
a story almost dead
Hagar to the wilderness afar
with a parched
pitcher and piece
of bread.

Translated by Yishai Tobin

HEBREW

Eli Bachar

Eli Bachar was born in Jaffa, Israel, in September 1954. He studied in various schools, as well as on a kibbutz. His poems were first published in the literary magazines of the daily papers and important literary publications in Israel. In 1978, after his military service, his first volume of poems, Black Coffee and All the Tobacco, *was published. This collection won him a special award from the Tel Aviv Art and Literature Fund. Since then he has continued writing for avant-garde publications in Israel.*

Room Poems

On a clothesline hangs the moon
grounds are strangled in a cup of coffee
my father, with meager talent, pretends to sleep
and through the window I see thoughts of his mother

Her heart is a mildewed carpet
climbing up the corners of the wall
and among all these sits my mother

Oh
mother
cloud of shyness
I go round from room to room
and under your feet the dry land blazes

Father
noon, now a terrorist, is upon you.
I found Valium in mother's purse
and in your pocket a shredded bill

Sometimes
when I leave the house
they cover the stains of my presence with clear dust

A Dawn of Jaffa Pigeons

I give rest to clear words
and dawn speaks to me in a heavy gray

Afterwards I speak with Arab pigeons
and water spoons open up
to close on angry sand

Jaffa peers with a whitish gaze
from the gap of the fountain
rise black angels in white robes
riding bicycles.

Houses, Past and Present

I
To my parents I am
a thick layer of innovation
no garlic, no onion will help in the house.

My brothers
are a lost train.

At times we renew ourselves
to speak for those who feel.

But at one time
we would wake up at night
and mother would wash our Eastern feet
with clean pains.

Now the filth lives outside the door
and my father reclines on the porch
wearing his wide shoes
for the coming year.

II
No garlic, no onion will help in the house.
Father puts on his glasses when occupied with himself
looking into his chilled vision.

Sometimes Natan plays with the block
sad balls move from his eyes,
and his journey's length
is in the palm of my hand.

The sofa will shortly
surrender its soul to disinfection.
In my mother's drawer lies a hair of her mother.

"In the end I don't go out anywhere,"
says my mother
as she puts on her apple apron.
In the kitchen she fixes seven meat balls
I eat two
and am full from the five.

Translated by Jeremy Garber

Yocheved Bat-Miriam

Yocheved Bat-Miriam was born in White Russia in 1901, attended universities in Odessa and Moscow, and settled in Palestine in 1928. Her verse has appeared in many anthologies and has been published in several volumes of collected works.

The Monasteries Lift Gold Domes

The monasteries lift gold domes,
crosses, crosses. I weary, seeing them.
I speak in parables and they are strange;
otherwise, I could not meditate.

The memory of the ancient generations
rises like a vision: a temple strong and splendid.
The roads are humming like encircling rivers,
an exultant throng draws near.

We have fled, today, the parables of Mount Hermon,
of Mount Gilboa and the fields of Carmel;
Sharon and Galilee mourn only in the adage,
the lordly cedar only in the proverb.

Left with my poverty, I envy
every sown valley rising like a song.
An exile, strange to every wind,
may I be given field and fallow land.

O may my home be like a kneeling camel,
my days move onward like yoked mules;
my silent soul howls like the jackals,
and cries out like the sea!

Translated by Robert Friend

Distance Spills Itself

Distance spills itself and grows dazzling and blue,
Silver lights like scythes flashing in the meadow.
Who is it that seems to call and answer, who is it
That seduces my heart, full of longing like a wild bird?

Sadness, so much sadness, a night without daybreak,
Sadness like the river mist towering over the river.
Let me kiss the mezuzah nailed to my doorpost and be gone,
Like the poor man that entered and suddenly was gone.

I will meet a man who will not hear me approach,
The beasts of the field will be slow catching my scent,
The footpaths will drone like bells for my sake
And I'll whisper to my soul in pure solitude:

Oh let me walk alone, hearing voices
Crying "Holy holy holy," let me say "Amen,"
And suddenly I'll whisper, "Blessed be your name,"
Scorched by the mystery, by amazing grace. . .

Sadness, so much sadness. The distance stretches out,
Reminder of all that lies beyond the borders.
Not to be, to be gone—I pray for this
At the gates of infinity, like a fey child.

Translated by Robert Mezey and Shula Starkman

Hayim Be'er

Hayim Be'er was born in Jerusalem in 1945 into a family that has been living there for about 150 years. He was educated in a religious school. He served in the army as a news correspondent. He now works as a literary editor and occasionally publishes literary comments in Hebrew newspapers. His first book of poems, Day to Day Delight, *was published in 1970.*

Tabernacle of Peace

In Kerem Abraham
Ada with the right hand of her righteousness
bakes cookies from the dust of the earth,
rejoicing in the world of His earth.

HEBREW

A little girl three or four years old
sitting in a sandbox in the morning
in the place where a century ago
the children of ancient and proud families
used to clear stones
and build unhewn stone walls under the guidance of the villagers
in the field of the missionary Mrs. Finn:
young Jews from the Old Settlement
who for their daily bread
earn three and a half piastres
from the wife of the English consul,
touching the Christian heart
by their strangeness and fragility,
and already several vines have been planted
and some mulberry trees
in the heat of the sun
in the yard of the Rachel Strikovsky Kindergarten
where I now see
Hebrew women yawning and sneezing,
holding their children by the hand
in the shade
beneath the mulberry trees,
for in Salem also is His tabernacle.

The Sequence of Generations

I am a child
of six generations here
under the sun of lower Syria
Mother and my aunts
during the World War
eat grass
and go begging for
colonial merchandise
little girls trapped
in poverty
waiting for General Allenby
a commander who is more like Wellington
than Napoleon
an Englishman who spent the last decade of his life
studying the lives of birds
and taking long trips
getting down from his horse at Jaffa Gate,

and in the Street of the Patriarch
the heathens say to them
Return return O Shulamite
eyes on them from every side
return that we may look upon thee,
and they run away and answer
What will ye see in the Shulamite,
hungry little girls in checkered blouses
who remind them of
the lady Mary, a Semitic woman
in Terra Sancta,
and I am a child,
little by little
in the world of actions
building the family tree
always as if walking
in happy light
There is nothing more enchanting in life than this,
to sit in the crusader East
and to see the sheep scattered upon the hills
and only the Lamb of God
standing and weeping
Dominus flevit—the Lord
in his Byzantine beauty
standing and weeping
on Mount Olivet
as he comes from Bethany
and on the threshing floor of Aravna the Jebusite
already the Mother of Zion hears
words of a husband to his wife
and laughs
Praise is comely

Love Song

In the light of the moon
birds fly over the paths—
wonderful to behold.
In the firmament
they make melody in honor of the moon,
make in her honor
ten different kinds of music,

lovely garments which clothe earth with grass
in the light of the moon,
as in "Let thy priests be clothed with righteousness."
Rabbi Nachman at the close of the Sabbath, before *havdalah*,*
explains the verse
"My beloved is like a roe or a young hart."
As we stand around him
in the little field behind the Italian Hospital
the blades of grass enter the Torah,
each blade pushing itself
to rise and be gathered in names of longing and affection.
Rabbi Nachman draws the speech of birds and beasts and the like,
drawings wonderful to behold,
draws the speech of palm trees
standing behind our wall
in the courtyard of the Ethiopian Church on the Street of the
Prophets.
Birds fluttering in the branches
make merry,
make a great laughter,
as night mocks at day,
so that the moon shouldn't fall into contraction
or hide herself from the world in clouds.
With one word of his the clouds
see her and they marvel
and are filled with consternation,
pushed away from the face of the moon,
die or become ill,
and so that there should be no diminution,
no blemish,
Rabbi Nachman blesses her with the gift
of good life

until it becomes day.

Translated by Stephen Mitchell

**havdalah* is the ceremony prepared to designate the end of the Sabbath.

Anath Bental

Anath Bental was born in Haifa in 1950. She was a student of English literature at Hebrew University at the time of her accidental death in 1975. Her parents are currently preparing a volume of her poems for publication.

Jerusalem in the Snow

White velvet covers the town
Like a *tallith,**
The canopy of clouds
Like a *chuppa*‡ above a bride
Dressed in white.
The wind ascends
With the sound and melody
Of crystal,
The fragile heart
Like a flake of snow.

Jerusalem
Is like this snow,
Beautiful at moments,
But muddy for hours and days
When it melts.

The Angel Michael

The Angel Michael visited my room,
Sat by my side
The whole night,
From midnight to dawn.
His words were full of comfort
And his arms embraced me,
Caressed me,
And he poured warm kisses over me.

*A *tallith* is a prayer shawl.
‡A *chuppa* is a bridal canopy.

The angel Michael spoke and I listened.
It seemed to me that I fell in love
With this angel
In one hour.
Then I struggled with myself
Like Jacob with his angel.
For I knew he was only an angel
And that at dawn
He would disappear.

Afterwards
I tried to recall
The image of his face,
But he is not here
And only his voice
Still echoes
Inside me.

Translated by Howard Schwartz

Avraham Ben-Yitzhak

Avraham Ben-Yitzhak was born in Galicia in 1883. He studied at the Universities of Berlin and Vienna, and became a lecturer in Hebrew and Psychology at the Jerusalem Teachers' Training College. He settled in Palestine in 1938. During his lifetime, Ben-Yitzhak published only eleven poems, although others have been discovered since his death in 1950.

I Didn't Know My Soul

In this vintage season, when the skies are full of movement,
Rays of light are thrown out by the earth,
Gray, wasting clouds are driven
Wide winged by the storm.
From the greenish black of the forest
Your house emerges doubly pale in its isolation,
Calling me with its windows:
In my heart
Is shelter from the storm.

When you are sitting by the earth,
And its gold dances
On the deep brown of your bent head,
Light flows between your fingers,
And the flame reflects movement
In the black silk of your dress.
Silently apples lie burning on your table,
Yellow grapes cluster thickly in their basket,
There is the full scent of blessing.

Let the forest thunder and roar,
Its song is sweet
In the stillness
Of your loved corner.

You and I,
With the sea's din
Over us,
Concealed
Like two pearls
In their soil
On the bed of the sea.

I didn't know my soul.
It took its fill of silence.
Look, my spirit's wings flutter.
The forest may roar and thunder,
The wind strike its waves,
While your quivering look rests on me.
In you is blessing
And comfort,
Though the storm cried at my soul,
Listen, there is a howling of breakers in the forest,
The whole earth is cried on;
The world has set all its soul bare
Before God in the storm.

HEBREW

Blessed Are Those Who Sow and Do Not Reap

Blessed are those who sow and do not reap
Because they wander far.

Blessed are those who give themselves freely, the splendor
Of whose youth had added to daylight
Though they flung off their glory where roads part.

Blessed are those whose pride crosses the borders of their souls
And becomes a white humility
After the rainbow's rising in the cloud.

Blessed are those who know what their heart cries out in deserts
And on whose lips silence flowers.

Blessed are they, for they will be taken into the heart of the world
Wrapped in a cloak of unremembrance,
Forever remaining without speech.

Psalm

There are a very few moments when you
Lift your soul within you like a drop of crystal.
The world is filled with its sun and broken colors,
Collection of sights and trembling objects,
And you perceive the world
As the drop of crystal.
Yet your world strains quivering to pour out,
Not to remain full,
Towards all limits, quivers.
You are given to all worlds.
The ends of stretches of air flow from your eyes,
Fears of darkness crouch in them,
Distant and close things find you
And demand your soul.

Stand, in night's silence,
On mountain summits,
Among the big cold stars lift your head.
The lives below you sink to the ground,
On the last burning of their grief
A black oblivion comes down.
You, though, wake to terrors
Above the darkness.
If a star drops
Through fear of the flamed roar
Rising from the distress of oblivion to the sky
It falls in the depths of your soul
And is consumed.

In the coming of morning
You are hovering over the face of the deep,
Drawing over it your profound heaven,
With the great sun in your hands
Till evening.

Translated by A. C. Jacobs

Hayim Nachman Bialik

Hayim Nachman Bialik was born in 1873 to a poor family in the Ukraine. He received the traditional Jewish training in Talmud. After establishing himself in literary and publishing circles in Odessa, Bialik translated classics of European literature into Hebrew, edited the Aggada and the Hebrew poets of Spain, established the Dvir publishing house and became the leading poet of the Hebrew national renaissance. Before settling in Palestine in 1924, he wrote in both Hebrew and Yiddish. He died in 1934. A translation of his selected poems by Ruth Nevo is in preparation.

When the Days Grow Long

When the days grow long, each one an eternity,
Each one as alike as yesterday and the day before it,
Just days, without much pleasure and filled with dullness,
And men and animals are seized by boredom,
A man will go out at sunset to walk on the seashore,
And see that the sea has not fled,
And he will yawn,

And go to the Jordan, and it will not flow back,
And he will yawn,
And see the Pleiades and Orion, not budging from their places,
And he will yawn;
And men and animals will sit, bored, together,
With their lives weighing heavily upon them,
And men will pluck the hairs of their head in distraction,
And cats will lose their whiskers.
Then the longings will rise,
Rise of themselves—like mushrooms raising a stench
In a decaying plank of wood.
The longings will fill all cracks and crevices,
As lice fill rags.
And when a man comes back to his hut for his supper,
And dips his crust and his salt herring in vinegar,
He will long,
He will drink his cup of murky, lukewarm water
And he will long;
He will take off his shoes and socks by his bed,
And he will long;
Man and animal both will sit in longing:
The man will wail in his dreams from his vast longing,
While the cat, on the tin roof, yells and scratches.
Then the hunger will come,
Growing, increasing, like nothing before it,
Not hunger for bread or vision, but for the Messiah.

And early in the morning, with the sun not quite showing,
The man, exhausted, shaken, glutted with dreams and empty in spirit,
The webs of an angry sleep still on his eyelids,
The night's dread in his bones,
Will get up from his bed, from the darkness of his hut,
And with the cat still wailing, its nails
Still grating on his brain and on his nerves,
He will hurry to his window and wipe off the steam,
Or he will get up and go to the entrance of his shack
And, shading his eyes with his hand, look out, blearily, fevered
And hungry for salvation, towards the little path behind his yard,

Towards the slope of the rubbish heap opposite his home,
Looking for the Messiah;
And under the blanket, the woman will wake, uncovering herself,
Her hair all wild, her body chafed, and her spirit murky,
And, pulling her shriveled nipple from her baby's mouth,
She will turn and listen very carefully:
Isn't the Messiah coming?
Hasn't anyone heard his donkey braying?
And the infant will look out of its cot,
And the mouse will peep out of its hole:
Isn't the Messiah coming?
Has no one heard his donkey's jingling bell?
And the maid, heating the kettle on the stove,
Will stick out her sooty face:
Isn't the Messiah coming?
Has no one heard the sound of his horn?

After My Death

After I am dead
Say this at my funeral:

There was a man who exists no more.

That man died before his time
And his life's song was broken off halfway.
O, he had one more poem
And that poem has been lost
For ever.

He had a lyre,
And a vital, quivering soul.
The poet in him spoke,
Gave out all his heart's secrets,
His hand struck all its chords.
But there was one secret he kept hidden
Though his fingers danced everywhere.
One string stayed mute
And is still soundless.

But alas! all its days
That string trembled,
Trembled softly, softly quivered
For the poem that would free her,
Yearned and thirsted, grieved and wept,
As though pining for someone expected
Who does not come,
And the more he delays, she whimpers
With a soft, fine sound,
But he does not come,
And the agony is very great,
There was a man and he exists no more.
His life's song was broken off halfway.
He had one more poem
And that poem is lost,
For ever.

Translated by A. C. Jacobs

Summer Night

True daughters of Lilith, night demons
weave and interweave with moonlight
gleaming silver threads, making one garment
for high priest and swineherd.

Once again a summer night begins,
houses empty, public gardens teem.
Once again, dreaming a giant dream,
men hasten to their little sins.

Impatient of spirit, in hope and desire blind,
"Stars," they implore (it is all their prayer), "be kind.
Shine nakedly in the heavens above, and show
the harlots shining nakedly below."

In public gardens, stirring sleeping streams,
a thin, a winding music breaks the hush.
Under a tree a ribbon whitely gleams,
a shawl-fringe flashes darkly by a bush.

The golden stars tip winks like bawd or whore
in calculation of a golden yield;
lust clings to every cobblestone and door
and to the sighing grasses of the field.

From river bank, from high balustrades,
from behind fences, murmurs and laughter float.
Naked arms reach up to lower shades
and quick hot breaths blow the slow candles out.

And now at midnight, reeking of sweat and spunk,
down stairs, through alleys, the world's lovers, drunk,
stagger, or vomit, and through the vomit roll,
suffering in the flesh pollution of the soul.

True daughters of Lilith, night demons
weave and interweave with moonlight
gleaming silver threads, making one garment
for high priest and swineherd.

Translated by Robert Friend

I Didn't Find Light by Accident

I didn't find light by accident,
I didn't inherit it.
I hewed it from the flint of my being
I quarried it from my heart.

One spark hides in the rock of my heart,
a small spark, all mine.
I didn't borrow it from anyone, or steal it.
It is my very own.

The hammer of grief strikes my heart
rock of my strength.
The spark flashes, flies to my eye,
from my eye to my poem

and from my poem to your heart
to kindle fire and disappear.
And I, marrow and blood,
am consumed in the flame.

HEBREW

Footsteps of Spring

A different wind, taller skies
clear spacious distances—
footsteps of spring on the hills!
Warm vapor, with the sun, in the yard,
on wet trees budding shoots.
A different wind.

Not yet full splendor, the bugle call.
A pure subtle song,
soft sundering light, half-hidden still,
till there burst forth the power of secret life,
till there flourish the vigor of youth
in all its fecund might.

How sweet the light, how sweet the wind!
Laughing faces wherever one looks
shining companionship everywhere
gold threads stretched over all things.
Soon that lavish youth will spill
flowers, a white aureole.

Soon, in white flowers my youth will overflow.
New youth and old dreams.
Through them too a different wind blows.
From a full heart I will speak.
With shining tears expel my black despair.
A different wind.

My Song

Do you know where I got my song?

In my father's house a lonely singer lived,
modest, unobtrusive, diffident,
a dweller in dark crannies, screened in chinks.
He knew one melody, familiar, fixed,
and when my heart grew dumb, and my tongue clove
to the roof of my mouth in silent misery
and stifled weeping welled up in my throat,
into my desolate spirit crept the song
of a chirping cricket, poet of poverty.

My father's want profaned the Sabbath feast.
His table carried neither wine nor bread;
his lamps were pawned and in their place there stood
a few thin ragged candles stuck in earth
flickering a smoky light upon the walls;
and seven kids, all hungry, half-asleep,
intoned a welcome to the Sabbath angel.
My mother listened downcast to the song.
My father, shamed, disheartened, cut black bread
and tails of salt fish with a damaged knife.
We chewed our salt and sour fare: all's one,
both tepid, and as tasteless as the tears
of deprivation and of wretchedness.
We raised our voices to our father's songs
with rumbling bellies and with hollow hearts,
and the cricket joined the dismal chorus then,
singing from his crevice in the dark.

In the long evening hours of rainy days
a voiceless gloom reigned in my father's house,
its rooms despondent like a silent seer
dreaming oppressive dreams beside some sphinx—
monster of dearth, and of repulsive want—
while seven souls raised their imploring eyes
in cheerless corners, choking back their tears.
Upon the stove the cat wailed hungrily.
The basket held no bread, the bin no yeast,

no coal to warm them, no groats in the pot.
Then through the cracked wainscot the cricket peered
and harshly rasped his arid, dreary song.
A moth devoured my heart, laid waste my soul.
There was no solace in his song, no rage.
He knew no execration, only wept—
as desolate as death, as my vain life,
trivial in its interminable grief.

Do you know where I got my sighs?

My widowed mother, with her orphaned mites,
was left without a source of livelihood.
Before her mourning ended, worry struck.
She looked about her at an empty world—
widowhood, orphanhood, filling all its space.
Even the ticking clock was muffled now
even the walls of rooms wept silently,
each corner hushed in pity and in rage.
"Lord of the world," the woman softly sighed,
"support me lest I fall, a widow alone.
Feed my chicks, poor worms; what is my strength?"
She went to market, blood and marrow spent,
returned at evening crushed to her last breath,
each cursed penny gained vexatiously
made moist with her heart's blood and soaked in gall.
At home at last, a harassed, driven beast
she did not put her candle out till dawn
but plied her needle, mending shirts and socks,
and dumbly sighing out her aching heart.
Each motion of the hand or nod of head
stirred the dim candle light as if, concerned,
it said, "Ah me. Poor thing. That a mother's heart
should wither and waste away in beggary."
When she lay down to rest her rickety cot
would groan from time to time beneath her weight
as if affliction might cause it to collapse.
The whispered feverish "Hear oh Israel, hear"
continued long to echo in my mind.
I heard her body's every aching joint
and in my heart of hearts I felt a scorpion's sting.

At break of day, at cock-crow, she arose,
in silence moved about her household chores.
In bed, in my dark room, by feeble light
I watched her bend her frail form to the dough,
her thin hands kneading, kneading, stubbornly,
the stool rocking beneath the baking trough.
Each pressure of the hand, each pinch, each rub
drove through the wall the whisper of a sigh:
"Lord of the world, support and strengthen me.
What strength have I? What is a woman's life?"
My heart knew well what tears fell in the dough;
and when she gave her children warm new bread,
bread of her baking, bread of her pain, her woe,
I swallowed sighs that seeped into my bones.

Translated by Ruth Nevo

I Scattered My Sighs to the Wind

I scattered my sighs to the wind,
and the sand has absorbed my tears.
Wind, if you find my brother,
tell him I am but a smoldering ember.
Tell him, a spring of tears welled up in me
and it has dried drop by drop.
Tell him, a flame burned intense in me,
and it has died down, spark by spark.
And now my spring is like a wound,
only bleeding and dripping now and again,
and my heart still smolders in hiding,
in ashes and in blood.

Translated by N. N.

The Sea of Silence Exhales Secrets

The sea of silence exhales secrets
And the world is silent;
And behind the millstones
The voice of the stream doesn't cease.

The night's darkness approaches,
Heaps shadow upon shadow, multiplies;
Silently into the sea of darkness
Star after star falls.

And when the world turns silent
I'll feel my heart awakening;
I'll feel one pure spring
Slowly murmuring and strengthening.

My heart secretly tells me:
"Son! Your dreams have come;
A star fell from the sky—
Believe me, it isn't yours.

Yours is still fastly embedded
And in its proper place it will shine;
Raise your eyes, look
It winks, hints to you a consolation."

And when the world falls silent
I'll sit and look at my star;
I have no world but one—
Set fast within my heart.

Place Me Under Your Wing

Place me under your wing
And be to me mother and sister.
And allow your breast to shelter my head,
The nest of my deepest prayers.

In time of mercy in twilight hours
Bend over and I'll disclose the secrets of my suffering:
They say, there is youth in the world
Where is my youth?

And one more secret I'll confess:
My soul burned in the flame.
They say there is love in the world.
What is love?

The stars lied to me,
There was a dream—it also passed;
Now I have nothing in the world—
I have nothing.

Place me under your wing
And be to me mother and sister.
And allow your breast to shelter my head,
The nest of my deepest prayers.

Translated by Gabriel Levin

Erez Biton

Erez Biton, an Israeli of Sephardic background, is the author of Moroccan Offering, *a collection of poems from which the following verses have been selected.*

Beginnings

My mother came
From a village of grasses,
Green, but a different green,
From a nest of birds who nourish with milk,
Sweet, but sweeter than sweet,
At the cradle of song, singing to me
A thousand nights, and still another night.

My mother knew how
To push trouble away
With a snap of her fingers
And beat of the breast
In the name of all mothers
A mother herself.

My father's concern
Was the world to come.
He hallowed Shabbat
In purest Araq
And knew, as no other,
The language of prayer.

While I as a child,
Separating off and apart
Withdrawing down deep
While all were asleep
Would go over and over
Inside and down deep
Short hymns of Bach
In Jewish
Moroccan.

HEBREW

A Bird's Nest

Small nests
On branches up high
Held together with a wish—
Sometimes winter water birds
Often the far-off cry of wolves
But never an eagle.
Yet when they arrive,
The birds from Europe,
We feel no special pride,
Come the first fine day, we know,
And south, off to Egypt, they fly,
Good fortune for us, our living here
At a station
Along the way.

Buying a Shop on Dizengoff

I bought a shop on Dizengoff
A way of purchasing roots
Of anchoring myself and finding a place
Among the Elite of Dizengoff Street
But
All these Elite of Dizengoff Street
Who are they, I ask myself
What is it with them, what do they do
These Elite of Dizengoff Street?
When they turn to me
Though I have not turned to them
I answer in purest tones
Yes, Monsieur
But of course, Monsieur
Whatever you say, Monsieur, to be sure
It is fine up-to-date Hebrew I speak
Unsheathing the language of Dizengoff Street.

But the houses that rise here above me
Towering high overhead
And the doors that stand open for them here
Have no doorways left open for me.

At the hour of dusk, then, I wrap up my things
To close the shop . . . on Dizengoff
For the journey back to a separate life
And to a very different Hebrew.

Translated by Judith Katz

T. Carmi

T. Carmi was born in New York City in 1925 and settled in Israel in 1947. He has lectured and read his poetry in Israel, Europe, and the United States. He has received the Shlonsky Prize for Poetry, the Brenner Prize for Literature, and the Prime Minister's Prize for Creative Writing. He has published eight volumes of poetry and has been translated into English. His Selected Poems *appeared in 1976.*

The Condition

First I'll sing. Later, perhaps, I'll speak.
I'll repeat the words

Like someone memorizing his face at morning.
I'll return to my silences

The way the moon wanes.
In public I'll hoist the black fowl of sorrow

Like a boy drawing his sword on Purim.
I'll court your closed hands

Like a lantern that is endlessly blackening.
So, I'll return, keep silence, weep,

And I'll sing. First I'll sing. I'll wrap the words
In paper bags, like pomegranates.

Later, perhaps, we'll speak.

Translated by Peter Everwine and Shula Starkman

The Author's Apology

I Closing Prayer: Yom Kippur*

The day draws to an end,
The gate is being locked.
O what a terrible outcry!
Can't you hear?
Open up, open up—
Someone is caught in the gate.

*In the Ne'ilah, the "Concluding Service" of Yom Kippur, the following poem is read (in Hebrew): "Open the gates to us when the gates are being closed, for the day is about to set. The day shall set, the sun shall go down and set—let us enter Your gates"—[Translator's note.]

HEBREW

II Order of the Day

Keep the children happy!
Keep the children happy!
Keep the children happy!

So they won't hear the screeching in our throats
or see the forest of antennae growing from our heads
or hear the tearing on all sides—
  clothing, paper, sheets, sky
So they won't hear the neighbor's eyes cocked behind their shutters
or see the camouflage beneath the skin of our faces
or hear the networks flashing in our bodies

We have to invent a grown-up's code
so we can talk about
  distant bell (fallen)
  green pine (missing)
  little cloud (captured)
  bird's nest (wounded)

Your commanding officer speaking:
A bird's nest, hovering
on a little cloud,
is landing in a green pine
to the tinkling of a distant bell.
Good night. Over and out.

Keep the children happy!
Keep the children happy!

III Sudden Remembrance

Adam, the first man, sits,
giving names to the animals,
breath to the words.

This morning I sit surrounded
by animals, flowers, sky,
and keep still,
unwilling to relinquish
the bit of air left to me.

IV The Neighbor

His shutters are locked.
Before? After?
His face is sealed.

The distant shouts of children
taking off, soaring,
chalk scratching
the blackboard of the sky,
the rattle of windowpanes.

He pulls a sheet up over the sounds
but the sand of the hourglass
pounds in his throat
grain by grain—
deafening timebombs.

V Anatomy of a War

1
I'm not ready yet.
One more day.
One more day.

Today my eyes crave
the tiniest creature,
the invisible motions of water,
the innermost rooms.
To see the pulse of a sudden crystal,
the first bubble at the brink of boiling.
To enter the eye of the blackbird
among twenty snowy mountains.
To hear the vines paling
on an autumn night,
an October night.

I'm not ready yet,
not yet.
One more day.

HEBREW

2
Repeat
Breach
Mother
Bulge
Widow
Mine
Father
Field
Orphan
Tank
March
Bridge
Zone
Repeat

3
Be for us a mouth
agape, a battered shoe, a breathing gunbarrel.

Be for us a hand
beating, a palm, a lined map, a text.

Be for us an eye
seeing.

Be for us an ear
hearing, a foot walking, a pomegranate brow.

Be.

4
During this war, I sat
in an air-conditioned room
and followed what was happening
on land, at sea, in the air.

I sat in the depths of the earth,
close to the well-informed sources.
Only from the eyes of those
descending and ascending
could I tell if it was day or night.

I knew all the codewords.
Like a man inside a fable
but not knowing the moral—
How can I make my point?

5
This is the author's apology:

I said to my face—
Stay with me.
But it widened suddenly like a lake
struck by rocks from the sky,
and it didn't return to me.

I said to my dreams—
The night is yours to rule.
But in droves they invaded my day.
The sun rose, the sun set,
and I couldn't tell.

I said to my name—
Stick with me.
I kept a signed snapshot in my pocket,
fingered it endlessly.
Too much, it seems.

I was stripped of face, of day, of name.

That was the author laying himself bare;
that was his apology.

6
Serpent, serpent,
go tell the Supreme Serpent
we're all choking underneath our old skins.

Serpent, serpent,
go tell the Supreme Serpent
our baby eyes are hardening in our foreheads,

our old hands are like rusty pliers,
our old mouths like shoes in the desert,
our old tongues like deformed keys,
the old venom seethes in our lungs.

Serpent, serpent,
go tell the Supreme Serpent
to give us back the seasons of the year,
summer and spring, winter and fall

and the moon at night.

VI

What happened—really happened
What happened—really happened
What happened—really happened
I believe with perfect faith
That I'll have the strength to believe that
What happened—really happened.

Translated by Marcia Falk

Abraham Chalfi

Abraham Chalfi was born in Lodz, Poland, in 1904. He came to Palestine in 1924. In 1925 he helped establish the Ohel Theatre, and later became one of the best-known actors in Israel. He published several books of poetry. He died in 1980.

My Father

I live my father's old age,
carry his years
in my flesh.
The two of us are like trees
with dreams huddled
in their branches
from fear of thunder.

Winter rains
fall on us, flood us
without bringing a blessing.
My father asks: what time is it?
I answer: lifetime, father.
And I give him the wine of hope
to drink, that benefits
every hour
and every breath.

My father is sad.

The One Who Is Missing

The one who is missing
was myself.
The one who had been
has left my shoes,
dispensed my coat, one sleeve to one,
one sleeve to another.
My pockets, filled with holes,
he gave away as memory.
Through them my deeds ran
like water.

Toast my memory
with an unsighed sigh
as I used to drink
when I sat among you
not long ago.

The one who is missing
was myself.

Translated by Shlomo Vinner and Howard Schwartz

Raquel Chalfi

Raquel Chalfi, born in Israel and reared in Mexico, is a poet, filmmaker, and playwright. Her first collection of poems was published in Israel in 1975, the same year one of her plays was published in Drama and Theatre. *She currently teaches film at Tel Aviv University and is a program writer/director for Israel Radio.*

Like a Field Waiting

I am like a field
waiting.
The earth
rolls in my roots
and lava streams
explode at the base of the globe.
I am like a field waiting.
Thistles in my flesh
and an olive tree, thick with generations
feeds off me.
At the field's edge
small animals lay an ambush for me.

I am like a field waiting.
My crops are meager
What are they
compared to the lava streaming under me
or the sediments of time
heaped one on the other
like dark mammoths. My
crops wither
and there are so many things
a field can wait for when
predators wait at her edge.

Translated by Myra Glazer Schotz

A Childless Witch

You dare not tell me
I'd be pregnant with a monster.
My belly can hold all the angels of the sky,
the little fiends of the abyss. My warmth
can blanket the earth with down—dig tunnels
of love for me inside.

You dare not tell me.
In the depths of my womb the bells
of the deep madly ring:
when my lover knows me, he knows me
till he loses himself in the oblivion
of a final fall. For him
I'm a ceaseless whirlpool
whose ripples spread over the words.
I'll sow shudders over the old
continents: the soft down of the sea
will stiffen with pleasure.

You dare not tell me. I'll swarm lizards
out of all this love, cover the earth
with flames if not with pink babies.
I'll unravel cushions of my love,
toss clouds of feathers into the sky.
I'll wipe out gravitation.
When a man sleeps with me,

God sleeps with me.
Put stones in my belly,
rend it like a wolf's.
First, though,
let me consume all
with a craving like this,
a craving like this.

Translated by Alexandra Meiri and Myra Glazer Schotz

A Witch Going Down to Egypt

Layer upon layer, with clay and bricks and hard work,
I have built myself Pithom and Rameses,
treasure cities at the mouth of an overflowing river,
granaries of wheat and stubble at hunger's mouth.
I was a mass of despised slaves,
I was clay and bricks and blood
unable to wash my wounds in the river.
Pithom and Rameses were dreams without an answer.
I drove my herd of slaves with hard whips
and I built and hoarded dams
at an overflowing river.
Year after year I ground my teeth to dust.
When I was a slave I shaved my head,
I shaved my head entirely, I was dust
and I was grinding dust and my meek body
was ground to dust and slowly my treasure cities
grew higher and higher and there
I buried my wheat, there I buried
a few grains ground by my ten thousand teeth.
I rolled boulders to their gates
and no one left or came to, came to or left my cities.
I was like tribes of old survivors,
dark and dry as parchment, sitting on top
of bold mountains, my eyes unused
to the white light. And neither Aaron's rod
nor the tongue of Moses saved my life,
only blood and locusts and lice and boils
and frogs and the ruins of exile
and my roasted body

my skull.

Translated by Mariana Potasman

HEBREW

Shlomit Cohen

Shlomit Cohen was born in Israel in 1946. She studied Bible and Hebrew literature at Tel Aviv University. Her collection of poetry, Six on the Left Hand, *appeared in 1975, and other poems have appeared in Israeli magazines and journals. She has also recently published a book of children's legends.*

The Same Dream

The same dream always—
They send me out of the garden
I take off on yellow sand
I see how the wind scatters the ashes of the phoenix with cold eyes
and in a transparent cloud, you,
wearing an embroidered shirt
your smile spellbound, your eyes evil,
an old abandonment written on your face.
My dream plagues my eyelids
wanting an answer—
my image was not on the cloud nor anywhere else.

An Unraveled Thought

There's definitely been a mistake. I wasn't
in the Valley of the Butterflies. I didn't ask
for silk threads or drawings
of filaments of grace.
I was here. I turned a key in the door.
I saw a spider leap with wretched lust
and spin a room.
Someone threw me a spool from the window
and spun thin threads becoming
ropes on my body.
Now, opposite a cracked mirror,
I weave my unraveled thought.

Translated by Myra Glazer Schotz

Wife of Kohelet

1
Wife of Kohelet, the fish in the pond are dead.
This is the fountain near the courtyard,
the house drawn from hollow stones,
the smiles hidden in autumn spider webs.
You have taught the bells their inner silence—
a cushioned melody—
Your eyes take in cracks and splinters
of the slanted roof
You aren't drunk, nor has your smile crumbled.

2
Your husband's grandfather labors over history,
a man of books and hacking cough.
You count fragments of sky in your fire,
other skies.

3
Your elbow at the window, cloistered woman,
you ponder the smell of the street waxing yellow
your shadow falling without choruses of affection
passed over without a glance.
Wife of Kohelet, at the window
your eyes burn to see
a dove turn blue
or seem to.

Translated by Yishai Tobin

Moshe Dor

Moshe Dor was born in Tel Aviv in 1932. He studied at the universities of Tel Aviv and Jerusalem. Since 1954 he has published ten volumes of poetry, three collections of children's verse, a volume of literary essays, and a book of interviews with foreign writers visiting Israel. He has translated into Hebrew Robert Graves, Jack London, and others. Maps of Time, *a selection of his poems in English translation, appeared in 1978.*

The Dwelling

on alien ground I dwelt and also
I ate on the Day of Atonement unatoned
not even heretic my
eyes are rubies my mouth beaten gold
purple the thread in my beard

I am lord over 127 provinces
and frost in my bones spreads and pitch
plasters my palms

when I determined to build an ark
in order myself to escape on
alien ground a dark bird
cried his dark voice

I did not learn his name as I sank to the depths

my eyes they are rubies my mouth beaten gold
and purple the thread in my beard
a day of atoning for sin
I have not even yet fearlessly
set forward my heresy there is no faith
in my bones I am lord
127 provinces

I wept remembering Zion in the cold
when kingdoms
fall and dark are the wings of the bird
its cries a sea
of darkness I do not know my name

Translated by Dennis Johnson

Small Bones Ache

Small bones ache. A small
pain gnaws, needing no metaphors. A
country small in its love grows towards
hunger.

Nights' candles are no candles
for the night. A map carved in the bones
is not valid when examined. Small
bones ache.

Names are being obscured. Hunger nags. Pain
calls with the voice of a small turtledove. With
fingers of grease and dust
blind people trace countries of light upon
a map of skin.

Candles are extinguished. Small bones
ache.

Translated by Ruth Fainlight

Among the Pine Trees

Among the pine trees
the voice of a dove as thin
feet run over cones, the countryside listens
with joy until

the first shot, then the next. A burst of shooting.

And there are figures taller than birds.
All birdsong muffled in their cries.
Silenced in the soft blue breath of their dying.

Thin and red are the feet of a dove
over needles and cones.

The countryside listens to the pause
and waits for sounds that wandered once
over pine-tree tops and can no longer
be heard. Although we listen sadly.

Translated by Elaine Feinstein

Nightingales Are Not Singing

Nightingales are not singing here,
but the veil of sleep caresses
the eyes beneath the casuarinas
and the mountain sun, stamping them
with spring, as with an ancient gold.

Once upon a time there was a war
and the eyes, guessing desperately
the sniper's bullet, burned

with salt sweat. Fingers
of the breeze test
the canopy of light. Even without

nightingales it is enough
that a turtledove should utter
the syllables of David and Michal
in gold brocade. But once
upon a time there was
a war, the dry throat pleaded silently,
and the reluctant limbs
charged as ordered among rocks, wild

wheat, the enmity of nettles. The shade
drips green forgetfulness.
Nightingales never poured out here

their magnificent throats, nor angels
passionately wept
at the melodies of any Orpheus
of the Middle Sea. But once
upon a time there was a war
and I am content with the redolence
of resin
that loosed in warm drops
soothes the tired eyelids,
mitigates the battles of salt and
gold.

Translated by Dennis Johnson

Anadad Eldan

Anadad Eldan was born on Kibbutz Beeri, one of the oldest kibbutzim in Israel, where he still lives as a teacher. He has published five books of poetry, among them The Flowing Darkness and the Fruit, Not by Stone Alone, *and* Interior Light. *In 1978 his* Selected Poems *was published in Israel.*

Words That Speak of Death

Words that speak of death
are frail and blind like chance.
Words that speak of death
drift slow as bubbles
through the fine veins of the heart.

Words you wrote in green
quietly implore
while the sunflower
turns its face.

The words that speak of death
are low as grass.

Wind in the reeds:
it is not words that speak of death.

Translated by Anthony Rudolf and Natan Zach

Who Will Give Cover?

Not a viper with milk beneath its tongue.
No plowshares.
Not even a leopard basking on the beach
and a little child to lead him.
No sea for the streams and for the wind
no ravine to reside in.
But the water receding and every day
a new scar on the ridge.
Who will give cover to the slope?
A passing raven screams: my olives are uprooted.
No dove, no ark will come back,
no grandpa Noah will return.

Samson Rends His Clothes

When I went
to Gaza and met
Samson coming out rending his clothes
on his flailed face rivers streamed
and the houses bent to allow him
passage.
His pain uprooted trees and clung
to the tangle
of the roots. Among the roots the locks
of his hair.
His head shone like a skull of stones.
The tramp of his tread tore my tears. I heard
how the earth groaned beneath his step,
how he crushed its belly.
Samson went dragging a tired sun.
Fragments of suns and chains sank
in the Gaza sea.

Translated by Ruth Nevo

Jakov Fichman

Jakov Fichman was born in Bessarabia in 1881. He left home at the age of fourteen and spent the next thirty years moving among various cities in Russia, Western Europe, and Palestine. He remained an adherent of the classical lyric tradition which was reflected in biblical poems, elegies, and the literary works which he edited in Warsaw and Israel. Fichman died in 1958.

Eve

I love Adam. He is brave of heart,
his blood is generous; and he, like God,
is wise. But the serpent whispers things
that are so strange. They hurt—and they caress.

When Adam sleeps, Eden lies desolate;
its birds are silent and its grass is wet.
And then *he* kindles, calling from the thicket,
a bonfire in my heart. "Pick it! Pick it!"

How good to feel at dawn Adam's warm hand
caress my flesh again, and in the hush
listen to the coursing of its blood,
But every bush of day that drinks the light
bends to a darkness. Eden is enchanted
only till night awakes the shadow in the brush.

Abishag

I waste my teeming age. I do not know
when crops grow golden and the earth brings forth.

Early the world arises there to blossom,
but here my days fall silently like leaves.

My woods of chastity grow taller daily,
rustling sadly—without a bird of song.

In castle splendor, in imperial purple,
a locust wilderness devours my bloom.

I leave my chamber, and like lips that burn
the dazzle of the white day welcomes me.

The heat of gardens, fronds dancing in the sun,
ignite a fire rising in my blood.

Peering from the secrecy of casements,
the unseen eyes of princes kiss my footsteps.

And then sometimes a tenderness floats in me,
my heavy blossom aches,

And all my unconceiving, unattempted flesh
—a vine neglected—yearns the gatherer.

But when night finds me sleepless and my eye
pierces the darkness of the frozen castle,

like a bird in its morning nest, a world then stirs,
the king's heart plays upon the fiddle strings.

This splendor hiding in wrinkles of pale day
rises from ashes when night's glory sings.

Night's castle sinks, and grief is drowned in grief
as wave is drowned in wave. And every sound

calling my poverty from the midnight dark
is gathered with it to the caves of song.

O song of midnight! in which my blood flows purely
(as sap in tender branches) to the dawn.

All of my warmth I give to the old King—
his heart plays the weeping of my Spring.

Translated by Robert Friend

Amir Gilboa

Amir Gilboa was born in the Ukraine in 1917 and traveled to Palestine as an illegal immigrant in 1937. Among his many literary prizes are the Prime Minister's Award for Creative Writing, and the Bialik Prize. A translation of his selected poems, The Light of Lost Suns, *was recently published.*

Isaac

It was early morning
and the sun walked through the forest
with my father and me,
my right hand in his left.

A knife flashed between the trees like lightning
and I was afraid, for my eyes
saw the blood on the leaves.

Father, Father, hurry to save Isaac
so that no one will be missing
at the next meal.

I am the one who is slain, my son;
my blood is already on the leaves.
And my father stifled his voice
and his face grew pale.

And I wanted to cry out in disbelief
and tear my eyes open.
And I woke up.

And there was no blood left
in my right hand.

Translated by Howard Schwartz

Moses

I went up to Moses and said to him:
Deploy the troops this way and that way.
He looked at me
and did exactly as I said.

And who did not see me then in my glory?
Sarah from my childhood was there,
in whose name I had planned to build a city.
The girl with the long legs was there, from the workers' farm.
Melvina was there, from Rabbat in Malta.
Dina from the Italo-Yugoslav border.
And Ria from the lowlands in the north.

And, very proud, I hurried to Moses
to show him the right way,
and suddenly I realized
that she who is clearly inscribed
inside my name—
was missing.

Moses Moses lead the people.
Don't you see, I am so tired,
and I want to sleep some more.
I am still a child.

Translated by Stephen Mitchell

Joshua's Face

And Joshua looks down on my face. And his face
is hammered gold. A dream embalmed. And cold.
And at my feet the sea strikes endless time.
I'm sick of its wailing. Perhaps, about to die.
But I am forced to stay alive
forever.
My brother's face rises in a cloud
to read my footsteps in the sea-washed sand.

The sea strikes and withdraws. Strikes and withdraws.
The wars of nature conditioned by laws.
Myself in the wind. Different. Running far.
Now Joshua also rests from war
and leaves his people a home
though he carved no tomb of his own
in the mountains of Ephraim.
Night after night
he walks the sky.
And I am sick, perhaps, about to die
barefoot in cold moon sand
on the shore
while the end roars in me, a roar
that strikes my own death at my feet
wave after wave—

high over many lives
may he be raised and glorified.

Saul

Saul! Saul!
I don't know if it was shame
or fear of a head with no body
but when I passed near the wall of Beit-She'an
I turned my head.

Then, when your boy refused you the sword you ordered,
I stood dumb, unable to speak
and blood drained from my heart.
I really can't say what I would have done
if I'd been your boy.

You are the king.
And you your majesty the king give orders.

And I really can't say what I would have done.

Saul Saul come back!
In Beit-She'an the people of Israel wait.

Translated by Shirley Kaufman

My Brother Was Silent

My brother came back from the field
In gray clothing.
And I was afraid my dream would be false
And began at once to count his wounds.
And my brother was silent.

Then I burrowed into the pockets of his tunic
And found a dressing with a dried stain,
And on a crumpled postcard his girl's name
Beneath a picture of some poppies.
And my brother was silent.

And I undid his bundle
And took out his things, memory after memory.
Hurray, my brother, my heroic brother,
Look, I've found your symbols!
Hurray, my brother, my heroic brother,
I'll shout your praises!
And my brother was silent.
And my brother was silent.

And his blood cried out of the ground.

Translated by A. C. Jacobs

HEBREW

Samson

And Samson grew old in days
and his sleep left him in the nights.
He was still a child when he picked up the world on its axis with one
hand.
When he grew up, he hoped he would die on the night that he was
seventeen years old.
He didn't want to die old: seventeen and a day.
That's why he tied firebrands to the three hundred foxes' tails,
to burn everything down.
In his twenties he planned to do wonders up to his death at the age
of thirty-three.
In the days when they gouged out his eyes
he prayed that he would live to see the weddings of his daughters.
At eighty he stopped growing up
and in the forgetfulness of his hours he daydreamed like a newborn
child.

And the gates of his Gaza are still asleep in the ore.

And Delilah

Seeds of Lead

A gray tiled roof.
Sloped.
Bullets were rolling off it
like beans.
Up against the wall
lay Father and my brother Joshua
protecting me—
my walls, my shields.

The sun stood and burned.
Strong. Silent as a bull.
Lighting up the whole mouth of noon
which stretched from the pear garden
to the crab apple hedge.

The well—
an open womb
taking in seeds of lead.
Early in the morning I sneak away to see
how stars, silver in its depths,
are born.

And the faces of Father and my brother Joshua
are like the distance—
statues a thousand years old or more.

After many years this became clear to me
in the gardens of big cities
and in museums.

Birth

The rain has passed.

And still from the roofs and from the trees
it sings in my ears
and covers my head
with a bluish bridal veil.

Good for you, my God,
the child is caught in your net.
Look, I will bring leaf to leaf
and I will see how leaf covers leaf
and how the drops blend.
And I will call the swallows down
to marriage from my sky.
And all my windows I will adorn
with flower pots.

Good for you, my God,
the child is caught in your net.
I open my eyes—
my earth is all one piece, engraved
with the stalks of flowers,
green.

O my God,
how embraced we have been!

Translated by Stephen Mitchell

HEBREW

Zerubavel Gilead

Zerubavel Gilead was born in Bessarabia in 1912, and has lived from early childhood at Kibbutz Ein-Harod. He has published eleven books of poetry, four books of stories, and four books for children. He is also the author of the famous "Song of the Palmach" and a collector and editor of documentary material. He has received several prizes, including the Prime Minister's Prize for Creative Writing.

Absalom

1

I galloped on a scarlet filly
like Absalom on
his mule:
my curls in the breeze and my heart
sang:
King of song, king of song!
The moon's light set dancing
the shadow of the terebinth
like the veil of a bride
in the forest's glade.
Young, young, young man—
Is it your voice my son
Absalom?

2

Your face paled
and your breath
and the palms of your hands embracing
my head.
A branch of a buckthorn blackened
suddenly in the window—
each leaf turned its face
and whitened in the terrible
silence.

3
I listen. I listen.
Stick my ear to the ground
as in an ambush. Lay my head on a stone
listen as in Beth-El.
From the treetop above me
a ladder of light
pallid.
I shake myself. Strain my eyes
brace my heart:
Did the border pass through Beth-El?
Why do you ask? Someone
caught in the thorn.

Pomegranate Tree in Jerusalem

1
The pomegranate tree in my garden adorns itself
with golden foliage like honey
of citrus. I remember your eyes
even the shadow of their lashes
amber.
"Tell me your name,"
I said to you when we met
suddenly in a deserted
lane. It was a hot day.
A hard wind. And you ever
new.
A moss-covered wall, silent
beside us,
bloomed at sight of you
with the song of bees.
"There are flowers
behind this wall," you said,
your eyes singing.

2
The electric light went out.
You lit
a Sabbath candle in a weekday
candlestick. Blue,
blue beat the shadow
of the pomegranate tree on the window and a song
bloomed from behind the wall
close as a tear.
And now the electric light!
The candle pales and the gold
of your eyes was shed, lost
between wall
and wall.

3
It is no longer a bush and not yet
a tree but
its blossom lights up in red fire
on a golden fire, and a pale green
thread of grace
despairing and tranquil.
"Stop, stop," you
whisper,
"Lest you wake the pain."

*Flying Letters**

I remember that before
I fell asleep
I put a marker between the pages.
But that seemed far off
and not real
when the black fire
caught the book
and the letters flew up
screaming.
Question marks tore
my skin
exclamation marks beat, beat—
until I sank
into darkness.

Translated by Dorothea Krook

*There is a Jewish legend that when the Temple was burned down the letters of the Holy Scrolls flew up to the sky.

Leah Goldberg

Leah Goldberg, born in Lithuania in 1911, became one of Israel's most popular poets and a distinguished critic. She arrived in Palestine in 1935 and began teaching Comparative Literature at Hebrew University in 1952. Her English-language Selected Poems *was published in 1976.*

*Heavenly Jerusalem, Jerusalem of the Earth**

1

Divide your bread in two,
Heavenly Jerusalem, Jerusalem of the Earth,
jewels of thorn on your slopes
and your sun among the thistles.
A hundred deaths rather than your mercy!
Divide your bread in two,
one half for the birds of the sky:
the other,
for heavy feet to trample
at the crossroads.

2

People are walking in the counterfeit city
whose heavens passed like shadows,
and no one trembles.
Sloping lanes conceal
the greatness of her past.

The children of the poor
sing with indifferent voices:
"David, King of Israel, lives and is."

3

Over my house
one late swallow.
All the other swallows
have already returned to the north.

*In the midrashic and Kabbalistic literature there is frequent reference made to a Heavenly Jerusalem that is the mirror image of the earthly one and after which the earthly one was modeled.

HEBREW

Over my head
towards evening,
in a city
weary of wanderings
in a city of wanderers,
small, trembling wings
trace circles of despair.

A sky of Hebron glass.
The first lamp of night.
Swallow with no nest.
Arrested flight.

What now?

A God Once Commanded Us

A god once commanded us to stand strong
under the terrible tree of life.
And in the black wind of the years we stood,
stricken with expectation—
perhaps the fruit would fall at our feet.
But nothing happened.

And on the day of secret reckoning
between him and us
we saw a hunched landscape, brown leaves falling,
and felt on our faces
a cold wind blowing.

Then said a Voice: this is your day of freedom.
This is everything. And this is good.

Now towards the flame of cutting cold, alone,
I take
a few steps only
until I meet
that flickering lantern
at the corner of the street.

From My Mother's Home

My mother's mother died
in the spring of her days. And her daughter
did not remember her face. Her portrait engraved
in my grandfather's heart
was struck from the world of images
after his death.

Only her mirror remains, sunk deeper with age
into its silver frame.
And I, her pale granddaughter, who do not resemble her,
peer into it today as if it were a pool
hiding its treasures
under the water.

Deep deep beyond my face
I see a young woman
pink-cheeked and smiling,
a wig on her head.
She is putting
a long earring into the lobe of her ear. Threading it
through a tiny hole in the delicate flesh.

Deep deep beyond my face
shines her eyes' bright gold.
The mirror carries on
the family tradition:
that she was beautiful.

Toward Myself

The years have made up my face
with memories of love,
adorned my head
with light silver threads
and made me beautiful.

Landscapes are reflected
in my eyes,
the paths I trod
have taught me to walk upright
with beautiful, though tired, steps.

If you should see me now,
you would not recognize
the yesterdays you knew.
I go toward myself with a face
you looked for in vain
when I went toward you.

Answer

To a questionnaire, which asked: What purpose does it serve to write lyric poems in our time?

And what are we to do with the horses
in this twentieth century?
And what with the gazelles
and the huge stones
of our Jerusalem hills?

Translated by Robert Friend

Uri Zvi Greenberg

Uri Zvi Greenberg was born in Galicia in 1896. His family was murdered in the Holocaust. He started to publish poetry in 1912, both in Yiddish and Hebrew. He settled in Palestine in 1923. His books of poetry reflect a nationalistic vision and a lyrical point of view, as well as a lament for the Jewish catastrophe.

With My God, the Smith

Like chapters of prophecy my days burn, in all the revelations,
And my body between them's a block of metal for smelting,
And over me stands my God, the Smith, who hits hard:
Each wound that Time has opened in me opens its mouth to him
And pours forth in a shower of sparks the intrinsic fire.

This is my just lot—until dusk on the road.
And when I return to throw my beaten block on a bed,
My mouth is an open wound,
And naked I speak with my God:
You worked hard.
Now it is night; come, let us both rest.

Like a Woman

Like a woman who knows that her body entices me,
God taunts me, Flee if you can! But I can't flee,
For when I turn away from him, angry and heartsick,
With a vow on my lips like a burning coal:
I will not see him again—

I can't do it,
                I turn back
And knock on his door,
Tortured with longing

As though he had sent me a love letter.

The Great Sad One

The Almighty has dealt bitterly with me
That I did not believe in him until my punishment,
Till he welled up in my tears, from the midst of my wounds.
And behold, he also is very lonely,
And he also lacks someone to confess to,
In whose arms he might sob his unbearable misery—

And this God walks about, without a body, without blood,
And his grief is double the grief of flesh,
Flesh that can warm another body or a third,
That can sit and smoke a cigarette
And drink coffee and wine,
And sleep and dream until the sun—

For him it is impossible, for he is God.

How It Is

I hear the sound of affliction. They are weeping,
It seems—human beings, male and female.
Once I heard only the joy of those who were married
To the juice and sweetness of life.

There's no need to ask why they weep—it's clear enough.
If women are weeping, it's a sign of their defilement;
If men, what could it mean but the loss
Of great faiths as powerful as the earth?

Souls that go forth gaily on their wanderings,
Adorned with their colorful visions,
How wan they are, and shrunken, when they come back!

The Valley of Men

I have never been on the cloudy slopes of Olympus.
In the living man's valley I grew with the bread.
Like other men, I drank the sweet water there,
Waters where cattle drank, whose flesh I ate.

The Queen's train my forefathers did not carry, amongst the
Gentiles.
The King did not call them, neither in sorrow nor in joy.
They were poor Jews, shining and singing,
Little more than the shepherd blows through his flute.

So I am pleased to carry myself from sorrow to sorrow,
As a shepherd his littlest sheep from pasture to pasture,
And he eats a few figs, to keep the breath in his body—

Red seamed are the ends of my days and nights.

There is a Box

There is a box and a coverlet, and a pair of black horses
Stepping forth heavily, in honor, of course, of the grief.
There is a spade, and a strong man, the digger,
White linen, and a girl who sews.

Adam is dust, the Rabbi must surely be rotting by now,
And what remains in writing—a doctrine of no death.
I speak of what feeds down there in the mire.
There is nothing in books, only a few words.

The Hour

The hour is very weary, as before sleep.
Like a foundling child, just in my white shirt,
I sit and write in space, as on a slate—
No matter, no matter.

Should the black cat come to the pitcher and drink
The remnants of white milk and overturn the pitcher,
I will close my eyes to sleep and sleep forever—
No matter, no matter.

On the Pole

Some clouds are rainclouds—
On my head like a mist the mercy of sorrow transpires.
It is good to command the boat of all longings:
Stop and anchor.

For here is the Pole--and joy is native
To the place of childhood, garlanded with beauty.
It is good to descend, to rake in the remnants of honey
And the white milk—in the final place.

Translated by Robert Mezey and Ben Zion Gold

HEBREW

Song at the Skirts of Heaven

Like Abraham and Sarah by the trees of Mamre
Awaiting the happy word,
Like David and Bathsheba in the royal house
That first night embracing,
My mother and my father rise martyred
On the sea in the west,
All the gleam of God's light upon them.
Slowly the weight of their beauty pulls them down,
Above them the mighty sea streams.
Beneath is their deep home.

No walls enclose that dwelling
Built of water in water;
The drowned of Israel swim there
Through spaces of sea;
In each mouth there is a star.
What they say
Is not revealed to song.
They know that in the sea—

Like a quenched harp, its radiant, flashing melody gone,
Am I their good son
Standing there by the shore, sharing its height with time.
And it happens when evening reaches my heart
Bringing the sea,
I walk out seawards
As if summoned to the skirts of heaven to witness:
The sun a sinking wheel,
At left and right revealed
My father and my mother,
He and she
Treading with naked foot
A running burning sea.

Translated by Zvi Jagendorf

Zali Gurevitch

Zali Gurevitch was born in 1949 and grew up in Tel Aviv. His poetry has appeared in several Israeli literary magazines and in 1978 he won the Hershon Literary Award at Hebrew University. Gurevitch lives in Jerusalem, where he is completing work for a graduate degree in social psychology.

Short Eulogy

They spoke
of the queen at night growing
into other scales.

In her palm she once resuscitated fluttering
birds, disheveling a hedge from her hair
she plaited braids from dark air
around her balcony.

One day her face turned.
Click, she locked her purse's lips, placed it
by her side, left an agitated tea to catch cold
had no mercy, not on a soul
and on herself. . . .

He who broke bread with her
tipped his hat.

Not Going with It

Not going with it to the end,
waiting, perhaps it will pass on the run
exchanging well-baked conversations
over a hot glass of tea near the usual table

who will go with me to the end?
I will—to the end and still
not thirty

age runs its course
it falls on me without a pinch of sweetness
when there isn't a chance to find
a person home,
nor a right place to sleep with me
it's like that—only tomorrow I could
write this.

Translated by Gabriel Levin

HEBREW

Haim Guri

Haim Guri was born in Tel Aviv in 1926. He studied at Hebrew University and the Sorbonne. While his early poems (1949) reflect the poignant passion of the war generation, his later poems are laced with a sense of estrangement and disillusion. Guri has published six books of poetry to date.

Isaac

The ram came last.
And Abraham did not know
that it answered the question
that had come first
in the sunset of his life.

When he raised his white head
he saw he was not dreaming;
when he saw the angel
the knife dropped from his hand.

The boy who was unbound
saw the back of his father.

Isaac, it is told, was not sacrificed.
He had a long life, a good life,
until his eyes went dark.

But that hour
he bequeathed to his descendants
still to be born
a knife
in the heart.

Translated by Naomi Tauber and Howard Schwartz

Anath

This translation is dedicated to the memory of Anath Bental, 1950-1975
—H. S.

Along the path where your light feet passed
your footsteps have been lost forever;
wandering sands have covered them without a trace.
That is the verdict of oblivion, Anath.
But my heart, which returns to you, remembers you upon a desert
land.
At night there are no frontiers between us,
there is no distance, no fences.
I pass with the winds, such is my way, unseen,
to every forgotten earth mound, to the most abandoned and lonely
of the ways leading to the mountain of God.
The terrible rocky desert, the visions of light, the wild landscapes,
the waterless and treeless desolation, facing skies of copper.
A place where you were betrothed to fire and lead;
a flaming marriage canopy to the melody of a band of hyenas.
I have accompanied the bridegroom to the light,
passing with the melody of your wedding,
gathering all distances, bearing all the adventures.
Anath, the ancients gazed upon you, on your nights.
From the temples of our sparse lines, the fire and lead.
Now all is silent. No one fires.
Stars emerge in the night, and facing them, speechless,
stands the dream of silence.
Animal tracks, stone walls in the sky,
and an abandoned cannon
silent as an iron tombstone,
and you are not there. Along these paths
your footsteps have been lost forever.
Only a lofty rock listens to a choir of jackals.
I pass and gather your bones into my pack,
into the tomb of my memory.

Translated by N. N. and Howard Schwartz

HEBREW

My Samsons

Behold, my Samsons are returning, and the gates of Gaza are on
their shoulders:
They pass, a smile, the blind sentries.
Satureja. Wind. Crickets.

Behold, my Samsons are returning, Delilahs at their feet;
They pass down my avenue.
I am awake.

Behold, my Samsons are returning, and they remember the lions
they held in their bare hands;
Barefoot, they tread lightly,
In the street no sound is heard, no flame is burning.

Behold, my Samsons are returning, and their ears still hear the frogs
of the valley of Sorek;
They go on their way, they always go on their way,
When was the last time I carried gates on my shoulders?

Behold, my Samsons are returning and the meat of the sacrifice-feast
is still between their teeth;
The wet bowstrings have been broken and the riddles have been
solved,
My first gray hair.

Behold, my Samsons are returning, no harshness in their glance;
They are returning to me from Gath,
Now that the firing has ended.

Behold, my Samsons are returning in the thick of night
Lit up by the flaming foxes.

Nine Men Out of a Minyan

Nine men out of a *minyan**, nine men who are thrown into a pit
Are not sold up above. As a caravan of Ishmaelites passes,
They stay in the pit.

Or else they crawl out or else they crawl out
In the dark, in order to breathe heavily.
In order to be silent in the rising dawn:
Now that it is day, where are they in this desert?

They do not move southward, to the Egypt of wheat
And dreams
To be a laughing stock and a puzzle,
To make pretenses in the king's palace.

Nor do they tread silently between divination and the magicians of
Egypt and royal purple cloth,
Between walls of basalt and silence.
Nor do they hear at night the feet of Potiphar's wife
On mute stones.

Nor are they helped by God
As they stand before the king's enigmatic riddles,
Until they become his right hand,
In war and in the grain storehouses.

They stay in the pit and in the desert
And climb up for the wars and climb up for the wars
To tear their teeth into the bread of violence and injustice,
To meet women who have no name.

To return to Jacob who awaits them in their dream.

**minyan*—a minimum of ten adult Jewish males, known as a *minyan*, are required to be present for congregational worship.

HEBREW

And on My Return

And on my return there are no traces on my face and on my clothes
Because this plague cannot be seen
Nor does it have horsemen galloping before it
Nor does it issue declarations of impending pallor.

And thus do I walk on and walk on and I know of other things
In another softer language
Soft as the silence that hovers over the empty city.

And my wisdom is profound and grows dark beneath my long
fingernails
And grows white in the hairs of my head,
As if I had exchanged my name and my family's name
And the very distant land of my birth.

Nor do I remember when I died
And when the ram's horn aroused me
To the rolling of the dead to resurrection and to Zion.

And on my return a very large sun hangs frozen in the metallic sky
As in a heavy heat wave above the towers
But I remember the names held fast within my clenched fists
And I have not forgotten the streets.

And on my return my face is creased with a great and glorious smile
worth the gold
Of these outstretched skies
For I have come from a land that is very low indeed.

And on my return to my city which I remember with tender grace
and mercy
I am like an angel
Before whom those who are afraid shut their eyes tight
But I am not an angel nor have I come in a dream.

Rain

He places his hand on her head as a hand placed against pain,
As the last hand in the world.
What remains to be said, and what remains to be heard?
What can she say to him? What can he say to her?

She says nothing, only his voice touches her,
Like a hand touching carefully and softly,
Like a hand asking whether she may be pitied,
Whether she may hear words of comfort that have not yet been
heard,
Slow, long words of comfort.
Warm as a mother, wise as a father.

Rain is falling hesitantly. Then it grows strong.
Most of it falls into the streams that flow to the sea.
And a little, falling on the leaves, becomes pearls waiting for the sun.

A Latter Purification

Without your knowledge they are turning your wounds into words
And your path upon the water's surface cannot be seen
Nor can the sea be heard.

Above you, slowly, the clouds move and change:
Islands and places and women's faces all of vapor
And the wind blows softly.

A marble city has returned to nestle upon the cliffs.
It doesn't ask what troubles you.

Your strange deaths have taken on hexameter form
They become more and more beautiful in the dark
You are slowly becoming lines that will outlive you.

And so you take leave of your movements
Take leave of the salty ropes, the shining swords
And the women whose hands follow you
Until you become a black dot.

You are a line and yet another line.

Translated by Mark Elliott Shapiro

HEBREW

Shimon Halkin

Shimon Halkin was born in Russia in 1898. He emigrated in 1914 to the United States, where he later served as Professor of Hebrew Literature at the Jewish Institute of Religion in New York. In 1949 Halkin settled in Israel as Professor of Modern Hebrew Literature at Hebrew University. Poet, novelist, critic, and literary historian, he has published numerous books. He has also translated works by Whitman, Shelley, and Shakespeare into Hebrew.

Do Not Accompany Me

The thorns have whitened along the way
to the burial.
Don't come with me any further:
the way is long for you,
for me it's short. My uncle
is standing there already in the dug-out grave,
the only one, during all my days among you
who really waited for me,
there in the earth tunnels.
Don't come any further.
The thorns have already whitened.

Against my will this time I go before you.
Believe me: only apparently first.
The dead are never angry, not even
for as long as the blink of an unseeing eye.
And I'm a bit embarrassed
you should feel unease
in thinking of the shroud
that crushes memory. No need. If you,
being only human, slip away
to find a pavement gloating in its shade,
don't be ashamed. Under the *tallit*
your dead one's already whitened. Like the thorns
along the way you find so long. And there's no shame
in turning glances from their pallid stalks
to greening patches
distant, on the horizon.
My uncle in the grave knew well
how my eye always sought green distant fields
before the stacking of untimely sheaves.
Always untimely. So let me seem to go
before you all
this time.

Soon only the innocent swallows will chirp
my requiem: O merciful God,
outside the house of eulogies. In foliage above it. Here
only they know
that a man wrapped in a shroud—
not owning even that—
is still not wholly prey to mourning rites
enacted by the pious clan of Cain.
The birds of the air know this, as do the dead,
who are by nature yielding. Especially one
who was like Abel in his field in life. In death
how much the more so. Blessed be the lark
who sings his praises and those of his uncle
growing towards him out of the open grave.
One of the uncles bred in village earth.
Whether they've vanished, or never were at all,
somewhere they still walk, those uncles
like trees from forests tangled dizzily
in sun or rain.

So perhaps it doesn't matter
that your shame accompanies me.
Soon, when you bury me you'll see one uncle
(or perhaps you won't)
growing towards me from the open grave:
here, from the hollow, half his body protrudes,
an abandoned hoe in his hand, expecting me.
It was always he alone who expected me,
as he rolled through cavities
from vanished villages right up to the trees
that edge the cemetery—a mere green patch
upon the outstretched sands.
He knew he would appear to me today,
here, a grass root in his beard, amazed
to find the earth a little damp even here
if you dig deep enough.
Damp, if you dig, even in this dry land
which thirsts for shade as I did
when I was still a sitter on pavement benches
rejoicing in tamarisk shade
on the short cut to the graveyard.
Trees? Thorns? We all of us, after all,
seized with vertigo, pine for shade
and find none.

Translated by Ruth Nevo

HEBREW

Hedva Harkavi

Hedva Harkavi was born on Kibbutz Degania in Israel. She has lived in Jerusalem since adolescence. She has a degree from the Bezalel Academy for Art in Jerusalem. She has had several exhibitions of her paintings and sculptures, and has published her poems in various Hebrew literary magazines. Her first book of poems won the Newman Prize in Jerusalem in 1973.

Talk to Me, Talk to Me

Talk to me. Talk to me.
I am so attentive.
Behold, a bird is drowning
on the edge of my soul
a bird to whom I have found no answer

darkness in space

and later on, my dreams . . .
and in them all, enveloped in shrouds,
the same woman cries for my dead.

Talk to me. Talk to me.

It Was Gentle

It was gentle.
Far away, the moon crumbled into the sea
and yellow waves, wrapped in ancient gowns,
turned, suddenly, into bells
of whitish silk.

The forests disappeared, and wild
transparent bushes came instead—bushes
of all colors whose arms embraced
a blue eternity

a fragile, dark eternity.

It was gentle.
Someone spoke softly about the death of the morning bird,
about waiting-without-flower, and how,
suddenly,
the white horizon turned into a wave
of strange and unexplained
delusions.
Someone else drew low tunes
on the underside of fear, and played
a yellow night
in another kingdom.

Whenever the Snakes Come

Whenever the snakes come
to die in caves
the man I never knew
stands on the rails
waving hats at me.

A king. I know he is a king.
Bells and wine hang from his neck.
All of his queens clean his face
and to his loins tie
white forests.

A king. I know he is a king.
Behind him a fairy plods along
with chariots of sun in her hands.
Behind him a bird rolls stones
and sand.

A king. I know he is a king.

Translated by Tova Weizman

HEBREW

Avraham Huss

Avraham Huss was born in 1924 in Poland and spent his early childhood in Germany. He came to Palestine in 1933. He is a graduate of Hebrew University in Jerusalem and served in the War of Independence. Since 1949 he has been a member of the staff of Hebrew University where he teaches meteorology. He has published one book of poems, With the Heavy Stone, *and additional poems and criticism have appeared in various journals.*

A Green Refrain

The rain falls and then vanishes.
The earth
Is devouring my mountain. A green refrain
Is bursting forth from the earth's throat:
the foliage of trees, cereals,
Bushes and wild grass. It is a law

That generation follows generation follows
many generations.
And again the yellow summer returns,
Returns and rests, like a cloud of locust
On the dust.
A dance that is endless.

An eternal dance. The wave of vagueness flails
The beaches of existence that are covered with
charming shells,
And the abundant silt-sand piling itself
layer by layer
Is the enemy of hills and the enemy of
mountains.
Indeed

All of our sane meditations will not escape
The empty conclusion that is rooted
In the convulsion of our lives. Our lives in captivity.

Time

What a fine tower the little boy is building with his blocks.
And the little girl consoles the doll that has fallen off the chair.
The ants are crawling in the dust and each of them bears its burden
between its teeth.
Listen, can you hear the clock's pendulum whisper
That there is no time for love?

How uncomfortable it is to learn seven times seven,
But the diligent little girl paints an anemone in her workbook.
A grayish-brown sparrow, serious and nimble,
Is picking out barley seeds among the great boulders along the road,
Because there is no time for love!

How beautiful is the smoothness of her neck, the youth moans.
And she closes her eyes and sees: a prince with a golden
Crown on his head galloping astride a white horse, a handsome
prince.
Clouds are carried off by the wind. White clouds. And they know
That there is no time for love.

An ordinary night descends upon a lovely apartment, so nicely
arranged.
The meal is over. And all the dishes that have been placed in the sink
Peacefully await the attention of the cleaning woman, who will come
in the morning.
The hour is late. They can't keep their eyes open.
Because there is no time for love.

Nocturnal Thoughts

Night, in the sweetness of his murky dominion,
Our spirit blossoms, but his sinews
Grasp the air, as if it were a homeland,
A solid homeland, an ancestral earth. And all his years,

Which are almost as long as eternity, seek
A day that opens with morning, that strides forth
With the confidence of a farmer's legs pounding the ground
And reaching the very steps of evening, and that descends

To rest in a niche of deep sleep.
But we
Have learned the flickering tongue of the candle's flame
And among holy pages we have placed our soul,
Which is now beyond recognition.

Our night is so rich and full
And he wraps us in a heavy and damp morality.
And he consumes us greedily.
And we have forsaken the day,
And we have forgotten.

A Classic Idyll

Something always remains a mystery.
Suddenly from among the reeds
Of a slumbering lake at midday
A mocking satyr emerges, and he is naked.

He embraces a white nymph.
Like a thin reed her body quivers,
And in her capering full of naive and wholesome charm
A drop of water slides from her breast.

The mocking smile vanishes from his face,
A light breeze whispers silently, and now
A billy goat's head with a thin little beard is secretly bowed—
And he kisses the drop as it falls.

And her entire body, in contrast to his, is full of excitement
In the saturated warmth of midday.
A merging of white and dark-brown,
And on her lips—the gauze of desire.

And suddenly, everything vanishes,
Except for the lake in the forest, dreaming
While facing the sun, which seems to be asking
Whether there was any meaning in this entire spectacle.

Translated by Mark Elliott Shapiro

Yehuda Karni

Yehuda Karni was born in Poland in 1884. He was active in the Zionist movement from an early age and settled in Palestine in 1921. His essays and poems voice his love for the homeland and his sorrow over the European Holocaust. His works include Gateways, In Thy Gates, O Homeland, Jerusalem, *and* Song and Tears. *He died in 1949.*

The Four of Them

The hills of Zion
poured loftiness into me,
and her valleys—
depth.

From an eagle
flying in the sky
like an orphan
I learned
loneliness.

And from the sycamore,
whose branches
are lopped off
and only her trunk sends forth
roots,
I sucked
rootedness.

Thus the images
of these four
are engraved
upon me.

HEBREW

Chambers of Jerusalem

Chambers of Jerusalem,
gray and dusty.
By day darkness lies there,
and at night
no lights are kindled.

Like daughters of one family
they all dwell together,
like a flock of ewes
huddling together
out of fear.

Chambers of Jerusalem—
lids on the mouths
of caves.
They brought in all the secrets,
frozen solid
over all that was
concealed.

It sometimes happens
that one small door
suddenly opens
and immediately shuts.
And nothing has changed.

Chambers of Jerusalem
made of clay—
they always seem to be
an altar
or a prayerstand.

If an old Yemenite
were to appear there
in the evening,
he would have the visage
of a prophet
or a priest.

Translated by Jeremy Garber

Rav Abraham Isaac Kook

Rav Abraham Isaac Kook (1865-1935) was a preeminent Talmudic scholar, a Lurianic Kabbalist, and a unique Zionist religious philosopher of his time. He was the first Chief Rabbi of Palestine. His writings include religious meditations and essays and one book of poems.

The First One Drew Me

The first one drew me with his rope
Into his palatial abode,
And I listened to his song
From the strings of his violin.

The sea of knowledge rages,
Its waves beat on me,
Thought mounts upon thought, like a wall,
And God stands above it.

One silent thought floats lightly
Like a cloud in the sky.
If I ask here below
Of the bewildered ones in the gates,
Whither floats this
Prisoner of the skies?
None can disclose the tale
Or even explain it in part.

Radiant Is the World Soul

Radiant is the world soul,
Full of splendor and beauty,
Full of life,
Of souls hidden,
Of treasures of the holy spirit,
Of fountains of strength,
Of greatness and beauty.
Proudly I ascend
Toward the heights of the world soul
That gives life to the universe.
How majestic the vision,

Come, enjoy,
Come, find peace,
Embrace delight,
Taste and see that God is good.
Why spend your substance on what does not nourish
And your labor on what cannot satisfy?
Listen to me, and you will enjoy what is good,
And find delight in what is truly precious.

When I Want to Speak

When I want to speak a word
The spirit has already descended
From its hiding place.
Before it came to strum the strings of my will
The roots of many souls,
The highest mysteries,
Were already reduced to finite forms
And became letters pressing
At the lower region of my soul
Close to the concerns of my worldly self
And linked to its essence,
And I am forced to speak.
I speak out of all treasures that live in me.
The words flow on,
The thoughts flourish,
The sounds reach out,
Sound meets sound.
The ascending stream from my mortal self
Joins the descending stream from the source of my soul,
And seeds of light
Fill the world, my whole being.

Translated by Ben Zion Bokser

Abba Kovner

Abba Kovner was born in Russia in 1918. He was a leader of Partisans in the Vilna Ghetto, helping to organize armed revolt and publishing the manifesto that urged the Jews to resist. After the war he settled on a kibbutz in Israel and fought in the War of Independence. He received the Israel Prize in 1970 and has been chairman of the Hebrew Writers' Association of Israel. Two volumes of his poems have been published in English.

Near

I. Abel

Light the candle I will return
to you: morning
rises and smoke on the face of the deep and I
in the field
alone
heaps of feathers
flutter under the sky and I can't
tell
if the birds
dropped them all when they died
or the quilts and pillows
when they were torn to shreds (I heard
one whistle
in the wind)
shed their entrails
outside
at dawn
very white feathers whine
there
between water and sky
if you have any
mercy
my God put them where the birds are

II. Cain

I swore that I didn't hear You
all day
calling me where are you and it's not You I feared when I escaped
but all the terrible noises
I remember a voice
coming from a shed like broken sounds of the *shofar*
(my house
between stables and eucalyptus trees) and her small braided head.
Your day did not open her
eyes

HEBREW

From sea to sea a land now rises around me
perfumed
a guilt offering of incense and through the whole world
like the radiance of the sky their innocence shines
on the desert of stone the pillar of man
in the image of a mushroom cloud. Light the candle
we will return to You: morning rises and there is no
messenger in the land but You
where are you
and me.

Observation at Dawn

The night is still silky. Curtains are drawn
from the edge of the dream in a slow rhythm.
Red silk. We are both awake
trying quietly to spin the thread
cut off between the ribs. I'm reluctant
to look at this rain
beating at the windows.

And inside, the night
is still silky. Your breath a soft thicket
guarding its border. When I count
the number of pulse beats, as if not believing,
and find signs in them, suddenly my eyes
discover my body (my arms stretched out) lying here
naked (must I retrieve them somehow?).

Rain
it's just rain! Like an oath I repeat
for the third time. Not your blood.
Then my finger taps on your throat
groping like a blind man's cane.

I Don't Know if Mount Zion

1

I don't know if Mount Zion would recognize itself
at midnight in the fluorescent light
when there's nothing left of Jerusalem
but its beauty
wakeful in the milky light that glides
over its limbs still wings
lift it from the sunken desert
slowly slowly higher than the stars
this strange shell that floats out of the night
transparent giant
so much sky
washes over it
I don't know if Mount Zion looks
into my heart holding its breath now in pain and pleasure
behind a barred window
and who it is meant for
at midnight

2

These olive trees that never knelt
their knowledge hidden
their wrinkles carved this whole blue fan
on the road of the Hinom Valley
I don't know if Mount Zion sees the things
that have changed our image
out of all recognition. Hands that touched it every day like a
mother's
touching the forehead of her son sank
dropping into the sleep
of the Dead Sea—
does it hear the cry
from the market of the gates or the rush of my prayer from the
shadow—
what's the use of friends who watch from the galleries
while our hearts struggle in the arena
and what's the sense of poets if we don't
know how to ask

Mount Zion does it really exist or
is it like our love that glows from another light
rising night
after night

Translated by Shirley Kaufman

HEBREW

Yitzhak Lamdan

Yitzhak Lamdan was born in the Ukraine in 1899. During World War I he wandered through southern Russia and rallied to the Communist cause during the Russian Revolution. However, he quickly became disillusioned and settled in Palestine in 1920. Lamdan's most famous work is the epic poem Massada, *one section of which appears below. Lamdan died in 1954.*

Massada

On an autumn night, lying restless, far from her broken homeland,
I watched my mother die.
A last tear froze in her eye, as she whispered her final blessing,
Before I left to battle in distant, foreign fields
With an army pack on my cowed shoulders . . .
On a Ukrainian road, littered with graves, destroyed by suffering,
My sadly gazing, sweet-hearted brother collapsed,
And was buried in unholy ground.
My father, my last dear one, clung to his sacred writings in the dust,
With God's name fell down, weeping a prayer.
And I
Fastening my cracking soul together
With its last ounce of courage
Escaped one midnight on a ship
Going up to Massada.

I was told:
The last miraculous revolt was raised there
That cried on sky and earth, on God and man:
"Repay!"
On tablets of rock obstinate fingernails
Engraved consoling words.
The steeled chest, with a roar
Against hostile generations, stood in relief there:
"This is enough!"
You or I
The fighting will force a last judgment
Here."

In tents of sanctuary, on the ramparts, tribes of Levites
Sing praise,
And echoes of tomorrow answer
"Amen."
On heights of the walls young priests
Stretch out tender arms to the orphaned
And sad night sky,
To pray for its injured moon.

I was told:
On the heads of the fighters
A divine presence falls scattering atonement.
Behind the future's screen a great dawn watches,
Keeping guard on Massada.

Translated by A. C. Jacobs

Jiri Mordecai Langer

Jiri Mordecai Langer was born in Czechoslovakia in 1894. He was a friend of Kafka, to whom he taught Hebrew. After the Nazi occupation he entered Palestine as an illegal immigrant. Langer published several volumes of poetry and a book of Hasidic lore, Nine Gates to the Hasidic Mysteries. *He died in 1943.*

On the Margins of a Poem

The poem
that I chose for you
is simple,
as are all my singing poems.

It has the trace of a veil,
a little balsam,
and a taste of the honey
of lies.

There is also
the coming end of summer
when heat scorches the meadow
and the quick waters
of the river
cease to flow.

You will find in it
many shattered vessels.
Indeed
they are pure,
but they are also
broken.

Riddle of Night

She floats
in a white shell
and the lake
is like
the secret heart.

She stretches
a crystal hand
and a silver harp
lays bare
its longing.

A sweet essence
shall be added
to a poem,
voiceless,
pure,
and calm.

A light cloud
brushing against it
passes quickly
and is gone.

And the secret
shall not be
revealed,
for should I think
of the breath
of beauty
until it passes?

Should I think
of beauty
until it passes
away?

Translated by Gabriel Preil and Howard Schwartz

Rena Lee

Rena Lee was born in Byalistok, Poland, in 1932 and came to Palestine in 1935. She has published poems, stories, and literary studies in magazines and literary supplements in both Israel and the United States. She is the author of three volumes of poetry, In a Nocturnal Avenue, Days of Wear and Tear, *and* To the Districts of the Sun. *She presently lives in New York City.*

An Old Story

And the snake was
talking to Eve
in his forked-tongue,
hissing into her ears
sweet words like
how s-swell she was-s
and how he wished
to s-swallow her all up.

"Come-on" he said
"I'll give you a taste
of real Eden."
His body shot as an arrow
in the direction
of the darkest tree,
and she darted—

Long hours they spent there
the two, on their plot,
perspiring conspiring,
as if rehearsing
overplaying
some future scene.

And all that time
Adam was
busy busy busy
dressing and keeping the garden
for God.

Translated by the author

HEBREW

Hayim Lenski

Hayim Lenski was born in White Russia in 1905. In 1935 he was sentenced to five years in a Siberian labor camp. Arrested shortly after his release, he died in another labor camp. In 1957 a package of his poems, written from 1927 to 1941, arrived in Israel. These poems have been published under the title From Beyond the Waters of Lethe.

Purity

Remote from our sordid world,
High above its sodden, moldy breath
You bloom, heavenly bush,
Seedling of fire
Bedded in the frozen void.

There in eternity your scions shine,
Your stars and galaxies, modest of glory,
A pure primordial radiance flows
Through gold channels
To the black watches of our nights.

Our ears have wearied of the day's din—
Where is there a stone that has not honed a knife?
A tongue that has not whetted a lie?
Bless us, O burning bush,
With your light, your truth, your peace.

Language of Ancients

Language of ancients, of Hayman, Halevi,
Some miracle made you mine, gentle-voiced Queen.
Your cadences kindled my soul, and your words
Burnt my lips like the kisses of passionate lovers.

From the shores of Euphrates and Jordan, you summoned your
    legions
And gave me command of them, made me your deputy, Queen.
Your letters stood upright all ready in ranks
Square-bearded like heroes of Asshur.

You issued an order: Call up the recruits!
So away pranced the horsemen in light-footed dactyls,
In iambics the infantry, the transport in trochees,
Zealous flagbearers leading them—the feelings incarnate.

Queen! From the Don and the Neva and the Nieman, my river
I brought over your cohorts—and I their commander.
So bring home my name across the waters of Lethe
Like the names of the ancients, like Hayman, Halevi.

Translated by Pearl Grodzensky

Upon the Lake

Upon the lake the dusk descends,
the fish seek depths in which to sleep,
birds come to roost—their chattering ends.
Dark is the rustling of the weeds.

What echo, whose echo now complains
amidst these reeds that slowly stir?
Desolate this shore since time began,
untrodden by a wanderer.

Of longing that can find no words,
of days whose sun set long ago,
of the migration of the birds—
reeds whisper to the lake below.

Translated by Robert Friend

Matti Megged

Matti Megged was born in Poland in 1923 and was brought to Palestine in 1926. He was active in Hagana and fought in the later wars. He is on the faculty of Comparative Literature at the University of Haifa and was awarded the Jerusalem Prize of Belles-Lettres. His works include poems, short stories, critical essays, and translations of Genêt and Beckett.

HEBREW

The Phoenix

The Phoenix,
Who returns time and again,
From his ashes,
Does not know the face of his father
Or mother.
The great fire
That has scorched his past
Is all that he remembers.

Tonight
I've heard his voice again
Breaking painfully out of his egg.
Naked, he ascends to the heights
And already the fire is scorching
His wings.

The Phoenix does not leave anything
To his descendants
But the memory of the fire,
The ashes,
And the eggshell.
But they, like him, will rise up
Out of the egg
And return,
With wings scorched.

White Bird

Then all became silent,
Blue sky holding its breath.
One white bird
(How did she wander here?)
Stayed a minute
And preened a feather
That fell
On me.

Suddenly I heard your voice
Calling me again
To come back.
Honey, I cried in my thirst,
Honey!
And you, fainting from desire,
Whispered, Jonathan,
Behold you are dying again
Inside me,
Jonathan, my Jonathan.

And I was greatly afflicted
With desire,
But a squadron of black birds
Shattered the silence
And I couldn't hear your whisper
Anymore—
Only the wind continued
To call.

*The Akedah**

When I was led again to the Akedah
(Not on foot, not on donkey,
Imprisoned in an iron womb)
My father's hand
Did not hold my own.
Nor did the angel come
To hold back the knife.

Alone,
Father and son,
The wind blowing over
My blood
Poured upon
Basalt.

Above me empty skies
Silent on the enigma of my life
And death.
Only from time to time I hear the voice
Of an old liar
Laughing at my
Extinction.

Translated by Howard Schwartz

Hayim Naggid

Hayim Naggid was born in Bucharest, Romania in 1940. He came to Jerusalem in 1948 but now lives in Tel Aviv, where he edits the literary supplement of the Israeli newspaper Ma'ariv. *He has published a book of poems and articles of literary criticism.*

*The *Akedah* is the binding of Isaac by Abraham at Mount Moriah.

A Snow in Jerusalem

The voice of King Solomon's nightingale
Is among the purple branches.
His voice is sweet to my tongue.

In the snowdrifts of Jerusalem
I went to school
And saw a white snow
Turning blue.

There was one woman,
Bad-tempered,
Who listened to the voice
With tired eyes,
Her face a rose, a rose that fell
Into the water.

And I went in the snow
That became mud
To the school
In the German Colony.

After the War

A memory of the face
Like a lost amulet.
Summer is twisted in the olive branches,
In the hard shell of the brain.
Barbed wire like stitches.
The earth is hungry for the dead.
Fertile.
Perhaps everything should be said
Differently.
The crowd is an illusion.
The earth betrays.
Dust, the color of honey,
Covers everything
Like the sweet sleep of the butterfly
In thin silk.

Like a Pearl

One day the tired sea will open to the sun
Like the petals of the white rose,
And I'll lie in the hollow of the light
Like a snail in its shell.
Intoxicated with song,
Choirs of angels will speak to me
In the sweet language of the sea,
And my song like the voice
Will be softened
And fade
Like the luster of a pearl.

Translated by Shlomo Vinner and Howard Schwartz

My Mother

Among our flocks of hard days
My mother padded about in woolen slippers.
(Aaron Aaron
Her voice bleached white in the streets)

I found gleaming pearls in my dresser drawer
One of my mother's remainders.
My days were quietly severed
From the silence of her pearl-perfect life.

Brought to the ground by the rage of my days
I attach myself to her memory.
Like a soft rain, it pours dimness on me.

In my sleep flags of blackness
Are folded and put away.

Translated by Rose Drachler

Dan Pagis

Dan Pagis was born in Bukovina in 1930. After World War II, during part of which he was in a concentration camp, he settled in Palestine. He teaches medieval Hebrew literature at Hebrew University. An English Selected Poems *appeared in 1976.*

The Last Ones

I am already quite scarce. For years
I have appeared only here and there
at the edges of this jungle. My graceless body
is well camouflaged among the reeds and clings
to the damp shadow around it.
Had I been civilized,
I would never have been able to hold out.
I am tired. Only the great fires
still drive me from hiding place to hiding place.

And what now? My fame is only in the rumors
that from time to time
and even from hour to hour
I wane.
But it is certain that at this moment
someone is tracking me. Cautiously
I prick all my ears and wait. The steps
already rustle the dead leaves. Very close. Here.
Is this it?

Am I it? I am.
There is no time to explain.

The Tower

I did not want to grow, but quick-fingered memories
which put layer upon layer, each one alone,
were mixed in the tumult of strange tongues
and left in me unguarded entrances,
stairs that led nowhere,
perspectives that were broken.
Finally, I was abandoned.
Only sometimes in the twisted corridor
a small speechless whisper
still rises in me and runs
like a draught and it seems to me
that I am a whirlwind
whose head is for a moment in the sky
and before I wake up
the mass of my burnt bricks
crumbles
and turns back to clay.

HEBREW

Instructions for Crossing the Border

Imaginary man, go. Here is your passport.
You are not allowed to remember.
You have to match the description:
your eyes are already blue.
Don't escape with the sparks
inside the smokestack:
you are a man, you sit in the train.
Sit comfortably.
You've got a decent coat now,
a repaired body, a new name
ready in your throat.
Go, You are not allowed to forget.

Translated by Stephen Mitchell

Scrawled in Pencil in a Sealed Railway Car

here in this transport
i eve
and abel my son
if you should see my older son
cain son of man
tell him that i

Translated by Anthony Rudolf

Draft of a Reparations Agreement

All right, gentlemen who cry blue murder as always,
nagging miracle-makers,
quiet!
Everything will be returned to its place,
paragraph after paragraph.
The scream back into the throat.
The gold teeth back to the gums.
The terror.
The smoke back to the tin chimney and further on and inside
back to the hollow of the bones,
and already you will be covered with skin and sinews and you will
live,
look, you will have your lives back,
sit in the living room, read the evening paper.
Here you are. Nothing is too late.
As to the yellow star: immediately
it will be torn from your chest
and will emigrate
to the sky.

Translated by Stephen Mitchell

Brothers

1

Abel was pure and woolly
and somewhat modest
like the smallest kid
and full of ringlets like the smoke of the offering
inhaled by his Master.
Cain was straight. Like a knife.

2

Cain is amazed. His big hand gropes
inside the butchered throat before him:
from where does the silence burst?

3

Abel stayed in the field. Cain stayed Cain. And since it's decreed
that he be a wanderer, he wanders diligently. Each morning
changing
one horizon for another. One day he discovers the earth tricked him
over the years. It moved, while he, Cain, marked time in one place.
Marked time, marched, ran only on a single scrap of dust, exactly
as big as the soles of his sandals.

4

One evening of grace he stumbles
on a fine haystack.
He dives in, is swallowed by it, rests.
Hush, Cain sleeps.
He's happy. He dreams that he is Abel.

5

Don't worry. Don't worry.
It's already decreed for the one who might kill you
that your vengeance shall be taken sevenfold.
Your brother Abel guards you from all evil.

Translated by Shirley Kaufman

HEBREW

Autobiography

I died with the first blow and was buried
in the stony field.
The raven showed my parents
what to do with me.

If my family is famous, not a little of the credit
goes to me.
My brother invented murder,
my parents—crying,
I invented silence.

Afterwards, those well-known events took place.
Our inventions were perfected.
One thing led to another.
And there were those who
killed in their own way,
cried in their own way.

I am not naming names
out of consideration for the reader,
since at first the details horrify,
though in the end they bore.

You can die once, twice, even seven times,
but you cannot die a thousand times.
I can.
My underground cells reach everywhere.

When Cain started to multiply on the face of the earth,
I started to multiply in the belly of the earth.
For a long time now, my strength has been greater than his.
His legions desert him and go over to me.
And even this is only half a revenge.

The Grand Duke of New York

Gabriel Preil, the Grand Duke of New York,
goes downtown every day incognito.
Disguised in a felt hat that sports a tiny feather
he walks among his multitudinous subjects,
lending them an ear. The stratagem succeeds.
They haven't recognized him now
for fifty years.
The skyscrapers erected in his honor
at the fringes of Central Park and farther south
keep constant watch: Where will he come from?
The police horses face every which direction.
The squirrels, tails erect, keep asking: Has he come yet?
And all the while he has been promenading
on Fifth Avenue, counting precious moments
in diamond-studded watches, granting pardon
to two or three thugs who by mistake
mugged him in an alley,
and finally arriving at his Hesperides,
a corner coffee-shop, and rests there from his labors.
Right away the waitress there lights up,
blossoms before this old habitué,
who likes to tease her now and then
with velvet softness.
But she, of little faith and overtired,
turns her attention to the hoipolloi,
so cannot know he deciphers in his goblet
a honied future for her.
Towards evening, the Grand Duke disappears
down the satanic subway, crosses the river
between drawn knives, is swallowed up
by an anonymous building block, and locking
his palace door behind him,
puts on majesty. An amber light
glows for him in his glass of Russian tea.
Now to make sure the city will go on existing tomorrow,
he composes a special night proclamation, which states:
Wrongs fade beyond the shore and time invites
*an easy confabulation.**

Translated by Robert Friend

*The lines in italics are from a poem by Gabriel Preil.

HEBREW

Israel Pincas

Israel Pincas was born in 1935 in Sofia, Bulgaria. He has lived in Tel Aviv since 1944. His books of poems include Fourteen Poems, Supper at Ferrara and Other Poems, To the Tropic, *and* About the House.

Mediterranean

From the hold of this ship
Making for distant places, I
Keep an intent watch.

The waters are taking pity. The evening now
Is like one a thousand years
Ago.

In this old sea of ours
There is no new thing.
Only the wind changes.

I do not think
I have missed anything.
Everything granted since then
Comes as a gift.

A Florentine merchant came
Once, offering
Red glass.
That was in the year
Fourteen hundred
And one.

I had nothing to give
For it, and he sailed away.
Now, I will buy it.

It's like a thousand years ago,
Now, this evening.

Translated by A. C. Jacobs

Berl Pomerantz

Berl Pomerantz was born in Poland in 1900 and studied in Vilna and Warsaw. He was killed by German soldiers in December 1942 while hiding with a group of fellow Jewish escapees in the forest near Janow. His first book of poems was published in 1935, and a second book followed in 1939. His later poems, written in occupied Poland, were never recovered and were probably buried with him.

End of Summer

End of summer tempts the mouth of the village
like a ripe fruit.

A sack-laden old man went begging in the yards,
an empty bottle in his hand for balance.

Boys lazed, wisdom filled their lips
and they knew what was inside the old man's sack—

"Sure, they are the emptied bottles
of all our seventy years."

Girls still carried pails of water,
a chain of pearls lay seeded in their tracks.

Their bare feet flashed on gray, drowsing steps—
like a dream of white marble, a Dream of Degrees.

Ample, handsome trees, as mushrooms in a wood,
their dark branches shook

like empty hands of age, spread above a passing head
muttering their blessing.

With darkness fires rose up from across
marking houses in the area.

Goats lolled at the doorways,
innocently spreading a smell of peace.

HEBREW

Young Virgins Plucked Suddenly

Young virgins plucked suddenly,
on a spring night, when the ice breaks up on the rivers;
and all the things they left behind
open a deep and silent source of sorrow.

One of them stood in a store,
showing shirts and ties,
her modest suggestion
influenced the buyer's choice.

One of them fluttered in a sweet shop,
serving tea and pastries,
the change from her hand
a guest would not count.

One of them woke the sick in a clinic,
giving sips of cool drink on burning nights,
and with her soft hands
tended the wounds.

Their treasure—a little money saved
and a bundle of special, pink-laced linen,
and in a secret corner of their daydreams—
a bridal canopy spread above them.

But their arms had not tasted the seal of joy,
nor had they bred a single hatred,
when death came to their pure cribs
and embraced them.

With black shawls and searching eyes
mothers nod silently on their path.
And wrinkled grandmothers weep bitterly,
who volunteered and were unwanted—

Young virgins plucked suddenly,
on a spring night, when the ice breaks up on the rivers—

Translated by Harold Schimmel

Gabriel Preil

Gabriel Preil was born in Estonia in 1911, but has lived in New York since 1922. He has published seven volumes of Hebrew poetry, including Landscapes of Sun and Frost, Candle Against the Stars, Maps of Evening, Fire and Silence, *and* Of Time and Place. *He has also published a book of Yiddish poems. Preil has been the recipient of many literary awards in the United States and Israel, including the La Med Prize for Hebrew Literature, the Jewish Book Council of America Award, the Bitzaron Prize, and the New York University Neumann Award. Two volumes of Preil's poems are forthcoming in English translation,* Selected Poems *and* Autumn Music.

Words of Oblivion and Peace

To Jenny N.

I once broke evening bread with the brown-faced, white-smiled
Prince of Siam.
He wore festivity and humility as the first skin of his body.
His talk touched on London and New York—large villages lacking
true wonders,
and his memory dwelt on the people of his country, small of stature,
eaters of pale rice,
and on the flowers there, high-tide huge, and summoning, ablaze,
the armies of their colors.
Lowering his low voice, "There is nothing," he said, "like the
absolute oblivion that Buddha gives.
No smallest eddy will ever ruffle its seas,
and there is nothing like the calm of the endless seasons that dream
in its orchards."

Suddenly, a wind blew from the corner of the street, a prayer spoke
from beyond the bridges
but as the flesh grew sad and silent in its fated valleys,
through the window-pane there poured a peach and northern
sunset,
and I saw Jenny, the villages of her peaceful words in flower.

HEBREW

Rains on the Island

After the first sudden rain,
the long pause after,
fleets of water anchored once again
before the window,
and we were like sad sailors of the dusk,
forsaken of all ports.

At home the coffee that we drank was bitter-hot
like the onslaught of the spring.
The bread we ate was good upon the tongue
as if the meadow-scent were in our nostrils.
The summer soon will knock upon our doors—
and we shall be
sailors of the dusk
drinking in its golden showers,
but sadder still.

From Jerusalem: A First Poem

Under these historic skies
I am older than Abraham and his stars,
and I am the young father of the children
playing among pink trees.

On Alharizi Street, on a violet afternoon,
such an hour of grace
gazes out of an arched frame
as sometimes whispered to the prophet
weary of fires,
who dreamed of a village
cool among the stars.

Arriving

My lines falter
on the downward slope,
but their defenselessness
begins to bare
first February shoots,
similar to those out of doors,
and wondering a little
about themselves.

Sometimes it turns spring.
Phrases of poems
hover in the air, tempting my hand
to seize them
as if they were the glimmerings
of a Talmudic proposition
in Grandfather's mind
or a geometry theorem
opening up like a field.
I am reminded
of that merchant of nightingales
in Isfahan
who bemoaned his lack of customers.
Weathers also exaggerate
and may lead one to forget
the peace found in a poem
living or lost
in a place without seasons.
It may be that what we arrive at
is the structure of the suggestive,
the space flowing between the lines.

Translated by Robert Friend

Autumn Music

for Asya

Jerusalem's autumn has prepared a text
clear and unclear, detailed and vague.
I survey passages and discover its music
that captures you with nets
and frees you with the waters.
This austere, seductive season

is like you. It prepares me to receive you
like a flickering prelude by Debussy,
like the wandering fire of Chopin.
I would free you from them for you
have been abducted
as if by a mirror that has captured your face.

Open and closed, you listen.
Perhaps you are not Scheherazade
weaving a thin, tenuous fabric of survival,
but I am surely the spellbound king
drawing out his reign
a little longer.

Translated by Howard Schwartz

Like David

Like David the pursued I raise my eyes to the mountains:
so slight are the differences of the valleys that indicate
the map of helplessness in his days and in mine.

Like David the submissive I raise my eyes to a woman:
so similar are the transitions in her blood and her flowering
in a city of love in his days and in mine.

From the mountains the rain beats, tall and dreary, like Goliath,
and even the sun, small as David the shepherd boy,
withholds its light from me.

Parting

She sat across from me and her eyes
were a deeper brown than the coffee,
more distressed than my body
when I tried to tell her
all the green things I had learned.
It's certain she did not listen;
she was trapped in a cage of estrangement
or she walked along a street
that refused to run
into another.

But I know that for a moment her eyes turned green,
they recalled an image of a garden praying in the rain.
So it seemed the aridity
of the brown valleys departed
and large stars
kept watch on the roads
for a little peace:
she cannot reach me.

Translated by Laya Firestone

Memory of Another Climate

My hand plunged into the waters of night,
awakened, salvaging fragments
of a dream that glimmered
like the wings of a gull.
In my room the mercury cooled
and began to sink,
while a house of song
floated toward me as on a sea
and someone briefly spoke
of the climate of another time:

Sun and moon were like prophets
preaching out of innocent skies
about the motion of repose
and the calmness of a storm,
and the landscape remained lucid in the eye
even in the rain.

HEBREW

A Summing Up

I spoke with a tangle-haired forester from Saskatchewan—
and in his words I detected a chorus of trees singing
under the stretched parchment dotted with stars;
I accompanied an artist ablaze with color,
probing mountain and river at sunset—
and on my private horizon burst forth a fire
primeval and untamed, plunging finally into
dormant marble, abundant with sadness;
I saw a monk from Siam, thin and ascetic as a reed,
perched on the spring of oblivion—
like him I was punished by scorpions of memory
and in the pale waters I purified myself;
and when I chanced upon the Greek cook, sober and round,
I learned from his mouth a lesson
of the spoon that stirs without pause
a broth of passion and boredom for the world.

Translated by Jeremy Garber

Giving Up on the Shore

In the open-faced river
inviting a boat for a chat
I cast my burden of desires
and he, forgiver of sins, tried
to envelop my city of clouds.
Above, the sky burgeons
like an overcultivated garden
and a bridge's arch catches
in its caliper the abundance of violet
passing through with calm lightning flashes.

Except for the small birds
on the way to summer
there is no one who will speak
of the moment that will break
into flame.

A Late Manuscript at the Schocken Institute

Prayerbooks return to Jerusalem
delicately colored, muffled whispers
which an untiring God absorbs in his heaven,
they repeat their prayers, sown like bread
soaring to Him, the appropriator.
I return from autumn ports
to a spring station among mountains

not in the image of a barely remembered Pentateuch,
not as one hanging his sadness on southerly trees,
nor as an itinerant warming a bird in the north:

Perhaps I am a sort of late manuscript,
uneasy in this garment of skin and bones
scorched by the words
of my progenitors—

they certainly are worthier than I;
I know their hallowed thirst
their frozen stream flowing
from Mantua to Amsterdam.

Translated by Gabriel Levin

Fishermen

The rain has been reciting
the same gray stories all day long,
and all day long the wind
has turned the pages.
But in the great library
we have southerly weather
as if fishermen were sitting
by the waters of a river
making song:

in their grip the glittery haul,
while overhead
the clouds are torn asunder
one by one.

Translated by Betsy Rosenberg

A Lesson in Translation

for Betsy Rosenberg

The translator attempted to bare things unsaid,
the modes of intent and disguise,
the groping and the discovery.
(Once she read something in my face.)

More than anything, perhaps,
she thought of plowing the foundations, to identify
the bristle of roots, the glowing shapes.
There were moments when she was attracted to an image,
to the incidental that orchestrates
a delicate irony, longings.

The original, we may assume, is still there.
She did not make it into her estate,
or into another vessel of mine.
Every stanza stands defended;
from autumn to autumn flows its credence.

With this I still question
how even a cool and careful text can turn sad,
can defeat the peace.
Did I learn a lesson in translation?

Translated by Howard Schwartz

Letter Out of the Gray

No one writes to me.
The books are as tired as I.
The pen still shakes on the paper
its dubious warmth.
It is a reed stuck in a faraway sea
or seized by a stranger
directing a line from right to left
as if by accident.
But sometimes, out of the gray,
a square letter smiles.
Blue and innocent,
it whispers:
I am the only one who loves.

Translated by Shirley Kaufman and Howard Schwartz

Biographical Note

It has been many years
since I was imprisoned
in the hothouse.
My bread is sour
and in my bones there grows
the rust of time.
Every desire turns to snow.

But when I beat my head
against the rock
of a poem
the fountain that springs forth
is sweet.

Had it not been for this
I could have been a knight
flickering and dying
in a forest of loves,
or one whose wrath
sets cities and villages
on fire.

Praise to the rock.

Translated by Howard Schwartz

Esther Raab

Esther Raab was born in Petah Tikva in 1899. She attended Teachers' Training College. Two books of her poems have been published.

Folk Tune

The great tiger
loved me—
and I loved him.
He had eyes
of an extinguished blue
with the skin sagging about them:
wrinkles, wrinkles . . .

I searched among the wrinkles
for the blue of his eyes
as for cold water
hidden in mist.
He smelled like a forest,
smelled like a hunter:
a hunter whose quarry
was wild beasts and women.
He lived
beyond time,
he was
"the eternal tiger"—
granter of visions,
dispenser of dreams,
collector of pain.

A Serenade for Two Poplars

Tonight I have a date
with two tall poplars
and a tall palm.
Man's dwellings beneath
murmur like beehives,
are cozy, are warm.
But I—
I feel good tonight
with two poplars
and a tall palm—
light clouds in their branches,
quince fragrance in hedges,
shadows on asphalt.

Translated by Robert Friend and Shimon Sandbank

Rachel

Rachel (Bluwstein) was born in Viatka, Russia, in 1890. After studying art in Kiev, she traveled to Palestine in 1909. Although she later went to France and Russia, she returned to Palestine for good. Many of her lyrics have been put to music. She died in 1931.

Rachel

For her blood runs in my blood
and her voice sings in me.
Rachel, who pastured the flocks of Laban,
Rachel, the mother of the mother.

And that is why the house is narrow for me,
and the city foreign,
for her veil used to flutter
in the desert wind.

And that is why I hold to my way
with such certainty,
for memories are preserved in my feet
ever since, ever since.

My White Book of Poems

Screams that I screamed, despairing, aching,
in hours of distress and loss,
have become a pretty necklace of words
for my white book of poems.

Hidden things not revealed to a friend
have been revealed,
that which was sealed in me with fire
has been laid bare,

and the grief of a heart
going under
everyone now
can calmly finger.

Translated by N. N.

HEBREW

Revolt

Like a bird in the butcher's palm you flutter in my hand,
insolent pride.
I stop your mouth,
I press together the wings of your back,
and I laugh at you.
I've got you at last.
This is revenge for the flowers you plucked in their early bloom,
for your fences that cut off my path,
for the world whose rainbow colors you made dim.
Lie down in your corner of darkness till I return,
till I return from him.

Translated by Robert Friend

My Dead

They alone are left me; they alone still faithful,
for now death can do no more to them.

At the bend of the road, at the close of day,
they gather around me silently, and walk by my side.

This is a bond nothing can ever loosen.
What I have lost: what I possess forever.

Translated by Robert Mezey

Perhaps

Perhaps it was never so.
Perhaps
I never woke early and went to the fields
To labor in the sweat of my brow.

Nor in the long, blazing days
Of harvest
On top of the wagon, laden with sheaves,
Made my voice rise in song.

Nor bathed myself clean in the calm
Blue water
Of my Kineret, O, my Kineret,
Were you there or did I only dream?

Translated by A. C. Jacobs

Yonathan Ratosh

Yonathan Ratosh was born in Russia in 1908. He traveled to Palestine in 1921 and worked as a journalist. His first and influential book of poetry caused a scandal because of its sensuality and innovative langauge. In addition to his poems and journalistic works, Ratosh translated Cyrano de Bergerac, *the* Fables *of La Fontaine, and other classics into Hebrew. He was one of the founders of the Canaanite movement, which sought inspiration in the pagan mythology of the Canaanites and attempted to de-Judaize Israeli identity.*

Lament

You did not suck at my mother's breasts,
brother,
nor did the same oil anoint us.
Only the grave
into which star after star falls
is one.
Each man and his star
disappear,
each man
and the pride of his heart.
For in those days
every man was his own king
and did that which was right
in his own eyes.

And each man shall pay with his blood,
and each one shall perish
with his brothers,
for each one sets forth
on the brink
of oblivion
at the crossroads paved
with bones.

You did not suck at my mother's breasts,
brother,
nor did the same death find us.
Only the distant crown
before which each head bows
is one.
Every man
and the fire of his anger,

every man
and the sword of the judgment
he makes,
for in those days
every man was his own king.

You were the first of the first,
the first to set forth alone,
the first to spill
your blood,
the first to dig your grave
with your own hands,
the first
in those days
in which every man
was his own king.

And each man shall be inscribed
with his own blood,
and each one shall be gathered
to his ancestors,
for each one sets forth
on the brink
of oblivion
to the call of the ram's horn
at the crossroads paved
with bones.

Translated by Howard Schwartz

Dahlia Ravikovitch

Dahlia Ravikovitch was born in 1936 and has worked as a journalist and a teacher. She has published four books of poetry, including The Love of an Orange *and* Third Book. *She lives in Tel Aviv. A volume of her work in translation,* A Dress of Fire, *has appeared in London and New York.*

A Dress of Fire

You know, she said, they made you
a dress of fire.
Remember how Jason's wife burned in her dress?
It was Medea, she said, Medea did that to her.
You've got to be careful, she said.
They made you a dress that glows
like an ember, that burns like coals.

Do you want to wear it, she said, don't wear it.
It's not the wind whistling,
it's the poison spreading.
You're not a princess, what can you do to Medea?
You must tell one sound from another, she said,
it's not the wind whistling.

Remember, I told her, that time when I was six?
They shampooed my hair and I went outside like that.
The smell of shampoo trailed after me like a cloud.
Afterwards I was sick from the wind and the rain.
I didn't know then how to read Greek tragedies
but the smell of the perfume spread
and I was very sick.
Now I realize it's an unnatural perfume.

What will become of you, she said,
they made you a burning dress.
They made me a burning dress, I said, I know it.
So why are you standing there, she said,
you've got to be careful,
don't you know what a burning dress is?

I know, I said, but I don't know
how to be careful.
The smell of that perfume confuses me.
I said to her, No one has to agree with me,
I have no faith in Greek tragedies.

But the dress, she said, the dress is on fire.
What are you saying, I shouted,
what are you saying?
I'm not wearing a dress at all,
what's burning is me.

HEBREW

Surely You Remember

After they all leave,
I remain alone with the poems,
some poems of mine, some of others.
I prefer poems that others have written.
I remain quiet, and the choking stops.
I remain.

Sometimes I wish everyone would go away.
Perhaps it's nice to write poems.
You sit in your room and the walls grow taller.
Colors deepen.
A blue kerchief becomes the depth of a well.

You wish everyone would go away.
You don't know what's bothering you.
Perhaps you'll think of something.
Then it all passes and you are pure crystal.

After that, love.
Narcissus was so much in love with himself.
Only a fool doesn't understand
he loved the river, too.

You sit alone.
Your heart grieves you, but it won't break.
The faded images wash away one by one.
Then the blemishes.
A sun sets at midnight. You remember
the dark flowers, too.

You wish you were dead or alive or
somebody else.
Perhaps there's a single country you love?
a single word?
Surely you remember.

Only a fool lets the sun set when it likes.
It always drifts off too early
westward to the islands.

Sun and moon, winter and summer
will come to you,
infinite treasures.

Requiem After Seventeen Years

The cantor was reading Psalms.
The trees whispered
like a flock of black priests.

We were not much taller than the gravestones
and we knew there would be
no resurrection in our day.

The ladder reached up from there
to the ranks of the holy and pure
who shine like sapphire
(most of them lay at our feet).

Our lives were like a grasshopper's
on the border of sun and shade.

But when the drowned girl passed through
all the chambers of the sea
we knew

it is the sea
that gives life to the rivers.

Translated by Chana Bloch

Abraham Regelson

Abraham Regelson was born in Minsk in 1896 and emigrated to the United States with his parents in 1905. He moved to Palestine in 1933 and continued to publish poems and prose in Hebrew journals at home and in America. He is the author of several large volumes of poetry and essays and has translated into Hebrew works by Milton, Blake, and Melville.

Moses on Mount Nebo

Not Canaan and its cities, the splendor of towers
And walls glittering in evening sun—
Not the green of gardens, rows of date-palms
And a river slow flowing to water with blessing
The fruit of fine vineyards and rich grain of fields
Till it kisses the lips of the sea glowing red—

HEBREW

Not these, my people's heritance, do my eyes see,
But multitudes of generations that will be born
And epochs and dreams that will be created—
Like blue mountains aspiring heavenwards,
Mount above mount and peak above peak,
Until lost from sight in mists of eternity.
And a drop of my heart's blood will reach and animate
Each dawn reddening a distant snowy head,
And the fire of the bush shown me by God
Will yet kindle sparks of dew in a morning to come.
Well I know I have darkened with smoke
The white of that fire, lest it blind
Dull eyes, I have sweetened the waters of my Law
To the palates of slaves who will not hallow truth
And a God invisible, to sacrificial rites averse,
Whom only the righteous dead may know.
And I send a blessing to future prophets
Who will distill fire from smoke, gold from dross,
The word of God from the words of my creed; my blessing
On the heads of all breakers-of-tablets after them,
Who with courage and toil and torments
Will lead a people in the wilderness to God. For
Like streams of fire petrifying on a smoky mount,
So freeze God's words in men's laws,
Till again a rebellious flaming current bursts
And smashes rocks of decrees and ancient altars
And raises a new law on their ruins.
Thus is the mount of man exalted to the heights,
To set his shoulder as a support for the stars
And immerse his head in mysteries supreme.
The vision fades. Now hosts of shadows
Cover the plain of Canaan and its vineyards,
And the moon's face gazes towards Jericho
And softens the pride of its walls. Night.
And a great calm settles on the desert
Like wings of slumber on weary eyelids,
And God's kiss descends, approaches,
And my soul trembles with the stillness.

Translated by Richard Flantz

I. Z. Rimon

I. Z. Rimon was born in Poland in 1889. In 1909 he traveled to Palestine, where he worked at various jobs until 1921 when, after savage mutilation by rioting Arabs, he retired in seclusion at the Synagogue of the Ari in Safed for three years. His poems reflect the religious influence of Rav A. I. Kook. In addition to poetry, he wrote commentaries on several books of the Bible and a book on Kook. He died in 1958.

I Am a King

I am a king
about to collapse.
My crown is broken.
My enchanted violin
has become silent.

I gaze at the streets,
I come to the bazaars.
I am not dreaming—
the world has been closed to me.

I have strange tears,
but my soul is not sad.
I am falling under torches of light
and my heart is wounded
and finds its peace
in pain
and in the flow of peace
its dying.

Translated by Shlomo Vinner and Howard Schwartz

HEBREW

David Rokeah

David Rokeah was born in Lvov in 1916 and came to Palestine in 1934. He studied law and literature, and currently works as an electrical engineer. He has written nine books of poetry, including Red Earth *and* A Town—the Time Is Summer. *Two volumes have appeared in English.*

Beginning

The poem begins
from night that flows through the windmill
on the way to Jerusalem.
From light on the spikes of stones
on the slope to the old well.
From thorns from fireflies between the thorns.
From earth that yields up legacies of sorrow
for those who truly love.
From the moon who reads the symbols of the cards
in the palms of the tellers.
From silence congealing
in rooms behind curtains.
From summer echoing
behind a wall behind a curtain.
In realities of flesh and desire
and a dream sprouting like grass
between roof tiles

I Am Like a Book

I am like a book
opened on a market stall.
The letters fly away from me,
the wind tears through the letters.
For many days now, I have accepted no invitations.
My friends conclude that summer
is the right time
for disloyalty.
The self-evident does not explain itself
in my poems.
Harder to run after kites aflame in the sun
than to water creepers in the yard.
The sea is steadfast in its laws—
time too, as it crumbles.

Translated by Robert Mezey

Hemda Roth

Hemda Roth is a young poet who lives in Jerusalem.

A Young Deer/Dust

*Rabbi Meir used to say: "the dust of the first man was gathered from the whole world" (Sanhedrin 20). "And he fashioned . . . man dust"—Rabbi Yehuda. Rabbi Bar Simon said: "A young deer" (Breshit Rabbah-14).**

I was never there.
But I know the cave
and the many slippery paths
to the pond.

(The mincing walk of the
does around it
left hearts
in the fine sand.)

A sloping wall, bubbling,
and the beating of drops.
A crack in the rock
and light on its way
to water.

Two wild goats
bent over to drink,
and a ruddy goat
raised his head.

The shadow of his antlers
in the pond—windows
with panes of softness.
(His kisses—a trace of colors
on the pond's skin,
like sand.)

*The poem, playing on the similarity, in Hebrew, between the word for "dust" (*ahphar*) and that for "young deer" (*ohpher*)—a similarity evident in the quotation—has for its Hebrew title the unvowelized letters *ayin-pai-raysh,* which can mean either one.

And one day my body,
living dust, forgot
all the places it was gathered
from.

And so a young deer awoke in it,
running, bleating,
calling to the places
that I was their dust
before they were
my one body:
so that many would come back
to me, come back
one by one.

Translated by Myra Glazer Schotz

Treason of Sand

Desert around. Desert
and the treason of sand.
How did the fish
get to the little stream
under the palm trees?

Once we swam in a distant sea,
once an old ocean was here, and
flying fish—
we'll fly
to find out, among the roots of the palm,
how the reflections of stars
blossom without fading

in the quiet of your hands,
sparks of compassion,
in the stream, at night.

The Song

The song! the song!
In the dark stream
the fish weave it around
their bodies and unravel
upon the water.

A silver fish sails,
pulling the threads, hanging
clouds on the wind.

Waves rise to become
fins of cloud
and fall to crawl upon the sand.

One more melody
is buried dumb
among the corals.

Look, the little fish burst forth
rising like bubbles

of the song.
It comes back into my body
night after night
unraveling in me like
dark water.

Translated by Mariana Potasman

HEBREW

Tuvia Ruebner

Tuvia Ruebner was born in Czechoslovakia in 1924. He has been in Israel since 1941. Ruebner has published several books of poetry and has translated S. Y. Agnon into German.

Among Iron Fragments

Among iron fragments and rusty dreams
I found you

lost in my astonished hands:
is this your face, your shoulders; this, the hair of night?

Dark flame and sleepy mouth
the years have forgotten your eyes

they rose up around you
with the sharpness of spikes

the fine, white dust above you
in winds that rose and died.

I found you
my wounded face in the wind and my arms open wide.

Translated by Robert Friend

First Days

Lost among secrets in a tangle
Of weeds by the stream
The newborn child is dreaming
His mother's dreams,
His eyes two rivers, seeking
Their place of birth
Back among hidden roots
In the blood of earth,
But his hands, like Moses beside the water,
Reach for the light, for Pharaoh's daughter.

Translated by E. A. Levenston

I Left

I left my temporary home and set off
To show my sons the source.
There, I said, I lay on the ground
With a stone for a pillow, lowlier than the grass
Like the dust of the earth—
All has been preserved there.
I meant to show my sons where I came from.

We passed mountains, woods, and cities that were
Caves. Water gathered in pools on the way and the roads got worse.
The car was forced to bump over the ditches.

In the fading light we arrived at my home town.
What is this sweet air? ask my sons.
What's this plaster falling off the walls?

Never mind, quoth the old woman at the window,
Here the future too is past. And she shut her dry eyes
Like a fowl that rises, and folds its wings and dives.

I was born here, I told my sons.
My parents and grandparents were born nearby.
Everyone is born. Here stood a house,
I told my sons, and the wind blew
Between me and the words.

I tried to show my sons where I came from and when.
Are we going to eat and where?
Are we going to sleep? ask my sons, and we are surrounded by
emptiness and there is no way out.

Translated by Betsy Rosenberg

Document

I exist that I may say

This house is not a house,
a place to spread fishnet, a barren rock, fear
there beside the square, did I say square?
a paved
wilderness.

I exist that I may say

This way is not a way,
its paths wind round, ascend in dream-rust
from the wood, I walk
the sand hill there, who walks? I'd
walked with child steps, in a sun
of ruin, hands stretched out, asking,
walking and asking my Father and Mother.

I exist that I may say

My father's history is coal,
ashes, wind
of my sister's in my hair blowing
back, back, night wind
in my day I exist that I may say
yes their night voices, yes their weeping, yes
the one astray in the house in their absence, falling
from the shadow of its walls
out of fear of my voice to say yes
in the empty space.

Translated by Harold Schimmel

Pinhas Sadeh

Pinhas Sadeh was born in Lvov in 1929 but was brought to Palestine in 1934. He has been writing for publication since 1945; his works have included poems, stories, and literary articles.

In the Forest

So, So. It is an old man sleeping here. Sleep here tonight,
they tell him. And the night wears on
towards the coming of Abednego, Meshakh, Shadrakh,
the forest wardens. Put leaves beneath your head. Rest
quietly. A squirrel passes by, looks, is astonished.
And the night wears on. Leaves fall. In the moonlight
the weed moves slowly in the dark water, gleaming.
Meshakh, Shadrakh, Abednego, how long till the night ends?
How much longer will the night last?
Sleep here, until the fall passes. Rest. Be still.
Look up: the troops of the Cross pass above the treetops.
Look east: Constantine! Look east. Guard the flank.
Heavily armed forces in the moonlight, wet with dew.
The quiet ones the holy ones. They glide by on high.
They take no spoil.
So, So. He sees a vision, the old man.
And then rises. See him: he is a child again.

In the Garden of the Turkish Consulate

I turned aside into the trees, among the shadows.
I wanted to take a shortcut across the field. (This
seems to have been Turkish territory in Tel Aviv. The garden
of their Consulate?) Among the trees then,
pine trees, I think, I saw dogs,
three or four, strays,
looking at me, in silence.
I hoped I could pass by them in peace.
I had not yet made out, it had not seemed to me,
that there were so many there. They slipped
out of the shadows, from behind tree trunks, wolf
dogs, gray. Slowly they began
to form a pack, coming closer and closer to me. Slowly,
quietly. Then I knew,
felt it, that there was no help.
If I went back, fled, it would be useless.
So, in silence, slowly, they surrounded me
and tore me to pieces.

Translated by Harris Lenowitz

Raya Brenner

Raya Brenner, is that you?
I wouldn't have believed
that I would meet you again.
How many years have passed since then!
It seems as if I'm dreaming.
Indeed, I know it is a dream.
But I intend to say that I dream
within a dream.
Now everything is intelligible and easy.
Now I know you understand me.
But then, to understand me, you could not.
I began to love you. I know
that I could have loved you very much.
Now there is nothing to reply.
Nothing to improve.
It is cold here. No, perhaps
it is not cold. A kind of a gray, sad
darkness. Are you still here?
Do you still hear me?
I don't see.
In life, as in death.
Nothing is.
And what was, as if it was not.
Nothing to reply,
nothing to improve.
I heard a rumor that you . . .
far away, in a strange city,
or was it perhaps at sea?
I no longer remember.
I, in a dimness, still, silent,
in the twilight before morning,
expired.

Elegy

While walking at dusk in a strange city,
he says to the girl,
"Walk in front of me,
bring me to the strange streets of evening,
among shadows and stone houses.
Vagrant lights, colors, names,
I don't know your name.
As a light mist, the back of your dress
in the half darkness.
Your hair is cold, your feet are golden.
The deep gold of the flames
of death."

Translated by Gabriel Preil and Howard Schwartz

Shin Shalom

Shin Shalom was born in Galicia in 1905. He lived in Vienna until 1922 and then traveled to Palestine, where he attended the Jerusalem Teachers' Training College. The influence of his philosophical training can be found in his poetry. In addition to ten volumes of poetry, Shin Shalom has written prose poems and dramas.

Splendor

I

Emerging from the inmost hideout,
from the pavilion of a throbbing soul;
I am the stratified alarm
of my people at the foot of Mount Sinai,
stunned by voices and lightnings
and thunderstorm clouds, my eyes,
inwardly open, reveal the hitherto
untraveled track. The deep blue
at the recesses of the retina
is cindered by purple, leaving a trail
of ashes. A searing wilderness
of light-years I have traversed,
an overwhelming desert, a cauldron
of brick-and-mortar, and on the other side
a vulture swooping on carrion
in the sand that burns my barefootedness,

and the serpent of derangement goes round
and round, gnawing at my heart.
Emerging from the inmost hideout,
from the pavilion of a throbbing soul,
a fire enwraps and consumes me,
a crucible of sapphire whiteness
cleaves in me wide-open spaces
pure and limpid as high heaven,
swings me upwards, tightens in me
the string of silent voices.
And the Splendor calls out:
"I."

II
There is no portrayal
of man's stature in this world
without a scrutiny of all spheres
and all worlds.
The light expands downward, fraught
with desire to add new dimensions
to the circumscribed soul.
Designated "The Light of Mercy"
its benevolence enriches the cosmos, the
entire process of creation, for it shines
upon all created entities.
But when they fail to return
light for light, the radiance
departs, ascends again
to its celestial origin. My learned friend
assures me that all we perceive
is only seen in the reflected light. . .
And that's why single, invisible persons
are daily burned on a hidden pyre
in all corners of the world
to become a splendor to new entities,
transcendent light to divine incandescence,
so that it should retain its radiant
zest to enrich the newborn souls
by the light of the former ones.

III
"*Unwitnessed,*" I heard at dead of night
the dream's reply to my query:—
"How shall I come by the grace
of the Splendor?" All of a sudden
shame seized me for the openness
of my mundane life.
So I sought a secluded corner
in the temple of the universe
to set out my prayer in peace
between me and my soul,
to shed the one true Light
solely in its own orbit.

IV
A moon on the bay's mirror.
Distant shores, blinking eyelashes
dazed by the plenitude of dormant radiance.
Ships, dinghies, ferryboats,
viewed through portholes of the
seven colors of the rainbow,
rest on pillars of translucent fire
that probe unfathomable depths.
Rows on rows of lanterns glimmer
along the boundaries of light-hills.
A city of tremulous afterglow
at the foot of a flaring mountain.
A sky with a myriad fixtures
girded by glowing horizons.
The air, rich with countless sparks,
breathed through azure inhalations,
is strewn with exquisite brightness.

V
"Before the operation I should like
to memorize three pieces: Bach's
Prelude and Fugue, Beethoven's
Hammerklavier Sonata, and one of
Mendelssohn's *Songs Without Words.*"

And just before she was wheeled into
the operating theater, she whispered to him:
"As long as these are with me
I shall fear no harm."
For three long weeks her fate
hung in the balance. With bandaged eyes
she lay in the ward while he sat
at her bedside.
But as soon as she was brought back home
with the verdict that her eyesight
was gone for ever, she asked to be seated
at the piano. Deep into the night he listened,
enthralled, and when the last chord died away she raised
her sightless eyes to him, drunk with happiness:
"I have played everything, everything. Not a single note
escaped me!"
And there was splendor on her face.

VI

A black gallery. A black carpet at
the doorway. The mainstays on either side
are black pillars of marble.
The footman—a black shadow
clad in a black mantle.
Black snowflakes falling
on vacuities of marble marvels,
hovering round or going
up the stairway of timeless Time.
All faces are black in the pictures.
Pieces of statuary are black
abstracts on a dark non-image.
Black-flamed lanterns pour out
weirdness from all directions.
Once in, one can never tell
the way in from the way out.
Alone yet not quite alone
his shadow has subtle nuances
inscribing him yet inscribed in him.
The stove cinders are frozen stiff,
the silence—a stifled wall.
Every parturient idea
gives birth to a black thought,

turns a canvas and it's naught,
turns a statue and there's nothing.
A black piano in an African pit.
The keyboard—all keys jet-black—
imprisons in dumbness and deafness
your black terror in the tempest,
your black despair in the ashes,
the black hailstones upon
your strenuous black strings—
I sought you from my soul's recesses,
O white sound of the Splendor!

VII
The rising morning sees
the spirit hold full sway.
Past, present and future
extend nimble fingers to play.
And the tune is your lips whose kiss
is the touch of a soul-taking bliss.
And the tune is your wine, strong and devious
that lures to a lasting oblivion.
And the tune is a fire-circled chariot
harnessed to snow-white lions
fuming and bristling: why tarries
my spirit to soar higher, higher.
And I, servitor to those true men
who renounce everything for the sake
of a spark that sublimely illumines
the hither-to-thither path, take
my pen in my hand to attest
that I've never been an offender
against divine Light and the test
of transmitting the innermost Splendor.

Translated by Abraham Birman

HEBREW

Aliza Shenhar

Aliza Shenhar was born in Israel in 1943 and received her Ph.D. in Hebrew Literature at Hebrew University. She has published three volumes of poetry and edited several books on Jewish folktales, and is presently the Chairman of the Department of Hebrew Literature and Folklore at Haifa University.

Trembling

At the crossroads
of my gaping dreams
Mother bends.
Her white smile
trembles.
With my eyes closed
I hear the
broken pieces
of her life
falling away.
I breathe
the pungent scent
of her terror.

Expectation

And the child, mine
and not mine,
sobs in secret between
the folds of darkness.
A light stream of blood
runs down the length of the leg
of time slipping away.
And your hesitant hands
on my expectant eyes
cease to foresee
the future.

Resurrection of the Dead

A thousand deaths a day
return to life.
Right eyelid closed
and a gaping mouth filled with symbols.
After all
the Torah did not speak
of the dead.
Awaken and be jubilant!
After all
nothing causes death
and nothing
brings to life.

The Drunkenness of Pain

A ladder ascends and descends
making itself holy
and self-afflicting.
The angels of God
whistle as they climb
its splintered rung.
Oh the drunkenness of pain,
of sweat and trembling!
The Foundation Stone
did not make its own back tremble
nor did it falter.

Sea-Games

My body is made of waves and foam,
warm, stormy,
your body is a battleship,
wide and deep.
Only a few
hours of anchoring
are left.
Light-house beacons
are lit.
Together
we will blow wind
into the folded sails
of your silence that is heard
beyond the sea,
and like the sea,
is wide, is deep.

The Akedah

The loudspeaker screamed
"Take your only one
the one you love."
And the altar is destroyed.
Wood of the burnt offering is scattered.
The youths roll balls of love
on the grass of their youth.
Their tongues are hot.
The knife is shining in the wadi
in the light of the moon
of mid-border.
The white angel, the one
who always cries
"Please don't lay a hand"
is on leave.

Song of the Closing Service

I will be exacting before the closing
of the silent gates.
My watch stopped . . . how
many years have passed since then . . .
The plaster pulled off from my eyes
and the sound of the wailing women
penetrating within.
My tears sprouted in my cheeks,
grass roams in my belly,
the moss blossomed.
Its flowers are bluish.

Translated by Linda Zisquit

Avraham Shlonsky

Avraham Shlonsky was born in Russia in 1900 and settled in Palestine in 1921. His influence on Hebrew poetry has been profound in terms of metaphor, rhythm, and lexical inventiveness. His poems have been published in a collected edition. Shlonsky translated many classics of world literature, mainly from Russian into Hebrew, and wrote books for children. He was the leading editor of his generation. He died in 1973.

Prayer

Forgive me, you whom they cast in a name,
You the confiding, the rising far yonder.
I am not to blame, I am not to blame,
That in language the words are bewildered and wander.

Many times now have our words probed in quest
Of all your creatures—but none would receive us.
Were we not born in the desert waste?
Perhaps he who was first—did not conceive us.

When from Edom the morning, flushed and tangled,
First trod on the heels of infinite night,
My father primeval, my father wrangled,
And roared out his words like a ram in its might.

Then rain to the meadow and storm to the fold
Would talk as they listened to Cain and Abel.
But what more shall we do, what more unfold?
In the flight of our words to nothing we babble.

Forgive me, you whom they cast in a name,
Forgive me my words, my bewildered features.
I am not to blame, I am not to blame.
Teach me a roaring like you to your creatures.

The Stars on Shabbat

The stars at their zenith, more tranquil than you—
You are sad today,
Sadness like desecration,
Eclipse of candles, hallowed by mother.

Did you not take a vow of silence,
That is distilled speech,
As honey is the pledge of a thousand roses,
As landscape, in which mountain, furrowed field, and broken stream
Have compacted, to dwell alone and together—
And do not struggle.

Assent to the times and to your generation's passing,
Go to your fate as the river goes
To the sea's assurance, that there is a shore.

Small children there knead loaves of bread
Out of wet sand.
There the seashell, innocent of speech,
Wheezes to your ear the mystery
Of ebb and flow.

The stars at their zenith, more tranquil than you—

Pledge

(This poem is engraved in the wall of Yad Va-Shem shrine in Jerusalem.)

By leave of my eyes that watched the bereaving
Add cry after cry to my crushed heart's burden,
By leave of my trust that taught me forgiving
Till the pall of days that seared beyond pardon,
I have sworn an oath: to remember each grieving,
To remember, never to harden.

Nothing, till ten generations* give way,
Till soothed is the rankling, annulled each pain,
Till the rods that punished are purged away.
I vow that the dark wrath pass not in vain.
I vow that at dawn I never more stray.
Lest now I learn nothing, again.

A New Genesis

The damp swell of dunes that turn into flour,
Saffron of sunrise on treetop and hair,
Filing past Adam, his body in flower,
The clamoring flocks are at morning prayer.

The honey is thick and crawls in the hives,
The flesh of the world, its infantile rose:
To speak with its Lord Creation revives,
Syllable by syllable, language grows.

Translated by Francis Landy

*The "ten generations" refers to Deut. 23:4: "An Ammonite and a Moabite shall not enter into the congregation of the Lord, even the tenth generation shall not enter the congregation of the Lord for ever. Because they did not receive you with bread . . . and because they hired Balaam . . . to curse you."

Dress Me, Dear Mother

Dress me, dear mother, in splendor, a coat of many colors,
And at the break of dawn lead me to work.

My land lies wrapt in light as in a prayer shawl,
The houses stand forth like frontlets,
The asphalt roads we laid with our own hands
Branch out like the thongs of phylacteries.

Thus does a graceful city
Offer up morning prayers to the Creator.
And among the creators, your son Abraham,
Poet-roadbuilder in Israel.

And toward evening, father comes home from his labors
And whispers, as if praying, with quiet joy:
Abraham, my dear son,
All skin and bone and sinew,
Hallelujah!

Dress me, dear mother, in splendor, a coat of many colors,
And at the break of dawn, lead me
To work.

Translated by Robert Mezey

David Shulman

David Shulman was born in Iowa in 1949 and moved to Israel in 1967. He taught himself Hebrew as a child and soon after began writing poetry, which was published in Israel. His book of poems was awarded the Neumann Prize in 1974. Shulman is presently an instructor at the Hebrew University in Jerusalem.

A Diary of the Sailors of the North

1

This anchorage will do,
our bellies full of memories of another earth,
our eyes tailing after the pathfinders

o all who have held fast the helm
and whose heads now drop in drowsiness—
upon the aging horizon there is a pillar of fog

and the star-men are saying: a journey of another
two days, or three,
beyond that, man's hand will never reach.
And yet, they are sailors, they are not
of the prophets

who threefold incant upon the lives of their offerings:
here our glory will rise up
here our continent will burst forth
here in lonely security our strength will be charmed to abundance.

2

But our hearts are all for the searching.
We have placed our all on the hands of the clocks,
our women we abandoned in
that other century.

Now our turn will come forever.
Our bodies stand taut in the wings
in a moment we shall be spewed forth,
in our wisdom, before the lights;
for us
the story of the future sea
is yearning.

Somewhere nearby that white gap on the map
has begun spreading like cancer its hidden lust:
we, only we, are sailing in your footsteps,

you who dwell at the foot of our misty encampments,
so defined and eroded—
soon your purity will pass.

3
That god in our knapsacks
is stolen.
If only we had been commanded to empty him out,
to hide him in the sand,
before we hid ourselves northwards—
then with pure hearts, with torches alit with fresh oil,
light-eyed, we could have sailed on our journeys—

but no! he has fled, escaped, been saved from our hands,
and where are his steps in the sands?
we scrape with our hands and have not found him,
our heart is cleft by the loss of our spoils

while the voices of sirens bless us in fury
with *his* anonymity
(why did we let him steal into our diary)—
"go forth in his peace;
be bound up in our spring of blood."

Translated by the author

Eisig Silberschlag

Eisig Silberschlag was born in Austria in 1908. He was educated at Vienna University where he received his Ph.D. and later settled in the United States, where he is Professor of Judaic Studies at the University of Texas. He has published poetry and essays in both Hebrew and English, and has been awarded the La Med Prize for Hebrew Literature and the Kovner Memorial Award for Hebrew Poetry.

Abraham

I shall go to Mamre's oaks.
I shall heed my God's command.
I may wither like a tree
Torn from the ancestral earth.
I shall not return to Ur.

My God has braced my hesitations
With his seasoned utterance.
I may err if I exchange
Patriate for expatriate lot.
I shall not return to Ur.

From oasis to oasis
I shall wander with my God.
I may succumb when I recall
Prior joy in vagrant grief.
I shall not return to Ur.

No bluffing priest, no tricky whore
Shall come between my God and me.
My God and I are ever one.
I shall go wherever I go.
I shall not return to Ur.

Proust on Noah

Noah sailed his ark and skimmed his inner world.
The outer world was locked with bars of water.
Noah did not fear his death.
He feared cessation of remembrance, death-in-life.

My spirit, Noah-like, slumbers in my room's ark,
Corked and isolated from the urban noise.
Remembrance is my life. Remembrance
Has restored the unlost times to utterance
With doubled joy, with doubled strength, with doubled splendor.

My rescued times resemble times
Of other men. My past, mixed with their past,
Drips into my present and their present
Like seasoned wisdom from the land of Lethe.

Translated by the author

HEBREW

Arye Sivan

Arye Sivan was born in Tel Aviv in 1929. He has been publishing his works since 1948.

Children's Song

Men went up on these sands along the sea,
built houses, and in the houses
brought forth children. They called this
coming to peace.
The children ran barefoot in the soft sand,
the sea crossing them like crimson thread
and the winds weaving a summer web in their hair.
The children grew, went to wars,
returned to the houses on the sand, so small:
six-by-nine, ten-
by-twenty. Now
they rest. Wherever they lie,
they rest. Just the houses
know no peace. They develop
very nicely. Some have
many stories—fifteen and twenty—
their thin figures grow tall
and the glass breaks
the sun into fragments.

In Jerusalem Are Women

In Jerusalem there are women whom I had, and children
that were not, sons
like hidden giants. In summer
a determined heat rises from Emek Refaim, the pine trees
like dogs break into my house
searching for cool shade. My women
draw back from them as in a dream
and my children draw back with them, transparent
as cistern water, along the wall.

How long can one sit so, in approval
that is like thanksgiving? They will go
to Mount Moriah, seeing there a father
lift his knife to the son he loves.

But perhaps they come to thank me, my children:
"That I was made a water child
and was not made a man of fire"
and the women whisper
"That we were not robbed of our children."

No, no, there is no holding on to the words
of a man who sits among his dead
like me, here, now.

Translated by David Shevin

Forty Years Peace

Forty years peace. Forty years.
Forty years the fig trees
multiply and replenish
the earth, like women whose breasts
touch and get caught everywhere,
and they do not care.
Forty years men sleep with their women:
their breath long and peaceful
like the breath of flutes
in the reeds by small rivers.
They allow the light of
the moon to envelop them:
men walk in peace, like sleepwalkers,
in fields of vines and pine trees.

To Xanadu, Which Is Beth Shaul

A man or woman walking today
to Xanadu, which is Beth Shaul,
reaches the black
eagles, perched
on high cliffs, they hover
in closed circles,
like new widows, round
and round. You can walk there
for hours in a silence
that does not speak,
contemplating the stolen
child, and his mother
running after him on
the mountain, wailing
in a terrible voice.

Translated by Anthony Rudolf and Natan Zach

Jakov Steinberg

Jakov Steinberg was born in the Ukraine in 1887, and emigrated to Palestine in 1914. He was a poet, story writer, and essayist. He also translated into Hebrew works by Daudet, Victor Hugo, Tolstoy, and others. His collected works appear in a two-volume edition. Steinberg died in 1947.

With a Book at Twilight

I sit by the window, reading a book.
My eyes absorb the pleasant word-drugs as if they were beams of
light.
The melting of lovely moments. Evening is drawing near.

A fiery figure in the window. Bright light on the leaves.
but only the torn fragments of the text are rescued from this light.
Some will be like fire, others like ashes.

A splintering imagination has overturned what had been delightful
and full of life,
A tender note, that has no equal, melts like a distant echo,
And my eye still gropes through blinding confusion.

Oh, foolish man, of what value are your labors?
A figure of joy, a figure without a name, has gone its own way,
And your fearful gaze embraces only the shadows of emptiness.

The World Is Not a Fenced-Off Garden

The world is not a fenced-off garden; on a shortened day when you have reached old age
Seven joys will press down upon your tranquil sorrow.

Old age will tread with gentle steps; even in the pastures of the aging
A cruel abundance teems with the scorpions of heresy.

You will sit in silence and reflect: my smoothly paved path has returned—
And on the other side arises a mob in tumult.

You will wake up in the morning and propound riddles: one cycle has been rolled aside,
And the children of the moth that are on its margins are already being shaken off into the abyss.

But when the clear evening turns silent, stars sing together,
And the only barriers between the stars are the lines that separate the subjects of parables.

Thus recluses never return; and he that is sentenced to decay
Sees the grave and is silent and restrains himself within his heavens.

A Donkey Will Carry You

A donkey will carry you day after day,
But put the household idols in the saddle—
There are those whose days are considerably lengthened
By even a tubercular fate.

Put makeup on your cheeks
And be the ignoramus in the eyes of everybody;
And friend and lover
Kissed each other without knowing for how long.

Flattery, which controls everything,
Will secretly understand and turn silent;
Only death will taste bitter
In the shameful ointment.

Translated by Mark Elliott Shapiro

HEBREW

Noah Stern

Noah Stern was born in Lithuania in 1912. After living briefly in the United States, he settled in Palestine in 1935. He worked as a newspaperman and high school teacher, and served in the Jewish Brigade during World War II. In 1960 he committed suicide after a long period of depression. His poetry received little recognition during his lifetime, but posthumous publications have stirred greater interest in his work.

His Mother's Love

His mother loved him. All the world of man
Held his life from him. And his mother loved him
And dead his mother left round his corpse
A web of boughs, boughs of love, and their moisture—his warm
blood.

And when his loneliness grew heavy and the daughters of Eve from
all sides provoked him—
He burst from his room and with knife-edge felled all the armor of
his boughs,
They dropped, decayed, then free of burden and father-fear,
He shook his dusty soul out and let it wander where it would.

Besides he even found a lover-friend and erected a house of love for
her
In order to rule her spirit and body, in order to flee and forget—
And his mother's love returned suddenly from the darkness of her
shut-up cave,
To her son's soul and her son's house returned, and again enwound
him and bowed low.

Moss and mold and sand split the base of the house of love from
under,
And demolished it fell before its master observed his virility's rite.
Barbed-shrubs spread about him and trees in a circle dark as fear,
Budded about him without release, buried his dwelling up to the
roof.

He then grabbed an axe and ran to hew them down, but the forest in
which he was prisoned
Then slowly extended crawling branches sodden in wormwood like
venomous tongues.
And when he climbed to the roof to view the face-of-the-world-of-
man, each one crept
After to scald him, until he fled despairing to his room—to the fist of
his cruel fate.

Grave at Cassino

Clusters of ruins on vine-shoots of steel,
ancient housing deviating from the line of landscape,
illusory death-orchards among reflected scenes
and a Star of David, perpendicular
at the edge of a field.
Now, we won't lament
the hardened soldiers in a train rushing past,
nor even refugees
carrying the destruction in their eyes.
In tranquil days that will come with light of lanterns
casting their lairs
in nighttime gardens, on unchoked happy life—
then each man, each person who grants his body to the grave,
will be remembered;
his trouble in days of depression, days without light
or desire,
his hardship in the tempest of steel, hopes
to his last day,
to the last minute of the meeting
of young life . . . and nothing.
To the right, the vineyard festivity—multi-
colored, inebriant and thriving,
and to the left, the mountain forests—fruit
of nature's limitless imagination,
and in the midst,
the grave of a victim.

Translated by Harold Schimmel

HEBREW

A. L. Strauss

A. L. Strauss was born in Aachen in 1892. He taught German literature at Aachen University until the Nazis took power, then fled to Palestine in 1935 and later taught at the Hebrew University. Strauss wrote poetry, short stories, and literary criticism. He died in 1953.

Lament for the European Exile

The thin mask of my sleep
Caught fire.
I woke
With my face seared.
I had seen the flames of the sunset,
But this was a new sun,
A red sun
That lit up the night
With a strange, cruel light,
In which I saw the heavens
Swallowing hell,
And the earth spawning out
Living death.

I knew that this sun
Was the blood of my people
Gathering in the sky,
Ripping the darkness
With a flaring cry.
For on the highways of the world
It poured along,
In the world's fields
It watered,
The blood knew no rest.
It rose
And split the night's calm.

The Angel of Death
Said to me:
"Thou art my son.
Today I watched thy birth."
And a new heart
Beat in me

Weak-voiced,
Jerking in agonies of death.
My flesh
Became dead flesh.
The blood flowed dumb
In my veins.

Can I mourn?
I am an elegy.
Lament?
My mind is lamentation.
Can I rise
With death heavy on my limbs,
Or see
When Nothing hangs at my eyelash?
I will mourn and rise.
Your look will ask in my eyes
Atonement for your blood
At the hands of the world
That shed it.

Translated by A. C. Jacobs

In the Discreet Splendor

In the discreet splendor of the moonlight,
my room dreams towards me. At my head,
a white and slender sentinel stands. The candle,
its light extinguished by a breath of night,
glows with a radiance that is the moon's.

On the Path

Every promised path ends in the Garden,
seraphs at its gate with flaming sword.
God, who bade me walk,
sets in my path an angel for my devil.

Voice in the Dark

What has risen in the dark and is?
I woke. How will I fall asleep again?
Was it a beast that cried with human voice,
or was it a human howling like a beast?
Did a beast cry from out the heart of night,
or the night cry from out the heart of beast?
The whole of darkness rose in me and is.

Translated by Robert Friend

Joshua Tan Pai

Joshua Tan Pai was born in 1914 in Kishinev, Russia, and came to Palestine in 1934. He was a kibbutz member, working as a laborer on roads and in orange groves. His first book of poems, From A to Z, *was published in 1937. His other books of poetry include* Variations on Spring, Songs of Darkness and of Seeing, The Entire Man, *and* Souls in My Grasp. *He has extensively translated poetry and prose from French, Russian, German, English, and Romanian. He has been working as a journalist for many years, and at present he is bureau chief of the* Ha'aretz *daily in Jerusalem.*

Trees Once Walked and Stood

The honor of God and man is not on
the olive that ceased giving its oil
and the fig that sought a pretext for its fruit—a pie
that changed its sweetness, a bitterness without taste
and the vine—an eternal forsaken shedding of leaves.
The joy of God and man stops
and only the bramble—ignited by a consuming flame.

Trees once walked and stopped without hope
and only the bramble—the uncut growth of thorns—
will move over all those who take refuge in the
kingdom crowned in dark smoke.
Woe to those who take refuge in the idle kingdom;
a word to the wood does not a king a stumbling-block make.

Honor and joy were lost in the shadow of the
question.

Tan Pai

My Soul Hovers Over Me

With every blow of the wind
my soul hovers over me,
like a garment over a woman's form,
and roars in confusion like the waves of the sea.

I was like the woman—
who plunges in a maddened sea
and to save her a crowd grasps at her garment
and brings back nothing but the garment.

So my soul—
like a rag that absorbed the entire sea
and was wrung out bit by bit
drop by drop
without restraint
forever—

The Life of Hard Times

The light of dimmed stars goes on
still goes on
until light ends from dimming stars

The rivers go from springs that have dried
still go on
until the water was gone from the dry spring
until every tongue cleaved to its roof

We go with the light
until struck blind
we drink from the trough
until broken

The life of hard times

Translated by Yishai Tobin

HEBREW

Shaul Tchernichovsky

Shaul Tchernichovsky was born in the Crimea in 1875. He received a degree in medicine in 1907 and served as a country doctor and a physician in the Russian medical corps. Following World War I he lived first in Germany and finally in Palestine. In addition to a volume of collected poetry which has been published in numerous editions, Tchernichovsky published stories, plays, and translations of the Greek classics into Hebrew. He died in 1943.

Man Is Nothing But

Man is nothing but the soil of a small country,
nothing but the shape of his native landscape,
nothing but what his ears recorded
when they were new and really heard,
what his eyes saw, before they had their fill of seeing—
everything a wondering child comes across
on the dew-softened paths,
stumbling over every lump of earth, every old stone,
while in a hidden place in his soul, unknown to him,
there's an altar set up
from which the smoke of his sacrifice rises each day
to the kingdom of the sky, to the stars,
to the houses of the Zodiac.
But when the days become many, and in the war of being
the scroll of his Book of Life is being interpreted—
then comes, one by one, each letter with its interpretation
and each symbol revealing past and future
that was inscribed in it when it was first opened.
A man is nothing but the landscape of his homeland.

And in that corner of earth where I was born,
in the vastness of the blue steppes,
the high places dreamed, the holy places,
on the backs of strange graves.
Nobody knows who spilled that earth, nobody knows when,
or who it is that sleeps for good in their laps.
And idols shrouded by the dust of many jubilees
look toward the mute grey borders,
like the steppes themselves before rain,
like the end of August when the earth cracks open
in a thousand places.

Kingdoms blossom and kingdoms sink into death
and the borders of states grow blurred and then sharp—
here on their beds they stand like headstones
on the back of a strange great past, forgotten forever,
faded away even out of poems and legends.

In that corner of earth where I was born
live the eagles of the field, lonely ones of the steppes,
giants with heavy wings and brown feathers,
like the sheaves of wheat the reapers left behind,
burnt by the east winds and eaten by heat and rain.
It happens sometimes that one comes down from the sky
and alights at the branching of roads, folding his wings—
a man will draw nearer and nearer
and then stop, and keeping his distance, stare at him.
And in his heart he will think: "What is this?
There is a sheaf and not a sheaf,
a bird and not a bird . . ."
When the eagle describes his pure God-circles in the sky
and hurls down from those heights his wild cry,
who will understand him? And who will know
why a bird calls out? Is it some kind of sigh,
or is it his song, childless,
without a listening heart, without an echo?
That cry is so lonely . . . dying over the steppes . . .

In that corner of earth where I was born,
there's an eternal fugitive;
there isn't a field he hasn't gone across
no road he hasn't stumbled on
or come to the end of.
From the wing of earth to the wing of earth
he rushes and passes by. Do you know what I mean?
It's the wind! Sometimes he drives clouds as heavy as lead,
and sometimes he goes wild in open space,
sometimes he chases dust till it darkens the sun
and sometimes exults among the treasures of ice and snow.
And there is nothing, he thinks, to stop him
and no one who can stand in his way.
But when he turns his face to the south . . . to the south,
longing to reach the southern seas,
the ancient cliffs and mountains suddenly
stand in his way.

And so in the shape of that corner where I was born,
my life's history was spelled out to me
and my fate was revealed.
I worked my dream in a semblance of its own image:
with a free soul, free of stain or tatter,
with a whole heart all its strings speaking in harmony,
I wandered alone in the congregation of my people,
bowed beneath the blessing
and the curse of the big graves.
And my poem is a stranger, an alien
in the heart of my nation, lonely,
lonely, coming lonely and going lonely,
without a listening heart, without an echo,
a savage cry ringing in solitude.
And like the wind that goes wandering forever,
I wandered from ocean to ocean all the days of my life,
but when I had to get to the southern seas,
mountains rose up before me and blocked my way . . .
And where shall I build my nest?

More open space, more roads! Give me my stick.
I am going.

The Grave

in memory of those fallen in the Ukraine

There are many like him here, without epitaph, without a mound.
The ox pulling a plow stumbles on him,
The peasant behind the plow swears at him furiously,
And his clearing will be the shelter of the locust.

The field, before autumn—and only a cloud weeps for him
With cold cries. A storm silences it
And thus he is mourned. No one to say Kaddish.
The path bends around him and does not cry, O father!

Even this year, look, his land is becoming green,
Awakening from sleep and turning its burning face,
Aftergrowth bursting up from everywhere,
And the stalks of wheat mock him with sighing and scraping.

And this fellow, struck down by fire, decaying in the soot,
He doesn't know why the spade dug him a furrow,
Nor why he lived his painful life,
Nor why he was cut down and thrown here before his time.

Translated by Robert Mezey and Shula Starkman

Saul's Song of Love

I descended in the evening to the fountain,
to the spring with a pitcher on my shoulder:
there I saw the mother of my dear one,
the sister of my darling:
his mother weeping—the tears ran down her cheeks—
and pale and sad his sister.
I did not ask the reason.
I put a seal upon my mouth. I kept my silence.
The Philistines came into the mountains,
the Edomites invaded, sacked and pillaged,
the Kings of the East and all their kindred tribes.
The nation was called up by families,
and my beloved went with all the others
the colors summoned.
The nation was defeated; many fell—
in the high places
brought low.
Some escaped; my beloved did not come.
At night upon my couch I wept and did not sleep.
In the day I was ashamed that I had wept,
and my sighs shamed me.
I washed my eyes at dawn in the cold waters,
the rills of the garden spring,
lest my mother see me,
my sister question deeply.
I wearied myself with sighs; I bit my pillow
so that my sighs should never reach the dawn.
The mother of sons is mourning, the wife of the husband weeping.
Shall then the virgins rejoice?

Translated by Robert Friend

HEBREW

The Death of Tammuz

Go forth and weep,
O daughters of Zion, for Tammuz,
For bright Tammuz, for Tammuz—for he is dead.
The days to come will be cloudy days,
Days of souls' eclipse, of untimely autumn.

At sunrise,
In the clear morning
Let us go to the grove that has grown dark with gloom,
To the grove that is hidden in dreams and mysteries,
To the altar of Tammuz, to the altar of light.

What dance shall we dance
Around the altar,
What dance shall we dance for Tammuz today?
Let us turn right towards him, then left,
seven times seven,
Let us bow, let us bow down to him: "Come back!"

Let us turn right towards him,
Then left, seven times seven.
But with stiff legs and very slowly—hands locked!
And we shall go forth and search for Tammuz,
The young men and young women in two separate groups.

On all the main roads
We have searched for Tammuz—
On the crossroads that are immersed in sunshine and light,
The crossroads whose calm and warmth please the heart,
Where the swallow soars and where she dips.

On narrow paths
Stretching through the fields of corn,
Paths strewn with thorns and wild poppies,
Beside wells and in fields of rusting reeds,
Where the springtime stalks sing.

We went down to the brook,
Through valleys did we pass,
Through bushes, along furrows, and in the valley of Bin-Adar.
Answer us, O wind that laughs through the green grass!
Partridge, turtledove, have you seen Tammuz?

We searched for Tammuz,
In the thicket among the fallen leaves,
In the cypress forests, in the entangled sumac,
Lest he sleep, lest the incense of cedars
And the smell of mushrooms joining the circle make him slumber.

We searched for Tammuz—
Yet we could not find him.
We climbed hills, we went down into valleys,
We set off in pursuit of mystery or marvel,
Any place where the living god was.

We saw the thicket
And the grove—full of flames,
The mysteries of the grove consumed by fire.
And yet the hungry nestlings encircling the altar
Cried out, and the altar was a wave of marble.

And on the waterfalls of the streams,
Where we said,
"Yet the winds pronounce a magical chant"—
The reed, dried to its very roots by the intense heat,
Grates and squeaks. Summer has returned.

And the she-devil's footprints
Could not be found in the meadow,
And the jester's voice has been stilled because of the wave's
mysteries;
And the meadow is grazing land for cattle, and goats gambol
Over to the water troughs in the dew-drenched mornings.

Go forth and weep,
O daughters of Zion, for you have seen
The sorrow of a world bereft of miracles,
For you have seen the sorrow of the world and the eclipses of its
soul:
Yes, Tammuz, bright Tammuz, is dead.

Translated by Mark Elliott Shapiro

Mordecai Temkin

Mordecai Temkin was born in Poland in 1891. He settled in Palestine in 1911 and pursued a career of teaching. His poems appeared in newspapers and periodicals over several decades. Six volumes of his poetry have been published as well as his translations of Mann, Kleist, Chekhov, and others. Temkin died in 1960.

Seal of Fire

By day your high gates are closed
with a seal of fire,
and by night the moon
like a gatekeeper
wordlessly turns a gray indifferent head
toward us.
You calmly devise evil against us
and in the shape of a tempest
You pass with a mighty mocking
above our bowed heads.
Why do you conceal Your face,
my Lord?

Foul Water

Forgive me, O Lord,
for I have spilled my life
on the ground
like foul water.
Forgive me, for all my wounds
are self-inflicted,
and with a weeping voice
like a beaten child,
I cry out to You
that You should bind them for me,
my Lord.

Hidden Bow

With a cry of fear
I broke through to Your world
like an animal into a clearing.
And all my days
I wearied myself
in hiding from Your face.
But Your snares on earth
became very numerous, my Lord,
and always, stretched out above me,
oh, fearsome hunter,
Your hidden bow.

Your Presence

You are naked and have no clothes,
yet You clothed me
with all that lives,
Your immense presence
like a garment
that I carry both in pain
and with delight.
But when my flesh shall be consumed,
and my pain cease,
You also will cease to be,
my Lord.

Translated by Jeremy Garber

HEBREW

Avner Treinin

Avner Treinin was born in 1928. He is a professor of physical chemistry at Hebrew University in Jerusalem. He received the Millo Award in 1969 and the Agnon-Jerusalem Award in 1979. His books of poetry are Hyssop on the Wall *(1957),* Mount and Olives *(1969),* The Blocked Gate *(1976) and* Periodic Table *(1978).*

The Cage

Return, light of wing,
my bars dream your back,
the down of your swelling breast,
the dance of heartbeats
against their bare dryness.
Come, bride of wing,
my trough envisions your face,
all my wires prepare
for your gentle, timid patter
on the slopes of my back.
My granaries are full,
my water flows.

Slammed, slammed the gates;
again you are a rib in my breast.

Hush, light of wing,
I enclose your beating heart.
Enclose, confine; the trumpets are still.
See, evening at the window,
all the trees betray,
go down to the rivers,
move, move to decay.
What would you do alone on branches
that hold out their arms to darkness?

Quiet, my bride, till morning comes
and your voice shall sound in the caves of my heart.

Translated by E. A. Levenston

Salmon Cycle

Where was the boundary between the bitter water
    —ocean mixing fins with salt and seaweed,
    a maw within a maw within a maw, above them eyes
    wide-open, aimless as if around a brutal arm
    stirring the bewilderment of my body—
and the water of the river, o sweetness of beginning
in whose existence I had already stopped believing,
a myth delivered to the ancients,
a covenant without a living witness
among the sharks and shards of war.

Suddenly the circle turned into a line, an arrow sent
flying toward the mountains; and what made birds of me
splashed me up to the summit, from shelf to shelf,
in the ascent of rock and waterfall,
as a chapter from the old religion regarding legacies,
the promised boundaries, the land I gave only to you—

from stair to stair, in the secret places of the stair,
glittering fish of joy, I come, leaping upon the mountains—
and as my body empties, my father's body in the standing
water crumbles in the shallows, touching me again
and giving me the sign. Again everything returns
from the beginning. Again the line becomes
a circle more encompassing, enclosing all my life,
from which I shall burst forth no more.

Translated by Robert Friend

Deserted Shrine

The god dwells alone,
his windows breeched.

In the doomed halls
silence crouches
and the prayers are speechless.

He is poised for revelation.
The spider weaves around him
threads of hope.

Along obliterated tracks
the daily steps shall return,
and the warmth of his hand . . .

And the priest still unrevealed.

Translated by E. A. Levenston

Shlomo Vinner

Shlomo Vinner was born in Jerusalem in 1937. He teaches mathematics at Hebrew University in Jerusalem. His first book of poems, For a Few Hours Only, *has recently been translated into English.*

Jerusalem

Jerusalem,
The former address of God;
Sometimes
They still imagine His silences
Between walls and bells.
To hear His heart
They call to Him over loudspeakers
And wait
Until everything dissolves.

And when the smoke clears the burnt house is revealed
And the bodies of the beloved.

The hearts of old trees are heavy as stone
And longings that last too long
Turn into thorns in the valley
While dreams are exchanged
For piles of rusted scrap.

At the end of the wars,
Amid new signs and arrows,
The birds leap on the grass:
Jerusalem 1967,
The former address of God.

In the Cabinet

Still playing:
God imprisons me in a cabinet
And leaves me the key.
I grope in the dark and breathe the scent
Of strange loves. Blindly I must wait,
But I know,
Even if he lingers,
He will not come.

With the deceit of artificial roses
They covered up his death,
Concealed his bones,
Scattered leaves where there were trenches,
Set up angels, chiseled faces
That would not hurt the stone too much.

The dust of ruins settles in my lungs,
The key in my hand.

Training on the Shore

Children
They teach to walk,
Soldiers
To crawl.
And between one lesson and another
They are shown the sand
God showed to Abraham
The hour He made him a nation
Wandering like sand.
They are shown the moon-struck sea,
Grass sprouting from the hearts of stones
That once were the wall of a temple.

And at midnight dew rises
From the beloved land,
The blessings of stars bring forth the grass,
The blessings of the grass
The stars.
Children
They teach to walk,
Soldiers
To fall.

Midnight and Ten Minutes

1
Because of long depression and a sudden urge
A star threw itself
From the seventh heaven.
We lament for it
But who will lament
For us?

2
The moon under the cover of planes
Sets out on its regular mission.
If it doesn't detect us
We will be able to stay
Another day at most.
If not, we shall be forced to uproot from here
And to camouflage our love
With sand.

3
Midnight and ten minutes,
And what else?
The anthem was played,
The clock set for seven exactly,
The stars remained without reason.
The angels have artificial wings,
Dusty,
And they lie in deep trenches.
The light on their face is masked in soot.
Only a blanket still covers
Our love.
And the hours
Pass over us
In silence.

The Need to Love

Therefore shall a man leave his father
and mother, and shall cleave to his wife;
and they shall be one flesh.
—Genesis 2:24

The need to love is the need to leave and move on.
That is how it is. Distant towers.
Giant letters of the announcement stuck in the clouds.
Buzzing of words in the electric air.
Pillars. Pillars.
The sweet sighs of the poplars in the wind.
And above all
The sudden whistle in the throat of twenty sirens
To announce an impending disaster.
If we put an ear to the evening
As to a seashell
It can still be heard.

The need to love is the need to think
Of all that one is forced to leave.
Years are growing thick in the pines.
Also in us time is calming down
As rain in dark cisterns.
Fever of the leaves in the fingers of the wind.
Preparations of ants in the unsettled dust.
Death in disguise is mentioned
In conversations of low bushes, in doctors' reports,

Signed on the trunks of olive trees.
And what remains unnamed, cannot be remembered,
Will be lost forever,
Until it is no longer remembered that it was lost.
And the ability to love is the ability to leave
And move on.
Fall will come again for the tired trees.
God will put them to sleep
As they anesthetize a patient
In dangerous surgery.
Thorns will die.
The earth will give a final response to those who search.

But the grass remains persistent.
Perhaps from habit.
Perhaps out of desire that cannot be measured.
There are no words left to explain.
This is how it must be understood,
To distinguish the sand and sand,
Sand and sea,
Our silence and the world itself.
To be moved by what is moved in me
When I say
The evening grows dark in us, crying,
And death passes.
Or when I say
The ability to love is the ability to leave
And move on.

Parting

1

A sword of light is unsheathed from the cloud.
This is a sign
For the doves and the evening
And the scaffold left by the building.
Jerusalem besieged between the walls
Sets free the bells
And the dark birds above us.
The crocus will blossom among thorns,
But it is doubtful
That we can do the same.
And on your forehead
The sign of parting is drawn
But concealed behind your hair.

2

Next summer
Your hair will grow longer
And the wind will blow it like a sail
In the direction of eternal wandering,
Of clouds and wind,
Sand and birds.
Even the pillars of a desolate house
Will be broken by standing too long,
And we shall have to move on
Or separate.
For between now and then
The evening descends,
The air trembles
And the sea floods the sand
With white shells,
Secret murmurings,
Garbled syllables,
Memories
And doubts
If we shall love again.

3
Our love will be left on the shore
Like a sailboat in winter.
The waves will wipe clean
The traces of our feet in the sand.
And see how the riverbeds
Have filled,
Dead leaves float in them now,
And on the bank,
Growing wild,
Visions of an autumn evening.

Translated by Laya Firestone and Howard Schwartz

Lullaby

Sleep now:
If not on the belly
On the back.
If not body to body
At least with thoughts about it.
But sleep.
No longer first or second,
Just the mattress and I
And outside
The sky spread above the ground
Like a giant net of camouflage.

Whoever observes us from above will not see
The heart covered
With its blankets, will not hear
The ticking of the clock,
The pining body;
Just sleep.

Translated by Laya Firestone

David Vogel

David Vogel was born in Satanov, Podolia, in southwestern Russia in 1891. After wandering through Eastern Europe for several years, he settled in Vienna from 1912 to 1925. He spent the rest of his life in Palestine, Berlin, and Paris. He was captured by the Nazis in 1943 and died in a concentration camp. Vogel's poems were collected in a volume entitled Before the Dark Gate, *edited by Dan Pagis. An English selection from this volume,* The Dark Gate, *appeared in 1976.*

Days Were Great as Lakes

Days were great as lakes
And clear
When we were children.

We sat a long time on their banks
And played,
Or went down to swim
In the fresh water.

And sometimes we wept
In our mother's apron,
For life was filling us
Like jugs of wine.

Our Childhood Spilled into Our Hearts

Our childhood spilled into our hearts
A deep, sweet grief—
How distant it is now!

The Talmud chant,
Heavy with dreams and longing,
Still rises at times,
Unsought, to our lips.

We look back
Anguished
At our vacant, innocent hearts
Almost in recognition.

We wander through life
Weeping,
With empty palms
Held out shaking
To every passer-by.

How Can I See You, Love

How can I see you, love,
Standing alone
Amid storms of grief
Without feeling my heart shake?

A deep night,
Blacker than the blackness of your eyes,
Has fallen silently
On the world,

And is touching your curls.

Come,
My hand will clasp your dreaming
Hand,
And I shall lead you between the nights,

Through the pale mists of childhood,
As my father once guided me
To the house of prayer.

Black Flags Are Fluttering

Black flags are fluttering
In the wind
Like the wings of caged birds.

All of us, for many days and nights,
Will go secretly,
Downcast,
Till we come
To the great, dark gate.

Like foolish children
We shall stand there nervously
Watching
For the opening
Of the great, dark gate.

Plain, Humble Letters

Plain, humble letters
A heavy hand labored to write
I have draped like decorations on my chest.

Your words sprouted in Bessarabian evenings
Like tough stalks of maize,
My dark sister.

In front of your door you dug a well:
Your neighbor's shaggy dog
Came to watch,
And in the evening
Your children tried to catch in it
A coaxing moon.

When I was a crawling baby
You kept me from falling
Off the table.

And now I speak strange words
Every night
To the surprised city,
Which doesn't know
I am talking inwardly to you,
My sister, hidden
In Bessarabian evenings.

When I Was Growing Up

When I was growing up, troubled and reckless,
My father told me, God, about you.

But I ran away from you
To play,
For there was so little time.

You
Always wisely kept hidden
So as not to spoil my games,
Till I'd almost forgotten you.

Now as I come back home alone
(All my companions fell asleep along the road)
I've made you out walking beside me,
Old and poor,
As I am today.

I'll lend you my stick
As far as a bench in the evening park.
We'll gently inhale the purple sunset
Of far-off skies.
And watch the children playing further
And further away from us.

Then we shall turn to the evening,
We two on our own,
To rest.

In Fine, Transparent Words

In fine, transparent words
Like silk scarves
I wrapped my life,

And when I unfasten them now
I can't recognize
My old passions.

All the old lures are laid out
In the market place,
And I have no wish
To buy anything.

Now as evening spreads
Our backs are bent low.
Even a little joy
Is too heavy for us to bear.

Now I Have Forgotten All

Now I have forgotten all
The cities of my youth,
And you in one of them.

Through puddles of rainwater
You still dance for me, barefoot,
Though you must be dead.

How I rushed galloping
Out of my distant childhood
To reach the white palace of age
That is huge and empty.

I can't see back
To the start of my journey,
Or back to you,
Or myself as I was.

The path of those distant
Days
Goes running on,
From nowhere to nowhere,
Without me.

Translated by A. C. Jacobs

Yona Wallach

Yona Wallach was born near Tel Aviv in 1944. She has published three volumes of poetry and is associated with the literary magazine Siman Kri'a.

Cradle Song

Imagine lamenting our longing, no,
we'd leave no room to mourn
and the bush is sprouting
wild to jazz rhythms.
What we hear in hysterical women
is the faint echo
of the voiced conclusion
a lullaby:
a butterfly net
and another song
another net.
And that's not what
will satisfy

my hunger no,
that's not
what
will calm me
no
that's not it.

When the Angels Are Exhausted

When the angels are exhausted
we fold their wings
with pleasure, with pleasure
prepare the whip
when the angels begin
and wound them
until dew floods the earth.

Death; She Was Always Here

It's not true that death is a lump like this, or a blow.
So much like a cloth veil, lifted,
like this she comes slowly, even like a bride.
The journey is private, it's true, listen
to what happens to me, what happens to you.
I'm not trapped here in any abstraction,
but all right, for me, death is like a bridal veil,
I don't speak, later, on the chariot,
there's this echo on the journey,
someone's disputing this theory,
I'm not involved when I pose a question
there's someone who keeps moving, and in poetry?

Oh, freedom, (my work, her work)
Oh, wind, where are you going, looking like the wind's soul,

You ask me later about her substance,
excuse me, but you seem to deafen yourself to her,
"How long ago was this?" only it's not a guess,
your journey, your death, the same carriage, it's
my death, the death I build, private, her privacy,
don't drop like fowl to her hand with no reply,
she was always here, an obverse view in my land, in her land.

Translated by Leonore Gordon

Manfred Winkler

Manfred Winkler was born in 1922 in Bukovina, Romania. In 1956 he started to write in German, and published three volumes of poetry. He immigrated to Israel in 1959, studied at the Hebrew University of Jerusalem, and received a degree in Hebrew and Yiddish literature. He has since published three books of poems in Hebrew. He has also worked as a translator, mainly from the German, Yiddish, and Romanian, into Hebrew. He has been employed since 1964 in the Central Zionist Archives, in charge of Theodore Herzl's archives and as an editor of Herzl's work. If My Hands Were Mute: Selected Poems of Manfred Winkler *is the first volume of his poetry to appear in English translation.*

One Goes With Me Along the Shore

I heard the sea murmur in my ears
wave after wave,
and the moon.
I heard the moon drown
like a pupil in alien eyes.
I heard the round voice of the moon
crushed between two waves of coal.
I wanted to give the sky to the woman,
to the child playing with crabs.
But the sea broke the moon
into many moons
and itself into many seas.
What does one give to the woman who never comes,
to the child who chases after crabs,
to the child who plays with crabs in the sky?
Cool saltiness of wind glides
over my eyes with the sand of night.
Frightened crabs flee on winding ways
as in a nightmare.
One goes with me along the never-ending shore
and whispers—one alone.

If My Hands Were Mute

If my hands were mute
they would cover us with tents
and we would again
be born under the tree,
would taste of the sweet and the bitter fruit and

lick the sweat of our soul,
would spit out our death
from the sweet and the bitter fruit
in the range of things-to-touch
and the winds would rise again
from the split of the sea
toward the beginning of the end of the way,
toward those simple words
of the chaos, and he would again
hover over the waters with hands of the primal deed
and his spirit would break the sluggishness of the flesh.
With rising reluctance he would begin a motion again.

Somewhere You Exist

Somewhere you exist
like a fruitful shadow
and aching light
somewhere I write you out of the flight
write in myself
write from the outline of a tower, not ivory.
All that I know
comes from an echo,
from things which have bloomed and which may exist,
from tensely drawn spiderwebs.
Sometimes I dream you
like a tiger in a cage of gold,
add much soul to the blood,
too much soul to the blood.
Somewhere the walls fall and remoteness comes,
remoteness of your angels,
and the pain pales
and becomes a transparent slave.
Somewhere there are circles of calm
where I can endure you
as the fire-keeping queen—
your velvety glances,
the glances of blind steel.

I Love What Is Not

I love what is not
in your power to give,
the morning which flees from my soul,
the stormy muteness, without which
we would not be, neither you nor I.

I love the autumn
which incessantly haunts
the rusty past
of longing,
the blue
in the haze of parting,
and the everyday feelings—
breathing the evening and awakening in gray.

I love what is not
in your power to give without giving yourself,
what my eyes feel beyond their bonds,
and if you leave, the world will become
emptier perhaps, or fuller
in nights and expectations,
in events which were never before.

I love what is not
in your power to give,
as you descend the paths of the earth
and the blood flows from the lands of the forest
with smells of animals and drying leaves.

She

I meditate long
in this place.
I—the last
of the suicides,
and she is dark.

I kiss
her twisted hands
before we part
for a very long time.

I shall bequeath her to a stranger
before we know what we were,
to a strange man
of our people,

or
to the son not born
of all expectations,
and from seed to seed
will remain last
one soul alone.

Translated by Mary Zilzer

Avot Yeshurun

Avot Yeshurun was born in Volhynia in 1904 and settled in Palestine in 1925. His three books of poetry, concerned with the common destiny of the European Jew and the Palestinian Arab, are The Wisdom of the Road, Re'em, *and* Thirty Pages.

The Poem on the Jews

The head of the congregation here stands at the head
of a long line of congregants who stand behind him.
A longer line than the one that departed and isn't.
Which—someone who has not seen it,

gradually the sight eludes him whereas
those other people, if not to resort to inhuman
idioms, why it can be said
with one word: they were the big ones when we were small.

At their hands each thing was cut they even cut
our slices of bread and they cut us
half an apple which voice of the apple we heard at the cutting.
And touched our cheeks and called our names.

They were in a closed circuit the masculine Jews we adored.
On holidays and on Sabbaths. With force they conducted
prayers and chanted hymns and acknowledged God.
And when Yom Kippur came kept packages of food for us at the fast.

After the holiday we still longed for the same holiday and
the same Jews to see them together. It's good to be among those who
are one
people who neither change "nor all their wrath awaken" and look
upon me as someone they didn't see awhile.

The Poem on the Guilt

Blest be Mother bind your hand on my head on the eve
of this day. I would have what would I have done
for Yom Kippur. Forests crash and you inside and at the center
of the land your soul and body you longed and did not arrive.

Your Father came in a dream to you.
Opened the glass cupboard; broke you a glass. A child of yours died
and you asked why. Your Father didn't reply and went out and you
meant to forgive
and lay on the floor and lay on the child and died of longing.

The Poem on Our Mother, Our Mother Rachel

And the two reservist guys went. Look, don't shoot.
And Jacob lifted his legs and went to the land of B'nei Kedem.
And Jacob said unto them: Ben Gurion and Nechemia Argov, my
brothers, from Whence?
From Ben Gurion and Nechemia Argov no reaction no response and
the two went off.

Ben Zvi's shack a wooden candelabrum
of local made carvings by Batia Lishanski,
and not a painting on every painting and not Chagall
on every France and presidential mansion rejoice and rejoice.

Inside sits Jacob
Esau stands outside.
From the window looks and wails
Esau's mother from the lattice.

Punished Earth.
You needn't start up with her. To speak
of her you need. To trick out her wardrobe. As meadows
wore sheep so we wore that Land.

Don't call her by many names.
Call her Rachel.
A man is born as a child and dies as a child.
All this close to the mother.

Punished Earth.
You needn't start up with her. To speak
of her you need. To trick out. As meadows
so we wore this Land.

Translated by Harold Schimmel

Nathan Yonathan

Nathan Yonathan was born in Kiev in 1923 and came to Palestine with his parents in 1925. He has studied at Hebrew University, Oxford, and Tel Aviv University. He has published numerous volumes of poetry and stories and produced several albums of his recited works. In 1975 he was awarded the Prime Minister's Prize for Literature.

Another Poem on Absalom

Cunning as a woman beautiful as a snake shy as an idol,
Always with his crew of cronies on horses in gold,
And now, tell me, where is the cunning of his women,
The beauty of his snakes, his shy idol?
The dreams of his kingdom—where are they?
A tree in the forest, that's all that's left of Absalom,
And the tears of a father, the old lover, man of wars;
Even his charioteer turns aside to weep;
Thus to break a father's back,
To make a joke of death, of everything!
Absalom my son my son Absalom
You couldn't wait,
You spoilt child, until we aged,
Until the crown brought us down in agony.
And your curls, what of your curls—
Didn't you know the danger that hides in such curls?

And why through the forest, of all ways—
Did you forget what happened to Jonathan?
Do you not know the terebinths?

Your father loved in you all that he was not,
See how this man trembles all over, why
Do you think I would not make you king—
Because of my concern for the people? Because
You were too young? If we'd only been able to speak of it calmly
You'd have understood that I'm no longer the same David,
Your mother's sorrow, but just an aging king
Going joylessly to his death,
With one last intrigue concealed in his heart:
To save at least one of his sons
From the crown and the wars.
I wanted, my little fool, only you, Absalom.

South Wind

If the tree fall toward the south, or toward the north,
in the place where the tree falleth, there it shall be.
—Ecclesiastes

For there is hope for a man
If he fall like a tree and if he fall in the north
In the place where he falls he digs his hands into earth
And a last wind of the north
On his branches will perch
Stolen from night to the dream
His wind of the north

And if he fall in the south
There too
Shall the wind rest on him
And spread the earth of his hair
And spread in his hair
Earth wherever he fall
A bird of night from the mountain of earth
Will revive his spirit
For ever
The wind of the south.

HEBREW

And the Silver Turns into Night

A woman is planting asters on the south wind side
Beside a sandmountain of dreams
And sea-green magic,
Like that dawn
Which divided his youth from east to west,
Now floods her.

Planting light in the gardens
While the sea still froths years
And thorns,
Asking herself where her flowers will be
When the asters light up in their godlike blue,
Where she will be
At the end of her love's summer.
To whom will her brambles turn?
There were nights when his shade still pursued her:
Then she fled to her enticements.
Now that it's evening,
Her face fills with the smells of April,
Sands grow cold,
An open well
And asters gleam in the darkness
Towards the face of the wise youth whom silence best suited,
His eyes the hue of the weeping sea,
He spoke not a word about love or sin.
Only the colors of time keep changing:

The sea-green into amber,
The black—into a graying man,
And the silver turns into night,
And the night into crimson,
The stars into asters,
Oblivion into happiness,
Memory into love,
And the next final flowering
Into a night-bird's last flight.

Translated by Richard Flantz

Natan Zach

Natan Zach was born in Berlin in 1930 but traveled to Palestine with his family six years later. He is presently Professor of Comparative Literature at Haifa University. His first book of poems was published in 1952. A pamphlet of his poems in English translation appeared in 1967, and a book is in preparation.

When God First Said

When God first said *Let there be light*
He meant it would not be dark for Him.
In that moment He didn't think about the sky;
but the trees already were filling with water,
the birds receiving air and body.
Then the first wind touched God's eyes
and He saw it in a cloud of glory,
and thought *It is good.* He didn't think then
about people, people in their multitude.
But they already were standing apart from the trees,
unraveling in their hearts
a scheme about pain.
When God first thought of night
He didn't think about sleep.
So be it God said. *I will be happy.*
But they were multitudes.

The Quiet Light of Flies

The quiet light of flies
sinks. The desert answers
with a faint drum of hooves.
Silk scarves
sway from the spines of cactus
and in the silvery tents
they are dancing the Dance of Jars.

Springs well up,
springs with their white stones,
springs with their musty deaths—
one bucket,

another,
and another,
they shiver in the wind like hanged men
and still there's time to rest,
the night drifts.

To Be a Master in Your House

To be a master in your house, to wrestle
against winds, to sit beneath the fig tree,

to be watchful of the foxes that spoil
the vines, to read in the book of dust,

to know the festivals of light cast down
at your feet, to taste gall sooner than a thief's honey,

to touch each bone twice, to sit a long time
and not look up at the clouds

passing overhead at night
on their way to the sea.

When the Last Riders

When the last riders disappear over the horizon
and even the dust of their horses no longer rises,
I will know then it is time to lock the gate.
The spent day will look at its hands and be content.
For me, the hour will be familiar. Come now,
I'll whisper to myself, it isn't the first time
you've seen them come and go.
The sun, of course, will be indifferent to my words.
Blood red, it will go down behind the far mountains
as if it alone were important. You have no other sun.
The Creator puts aside his handiwork,
the angels' verdict is in the locked book.

The gate must be closed, logic tells me. At night
the dark is darkest.

In This Deep Darkness

In this deep heavy darkness
remember me who stood before you—
thirty-two years, to the day,
in this deep heavy darkness.

Remember me when you climb the watchtower
at evening in a bloody swirl of light.
Remember me when you drive away the clouds
from this world down into another

where clouds vanish and are forgotten.
Remember me among your flocks;
remember me more than you remember all your orphans
in this deep heavy darkness

where I am lost more than an orphan,
more than a lamb, for my eyes are open
and I see how the blue darkens. I am not deceived:
I see how blood thickens, the voice stumbles,

how at evening everything rises and returns
with its memories, and is a mouth to all
that has ever been since time's beginning,
all that is forever homeless
in this deep heavy darkness.

A Short Winter Tale

The apprentice in the shop across from me
—blacksmith or carpenter—
had a girl.
Each day at the close of work
(I finish my work at eight,
then take a long or a short walk)
I'd see her sitting on a stool
in her woolen cap, swinging her leg
to some hidden song,
while the boy finished his work,
an hour late, as usual.

Now the girl has gone, and I don't know
who or what takes place at the blacksmith's
or the carpenter's shop. But I know this:
Winter passed. The spring nights ooze like honey
from the lamp. And one must find, without delay,
rest equal to each pain, sadness for each lover, a just abundance
for a night of thanks.
And to do this, time is very short
and the task is great.

Perhaps It's Only Music

Perhaps it's only music. Since the emotion is obscure,
call it what you wish.
Only music, perhaps. Yet here it is
—hesitant, complete, on an evening
otherwise uneventful. An evening, perhaps,
such as one when David played. Yet Saul wasn't suspicious.
Manly and confident he threw his spear
as if there stood forth in David's song
matters that are judged and cleanly cut
like the severed head of Goliath.

A Peaceful Song

A peaceful song. On such an evening, God, as this,
that falls like a truce, if I could sometimes sing
also a peaceful song, if I could ask you
to turn the light of your face unto all
your worms, crawling wherever they are, loved
and unloved, appeased
and unappeased, God
and unGod.

Translated by Peter Everwine and Shula Starkman

As Sand

When God in the Bible wants to promise
he points to stars. Abraham goes
through the opening of his tent at night,
and sees lovers. As sand on the sea's
shore, says God, and man believes.
Even though he knows that
as sand, is merely the language
man can understand.

And since then, sand and stars remained
linked in the net of man's similes.
But perhaps there's no point in
mixing man in here;
it wasn't man that was
then spoken of.

And yet it's explicitly said
as sand, which implies, of course,
the capacity for suffering.
Or maybe it's possible to imagine that
all was then permitted: and no words made
a difference any more.

As sand on the sea's shore. But nothing is said there
about water. And yet explicitly
God mentions seed.
But this is heaven's way,
and possibly, nature's.

Against Parting

My tailor is against parting.
That's why, he
said, he's not going away;
he doesn't want to part
from his one daughter. He's definitely
against parting.

Once, he parted from his wife, and
she he
saw no more of (Auschwitz).
Parted
from his three sisters and
these he never
saw (Buchenwald).
He once parted from his mother (his father
died of a fine, and ripe age). Now
he's against parting.

In Berlin he
was my father's kith and kin. They passed
a good time in
that Berlin. The time's passed. Now
he'll never leave. He's
most definitely
(my father's died)
against parting.

Translated by Jon Silkin

No

Not at night, no, altogether, tomorrow,
she will not come today, today it's cold,

no, if at all, not in the dark, alone,
shadow on the wall, hand on heart, not a trembling heart,

not in fear, no, if at all, not in the rain,
not like a spear, no footsteps in the rain, not a net

of water, not black clouds, not a cloud,
not overcast, not now, under a flourishing tree,

not in the street, if at all, not in the entrance of the house,
not by hand, not slowly, not in heat, under an olive,

not today, not hard, not from necessity,
not in sunlight, not like a blessing.

Listening to Her

I must go. I must gather my few things
and put them in the open suitcase. I was here
for a good year. Now I must go.
At dusk the feeling came.
Not for a moment did it occur to me to complain.
The element of time for me is not one of pain.

The colors come. Welcome silent ones. The air
passes through the cricket trees
like glowing coals—
pearls on a glass covered with branches and leaves.
I must go while there is still light: night babbles
and returns the world to its safe like a treasure
to the darkness of a miser.

Every vein in me calls to her now, and I ache,
passing my hand over my face, to pass my face
over her hands, to listen again
next to her ears, how night arises from her words, keeps
sleep from the eyes, to listen to her
otherwise unheard, at least now.

A Foreign Country

Her body dances in my dream, and my body
moves, it also dances. In her dream
I am not. A gentle night wind plays
the curtains in the room. If only
I were back home again
whispering words of love
to you.

Translated by Laya Firestone

HEBREW

Zelda

Zelda was born in Russia in 1914 and settled in Palestine with her family in 1926. She studied at Mizrachi Teachers' Seminary and later taught in religious schools for girls. Though she had been writing for a long time, her first collection of poems was not published until 1967. Her books of poetry are Leisure, The Unseen Carmel, Be Not Far from Me, *and* Behold the Mountain, Behold the Fire. *An English selection is in preparation.*

I Stood in Jerusalem

I stood
in Jerusalem,
Jerusalem suspended from a cloud,
in a graveyard with people crying
and a crooked tree.
Blurry mountains
and a tower.
You are not!
Death spoke to us.
You are not!
he turned to me.

I stood
in the midst of Jerusalem,
Jerusalem checkered in the sun,
smiling like a bride in the field,
slender green grass
by her side.

Why were you frightened
yesterday in the rain?
Death spoke to me.
Am I not your quiet
older brother?

The Moon Is Teaching Bible

The moon is teaching Bible.
Cyclamen, poppy, and mountain
listen with joy.
Only the girl cries.
The poppy can't hear her crying—
the poppy is blazing in Torah,
burning like the verse.
The cyclamen doesn't listen
to the crying—
the cyclamen swoons
from the sweet secrets.
The mountain won't hear her crying—
the mountain is sunk
in thought.

But here comes the wind,
soft and fragrant,
to honor hope
and sing—
each heart
is a flying horseman,
an ardent hunter
swept to the ends of the sea.

In the Dry Riverbed

In the dry riverbed
barefoot desire
trumpets to the heat wave
with a horn of gold.

The heat wave goes wild,
kissing the sun.
The world darkens,
dust swallows us up.

Only the jasmine
whitens
in the dark,
and Cain's eye flashes fire.
Women faint from sweet scents
and hot fear.

With My Grandfather

Like our father Abraham
who counted stars at night,
who called out to his Creator
from the furnace,
who bound his own son
on the altar—
so was my grandfather.
The same perfect faith
in the midst of the flames,
the same dewy gaze
and soft-curling beard.
Outside it snowed,
outside they roared:
There is no justice,
no judge.
And in the shambles of his room
angels sang
of the Heavenly Jerusalem.

Light a Candle

Light a candle.
Drink wine.
Softly the Sabbath has plucked
the sinking sun.
Slowly the Sabbath descends,
the rose of heaven in her hand.
How can the Sabbath plant
a huge and shining flower
in a blind and narrow heart?
How can the Sabbath plant
a bud of angels
in a heart of raving flesh?
Can the rose of eternity grow
in a generation enslaved
to destruction,
a generation enslaved
to death?

Light a candle!
Drink wine!
Slowly the Sabbath descends
and in her hand
a flower,
and in her hand
the sinking sun . . .

Translated by Marcia Falk

Ezra Zussman

Ezra Zussman was born in Odessa in 1900. His first Hebrew poems were published in 1925, but his first book did not appear until 1968. In addition to his poetry, Zussman worked as a literary critic and translator. He died in Tel Aviv in 1973.

At Dante's Grave

Stilled is the quarrel over his bones.
Forgotten, quite forgotten, both friends and foes.
The Divine Script is closely guarded.
To what avail?
The eagle broods
Over the grave.
To love a little girl
And write her Tuscan sonnets.
After her death to set out on a journey
To Hell and all its circles.
All has turned to stone.
But what can stone
Avail against her gaze
What—
The nether circles he explored.
The sad eagle, eagle in love
Stares with stony eyes.
The eagle droops.
I'm alone with him. I'm afraid.
Beyond his grave
Falling quietly to earth
A hushed shower descends.

Not the turbid drench
That fell in Hell's third circle.
Pigeons drink out of the font of faith.
Submissive, overcome
Animals and Lucifer are silent
Remembering the day on which arrived
Salvation—
His journeying
Into the sun the fire the smoke the darkness
The rivers and forests
Towards his Beloved
To fade away into that gaze
"That moves the sun and the other stars."

The Last

And that question which I have not asked
nor shall ask
because of all the commotion around
all the killing around
and other peoples' voices
and the sea in its tumult
and the sea in its silence
and the dahlias flowering at my side
and the dew dyingly shining
and the vapor of the earth
rising to my face
and the softness of the earth
under my steps light and fleeing
for to ask would mean
no longer to descend
to that calm and that silence
which have, for long now, been
my true estate
and because of other disturbances
not to be nailed by name.
I have not asked
one of the questions
I should have asked
And I listen to your questions
—marketable ones—

and I listen to your answers
as though they were indited
in the mystic Book of Raziel.
But rather than ask
I should have gone on my knees
in the benediction of thanksgiving
in the prayer of one spared
the green cap covering
the head of the one tormented
whose question I should have asked
not asking who listens in
not asking who looks on
with such compassion, now,
into my innermost heart
in my awaking as in my sleep—
to the end of all questions
until the sealing of my lips
that are silent
that whisper
that beg
that keep repeating the beloved name
that know without asking
the last of the light
the last of the candle
the last of the voice
the last.

Translated by D. Shnayorson

II *Yiddish*

Introduction to Book II
by Ruth R. Wisse

It is interesting to speculate what might have been the achievement of Yiddish poetry had the Jews enjoyed anything resembling a normal existence in Europe. The first major works of old Yiddish poetry, contemporaneous with the beginnings of vernacular literatures in France, Italy, and Germany in the fifteenth and sixteenth centuries, are so broadly similar to the romances and verse adventures of those areas that one can readily imagine the Jewish vernacular flowering into its own renaissance, and producing a cumulative body of literature from that day to this. If Eliohu Bokher's *Bove Bukh* and the anonymous *Shmuel Bukh* of that period are any example, the adventures of errant princes were wonderfully adaptable to the cultural expectations of Jewish readers, and indigenous Jewish—in this case, biblical—material could be well exploited for new literary ends. As long as Jews lived among literate peoples, with interaction between the communities, Jews could be expected to produce their own homologous artistic works.

But the expulsions of Jews from Western Europe forced a great migration to the east, compelling Jews to adapt to wholly new surroundings. Jewish literacy was an exceptional phenomenon in Poland of the seventeenth and eighteenth centuries, where even the *Szlakhta*, the feudal lords, could rarely read or write. Turning inward, Jews enjoyed a vigorous intellectual life centered on Talmudic study while the heart's needs were met by Jewish story collections, prayer anthologies, martyrological poems, and books of advice, which amused, comforted, inspired, and instructed women and men without access to rabbinic texts. Though in the Western sense there was little of *belles-lettres*, Jews developed their own rich literary culture in both Hebrew and Yiddish, and a strong Yiddish folk culture that owed much to the surrounding Slavic peoples.

It was not until the end of the eighteenth century, when Western influence began to penetrate into Eastern Europe, and Jews reached out to the Enlightenment—the Haskalah—as the key to their anticipated emancipation, that Jewish writers again looked eagerly to European literature for models. At first the enlighteners resisted Yiddish, which was not only the lower-status language in relation to Hebrew, but the reviled object of the Berlin Enlightenment, which considered Yiddish no more than a debased form of German. But the vitality of Yiddish and simply its prevalence (even in Germany) as the spoken language of the Jews made it a choice logic could not overrule. The reluctance to use Yiddish abated as soon as the first masters, Mendele Mocher Sforim, I. L. Peretz, and Sholem Aleichem in particular, showed how the very "lowliness" and fluidity of the language could be used to precious advantage.

This perception of Yiddish as a vernacular, so long after all other European vernaculars had become national languages with strong literary traditions, was to have a marked effect on the development of the new literature, particularly on the poetry. Certain modes were immediately acceptable: the poetic fables or satires of Shloyme Ettinger seemed a natural outgrowth of the homey homiletics of the preachers; the neo-folk songs and ballads of I. L. Peretz, Sh. Frug, and later Abraham Reisin and Mordecai Gebirtig derived from equally familiar folk songs and recitations. But when Yiddish poets around the turn of the century began to experiment with the subjects and forms of modern European verse, they were mocked for their pretentious, artificial borrowings. Many efforts of Yiddish poets to "catch up" with German, Russian, and French poetry were indeed derivatively stiff. One could not effect at will, overnight, the evolution that had matured European literatures over hundreds of years. The creative impulse of modern Yiddish poetry derives from just this tension between the cosmopolitan openness to all the varieties of contemporary expression and the claims of the tradition that generates its own standards of authenticity.

Perhaps because of its distance from the heartland of Yiddish, America proved an exceptionally fertile ground for modern Yiddish verse. By the end of the first decade of this century there were dozens of young Jewish immigrants on New York's Lower East Side, working in small factories and shops, with writing as their real vocation. The freedom of America seemed to fire their dreams of literary grandeur, while the painful process of adjustment to such a raw, unfamiliar environment sought expression in the familiar language, resonant of home. There was a run of little magazines and anthologies crammed with new poems and glimmers of talent.

The young writers—*Di Yunge,* as their group came to be known—broke away from the social and national poetry of statement that their immigrant elders preferred. Their literary manifestos proclaimed a private, allusive poetry that required nothing more for its justification than the sounds and images of individual truth. Yet the "truths" of the poems bore little obvious relation to the lives their authors were living. In contrast to the noise, energy, and activism of the teeming immigrant neighborhoods, the poems drew upon landscapes of silence, wintry plains in the Ukraine, and languid summer afternoons on grassy knolls. In place of the harassed young husbands with their meager pay for endless hours of tedious work, the poets presented themselves as solitary brooders, disaffected and bored. One feels in these early lyrics the heavy influence of Russian poetry with its plaintive sweetness and its image of the poet as solitary genius. Poetry was at first the softening, the ordering, the taming of a reality that was all too shrill and chaotic.

Mani Leib and Zishe Landau were the two most influential voices of this new sensibility. Using assonance, alliteration, and sounds of softness, Mani Leib wrote musically affecting poems of love and remembrance that freed Yiddish verse from an automatic association with folksiness, wit, or rhetorical bombast. Despite the harsh circumstances of his personal life, he struggled to achieve, at least in his art, a vision of essential harmony and serenity.

Zishe Landau, the programmatic aesthete of the Yunge, deliberately provoked new attitudes to poetry and to life. The very title of a poem like "Tuesday" indicated that Landau was not going to celebrate the sanctified and ritualized moments of the Jew's existence, the Sabbath, but the ordinariness of midweek when nothing essential gets done. The natural diction and deliberate casualness of Landau's style were as much of a goad to the expectations of Jewish readers as his asocial irony.

Not all the young, however, adopted this new understated style. H. Leivick, who escaped to America from a life sentence of exile in Siberia for his part in the Russian revolutionary movements, wrote with deliberate pathos and great moral fervor. Even the softest of his lyrics seem to speak for the collective pain and sorrow of the age.

And Moishe Leib Halpern struck the pose of a street-drummer in a coarse and taunting kind of verse. Drawing more from Heine than the Russian Symbolists, Halpern uncovered the sharp disharmonies in both the old home and the new. He saw the dreamy Yiddish poet, with his intimations of immortality, as a jarring, comical misfit in the American metropolis. If some of the Yunge succeeded in forging beauty out of their sore experience, Halpern's longing for beauty was snagged by the crude competition and wicked hypocrisies he felt around him.

In Europe, what was still entrenched of the old Jewish way of life gave way by 1920. World War I and the long-anticipated Russian

Revolution forcibly hastened a process of change that had begun somewhat tentatively, had gathered momentum for some fifty years, and was now sealed by massive political and demographic upheavals. The Great War—in which Jewish soldiers fought on both sides—the Bolshevik seizure of power, the terrible pogroms of the Ukraine, all brought a glimpse of the apocalypse, the bloodshed which was thought by some to presage a messianic age. Jewish writing registered the destructive energy of events, but there was also a wild release of hope, as if this horror must usher in a better world.

The contradictions of this period were caught by young writers who banded together in the postwar Warsaw group *Khaliastre,* "the gang," dedicated to the "savagery in song; the chaotic in image; the clamor of blood." For Melech Ravitch, just out of uniform, poetry was an ethical quest that he defended in violent manifestos and polemics. Though his poems were rich in descriptions of man's "prehistoric landscapes," the primitive passions and needs, he reached out to a humanistic ideal that would untie the knot of good and evil:

> Man is evil, but who else sings to God
> about turning the other cheek to the oppressor—
> while under our jackets, barely concealed,
> we clutch the freshly sharpened axe.

Peretz Markish, Ravitch's colleague of those years, was almost his exact antithesis. Spontaneous and fresh, rooted in the Russian soil and in the simple rural life of his childhood, Markish wrote in long and robust lines, and his poems throb with discovery. For him, the Russian Revolution was not simply a change of regimes, but the wellspring of a new Yiddish (as well as Russian) poetry that should be wholly dynamic and freed from its debt to the past. The "Byronic" beauty of Markish, and his impulsive romantic temperament, exerted a strong influence on younger writers who drew from him their conceptions of poetry and the poet.

Some of this legacy can be felt in the work of Moishe Kulbak and Rachel Korn, natives of tiny hamlets in Lithuania and Galicia. Kulbak glorified earthiness, the rough-and-ready Jews of the soil and smithy. As against the Jewish emphasis on self-restraint and intellectual discipline, Kulbak rejoiced in yielding to momentary impulses and sensations. His sharp eye for the gap between romantic ideals and reality made Kulbak a wonderfully comic observer of the Jew's eagerness to modernize and of socialism's eagerness to modernize the Jew.

Rachel Korn, whose long and difficult odyssey brought her finally to Canada, made her reputation as a master of domestic detail and of rich emotional nuance. Drawing, like Kulbak, from a firsthand knowledge of land and nature, she uses natural imagery in lyrics of great formal control to describe the bonds between generations, the elemental moments of parting and love, the conflicts between life and art.

While the romantic strain in Yiddish poetry expressed itself in an attachment to soil, there was also a strong current of social realism, and an identification with the suffering masses of Polish Jews. The Yiddish writers of interbellum Poland felt themselves a solid part of the striving for national dignity and working-class survival. The poems of Yisroel Shtern, Kadya Molodovsky, and other young Polish writers recall the drawings of Kathe Kollwitz in their open sympathy for the miserable and neglected.

By the mid-1920s the variety and quality of Yiddish publications in Poland, Russia, and America offered abundant proof that Yiddish poetry had passed its infancy and come to unexpectedly rapid maturity. New bibliographical and literary journals like *Bikhervelt* ("Bookworld") and the influential *Literarishe Bleter* of Warsaw provided high standards of criticism and forums for serious discussion of art. In the Soviet Union, Yiddish poets enjoyed a singular period of encouragement. So attractive was the governmental recognition accorded to Yiddish culture, education, and literature in the first post-Revolutionary decade that Yiddish writers like David Hofstein and Peretz Markish "came home" from Palestine and France to benefit from and contribute to the buoyant renaissance. Only gradually, beginning in 1928 and then with increasing force, did the vise of state censorship squeeze first the art and finally the artists to their deaths.

In America, Yiddish writers faced benign neglect. Unlike Poland where indigent writers shared the fate of the impoverished majority, America allowed immigrants fair opportunity of advancement to the degree that they could adapt to new conditions—including English, the host language. As the postwar immigration laws restricted new arrivals from Europe, and the process of Americanization pried Jews loose from their roots, the local Yiddish writers felt increasingly isolated. "And here am I," wrote Mani Leib in the sonnet "To the Gentile Poet,"

> Unneeded, a poet of Jews . . . .
> Singing in an alien world the tears
> of wayfarers in a desert under alien stars.

Yet as though in demonstration of a principle of physics, the contracting Yiddish world in America became more active and volatile. Political differences between social democrats and communists hardened. The organization *Proletpen* was the rallying point for a literature of social commitment, universalism, and broad accessibility. At the same time modernists like Jacob Glatstein, Abraham Glanz-Leyeles, and B. Alquit wrote provocatively experimental and intricately personal poems that cultivated and demanded a sensitive and educated readership.

A special dimension was also added to Yiddish poetry, particularly in America, by the women poets, whose short and precise lyrics spoke with candor and in deliberately female imagery of their wrestling with man, world, poetry, and God.

In addition to the regionalism of politics, Yiddish poetry was also affected by differences of regional sensibility. Romania, one of the richest repositories of Yiddish folklore, birthplace of the Yiddish theater and cabaret, also brought forth two great neo-folk poets, Eliezer Steinbarg and Itzik Manger. It is obvious how much Steinbarg's poetic fables owe to Jewish fabular and midrashic literature. As for Manger—who wrote under the name Itzik, rather than the more respectable Yitzhak—he candidly shapes his poems and ballads from the material of Jewish Aggadah and earlier folk bards and singers. Yet the work of these two poets shows how deceptive the concept of "folkishness" can be. Much of the humor and charm of Manger's ballads derive not from their simplicity, but from their wicked juxtaposition of cultivated European ideas and forms with the idiomatic usage of marketplace Jews and the worn coin of fairytales. Steinbarg, whose unyielding perfectionism kept his work from publication throughout most of his life, achieves spectacularly witty and dramatic effects under the guise of spontaneous narration. Paradoxically, the neo-folk poets are the most refined of all modern Yiddish literary craftsmen.

In the period between the wars there was a conscious drive to write long poems (prevented, for reasons of space, from inclusion in this volume) that would prove the suitability of Yiddish for sustained dramatic and philosophic verse. The thundering prophecies and the idylls of Peretz Markish, the ambitious sagas of Menahem Boraisho and I. I. Schwartz, the historical dramas of H. Leivick and A. Glanz-Leyeles, enshrine the myths and themes of Jewish history and contemporary experience in a poetry of the highest national resonance. The work of Aaron Zeitlin in particular seems like the modern voice of Jewish tradition; his poems of mystical quest and religious groping read like modern prayer.

One of the last literary groups to spring up between the wars was *Yung Vilne,* a local fraternity of writers and artists that included the animator of nature Elkhonon Vogler, the zany iconoclast Lazar Volf, and the mischievous wordsman Abraham Sutzkever. The artistic confidence of these young writers, even in their very first appearances, owes much to Jewish Vilna itself, a poor community bursting with vitality. To study the work of young writers like these on the eve of the war is to wonder, as I said in beginning this brief introduction, what might have been the weight and future of Yiddish poetry had modern Jewish history been less calamitous.

Abraham Sutzkever, who miraculously survived the war, belongs to the cosmopolitan brotherhood of art. So susceptible is he to the inspiration of the natural world that its beauty shines through even the bleakest ghetto poems. As in Sutzkever's metaphor of the plum in the lyric "Poetry," the finished poem is conceived as a wholly ripe and full emotional offering, but one that is ultimately impersonal, the product that has transcended its own generative process.

Among contemporary Yiddish poets, the majority included in this volume have come from Poland or Russia or America to settle in Israel, in kibbutzim, in the cities, or in smaller towns. The landscape of Israel permeates not only the work of writers like Rachel Fishman and Moshe Yungman, whose lives are closely bound to the soil of Beit Alpha and Safed, but also the work of Diaspora writers for whom Israel as much as the shattered world of Europe is now the interior landscape. Israel sometimes figures as the very concrete reality, sometimes as the fulfillment of promise, and often as the touchstone of longing. Inevitably contemporary Yiddish writing includes the dimension of absence. Some poets yearn, in age-old ways, for the Messiah. Others, with a perfect sense of irony, reach back from the heat of Jerusalem and Tel Aviv to the snows of their past. For Yiddish poets today, art confirms not only the world they inhabit, but the world they have lost.

Ruth R. Wisse was born in Czernovitz, then Romania, now Russia, and has lived most of her life in Montreal except for two years in New York and two years in Israel. She is Professor of Yiddish Literature at McGill University and Visiting Professor of the Max Weinreich Center of the YIVO Institute for Jewish Research. She is the author of The Schlemiel as Modern Hero, *editor of* A Shtetl and Other Yiddish Novellas, *and co-editor with Irving Howe of* The Best of Sholem Aleichem.

B. Alquit

B. Alquit, the pen name of Eliezer Blum, was born in 1896 in Chelm, Poland. He emigrated to New York in 1914, where he worked as a tailor. Known as an Expressionist poet, he was a co-editor of the anti-realist Yiddish literary journal Inzich *during the 1930s. He also wrote articles and essays for the New York Yiddish* Morning Journal. *His one collection of verse,* Two Paths and Other Poems, *was published in 1931. He died in New York in 1963.*

The Light of the World

The soundless
light drifts over
the distant
sea.

The white
body of a woman
lies upon the silent
earth,
over the layers of frozen
treasures.

Only
the unspoken
word fills itself
on silence.

The hand of creation
weeps.

Wandering Chorus

In the West
circles a wheel
of fire, the glow
of the scarlet
hour.

Shadows
of black loam
rise like a wandering
chorus; the shadow of the East
stands guard
at the far-flung
gates.

And the West pours
red wine
on the white
banner
of silence.

Translated by Howard Schwartz

Asya

Asya (Gay) was born in Vilna, Lithuania. After working in a Russian labor camp in 1941 she was repatriated in Poland until she went to Israel in 1951 with Youth Aliyah. She presently lives in Jerusalem. Her poems have appeared in a variety of magazines and have been translated into Hebrew by Shimon Halkin, among others. Her book Trembling of Branches *was published in 1972.*

The Deer

for Jacob Glatstein

I don't know whether the gray deer knows
That his horns can wound,
But he surely knows the sources of clear water.
In his kingdom,
Where the Divine Presence and danger live side by side,
He is not afraid to risk breaking his slim leg
When thirst gives him wings.
And he does not pursue the shepherdess,
Whose pitcher gives drink to the passerby.
His sense of smell, polished by the wind—a sail
Bearing him upon the waves,
And when he raises his head, drenched with water,
His horns dip into the sun.

Celan

Float up again.
We will descend to our own depths.
Give the seadeck to the preying fish
With their rough scales.
Take your head out of that strange dishevelment.
Put on the blue *yarmulke** —the sky of your city,
Her beams wrapped in psalms.
See how the East flames up,
An eternal candle.

Pause a Moment

Pause a moment
At the well coming toward you.
Purify your palate and body.
A drought lies upon the roads;
The southwind hurls hot days and nights.
You will not slake your thirst in the desert.

And before the bucket ceases to beat
In the throat of the well,
Lower your eyes
And look into the depth
That does
And does not
Let itself be drawn.

Then the face you see
Floating up
Will fall into a stillness
That remains within
Its shores.

**yarmulke*—a skullcap worn by religious Jews.

My True Memory

If you stop caressing me
I will forget your hands,
Because as soon as I began to see,
To recognize the world,
I learned quickly to forget
Those closest to me.

By nature, from birth,
The sense of smell
Is my true memory,
And that which has drawn me to you
I will seek at another door.

And so jumping up from his lap,
Arching her back,
She hissed
And slipped out of the house.

My Strawlike Hair

They are disturbed even by my hair,
Which I inherited.
Had it not been for the strawlike hair
Which envelops me,
They would not have suffered such disgrace,
Accepting me as one of their own;
They would not have to break their teeth
Deciphering ancientness,
My name,
And suddenly recognize
Who I am.

A Grain of Moonlight

Such a sad celebration
As if a grain of moonlight
Had slipped into the blood
And sailed away
On lakes of tears
That have not yet been shed.

Every cell is an eye watching,
An ear listening
From deep within
As if enveloped
By veils of sleep.

This may be fear,
Or may be voices calling
Each other
From above and below
As if before
Being.

Translated by Gabriel Preil and Howard Schwartz

Ephraim Auerbach

Ephraim Auerbach was born in Bessarabia in 1892. He joined the pioneers in Palestine in 1912 and remained until 1915, when he was expelled by Turkish authorities and emigrated to the United States. His poems and essays were published in the Yiddish dailies until his death in 1973. Auerbach published several volumes of poetry and has been translated into Hebrew.

Seismograph

In my fingers the world can be grasped.
I am a net of wire,
pulse of a thousand pulses,
seismograph
of world quakes.

In the East
the sun rises in me;
in the West the sun sets.
Morocco storms my fortresses;
hurricanes devastate my fields;
on Broome Street I perish in flames.
The black Hudson
drags me to its bottom;
I kindle the world
in the fire of decline.

With hungry eyes and angry fists
the world convulses in my fingers
as I advance,
and I with it,
sullen and sad.

Translated by Howard Schwartz

Rachel Boimwall

Rachel Boimwall, daughter of playwright and director Yehudah Leib Boimwall, was born in Russia in 1913. She was evacuated to Tashkent during the Second World War. Several years later she emigrated to Israel, where she now resides. Her poetic works, written in Yiddish, include a book of children's poems, Pioneers *(1934),* Tarah *(1934),* Poems *(1936), and* Love *(1947), all of which were published in Moscow.*

Diaspora Jews

When the Druzes come together
they sing.
When the gypsies come together
they dance.
When Englishmen come together
they are silent.
When Frenchmen come together
they laugh.
And what about the Jews?
Alas, when Jews get together
they sigh.

Translated by Gabriel Preil

Lifelong

All the days of my life
I destroy wholeness.
I bite into an apple
and I break off a twig.
I break the stone into little pieces
and I cut through a mountain.

All the days of my life
I imprison the deer.
I stop the stream from flowing.
I capture the bird
and I harness the wind.

All the days of my life
I create things
that are against nature,
and it revenges itself on me.
My wholeness is being destroyed
through the swift passage
of time.

Round

Everything is round,
the apple and the plum,
the earth,
a drop,
the base of the tree,
the times of day and night,
times of the year,
and another thing,
every concept
is round,
and every deed,
if one looks deep enough.

The logical sequence itself
is a circle.
The return from going away
is the prize.
Birth and death,
laughter and weeping,
and then the understanding
that we cannot understand.

All right,
I will not discuss it anymore.
A round tear
drops from your eye.

At Night

Without a door, through the smooth wall,
somewhat blue,
comes my murdered father
who looks silently into my eyes.

Enters my grandfather, also murdered,
and remains standing
not far from my father.
A bit late, and following them both,
my grandmother comes in,
covered with wounds.

My brain then fails
because of my bitter labor
to understand
what it means not to die a natural death,
but to be shot, to be shot.

Three frozen, bloody heads.
Three mournful, glazed pairs of eyes.
The wall has pulled them back
into itself,
and covered them over with blackness.

Translated by Gabriel Preil and Howard Schwartz

Nahum Bomze

Nahum Bomze was born in eastern Galicia, which was then part of the Austro-Hungarian Empire, in 1906. His first poem appeared in the Warsaw Yugent Veker in 1929, and he was a member of the Lemberg literary group Tsushtayer ("Contribution"). He fought in World War II in the Russian army, and settled in the United States in 1948. He published four collections of poetry: In the Days of the Week *(1929),* Barefoot Steps *(1936),* A Visitor at Dusk *(1939), and* An Autumn Wedding *(1949). He died in 1954.*

Pshytik

The last hour nears
on the scarlet horizon.
I could not recognize
the walls of my house.

In my house the walls are red,
not blue,
so I could count the minutes
of my last hour.

In my own house lurks
a deep fear.
My neighbors are sharpening
bright, shining axes.

Bright, shining axes,
in sunset red.
Beyond blue walls
black death is waiting.

Translated by Gabriel Preil

City of Light

Let us leave behind this city
of light.
Too much light has blinded me,
I cannot find my way
to you.
Oh, lead me, lead me
with your pale hands
to the dark side
of the light.

Translated by Gabriel Preil and Howard Schwartz

Celia Dropkin

Celia Dropkin was born in Bobroisk, a town not far from Minsk, in 1888. She received an education in both Yiddish and Russian, though after her emigration to New York in 1912 she chose Yiddish as her language of literary expression. Critics see her as one of the first of the modern Yiddish poets in America. Her book of poetry, In a Hot Wind, *was published in 1935. She died in New York in 1956.*

A Circus Dancer

I am a circus dancer
dancing among daggers
that circle me
with their points turned up.
Barely,
barely touching the edges
of the knives,
my light body avoids death
from falling.

With bated breath
they watch my dancing
and someone prays to God for me.
Before my eyes the points glow
in a fiery circle.
And no one knows
how much I would like
to fall.

Translated by Howard Schwartz

Lazer Eichenrand

Lazer Eichenrand was born in 1912 in Demblin, Poland. In 1937 he emigrated to Paris, joining the French army at the outbreak of the Second World War. He was captured by Nazis and taken to a prisoner-of-war camp, but managed to escape to Switzerland in 1942, where he now resides. His book of poems, From the Depths, *was published in Paris in 1953.*

The Mute City

Alone, alone
you are the eyes of midnight
that fall deep
within themselves.
Your walk resounds
between this world
and the next
and does not echo
in either.
Your fear quenches the light
which reigns supreme
on the other side of the dead,
and you become the voice
which bears you up
and carries you afar
from a beginning
to a beginning
which has long ago
passed.
And the secret of the earth
falls to you
and cries out a mute cry,
a cry of which
nothing remains.

Prologue

In your words
wolves mix up their blood
with the night.

A dark sun is your silence.
All winds from the poles
continue to arrive.

Sated, in a red calm,
nest the snakes of your heart.

Upon the cliffs of the day
your eyes are birds
of prey.

Always, when from your hand rises
everyman's death,
there rains heavily
above God
the sorrow of the moments
of His creation.

From Life

The swallows hide
in the nest of the day
when the old man walks by
who carries the light of tombs
in his hands
and does not see it,
even though his spirit
walks before him
and engraves itself
on everything.
Perhaps silence
already climbs up the hour
as the rain climbs upon
the lightning.

Translated by Gabriel Preil and Howard Schwartz

Rachel Fishman

Rachel Fishman was born in Philadelphia in 1935. She moved to Kibbutz Beit Alpha, in the north of Israel, in 1954, and she continues to reside there. Her collections of poetry include Sun Over All (1962), Thorns After Rain *(1966), and the bilingual Hebrew-Yiddish collection* Wild She-goat *(1976).*

In the Beginning

In the beginning
There was the sun
This valley is a charmed
Dimple on her face
All the pomegranates
Are her breasts
And the grapes
Are her fingertips
Whereas her toenails
Are thorns in the field
And the small bones of her
Raised fist is the Gilboa.

When the sun
Unties her braids
And the dark hair
Spreads itself out
On the pillow
It turns to night,
But we know:
Her pink ear
Will move itself
Out from beneath
Its cover
This is the dawn
The beginning
Again.

Translated by Gabriel Levin

Even If

Even a cloud
does not have as many
thirsty mouths
as I do.

Even a cloud
does not have
such damp eyelashes
as I do.

Even a rain
does not disturb
my dream like this
in the night
as you do.

Even a rain.

Translated by Gabriel Preil and Howard Schwartz

A. Glanz-Leyeles

A. (Aaron) Glanz-Leyeles was born Aaron Glanz in 1889 in Włocławek, Poland, and emigrated to New York in 1909. His prose essays and articles for the Yiddish daily The Day *appeared under his own name, while his poetry appeared under the pseudonym A. Leyeles. In 1919, together with Jacob Glatstein and N.B. Minkoff, he founded the* In-Zich *movement of Yiddish poetry and the* In-Zich *journal. His books of poetry include* Labyrinth *(1918),* Young Autumn *(1922),* Fabius Lind *(1937),* A Jew at Sea *(1947),* At the Foot of the Mountain *(1957), and* America and I *(1963). He wrote two dramas,* Shlomo Molkho *(1926) and* Asher Lemlen *(1928), and published a collection of his essays,* World and Word, *in 1958. He died in 1966.*

Castles

Castles—
Castles built of iron and granite
Castles of marble and of malachite
Castles of bronze and cast steel
Castles and castles no tongue can tell.

Castles—
Libraries and museums,
Monuments, mausoleums,
Temples, churches, cathedrals—all
Castles now
Fall, fall, fall.

But my castles
Built of yearnings,
Nightly fears, daily burnings,
Stirrings, visions,
Ambitions, desires,
Twisted and spun
By a far moon and a further sun,
By the heart's endeavor
That never
Stops streaming from the heart:
My castles shall
Never fall, never fall, never fall.

White Swan

Girl, your young loveliness
Is a white swan
Winging above me, casual in triumph.
In swooning oblivion I lie
And it
Quite unaware of what it does
Pecks at my heart
With pink and tender bill.

Madison Square

1
No rooftops to rest on.
Lines soar and are lost on
The heavens they thrust on.
        Severe and male.
The feeling—chaotic,
Cooped up, anti-gothic,
Commercial-quixotic.
        Mere chance for style.
Pent energy crouching.
Trapezes high-pitching.
From wills overreaching.
        Anxiety-state.
Grandiose in its plainness.
Derisive of meanness.
Diverse in its oneness—
        New York the Great.

II

Manshape, Flatiron Building, proud wonder,
You cut into the Square, a hero-juggler,
Your hands and feet flung back, head to the fore
For take-off—but manlike you check your desire.
Straight up your line shoots, Metropolitan, the thunder
Of your song thrills every poor man's dream on the Square,
Your mocking laughter lands on asphalt under.
Carved forms crowd round, each one an obelisk,
Heroic towers puncture the solar disk,
And through a gap a corner of the Garden is slender,
Fame of a former generation that more and more
Loses itself in New York and runs from care and risk.
But Fifth Avenue laughs and Broadway flaunts a smile,
With neither will nor time to ask is it worthwhile
To change their form or style.
They change. The Square—a chance halt, a surrender
Whose passion in one stormy moment spent
Bore giant sons of iron and cement.

Translated by Keith Bosley

Jacob Glatstein

Jacob Glatstein was born in Lublin, Poland in 1896. He emigrated in 1914 to the United States, where he helped found the Introspectivist (In-Zich) group of Yiddish writers. Glatstein published thirteen volumes of poetry. He died in 1971. His Selected Poems *have been published in the English translation of Ruth Whitman.*

The Poet Lives

The poet lives. The Jewish coffin-birds snap.
Your song is a charm against their teasing.
The coffin-birds won't grab you
on this your living morning.

The sun mirrors your image.
Your years disappear with a wipe.
Necktie your neck with the prettiest colors.
Don't be afraid. The Jewish coffin-birds won't collar you.
They won't even give the time of day to a living poet.

Now they're honing their beaks to tease you,
they're whistling up your obituary,
not for your sake, but hoping your death will engrave
their arrival from all swampy corners,
from all our moldy stinks.

Be calm, living poet.
Cry, laugh, in solitude tear your hair.
The coffin-birds will peck at you
but they'll never, God forbid, wish you a living year.

Mozart

I dreamed that
the gentiles crucified Mozart
and buried him in a pauper's grave.
But the Jews made him a man of God
and blessed his memory.

I, his apostle, ran all over the world,
converting everyone I met,
and wherever I caught a Christian
I made him a Mozartian.

How wonderful is the musical testament
of this divine man!
How nailed through with song
his shinging hands!
In his greatest need
all the fingers of this crucified
singer were laughing.
And in his most crying grief
he loved his neighbor's ear
more than himself.

How poor and stingy—
compared with Mozart's legacy—
is the Sermon on the Mount.

YIDDISH

I'll Find My Self-Belief

I'll find my self-belief in a dustpuff of wonder
flecking my view back
as far as dim sight
can imagine, can see.
In the bobbing
kindled dark
there rises up
a salvaged half-star
that managed not to be killed.
A chunk of exploded planet
that once had life,
green abundance, grazing luxury.
Witnesses: my tearfilled eyes,
the distant flora, grapestained with blood,
under a sky eternally sinking;
leaves rocking like bells
deafened, soundless,
on unlooked-at trees
in an empty world.

I'll be stubborn,
plant myself
in my own intimate night
which I've entirely invented
and admired from all sides.
I'll find my place in space
as big as a fly,
and compel to stand there
for all time
a cradle, a child,
into whom I'll sing the voice
of a father drowsing,
with a face in the voice,
with love in the voice,
with hazy eyes
that swim in the child's sleepy eyes
like warm moons.

And I'll build around this cradle a Jewish city
with a *shul,* with a God who never sleeps,
who watches over the poor shops,
over Jewish fear,
over the cemetery
that's lively all night
with worried corpses.

And I'll buckle myself up with my last days
and, for spite, count them in you, frozen past
who mocked me,
who invented my living, garrulous
Jewish world.
You silenced it
and in Maidanek woods
finished it off with a few shots.

In a Ghetto

In a days-and-nights ghetto
our rescued life is lying,
everything that happens,
fated and accomplished,
is Jewish through and through.
We haggle away our days
borrowing and lending,
then we turn on
the frightened night-time lamps
of our line burdens.
Too bad, Yiddish poet,
you're not fated to become
a fortress of quotations.
The Old Testament that they threw back at you
over the fence
I picked up long ago, already converted.
Now you're alone again.

Alone.

YIDDISH

Poet, take the faintest Yiddish speech,
fill it with faith, make it holy again.
All your virtuous deeds huddle at your feet
like trusting kittens;
they look in your eyes
so you'll stroke them and fulfill them.
You don't realize everything's at stake.

So you'll fulfill them.

Be on guard. The wasteland calls again.
A wild plow grinds a great surfeit to dust
and finds a skeleton's heart.
And if you can talk yourself into believing
that a skeleton has no heart
then you must know, sick boy,
that the whole glowing
incandescent life
on the other side of the fence
can't strengthen you, can't exalt you
because it's a skeleton-heart
with all its joy,
pity and chimes of faith.

Poet, what of the night?
Our liberation is tiny,
unguarded, unprotected.
Become the watchman; guard,
preserve—
this believing-hoping happily-ever-after myth
of a next year,
which is forever,
is bitten into your believing bones.

Loyal Sins

My loyal sins,
I've never really committed you
and never even done you
as one does good deeds.
I've mumbled you off dutifully,
you never even penetrated me,
teased me to the bone
like good deeds that
flap in the memory
like a fine apt proverb.

Blessings on your dear eyes
that have good-deeded me
pieces of raw life, pieces of grass
where I now rest my head
and dream sharp dreams.

You're my fate.
My blessing.

Like Weary Trees

Naked Eve shared the last bite
of the apple with me.
God, bashful, disguised himself
as an electric button.
I touched it
and there was light
between her and me.

Blessings on you,
I said to her.
Wearily, with my limbs
full of first darkness,
I dreamed of a
single moment
out of the treasure of those numbered days
that, with every step of the way,
slowly gathered
into pieces of time; dreamed
of those crude stammerings
that became eloquence.
Do you remember?

Do you remember
how we rose early
and came, in our newness,
but God had already prepared
everything for us?
No matter how early we came,
He came a little earlier.
We always asked:
Who was first, He or we?

We already had
a whole forest of singing birds,
strong beasts, faithful light.
And all the time He kept turning up
unexpectedly between us.

Do you remember?
We sat on the ground,
ate the first fruit of our sweat.
Prattled. Drowsily
He listened.
It was just barely first,
nothing had yet happened.
Like weary trees,
interlaced,
shadowy we fell asleep.

Memorial Poem

Strangers' eyes don't see
how in my small room I open a door
and begin my nightly stroll among the graves.
(How much earth—if you can call it earth—does it take to bury
smoke?)
There are valleys and hills
and hidden twisted paths,
enough to last a whole night's journey.
In the dark I see shining towards me
faces of epitaphs
wailing their song.
Graves of the whole
vanished Jewish world
blossom in my one-man tent.

And I pray:
Be a father, a mother to me,
a sister, a brother,
my own children, body-kin,
real as pain,
from my own blood and skin,
be my own dead,
let me grasp and take in
these destroyed millions.

At dawn I shut the door
to my people's house of death.
I sit at the table and doze off,
humming a tune.
The enemy had no dominion over them.
Fathers, mothers, children from their cradles
ringed around death and overcame him.

All the children, astonished,
ran to meet the fear of death
without tears, like little Jewish bedtime stories.
And soon they flickered into flames
like small namesakes of God.

Who else, like me, has
his own night-time
dead garden?
Who is destined for this, as I am?
Who has so much dead earth waiting for him, as for me?
And when I die
who will inherit my small house of death
and that shining gift,
an eternal deathday light
forever flickering?

YIDDISH

Move On, Yiddish Poet

Yiddish poet,
poorest of all poets
in the whole world,
give up your pretense of Parnassus,
that warm little space
with its many pleasures.
You'll never be
one of the high and mighty.
Find a little alley in Safed,
let it correct your ambition,
fulfill yourself
by making Safed your Jerusalem.

Listen, just as there is a concealed light
ready to flood the world
at the end of time,
so is there a concealed dark
which the Holy Ari
unsheathed to gild
his crown city of Safed.

Listen, poet, and get it straight:
you must stand against the sunset,
and wait for the hour
when that concealed dark will descend,
singing,
kindling with pity
everything that lives, is silent,
everything that suffices without words,
all meaningful questions:
you'll be filled through, skin and bone, with dark,
and you'll know, unafraid,
that death exists.

So come down, Yiddish poet,
from your vain Parnassus,
and slip into the poverty
that suits you.
Veiled in her royal darkness,
your crown city of Safed
is waiting for you.

Translated by Ruth Whitman

Evening Bread

A fresh bread on the table, pregnant, whole.
Unspeaking guests at table—
I and she and one more she.
The mouths silent yet the hearts strike.
Like small golden watches strike the hearts of the guests.
And by the bread, a keen knife, quieter still than the guests
Whose striking is more restless
Than mine, than hers, than the other hers.

The door lies open to the setting sun.
Flies, day-worn, drowse on the ceiling
And the windows glow astonished, expectant and afraid,
Afraid and expectant of evening bread.

Tightly, the knife and I embrace each other's fright.
I flap around the bread with trembling hands,
And I think of my warm love of them.
Of my deadly hatred of them.
The knife faints in the grip of my hand
From fear and danger of evening bread.

She takes up the knife and looks at me, at her:
Two dead guests sitting silent at table.
And in her heart the knife blade sings
A song of danger of evening bread.

The other she plays with the blade of the knife
Lightly, joyfully, and with words that have no life;
And her love of us and her hatred of us
And her love of me and her hatred of her
Sings out through the gaping door
To the setting sun, to the sun, to the sun
With longing for evening bread.

Windows flooded with song and color.
The knife exhausted from red desire.
Unspeaking guests sit at table—
I and she and one more she.
The knife dances from me to her, from her to her.
And unspeaking we eat of love and hatred.
Evening bread.

Translated by David G. Roskies and Hillel Schwartz

Praying the Sunset Prayer

I'll let you in on a secret, Nathan,
about how one should pray the sunset prayer.
It's a juicy bit of praying,
like strolling on grass,
nobody's chasing you, nobody hurries you.
You walk towards your creator
with gifts in pure empty hands.
The words are golden,
their meaning is transparent,
it's as though you're saying them
for the first time.

Praying the sunset prayer
is quite a little business.
Nathan, if you don't catch on
that you should feel a little elevated,
you're not praying the sunset prayer.
The tune is sheer simplicity,
you're just lending a helping hand
to the sinking day.
It's a heavy responsibility.
You take a created day
and you slip it
into the archive of life,
where all our lived-out days are lying together.

The day is departing with a quiet kiss.
It lies open at your feet
while you stand saying the blessings.
You can't create anything yourself, but you
can lead the day to its end and see
clearly the smile of its going down.
See how whole it all is,
not diminished for a second,
how you age with the days
that keep dawning,
how you bring your lived-out day
as a gift to eternity.

What else did our forefathers do
when they went out into a field
to stroll through a prayer?

I used to indulge in fasting, Nathan,
punishing my flesh,
until once in the middle of a sunset prayer
I heard scornful words.
It was my grandfather's voice,
I'd know it anywhere.
Why are you fasting like this?
Why are you punishing your body?
Because it gave you
an occasional crumb of pleasure?
People who look better than you do are already in their
graves.
What are you doing to the human image?
Who cares about your sins anyway?
Who gets the worst of your transgressions?
How can it be right to torment yourself
until you have no strength left
for even a thought of penance,
my precious penitent sinner?
A healthy fat *Tsadik*
could knock you over with a sneeze.

Nathan, right after than sunset prayer I broke my fast
and said to myself:
First I have to bargain with the divine world
about the value of my good deeds.
A good deed here, a good deed there,
it's like haggling over a ducat.
But I mustn't put on airs
about my little transgressions.
One must be man enough
to be able to forgive himself.

Translated by Ruth Whitman

YIDDISH

Naftali Gross

Naftali Gross was born in 1895 in Kolomea, Galicia. He joined an uncle in Montreal in 1913, and there published his first poems in the Yiddish press. Shortly afterward he moved to New York City, where he made his home until his death in 1958. He is the author of the extensive collection of Yiddish folktales, Ma'aselech un Mesholim, *which is the subject of Haim Schwarzbaum's major work,* Studies in Jewish and World Folklore.

The Fire Goes Out

The fire goes out in the oven.
It grows dark on the walls.
Someone was in the house
When the fire was burning.

Someone sat beside the fire,
Smiled and spoke softly,
And with pale white fingers
caressed me.

The fire goes out in the oven.
It grows dark on the walls.
Someone was in the house
When the fire was burning.

Where Rests the Wind

Where rests the wind when it does not blow?
Where rests the wanderer when he does not go?
And where will you rest, my soul,
When I will be here no more?

Translated by Jeremy Garber

Just Because

Moishe Leib stood up
in the middle of the night to think out the world.
He listens to his own thinking—
someone whispers in his ear
that everything is straight and everything is crooked
and that the world spins around everything.
Moishe Leib picks at a straw with his nails
and smiles.
Why?
Just because.

He picks at a straw in the night,
and then he has another thought.
He thinks—he listens again—
someone whispers in his ear
that nothing is straight and nothing is crooked
and that the world spins around nothing.
Moishe Leib picks at a straw with his nails
and smiles.
Why?
Just because.

Go Throw Them Out

When people come with big muddy feet
and open your door without a by-your-leave,
and begin to walk around inside your house
like in a whorehouse in a back street—
then it's the heart's finest joke
to take a whip in your hand like a baron
teaching his servant how to say good morning,
and simply drive them all away like dogs!

But what do you do with the whip when people come
with corn-blond hair and heavenly blue eyes,
bursting in like birds briskly flying,
lullabying you as though with lovely dreams,
and meanwhile stealing into your heart,
singing, taking off their tiny shoes,
and, like children paddling in summer brooks,
dabble their pretty feet in your heart's blood?

YIDDISH

Memento Mori

And if Moishe Leib the poet should tell
that he saw death in the waves,
as one sees oneself in the mirror,
in the morning, of all times, around ten o'clock,
would they believe Moishe Leib?

And if Moishe Leib greeted death from a distance
with his hand, and asked, How's it going?
precisely at the moment when thousands of people
were having the time of their life in the water,
would they believe Moishe Leib?

And if Moishe Leib, weeping, should swear
that he was drawn to death as much
as a fellow mooning around in the evening
at the window of a lady he's made holy,
would they believe Moishe Leib?

And if Moishe Leib should picture death for them,
not gray and dark, but gorgeously colorful,
just as it showed itself around ten o'clock,
there, far away, between sky and wave, alone,
would they believe Moishe Leib?

Translated by Ruth Whitman

Zlotchev, My Home

Oh Zlotchev, my home, my town,
With your steeple, *shul* and bathhouse.
With your women of the marketplace,
With your little Jews who scurry
Like dogs after the peasant carrying
His basket of eggs from Sasover Mountain—
Like springtime, my life awakens in me
My poor, little yearning for you—
My home, my Zlotchev.

While yearning, I also recall
Rappaport the rich man carrying
His prominent belly to *shul*,
And Shaye Hillel, the pious bigot,
Who would even sell the sunshine
Like a pig in a sack—
That's enough to extinguish in me,
Like a candle, my longing for you,
My home, my Zlotchev.

How does the story go about that dandy:
How once at dusk he saw
An endless stream of angels around the sun,
Until a *goy*, a drunk with an axe,
Gave him such a blow through his vest
That it almost killed him—
That *goy* with the axe is the hate in me
For my grandfather and for you—
My home, my Zlotchev.

Your earth knows I'm not inventing.
When my grandfather used the police
To throw my mother out of the house,
My grandmother stood with her legs apart,
Smiling almost sweetly as honey,
Like a *shiksa* between two soldiers—
I curse the hate in me,
Reminding me of her and of you—
My home, my Zlotchev.

Like a bunch of naked Jews
Surrounding a scalded man in the bathhouse,
Onlookers rocked and petted their beards
Around the tossed-out packs,
The rags and tatters in bundles,
And around the pieces of a poor bed—
My mother still cries in me,
Just as she did under your sky, in you—
My home, my Zlotchev.

Yet marvelous is our world:
Crossing a field with a horse and wagon,
You drag yourself to the train,
Which tears like a demon over fields,
Depositing you into steerage;
You're borne over water to downtown New York—
And that really is my only comfort,
That they won't bury me in you—
My home, my Zlotchev.

Considering the Bleakness

Considering the bleakness
And the hoarse animal roar,
You would think it a desert
Where a sick, old lion
Crawls around a rock,
Looking for a place
To lie down and die.
In truth, it was a vacant city
Where a madman, on all fours,
Was crawling around,
Circling a collapsed house,
Dragging from behind only
A skull on a rope
Tied to his belt.

Translated by Richard J. Fein

Isaac Leybush Peretz

1

And you are dead. The earth has not yet covered you,
And through a thousand distant streets like racing hooves
The news spreads. Headlines, quick as telegrams,
Cry out at us that your heart doesn't beat.
And like a garish advertisement, your gray head
Is framed in black. And we, the bigshots who should now be dumb
And prostrate, circle around your spirit
Like husky girls in a saloon around a rich old drunk.
And we have tears and speech like round smooth pearls,
Like big gold coins. And everyone who has a tongue
Drums out a rhythmic dirge, lamenting like a cobbler-boy
Pounding a thick nail in an old shoe's heel.

And every sound is full of filth and sweat,
Like a slave's skin, and everything is merchandise—
We deal in all that can be bought and sold—
Torahs and hog-bristles, men and devil's dirt.
It's amazing that we haven't cheated Death
Of his death-tools with copper coins and schnapps!
We are the flesh and blood of that great hero, Jacob,
Who bought his brother's birthright for a pot of lentils;
And one of us, a great god (some believe),
Was sold for thirty shekels' pay;
And if this all is fact, why shouldn't we
Deal in you today? You, dust of our pride,
What, then, were you to us? A last charred log at night
Smoldering on the steppe in a gypsy camp;
A ship's sail struggling with the wind and sea;
The last tree in a mazy wood
Where lightning cut down at the roots
Oak giants, thousands of years old. What are you now?
A man in the cold earth, as still as
Marble in the shine of a death candle. A beginning-end;
An image—only a moment's vision in that long sleep
Depriving us of day and night, that bit of life
Containing all the beauty of the world. Can this be peace?
Is this the hope of our dark way?

2

Why, then, does man fall prostrate at the thought of death?
Why does he wail like a small child alone in the dark night?
Who guides the world? Who calls the spring to blossom and depart?
Who drives the wind through waste and wood in autumn days?
And when the eagle fails in flight and falls,
Why must the raven gouge its eyes?
Why must a hand stretch out fearlessly
To the dead lion? Doesn't the lion's soul cry out
From its flayed hide—the kingly soul from the carcass?
Forgive me for my asking. Pardon me. Forgive.
But what else can I do? I too love life,
And I have eyes, and they are open. I am blind.
But I am just a common merchant's child.
And like the thirsty earth that longs for coming rain,
I tried to purify my life within your light.
And like the poor man's hand that trembles after bread,
Vainly I hope to see your spirit, which has turned away.

But I see only night in you and death in you,
And desolation, which without you is aridity in me.
He who believes in an afterworld is blest.
He has some solace. I have nothing, nothing at all.
I'll have only a candle lost in smoke.
I'll have a gravestone sinking in the earth.
Again I'll see the riddle that is death,
Its sickle glitters near me like red fire,
Like red fire,
Like gold,
Like blood.

That's Our Lot

Young fisherboys sing like the endless sea.
Young healthy blacksmiths sing hot as the fire.
Razed buildings on abandoned streets, we sing
Like the emptiness there when it rains.
In parks the children play and sing together.
In their song lives the love of a good mother.
But we, it seems, were not born of a mother.
Misfortune, singing, dropped us in the road.
We sing unlucky songs for no good reason.
Perhaps like parrots swinging inside cages,
Like frogs at dusk between the swamp and grasses,
Or laundry outdoors when the winds are blowing;
Or else like scarecrows, that have been forgotten
In fields, when fall has preyed on everything.

Translated by Kathryn Hellerstein

Sacco-Vanzetti

You can tear a gray hair out of your head
When sometimes it comes too soon from grief that is too heavy,
But whoever in his grief imagines
That his head's heavy with skin and hair,
Like something he can no longer carry
On these two poor bones, shoulders—
So we humans call them—
He shouldn't stop then with gaping eyes and mouth
As if in some madhouse;

And also the stone of the wall is harder than his head
And banging it against the wall just brings a lump
No larger than an apple on a withering tree
With no one to pluck it in time.
And after all, today there's an easier way out
If you're looking for one:
Just be quiet for a while
And, like a plague victim, bend your head to him who shaves.
After all, he is a brother
And why be angry with him,
If he leaves your skin intact.
He's only doing what he's told and only when he's paid.
And also the death suit,
This too was sewn by a brother who is hungry.
And as the poorest child
When dressed in a holiday outfit
Is held by the hand wherever it is taken,
So you may let yourself be led to the death-chair which awaits you,
However old you are.
And since the deadly copper is already gleaming on your head,
What obstacles remain?
A king—when all his people cry before his throne—
Must be silent at his coronation.
And since the crown upon him—the chosen one—is made of fire,
It is a wonder-crown in this so desolate world.
And only the wolf who is lurking, wild,
And only the robber in the darkness
Shrink from the fire.
Still speechless infants
Whose open eyes see nothing yet
Grab for the fire.
And only the butterfly that longs for light
In the darkness of the night
With wings outspread forever greets
Death in fire.

Translated by David G. Roskies and Hillel Schwartz

YIDDISH

Mordechai Husid

Mordechai Husid was born in Bessarabia in 1909. His first book of short stories was destroyed in the Vilna Ghetto, and it was not until 1969 that his first collection of poems, The Cry of Generations, *was published. Husid presently lives and teaches in Montreal.*

On The Way

Someone walks my father's way,
and sadness disarrays
light steps
and footprints.

Tossing images upon the window
the day gambles
away avenues so they tumble
and disappear into rivers.

The day hauls up city twilight
to the *shtetl* shrinking on the eve of death,
tears yesterday's stale bread
from the clutching hands of dreams.

Day grabs away what the child hoards,
even steals maternal tears
and leaves no motherly face
to bewail and cry.

Sadness, grief, rub out my footprints,
erase my traces—who is it
on his way now moves
and plays havoc with my footsteps?

The Cry of Generations

I have set out to follow the day
and bring up my wagon filled with wood bound for sacrificial fires.
God, I will not be chased away
by all your winds.

Does one also need crematoria
now that the blazing horizons surround us?
Congregations of Jews follow after me
and silent ash from chimneys.

I entrust myself to the demands of my voice.
Prepared as I am to be the messenger
how can I stop to unload this burden
when the cry of generations drives me on.

Windows

I will install windows in my dream
before they get smashed;
hungry shadows cannot keep still
and have crept up to the sills.

Clenched fists
are packed with stones—
for frightened birds?
to scatter feathers and break bones?

To the dream I will bring windows,
windows with broken frames
that were once strong.
God, how have we led ourselves astray and gone wrong?

Translated by Seymour Mayne and Rivka Augenfeld

Rachel Korn

Rachel Korn was born in Podliski, Galicia in 1898. She lived in Lvov until 1941, when she sought refuge in Soviet Russia. She remained in Russia for several years after the war until emigrating to Canada. Her collections of poetry include Village *(1928),* Red Man *(1937),* Home and Homelessness *(1948),* Predestination *(1949),* From the Other Side of a Poem *(1962),* The Mercy of a Word *(1968),* On the Edge of a Moment *(1972), and* Bitter Reality *(1977). At present she lives in Montreal.*

I'm Soaked Through with You

I'm soaked through with you, like earth with spring rain,
and my fairest day hangs
on the pulse of your quietest word,
like a bee near the branch of a flowering linden.

I'm over you like the promise of surfeit
in the time
when the wheat comes up even with the rye in the field.

From the tips of my fingers my devotion pours on your tired head
and my years
like sown acres
become timely ripe and gravid
with the pain
of loving you, beloved man.

Longing

My dreams are so full of longing
that every morning
my body smells of you—
and on my bitten lip there slowly dries
the only sign of suffering,
a speck of blood.

And the hours like goblets pour hope,
one into the other,
like expensive wine:
that you're not far away,
that now, at any moment,
you may come, come, come.

My Body

My body's like a tree trunk in the woods—
it stretches to the sky with all its branches,
its longing green again
with each young love—

But my shadow
like a veil
stitched of thinnest mourning,
already takes my measure
for waiting earth,
for moist grass.

The summer day turns icy
in the hoop
of the narrow cask of shadows,
and the grass darkens
at my feet,
as though it were just touched
by a first breath
of autumn.

My shadow
like a veil
stitched of thinnest mourning
already takes
my measure
and sisters me
with waiting earth,
with moist grass—
and in my blood
I hear the world's weeping
and my unborn song.

A Letter

You know, sweetheart—
today the day is as sunny and tart
as a yellow-gold fruit.
I'd like to take it
slowly and tenderly,
so as not to erase its translucent color,
and wrap it in the soft flax of my dreams
and send it to you
like a letter.

But I know
you'd send the "letter" back immediately
with a note on the margin, all neat and fine,
that, I swear, you don't understand what I mean
(it's always like this with you, Rachel, always)
and you're angry,
yes, you're even angry.
Because the envelope—is empty.

YIDDISH

Sometimes I Want to Go Up

Sometimes I want to go up
on tiptoe
to a strange house
and feel the walls with my hands—
what kind of clay is baked in the bricks,
what kind of wood is in the door,
and what kind of god has pitched his tent here,
to guard it from misfortune and ruin?

What kind of swallow under the roof
has built its nest from straw and earth
and what kind of angels disguised as men
came here as guests?

What holy men came out to meet them,
bringing them basins of water
to wash the dust from their feet,
the dust of earthly roads?

And what blessing did they leave
the children—from big to small,
that it could protect and guard them
from Belzec, Maidanek, Treblinka?

From just such a house,
fenced in with a painted railing,
in the middle of trees and blooming flowerbeds,
blue, gold, flame,
there came out—
the murderer of my people,
of my mother.

I'll let my sorrow grow
like Samson's hair long ago,
and I'll turn the millstone of days
around this bloody track.

Until one night
when I hear over me
the murderer's drunken laugh,
I'll tear the door from its hinges
and I'll rock the building—
till the night wakes up
from the shaking coming through every pane,
every brick, every nail, every board of the house,
from the very ground to the roof—

Although I know, I know, my God,
that the falling walls
will bury only me
and my sorrow.

A New Dress

Today for the first time
after seven long years
I put on
a new dress.

But it's too short for my grief,
too narrow for my sorrow,
and each white-glass button
like a tear
flows down the folds
heavy as a stone.

Translated by Ruth Whitman

The Thirty-one Camels

Thirty-one camels
trudge through the white burning sands
of the Sahara,
laden with the load
of my longing,
the treasure of my sacred hope.

Against them
Sahara stretches her feverish brown body
indolent and weary.
Eagles fly over her with flaming wings
and lions soothe her with lullabies
on starry nights.

Thirty-one camels
trudge among white caravans
of bleached skeletons
with annihilation
in their eyes.

Thirty-one camels
make their way
without a leader,
without a guide.

Translated by Howard Schwartz

Too Late

It is too late for the word
I chose for you,
yet perhaps it is too soon
for that stillness that opens
the distance between us.

There is no way now
to follow you—
the ash which was your glance,
the smell of your hair

have risen up again
with the planted wheat—
but the smoke
that rises and curls in the air
tries the sky,
becomes a chain,
and forms itself
into the letters of your name.

Put Your Word to My Lips

Put your word to my lips
like a signature at the end of a page.
Send me—where? I don't know—
for who waits there but the dark syllable?

I have been anointed with sadness
like the queen of endless night.
She does not know whether she is in a dream
or someone has imagined her.

Perhaps she has only been gambled away
to Fate's winning hand—wagered
as a stake and forfeited,
abandoned to the wind, to the unknown?

Put your word to my lips
and lead me like a child by the hand
to the border outlined by tears,
frontier at the country of night.

With Poems Already Begun

With poems already begun
every line
pulls in another direction.
Each tries to trick me
into its own time and place.

Summer, autumn, winter pass.
Only spring is hesitant
to appear here among these words
as if it were afraid
for its blossoms,

as if it were agonizing
whether to entrust
its treasures
and the promise of May
to my frost-silvered lines.

From Here to There

From here
to there—
is it far?
Just a step.

Everything is prepared,
all is ready:
even the angel
with wings folded
like tired arms,
waits at the crossroads of time
to kiss my forehead—

that I should forget all,
that I should become
like him,
without smile,
sadness,
or tears.

Translated by Seymour Mayne and Rivka Augenfeld

Moishe Kulbak

Moishe Kulbak was born in Smorgon, Lithuania, in 1896. He initially wrote poetry in Hebrew but soon switched to Yiddish, publishing his first book of poetry, Songs, *in 1920. His expressionistic style is apparent in his poetry and in his prose works* Messiah, Son of Ephraim *(1924) and* Monday *(1926). He emigrated to Byelorussia and became associated with the Minsk group of Soviet Yiddish poets. He exchanged his expressionism for the only style acceptable to the Soviet regime, socialist realism, in his novel* Zelmenianer *(1931) and in his comic epic* Childe Harold of Dissen *(1933). Nevertheless he was arrested in 1937 and sent to a slave labor camp, where he died in 1940. In 1956 he was rehabilitated by the Soviet regime and his books once more appeared.*

I Just Walk Around, Around, Around

I just walk around, around, around
for a year, and two, and three, and maybe more;
I arrive uninvited everywhere, everywhere,
and everywhere it's void and empty. . .

It's void and empty,
and lonely,
and terribly boring,
brrr! . . .

Spring

My barefoot steps lie broad and big
on the field, on the black field.
My flesh is the earth, I'm the ryebread-song
in its heart.

My hungry walk inundates the morning.
I spread my arms:
tra-la-la, tra-la-la!
The luminous world has no walls.

Hey, down with the feet that trample me,
hurray for the drunken life . . .
I strut and laugh into every door:
Haven't you seen anything?
Haven't you heard anything?
The world has surrendered to me.

Summer

Today the world unwrapped itself again,
fat bud, full earth, green whispering,
everything trembled the way taut girl flesh
trembles with the sharp joy of becoming a wife . . .

Like a cat I lay in the middle of the field
where it splashed, flashed, sparkled and glistened,
one eye smeared with sun, the other—closed,
and silently rejoiced, silently laughed . . .
over miles of plain and forest and valley—
here's where I lounge about—a splendid hard steel.

YIDDISH

Two

Two people live side by side;
two neighbors, two tall boys—
a girlish one and a pale creature
(in me, in me, in me).
Two people live side by side.

I'm asleep. Suddenly someone's hands start . . .
(when one goes to sleep, the other awakes)
he unrolls a shadowy ladder
and climbs up the walls, up the walls, up the walls.
I'm asleep. Suddenly someone's hands start.

Sometimes when I sit with a glass of wine
(it happens, it happens, if only it didn't),
the little man opens a tiny door
and spits in my face . . .
O, sometimes when I sit with a glass of wine.

Two people live side by side;
two neighbors, two tall boys—
a girlish one and a pale creature
(in me, in me),
two people live side by side.

Translated by Ruth Whitman

Vilna

1

Someone in a prayer-shawl is walking over your ramparts,
Gloomy, and the only walker in the nightly city.
He listens: The old veins of gray courtyards and synagogues
Are awake and astir like a hoarse and dusty heart.
You are an open psalter cast in clay and iron;
Every stone is a prayer, every wall is a chant,
When moonlight oozes down to your Caballah streets,
And the cold and ugly splendor bleaches forth, naked,
Your joy is sorrow—the joy of deep basses
In orchestras, your funerals are festivities,
And solace—the clear and radiant poverty,
Like quiet summer-fogs on the city's corners.
You are a cameo darkly set in Lithuania,
Written gray and old in moss and lichen;

Each stone a scripture, each wall a parchment,
Secretly opened and consulted at night,
When a frozen water-carrier, his beard tucked in,
Stands at the ancient synagogue and counts the stars.

2

Gloomy, I, the only walker in the nightly city.
No sound. The houses freeze—heaps of rags,
But somewhere aloft, a tallow candle drips and flickers,
A Cabbalist is sitting in an attic, woven fast,
Like a spider, and drawing the gray thread of his life:
Is there anyone in the vast cold wasteland
Whose lost shrieks we, the deafened, hear?
And before him, in the darkness, Raziel
Stands leaden, with old and threadbare parchment wings,
And eyes that are graves choking with sand and cobwebs:
Gone. Sorrow is all that abounds!
The candle drips. The green and stony Jew is listening
And sucking darkness from the angel's sockets,
And garret over garret draws a breath—the lungs
Of the hunch-backed creature drowsing in the mountains.
City, you may be a Cabbalist's gray dream,
Drifting through the world like early webs in autumn.

3

You are a psalter cast in clay and iron,
And your faded letters range and ramble:
Men stiff as wood, and women like loaves of bread,
Cold, mysterious beards, the shoulders hammered out,
And long eyes wobbling like skiffs on a river—
Your Jews buy a silvery herring late at night,
Beating their breasts: Oh God, we sin, we sin. . . .
And the moon, like a white eye, ogles through the windows—
Where the rags turn silver as they hang on ropes,
The children in the beds—yellow, slimy worms,
And virgins, half undressed, with bodies like planks—
Narrow as the alleys are your gloomy Jews:
Mute foreheads, like the wide and rigid walls of your synagogue,
And eyebrows, mossy, like the rooftops of your ruins.
You are a psalter written on the meadows,
And like a raven I sing about you in moonlight,
For never has the sun gone up in Lithuania.

4
Your joy is sorrow—the joy of deep basses
In an orchestra, your quiet spring is black.
Saplings grow from the rampart, grass from the walls;
The grass blossoming drowsily crawls from the old tree
And the cold and muddy nettle stands upon the soil,
Only filth and frozen walls in the wetness,
And sometimes at night a breeze puffs dry and terse
On rooftops, and a shape of waterdrops and moonlight
Steals through the streets in silvery and trembling fantasies—
The Vilna river has arisen cool and foggy,
And fresh, and naked, with long and watery hands,
Has risen into the city. The blind windows squint askew.
The arching bridges flung upon the ramparts,
And no one will open a door and stick his head out
To the Vilna and her thin, blue nakedness.
Like the surrounding mountains, the bearded ramparts stand agape.
And silent, silent—

5
You are a cameo darkly set in Lithuania
And shapes are barely glowing on your restless ground.
The white and radiant geniuses of distant light
With hard and narrow bones sharpened by drudgery.
And Yiddish is the simple wreath of oak leaves
Over the city's secular and holy gates.
Gray Yiddish is the candle glinting in the windows—
Just like a peddler stopping at an ancient well
I sit and listen to the harsh voice of Yiddish.
I am the city! The myriad narrow doorways to the world,
Roofs upon roofs toward cold and muddy sky.
I am a black flame, starving, licking up the walls,
And gleaming in the sharp and cutting eyes of Jews abroad.
I am the grayness! I am the black flame! I am the city!

6
And on the ancient synagogue, a water-carrier,
Frozen, his beard tucked in—He stands and counts the stars.

Translated by Joachim Neugroschel

Leib Kwitko

Leib Kwitko was born in Russia in 1890. He was orphaned while very young and had to earn his living from the age of ten. He was regarded as one of the "Kiev triumvirate," along with poets Peretz Markish and David Hoffstein. In 1920 Kwitko left Russia and settled in Germany, until 1925, when he returned to Russia to live in Moscow. There his works were translated into many of the languages of the Soviet Union, and about eleven million copies were printed. In 1939 he was awarded the Red Worker's Banner. Arrested in the Stalinist purges in 1949, Kwitko was executed with about thirty other Yiddish writers in 1952. He was "rehabilitated" in 1954 as an innocent victim of injustice.

Esau

Esau,
Shaggy, blest with a fragrant field!
I bring you an age-long debt,
It lies sunk in my heart,
Buried among my lost treasures.
Esau,
Silently behind your back,
Silently I have sucked the riches of your lot,
The powerful drink
Of you, Esau, fragrant field.

Esau,
Hairy, with your father's blessing
Upon your mild, blond
Forest of a head—
Don't tell me off . . . don't tell me off—
Drop by drop you have seeped
Into my age-long sorrow,
Drop by drop oozed out
With all the thousands of souls
Upon the ash of going
Upon the ash of being . . .

Esau,
Over the wide, wide plains of musty ancient woe
Is spun,
Woven,
Embroidered
My ancient heart,

My age-long dream,
My darkly shining gaze:
Seek there, seek,
Esau,
Return to your sheep,
To your fragrant springs,
Lay your hand upon them,
Your old, hairy hand.

My Fiddle

Let me just finish off my slender fiddle
I carve and chisel all the morning through:
From matchboxes, my fingers in a fever,
I carve and chisel all the morning through.

Fierce tempest, wait awhile in the beyond!
I've yet to chisel out the lower part,
And you, Death, on the threshold stand awhile,
Keep watch: I've yet to plane the upper part.

Now to put pegs into the thin, smooth neck
And draw fine hairs down all its lovely length.
The mob is howling in the yard outside
And even now is glancing at my door.

One more hair for the fiddle from my head . . .
Darling, don't tremble—there, just one more hair . . .
A tiny fiddle for the poor pale child:
May it be his for many a long year!

Translated by Keith Bosley

Zishe Landau

Zishe Landau was born in 1889 in Plotsk, Poland, to a family of distinguished rabbinic lineage. Orphaned as a child, he emigrated to New York in 1906 and by 1911 was affiliated with the Yiddish group Di Yunge. The news of the pogroms in Poland, Russia, and the Ukraine caused him to turn to Jewish national and American patriotic themes. A collection of his comedies, Nothing of Any Importance Happened, *and his collected works both appeared in the year of his death, 1937.*

I Have a Big Favor to Ask You, Brothers

I have a big favor to ask you, brothers . . .
Namely, it has to do with the fact that you
with your deep wisdom and understanding,
might tell me if I am right—
Lately, brothers, I have a feeling: of all the lips
that stand ready in the world to be kissed,
the sweetest are those that are a little bit faded,
that are pale, crumpled, and discolored. In short, those
that are kissed out, kissed up, kissed through and through.
So far as a man can understand his own heart,
the feeling in me stems from my
sticking to my opinion: in our condition, in our years,
sixteen-year-old blood is nonsense: I've tried more than once
to take a sixteen-year-old by the chin
but it gave such a shudder in my hand
that my own hands began to shake
as though I were holding a little mouse by its tail.
O brothers of mine, your brother doesn't want to
risk his daily bread!
That's why he turns to you now for advice,
to your deep wisdom and understanding.

Parts

A man's parts tell us such a lot!—
A hand someone put on his knees, like this,
a neck, a shoulder that you notice
in a noisy cafe, in a bus, perhaps a theater.
How many times your heart is jolted by lips
you suddenly meet;
hair and bellies speak, glances speak,
things that words can't say!
How feet can shake your heart!
Light women's feet skimming by!
But I love those best that are thick and clumsy,
they remind me of good friends, old letters,
and of her who gave me my life.

YIDDISH

Tuesday

I drank up two glasses of hot tea and milk,
ate up three or four zwieback:
then I sat at the table for a long time,
smoked and looked at a nail on the wall,
translated four poems from German
and lay down tired on the sofa,
put my hands behind my head
and spat three times up at the ceiling.
I felt heavy
because the summer was over.
Otherwise I'd now go for a walk in the park,
or even hang around the house catching flies.
Again I spat up at the ceiling three times,
and missed all three times,
then I fell asleep.

Of Course I Know

Of course I know today is Sunday
and tomorrow will be Monday
and after spring comes summer
and our system is a bad one,
and in New York lives Opatoshu,
the pride of France is Jaurés.

I also know many deep secrets:
the Duke of Abruzzi is
no duke. He's our equal,
and often goes walking down the street
on nice days; his coat over his arm.

I also know: Darwin guessed right,
Copernicus was right,
but best of all I know:
I
am
lost forever.

The Little Pig

The little pig with its sawed-off snout
dug so deeply into the garbage that steam rose up.
And then it examined me
with two mild charming almond eyes.
A warmth flowed through me when I
saw how it twirled its little tail into a point.
O how much charm there lies in a pig's tail!
O how much tenderness, O how much grace and innocence!
It's as graceful and charming as that curl that in my youth
robbed me of more than one hour of rest!
And it's as tender and as innocent
as your lines, divine Verlaine!

Translated by Ruth Whitman

Mani Leib

Mani Leib (Brahinsky) was born in Nyezhin, a Ukrainian town near Chernigov, in 1883. He arrived in New York in 1905 after a period of involvement in the Russian revolutionary movement. He published many poems in the anthologies of the "art for art's sake" group of American Yiddish poets, Di Yunge. His collections of poetry include The Song of Bread, Ballads, Jewish and Slavic Motifs, *and* Poems, *all published in 1918, as well as* Little Flowers—Little Wreaths *(1922), a book of children's poems entitled* Clever Little-Tongued Boy *(1922), and* Wonder upon Wonder *(1930). Mani Leib died in New York in 1953.*

The Pyre of My Indian Summer

The pyre of my Indian summer burns
Out now in rings of smoke and drops of gold.
I am dumb and devout as my hand turns
The ash upon the last coal-star gone cold.

And night and villages. The crickets play
On moon-flutes to my soul a mournful tune.
Upon white grass at fences going gray
The pumpkins are as yellow as the moon.

And trees—blue wax—in the void's brightness cool
Like erect candles, full of holy dread.
And silence keenly marks the sere leaf's fall,
And keener still the unrest of my tread.

Winter

Before my bright window
The snowy rooftops
Rise higher and higher
In silvery caps.

Before my bright window
Above the high roofs
Smoke curls even higher
Like silvery doves.

In Little Hands

In little hands she holds an open book,
Her head is leaning back, becalmed in grief,
The sun sinks at the window, sends a brief
Red glow across the pages of the book.

Where is big sister? She has gone away,
Away—why and for how long no one knows;
At home that evening as she always was,
By night she had for ever gone away.

And afterwards the mother wrung her hands
And with a kerchief covered her old face;
She lit the candles, stuck each in its place,
Wept without tears and wrung and wrung her hands.

And everyone at home was grieving then
And everyone at home was watching mother
And quieter grew their tread about each other
And everybody's talk grew quieter then.

. . . The book falls from her little hands. She weeps.
Her childish lips are quivering with fear.
"Like my big sister I shall go from here
As soon as I am grown up. . . ." And she weeps.

Translated by Keith Bosley

A Plum

In the cool evening the master
Tore a ripe plum straight off the tree
Together with its leaf, and sank his teeth
In the dewy blue skin. From its fetter

The sleeping sap flowed out and up
With cool foam. And to lock in all
Its sap—and let no drop fall—
Slowly, as one carries a cup

Of wine, in both full hands he carried home
The plum to his wife and gently
Brought it to her lips. She, with a kind

"Thank you," began to suck the plum that lay
In his hands. Until there remained in his hands
The skin, the pit, and clinging foam.

Psalmodist

Let shrieking steel and gray stone be set
For green grass; the clash of hammer and tongs
And the rush of wheels—birdsong;
Grating of saws—the summer cricket; the pious poet—

The merchant. And as in earliest and early days
The grass will shoot its stalk through the rock
In rhythm with the cricket; and over the clanging shock
Of steel—the bird's song will range far and away.

So too the poet: pious, from market noises,
From business bustling and the wheels' clatter
He will move apart with parchment, ink and feather

To the holiness of the word, which in its commonness
Is strong—to stitch prayers for the world: to knit
The heart to God, to unbind the sorrow on silent lips.

YIDDISH

From the Crag

You have granted me my full share of days,
The crown of old age—proud silver in my hair;
Hindsight to see clearly everywhere
From my crag, at the glint of memory:

The valley, the chasms through which I rode
With the chariots of my breaking dawn,
Through red summer, golden autumn,
To winter's white truth, when the wheels froze

The lines on my forehead from appreciated pain,
From passing through on your earth, suspecting your grace
Has everywhere stood by me and given solace

That just as your hand leads the sun into day
So too your hand strengthened my old wing,
Raised me to praise you from the crag where I cling.

They

There they were many, O God, so many,
Such vital ones and unafraid,
Such noble ones, with beard and braid—
And talking in a marvelous strange way.

And under every roof they would sing—
With Torah chant and scripture cymbals—
Such rare songs, proud and boastful:
Of the golden peacock and Elimelekh the king.

But above their heads only the sun in its stare
Saw the raw fury, the killer's cold blade,
How with wild force it descended,
And what massacres were there.

Now they are but a trace of that fury:
An axed forest, a couple of trees.

Translated by David G. Roskies and Hillel Schwartz

H. Leivick

H. Leivick was the pseudonym of Leivick Halpern. He was born in Igumen, Byelorussia, in 1886. Leivick is best remembered for his verse drama The Golem, *published in 1921. With the help of friends, Leivick escaped in 1912 from a sentence in Siberia and emigrated to the United States, where he became a member of the Di Yunge group. He died in 1962.*

How Did He Get Here?

How did he get into this sickroom,
the philosopher from Amsterdam?

I look at him—there's no uncertainty.
It's he, it's he.

The full lips. The long nose.
The whole head as though under glass.

His sick chest heaves, straining,
racked, racked, by fits of coughing.

Three hundred years—as though one minute.
A drop of blood dots his lip.

Three hundred years of moonlight fall
on his head and pillow. Fall.

Holy one, I touch your sleeve.
Wake up. Rise up. Recognize me.

Two Times Two is Four

(Spinoza Cycle, No. 11)

My body's passion-hide
is stripped away. My pure
soul, what does she do?
She counts, she counts.

Two times two is—four,
I times I is—you,
you times you is—me,
death times death is—rest.

My head is in the east,
my feet are in the west;
drive quicker, don't get lost—
near times near is—far.

Tap the door.—Knock, knock.—
It's open, come right in—
kindle the last look—
death times death is—being.

Through the Whole Long Night

Through the whole long night the rain stormed down,
the old apple tree twisted with cold,
pounded for help on the canvas tent
as though saying goodbye to his deep old age.
But at dawn when the east on the world's edge
came face to face with the rising sun—
the tree came to meet it with instant joy,
as though his smallest leaf had not fallen away.

In the tent a man slept, as though under a spell—
not hearing the clatter of tree or rain,
and at dawn, his eyes still clogged with sleep,
he gazed at the fresh pools on the ground,
while over his head, through sun-streaked mist,
the morning apples clanged as they fell.

Translated by Ruth Whitman

I Hear a Voice

The sun rose over a mound of corpses
And one, who witnessed it, asked:
—Are you not ashamed to rise, sun?
He asked and received no reply,

For in that moment he said to himself:
—Are you not ashamed to live on?
And he sat down opposite the mount,
And looked at the bodies as they lay,
Some face down to the ground
And some face upward to the sun.
And again he asked:
—Are you not ashamed to look at the sun?
And in that moment he said to himself:
—Are you not ashamed to sit while they lie—
And he lay down, like one of the dead,
Face up, and lay this way for hours.
While he lay there, a melody rose within him
That sang of his own shame,
And the melody began to sing out from within,
he stood up
And allowed the melody to spread
And the mount of corpses
Picked up his melody
And answered with an echo
Like a resounding choir.

Translated by David G. Roskies

Malka Locker

Malka Locker, the wife of Labor Zionist leader Berl Locker, was born in Eastern Galicia in 1887. In addition to a biography of Rimbaud and essays on romantic writers, she has published several volumes of her own poetry in Yiddish and has been translated into Hebrew.

Clocks

Clocks—
the most prominent reminder
of destruction:
standing motionless
with silent faces
without complaint,
their hearts knocked out,
they stubbornly show the hour
it occurred.

Drunken Streets

The streets are a bit confused,
truly drunk. They fall off their feet.
The corner streetlamp
stands bewildered and alone,
oblivious to itself.

Houses, emptied of their contents,
are stationed before them,
petrified like skeletons.

Translated by Jeremy Garber

Itzik Manger

Itzik Manger was born in 1901 in Bukovina, where he acquired a great interest in Yiddish folklore and German literature. He was strongly influenced by Rilke. His first collection of verse was published in 1929. In addition to writing several volumes of poetry, Manger applied his bardic talents and his passion for religious and Biblical themes to modernizations of Biblical motifs and plays. After fleeing the Nazis, he lived in London until 1951, then in New York. He moved to Israel in 1967 and died there in 1969.

Rachel Goes to the Well for Water

Rachel stands by the mirror and plaits
her long black braids,
she hears her father cough
and wheeze on the stairs.

She runs up to the windowseat:
"Leah! It's father! Quick!"
And Leah comes to the door,
hiding her trashy book.

Her face is drawn and ashen,
her eyes red and weepy.
"Leah, you'll ruin your eyes,
you've read enough today."

And Rachel takes the pitcher
and starts off towards the well—
the twilight is blue and mild,
it makes you want to cry.

As she crosses the dark field
a rabbit flashes by.
Chirik!—a little cricket
chirps in the deep grass.

And in the sky there shimmers
an earring made of gold:
"If only there were two,
I'd like to have them both."

A piper whistles near her:
tri-li, tri-li, tri-li—
The air is full of dusk and hay
from all the cows and sheep.

She runs. It's late. The Good Book says:
a guest waits near the well,
today the cat has washed her face,
today she fasted too.

She runs. And high up sparkles
the earring made of gold:
If only there were two,
she'd like to have them both.

Abishag Writes a Letter Home

Abishag sits in her room
and writes a letter home:
Greetings to the calves and sheep—
she writes, sighing deeply.

Greetings to her old mother
and the old linden tree;
she sees both old folk
in her dreams frequently.

Greet the handsome miller
who works in the mill—
and the shepherd Oizer, whose
piping she cherishes still.

King David is old and pious
and she herself is, "oh, well"—
She's the king's hotwater bottle
against the bedroom chill.

She thought—but who cares what
a village girl may think. . .
more than once at night
she softly mourned her fate.

True, wise people say
she's being charitable.
They even promise her
a line in the Bible.

A line for her young flesh,
the years of her youth.
A line of ink on parchment
for the whole long truth.

Abishag puts down her pen,
her heart is strangely bitter,
a tear drips from her eyes
and falls on the letter.

The tear erases "mother"
and erases "linden tree"
while girlish in a corner
a dream sobs tenderly.

Alone

Nobody knows what I say,
nobody knows what I need—
seven mice and a mouse
are on the floor asleep.

Seven mice and a mouse
I think make eight—
I put on my hat
and I say goodnight.

I put on my hat
and I start to go.
But where to go late at night?
All alone?

A bar in the market place
winks at me: "You fool!
I've a firkin of wine,
a firkin of gold."

Quickly I open
and fall through the door:
Greetings to all,
whoever you are!

Nobody knows what I say,
nobody knows what I need—
two drunkards and a bottle
are on the floor asleep.

Two drunkards and a bottle
I think make three.
Shall I make a fourth?
Not me.

I put on my hat
and I start to go.
But where to go late at night?
All alone?

Autumn

September. The gypsy and the nightingale
don't know what to do with themselves.

A moonwalker sleeps near the cool river,
stripped of all his dreams.

Ophelia, sick Ophelia!

Weariness in a silk dressing gown
smooths the gray valley with her fingers.

She smooths and says incantations and wakes
the blue marvel of once upon a time.

Ophelia, sick Ophelia!

The green eyes of the September night
look wearily through the windowpanes.

In those eyes—cries of wild cats—
what are those eyes to us?

Let's run away. But where can we run?
The blind lantern stands and watches,
and the doors and windows are closed—

Repent, Ophelia!

This marvel took off
from Aladdin's magic blue lantern,

and the gypsy and the nightingale
don't know what to do with themselves.

And Itzik Manger sleeps on the hard ground,
stripped of all his dreams.

Translated by Ruth Whitman

Abraham and Sarah

Avremele, when will we have our own child?
We've already reached our old age,
A woman who has lived as long as I have,
Has by now mothered many a babe.

Father Abraham smiles and thinks,
And smoke from his pipe fills the air,
Faith my wife, if the Holy One wants,
Even a deaf mute can hear.

Avremele, you hear how every night,
My body and soul are torn with strife,
And Hagar is only your servant girl,
And I am your loving wife.

Often I think that the stars and the dust
Form the soul of our child unborn,
Who wanders around night after night,
Through the rain and the wind and the storm.

Father Abraham smiles and thinks,
And smoke from his pipe fills the air,
Faith, my wife, if the Holy One wants,
Even a deaf mute can hear.

And when I see how Hagar's child
Plays all day in the sand,
And I gently stroke his curly head,
I feel the hurt in my hand.

And when I take him on my lap,
And he smiles so warmly and smart,
My eyes grow large and fill with tears,
And I feel the ache in my heart.

Avremele, when will we have our own child?
We've already reached our old age,
A woman who has lived as long as I have,
Has by now mothered many a babe.

Father Abraham smiles and thinks,
And smoke from his pipe fills the air,
Faith, my wife, if the Holy One wants,
Even a deaf mute can hear.

On the Road There Stands a Tree

On the road there stands a tree,
It stands there all bent down,
And all the birds from that tree,
Have long since left and gone.

Three flew eastward, three flew west,
Three southward before the storm,
And the tree was left alone,
Abandoned and forlorn.

YIDDISH

Said I to mama, "Listen well!
I'm not to be disturbed,
Because now mother you will see,
How I become a bird.

I will sit there in the tree,
And guard him the winter long,
Through the snows I will console him,
And sing him a lovely song."

Said my mother, "No my child!"—
And she begins to cry—
"You might catch a cold up there,
And, God forbid, you'll die."

Said I, "Mother, 'tis a shame,
Your dark and lovely eyes,
But no matter what you say,
I'll fly across the skies."

Cries my mother, "Itzik dear!
Take—I beg you please,
Take at least a little shawl,
So that you will not freeze.

Take along galoshes too
The winter's long and hard,
Be sure to wear your woolen cap,
Woe is me! My aching heart!

And take along your winter coat
Put it on, you empty-head!
Unless of course, you want to be
A guest amongst the dead."

I try to lift my wings and fly
They're so heavy Oh my word!
With the clothes my mother put
On the small weak bird.

I look sadly in her face,
Tears fill up her eyes,
Her love prevented my one dream,
To soar across the skies.

The Strange Guest

The strange guest in the dark asylum
Looks at the darkened walls and doesn't understand,
Where the blackened host clamors and claps,
And nails the shadow-king together in his hands.

Through the open window lies a road
And then a second one bears left
And the guest stands there at the end
Sphinx-like without a friend.

Then all at once there shines in him a light,
A joy which he did not anticipate
And he is aware that on the other side
The great and holy Baal Shem Tov awaits.

Dying Thief

The thief is dying in the moonlit night—
A Jew falls upon him in the woods,
And takes his sack of gold—all his worldly goods,
Then turns into the woods and out of sight.

The moon's a great wild poppy flower,
The forest—a choir of sickly nightingales singing,
Riders on horseback. And the echo of far-off horns ringing,
The willows crookedly hang in the late night hour,

And fear lurks there mixed with dread,
An old Jew, bent with gray and hoary head,
Carries off a sack of golden ducats.

The thief is dying. The red poppy flower fades,
And then expires in the open glades,
And singing still the nightingales die.

Translated by Stephen Garrin

YIDDISH

Fairy Tales

Beggars in the stories of old
wandered ragged up and down
from town to village, back to town,
from one house to another.

And the stories always ended
with the children being told
how the beggars were rewarded
with crowns of purest gold.

Evening

Evening's barefoot monk
descends from the church on the hill
his long shadow falls
across the empty market place.

The turtledoves in the dovecote
murmur to each other sleepily
and our house breathes the peace
and piousness
of ryebread and evensong.

Under the Ruins of Poland

Under the ruins of Poland
lies my fair-haired dove,
her dead face, my fallen city,
are more real to me than love.
My fate, my sorrow.

The squire's pretty wife
confessed her trifling sins,
she wakened the next morning
new, redeemed and cleansed.
My fate, my sorrow.

Across the ruins of Poland
the snow lies thick and deep,
but the headache of my darling
will not mend with sleep.
My fate, my sorrow.

Her death sits down beside me
to write letters to the world,
but words to tell her suffering
are worn-out and cold.
My fate, my sorrow.

Above the ruins of Poland
a hawk flies high and stays,
that bird of giant darkness
shadows all my days.
My fate, my sorrow.

That bird of huge ill-omen
has seized my heart, its prey,
and carries the sad tidings
of this song eternally,
My fate, my sorrow.

(Under the ruins of Poland
lies my fair-haired dove,
her dead face, my fallen city,
are more real to me than love.
My fate, my sorrow.)

Translated by Miriam Waddington

A Dark Hand

A dark hand engraved
A question mark above my night:
Until now, so; and after, what?
You don't go through life just like that,
You can't forever be pals with the wind—
A cradle yearns for you,
A child yearns for you,
A woman yearns for you.
You can't forever be pals with the wind
And you don't go through life just like that.

God my God! My pale hands
Quiver, nervous for murder and thieving
Though my soul is as blue as April
And coos in the nests like a dove.
My eyes are blind from seeing too much,
They cry: "Young-old one, believe."
But my fingers twitch, nervous,
Set for blood and murder and thieving.

So how then can I come and say: here,
At this very place, I have my tent unfurled?
How can I play with a drop of light
And say, it is all the world?

How can the head of a young woman
Sleep quietly on my chest, so,
When my fingers twitch, nervous,
So . . . so . . . I myself don't quite know.

You, God, whose only greatness is
To be alone from creation onward,
See! In the folds of your robe
I cast off my cry as I would a bastard.
Hold it close, choke it, cradle it, rock it to sleep—
Whatsoever you think best will be good.
I know that soon I will stand before you
And spit at your face with my blood.

Translated by David G. Roskies and Hillel Schwartz

Anna Margolin

Anna Margolin (the pseudonym of Razel Lebensboim) was born in the Lithuanian town of Brisk in 1887. She was raised in Odessa and Warsaw, two centers of the Jewish intelligentsia. As a young woman she visited London, Paris, New York, and Palestine, and for a time was the secretary of Chaim Zhitlovsky, the Diaspora nationalist and Yiddishist. In 1914 she settled in New York, where she wrote for the Yiddish daily The Day. *Her book of Yiddish verse,* Poems, *was published in New York in 1929.*

Ancient Murderess Night

Ancient murderess night, black mother in need, help me!
Beguile him, entangle him, swallow him, beat him to death!

And I,
whose drink was tears,
whose bread was shame,
will drink swooning
greedily and long
like a lovesong
his wife's crying,
his children's silence,
his friends' whispering
over his corpse.
I'll get up like someone who's long been sick,
a black figure in morning-red,
and I'll bow to all four corners of space
and sing and sing and sing to life
my praise of death.

Years

Like women who are loved very much and are still not sated,
who walk through life with laughter and anger,
and in their eyes shine fire and agate—
that's how our years were.

And they were like actors, playing
Hamlet out of the side of their mouths in the square;
like grandees in a land, a proud land,
who seize rebellion by the scruff of the neck.

But now see how submissive they are, my God,
as silent as a smashed piano,
and they take each blow and taunt as a caress,
and seek you, not believing in you.

Translated by Ruth Whitman

My Kin Talk

My kin:
men in satin and velvet,
faces long, silky-white,
yearning, passionate lips,
thin hands patting yellowed folios
talking at dead of night with God.

Merchants from Leipzig, Danzig,
clean cuffs, refined cigar smoke,
jokes from the Gemara, manners
from Germany,
their glance astute and dull,
astute and overfed:
Don Juans, tradesmen, seekers after God.

A drunkard,
a few renegades in Kiev.

My kin:
idol-women decked in diamonds,
stained red with Turkish shawls,
heavy folds of satin-de-lyons:
but their bodies are weeping willows,
like withered flowers their fingers in their laps
and in their faded, veiled eyes
desire is dead.

Grandams in calico and linen,
broad-boned, strong, lively,
their laughter light and contemptuous,
their talk quiet, their silences uneasy:
before dark at the windows of their humble houses
they sprout like statues
and through their twilit eyes
grim desire stirs.

And a few
I am ashamed of.

My kin:
all of them,
blood of my blood,
flame of my flame,
dead and living jumbled together,
sad, grotesque, fat,
tramp through me as through a dark house,
tramp with prayers and curses and wailing,
shake my heart like a copper bell:
my tongue quivers,
my voice is not my own—
my kin talk.

Homecoming

Houses are swaying, swimming in gray light
With damp gardens, alleys silvery-bright,
And people in doorways
Are bowing, smiling, fading,
Everyone appears and disappears
Through the rainbow of tears.

A child sits at the window.
In the moonlight her hair streams like dark rain.
Persistent, clear,
Her eyes search as through a forest
For my own distant form.
Oh why do you tremble, child, as I draw near?

Mother Earth

Mother Earth am I, much trampled and sun-washed,
Dark slave and mistress,
O loved one.
From me, the lowly one, the pushed and shoved one,
You sprout a mighty stem,
And like the eternal stars and the sun's flame
I circle in long blind silence through
Your every root, your every bough,
And half awake, half dreaming I
Aspire through you to heaven on high.

Translated by Keith Bosley

YIDDISH

Peretz Markish

Peretz Markish was born in Russia in 1895. His first book of Yiddish verse was published in 1917. With a large group of other Jewish writers he was arrested and killed during the Stalinist purges in 1948. Much of his poetry portrays Jewish heroism during the Nazi period and pays tribute to the Jewish heroes of the Warsaw ghetto.

In the Last Flicker of the Sinking Sun

In the last flicker of the sinking sun
Alone
On roads beneath night's mask
What can I ask?

In the black embers of the dying day
Astray
On peaks that point still higher
To what can I aspire?

In the black forest of tranquillity
Where black shapes tangle and throng
Who is approaching me?
To whom can I belong?

Your Burnt-Out Body

Your burnt-out body festers still,
And still to strip and flay your shadows track
And hound you, and the winds of autumn steal
Up on you in a starving, wolfish pack;

Now lambs of snow seek white wool for your shelter,
And somewhere now a royal frost sucks up
The Dnieper's dream, the Volga's helter-skelter,
And sips a white salve all your rivers yield . . .

And everywhere you halt, there bows a hope,
A wayside hamlet on your twilit field . . .

Translated by Keith Bosley

Kadya Molodovsky

Kadya Molodovsky, born in Lithuania in 1894, received her early education from her father. In the 1920s and '30s she was active in the progressive Yiddish education movement. She taught in Yiddish schools in Warsaw, writing light verse, ballads, and poetic tales for adults and children. In 1935 she emigrated to New York. She wrote several collections of poetry, including Angels Come to Jerusalem *(1952) and* Light of a Thorn Tree *(1965), and a book of children's stories and poems,* Marzipans *(1970). Her other works include a drama,* Toward the God of the Desert *(1949), and a novel,* At the Gate *(1967). She died in New York in 1975.*

In Life's Stable

My poor Pegasus must go on foot.
Both he and I—we've clean forgotten how to fly.
The world is very small,
the sea is drying up.
I've tied up this wild pony in the stable of life.
Now both of us drag our feet.

Who shot away his wings?
Who gnawed the point off my pen?
The sun sinks down, the windowpanes shine bloody.
The sun comes to an end. My sight comes to an end.

Come, lines, arrange yourselves, raise me up.
You're my bodyguard, my generals.
I can't cross over this fence of webs and dust,
the whole field darkens, narrows.

What good is boasting, what good is it?
What's the good of kneading out story after story?
Pegasus, don't stand too close to your stack of hay.
God forbid, you might become a donkey with epaulets.

YIDDISH

Night Visitors

One night a bird came to me
and knocked with its wings
on my window and door.
—Come in, feather-fiddle, kind musician of my child-song,
I've saved you some water and bread,
come in, be my guest, be honored.
We're both destined to live and to die.

And a cat came, wandering in the night,
scratched with its claws,
scratched and scraped.
—Come in, kit-kat, frightful beast of my childhood,
I've often been spanked because of you.
Come in, be my guest, be honored.
We're both vagabonds destined to roam.

And a nanny-goat came, with its pointed beard.
It knocked with its hoofs,
scratched with its horns.
Come in, nanny-granny, short-beard, milk-in-mug.
Your song still makes a cradle of my bed.
Come in, be my guest, be honored.
We're both destined to teach for a living.

One night a man stood at my door,
and a terrible fear
took hold of me.
Who are you? Is that a knife in your hand?
Are you a betrayer? A firebrand?
And I locked and barred and bolted the door,
and fell, hiding my face in my hands.

And the night was dark, almost blind.
And my floor became hard as a stone,
and outside the door the man was standing
and outside the door I heard him crying.

Translated by Ruth Whitman

And Yet

My skin is so thin
that a single bullet,
one small steel bee
can kill me,
can kill you,
can kill him,
my dears.

My heart is so small
that it won't hide all
of my tears,
and if even one drop spilled
it would choke me,
it would choke you,
it would choke him,
my dears.

My life is so hard
that no boats at sea
or trains on the land
can ever take me
where I want to go,
my dears.

And yet—
with death stalking me,
hiding my tears,
desperate—
I am an arrow set in the bow
and my will is the hand

that aims me
where I will go
and will arrive,
my dears.

Translated by Seymour Levitan

YIDDISH

Mendel Naigreshel

Mendel Naigreshel was born in Nai-Sandz, Galicia, in 1903. Growing up in Vienna, he became a district attorney in juvenile courts. After the Nazis annexed Austria, he was imprisoned in the concentration camps of Dachau and Buchenwald. Nine months later, however, he was permitted to emigrate to Brazil, where he lived for two years until coming to America. His collections of poetry include In Black Realms *(1924),* Tents *(1930), and* Round Days *(1935). He died in New York in 1965.*

What Will Remain After Me?

What will remain after me?
A door standing ajar,
a shelf of books,
old and dusty,
and an empty chair—
where I dreamed forth my poems,
that I believed in.
Poems that will lie hidden in a wooden drawer,
mute,
like unfinished letters.

What will remain after me?
Shoes and socks,
a shirt that once covered
a terrified heart.

What will remain after me?
A sunbeam
flickering at twilight
on a wall in a courtyard.

Nation

He is the primal rock. Gray, wise, and old.
I am a blond and singing wood.

He is the primal rock. Forged gray and hard.
I am a green wood murmuring its song.

He is the primal rock. Unmoving. Mute.
I am a wood that withers and wears out.

And He—is eternal. The starry night
drips cryptic writing on his face.

The moon bows silently to him. And when
the sun returns he radiates violence

whose breath is of the strength of all beginning.
He is the primal rock.

Translated by Joachim Neugroschel

Leib Neidus

Leib Neidus was born in Grodno, a predominantly Jewish town in Russian Poland, in 1890. Born of wealthy parents, he attended a Russian gymnasium, but was expelled in 1905 for taking an active role in the Jewish Socialist Territorialist movement. From the age of ten he wrote poems in Hebrew, Yiddish, and Russian, but as he grew older he wrote chiefly in Yiddish. His first book of poetry, Lyrics, *was published in Vilna in 1915. In 1917, he translated some Pushkin stories for use in the emerging Yiddish schools. In 1918 he published two collections of poetry,* The Pipe of Pan *and* The Awakened Earth. *He was a prolific writer in his last years, spurred on by the knowledge that he was dying of heart disease. He died in Grodno in 1918. His small collection* Intimate Melodies *appeared posthumously in 1919.*

In an Alien Place

For whole nights—(don't ask how many)
I was rich with suffering and dreams . . .
I longed for you as a sailboat longs
for the cool swell of the river.

I longed for you as a dark soft curl
of woman's hair longs for a flower,
as the blueness of the sky longs
for the rhythmic fables of bells.
Longed, as an empty cradle longs
for someone's tremulous sleep,
as the mirror longs for reflection,
as the beginning longs for the end.

I Often Want to Let My Lines Go

I often want to let my lines go without beat, without measure,
without squeezing my heart into iamb or trochee,
I want to speak in a language that's simple, direct,
and not file down my joy and my pain.

And the meter's so tight, it's four ells long,
let my lines go free, let out the reins,
clear and candid as a mother's look,
unrestrained, wild as life itself.

The muse kicks off her dainty cramped shoes,
surprised by the new unexpected feeling,
she runs barefoot, free, with a wild delight,
and sings when she chooses, her own melodies.

Translated by Ruth Whitman

I Love the Woods

I love the woods that stretch far back
And lean against the sunny sky:
No, not the woods—the lonely track
That cuts into it secretly.

I love the track bedecked with moss
And thick with flowers that men call weeds:
No, not the track—the lonely house
To which the winding trackway leads.

I love the house brightly arrayed
With blossom, hidden under green:
No, not the house—the lovely maid
Who lives there quiet and serene.

Translated by Keith Bosley

Melech Ravitch

Melech Ravitch (the pseudonym of Zekharye Khone Bergner) was born in Radymo, Galicia, in 1893. After World War I he moved to Vienna, where he was influenced by German Expressionism. In the early 1920s he moved to Warsaw, where, together with Uri Zvi Greenberg and Peretz Markish, he struggled against the realism obligatory in Yiddish poetry. In 1941 he settled in Montreal. His collections of poetry include the selection from his earlier volumes The Songs of My Songs *(1954), and* The Main Thing . . . I Forgot *(1969). Ravitch also compiled a three-volume biographical encyclopaedia of Yiddish writers,* My Lexicon *(1945-58), and wrote a two-volume autobiography,* The Story Book of My Life *(1962-64). He died in Montreal in 1976.*

Twelve Lines About the Burning Bush

What's going to be the end for both of us—God?
Are you really going to let me die like this
and really not tell me the big secret?

Must I really become dust, gray dust, and ash, black ash,
while the secret, which is closer than my shirt, than my skin,
still remains secret, though it's deeper in me than my own heart?

And was it really in vain that I hoped by day and waited by night?
And will you, until the very last moment, remain godlike-cruel and
hard?
Your face deaf like dumb stone, like cement, blind-stubborn?

Not for nothing is one of your thousand names—thorn, you thorn in
my spirit and flesh and bone,
piercing me—I can't tear you out; burning me—I can't stamp you
out,
moment I can't forget, eternity I can't comprehend.

A Poem—Good or Bad—A Thing—
With One Attribute—Flat

(Poem for people in the poetry-business—and not even all of them will understand.)

What's a poem? A flat piece of paper,
dotted with endless letters,
and you often take many such poems
and bind them into a book—and a book's flat too.

And the life the poem sings about projects and has endless forms,
has sound and motion, and is in you and outside you,
sometimes concave like a deep valley, sometimes convex like a
mountain peak,
and it streams like Niagara, roars like thunder, flashes like lightning.

Yet the world—a plague on it—
is made in such a way that the living truth fades away, fades away,
but a poem—simply a piece of paper, boneless, soft, and flat besides,
is indeed an eternal and lasting thing.

And everything that projects, moves within itself and around its
shape
can become eternal only when it's "eternalized"
into a poem on a piece of soft flat paper—
doesn't that make you burst?—and this projection around which you
led your life

becomes straightened out, softened out, flattened out on paper—
and only then can it live endless years.
It seems that God-world-man, this three-in-one thing
likes to pass into flatness. And what can be flatter than a flat poem?

Translated by Ruth Whitman

Twilight Thoughts in Israel

I lifted my eyes to the sky.
Twilight, and the sky was blue.
There is no place on earth where the sky is as blue
as it is here
at this hour.

A little cloud, a solitary lamb,
suddenly appeared in the sky,
its head bent to the blue pasture,
and step by step moved toward the setting sun,
quietly grazing.

But the sun was red, and the horizon red,
red as the border, as blood, as the front,
and only the grass in the lamb's mouth
was still blue, blue, blue.

Little lamb, why am I so sad?
Sad as a solitary stone
that weeps
and is unable to hear itself weeping.

Where did the night come from?
And where are
the last rays of light
or even the shadows
that retained at least some of the light?

Like the lamb in the blue sky,
I lowered my head dreamily
to the night
and said, or perhaps only thought
in my heart:
the suddenness of the night.
But what is suddenness?
Where does it fall from?

And I lifted my head
to the sky again,
and the moon was there,
looking about in amazement
at this alien century.
And her eternally smiling mouth
asked audibly:
Where am I?
But I couldn't answer.
What could I say that the moon doesn't know?

And then below on earth
I heard a small voice.
A blade of grass
growing in a clod of earth was talking to me.

The clod of earth clung to a stone,
and a drop of dew clung to the blade of grass,
and in the drop of dew was blue,
and the blue was a moon,
tiny as a grain of sand, a single poppy seed,
and the whole small universe
trembled in my hand.

I held it
and my hand moved,
and I thought:

YIDDISH

Is the clod of earth trembling?
Or is it my hand?
Or is the whole world trembling?
Then the clod of earth fell from my hand,
and I heard a child weeping.

Where was the weeping coming from?
From the deep empty pit of darkness?
Did the child fall into the dark?
And how could it live there,
when there was no one there
to give it
water, bread, and light?
How could it survive?

And the weeping came closer and closer
out of the night.
It was no longer coming from the pit,
the child was here,
wandering the world alone.
And I bent down and asked the child:
Who are your father and mother?
Tell me, my child, don't be afraid. Tell me,
and I will take you away from this place,
and if you are tired, I will hold you in my arms.

The child answered:
My father is dead, my mother is dead,
and my home is a place where miracles happen,
and I am going to it.
Then the child departed
and left the fear with me.

And then I realized that I hadn't heard a child's weeping,
that I was weeping,
that I was the one waiting for the miracle.

Translated by Seymour Levitan

Let Us Learn

Let us learn from the animals in the forests
to move in the path of the blazing sun,
living in the very present
not knowing that this day is now.

Let us learn from the birds—
isn't everything flight and song?
Why not live with narrow heads,
bright, multicolored, and without a thought?

Let us learn from the trees and grass
to sink roots into mud, water, and around stone.
Let us give up thinking, be as absolute
as growing things. After all, what is there to understand in the
world?

Let us learn from the omnipotent Being
who shrivels things and lets them grow, who builds and destroys,
who is eternal because He knows the secret of secrets,
most simple of all: there is no difference between life and death,

as it follows, no difference between death and life,
none between revelation and secret.
All that was, will be—YHWH—
and nothing comes between the sons of Adam and God.

Verses Written on Sand

In the garden. Summer's end. Evening. On a bench.
The second highest tower burns in the west.
The night wind has risen and with the rake
I begin to compose a poem in the sand:

We are destructive, and friends' blood
is as thin as water to us.
Can I ask God or man why this is so?
It seems relatively easy to be good.

Like the slaughterer's knife
we are always in the right.
I ask you again, God or man.
It seems so difficult to fully give way to strife.

We destroy, but who else sings on
about turning the other cheek to the oppressor—
And under our jackets we can hardly hide
the newly acquired weapon.

In the garden. Summer's end. Evening. I rise from the bench.
The darkness has eclipsed the last of the towers.
I simply say farewell to the emptiness
and in the darkness trample on my poem written in the sand.

Translated by Seymour Mayne and Rivka Augenfeld

Conscience

Like a dog before the dog-catcher's sling
I dash along
Before my own conscience,
With ears drawn in, flat out upon all fours,
Across the gaping town,
Down narrow alleys, between two high walls
I pant and ponder: what a frightful hunt!
Suddenly I am gripped by the neck:
Lost, all is lost! I shriek,
Shriek loud again when the grip is gone,
And at the dog-catcher's feet lie down—
And cower in silence
Before my conscience.

Fear pounds my brain, sparks glow before my eyes:
Oh might I go flat out upon all fours
Across the town once more . . .
Fear burns my brain, sparks glow in my doggy eyes.
The dog-catcher—now I see what I have so often heard—
Holds an iron hammer before us dogs, an executioner's sword;
And my skull is soft bone,
Will be smashed with such ease,
And brains will spurt out of my eyes.

I cower in silence
And in anguish
Lick the boots of my burning conscience.

Translated by Keith Bosley

Abraham Reisen

Abraham Reisen, poet and short-story writer, was born in Kaidonovo near Minsk in Byelorussia in 1876. His was a literary family, with his father, Kalman, his brother, Zalman, and his sister, Sarah, all writers. Along with Sholem Asch and N.D. Nomberg, Abraham Reisen was one of the main followers of Peretz. In 1914 he settled in New York and became a prolific contributor to the Yiddish daily newspapers. His poems, stories, and sketches were marked by compassion for the simple, often exploited Jews rather than by satirical attacks as was common among Haskalah *writers. Reisen's collected poems and stories were published in twelve volumes in 1917, though the following years added several additional volumes to his corpus. Reisen died in New York in 1953.*

The Family of Eight

Only two beds
For a family of eight—
Where do they sleep
When the hour gets late?

Three with the father
And three with the mother,
Small feet and fingers
Entwined with each other.

And when it comes time
To prepare for the night
Then Mama starts wishing
Her death were in sight.

And is it surprising
She'd rather be gone?
The grave's narrow too
But you lie there alone.

Translated by Marcia Falk

What Is the Case in Point?

What is the case in point. . . ?

What's the point of the rain?
Like dismal tears, the drops
Skid down the window pane.
My boots are torn
Just when the streets are soaked;
Soon winter will be blowing in,
And me without a warm capote. . . .

What is the case in point. . .?

What's the point of the candle flame?
The tallow drips and splatters
Until the light is gone.
So I flicker in this study house,
Just like that candle, dim and small,
Until the time I'll quietly die,
Cornered, near the eastern wall. . . .

What is the case in point. . . ?

What's the point of the clock
With its yellowed face,
Its wheezing tick and cursing tock?
But it isn't alive,
It's only a wound-up thing
Without desire or will.
The hour comes, it must ring. . . .

What is the case in point. . . ?

What's the point of my whole being?
To rot, to wither in my youth,
Long before I'm old and dying.

Eating charity and swallowing tears,
Sleeping on my fist, hard as stone,
Killing my life here,
Waiting for the life to come. . . .

Translated by Richard J. Fein

Newcomers

It was a foreign ship that sailed
    And brought us all this way;
A foreign captain guided us
    Across the wide wide sea.
The ship it rocked both to and fro,
    From side to side did sway,
And if it rocked a man to sleep
    He slept uneasily.

A new land and a foreign land—
Who are those people, who?
Someone has left a wife bereft,
With little children two,
A tiny cot, a garden plot,
A father white as snow,
And every heart is torn apart
By its own private woe.

How long will the ship sail, how long?
Each one began to brood.
We asked one of the sailors: he,
A foreigner, laughed out loud.
The night turned into day, the day
Returned beneath night's shroud,
Until the foreign captain steered
Us where a shoreline stood.

A foreigner came up to us:
"Healthy?" he snapped, and frowned;
And he inspected each of us
As you'd inspect a hound.
He looked into our eyes, our mouths—
Good reason might be found:
Had he but looked into our hearts
He would have seen a wound.

We shook each other by the hand
But our farewells were dumb—
And should we ever meet again
In all the years to come?
The city threatened from afar,
Frightening with its hum;
Dozens of languages we heard
And walked amid them dumb.

An Endless Chain

Widely we are scattered
Over hill and plain,
Each a link belonging
To an endless chain.

By all rivers—not of
Babylon alone—
Looking for a homeland
We have sat us down.

Nowadays we cherish
Every continent:
On the farthest shoreline
We have pitched a tent.

Vistula and Rhine are
Precious to us now,
And the wide, wide Dnieper
Murmurs sweet and low,

And the Hudson bids us
Welcome to the West:
Here upon its banks we
Shall at last find rest!

We can sing the tune, no
Matter what the song,
Any purling river
Makes us ache and long,

Any flag that flutters
Greets us as a friend,
Any ship that sails goes
To a brother's land!

Girls from Home

a New York picture

I walk along the bustling streets,
The sun is dipping in the west:
In dark processions Jewish girls
Are trudging to and fro, hard pressed.

O Jewish girls in factories!
I can see hidden by your gloom
The sweetness of the Jewish *shtetl,*
The brightness of the distant home.

You walk now upon streets of stone,
The earth, the sky are both concealed,
And yet your clothes are breathing still
The fragrance of the *shtetl* field.

And more and more I see as I
More closely concentrate my look:
The crowns of many thousand years
Are shining from beneath the yoke.

For you are all princesses, your
High birth sits in your gaze serene:
What slaves you have become now! Who
Shall take you to the King again?

Translated by Keith Bosley

Joseph Rolnik

Joseph Rolnik was born in Lithuania in 1879. He settled in New York in 1908 and began writing poems which broke away from the didactic social verse which dominated Yiddish poetry. He wrote of simple feelings and emotions. A major theme in his three volumes of poetry entitled Poems *(1915, 1926, 1935) is nostalgia of the New York tenement poet for his rustic Lithuanian home. Rolnik died in 1955.*

In Disguise

Each day, a certain hour:
I doff the royal mantle,
Take up the wanderer's staff,
Step out beneath my lintel.

I roam through markets, streets,
Past each walled house alone;
Each watchdog barks at me,
Each youngster throws a stone.

Strange latches scorch and scald;
Wounds come when the stone flies—
By now more than one king
Has wandered in disguise.

I'm Not Rich

I'm not rich: I've one coat for home,
For synagogue and for the road;
I trade in it on market days,
On feast days pray in it to God.

The dust of summer falls on it
And all the mud from autumn rain
And gutter-splashes: all the soaps
Will not wash off a single stain . . .

To parties and to funerals
I wear the same. I'm not rich. And
With all these stains upon me I'll
Arrive in heaven's promised land.

At God's Command

At God's command! Let him lead me
Wherever, however he wants . . .
I will not stand against him, but
Walk after him with confidence

On mountaintops, in deep ravines,
With my eyes open—and yet blind;
In wild beasts' lairs; the Father leads—
And the child softly treads behind.

Translated by Keith Bosley

Leah Rudnitsky

Leah Rudnitsky was born in Lithuania in 1916. She was active in Yiddish cultural life in the Vilna Ghetto, where her poetry won public acclaim. During the liquidation of the ghetto in 1943, she perished in either Maidanek or Treblinka.

Birds Are Drowsing on the Branches

Birds are drowsing on the branches.
Sleep, my darling child.
At your cradle, in the field,
A stranger sits and sings.

Once you had another cradle
Woven out of joy.
And your mother, oh your mother
Will never more come by.

I saw your father fleeing
Under the rain of countless stones,
Over fields and over valleys
Flew his orphaned cry.

Translated by David G. Roskies

Beyle Schaechter-Gottesman

Beyle Schaechter-Gottesman was born in Vienna. She spent her youth in Cernauti, Bukovina. After the war years under Nazi occupation, she came to the United States in 1951. Her first collection of poems, Foot-paths amid Stone Walls, *was published in 1972. She is presently editor of the Yiddish periodical* Kinder Zhurnal *and co-editor of* Afn Shvel.

Meditation

Overflowing eyes,
Heavy talk,
Thought penetrates
Every last corner.
A dark glow,
A yellow spark,
The world a flaming pyre.
Gloom runs over
The inklike night
And burns.
Thought and sorrow
Clasp hands—
Companions of long ago.

Translated by Gabriel Preil

YIDDISH

Jacob Isaac Segal

Jacob Isaac Segal was born in Solovkovitz, Podolia in 1896, of a family of scholars. He emigrated in 1911 to Montreal, where he worked as a tailor and later as a teacher at the progressive Yiddish school. As a child Segal wrote in Hebrew and Russian, but after 1916 he wrote almost entirely in Yiddish. In 1918 he published his first book of poems, From My World. *Later, he published two Yiddish literary journals which saw a total of four issues,* Nuances *(1921) and* Epoch *(1922). He wrote articles for the Montreal Yiddish paper* The Canadian Eagle *and for many years was president of the Canadian Jewish Writers Association. His books of poetry include* Poems and Praises *(1940),* A Jewish Book *(1950),* The Last Poems *(1955), and* Songs for Jewish Children *(1961). Segal died in Montreal in 1954.*

Candle

Your innocence snuffed out,
your frail thinness curtsied to Death—
today at the corner store I bought
a bit of wick for just a penny.

Pour a shard full of oil,
dip the white wick:
for the broken twig,
for my daughter's young body.

Memory sweeps up like a mist
from the roads and fields.
Sweet, the mouth of the fresh rain
in the new summer's sun.

My daughter, little bride,
in your white silk and silver veil
we must give you away.
From the night's distances
the young summer's wind
blows against my dark windowpane.

Rest

Such a calmness
upon your face—
Your every word
is a translucent song,

thin, perfect,
scintillating,
sharp as October's
crystal ring.

A breeze freshly blossoms
over your weariness,
a guest blows in—Death,
clothed in the lightest snow.

Throwing off his hat
and coat, he holds up
his grayish
proud head,

joins us at our table,
crosses his legs—
on a silvery afternoon
talk is filled with light.

Translated by Seymour Mayne

Zvi Shargel

Zvi Shargel was born in Chelm, Poland in 1905. He left for Palestine in 1926 and since 1961 has been cultural administrator and manager of Petach Tikva. His books of poetry include In Blue Light *(1937),* Sunny Doorsteps *(1968), and* Gates in the Mountains *(1973). He has also published two volumes of essays, one dealing with prose and one with poetry.*

Pictures on the Wall

Painted stars
make my mood heavy.
A drawn blueness wants to obscure the sky.
Trees, flowers, grass,
want to escape from the watercolors
and stand about me in the twilight.
Sheep and lambs run down a mountain,
tell of an imaginary shepherd,
and hear a market place,
and hear a forest,
and you may imagine
a young woman with singing limbs.

But the melody of the end of summer
casts off the veils
and brings in a sadness
of stalks cut down.
Changing visions arrive and depart
with the early rain
through closed panes.
Gray pigeons fly out of the frames,
and forbid me to look out the window.

So my eyes dip into cloudy rivers
and ask grace from the vibrant colors:
If you can't show me the sky,
show me the other side of passing,
the other side of death.

I Will Go Away

I will go away
and the table will remain bare,
uncovered.
The chair in brown and green
will await my eye, my hand.
I will go away
and the floor will remain behind,
waiting like a lamb.

In sleep my lurking
will seeth and storm,
will tear from gate to gate
and waken the delight
of rising up.
But I will already be behind the mountain,
caught by the wind,
calm,
and I will show you my way
if you have not seen it yet,
until today.

Dreams are guarding my departure.
My grief is being cut into beams
and the birds fly away.
But the great cloud
obscures the sun for me,
and the night bites into the stars.
I follow in the steps of the sheep.
No one will see,
no one will hear
anything.

Translated by Gabriel Preil and Howard Schwartz

Let Us Laugh

Let us laugh then, you and I.
Let us look into each other's eyes
as if we were lovers.
You, with a thousand eyes,
and I, with my two tired eyes.
Look,
look,
until the grief is gone.

Until the grief is gone
and you, its messenger,
and I.

Translated by Gabriel Preil

Eliezer Steinbarg

Eliezer Steinbarg was born in 1880 in Lipkany, a small Bessarabian town. Like his cousin, the Hebrew author Judah Steinberg, he became a teacher, and he directed the Hebrew-Yiddish school of Lipkany until 1920. He was known primarily as an author of mesholim, *or parables, which became quite popular in Eastern Europe in the 1920s through the dramatic public readings of Herz Grossbart. At the time of his death in 1932, Steinbarg was a leader of the cultural activities of the Jews of Czernowitz, Romania. His book of parables,* Mesholim, *was published a few months after Steinbarg's death.*

Where Is Justice?

It happened
In a second:
The door snapped
Shut and trapped
The mouse
In the house
Outraged
And caged!
(What luck! declared
Miss Sarah Baird)
Now a hungry cat
Out stalking a rat
With claws to scratch
Peeked through the latch
And began to meow
And curse and meow,
"What's the meaning of this!
Where is justice?
In that fancy house
That lucky mouse
Lives like a prince—
Which made him wince—
And I the noble cat am poor
And left to crouch beside the door!"

Shatnes *or Uncleanliness**

I'll tell you everything, I give you my word!
About a pillow made of silk and one
That's made of wool.
Wool?
Why that's absurd!
People must be gullible! It has more cotton
In it than anything else, I've heard!

*According to the *Halakah*, the traditional Jewish law, it is forbidden to weave wool and flax in the same cloth.

And what about the silky little pillow?
Threaded through with a golden fish and also
A turkey followed by a capon with a crown.
What's inside it?
What pious grandmas plucked:
the down
From feathery chickens slaughtered for the Sabbath.
The pillow is so soft and so exquisite.
It knows, of course, so don't remind it on a visit!

Addressing the woolen pillow in a nice
Soft silky voice—made to entice—
It whispered, "Do pardon me, but could you move away
And never, never touch me please!"
"But why?"
"Because it's not proper, I say."
"Oh, please!"
"When I say, 'it's not proper,' you have my word of honor!"
"Still, how dare you say such things?
Such words are not shed lightly, it stings!
Unless you mean to tell me even more?"
"Well, if it's all right? . . .
You are . . . don't take it amiss for I'm not libel
It's . . . what can I say . . . it's written in the Bible!
It's a law one never can relax.
You are a *shatnes*, a sin, a *mésalliance* of wool and flax!
Your pedigree is most unsavory, a blight!"
"Oh, I see, I see now, but wait!
If you are made of sweetness and I am drawn from mud—
A *shatnes*, then don't forget, remember what I state:
How many chickens, for your sweetness, paid in blood!"

Translated by Seth L. Wolitz

YIDDISH

The Umbrella, the Cane, and the Broom

Sing to whom a hallelujah? Whom endorse?
The umbrella! No one else, of course.
So worthy, well-to-do and ample,
Over us he spreads his wings. For example,
If he wants to fly to heaven's sector
Or be our true protector
Rain or shine, he can! To be brief indeed,
He is our watchman and our friend in need.

The cane comes up to the umbrella:
"The world, it leans on me," he yells, "I'm the older fella.
And my grandpa, bless him, it was he who split
The Sea of Reeds. So doff your hat, for I can hit!
If you don't obey me now, watch out!"

"*I* won't obey," the broom says with a shout,
"Me you'll never frighten.
I'm bigger than both umbrella and cane. I'm a titan!
Here I'm boss," he bays, "I'm big and wide.
Whoever I've no use for—swish—I sweep outside."

The master of the house, peeved,
Overheard them in the room.
"Are they masters, too, the cane, umbrella, *and* the broom?
What then's *my* worth here? Where's *my* prestige?" he grieved.

"You," they yelled, each of the three,
"God made to cater unto me!"

The Horse and the Whip

"May an unforeseen disaster
Overtake your worthy master,
The wagoner, Reb Benjamin,
And strike at you along with him,"
The horse was saying
to the whip and neighing,
"Did you ever
Hear of such a thing? I never . . .
Tell me why I'm always beaten.

And for nothing, too! You think it's fun to drag this dray?
Remember, first of all, I haven't even eaten
Half a barley grain today.
Not to mention oats! Poor
Me! But go talk to a whip, a boor!
If your hide felt this stinging tanning
You'd stop that fanning,
Flogging, flaying.
What, again . . . . ? I'll raise a rumpus on the streets by neighing . . ."

"Shut up," the whipstick crackles its long tongue.
"It's true, that draggin' this here wagon,
And to top it off, on an empty stomach, naggin' . . .
Well, it's possible to pop a lung
But when I whip, you see—
Just between . . . um . . . you and me—
It's not 'cause you don't want to drag
The wagon. They ought to chop your head for this:
You ass! Your horse-sense went amiss!
You let yourself be harnessed—nag!"

The Bayonet and the Needle

A man (a Tom, a Dick, or some such epithet)
Comes from the wars with gun and bayonet,
And in a drawer he puts them prone,
Where a thin needle had lain alone.

"Now there's a needle hugely made,"
The needle ponders as it sees the blade.
"Of iron and steel, no doubt, it sews metal britches,
And quickly, too, with Goliath stitches,
For a Gog-Magog, perhaps, or some other giant."

But the bayonet is thoughtfully defiant.
"Hey, look! A bayonet! A little midget!
How come the town's not all a-fidget
Crowding round this tiny pup?
What a funny sight! I've got to tease this bird!
Come, don't be modest, pal! Is the rumor true? I heard
You're a hot one. When you're mad the jig is up?
With one pierce, folks say, you do in seven flies!"

The needle cries, "Untruths and lies!
By the Torah's coverlet I swear
That I pierce linen, linen only . . . it's a sort of ware . . ."

"Ho ho," the gun explodes in laughter.
"Ho ho ho. Stabs linen! It's *linen* he's after!"

"You expect me, then, to stitch through steel?"
The needle asks. "Ah, I feel
If I, like you, were bigger . . . "

"Oh my barrel's bursting," roars the gun, "my trigger—
It's tripping! Oh me! Can't take this sort of gaff."

"Pardon me," the needle says. "I meant no harm therein.
What then *do* you do? You don't stitch linen, you don't stitch tin?"

"People! We stab people!" says the bayonet.

But now the needle starts to laugh,
And it may still be laughing yet,
With ha, and hee, and ho ho ho:

"When I pierce linen, one stitch and then another, lo—
I make a shirt, a sleeve, a dress, a hem.
But people you can pierce forever,
What will you create from them?"

Translated by Curt Leviant

Moishe Steingart

Moishe Steingart was born in Poland in 1912. He came to the United States in 1927. His poems were published in various Yiddish journals here and abroad. His first book of poems, Alein, *appeared in 1950. In 1979 he was awarded the Harry & Florence Kovner National Jewish Book Council Award for his second book of poems,* In Droise Fun Der Velt.

The Last Fire

The sun burns out
From singed trees—
The leaves wither away the day.

I hear the clouds rising,
An open world—
All is awake.

The sky is limpid—
I thinner—more transparent—
Become pure awe.

The eyelids droop
The heart gives out
Silence.

God, You are too much!

Generations

The generation before me departed too soon.
And I suddenly am old.
Slowly day by day I am diminished.

The horizon grows narrow and narrower,
Where the sun sinks, day falls.
Curiously I look about me.

The more the days pile up on me
And brighten the silver in my hair
The closer I come to a lost generation
And see myself reflected
At every step and turn.

Twilight increases. The dusk sharpens.
The silver in my hair brightens the way.
With head straight and hesitant step
I go where the sun with its colors falls down.

Translated by Gabriel Preil

YIDDISH

A. N. Stencl

A. N. Stencl was born in 1897 near Sosnowice in Poland. In 1919 he went to Holland, and in 1921 he traveled the German countryside and worked with peasants. He published his first book of poems in 1923. Since 1934 he has lived in London. His books include Whitechapel Shtetl of Britain, *a selection from his previous books, published in 1961.*

Ezekiel

Terror swoops down on his heart like a vulture.
Wheel within wheel in the heart of him quivers,
Everything seen shatters in fragments,
And as in a water-mirror shivers.

Pinions over him and within him,
An eagle his soaring head of hair,
His bowels squirming eels in the gullet
Dribble transparent and clear.

By his own blood he counts the days,
But each drop means something else.
By the paw of a lurking lion
The coming days he tells.

That face there among the waves
With furrows quaking with awe,
How it convulses and churns
With its twisted slavering jaw!

The fists filled thick with hair,
And the lips naked, without beard,
Wheel within wheel wild creatures!
Doing—the unspoken word!

How easy now to endure all things.
A repeated word is Israel!
And how easy it will be to endure
What the coming days foretell—

Terror swoops down on him like a vulture,
Wheel within wheel his blood quivers with dread,
And the lurking beast behind him
With his heart is being fed.

Silent are the harps, silent the willow trees.
Only in his ears the clanking of a chain,
And in the link-in-link, the iron,
The coming days he sees.

Translated by Joseph Lettwich

Abo Stoltzenberg

Abo Stoltzenberg was born Abraham Abo Stoltzenberg in Glina, Galicia, in 1905. As a youth he participated in amateur Yiddish theater productions of his father. He studied in a heder *and in a Polish gymnasium. In 1923 he emigrated to New York, where he was persuaded to write in Yiddish instead of Polish. He worked in a variety of jobs from garment worker to messenger boy. His poetry had much in common with Di Yunge, the avant-garde group of Yiddish poets. He died of cancer in New York in 1941, only a few days before the appearance of his first collection of poetry,* Poems.

In Vistas of Stone

In vistas of stone
we blossom like jasmine,
becoming green like May;
on evening walks
we rustle like forests,
and blossoms fall from us
like snow.

At night,
tense as wounds,
we glow like glowworms
in a field,
by all our roots connected
with the deepest wells
of the world.

What Am I?

A weeping tree,
a barren field,
a thorn blazing up,
a lazy beast
ignorant of its fate,
an ox
bound to God's yoke.

YIDDISH

The French Mood

When the snow starts melting
and the mud begins to flow,
there comes into the city
an aristocratic little lady,
rich feathers and black flowers
on her hat,
but with no shoes on.
And barefoot
she walks in the mud.

She is the French Mood
and she is worse than a skunk.
Chickens die as she passes;
barrels of water become unclean;
broth turns sour,
and children come down with measles
in every house.

She prefigures
a great conflagration,
and people curse her
and avoid her steps.
Master of the Universe,
You who preserve us
from all troubles,
preserve us also
from the French Mood.

Translated by Gabriel Preil and Howard Schwartz

Abraham Sutskever

Abraham Sutskever was born in 1913 near Vilna. He was a leader of the Young Vilna group before the war and escaped the Nazi occupation by fleeing to Russia. Influenced by Moishe Leib Halpern and the Introspectivists, Sutskever is editor of the Yiddish literary magazine Goldene Keit. *He lives in Israel.*

On My Wandering Flute

A barefoot tramp on a stone
in evening-gold
brushes the dust of the world away.
A bird in flight
darts out of the wood
and grabs the last tatter of sun.

And there's a willow near a pond.

A path.
A field.
A trembling meadow.
Hidden footprints
of hungry clouds.
Where are the hands that make miracles?

And there's a fiddle that's alive.

What can I do in such an hour,
O my thousand-colored world—
except
gather this red beauty
into the wind's purse
and bring it home for supper.

And there's desolation like a mountain.

Song for a Dance

I invite you, child, to dance. You come. I bow my blond head,
bending it down to the ground.
Eager, warm, this is how I see you:
a yielding ear of wheat, your arm, your knees,
the singing outlines through your skyblue dress
and—your eyes—velvet joy—
I forget where I am. I become a springtime stream,
singing my heart out through every atom
of my blood. And then, and then—and only this is real—
we twine our hands together and we both
are equal in our dance.

And suddenly we go, a stormy journey
through big dark woods, over night and day,
over time. The world hides somewhere in a corner.
I don't know who I am. I think: I'm evening gold, I'm you,
I'm even a swallow. . . . Shouts fly by, rivers, cities,
everything—in our dance, with red and violet
and green. You cry. I listen. Your look falls on me like fire.
I think, you're a sailboat somewhere on the sea
and I a salty wind, in a duel with you.
You struggle. I spank you with foam. And we both
are equal in our dance.

Landscape

The sky—like a lunatic's dream—
has no sun in it. It blooms and laughs in a
hot full wild
rosetree in the meadow.
The wind is a magician. It buttons
day to night.
A root babbles something to a root.
A cloud laughs
in its sleep. A lightning eye blinks from the wood.
Birds fly by like falling stars.

Songs to a Lady Moonwalker

1
I've known you since the time
you were amphibian.
I remember our sin's firstness.
you love me?—I love you, yes.

We paired ourselves together
under silver weather.
Our love increased
as though it rose from yeast.

2
With a silver broom
you sweep the dust from my dreams,
cleaning the little room. Through the pane
a twig of lilac gleams.

You stretch your hand to salve
and smooth my forehead clear
as your nightgown flutters in folds
and buttons your breast to a star.

3
Stormbent I'll brush your secret
as a sail brushes a wave—
but your secret is tight with guilt,
the sealing wax of love.

My lust is: I must unveil
that landscape of terror and good.
Your secret that sings like a fiddle
must yield to my winging blood.

4
Who is he, that third one, as soon
as I fondle you, dares to protest?
It's your crazy love in the moon
who rules from a silver throne
on the blackest twig in the forest.

There can't be three of us
when quicksilver fills us with chills.
My envious skin will ripple
when that moonnik sucks out your pupil
and kisses your footsteps with pearls.

Choose, for choose you must.
Get rid of that bane of my life.
Nothing him less than dust,
let him burn in a silver log,
you bird, you dream, you wife.

YIDDISH

The Banks of a River

From a high mountain I see how the banks of a river
shimmer. In the distance
near the horizon they darken and wrangle,
then light up silvergreen and violet,
then darken again. I look down
into the river where my face's tinder is quenched
and my body shines clear, transparent,
and I say to the east, west, north, south:

Look and see
how beneath choked leaves and houses
in cold riverwriting my name is written.

Broadcast it all over the world.
Amen.

How

How and with what will you fill
your cup on the day of freedom?
In your joy are you willing to feel
yesterday's dark screaming,
where skulls of days congeal
in a pit with no bottom, no floor?

You will look for a key to fit
the lock shivered in the door.
You will bite the streets like bread
and think: it was better before.
And time will gnaw you mute
like a grasshopper caught in a fist.

They'll compare your memory
to an ancient buried town.
And your alien eyes will tunnel down
like a mole, like a mole . . .

Song of Praise for an Ox

(from the African Cycle)

Come marvel at my ox.
He has no equal.
His father was the sun,
his mother—the moon.

Whiter than the first spurts of milk
from a woman
giving suck, so is the whiteness of his brow.

In his eyes you can see the future,
but don't pry them open
if they're drowsy at the moment.

His horns are the masts of a ship
carrying great treasure in its belly.

Girls are transformed in the shimmer of his splendor.
They feel in their blood
the warmth of unknown mouths.

Come marvel at my ox.
He has no equal.

Wherever he bathes—the rivers become sweet.

Poetry

The last dark violet
plum on the tree,
delicate and tender as the pupil of an eye,
blots out in the dewy night
all love, visions, trembling,
and at the morning star the dew
becomes airier—
that's poetry. Touch it without
letting it show the print of your fingers.

Under the Earth

Are there birds twittering under the earth,
choking back
their holy tears in their thin necks,
or is that throbbing under the earth
once-used words that seem invisible birds?

Wherever my feet have the wisdom to walk,
over snow, over hay, over drunken fire,
they feel words,
the souls of words,
it's a pity my feet can't hold a pencil . . .

Like a snakecharmer
I stop my feet in their going:
here and here and here
here they are, here.
Once-used silence.
Once-used places.
And I dig with my hands—bony spades,
down to where the black
palaces burst,
where words throb
hidden in violins.

Translated by Ruth Whitman

Yiddish

Shall I begin at the beginning
like Abraham
my namesake and hack the idols to bits?
Shall I let myself be translated alive?
Shall I plant my tongue
and wait for it to turn
into legendary
raisins and almonds?
Why the cutting
jibe
from my brother-poet
that my mother-tongue is dying?
Surely we'll sit by the Jordan
a hundred years from now and speak it.

For there remains
the nagging question
Where? If you can see it,
show me where
the Berditchever's prayer,
Yehoash
and Kulbak's song
are straggling toward destruction.
Show me where the language is going under.
Is it at the Western Wall?
If it is, I'll go there,
and like a lion
clothed in fire,
I'll swallow our language alive before it goes under
and wake the coming generations with a roar like thunder.

Toys

Love your toys, my darling,
your toys even smaller than you.
And at night when the fire is sleeping
cover them up with stars.

Let the little gold horse put his nose
in the cloud shadowed grass so sweet.
Put the little boy's shoes on his feet
whenever the sea eagle blows.

Put the panama on your doll's little head
and a little bell in her hand.
For not even one has a mama,
and they cry to God in their bed.

Love them, your heirs to the crown,
I remember a day of woe—
seven little streets with dolls in each one,
and not one child in the town.

Translated by Seymour Levitan

YIDDISH

A Cartload of Shoes

The wheels hurry onward, onward,
What do they carry?
They carry a cartload
Of shivering shoes.

The wagon like a canopy
In the evening light;
The shoes—clustered
Like people in a dance.

A wedding, a holiday?
Has something blinded my eyes?
The shoes—I seem
to recognize them.

The heels go tapping
With a clatter and a din,
From our old Vilna streets
They drive us to Berlin.

I should not ask
But something tears at my tongue
Shoes, tell me the truth
Where are they, the feet?

The feet from those boots
With buttons like dew—
And here, where is the body
And there, where is the bride?

Where is the child
To fill those shoes
Why has the bride
Gone barefoot?

Through the slippers and the boots
I see those my mother used to wear
She kept them for the Sabbath
Her favorite pair.

And the heels go tapping:
With a clatter and a din,
From our old Vilna streets
They drive us to Berlin.

Translated by David G. Roskies

To My Child

Out of hunger
or out of great love—
but your mother can witness to it—
I wanted to swallow you, my child,
when I felt your small body cool
in my fingers,
as if I pressed in them
a warm glass of tea
and felt it turning cold.

Since you are no stranger, no guest,
on our earth one does not birth another:
one births oneself like a ring
and the rings link in chains together.

My child,
who in words is called: love,
and who without words are yourself love,
you—the seed of my every dream,
the hidden third,
who from the wides of the world
with the wonder of an unseen storm
have made two meet and flow together
to create you and complete our pleasure:—

Why did you darken the creation
as you did when you shut your eyes
and left me outside like a beggar
with a world blanketed in snow
which you shook off?

No cradle, whose every motion
holds within the rhythm of the stars,
had brought you joy.
The sun—for you have never seen it shine—
might as well crack and shatter like glass.
A drop of poison burned out your faith.
You thought
it was warm sweet milk.

I wanted to swallow you, my child,
to know the taste
of my anticipated future.
Perhaps you will blossom as before
in my veins.

But I am not worthy to be your grave.
So I bequeath you
to the summoning snow,
the snow—my first respite—
and you will sink
like a splinter of dusk
into the quiet depths
and bear greetings from me
to the small shoots beneath the cold.

Vilna Ghetto, January 18, 1943

Translated by David G. Roskies and Hillel Schwartz

J. L. Teller

Judah Leib Teller was born in Tarnpol, Galicia, in 1912. He emigrated to New York in 1921 and studied at Rabbi Isaac Elchanan's Yeshivah, City College of New York, and Columbia University. His books of Yiddish poetry include Symbols, Miniatures, *and* Poems of the Day.

Lines to a Tree

Around us speeches of birds. I tremble
with the passion before pairing.
We are both of one tribe.
My fingers dig in like roots
to the cool, dark depths.
For both of us the bark bursts,

the sap strives to emerge
and also the book.
The book and I, rooted like you,
with fear and trembling, involved
with rivers, earth and sun.
All nests are warm with whispering;
the birds tremble awake;
my hands on you, I seek your
knowledge, find your
longing.

Minor Key

The night lies blue and white
across the blanket.
My wife is porcelain
and I am like hail
in the windows.

Our dream repeats
our day.

You are right, comrades.
You smell of the revolution
like whiskey.
Your heads do not even turn.
When your stones hit my window
I won't care.

To the Divine Neighbor

I turn to You
not at noon,
but at twilight,
when smoke writes in the air
and is at the same time
erased.

Translated by Gabriel Preil and Howard Schwartz

YIDDISH

Malka Heifetz Tussman

Malka Heifetz Tussman was born in the Ukraine in 1896 and emigrated to the United States in 1912. In addition to several volumes of her own poetry, she has made translations of Dylan Thomas, Akhmatova, and Tagore into Yiddish. Ms. Tussman now lives in Berkeley, California, where she continues to publish in Yiddish journals and magazines.

At the Well

My whole life
pushing and straining,
and but a crack
I moved the stone
from the well
where in darkness
the water
was clear.
And now
when a star
blinks there,
at once
I taste tomorrow's
tears.

I Say

I say to the Almighty:

Ever-homeless Wanderer,
I would,
if but my heart were pure,
invite
you in, to spend the night.

Thou Shalt Not

for Yudka

In fire-script
a strict law raged against me.

The West in the background
crinkled
like a burning sheet.

Magically the script
wound itself around me
and annulled me completely
when I, a needle-ray,
descended
into the abyss of secret self.

Water Without Sound

The sea
tore a rib from its side
and said:
Go! lie down there, be
a sign that I
am great and mighty.
Go
be a sign.

The canal
lies at my window,
speechless.

What can be sadder
than water
without sound?

Love the Ruins

With one letter of your many names
you broke in—
and now you live
your own hot life in me.

With one sound of your many names
you pierced yourself in me—
and now you feed
on my heart's blood.

Soon
you will shatter me
from within.

Then gather up the splinters,
and love the ruins,
my God.

Songs of the Priestess

I. The Dream

What shall we do
with our God-kissed boy?
What shall we do?

He chases madly
with poison on his lips—
God's kiss—
like Tristan with the magic potion,
and sets nightmares ablaze
at the head of Isolde
and puts out the saintly smile
of the other,
sapping the life
from her white fingers.

What shall we do
with our God-kissed boy?
What shall we?

Soon he'll overcome the strongest guard
watching over the priestess.
Soon he'll break in
to her strict untouched seclusion.
Tonight the priestess saw him
in a dream,
and cried.
She cried at night.

What shall we do
with our God-kissed boy?
What?

He is God-sick, our boy.
He is death-sick, our boy.
It pursues him so—
God's kiss on his lips.
He keeps seeking the mate
of the kiss.
The mate of the kiss.

But God kisses only once.
Only once.
With the second,
He takes back the breath.

Should we pray for the death
of our boy?

II. Her Plea

Gather me up
like wheat.

Cut quickly
and bind me
before autumn's whirlwind
sweeps me away.

Hurry—
I am fully ripe
and all the fences are down.

Don't be afraid—
I don't have to grow any more.
The rain is yours.
I have been through
my rainstorms.

Gather me up
like wheat.

III. Her Lament

Love
drained me pale
and I became still
and I became thin
and weightless.

Flesh
toppled me over
and I became swollen
thick and heavy
with passion.

God,
where are you
not!
Even in the unclean
fires of hell,
I see the shadows
of your lashes.

And flesh is
a golem,
staring,
dumb,
and when it cries—
what a pity,
what a desolate
pity.

IV. Cradlesong

Rest, priestess,
at the crossroad
where
you were led
by your senses
and he
by his longing
for the last kiss.

Eternity?
That's what you sought?
And when you found a path
to the secret well,
you fell
as one falls
before the light of the Shekhina.
You scooped up a handful
of water
and it flowed out from your fingers.
You tasted only
a drop.

There is
no more.
And know
That even death
is not eternal.
There is only a moment
when a stumble bends your knees
and there is
no more.

Rest,
sleep,
swaddled in your own
two shuddering wings,
cradle your tremble
to the end.

Translated by Marcia Falk

Miriam Ulinover

Miriam Ulinover was born in Lodz in 1890 and died in Auschwitz in 1944. Much of her poetry has to do with Yiddish folklore.

Havdolah Wine

Everyone drinks Havdolah* wine
So I drink a few drops too.
Says Grandma sweetly earnest:
"My dear child: I must warn you

A girl who drinks Havdolah wine
Will grow a beard in no time,
So is it written in books
Over there in the bookcase."

I break into a cold sweat
And tap the edge of my chin:
Oh Thank God, still smooth and soft . . .
Only fright can make it bristle.

In the Courtyard

Summer morning—five o'clock
The courtyard's awake
Everyone's bustling about
Time to feed the hens.

Drawing the girl close to him
By the chicken coop
He gives her a tender kiss
And then a caress.

Frozen to the spot, the girl
Doesn't know what to do
And blood rushes to her face
The yellow hen gapes.

*Havdolah is the ceremony concluding the Sabbath.

Should the hen peck a red dot
From her blushing eyes
Then all the egg yolks will bear
The dreaded blood spot.*

Translated by Seth L. Wolitz

Moshe Yungman

Moshe Yungman was born in Eastern Galicia in 1922. He was taken prisoner by the Russians in World War II and worked in a forced-labor camp. After the war, he returned briefly to Poland, soon migrating to Italy, where he led Zionist groups. He emigrated to Israel in 1947. His collections of poetry include In a Daze *(1947),* In the Homeland's Shadow *(1954),* White Gates *(1964),* Smiles from the Holy Land *(1969),* Rainbows at the Head *(1973), and* In the Land of Elijah the Prophet *(1977). He lives in Kfar Tiv'on, outside Haifa.*

The Sacrifice

Links of fear
slowly become a chain,
binding my hands and feet.

My father never wanted
to lead me to the sacrifice.
He was bound as I was.
But he led me.

Now I lie on the altar,
my father inside me,
my grandfather inside me.

There is no escape—
no escape.

*A blood spot in an egg makes the egg unfit to eat, according to the laws of *Kashruth*.

Don't Say

Don't say I'll have to search farther for
a blade of grass,
a piece of sun.
Don't place me face to face again
with thorns
that men have designed for me.
Don't burn into me again
knives,
eyes,
fear of not being able to raise a hand.
Don't lay me down again
under everyone's feet.
Don't wake me up.

Translated by Marcia Falk

The Messiah

The streets also have eyes:
They stare out at night and stare,
Their fevered cobblestones glaring.

Will the Messiah sometime
Ride in on them with his following,
Their faces flushed, all of them singing?

Still . . . on the dark cobblestones
Of the streets two blind old Yemenite grandfathers
Drag heavy bundles of dreams to their Moriahs.

Translated by David G. Roskies and Hillel Schwartz

Encounter in Safed

Here the Messiah lives.
I walk down a small street
and stand enchanted before a wall—
the end of the world.

On the other side the Messiah stands.
Perhaps he has already forgotten
that he must come.
He has hidden himself behind a rock.

So I knock at the gate:
I am pure and without sin
and the sorrow of a thousand water-bearers
burns in me.
"What is it you want?" calls a voice from the depths.
I hear a cough, the sound of sandals.
Someone comes close.
"It is I." My breath is taken away. I stammer.
An icy chill runs down my hands.
In but a moment the little door will swing open
and the Messiah will appear in his splendor.

Safed. The sunset flickers in the deserted street.
An old woman stands in the narrow doorway
as in an old frame: "A Jew . . . who wants to be fed."
And she stretches out a half-dried bread:
"Take."

Melons

On small donkeys they bring in suns,
melon-gold which strains at the sacks.
The donkeys walk step by step
with slumbering chins
and drop the sound of bells note after note.

The street swallows the taste of melons.
And from barns, doors,
the donkeys are standing in pairs.
The entire world is suddenly sunny and bare.
And it is small and good and warm to touch.

So drunk they walk about with melon suns.
The sewers overflow with gold.
And the mountains in the distance.
With small suns they are riding toward evening.

And suddenly nothing. The sacks are empty, extinguished.
The driver busies himself by his donkey,
and looks around for someone to come
to redeem him.

Translated by Gabriel Preil and Howard Schwartz

YIDDISH

Aaron Zeitlin

Aaron Zeitlin, son of the Hebrew writer and mystic Hillel Zeitlin, was born in Gomel, a large Jewish town of the Ukraine, in 1898. As a youth he wrote both in Yiddish and Hebrew. In 1939 he was invited to New York from his Warsaw home to prepare for the premiere of a play he had written. Shortly after his arrival the war broke out; his wife, children, and parents, all of whom remained in Warsaw, were killed. His collections of poetry include Shadows on Snow *(1922),* Metatron: An Apocalyptic Poem *(1922),* Between Fire and Deliverance *(1957), and a definitive collection of all his poetry in two volumes published in 1967-70, including* Volume 1: Songs of Destruction and Songs of Faith, *and* Volume 2: Further Songs of Destruction and Faith and Janus Korshak's Last Walk. *He also wrote several dramas,* Yakov Frank *(1929),* Brenner *(1929), and* In No Man's Land *(1938), and a novel,* Burning Earth *(1937). Zeitlin died in New York in 1973.*

A Dream About an Aged Humorist

Last night I had a dream
whose paradox followed me
late into the day: a woman was
walking with an ox.

The ox—as I knew—is an acquaintance of mine,
a Jew, a humorist. He's in trouble,
senile, deaf, and half-blind
with the face of an old eunuch.
They don't laugh at his jokes. He smells of the grave.

Now he, that big ox, red, fat,
was walking proudly—and the woman with him
had the look of a flirt,
until he left her behind
and violently
rushed off to meet some kind of
bullish adventure.
He strutted about joyful and fresh
but I knew perfectly well it was he—
the worndown humorist, the ex-talent,
old and sadly wrinkled all over,
and when I thought of his new joke in my sleep,
I shuddered.

Text

We all—
stones, people, little shards of glass in the sun,
tin cans, cats and trees—
are illustrations to a text.

In some places they don't need us.
In some places they only read the text—
the pictures fall off like shriveled parts.

When a death-wind blows in the deep grass
and clears off from the west all the pictures
that the clouds set up—then
night comes and reads the stars.

The Empty Apartment

I was drawn to look at an apartment
where I once lived.
It stood empty,
dreaming of a person
who once made his home there—
me.

Lines
I wrote there
gathered themselves
around the windows
in flocks, like birds before flight.

Crawling
and quietly seething
was the astral body of an insect
I once squashed.

All kinds of almost nothings
were stuck
in the corners, in the shadows,
like dust under a brush,
looking with mousey fright
for a crack to escape into.

A very small imp
who lay naked under a wall,
jumped up at me:
Papa, how are you?

In the middle of the room stood a thought.
She stood there lost in thought
about the one who once thought about her
here one evening:
about me.

And when she noticed me,
she tore herself from the spot
and began to revile me.
You are, she said, a dark betrayer,
a runner-away, a disappearer,
a begetter
who abandons his offspring.

Translated by Ruth Whitman

Ode to Freedom

I love you, not because I love the guillotine
And not because I wish to flay the flayers
And not because I—like those sons of yours—
Have learned from wolves to gnash my teeth.
No, no, their red flag, their black wrath,
Their envy's fangs buckled with spleen
Whetted against what does not please the herd—
All this I always loathed and still shall loathe.
For this more likely would have stirred
Not love but hatred for your crown, O queen.

Your rabble's crazy laughter suits me ill
And foreign to me is its unjust will
That stops at nothing to achieve its ends
And in whose heat justice with iron blends.

My heart is not with those who drag before you
The tyrant's severed head or bleeding trunk;
I am not moved by struggling sansculottes
Whom hunger makes heroic, hatred drunk:
They will behead you swearing they adore you!

My heart is not with those who put up barricades,
Who kindle and burn in your exalted name;
And not with tribunes who can so inflame
Men's hearts with skillfully composed tirades
That they cry out for blood—and the herd soon
Puts executioner's apparel on
And to each sovereign's head lays bloody claim
And smashes and destroys the very thing
Which he, the slave, was lately worshipping
And bowing deeply down before their crown!

Nor yet, O Freedom, am I glad you take
Lodging among us because for your sake
The herd gives up home joys, and rears instead
An altar to the happiness of all!
I know: tomorrow it will wait to sell
Your head to Satan, and to change as well
Your heights into a vale of mortal dread
And your white temple into a red stall.

Only for this, O Freedom, are you dear:
That through the smoke that rolls into the sky
Above your bloody altar will appear
God's Kingdom! You are dear to me because
Your thunder brings us close to heaven on high,
Because hearts feel that nearer the day draws
When one who sifts the times will come, whose sifting
Mankind renewed towards God will be lifting,
And that above we have been spared a thought,
That earth has not been utterly forgot
Like a bad dream on memory's ebbtide drifting.

Translated by Keith Bosley

YIDDISH

Rayzel Zychlinska

Rayzel Zychlinska was born in Gabin, Poland, in 1910. She left her home in Warsaw during World War II and took refuge in Soviet Russia. In 1947 she returned to Poland, but left after one year for Paris. In 1951 she emigrated to New York. Zychlinska has published several volumes of her poetry, including Poems *(1936),* The Rain Sings *(1939),* To Fair Shores *(1948),* Silent Doorways *(1968), and* Autumn Squares *(1969).*

Remembering Lutsky

Today I was awakened by the moon
that suddenly remained
in the empty sky,
and maybe by the dead poet
who still makes his rounds
in the cafeteria.
In his green bow-tie,
with his book in his hands,
he makes his rounds
in the cafeteria.
He reads a new poem to colleagues,
asks their advice,
quarrels,
erases.
I still go there, looking for him
among the empty tables.

The Clothes

The clothes in which you saw me—
they'll never get old,
with all their colors
they go on blossoming in my closet.
The violet dress is whispering to the green
a green and grassy secret,
the rose clings to the yellow
and at their hems
flowers continue to blossom.
Removed and special in a corner of its own,
its arms thrown over its shoulders,
my blue dress is dreaming of you.

My Mother's Shoes

At night my shoes look at me
with my mother's tired eyes,
the same look
of having gone through it all, and not arrived,
of having chased after luck, and missed it.
I go up into skyscrapers
and sink down in the valleys between them.
At night I come back
in my mother's shoes
bedecked with the patient dust of years.

Translated by Marc Kaminsky

III *English*

Introductions to Book III
by Howard Schwartz and Anthony Rudolf

The United States, Canada, Israel, South Africa, Australia, India and Sri Lanka
by Howard Schwartz

I The United States

The situation of the modern Jewish poet in America is one deeply connected to the nature of Jewish life in the United States. From the beginning of this century until at least 1960 the primary ambition of most American Jewish poets was to make a contribution to the rich English language literary tradition. With a few exceptions of poets such as Charles Reznikoff, Karl Shapiro and Alter Brody, most poets of the older and middle generations saw Jewish life and tradition at the periphery of their lives, and in some cases there was even a shrinking away from it. In most cases, however, these poets chose to write only a few, usually deeply felt, poems on Jewish themes. They simply did not regard themselves primarily as Jewish poets, but rather sought to define themselves as American poets. Delmore Schwartz, for example, was the very model of the New York poet, and the three poems included are virtually unique among his writings. And even these poems do not attempt to resolve any issues of his cultural heritage, but are based on biblical sources in the classical manner.

Unlike the Hebrew or Yiddish poets of the same generation, American Jewish poets did not have a uniquely Jewish language to write in, nor was the cultural context in which they lived primarily a Jewish one. Furthermore, these poets, as most of the Jews of their generation, had abandoned the rigorous demands of the Orthodox Jewish lifestyle, largely losing touch with all but a few remaining rituals and traditions. Perhaps the decisive factor was the desire on the part of most Jews to blend into the American culture and to succeed as part of it, on its terms.

The first things to be discarded were the external signs of the foreigner—the dress and language of the European Jews. The film *Hester Street* accurately conveys the prevailing social pressures dominant during that period in which recent immigrants did not hesitate to make disparaging remarks about the Old Country style of the newest immigrants. The transition from the Old Country mentality to that of the New World took place remarkably swiftly, within a single generation. And of course such a transition had its price.

One tragedy of this rush towards cultural assimilation was the abandonment of the Yiddish language. The new immigrants almost universally chose not to pass their native Yiddish tongue on to their children. Instead, every effort was made to speak English, at least in the presence of the children. And the children, of course, were more than happy to make the new language their own, as children are even more susceptible to cultural pressures than their parents. As a result the "awkward and embarrassing" Yiddish was lost in a single generation and now faces the likely fate of shortly becoming extinct.

Although those caught up in this drastic cultural assimilation were not aware of it, they had set the scene for an intense longing for the lost world that manifested itself in the third generation. This nostalgia, coupled with a growing sense that the illusion of being Americans and nothing else was starting to wear thin, led many young Jews, and among them many Jewish poets, to attempt to find some kind of foothold in their cultural heritage. Such longing is the stuff out of which poetry is written. This sense of absence and loss led to the desire to seek out in memory, ritual and the written record something which would ease the pervasive sense of cultural dislocation which many young Jews felt. And of course they did not have to look very far back in order to find what they were seeking: a rich cultural tradition that had an abundance to offer even to those who refused its more ascetic and rigorous manifestations.

For these reasons, therefore, there are sharp divisions in the attitudes and use of Jewish thematic material among the generations of

American poets, for what the older generations were only too willing to discard, the younger generation found to be immensely valuable. At the present time there does not exist anywhere a Jewish cultural and religious revival to rival that of the current generation of American Jews from the ages of fifteen to thirty-five. Although the numbers involved in this revival are small in terms of the total number of American Jews, and located in definite centers, such as New York and Boston, the trend is quite apparent. Perhaps the most intriguing forum of this religious/cultural revival is the emergence of the *Havurah* in which the younger generations of Jews have sought out a form of Jewish affirmation at odds with the increasingly stagnant modes of Conservative and Reform Judaism. And already there has been a rich early harvest from those associated with this revival in practice and in spirit. The writings of young poets such as Joel Rosenberg, Gary Pacernick, Stephen Mitchell, Marcia Falk, Gerda Norvig and Jack Myers, to name only a few, hold the promise of an emerging generation of poets who regard themselves as Jewish American writers, rather than the reversed emphasis of the older generations.

In their search for models among the older generation of American poets, these younger poets rediscovered Charles Reznikoff. In his long career, Reznikoff's work had gained some attention in the 1930s, only to fall into obscurity until the appearance of *By the Waters of Manhattan* in 1962. Reznikoff's reputation has grown steadily since that time, and by the time of his death in 1976 he had finally become recognized as the first major Jewish American poet, in the sense that Jewish concerns were central to his work.

Reznikoff's unique role as a poetic chronicler of Jewish events can best be understood when his writings are seen in the context of the Jewish writings of the period. It is not hard to imagine that had Reznikoff not been born in Brooklyn, he might easily have become a Yiddish poet, for both in his subject matter and poetic rhythms his poetry has much in common with Yiddish literature. There is the same tendency to divide poetic effort between short lyrics and long narratives, and Reznikoff is a master of both forms. Usually the lyrics convey his personal perceptions, and the narratives describe the lives of his fellow Jews in America or Israel, or, as in the epic poem "Holocaust," the Jewish suffering at the hands of the Nazis. And as with the Yiddish poets there is the same blend of openly nationalistic feelings and an acute awareness of the flaws and pressures of the environment.

Ever since the days of Ezra Pound, American poetry has suffered from an excess of labeling. Pound initiated the Imagist Movement and then a succession of other movements, such as Vorticism. Other poets of the period felt compelled to do the same, primarily as a device for gaining attention for their work. Thus, with Louis Zukofsky taking the lead, Reznikoff became a member of the Objectivists; the other members, beside Zukofsky, were George Oppen and Carl Rakosi, all of whom are represented in this collection. Zukofsky's definition of their goal was the "desire for what is objectively perfect, inextricably the direction of historic and contemporary particulars." But it is Reznikoff's down-to-earth definition of their objectives that probably comes closest to the truth: "The Objectivist Press is an organization of poets who are printing their own work and that of others they think ought to be printed."

In truth, Reznikoff's poetry had little in common with that of the others, and this grouping makes no more sense than including the poetry of both Robert Duncan and Robert Creeley under the category of "Black Mountain Poetry." But the persistence with which such labels cling once they have been made is astonishing, and explains why Reznikoff's work was lumped together with the other Objectivists as an historically interesting but essentially minor footnote to the Poundian era. Actually, nothing could be further from the truth. It is to Reznikoff's everlasting credit that he continued to draw his inspiration from very unfashionable Jewish sources, despite the evident embarrassment with which it was received.

Far more loyal to Poundian principles and experiments were the other three Objectivists. Louis Zukofsky, the founder, was, even for our own time, a radical experimenter. His central work, *A*, was developed over a long period, much as Pound's *Cantos* were, and is an obscure and difficult work. The poems of Zukofsky included here were selected from the first volume of the poem *A* to appear. These selections show a familiarity with and understanding of traditional Jewish sources, especially the Talmud. The poem "Expounding the Torah," in particular, has the structure of a Talmudic discussion.

George Oppen is another highly idiosyncratic poet whose poetic style presents great difficulties for the novice reader. Oppen's use of the techniques of association and juxtaposition is the dominant element in his poetry, and the long poem included here, "It All Went Up in Smoke," inspired after a visit to Israel, is a good example of how effective his technique can be. Carl Rakosi, on the other hand, is more a poet of individual moments and impressions, and in fact he uses words much in the way the French Impressionists used paint.

One other poet of Reznikoff's generation deserves to be ranked in the forefront of Jewish poets concerned in particular with their Jewish heritage. This is Alter Brody, whose long poem "A Family Album" is certainly one of the major discoveries included here. This poem has long been out of print, but it has the energy and distinctive vision that is characteristic of the finest poems. And so sustained is it that it can only cause the reader to marvel.

Of the next generation of American poets, many of them born in 1913, the first widely recognized American poet to publicly declare himself to be a Jewish poet was Karl Shapiro, who titled one important book *Poems of a Jew.* Shapiro was also one of the first American poets to seek out images and symbols from the treasure house of Jewish legend, the Midrash. In his poem "The Alphabet," for example, Shapiro makes use of legends associated with the letters of the alphabet and of the legendary Book of Life that is said to be kept in Paradise.

It should be understood that this propensity for Jewish subject matter was still very much the exception. Far more common in the period of the Twenties until the Forties was the use of the usual Greek-Western system of literary allusions, as best exemplified by T. S. Eliot. And even this was not the predominant trend, as the majority of poets writing at that time attempted to shake off all mythological and religious systems and chose to play down the religious elements in their lives and work. Thus for the primary Jewish poets of this period, such as John Hollander, Irving Feldman, Anthony Hecht, Stanley Burnshaw, Howard Moss, and Arthur Gregor, the Judaic material is primarily essayistic or elegiac. It is only in recent years that these poets have turned to what Harold Bloom has termed "diasporic Jewish myth-making."

Only in the cases of two other well-known poets of this same generation, David Ignatow and Muriel Rukeyser, and of two others whose work has only recently emerged, Rose Drachler and William Pillin, is there to be found an unabashed use of this very same "Jewish myth-making." Ignatow's poetry is pervaded by his sense of his own Jewishness, and Yiddish echoes can also be found in his work. Nor are these echoes an accident, as Ignatow is a cousin of the Yiddish poet Dovid Ignatow. Muriel Rukeyser's poetry, on the other hand, is written in a myriad of styles and voices, although Rukeyser manages to preserve her identity no matter what form or style she has put her hand to. Her central Jewish poem, "Akiba," included here, is an epic response to the biblical and talmudic traditions. Rukeyser's *Collected Poems,* recently published, is a remarkable testament to her long career. Because she has never been associated with any school or group of poets, her work exists as something of an undiscovered continent to the reader who is fortunate enough to come across it.

Rose Drachler, whose work was clothed in obscurity until the last ten years, writes poems that have a spareness and authority that is rare among American poets. Her voice is as distinctive as that of an oracle, and it is clear that she is speaking from emotional depths in her poems, which resonate for long afterwards. She may well be one of the finest women poets writing in English, and her work is surely destined to become much better known.

Another poet who certainly deserves to be better known is William Pillin. Pillin's books have all been published in small editions that have reached a small but select audience, among whom his work is widely admired. Pillin's poetry is distinctly and uniquely his own, and it it almost impossible to read in it the influence of other poets. Rather, Pillin seems to be a poet who, like Blake, thrives and grows in private, and emerges one day with a fully matured poetic voice and a coherent vision of the world.

Still more open and flexible in their use of Judaic material are the poets born at the end of the first generation of American Jewish poets, between 1920 and 1935. These poets, whose influence is currently in its prime, include Philip Levine, Robert Mezey, Donald Finkel, Marvin Bell, Bert Meyers and Harvey Shapiro. All are powerful poets who have tried hard to break away from the overly academic attitudes of the earlier generation, and their poems are characterized by open expression of a wide range of emotions, from the despairing to the ecstatic. Although these poets have all retained their primary identity as American poets, they are open in their frequent disenchantment with the world they live in and convey a sense of pulling away from their native culture rather than of being attracted to it. While each of these poets has devoted only a small portion of his work to poems based solely on Jewish themes, these particular poems are usually exceptionally beautiful and moving, and reveal an intensity of feeling for their heritage that is missing from their considerably cooler predecessors. Furthermore, it is apparent that what can only be called an intrinsically Jewish outlook on the world pervades all of their poetry and has deeply influenced the essence of their poetic voices.

Perhaps the finest of these poets is Philip Levine, whose development reveals much about the poetic currents of the past fifteen years. Levine's first book of poems, *Not This Pig,* is characterized by a down-to-earth, almost brutal attitude toward existence. But by the time of the publication of *They Feed, They Lion,* ten years later, Levine has obviously been affected by the brand of Surrealism practiced by poets such as Zbigniew Herbert and Pablo Neruda. Yet Levine does not allow himself simply to imitate these styles, but rather to create a fusion of his own realistic voice with the unexpected surreal turns that characterize so much of contemporary European poetry. The product of this fusion is some of the finest and most original poetry written in recent years.

Somewhat less intense is Levine's next book, *1933*, which is primarily a work of reminiscence. It is from this book that the title poem "1933" is taken, which brings together all the complex emotions of Levine's relationship with and memories of his father, and yet remains a remarkably sustained and lyrical poem. In his most recent books Levine seems to have come full circle to the charged, realistic poetry he began with. Some critics have voiced disappointment with this development, but Levine remains an unpredictable poet of great power who can write convincingly and preserve his own voice no matter what style he chooses to write in.

Although the body of Robert Mezey's work is slim, some of his poems are extraordinarily lyrical, and at least two of them, "New Year's Eve in Solitude" and "I Am Here," must be reckoned as masterpieces.

Another extraordinary poet is Donald Finkel, who is able, more so perhaps, than any other American poet, to capture the primitive and elemental aspects of myth and experience in his poems. Good examples of this ability are demonstrated in his poems "Genealogy," "Finders Keepers" and "How Things Fall." Finkel peers into the fire burning inside the cave and his poems report back the visions that take form in the flames.

Marvin Bell is another poet of the same generation as Levine, Mezey and Finkel, and, in fact, all four attended the Poetry Workshop at the University of Iowa in its founding days. Bell's poems are dense and tightly written, and over the years his vision has been transformed from a realistic one to one that is far more visionary. Bell's sense of identity with the victims of the Holocaust in the poems "Getting Lost in Nazi Germany" and "The Extermination of the Jews" is extraordinarily complete, as is that in Mezey's "Theresienstadt Poem."

Bert Meyers also produced a very small body of poetry before his death in 1979, but it has the intricacy and focus of fine miniatures. His poem "When I Came to Israel," for example, has the kind of profound simplicity that is associated with Blake's *Songs of Innocence.* It is likely that Meyers' reputation will grow as his work becomes more widely known.

Harvey Shapiro is a poet successful both in brief poems that read like intricate miniatures, and in longer, narrative-like works. Each of his poems is remarkable in how well it preserves the original emotion that impelled the poet to write it down. His poem "The Six Hundred Thousand Letters" is a midrash in itself, linked to the traditional legends of the six hundred thousand souls that God is said to have created, and to the number of Israelites present at Mount Sinai when the Torah was given to Moses.

Some of the poets of this same generation whose work has only recently become more widely read are Linda Pastan, Stephen Berg,

Benjamin Saltman, Barbara F. Lefcowitz and Myra Sklarew. Linda Pastan has a particular ability with a lyric, and even her solemn poems never lose their lyric quality.

Stephen Berg has an ability to weave narrative into a poem that still is able to retain its surreal mystery. A good example of this is his poem "Desnos Reading the Palms of Men on Their Way to the Gas Chambers." This remarkable poem is based on a true incident in which the French poet Robert Desnos (who was not Jewish) read the palms of prisoners on their way to the gas chambers at Buchenwald, and predicted good fortune for them.

The poems of Constance Urdang are very clearly drawn, and even her surreal poems are vividly clear visions. In addition, her ability to condense her poems makes each one a miniature epic, in which each word and image are drops of water out of which oceans emerge.

Benjamin Saltman has turned almost completely to European sources, and especially to the French Surrealists for his inspiration, and the blend of the traditional and the surreal in his poem about phylacteries has a powerful effect.

Barbara F. Lefcowitz took up writing poetry in her late thirties, and emerges as a fully developed voice. Her poem "At the Western Wall," for example, captures the religious awe so rarely expressed by poets in the West in the presence of the Wailing Wall, and taking a leap of faith that makes the legends live, she creates in our imaginations an authentic religious experience. Her poem "Driftwood Dybbuk" reveals the age-old Jewish tendency to project personae on every object and to regard the world as filled with demons of every kind. Here she recognizes a demon's face in a piece of driftwood, and before long we all fall under the power of the demon, who comes alive in our imagination.

Myra Sklarew is also a late bloomer among poets, but in her book *From the Backyard of the Diaspora* she emerges as an important voice and vision among modern Jewish poets. Her poem "What is a Jewish Poem" addresses itself not only to the subject matter of the Jewish poem, but to the very nature of being a Jew in the Diaspora, remote from the rituals that were so central for our grandparents.

An important poet in a class by himself is Allen Ginsberg. Ginsberg almost singlehandedly restored the expansive voice of Walt Whitman to American poetry and is the father of a generation of Beat poets. The raw power of his poetry is unquestionable, but when it is blended with the bittersweet pathos of a tribute to his mother, Ginsberg's "Kaddish" manages to soar. That Ginsberg should have chosen the structure of a Kaddish, the traditional Jewish prayer for the dead, clearly reveals his attachment to and understanding of his native tradition. Ginsberg is represented here by the first long section of this already classic poem.

Ginsberg was also indirectly responsible for the evolution of a West Coast locus of Jewish poets who look to the free forms of Beat poetry in which to cast Kabbalistic themes and autobiographical expressions. This is perhaps one of the strangest and most interesting chapters in the history of Jewish American poetry. Ginsberg was a direct influence on two San Francisco poets, David Meltzer and Jack Hirschman, and a considerable influence on a poet and editor closely linked to this group, Jerome Rothenberg. Meltzer became one of the leading Beat poets, and then, in the mid-sixties, turned his back on Beat poetry and immersed himself in Jewish studies. In 1967 he published the first issue of *Tree* magazine, which became a central vehicle for the transmission of a Kabbalistic revival among Jewish poets. Meltzer soon established a close working relationship with Hirschman and a great many other younger Jewish poets, and turned *Tree* and Tree Books into an important forum for the movement. Most of these poets had developed with Ginsberg as their primary model, and they were now led by Meltzer's own poetry and that published in *Tree* magazine to discover their heritage on their own terms. The results were stunning. Some of these poets, such as Stuart Perkoff, J. R. Willems, Michael Castro, Harris Lenowitz and Rodger Kamenetz have produced poetry that, if it is read on its own terms, which reflect the ethos of the Beat poets, is itself in keeping with the ancient Jewish literary tradition, and proof that it is still alive. These poets have managed to fuse the frank, open rhythms of the Beat poets with their own intense awareness of the sense of absence that pervades the lives of so many Diaspora Jews into a poetry that is uniquely their own.

One aspect of the Kabbalistic tradition that seems to hold an especially powerful sway over these poets is the very existence of an important role given to the Shekhina, the Divine Presence, who becomes transformed in the Kabbalistic literature into the feminine aspect of the Divinity. Edouard Roditi, one of the many poets brought back to prominence by *Tree,* has written an important poem on this subject, "Shekhina and the Kiddushim."

Another legendary figure that these poets are drawn to is Lilith. According to the legend, Lilith was Adam's first wife, a very independent creature who rebelled at Adam's sexual dominance, dared to pronounce the secret Name of God and flew out of the Garden of Eden to the Red Sea, where she found new lovers among the demons who lived there. The story goes on to say that Adam complained to God, and God sent three angels, Senoy, Sansenoy, and Semangelof, who ordered Lilith to return to her husband. But even when they threatened to kill one hundred of her offspring daily, she refused to return. It is at this point in the legend that God rectified His error by creating a second wife for Adam—Eve.

Nor does the infamous history of Lilith end there. She was believed to be jealous of Eve's ability to have human children, while her own were merely demons, and thus she was held responsible for the high percentage of infant mortality that prevailed. It became necessary to protect pregnant women and newborn infants from Lilith's vengeance by having them wear amulets to ward her off. Furthermore, Lilith's lust was believed to have been so great that any time a man had sexual dreams or fantasies, he was believed to have intercourse with Lilith, and the offspring of this union are all the demons that populate the world. It was even believed that a man must recite Psalm 91 at the funeral of his father to ward off his demon offspring, who would otherwise try to steal his inheritance.

This remarkable legend has become one of the favorite themes for a great many Jewish poets. For many of these poets, and especially for women, Lilith replaces the missing pole of passion that Eve is not permitted to display. But for the poets connected to the *Tree* movement Lilith and the Shekhina become symbolic of the feminine poles they were attempting to explore in themselves. That is largely due to Jung's notion of the *anima*, a feminine aspect of every man, having been widely accepted among modern poets, along with Robert Graves' theory about an omnipresent "White Goddess" in all poetry.* These theories have given rise to a great many "anima poems." For Jewish poets, in particular, Lilith and the Shekhina came to represent the primary aspects of the Jewish anima and came to serve as a great source of inspiration. Among the poets whose poems on Lilith are included in this section are Ruth Feldman (who also translated Primo Levi's poem "Lilith," which appears in Book IV), Jascha Kessler, Allen Grossman and Donald Finkel. Of these poems, the most vivid is probably Finkel's "Lilith," whom he identifies as the personification of lust who "held open house/in her round bed/without a foot/without a head."

For Jack Hirschman, though, it is the Shekhina, not Lilith, who is most closely identified with the muse. It is in this role that he is best able to recognize and come to terms with her. And because the Shekhina is far less accessible than Lilith, Hirschman is almost never able to identify her with his earthly lovers; the "she" grows remote from the world, has an existence only on the inside, in the recesses of himself, until this religious concept is translated into a psychic reality, a living anima figure or muse with whom Hirschman shares his soul. Both of Hirschman's poems included here, "Zohara" and "NHR" concern his seeking out of his own Shekhina/soul.

Like the poets of the Beat school who were his original models,

*Jung also postulated a masculine aspect of every woman, which he called the *animus*.

ENGLISH

David Meltzer is a master of the long breath. He has developed his own type of sequence poem, which clusters images around an imaginary center, so that the reader can understand the subject in light of the Kabbalistic process of emanations. Meltzer has written many such long sequence poems, including *Lil,* which is about Lilith. He has also published a long autobiographical poem entitled "The Eyes, the Blood." This poem traces in the sharpest detail Meltzer's childhood in a traditionally Jewish neighborhood in Brooklyn, and includes descriptions of people and places that often come alive on the page. Another aspect of his poetry, that of the poem as prayer, is demonstrated in his fine poem "Tell Them I'm Struggling to Sing with Angels."

Heavily influenced by the trends of both Beat poetry and the European poetry of Paul Celan, Edmond Jabès and others is Jerome Rothenberg. Rothenberg's vision is less mystical than that of either Meltzer or Hirschman, and tends towards the boldly realistic. His greatest success in books such as *Poland/1931* comes in creating an atmosphere in which we revel in his breathless recounting, endless lists, and a multitude of detail. One of the poems that he is represented with here, "The Alphabet Comes to Me," which apparently recounts a dream, has a strong echo of a Kabbalistic legend of the alphabet found in the Zohar. The other is a tribute to the poet Paul Celan, whom Rothenberg was one of the first to translate into English.

With the aid of *Tree* magazine and other journals, such as Daniel Weissbort's *Modern Poetry in Translation* and Andreas Schroeder's *Contemporary Literature in Translation,* many obscure and half-forgotten European poets, such as Edmond Jabès and Paul Celan, came to the forefront in the late 1960s. One of the clearest examples of creative inspiration between poets is the obvious influence exerted by Celan on the young American poet Paul Auster. Auster's poems are not an imitation of Celan, but rather new works written in the same Hermetic language Celan invented, which critics had assumed to be a dead end, as was the language invented by James Joyce for *Finnegan's Wake.* Auster also captures the powerful Hebraic essence that is at the core of Celan's vision, conveying a sense or impression that provokes a vivid sensation by the use of a fragmented, obscure syntax.

Such a fragmented syntax is also the mark of another poet included here, Larry Eigner, who carries the experiment begun by Charles Olson to its logical limit, and the results are poems that are pure evocation and resist any attempt at reconstruction of their movement of inspiration.

Among other U.S. poets who have been highly influenced by European models are Suzanne Bernhardt, whose poetry also recalls the French surrealists; Willis Barnstone, whose broad experience as a translator has exposed him to avant-garde developments in Spanish and

French poetry, and yet who is able to cast these influences in that most traditional of forms, the sonnet; Stephen Levy, who has been inspired by his Sephardic tradition, and has sought out models in Judezmo* in both folksongs and modern poetry; and Nathaniel Tarn, who has spent most of his adult life in Europe and has sought his models almost exlusively there.

Among the poets included in this American section are two who are better known as novelists. These are Cynthia Ozick, author of *The Pagan Rabbi* and *Bloodshed,* and Susan Fromberg Schaeffer, author of *Anya.* Both prove themselves to be accomplished poets as well. Ozick's "A Riddle" makes good use of Talmudic phrasing and imagery, and "The Wonder-Teacher" reveals a deep sympathy and understanding of the Hasidic tradition. Schaeffer's poem is a moving elegy which accurately reflects the kind of meditation encouraged on the *Yahrzeit,* or annual day of remembrance, of one who has died.

There are a substantial number of young poets who were molded by the famous Boston *Havurah* out of which was edited *The Jewish Catalogue.* Some of these poets are Stephen Mitchell, Joel Rosenberg, Danny Siegel and Barry Holtz. Marcia Falk was also connected to this movement. These poets all demonstrate considerable knowledge of Jewish traditional sources, especially of the legends of the Talmud and the Midrash, of which they make good use in their poems.

It is also interesting to note the unusual precedent established by David Rosenberg. At one point Rosenberg decided to utilize all of his poetic powers in creating modern, free verse adaptations of books of the Bible. To date several volumes have been published to wide acclaim. It is Rosenberg's accomplishment to have preserved both the primary meaning of the Biblical passages in his versions of them, and also his own voice and integrity as a poet. Rosenberg's success at revitalizing the Bible for readers of modern poetry suggests possibilities of other poets approaching other portions of the sacred and secular literature and making them new and vital for modern readers to appreciate again.

A number of poets divide their time between writing their own poetry and translating a considerable amount of poetry from other languages. Among them is Willis Barnstone, editor of *Modern European Poetry,* whose poems obviously arise out of the wide range of European poetry in which he has immersed himself. Another of these poet/translators is Ruth Whitman, editor and translator of *An Anthology of Modern Yiddish Poetry.* She has obviously been influenced by the Yiddish poets she has translated, especially Jacob Glatstein. Her poem "On Translating" is one of the finest statements on the subject.

*Judezmo is the modern spoken and written form of the Judeo-Spanish language known as Ladino.

Chana Bloch is another poet deeply involved in translation. She has especially devoted herself to the Hebrew poet Dahlia Ravikovitch, and the resulting translations succeed in bringing the Hebrew poems to life in English. It is interesting to note that Bloch's own voice is much calmer and restrained than is the voice of Ravikovitch, and that she is convincing in both voices.

Still another poet/translator is Marcia Falk, who is drawn equally to ancient and modern Hebrew poetry. She is the translator of a fine modern version of *The Song of Songs*, and is also the primary translator for Zelda, a Hebrew poet, and Malka Heifetz Tussman, a Yiddish poet. Her own poems have the clarity that is the hallmark of both of the poets she translates, and they are also distinctly her own.

Joachim Neugroschel, a highly accomplished translator of more than eighty books, is also a poet and editor. Both of his poems included take the form of being midrashim on ancient themes. Neugroschel's broad knowledge of European literature is an obvious influence on the style of his poems, which owe a particular debt to German poets such as Georg Trakl and Paul Celan. Neugroschel has translated two volumes of Celan's poetry into English, including the landmark collection entitled *Speech-Grille.*

Finally, it is important to note the presence of the considerable number of young poets who have emerged in the past five years. Most of these poets have published only their first book of poems, and in some cases have as yet published only in magazines. All of them seem authentically inspired by their Jewish heritage. In general they are more attracted to Jewish rituals, legends and traditions than to Jewish history, although the Holocaust and the State of Israel are common themes. Of course it is impossible to predict a poet's career, but virtually all of these poets seem exceptionally promising. They include Gerda Norvig, Laya Firestone, Marc Kaminsky, David Shevin, Susan Litwack, Sol Lachman, Anita Barrows, Emily Borenstein, Dan Jaffe, Kim Chernin, Melvin Wilk, Jerred Metz, Molly Myerowitz Levine, Elaine Dallman, Lucille Day, Martin Grossman, Martin Robbins, Arlene Stone, Maxine Silverman, and Linda Zisquit.

The shift in adjectives from American Jewish to Jewish American is not merely a change in emphasis. Instead it is a recognition on the part of many of the younger Jewish poets that an opportunity exists to contribute to a tradition other than the contemporary American one. Far more inspiring is the sense of writing in a tradition that has existed for thirty-five hundred years, and the invigorating sense of giving this old tradition new life. In a time when publishing a book of poetry can be like tossing a rose petal into the Grand Canyon and waiting to hear it drop, the opportunity of addressing an audience hungry for the kind of Jewish experiences they can identify with seems almost heaven-sent. At this time Jewish readers are only beginning to discover this newly created addition to the ancient canon, but the potential exists for these poets to serve as vessels for this ancient tradition, and to perform the necessary task of receiving and then transmitting what they have received. And in this way it is also possible for them to leave their human imprint on that which they transmit.

II Canada

Outside of the United States and England, the primary locus of Jewish poets writing in English is to be found in Canada and Israel. It is interesting to note that poetic circles in these and most other countries tend to be focused primarily on the writers of their own nation. That is to say that the dominant and most influential poets in Canada are Canadians and not the American poets south of the border.

Like the American poets, the Canadian poets have had three generations of poets that are distinctly different. Among Canadian poets, A. M. Klein and Irving Layton are regarded as the central establishment figures on the Canadian literary landscape. Klein, Layton and Miriam Waddington belong to the older generation, and the middle generation is represented by Leonard Cohen, Phyllis Gotlieb and Deborah Eibel, while the primary poets of the younger generation are Seymour Mayne, Sharon Nelson and Joseph Sherman. One primary difference between these poets and their American counterparts is that Canadian poets were never as self-conscious about being Jewish as were the first and, to a lesser extent, second generation of American poets. This is because the Jewish communities in Canada long resembled the *shtetls* of Eastern Europe since there was less pressure to assimilate than in the United States. And for the same reason Canada has remained one of the last bastions of Yiddish, so that even today it is not unusual to find young Canadians who speak Yiddish. (It is worth noting that Canada is also the home of several important Yiddish poets, including Rachel Korn and J. I. Segal.)

Although not as heralded as Klein or Layton, the finest Jewish Canadian poet may well be Miriam Waddington. Her poems are exquisitely well-controlled and convey an emotional intensity that is rarely encountered in the poems of either Klein or Layton. Leonard Cohen, better known for his songs in the United States, is highly respected as a poet in his native Canada. And among the younger poets, the one who seems to be most fully identified with the Jewish literary tradition is Seymour Mayne, who has also spent a considerable amount of time living in Israel. His poetry makes use of traditional Jewish imagery, and his poetic voice seems able to shift from the oracular to the conversational.

ENGLISH

III Israel

The English-language community in Israel is made up almost entirely of immigrants to Israel from the United States, England and South Africa. The poets among these immigrants are, of course, familiar with the poetic traditions and trends of their native countries, and tend to reflect these in their poetry. At this time it cannot be said that these poets have as yet developed their own literary tradition, but that is because English is a secondary language in Israel, and most literature is written in Hebrew. However, there is a strong sense of community among the English language writers in Israel, and many of these writers devote themselves to translation, especially from Hebrew into English. The result has been an abundance of fine translations, many of which are included in this anthology.

Perhaps the best known English-language poets in Israel are Shirley Kaufman and Dennis Silk. Before emigrating from the United States, Kaufman had become recognized as one of the most highly respected poets of her generation. In recent years Jewish themes have become increasingly predominant in her poetry, and her work is a fine example of the fusion of two literary traditions, the ancient and the modern.

Dennis Silk emigrated from London in the early 1950s, and has been a fixture on the Israeli literary landscape ever since. His poetic vision is pervaded by his awareness of the juxtaposition of the ancient and modern in Israeli life, and of the inevitable ironies that result from such a combination.

Another American emigrant, Harold Schimmel, has in recent years switched from English to Hebrew as his primary written language. Schimmel is closely identified with the avant-garde movement among modern Hebrew poets, and he has translated many of them into English, including Avot Yeshurun and Israel Pincas.

There are also a substantial number of young poets writing in English whose work holds great promise. Among these are Gabriel Levin (son of the novelist Meyer Levin), Paul Raboff, Betsy Rosenberg and Myra Glazer Schotz.

IV South Africa

As might be expected, the literary life in South Africa is largely self-contained, due to that country's geographical and political isolation. Also, many South African authors have left that country and immigrated to other nations, especially to England and Israel. Of the six South African poets represented, only two are currently living in South Africa, Mannie Hirsch and Allan Kolski Horvitz.

Perhaps the best known among these poets is Sydney Clouts, whose work has much in common with other contemporary British poets, among whom his poetry is held in high esteem. Clouts presently resides in London. Although his poetry does not in any way engage his Jewish background, that of the other South African poets reflects an intense awareness of their Jewish heritage and a desire to regard themselves primarily as Jews rather than South Africans.

V Australia

Due to the considerable physical isolation of Australia from the rest of the world, little is heard in the West of the considerable Jewish community that makes its home in Australia. That this community has had to struggle to maintain its Jewish ties is apparent from the poems included here. Those of Nancy Keesing and Fay Zwicky are concerned with the history that led their ancestors to settle in Australia, and David Martin's poem "I Am a Jew," is clearly intended to serve as an affirmation of his Jewish heritage.

VI India

The sole representative of Jewish poets in India in this volume is Nissim Ezekiel, of a family that has made India its home for many generations. Ezekiel is regarded as one of the central figures among English-language poets writing in India, and his work has also appeared widely in journals in England and the United States. It is apparent from his poems that, despite his isolation from the other Jewish communities in the world, he has retained a powerful Jewish identification.

VII Sri Lanka

Perhaps no poet is as isolated from Jewish communities as is Anne Ranasinghe, who has chosen to live in Sri Lanka. Her poetry, however, is dominated by themes related to the Holocaust, in which she lost her mother. We are grateful to have had the opportunity of uniting Ms. Ranasinghe and these other far-flung Jewish poets under a single roof in this anthology.

ENGLISH

England, Scotland and Wales
by Anthony Rudolf

1.

Before Isaac Rosenberg there was virtually no poetry of any quality written by Jews in Britain. And not until the Second World War do we find the beginnings of a real poetry. There was verse, some of it in Yiddish. There was not a poetry, though Joseph Leftwich in his tercentenary survey of Anglo-Jewish poetry (*The Jewish Quarterly* 1956) made a valiant attempt to find one.

The example of Rosenberg shows that poetry is not bound by ineluctable sociological laws, but it is safe to suggest that circumstances were not propitious for the creation of an English-language poetry by Jews. The older generation of the great immigration from Russia, Poland and the other countries spoke Yiddish and this was the language their children were born into. The German immigration did not begin in earnest until 1933 and though it brought with it some who made an immense contribution to British intellectual and scientific life, there was little poetry. As for the old Sephardi families (whose only scion in this section of the book is A. Alvarez) they were busy in the City of London—physically adjacent to the East End but spiritually and culturally continents away.

Britain is not America. Even today, multi-communal Britain (now happily *explicit* as a self-image notwithstanding pre-lapsarian imaginings in certain quarters for an England that never was) lives its life according to societal rules of its own—that are not America's—under what has become an old post-imperial, de-industrialising offshore island monarchy whose Jewish community is as English as French Jews are French and Israeli Jews are Israeli. This means that an Anglo-Jewish literature along the lines of American Jewish literature is not possible—unless the Jewish community, forgetting it is English, does some thinking and redefines itself. Anyway, with the community a product of the days when philistine England was busy with Empire, only a small minority reads its novelists and of that minority an even smaller minority reads its poets. And therefore you will not find the community in the poetry. In the production of English-language poetry, British Jews have been a generation behind America.

Self-awareness of Jewishness is a radically different affair from awareness of Jewish history, though in *English* the presence of the Bible as part of the native literature makes the situation more complex than in other communities—apart from those speaking Hebrew, Yiddish and the Jewish dialects. Identity is involved, and with identity—identification. There are structures of shared feeling and common perception bequeathed by a dynamic heritage; there are psychic tensions created and psychic energies released (blocked too in certain quarters) by the dialectical components of that heritage. Self-awareness of Jewishness leads, as it must, to commemoration and remembrance; and to a tone of voice. For history and myth are father and mother of the poem, whose midwife is the language of the Jew's current abode.

But Jewishness, inasmuch as it affects the poet, is one virtual reality among many, of his or her being; and it has manifold dimensions: religious, social, familial, psychological, ethical, political. After the attempted genocide by the Nazis and the creation of the State of Israel, Jewishness took on a new depth and intensity and became a renewed source, a root/route—but the immense practical problems of post-war resettlement, regrouping, defence and psychic repair as well as the lamentable failure of orthodoxy to address itself to other worlds both Jewish and non-Jewish have made inevitable a muting of the impact of the Jewish *word*. Its time will come.

Some thirty years after the death of Rosenberg, Anglo-Jewish poetry began to flow in the wake of the Second World War. The manifold dimensions of Jewishness form the background or foreground to the individual psychodrama which is the making of poems, written within or against the ancient tradition of English-language poetry, sometimes mediated through other European languages, or through the Hebrew or Yiddish traditions. Jewishness does not affect every poet in equal measure. The other virtual realities: nationality, class, region, age, occupation, sex, etc. naturally play their part too. A glance at the biographical notes on the poets throughout the book will reveal some aspects of their heterogeneous backgrounds—and a more complex interplay between national and linguistic frontiers than in any other imaginable anthology.

The poets work towards a time, Messianic, when in the words of Rabbi Leo Baeck "there will be no division between commandment and grace." For, as Samuel Beckett—consciously or unconsciously alluding to a phrase of Kafka—has written: "all poetry, as discriminated from the various paradigms of prosody, is prayer." Remembrancer of an ancient promise, the Jewish poet defies spiritual imperialism.

2.

Isaac Rosenberg, a radical Jewish working-class private soldier from a Yiddish-speaking home, is the grandfather of Anglo-Jewish poetry. His death in the First World War, at the age of twenty-eight, makes it easy to forget that he was born only four years before Charles Reznikoff and Uri Zvi Greenberg. And concentration on the great trench poems also makes it easy to forget that he was a fully-fledged poet before he went to France. Nor was he a war-poet in the way Owen was: "my subject is war," wrote Owen, "and the pity of war."

Had Rosenberg lived, his presence would have had a profound effect on new generations of Jewish and non-Jewish poets writing in English. "I am determined that this war, with all its powers for devastation, shall not master my poeting; that is, if I am lucky enough to come through all right. I will not leave a corner of my consciousness covered up, but saturate myself with the strange and extraordinary new conditions of this life, and it will all refine itself into poetry later on," he wrote in Autumn 1916. And there are strong suggestions in his letters that he would have written a devastating prose account of the war which he despised and hated, including his treatment in England at the hands of his senior officers. As it is, we must remain grateful for the extraordinary poems written in the trenches as well as many of the earlier poems. No reader can fail to be overwhelmed by the Keatsian pathos of this "half used life" and death.

The allusion to Wordsworth's Lucy poem in *Dead Man's Dump* ("The grass and coloured clay/more motion have than they") is one of many indications that Rosenberg, a great English poet by any reckoning, had read his Blake, Keats, Donne and other major poets: Rosenberg's themes (which, as with all true poets, emerge—to quote Goethe on Homer—"in a language that in and by itself makes the poetry and does the thinking") often echo the preoccupations of the English poets from Shakespeare to Browning, but he never loses the edge of his Jewish specificity, his Jewish radicality. "Root" in the work of this poet whose "heart utterance was Lilith" is an energising ideational symbol and image, while "God," like war, is to be revolted against: "Ah this miasma of a rotting God."

The image of Absalom in *Chagrin* "articulates the rootlessness of the Diaspora Jew," to quote the major essay on Rosenberg by Jon Silkin, the Jewish diaspora being the collectivity Rosenberg knew best. But the image of rootlessness surely applied, in Rosenberg's mind, to *all* existing communities, the Jewish one serving as a peculiarly complex and appropriate emblem of what was, is and probably will be a universal condition, pending the Messiah. Yet, it is evident from his writings that Rosenberg would later have imagined and perhaps helped to create a community whose structures would be rooted in a lived vision of human fulfillment (would he, like Kafka, have considered living on a kibbutz?), but the civilisation he was born into created the monstrous progeny of a war that destroyed not only the poet but the hopes that he and others nurtured.

3.

Three of the five United Kingdom poets included here from the next generation were born outside England. All five were in the Armed Services during the Second World War. Dannie Abse is Welsh, and the qualities of warmth, loquacity and good humour (very evident in his prose books as well as his verse) traditionally associated with Wales reinforce and are reinforced by his Jewishness. The two poems included here are from opposite ends of his collected poems. Dov Shamir and Rabbi Schatz link hands. If Jewishness is less evident in Abse's poetry than in, say, Silkin's, could the explanation be that Englishness has less influence over the English poet than Welshness has over the Welsh poet? And this despite the fact that Abse writes in English and not in Welsh? Or is it that, like Feinstein (see below) much of the concern with these matters is found in Abse's prose books?

Michael Hamburger, like Yehuda Amichai, was born in Germany in 1924. Hamburger's pre-eminence as a translator of—mainly German—poetry has led, until very recently, to neglect of his own work as a poet, which has become remarkably supple and subtle since he bade farewell to traditional forms with his long Holocaust sequence, *In a Cold Season.* The plangent cadences of *At Staufen* are his own characteristic music, the music of a melancholy Jewish poet whose assimilation to other ways does not extend to his memories, to his origin ("mors, mors") which is survival amid the ruins of the German-Jewish symbiosis.

Asa Benveniste is America-born though settled now in England as a naturalised citizen. His main work as a Jewish poet is rooted in Kabbalistic and Sephardi perceptions but, as with many poets in this book, there is implicit a pained awareness that Jewishness is a condition of great psychic and existential potency, and therefore can be a gift to poets: at the same time, in personal terms, divorced from Judaism it can create problems capable of no resolution.

Emmanuel Litvinoff and Edward Lowbury were born in Rosenberg's lifetime, and Litvinoff grew up in Rosenberg's world: the Jewish proletariat of London's East End—what the Yiddish poet A. N. Stencl called the *shtetl* (whose streets Stencl still walks). Litvinoff appears to have concentrated on prose since the early sixties—drama and novels. The voice in his poems speaks anguishedly from the whirlwind of the Holocaust and the Second World War. It is direct and unmediated, the historical and psychic pressures on him being too strong for English proprieties. T. S. Eliot never permitted *After Strange Gods* to be reprinted. Litvinoff's *To T. S. Eliot* may or may not have been one of the causes, but it is certainly one of the most powerful rebukes—not least because it is written as much in sorrow as in anger—ever made by one poet to another.

ENGLISH

Edward Lowbury's poems are generally statements whose tone implies a world view instinct with moderation and reason but the Prague poem, surely his strongest poem in any book, is fraught with the emotion that a Jewish origin so often yields under involuntary and untranquil recollection, an emotion that Osip Mandelstam, in his magnificent essay *The Noise of Time* voices: "as a little bit of musk fills an entire house, so the least influence of Judaism overflows all of one's life."

The next group of poets are old enough to remember the Second World War. A. Alvarez is an unprolific poet, which may or may not be connected with his work as a novelist and highly influential critic. One would not have predicted his wistful and autumnal tone given his personal pantheon of American poets: Plath, Berryman, Lowell. We find, as in Lowbury and several other poets in this book, the sentiment expressed: "There were Hebrew prayers I didn't understand." Ruth Fainlight and Elaine Feinstein (the former born in America, the latter a novelist and translator) are the best known Jewish women poets in the United Kingdom. The puritanically measured gravitas of Fainlight's line, her exceptionally high use of nouns, slow down her tread, bring her deliberately close to prose without, as it were, crossing the line. She treats Jewish themes directly, intellectually (though the recent sequence about various sibyls heralds a release, an inwardness, a breaking of the vessels for this poet). On the other hand, Feinstein—perhaps because her prose, like Abse's, elaborates and treats of Jewish themes more fully—generally writes a poem more driven by nervous energy, breaking lines and the flow in a jagged, edgy way. What George Oppen calls the "lyric valuables" are in her work rough diamonds rather than the string of pearls Ruth Fainlight displays. Like Michael Hamburger, though younger, Lotte Kramer comes from Germany. Her poems, uncollected so far, are, for the most part, lyrical emanations of loss and of grief.

The note written by himself on the cover of A. C. Jacobs' book of poems "The Proper Blessing" begins: "There are a great many blessings in Judaism." And ends: "One is very conscious . . . of the need to say the appropriate blessing when its situation arises. The poems . . . are, from one aspect, about living in a world in which there is no certainty about which blessing to say when, or even whether one can bless at all." Such an unembarrassed rootedness in Judaism as a religion as distinct from ethno-cultural or similar dimensions of Jewishness is indeed rare in this book. Jacobs, like his *Yiddish Poet,* regrets the passing of the old ways but like the Jew in his poem *Painting* "what he utters/Will touch/The depth of survival." *Poem for My Grandfather* contains a Scottish word and several of Jacobs' poems reflect his Scottishness. The language of his poems, like that of Fainlight, is direct and they often make their points with the peculiarly Jewish humour and irony that can be found in several poets in this book.

Jacobs is also admired as a particularly talented translator of Hebrew poetry. His exact contemporaries—Jeremy Robson and Daniel Weissbort—the former a pioneer in the poetry-and-jazz movement, the latter a major translator and editor of Russian poetry, also work with Jewish themes, albeit to a lesser extent. Robson is apparently more integrated and secure than Weissbort, though he too refracts Judaic anxieties from time to time. The persona in Weissbort's *Walking Home at Night,* who observes that "the small synagogue is alight, full of conspirators" is engaging, a sad clown.

Jon Silkin has always been deeply aware of his Jewish heritage and has been preoccupied with the place of the Jew within Christendom (if not within Jewry). His books return regularly to the theme of suffering, but not only the suffering of Jews: the sufferings of English working men are documented in powerful poems like the Kilhope Wheel sequence. Silkin has *not* sought to merge poetically the identity of Jews and these working men (not even by writing about proletarian Jews). And Silkin, unlike Rosenberg about whom he has written with such empathy and perception, is not working class, but he is a Jew true to the prophetic tradition of Judaism—which is the inspiration or origin of many radical social movements. Such a Jew, virtually by definition, is aware of human and animal suffering and—if a poet—given to the articulation in poems of a theodicy or at least the rejection of alien justifications for evil. He would inhabit "a peaceable kingdom"—the title of one of Silkin's books. Optimism would be seen in Walter Benjamin's terms: "only for the sake of the hopeless ones have we been given hope." To this Silkin would add love and the need to write a poetry of commitment to values that will underlie a viable and principled politics of communitas. Only if good works (political, literary etc.) announce or prefigure the Messiah can we read meaning into or out of our world. Certainly, absence of Messiah is a key figure in Silkin's poetry.

It is difficult to select well from this wide-ranging and difficult poet. The group begins with the early and great poem *Death of a Son* which, in the context of this book, takes on the status of a kaddish. This most powerful and charged universal statement of paternal love and loss becomes a Jewish requiem for a son, though it would be a mistake to extend the personal, individual nature of the lament to a comment on *history.* In *Resting-Place,* Silkin returns to the theme—the unremembered massacre of the Jews of York—of a poem written twenty years earlier, *The Coldness. Resting-Place* is a more inward reflective poem than the earlier one; less spelled out, it is more sorrowful than angry. Its movement is freer than some of the crabbed, congested poems written between the two York ones. Or, perhaps, his Jewish poems draw on a wellspring that nourishes the roots of language in such a way that the poems yield themselves more openly. *A Word about Freedom . . .*is notable from this point of view in the context of the book where it first appeared. And the same goes for *It Says.* Diction, rhythm, structure, all the registers of poetry are fully stretched, entangled, then released in the strong poem *Jerusalem.* It demands close attention from the reader, who in the process becomes a lover or a worshipper. And it ends with a proud Judaic paradox: "Flesh sings as if spirit;/would to God it were, but then, no. All/I have to do, where clashes/of serene absence whiten blank stone/is lift you to where this illumination/overfills with space."

The final group consists of poets born during or after the Second World War. Like many Jewish poets, Richard Burns oscillates between his own version of what Matthew Arnold and other thinkers have seen as the two poles of Western civilisation, Hebraism and Hellenism, between Jerusalem and Athens. (The greatest Jewish poet cursed or blessed with this bipolarity explicitly within himself was Osip Mandelstam). Sometimes it is synthesized; sometimes not. Either way, it is a *figure* of many modalities. Bearings can be taken from both poles in Burns' *Angels,* but England is not enamoured of his rich rhetorical mode, something that was also objected to in Nathaniel Tarn, now an American. Burns takes the Jewish heritage as myth rather than history, not least in his concern with language and Babel.

The mythic dimension of the Judaic religious civilisation (to employ the terminology of Reconstructionism—a movement which regrettably has had little or no influence in Britain) is also found in the work of Anthony Barnett, Tali Loewenthal and Gad Hollander, the last two born in Israel. The shade of Paul Celan hovers over Barnett and Hollander; it mediates a tradition that Loewenthal, a Lubavitcher Hasid, apprehends directly. Tom Lowenstein, Asher Mendelssohn and Anthony Rudolf appear to be more concerned with the geo-historical layers of the Jewish past. Francis Landy, in his *Lament for Azazel,* brings together historical and religious truth as one inward parabolic myth of revelation. It is a holistic visionary poem where the "festive wool . . .sews a yellow star for Azazel," where Azazel's wilderness is heaped with "the ashes of the Inquisition/ the ashes of Dachau." The poem concludes: "They cast lots on the Day of Azazel/They cast lots between blood and blood/Both are for Azazel." The darkness of the night of Jewish Europe contains even the joy earned by some of our poems.

UNITED STATES

Paul Auster

Paul Auster was born in Newark, New Jersey, in 1947 and studied at Columbia University. He is the author of three books of poetry: Unearth *(1974),* Wall Writing *(1976), and* Fragments from Cold *(1977). He has also published numerous translations of French poetry and has published reviews and essays in many journals.*

Scribe

The name
never left his lips: he talked himself
into another body: he found his room again
in Babel.

It was written.
A flower
falls from his eye
and blooms in a stranger's mouth.
A swallow
rhymes with hunger
and cannot leave its egg.

He invents
the orphan in tatters,

he will hold
a small black flag
riddled with winter.

It is spring,
and below his window
he hears
a hundred white stones
turn to raging phlox.

ENGLISH

Hieroglyph

The language of walls.
Or one last word—
cut
from the visible.

May Day. The metamorphosis
of Solomon's seal
into stone. The just
doom of the uttered
road, unraveled in the swirl
of pollen-memory
and seed. Do not
emerge, Eden. Stay
in the mouths of the lost
who dream you.

Upon thunder and thorn: the furtive air
arms
the lightning-gorse and silence
of each fallow sky
below. Blood Hebrew. Or what
translates
my body's turning back
to an image of earth.

This knife
I hold against your throat.

Song of Degrees

In the vacant lots
of solstice. In the light
you wagered for the rubble
of awe. Sand-heaps:
retched into prayer—the distance
bought
in your name.

You. And then
you again. A footstep
gives ground: what is more
is not more: nothing
has ever been
enough. Tents,
pitched and struck: a ladder
propped
on a pillow of stone: the sheer
aureole rungs
of fire. You,
and then we. The earth
does not ask
for anyone.

So
be it. So much
the better—so many
words,
raked and murmured along
by your bedouin knees, will not
conjure you home. Even
if you crawled from the skin
of your brother,
you would not go beyond
what you breathe: no
angel can cure you
of your name.

Minima. Memory
and mirage. In each place
you stop for air,
we will build a city
around you. Through the star-
mortared wall
that rises in our night, your soul
will not pass
again.

ENGLISH

Covenant

Throng of eyes,
myriad, at sunken retina depth: the image
of the great, imageless one,
moored within.

Mantis-lunged, we,
the hirelings, alive in juniper and rubble,
broke the flat bread
that went with us, we
were steps, wandered
into blindness, we knew by then
how to breathe ourselves along
to nothing.

Something lost
became
something to be found.
A name,
followed through the dust
of all that veering, did not ever
divulge its sound. The mountain
was the spoor
by which an animal pain
hunted itself home.

All night
I read the braille wounds
on the inner wall
of your cry, and at the brink
of the thick, millennial morning, climbed up
into you again, where all
my bones began
beating and
beating the heart-drum
to shreds.

Willis Barnstone

Willis Barnstone was born in 1927 in Lewiston, Maine. He graduated from Columbia and Yale Universities, and currently teaches in the Comparative Literature and Latin American Studies departments at Indiana University. His books of poetry include From This White Island, China Poems, Anti-Journal *and* Sonnetbook: A Rose in Hell.

The Good Beasts

On the first morning of the moon, in land
under the birds of Ur, before the flood
dirties the memory of a couple banned
from apples and the fatal fire of blood,
Adam and Eve walk in the ghetto park,
circling a tree. They do not know the way
to make their bodies shiver in the spark
of fusion, cannot read or talk, and they
know night, noon, but not the enduring night
of nights that has no noon. Adam and Eve,
good beasts, living the morning of the globe,
are blind, like us, to apocalypse. They probe
the sun, deathray, on the red tree. Its light
rages, illiterate, until they leave.

The Worm

My fathers come to me in an old film:
a peddler and tailor in the new world;
in the old, the image blurs, unknown.
I must be a bit like them. Old photos
say, look, here you were with a white beard,
black hat, a dark faith in the One God.
But they stood dully in the light and were
despised. They wandered here. It seems
impossible—here where I work and now
a plane hangs like a shiny wasp
in the air. With no God or fear I am
a free son: with the worm eating my heart.

Grandfather

Born over there, in mist, not even God
or Germans have a record of the house
or village outside Vilna. Here, he is the odd,
poor tyrant whose work is stitching a blouse
or shirt. He finds a black woman to live
with when his wife dies. My smart father sells
papers in the Boston subways and won't forgive
the whippings, which embitter him. The smells
of steam and cooking mix with yellow cheeses
while the tailor sews. Suddenly he seizes
a bar and pounds the son for rotten grades.
Last assault. Twelve years old, enraged, he leaves
school and the house for good. The tailor fades
from all of us, forever, stitching sleeves.

Gas Lamp

In old commercial Boston down on Milk Street,
up two flights, near the gas-lamp, the dark tailor
nervously waits for the midwife. August heat
has worn the woman out. Amid the squalor
she looks around the bed, clutching a cape
she brought from London as a child. It's dawn
and dirty. The dark tailor wants to escape
to his tiny shop. The woman's sheets are drawn
below her waist. She isn't hollering now;
her eyes are dark and still; blood on her thumbs.
Her name is Sarah. No. I'm guessing. How,
untold, am I to know? Hot day has worn
into the room. The midwife finally comes.
It's 1893. Sarah dies. My father's born.

Miklos Radnoti

Because time is a fiction in the mind,
I don't want to die, that is, in July
or Friday or last year. Farms and haystacks
are burning today. I Miklos Radnoti
write you a postcard with a poem. Darling,

I say to myself I won't lie down. The ox
drools blood. The shepherd girl is an orphan
when the troops stray over the wheatfields.
Wife, after they beat me to death, look through
my trenchcoat, in the mass grave, for the poems.

Maybe in two years, by 1946,
you will find our bodies. Today all over
Hungary and Poland I am dying. In taverns
I am already forgotten. How could the smell
of my hair linger? I hid in cellars too,
smoked in darkness, kissed kisses of the taste
of blackberries. When peace comes I won't be
at the Writers' Club. Angels drink artillery.
Peasants dream among fleas, among worms. Wife,
the poems are time's wings. Spread them darkly.

Paradise

The old Jew
sat alone

on his bench
in the dark

drawing charts
of the soul.

Daylight fell
on his beard.

He saw flame
he saw flame.

ENGLISH

Anita Barrows

Anita Barrows was born in New York in 1947 and presently lives in Berkeley, California. She has been poetry editor for a radio station in Berkeley and has been published in journals in the United States and Great Britain. Her poems have been anthologized in No More Masks *and* Rising Tides: 20th Century American Women Poets.

Avenue Y

for my mother's father

1
A room where someone
lies ill for many nights
A room the dogs
refuse to enter
A room
          that sways, sways

   Like an old
Jew, he said
Like a train

               To awaken
like this, he
said, to remember
                         the place one
watches for

2
And that other
where one boarded

Is it
possible, it seems
       possible

               Women in the streets
carrying loaves of bread
their brown coats, a language

among them

3
Here is a blessing: ignore it

The stops are less frequent now
From the window the names

        of streets illumined
by streetlamps
                        Bind these
to your forehead, and twice

around your arms

4
(the rabbis translate him but do not hear him)

He says, *water*

        They say, *He is ready now, he is about to cross*

Bread, he says, *a little bread*

        They ask him for payment, the rabbis
        say, *he tells us*
        one does not enter that place empty-
                handed, without gifts

The window, he says, *I would like it opened*

        This is a miracle: he says
        he will not forget us, nor keep
        what he learns there secret from us

5
(his voice)

I have been perhaps too simple
have walked always the same
streets

My habits the dog
knows as well as myself

What does a poor
man count? I could say
what my hands have loved

Or my feet, old
leather, the reticent
grass

6
(my prayer)

You, trees

If no one else will listen
If the wise men, the children
won't listen

You, trees
Because my grandfather
walked tenderly among
you, grieved
for your dead young

Tenderly, as first
in his own country
Lena, dark
new-breasted girl
—his wife

So he touched pearblossom, appleblossom

The Ancestors

for Yehuda Amichai

1

There is one who sits in his room
all day, and a dog sits under his table.
Perhaps the dog is also praying; or perhaps
the drone of the man's voice
is something the dog understands.
His muzzle pressed to the floor, he makes
low, crooning sounds, sighs
when the man sighs, and when the man
rises, the dog also rises. Maybe prayer
is the imitation of one's God? The man's
eyes are closed, he doesn't think
about the dog, but hears the low
wind moving over the roofs
of the troubled houses.

2

There is another, who lives
near a park. He speaks English
to his child, and if he wants the child
not to understand, he speaks Yiddish.
When the child learns Yiddish, the father
speaks Russian; then Polish; then the child
grows up, and he has never learned
what it was that was such a secret.

3

As you grow older you grow more simple.
Your flesh has stopped arguing
with your bone, and your eye
has resigned itself to its two directions.
You are like a telegram
someone has sent, and left out all the extra
words, because of the cost: Love,
you say. Candle. Good-bye.

4
I think of a field
where the trees lean even in still
air to prevailing
wind, but in the split trunk
one year of fire, one
of late frost. The simple
leaves, lifted like faces
to sunlight, so slenderly
joined to the world. Their falling
is like the death of children
who have learned nothing, only birds
and shadow. Who can tell
nothing, and go
down unanswered. But wood who has
held them grieves and remembers
and wears a ring to record each
mute generation.

5
I saw a man rocking back
and forth, as though all the restless
unborn were asleep
in his arms. "Wait,"
he sang, "Sleep. The earth

your mother is also tired.
Your brother builds a house of his bone.
Your sister weaves a cloth of her hair.
But you will walk

cold and uncovered, will bruise
your hand on the softness
of the world, will make

of nakedness
also a prayer."

Marvin Bell

Marvin Bell was born in New York in 1937. He presently lives in Iowa, where he is on the staff of the Writers Workshop at the University of Iowa. His book A Probable Volume of Dreams *won the Lamont Poetry Selection Prize.* Stars Which See, Stars Which Do Not See *(1977) was a National Book Award nominee.*

Getting Lost in Nazi Germany

You do not move about, but try
to maintain your position. Would you eat
the fruit of the corpses?—You would.
Your friends are the points of a star
now a golden, unattainable "elsewhere"
because there is no elsewhere for a Jew.

Men have closed their daughters to you,
and now the borders like neat hairlines
limiting your ideas to hatred and escape.
This way, they have already begun
the experiments with your brain—
later to be quartered and posted.

Cremation of what remains?
In a dream like this one, a weathered face
will drive you off under a load of hay
at the very moment the Commandant calls.
You could swear the voice you hear is kind,
calling you home, little Jewboy in alarm.

The Extermination of the Jews

to Donald Justice

A thousand years from now
they will be remembered as heroes.
A thousand years from now
they will still be promised their past.

Objects of beauty notwithstanding,
once more they will appear
for their ruin, seeking a purse,
hard bread or a heavy weapon

for those who must survive,
but no one shall survive.
We who have not forgotten,
our children shall outremember:

Their victims' pious chanting—
Last wishes, last Yiddish, last dreaming—
were defeats with which the Gestapo
continues ceasing and ceasing.

The Israeli Navy

The Israeli Navy,
sailing to the end of the world,
stocked with grain
and books black with God's verse,
turned back,
rather than sail on the Sabbath.
Six days, was the consensus,
was enough for anyone.

So the world, it was concluded,
was three days wide
in each direction,
allowing three days back.
And Saturdays were given over
to keeping close,
while Sundays the Navy,
all decked out in white
and many-colored skull caps,
would sail furiously,
trying to go off the deep end.

Yo-ho-ho, would say the sailors,
for six days.
While on the shore their women moaned.

For years, their boats were slow,
and all show.
And they turned into families
on the only land they knew.

Stephen Berg

Stephen Berg is the author of The Daughters *and* Grief: Poems and Versions of Poems *and is a founding editor of* The American Poetry Review. *He has also written* Nothing in the Word, *versions of Aztec poetry, poems from the Aztec, and is a co-translator of the volume* Clouded Sky, *poems of the Hungarian poet Miklós Radnóti. He was awarded the Frank O'Hara Memorial Prize in 1971 and a Guggenheim Fellowship in Poetry in 1974. He co-translated with Dishkin Clay,* Oedipus The King. *His book of poems* With Akhmatova at the Black Gates *was published in 1980. He presently teaches at the Philadelphia College of Art and Princeton University.*

Desnos Reading the Palms of Men on Their Way to the Gas Chambers

Our suffering would be unbearable
if we couldn't think of it as a passing
and sentimental disorder.
*—Robert Desnos, March 28, 1944, Buchenwald**

Maybe I should go back to the white leather
sofa and bull terrier
of my childhood, when my grandfather died,
but I can't.
It rained and there were beaks of light.
Who was it
picking my hand up where it hung
against my naked thigh?
What matters is how we act before we die,
whether we have a joke ready
and can make all the terrified sad faces
around us laugh and weep,
whether we can make everyone kiss.

Who was it? Who holds us here?
Whom should we touch?

*It is reported that the French poet, Robert Desnos, broke out of a line of naked prisoners on their way to the gas chambers at Buchenwald and went from prisoner to prisoner reading palms, predicting good fortune and happiness. My friend, Bill Kubik, who has translated Desnos' poetry in his book *The Voice* told me this story.—S. B.

ENGLISH

You squeeze my hand.
The orchestra's notes from across the road
weave upward in the smoke,
the frozen eyes, the brown angular light
off center, rows, stacks, glasses
without anyone's eyes behind them
and nothing except
the smile of a boot,
the eyes of gloves,
the mouth of a belt
and the holes.
Holes.
I squeeze your hand.

You don't love anyone.
I'm sorry. You never loved anyone.
Probably it's because your planets
are mixed, or Jewish.
But there's a cross down by the wrist
on the edge of the mound of Venus
and lines tangling violently
along the third finger.
You're a sexual person.
And, those lines webbed
under the thumb are bright.
The agony is false.
The earth has been here beneath us
less than an hour
and we are shuffling forward.
Nobody looks at us.
Say anything,
say we are somewhere else,
each violin has
long curved eyes
tilted seaward and up
like your hand in mine.

And yours, little boy with dark brown eyes,
is wetter than the fake soup
of urine and grass the Nazis give us.
You hide your penis fearfully
behind it, making a pathetic cup
while the other hand dangles

like a noose
that will open on no one,
close on no one.
But I predict one last moment
of incredible joy
when you see yourself melt
into the hundreds gasping around you,
and the doors are pulled
and the gas sighs once, reminding
the Father of you.

Nothing is lost. One guard sprouts wings
in his sleep. He is given a robe of
spun blond hair and a throne
of tiny nuggets.
In the morning on the parade ground
he opens his fly and prays for us
as he shows his penis,
and is shot
and chopped up for the dogs.
But the next night he returns,
an amputated wing
branding its shadow in miniature
on twelve foreheads.

Like a blind clown I dance between
rifles and the laughter of guards,
and it must be my withered cock and balls,
the color of stone walls,
that cause so much happiness
in the ranks
as I stumble through the prisoners to hold them,
needing to touch as many as I can
before I go.

There's a shallow hole over the bunkbed
on the wall behind my head
where my dreams live on
after I have waked and knelt
and bled
thousands of times.
I look into it and if I concentrate
I see bodies decorated with

ENGLISH

God's toil and ashes.
They drift
into the mouths and eyes
of the living
until there is nothing
but children
like us
here.

Shaggy grains of frost
cling to the ground.
The barracks glitter, the sky hugs
itself like a girl whose arms
have been hacked off, and the wire
hums invisibly in the night air except when a
strand goes white for a second
from no source.
O I want to be that thread, tiny
barrier, bodiless vein, line
that the wind reads.
When I chew on what looks like a finger
and tastes like sour wine
I remember you running, stretching your arms out
to be caught or to fling yourself
through space into my arms
until your laughter choked in the sand.
I remember nothing.

You ask me why.
I stand facing you
and speak your name,
whatever it is.
Your name over and over
like a lullaby
until we kiss.
I put my hand on your breast.
It is beautiful, and ugly,
and as empty
as we will be soon.
Lights begin passing
in your eyes
like cities going to sleep

or like those thick lamps on the masts
of fishing boats.
I love you more than I
growing smaller, smaller
have loved anyone.
You touch my hair and cry.

Are you different from the one
I just touched? Who are you?
Everyone looks so young suddenly
as if this were the beginning
of the world.
Everything is as silent as this hand
laid up in my palm,
except for a slight hissing somewhere.
What would you say if I spoke?
I will marry a beautiful woman
named Youki,
have children, a cottage
in the forest near Compiègne
and live many years?
I will marry and have children.

Sometimes a message flutters down,
and someone picks it up
and reads:

then goes back home.
The wheels clack

Unbearable, the wrong parents, the sun
funneling down like the wings
of judgment. Love suffers.
I
dance in any direction now,
kissing the guards, soothing their faces
with my torn hands, singing like a child
after a long illness
who is here, here and here,
knowing you by the lost warmth
of your hands
in Philadelphia, Cape May,

ENGLISH

New York, wherever I could not be.
Who is it?
I slide under the uniforms
and fill them,
and as I swim the sorrow and depth
of a stranger's blood, of
a belly held in by a bulletproof vest,
I know it was not a mistake
to be here.

I am my sister, but I have none.
My brother, but I have none.

Living men, what have you done?
In a strand
of invisible scorched nerve
scenes we mustn't remember
never stop flashing toward us,
unreceived,
like us.

The last wisps of gas
rise from our sleeves

and what I danced is danced again where
you smile about love
and eat with friends
the last smile is smiled first
and I am both of them
on the last mouth

I am the light you see by
fingers tracing the breast
a cloud chilling the street suddenly
what you need, say, lie down
next to in hours
of common terror
I am the face
touch   touch

and who it is is who it is

a boot's O empties itself eternally
as radiant in the holiness
of presence as
any

I go back
and can't

but I hear myself
call the flesh
call what I love
what I love is not listening

Don't you hear it?
It says "The pain will soon be over"
It says "The lovely season is near"

Don't you hear it?

Suzanne Bernhardt

Suzanne Bernhardt was born in 1946 and earned degrees in English literature at the State University of New York at Binghamton. Her poems have appeared in a number of magazines and journals. She is presently living in Rochester, New York.

In a Dream Ship's Hold

some steerage
before Jerusalem
in a ship's
shell

we were being dipped three times
in salt water like a bunch of
greens

in a bitter sea

choking,

then breathing water
smug as fish.

Three times.
Nothing flashed before us
but rescue;

we talked and were still.

Dry breath
the smell of toast
a telephone ringing

salt end
of the sea dream's
seder
night.

The Unveiling

In the custom of the Jews
a name & dates
have appeared

you show me your face
everything is revealed

a lily, a wash of roses,
a fish, a thrust of angel
rising from the earth
wrestling to the ground
the sky the Christian heaven.

It is always raining

your rent sleeve
groans with pain.

Your parents are stunned;
blocks of Hebrew
fly thru the air
each letter
dipped in gall;

umbrella wind
tugs us both
to blow us away
feed us secret
honey on the heights
sweet raven of mine

your mother weeps Yiddish
your father sneezes
ashes & gold.

Chana Bloch

Chana Bloch was born in New York City in 1940. She studied at Cornell and Brandeis, and the University of California at Berkeley. She now lives in Berkeley and teaches at Mills College. Her translations from Yiddish and Hebrew include a selection of Dahlia Ravikovitch's poems, A Dress of Fire. *A volume of her own poems,* The Secrets of the Tribe, *will appear shortly.*

Paradise

1
Adam is clay, the dumb
stuff of kids'
games. His eyes
are stuck asleep.
                    Day
wheels out from the blue,
a yellow tongue of beach
licking the sea.

2
In the grass of Paradise, shadows
are blue. Eve's hair
is blue, Adam's hollow eyes
blue fears.
            The fruit
red as an eye.

3
Once they were tall as the trees.
The sun spoke in the branches, the hand
reached, the round
gourd of the hand grew full
when it wanted.

Now the trees close over us, slowly
we carry
everything with us, scored
in the private
softness of our hands.

We keep our heads down like burrowing animals
that can't see in the daylight.

Noah

1
The ark noisy with children,
angels, birds—dim, stuffy,
close, the nest of home
where Noah broods,
at sea.
How can one think
in such a place? The world
presses around, and God
breathes down his neck.

2
The ark, at least, is
warm. Outside,
a square of blue, pale, tentative,
perhaps still wet.

Noah gropes, but the brave
animals sniff land:
the dove
a fist of light.

3
Yawning, the rain still drips
from memory,
damps the small dust down.

Sun buds in the sky.
Trees shake out their tails.
Birds sing, gingerly,
rolling the last drops off their wings.

New grass whets its blades.

4
The great hulk of houseboat beached
on top of Ararat.
Drying, the timbers crack.
It will stay there forever, shrinking invisibly.

On land our stiff
white birds' legs
wobble,
remembering the ocean's push.

The last
waters go on rocking
in the conch of the ear.

The Sacrifice

1
The patriarch in black takes
candle and knife
like cutlery,
rehearsing under his breath
the Benediction
on the Death of an Only Son.

Isaac stoops under the raw wood,
carries his father on his back,
candle, velvet and all.

2
On the woodpile
Isaac's body waits
as women wait,
fever trilling under his skin.

He will remember the blade's
white silence,
the waiting
under his father's eyes.

Yom Kippur

Our new clothes fool no one.
A year of days.
The fingernails keep growing,
even in life.

We are tight for winter, brooding
in this vat of used air.
As if we could hatch
some glory out of our sitting still.

What shrinks inside us, these stones
that rattle in our throats
tell us only
to go on getting older.

But the eyes want, the fingers, the emptiness
of the mouth
wants something to speak to, some lost
horn of a mouth with its unpredictable answers.

On the eastern wall, the lions
stand on end,
raising their braided heads,
their gold tongues whetted.

Emily Borenstein

Emily Borenstein was born in Elizabeth, New Jersey, in 1923. She was a student at the Juilliard School of Music. She has degrees in comparative literature and English literature from Columbia University and New York University. Her books of poetry include Woman Chopping, Finding My Face, *and* Cancer Queen.

Life of the Letters

Can you hear the music of the letters of the alphabet?
Listen to it
and follow it into the darkness that precedes creation.
Like the scrolls of the Torah the letters assemble into waves
rolling out into the world through the generations.
They rise into a great yearning wave covering the centuries.
As the waters recede each letter becomes a tree of knowledge
that bears fruit.
The letters dwell in their names like the heads of giraffes
nuzzling among leaves.
Each of the letters is peculiarly haunting and has about it
a magic spell.
The letters capture the susurrus of waves.
They combine into words held together by a string of plot,
words that *are*, words that are *not*.

Alter Brody

Alter Brody was born in Russia in 1895 and came to New York in 1903. He has published A Family Album *and* Lamentation: Four Folk-Plays of the American Jew, *which are interpretations of his life on the Lower East Side. It has not been possible to determine what became of Brody after World War II.*

Lamentations

In a dingy kitchen
Facing a Ghetto backyard
An old woman is chanting Jeremiah's Lamentations,
Quaveringly,
Out of a Hebrew Bible.

The gaslight flares and falls . . .

This night,
Two thousand years ago,
Jerusalem fell and the Temple was burned.
Tonight
This white-haired Jewess
Sits in her kitchen and chants—by the banks of the Hudson—
The Lament of the Prophet.

The gaslight flares and falls . . .

Nearby,
Locked in her room,
Her daughter lies on a bed convulsively sobbing.
Her face is dug in the pillows;
Her shoulders heave with her sobs—
The bits of a photograph lie on the dresser . . .

Ghetto Twilight

An infinite weariness comes into the faces of the old tenements,
As they stand massed together on the block,
Tall and thoughtfully silent,
In the enveloping twilight.
Pensively,
They eye each other across the street,
Through their dim windows—
With a sad recognizing stare,
Watching the red glow fading in the distance,
At the end of the street,
Behind the black church spires;
Watching the vague sky lowering overhead,
Purple with clouds of colored smoke
From the extinguished sunset;
Watching the tired faces coming home from work,
Like dry-breasted hags
Welcoming their children to their withered arms.

A Family Album

I

Worn and torn by many fingers
It stands on the bedroom dresser,
Resting back against its single cardboard buttress,
(There were two),
The gilt clasp that bound it, loose and broken,
The beautiful Madonna on its cover, faded and pencil-marked,
And the coarse wood of its back showing through its velvet lining.

II

I remember the time that my sister Pauline bought it for the house
(300 Cherry Street, fourth floor, right-hand side, front)
Thirteen years ago,
With the proceeds of her first week at the factory.
It was beautiful then,
The golden-haired, grave-eyed Madonna that adorned it.
Her blue eyes were ever so much bluer and clearer, and so sweetly
pensive,
Her golden hair fell forward over her bare breast,
Brighter and yellower than gold,
And there were no black pencil marks across the pure white of her
brow
Or the delicate pink of her cheeks.
She was beautiful . . .
And my father,
I remember my father didn't like that album,
And murmured against the open-bosomed female on its cover,
"It is sinful to have such a picture in a Jewish home!"
But I,
I loved that album because of its glorious, golden-haired Madonna.
And when I was left alone in the house
I would stand in the parlor for hours
And gaze into her ecstatic face
Half reverently, half tenderly.
And sometimes,
When I was doubly certain of being alone,
I would drag a chair up to the mantelpiece
And get on top of it,
And, timidly extending my hand,
Touch with my trembling fingers the yellow threads of her hair as
they lay across her breast,

Or the soft slope of her breast into her loose robe.
And once, I remember,
Ashamed of my feelings, yet unable to repress them,
I drew the picture closer to my face.
And pressed my lips passionately on that white bosom—
My first kiss . . .

III

Somehow I never cared to open the gilt clasp of the album
And look through the photographs that were collecting there:
Photographs brought here from Russia,
Photographs taken here at various times,
Grandfathers, grandmothers, aunts, uncles, cousins,
Sisters and sisters-in-law, brothers and brothers-in-law;
Photographs of some of the many boarders that always occupied our bedrooms
(The family usually slept on folding beds in the kitchen and parlor
Together with some other boarders);
Boarders-in-law; sweethearts, wives, husbands of the boarders;
Group pictures: family pictures, shop pictures, school pictures.
Somehow I never cared to open the gilt clasp of the album
And look through that strange kaleidoscope of Life.
But now,
As I find myself turning its heavy cardboard pages,
Turning them meditatively back and forth,
My brain loosens like the gilt clasp of the album,
Unburdening itself of its locked memories,
Page after page, picture after picture,
Until the miscellaneous photographs take to themselves color and meaning,
Standing forth out of their places like a series of paintings;
As if a Master-Artist had gone over them with his brush,
Revealing in them things I did not see in the originals,
Solving in Art that which baffled me in Life.
And all the while as I go through the album, supporting the cover with my hand,
The yellow-haired Madonna gazes at me from under my fingers,
Sadly, reproachfully.

IV

Poor, warm-hearted, soft-headed, hard-fisted Uncle Isaac
In his jaunty coat and flannel shirt,

Stiff and handsome and mustached,
Standing as if he were in evening dress—
His head thrown backward, his eyes fixed forward;
Conscious of the cleanliness of his face and hands,
Fresh washed from a day's grime at the coal cellar.
When I look at his bold, blank face
My mind tears through the dense years,
Along the crazy alley of his life,
Back to a Lithuanian village on a twig of the Vistula.
Kartúshkiya-Beróza (what a sweet name—
Beróza is the Russian for birch trees)
And from a background of a dusty road meandering between high,
green banks of foliage
I feel two black eyes looking at me strangely,
Two black passion-pregnant eyes
Nestling in a little dark face.

V

Every Saturday afternoon in the summertime
When the town was like a green bazaar
With the houses half-hidden under leaves and the lanes drifting
blindly between the dense shade trees
After the many-coursed Sabbath dinner and the long synagogue
services that preceded it
Mother took the four of us over to Grandpa's
A few houses up the lane
Where the aunts and the uncles and the cousins and the nephews
and the nieces
In silk and in flannel and in satin and in linen,
Every face shining with a Sabbath newness,
Gathered on the porch for the family promenade:
Up to the lane and across the Gentile quarter and around the
Bishop's orchard;
Through the Polish Road past the Tombs of the Rebels to the haunted
red chapel at the crossroads—
And back again by cross cuts through the cornfields,
With the level yellow plain mellowing mystically around us in the
soft sunshine,
And the sunset fading behind us like the Sabbath,
At twilight—just before the evening service—
Every Saturday afternoon, in summertime.

ENGLISH

VI

They rise in my brain with mysterious insistence
The blurred images of those Sabbath walks—
Poignantly, painfully, vaguely beautiful,
Half obliterated under the cavalcade of the years,
They lurk in the wayside of my mind and ambush me unawares—
Like little children they steal behind me unawares and blindfold me
with intangible fingers
Asking me to guess who it is:
Across a wide city street a patch of pavement like a slab of gold;
A flash of sunlight on a flying wheel—
And I am left wondering, wondering where I have seen sunlight
before?
By a holiday-thronged park walk, a trio of huge trees thrust their
great, brown arms through uplifted hillocks of green leaves—
And I stand staring at them penetratively;
Trying to assure myself that they were real,
And not something that had swum up in my mind
From a summer that has withered years ago—
In the beaches by the wayside on the Polish Road,
Isled among the birch woods,
As you come out of Kartúshkiya-Beróza.
On my bed, within the padded prison-walls of sleep, lurching
through a night of dreams;
I am awakened by a shrill wide-spreading triumphant outburst of
incessant twittering—
Under my window in the park,
Catching like fire from tree to tree, from throat to throat
Until the whole green square seems ablaze with joy,
As if each growing leaf had suddenly found tongue—
And I raise myself in my bed, dreamily, on my elbows
Listening with startled attentiveness to a sweet, clear twittering in
my brain
As of a hundred populous treetops vying with the pebble-tuned
waters of a brook
Gurgling timidly across a wide road.
In a hallway among a party of girls and young men tripping
downstairs for an outing on a Sunday morning,
The coarse, keen pungency of satin from some girl's new shirtwaist,
Through my nose into my brain pierces like a rapier—
And suddenly I am standing on a sunny country porch with
whitewashed wooden columns,
All dressed up for a Sabbath walk,

In a red satin blouse with a lacquered, black belt
With my mother in her blue silk Sabbath dress and grandmother
with a black lace shawl around her head
With my sisters and my brother and portly Uncle Zalman with his
fat, red-bearded face
And my grandfather stooping in his shining black capote with his
grizzled beard and earlocks and thoughtful, tiny eyes
And poor Aunt Bunya who died of her first childbirth, with her
roguish-eyed young husband
And smooth-shaven, mustached Uncle Isaac half-leaning, half-
sitting on the banister with his little girl clamped playfully
between his knees
And his wife Rebecca, with black eyes and pursed up scornful lips
standing haughtily aloof
And my cousins Basha and Miriam and little Nachman clutching at
Uncle Zalman's trousers
And their mother, smiling, big-hearted, big-bosomed Aunt Golda,
offering me a piece of tart
As I am staring absently sideways
Into the little dark face rimmed lovingly between Uncle Isaac's
coarse hands.

Stanley Burnshaw

Stanley Burnshaw was born in New York City in 1906. He taught for a time at New York University and has had a long career in publishing, serving as vice-president at Holt, Rinehart and Winston until 1968. His best-known works are The Poem Itself, The Seamless Web, Varieties of Literary Experiences, *and* In the Terrified Radiance. *Burnshaw currently lives on Martha's Vineyard.*

Isaac

The story haunts this tribe that cannot wipe from its eyes
The flashing hill, the trembling man tying his son in his arms, the
bewildered ram
Bearing twigs and firewood. They think it again and again
Through forty centuries. Even now when they look at a chance
hillock
Under the sky of an unmysterious day, the eyes
Of their poets hang it with flame—
"Father, father, save Isaac!"

One of them hears his night cry out, as though the indifferent cloud
Were sown with seeds of blood bursting to flutter
Over the boiling stones.
                                        Even my own father
One morning of my longago childhood helplessly
Watched his thought slip through the Hegelian chain
With which he wrestled the world, to relieve the curse
Thou shalt not raise thy hand . . .
                                                    Nor yet can a generation
Die without shouting once into the air to purge its heart
Of the blind obsessive tale, as though for always unsure
Of the wrong of worshipping the blood's terror of sacrifice.

House in St. Petersburg

If my mother had never been the protected child
Of a dreamy scholar in a protected house,
          I would not be writing these lines—

If the sign hung in the window of that house
Had told a different lie from the lie it told,
          I would not be writing these lines—

If the bribed police who winked at the sign had lived—
If the old one had not choked in a swilling night,
          I would not be writing these lines—

If the young recruit had been briefed with the well-bribed
            word
By his well-bribed captain before he walked by the house,

Or if he had never tripped on a cobble of ice
And ripped his shirt as he sprawled on a gashing stone,
          I would not be writing these lines—

If he had not then remembered the house with the sign
Because of the word it had always said to the street,

Or if when he asked the service of needle and thread
Father or child could have brought him needle and thread,
          I would not be writing these lines—

If the suddenly tongueless man of a stricken house
Had dared to speak with his eyes and a bag of gold,

Or if the gold had said to the young recruit
What it always said when the hunted spoke to the law,
I would not be writing these lines—

If the young recruit had not shouted guilt in the street
So that passersby turned round to assault the house,

If he had not screamed the name as he climbed the steps
To the barracks and flung his find in his captain's face,

Or if when the captain scanned the innocent's eyes
He had found a gleam that confessed it was not too late,
I would not be writing these lines—

If the innocent had not shouted again and again
And again—if the captain could have closed up his ears,

Or if his major, cursing his luck and loss,
Had never signed the papers to pillage and seize,
I would not be writing these lines—

If the child and father, clinging with dread in the snows
Of night, had failed before they reached the frontier,

Or if their boat, lost in a wild North Sea,
Had not been sighted and saved on a Scottish shore,
I would not be writing these lines—

Or, when they voyaged again, if their battered ship
Had not groped through its trial to the promised port,

Or if when they saw the sun of a friending earth
They had not danced in the recklessness of its air,
I would not be writing these lines—

If the father after the years of dancing and grief
Had sought his sleep on an alien hill of Home,
I would not be writing these lines—

Or if my mother, walking in tears from his grave,
Had not returned, one April, to join his sleep,
I would not be writing these lines—

And if she herself, before, in a long ago,
Had never told this tale to a young one's eyes,
I would not be singing her song.

Talmudist

Gloat, glittering talmudist,
With your eastern eye, your northern eye, your western eye;
The days are a fog of clashing words: cleave
If you can—warp with your buzz-saw brain a light-filled
Path shallow enough for a heart to follow.

Why do you fist your words
With your merchant's hand, your scholar's hand, your toiler's hand?
Is a god you smother the dynamo of your fury
Or a wraith you reasoned into existence in hope
It would pierce your eye with joys? Or a heartsick need

For a heaven-on-earth perfection
That drives you, though you have found there can be no right
Unmixed with wrong. Where will you go when the moment
Strikes and your arms, defying brain, reach out
To your brothers' will, your homeland's will, your body's will?

Michael Castro

Michael Castro was born in New York in 1945 and attended the State University of New York at Buffalo and Washington University. His poetry has appeared in several small magazines, and he has published three books of poems, The Kokopilau Cycle, Ghost Hiways and Other Homes *and* Cracks. *He edits the magazine of poetry and art,* River Styx.

Grandfathers

One chain-smoked cigarettes,
rolled his own
with slow, deliberate movements,
never wanted matches,
lit each new smoke
with the butt of the last.

Worked as caretaker
of a club for rich French
& German businessmen
in Salonika,
by the Aegean Sea,
where he watched
the Greeks & Turks unite
to drive out the Bulgarians.
They'd shoot at
the Bulgarians,
driving them back,
street by street.
Then they'd shoot at
each other.

Like most who lived there,
this grandfather
didn't give a damn
who won.
But the Germans,
the Germans cared,
& so they tried out their bombers
over the city,
warming up
for 'The Great War.'

The city smoked
with this grandfather.
But each work day
ended the same way for him.
He'd sweep up his own butts,
throw them away in the trash,
& consign it all to flames.

ENGLISH

He was a disgrace
to the family,
for he worked on the Sabbath.

His grandfather
had been head rabbi
in Palestine,
& his brother
was a rabbi in Salonika,
who changed money on the side.
He had a little booth
on a busy corner.
My father,
who is now a grandfather,
remembers it well.

This brother was thought
highly of
by the family.
But my grandfather, the black sheep,
saved his money.
He left for America by steamship
with his oldest son, Alberto,
to keep the boy
from being drafted.

My father, the grandfather,
the orphaned son,
stayed behind with his sister.
He slept five in a bed
with uncles & cousins & aunts,
& sold needles & postcards
to soldiers' outstretched hands
through barbed wire fences.

He was in Salonika
during the Great Fire of 1919.
He saw British troops,
a few blocks ahead of the blaze,
spraying buildings in the Jewish quarter
with gasoline.
They preferred to destroy the city

than to let the Germans have it.
People jumped into the harbor
to escape the conflagration.

All that smoke.

When my father came to America
he took up cigars,
& eventually opened a cigar store
on Chambers Street,
near the Immigration Bureau.
His grandfather
died of Nazi gas,
age 101.

On the other side
more smoke.

My mother's father
was from Jannina,
from an ancient line of Greek Jews.
In America, this grandfather
worked in a cigarette factory
& lived in Harlem.
He is best remembered for
his big, beautiful brown eyes,
& for the love he showered on his wife,
his children,
& on distant relatives
arriving by boat at Ellis Island.
He died
in the influenza epidemic of 1919,
while Salonika went up in smoke.
My grandmother followed him,
dying in Harlem
six months later
of a broken heart.

For years
my mother thought the "deathbed"
was a special bed.

All those babushka'ed aunts
& kimona peddling uncles
wept at the funerals,
but none took in the children.
Somehow my mother, the grandmother,
survived, taking care
of her two younger brothers,
shuffling from foster-home to foster-home
& back again
to the Hebrew Orphan Asylum.

She met my cigar smoking father
&, about the time his grandfather died,
made him a son.

The son worked in the smoke shop,
handed over Turkish
blend Camels
to hacking chain-smokers
(old proverb of Jannina Jews,
"The camel doesn't see his own hump,"
echoing in his brain),
swept up their butts
as they disappeared
out the door in their own smoke,
didn't smoke himself,
didn't think he knew
his own grandfathers,
but somehow,
with a little help, was able
to make
his father one.

Percolating Highway

I'm running from myself down this percolating highway
I got coffee cups balanced on my palms, saucers in the sky
The moon's my cream, & sugar crystal stars
I'm running from myself & my hands are burning
I got blood spurting from wounds that never heal
I got lizards licking me behind, roadrunners up ahead
Sirens spinning in my head

I'm running from myself & I feel like dying
I feel like lying down & letting fire-ants put out my flame
I got fenceposts down my trousers, & jail bars up my sleeves
I got everything in writing, but I can't recall my name
I got a desert rat feeling, got the rattler shakes
Got a king in the hole, a joker in my soul
Searching for seven cities until this gold fever breaks
I'm running from myself down this percolating highway
I got the caffeine sweats
I'm gonna collect all bets down in White Sands tonight
When the mushroom billows I get a flash of white light
Yes I got a stone slab pillow for my head
Cactus needles for my bed, a saddle for my horse
A limp body for my cross—
I'm running from myself & I feel like dying

Eric Chaet

Eric Chaet was born in Chicago in 1945. He presently teaches at Nebraska Western College. He is the author of two books of poems, Old Buzzard of No-Man's Land *and* Counterattack, *and of one novel,* Unraveling Smoke.

Yom Kippur

I throw off all the ceremony
to get to the kernel of the wheat,
the germ, to get to the
repentance itself;
pardon me, I am not trying to get organized,
I am trying to operate
from the fire that is the bush.

A Letter Catches Up with Me

I'm more afraid of those I love than dying.

A letter catches up with me
where I've taken refuge from storm & moon
at fragrant family table.

They say: O, a letter.

ENGLISH

I leap to my feet
& out into pouring rain & forked lightning
biting my nails
searching for a phone booth
gulping my pride
longing
to whisper all the old honesties.

Therefore:
I'm more afraid of those I love than dying.

They don't dare say:
drop everything & come to me.
Only death dares.

I don't regret those who can't bear my love close up.
Only I'm dropping everything.

Sky writes no suicide notes.
It storms, it clears, it's blue—
it drops everything, that's all.

I'm in no hurry to die.
I like happening & watching.

These bruises on my heart are grateful for their chance to be.

Listen, you who wonder what all this dying's for:
this bright, ripening gift, you mean?
They used to call it God, there's that.
& who knows? they may again.

I hang around behind warehouses
where tumbleweed lies on shining rails
just for pleasure.

Fellow fossils:
crow who comes from sky is one of us.
Stranger: welcome all strangers.
In some languages, this is called celebration.

So: I'm more afraid of those I love than dying.

As for love: it overwhelms my fear.

Kim Chernin

Kim Chernin was born in 1940 in New York City and presently lives in Berkeley, California. She has written six books of poetry: The Tribes of Inheritance, A City Not Forsaken, The Army of Horsemen, Awake, Psaltery and Harp, A Way for the Ransomed, *and* When I Remember These Things, *all as yet unpublished.*

Eve's Birth

Was I summoned
or did I rise
from my own emergency?
Dreaming of a dark and formless thing
that had no eyes
and fashioned mine.
Remembering:
waters, the disquieting wind,
dark earth and dismembering fire:
a servile arc
that roared disquietude,
wakened from slumber;
and breath,
ribbed with mortality.

Elaine Dallman

Elaine Dallman was awarded her Ph.D. in creative writing from Southern Illinois University. Her poems have had broad acceptance in literary anthologies and journals.

From the Dust

There were only Adam and Eve.
The snake came from a slit
in Adam's mind.
Moving outward, soft coiled skin,
the uncoiling intuitive search for a tree
to be glossy like a beast in.

Released from Adam, evil spread in flicking colors
a red sun,
opaque;
the pigmented world set hard.

Souls, bodies, are spaced on a
clay wheel. Below it,
the serpent dances, ends time.
I know what Hecuba is to me:
a fist that knocks twice on clay.
One after another,
women make fists, knock twice;
each knock is the desire
to re-enter.

When my dark hair blows in the wind,
I would lift.
I try to knock on earth's air.
The second time, I make a tighter fist.
I breathe dust spreading down in
a great wing.

Lucille Day

Lucille Day was born in Oakland, California, in 1947. She is currently working toward her Ph.D. in science/mathematics education at the University of California-Berkeley. Her poems and stories have been included in Berkeley Poetry Review, Epos, *and* Contemporary Women Poets: An Anthology of California Poets.

Labor

All night the Shabbos candles
beat like twin hearts.
I awoke every hour
and when they finally went out
I got up.
It was still dark.

Now, clouds blister the sky—
a terrible rash, all white.
The sun is no poultice,
but the wind
soothes and soothes.

Soon the pain will be over.
I am going to find a room.
It will be all white
except for my blood
and one lamp
burning like a small sun.

I will not notice it.
Cool drafts will cover my body.
Outside the sky will clear.
By noon
someone will be born.

Yom Kippur

Kol Nidre

The cantor sings.
The congregation responds.
This prayer is the long
melodious chant of swallows
that rise sunward, beating
like a thousand hearts.
They sing of the wound
and blood's dark tendrils,
of the hidden nest
and the slow healing.
Darkness unfolds. They land
in a field of blue flowers
as cold stars settle.

Torah

It happens again.
There are two goats.
One is to be sacrificed:
straight bones and firm
muscles will burn.
The other receives the sins
of the people, goes free.
The burden twists him;
skin and muscles rip.
He wanders alone, blind,
edging into dusk.

Ne'ilah

Again the day rolls
into darkness; the sky
spills its pinks and purples,
draining to blackness. Deep
inside there is a closing,
a small gate
swinging shut in the mind.
Those few last thoughts
rush through, and a life
is sealed. Outside the temple
a lone bird sounds its call,
waits for response.

Rose Drachler

Rose Drachler is a graduate of Hunter College with additional studies at Columbia University and the New School. Though she writes in English, her poems display a fondness for the Yiddish, Polish, Russian, and Hebrew with which she is familiar. Her poems have appeared in numerous journals and have been published in two books, Burrowing In, Digging Out *and* The Choice.

Isaac and Esau

Who comes to us in our dark
Smelling of innocence?

The tent being full of dream sheep
We need no increase of real flocks.

Is there a dream we can give the child
Plain as hunger?

We hear him weeping, helpless
Against eyes that cut through sky

For the customary ram
Familiar to our darkness.

The Dark Scent of Prayer

In the tunnel
Light is haloed
Sound dissolved
The skin of separation
Is softened

Thought approaches
Airy and bright
Soft but pervasive
It penetrates rock

Where no edges are tight
The despairing hornet
Can fly through
Stained glass

Frightened sparrows
Can soar through clouds
Painted on the ceiling

The striped wasp
Confused by the Book
Can thrive on
The dark scent of prayer

Under the Shawl

The great beasts rumble and sway.
It is dark down here under my father's shawl,
Sweet and familiar behind his knee.
I play with the fringe and look up into
The forest of nostrils and beards.

A careful power lifts my child-bones up
To the lectern where the smell of snuff
And the peppery man-smell, the great rough hands
And the coarse grandpa clothes comfort me.

The place smells the same as once
And drones too as I remember.
My bones feel small. I am lifted easily.

ENGLISH

Zippora Returns to Moses at Rephidim

By the wells
Alone and running
You found my dark skin a comfort
A home of maternal wetness

Now I bow, since I must
To your unseen Lover

My son is well named a stranger
For me

If there are others
You may cut them
Before they have learned to suck
Using bronze not stone
Oh bitter husband to me

Distracted lover
I shall sleep in your tent alone

My father has brought me back
He will stay to teach you
To govern your inconstant people
Constant only in revolt

It was his craft brought you this far
His and the hand of your Bridegroom

No more shall I be troubled
By the smiles of my six glutted sisters

Send your Nubian concubine to me
We shall both be darkly forsaken

While you fast
And adore in the wind
You jealous
Bridegroom of blood

As I Am My Father's

based on a work of Achad Ha'am

I am my own
My opinions and feelings
Are my own

I do not conceal
Or deny what I am
What you put there

In the end
At the end of days
You will be just

Like Balaam
Who beat his ass
For seeing

What was there
You beat us
These many times

But in the end
You will see the angel too
Since you put this angel
In our way

You will be just
Since justice is your name
I do not speak of mercy
Which is your name too

The Letters of the Book

Aleph the cow with wide horns
Her milk in the night sky
Walks slowly on clouds
Aleph to the tenth power
She leads with symbolic logic
To the throne of milky pearl
Aleph the sky-cow with lovely eyes
Wide-horned giver she gives mankind
Her sign of is-ness

ENGLISH

Bayz the house snug
Under the heat of the sun
Out of the rain and the snow
We curl up in a corner
Under the roof of Bayz
Out of the daily sorrow
Bayz the comforter
Inhabited by humanity
Cat-like and childlike
Inside of his Bayz

Ghimel the camel
Carries man into the book
The leaves and waves
Of the forest the sea of the book
Boat of the desert the camel
Long traveler drinking the task
Ghimel drinks the dry road of daily observance
It slakes the thirst for communion

Daled the door like a wall
No hinges no handle
Daled the mysterious opener
Into a place with a road
The six hundred and thirteen small roads
Of derekh eretz

I have swallowed Vav the hook
It had something tasty and nourishing on it
A promise of plenty and friendship
With someone more than myself
I've got Vav the hook in my gut
I shift to rearrange the discomfort
Like a sharp minnow inside
When he draws up the line
Attached to the hook
When he rips the Vav out
There will be strange air around me
Burning my gills

Yod the hand
And Koff the palm
Rested gently
On Raish the head
Of Abraham our father
Who crossed over
Burning the idols
Behind him in Ur
He looked upward
At stars sun and moon
Then looked further
For a pat on the head
From Yod and Koff
The unseen hand and palm

In the crook
Of the Lammed leaning forward
I put my neck when I pray
My shepherd makes me meek
He makes my knees bend
He guides me I follow
With the loop of the Lammed
On my throat
I go

Mem is the water
Sweetly obeying
The red-raging water
Which parted
Mem came together
And drowned the pursuers
Stubborn refusers of freedom
The enslavers Mem drowned them
Mem was the water
Brackish tormenting
Sweetened with leaves
By our Moses
The waters of trust
Which he struck from the rock
Mem mayim water

The jelly-glowing eye full of love
Sees past the eye the Ayin
Like a dog it perceives the hidden
It turns and stares at its master
It pleads with him to come home
The longing for certainty
Fills him too full
Return, my master, he says
Your eye to my eye
Ayin

Peh the mouth speaking hastily
Praying easily fast without reverence
Full of gossip causing estrangement
Let my soul be as dust to Peh
The loud quarreler the prattler
The carrier of tales to and fro
The beguiler the mouth Peh better still

Shin is the tooth
It chews on the word
(With the dot on the left
It is Sin)
So much sharper than Shin the tooth
Is learning in the study
Together by dimlight
Chuckling together at the tooth
The horn that was known to gore
The tooth for a tooth in our story
The sharp-toothed father
Of our fathers
Who was wont to gore in the past

Larry Eigner

Larry Eigner was born in 1927 and currently lives in Swampscott, Massachusetts. In addition to being included in major anthologies of modern American poetry, Eigner has published the following books: Selected Poems, Another Time in Fragments, Words Touching/Ground Under, *and* Anything on Its Side.

The Closed System

The closed system
Of earth
Of the Ark
Love
Mercy

shut him up carefully
in it like involved self the
wandering spot with
the man family beasts

the needs after predictions of
your own acts

rise up go forth
on the water beyond
the walls that
can be made
creation
and the floods
the more there is the more
begins
a kind of chain
firecrackers or
burning woods
having defined a thing
and called it Evil
in all proportion
the outsized Men

Remember Sabbath Days

Remember
Sabbath days to
keep time still
how multiple clothe
the past it's
not bare but
it takes time
to look eat
and prepare darkness
among the stars

ENGLISH

Marcia Falk

Marcia Falk was born in New York City in 1946. She has studied at Brandeis and Stanford, and currently teaches Hebrew and English at the State University of New York in Binghamton. Her poems and translations from Hebrew, Yiddish, and Spanish have appeared in literary magazines and anthologies in the United States, England, and Israel. Her translation of The Song of Songs *was published in 1977. A collection of her own poems is now in preparation.*

Shulamit in Her Dreams

Day and night she dances,
between the suns
she dreams

By day she is the moon
turning
on the underside of earth

At night she is the windmill
waving
above the city walls

Dusk, she is
Shulamit

As she turns
the warriors chant her praises,
her thighs spin like jugs
on the potter's wheel,
her belly is round
with promise

Everywhere she moves
she captures
kings in the moats
of her eyes,
worlds in the locks
of her hair

Day and night she dances,
between the suns
she dreams

Modern Kabbalist

You tug at words
like weeds,
severing stems from roots,
until your hands are lined
with graphic signs.

Then you come to my house,
your hands open
and dumb—
like the neighbor's cat,
proud
with its prey
at my door—
and scatter on my floor
a pile of thorns
in the shapes
of things.

What shall I do
with these
small
inviolate
knives
that scar the mind.

Woman through the Window

For a year, she walked past my window
every morning singing
in the heat waves, in the rain,
her basket of mint and parsley
balanced surely
on her thick black hair.
Her head straight,
her eyes forward,
her voice slipped quickly
around the corners,
and if she felt the weight
of her bundles
it showed only in the slope
of her breasts,

heavy beneath black linen.
Till one day this April
she stopped coming.

In the summer, the steaming Arab market,
draped with lines of carpets,
embroideries, old clothes,
will swarm with young Europeans.
Which one will soon be wearing
the darkly woven patterns
of her dress?

Irving Feldman

Irving Feldman was born in Brooklyn in 1928 and was educated at the City College of New York and Columbia University. He currently teaches English at the State University of New York in Buffalo. His volumes of poetry are Works and Days, The Pripet Marshes and Other Poems, *and* The Magic Papers and Other Poems.

The Pripet Marshes

Often I think of my Jewish friends and seize them as they are and transport them in my mind to the *shtetlach* and ghettos,

And set them walking the streets, visiting, praying in *shul*, feasting and dancing. The men I set to arguing, because I love dialectic and song—my ears tingle when I hear their voices—and the girls and women I set to promenading or to cooking in the kitchens, for the sake of their tiny feet and clever hands.

And put kerchiefs and long dresses on them, and some of the men I dress in black and reward with beards. And all of them I set among the mists of the Pripet Marshes, which I have never seen, among wooden buildings that loom up suddenly one at a time, because I have only heard of them in stories, and that long ago.

It is the moment before the Germans will arrive.

Maury is there, uncomfortable, and pigeon-toed, his voice is rapid and slurred, and he is brilliant;

And Frank who is goodhearted and has the hair and yellow skin of a Tartar and is like a flame turned low;
And blonde Lottie who is coarse and miserable, her full mouth is turning down with a self-contempt she can never hide, while the steamroller of her voice flattens every delicacy;
And Marian, her long body, her face pale under her bewildered black hair and of the purest oval of those Greek signets she loves; her head tilts now like the heads of the birds she draws;
And Adele who is sullen and an orphan and so like a beaten creature she trusts no one, and who doesn't know what to do with herself, lurching with her magnificent body like a despoiled tigress;
And Munji, moping melancholy clown, arms too short for his barrel chest, his penny-whistle nose, and mocking nearsighted eyes that want to be straightforward and good;
And Abbie who, when I listen closely, is speaking to me, beautiful with her large nose and witty mouth, her coloring that always wants lavender, her vitality that body and mind can't quite master;
And my mother whose gray eyes are touched with yellow, and who is as merry as a young girl;
And my brown-eyed son who is glowing like a messenger impatient to be gone and who may stand for me.
I cannot breathe when I think of him there.
And my red-haired sisters, and all my family, our embarrassed love bantering our tenderness away.

Others, others, in crowds filling the town on a day I have made sunny for them; the streets are warm and they are at their ease.

How clearly I see them all now, how miraculously we are linked! And sometimes I make them speak Yiddish in timbres whose unfamiliarity thrills me.

But in a moment the Germans will come.

What, will Maury die? Will Marian die?

Not a one of them who is not transfigured then!

The brilliant in mind have bodies that glimmer with a total dialectic;
The stupid suffer an inward illumination; their stupidity is a subtle tenderness that glows in and around them;
The sullen are surrounded with great tortured shadows raging with pain, against whom they struggle like titans;

ENGLISH

In Frank's low flame I discover an enormous perspectiveless depth;
The gray of my mother's eyes dazzles me with our love;
No one is more beautiful than my red-haired sisters.
And always I imagine the least among them last, one I did not love, who was almost a stranger to me.
I can barely see her blond hair under the kerchief; her cheeks are large and faintly pitted, her raucous laugh is tinged with shame as it subsides; her bravado forces her into still another lie;
But her vulgarity is touched with a humanity I cannot exhaust, her wretched self-hatred is as radiant as the faith of Abraham, or indistinguishable from that faith.
I can never believe my eyes when this happens, and I want to kiss her hand, to exchange a blessing

In the moment when the Germans are beginning to enter the town.

But there isn't a second to lose, I snatch them all back,
For, when I want to, I can be a God.
No, the Germans won't have one of them!
This is my people, they are mine!

And I flee with them, crowd out with them; I hide myself in a pillowcase stuffed with clothing, in a woman's knotted handkerchief, in a shoebox.

And one by one I cover them in mist, I take them out.
The German motorcycles zoom through the town,
They break their fists on the hollow doors.
But I can't hold out any longer. My mind clouds over.
I sink down as though drunk or beaten.

Ruth Feldman

Ruth Feldman lives in Cambridge, Massachusetts, but spends much of her time in Italy. Her poems and translations from Italian to English have appeared in many major literary journals. A number of her poems have been published in Italy in translations by Italian poets. Shema: Collected Poetry of Primo Levi *won her and her co-translator, Brian Swann, the John Florio Prize in 1976. A collection of her poetry entitled* The Ambition of Ghosts *was published in 1979.*

Lilith

Half of me is beautiful
but you were never sure
which half. You lay with me

of your own free will, then fled
back to her chaste bed.
The mother of your real children

hangs an amulet with magic syllables
over their cribs,
to ward me off.

Sitting beside her
on the Sabbath bench, you
exorcise me. I come back, riding

the wind's wing, slip through
the walls and steal into bed
between you. You wake spent.

Each time your loins
twitch with desire,
my womb swells with a new burden.

Our children multiply like seeds.
They will wail at your deathbed
and crowd her children out. But not

for long. Robbed of their birthright,
my frail progeny will fade and die
as her brood grows rosier.

ENGLISH

Donald Finkel

Donald Finkel was born in New York City in 1929 and graduated from Columbia University. Since 1965 he has been poet-in-residence at Washington University. He has published eight volumes of poetry, including A Joyful Noise, Answer Back, The Garbage Wars, Adequate Earth, Endurance, *and* Going Under.

Genealogy

Fire was first
out of fire came fist
out of fist, teeth

teeth begat mouth
and mouth, stone
stone begat worm

worm took his tail in his mouth
and wind was born
out of wind came foot

foot begat running
running, water
water, womb

then
out of womb sprang meat
and meat went into his mother

and begat
and begat
and begat

Lilith

She hissed in my ear
What can you lose?
she wasn't bad
but for the nose
that battle axe
long loose black hair

black arrogant eyes
generous mouth
great creamy boobs
on the frame of a boy
she laid for dwarfs
and garbage men
fucked like a snake
beak like a hawk
held open house
in her round bed
without a foot
without a head

where is she now
slithering across what
littered moonscape
stirring with that
irreverent snoot
the dreams of virgins
dry gritty
snatches of spinsters
night lizard
demon of lonely sleepers
while we tumble and turn
in our four square bed
between us a field
a flock a house
two grumbling boys
twenty years
of sweat and bread
and everything to lose

Cain's Song

First was Eve
the heavy mother
first the egg
cruising the borderless
kingdoms of water
gliding dividing
leaving herself behind
she was everywhere

coming and going
she met herself
she was bored
boredom is the root
of the sorry tree
I am the fruit

The air was not, nor the sky above it. What kept closing in? Where? And whose enclosure? And was the plunging abyss all water?

out of boredom
on her placid brow
heavy mother
grew a root
like a twisted horn
she looked about
there was no one
to bury it in
but herself
out of boredom she fell
into sleep
the root did not

And why shoulde I not commen more familiarly with you, accordynge to my custome? I praie you, is it the head? the face? the breast? the hands? or the eares? which parts of the body are named honest, that engendre gods, and men? I trow no. Naie, it is euien that selie membre, so fond, and foolisshe, as maie not without laughter be spoken of, which is the onely planter of mankynde. That, is the onely fountaine, whens all thynges receiue life, a great deal sooner than from Pythagoras quaternion.

on her smooth brow
the twisted root
sprang to life
divided not quite
grew roots of his own
and leapt fully armed
with his hump and his flute
Adam the forked
Adam the clown

first was Eve
Adam the bone
he raised his flute
and played her awake
she swayed before him
watching the instrument
turn in his hand
to a tree to a snake
to a snail to a plow
he plowed a furrow
in the water
and called it land

Every so often this Humpback Flute Player would stop and scatter seeds from the hump on his back. Then he would march on, playing his flute and singing a song. His song is still remembered, but the words are so ancient that nobody knows what they mean.

thence to a lily
to an ear of corn
to a needle an arrow
an iron bar
he raised it high
about the tip
glinting swirled
a rose of dust
he brought it near
and stroked her breast
she felt her atoms
swivel in their flaming sockets
he called that direction

divided against
herself forever
heart against head
longing
loathing
heavy mother
took to her bed
he juggled it back
to a flute and played
her whole again
Adam the natural
Adam the clown

The syllables of a good double strophe are as follows: Zizozozizizizizizizizizi-rreuzipiah totototototototozissskutziah.

thence to a stick
beat time on her brow
thence to a feather
plunged in her belly
drew out a worm
she dreamed again
could feel us already
flailing away
with our knouts truncheons
nightsticks pikes
he called us Abel and Cain
things would never
be the same
heavy mother
moaned in sleep

"It is a sound," say the Mullers, "that blends the deepest lowing of cattle with water splashing and something like sighs."

it is a sound
Cain will remember
till he dies

Lame Angel

Lame Angel slumps at his desk
his basket is empty
but his hand
clasps and unclasps the indifferent air
like an embryo practicing its grip

like an embryo
he practices everything
swimming creeping chinning himself on the cord
even flying in place

under his shirt his downy shoulderblades
throb like a deer's first horns
he scrapes them against his chair

sometimes in high places
he goes to use them
as a one-legged man might run from a burning house
he'll die before they sprout

clenched in his teeth perhaps
a morsel of wind
a worm rehearsing perpetually the life of a butterfly
but a worm to the end

Finders Keepers

In that tribe the priests are chosen
for memory alone
they have forgotten nothing
can give the gods their testimony
twelve nights running
chanting to each of the four winds in turn
that none be insulted

whereas the poets have memories
so frail
rising they remember neither
the nightmare nor the night before
wake without history
forebears
crying
ma ma
a lamb on a stone

each day
they construct anew
not merely their own
truncated lives
but the language of the tribe

Feeding the Fire

The children know how to do it
they kneel to it tenderly
crooning, *Eat little fire*
here is a scrap of paper, a handful of thorns

and the moth knows
wrapped like a monk in saffron flame
and the log
serene in his iron cradle

now the fire has eaten the thorns
a girl approaches, gift outstretched
eyes averted, sidling warily
the fire snatches it from her hand

it has grown, it is
hungrier than ever

How Things Fall

Shoes fall on their feet
angels fall to their knees
the note falls due
the words fall short
the butterfly falls to a blade of grass
and clings, still flittering

dust settles, stars decline
curtains plunge and splendor sprawls
the day falls into place
the sleeper falls back on his dream
princes fall out and troops fall in

a pound of feathers falls like a pound of flesh
the balances pitch and tremble
leaves fall like lovers, suicides like snow
drifting reluctantly plummeting eagerly
whispering in the wind they make

when the temple falls
every shard becomes a temple
when the city crumples
won't the masons have their day
a feast of heavenly mortar
an orgy of stones

Laya Firestone

Laya Firestone (Seghi) was born in St. Louis, Missouri, in 1947. Since then she has lived in Israel, Wisconsin, Illinois, and Canada before returning to live in Missouri. She has worked as a Hebrew teacher and translator. Her translations from the Hebrew have included poets such as Yehuda Amichai, Gabriel Preil, Shlomo Vinner, and Natan Zach.

Listen to the Bird

Listen to the bird
Flying
Singing
Signaling with sound
Or song
Traveling from one heart
To another.

After many miles of silence
A sound
One small signal
Starts circulation
On the desert of the soul.

The wagons have been dismembered
Wheels rolled into sand
Bones unburied
And what was once owned
Strewn about, no longer
Part of household or home.
Dried wood lies bleached in the sun
And there are no words
To leap like birds
With messages of how the world turns.

What is the sound?
Simple beyond recognition
It persists
Like water hitting the stone
And wherever the sound rings
The shape of the land
Takes form.

Thoughts for My Grandmother

The sound of your lips beating
Against each other in prayer
Like the flapping of wings
Preparing for flight,
And the power in your stare—
Your every movement was strength.
Even the clenching of your teeth
Was as deliberate a command as I'd ever heard.

But I didn't understand your ways.
I cried for days.
Only now do I begin to see
How you boomed,
Vibrated, shouted
In utter self-restraint.

Crow, Straight Flier, But Dark

Crow, straight flier, but dark;
Water, muddy and clear;
Wood, good to burn and would you burn it?
Trees, good to hold and hold on, they can hold you.
Holes, find one and hide.
Now let's start over.

Hole, come out of one;
Tree, hold onto one;
Wood, pick some up and start a fire;
Fire, heat your body and find warmth;
Stones, heat your stones on the fire,
Watch out—you may cause an explosion.
Let's start over.

Hole, come out of one,
Look at the light without fear.
Rain, let it fall on your eyes and into your ears.
Now you can hear and
See, the lights are shining,
Each one a star,
Every star a soul,
Every name a soul connected,
A chain of souls connected by
Names.

For Gabriel

Touching books,
You finger pages and words.
You reach out to feel
Even the letters,
As if to greet the meaning,
To welcome each and every message
With your hand.

Allen Ginsberg

Allen Ginsberg was born in Newark, New Jersey, in 1926 and studied at Columbia University. He was co-winner of the National Book Award in 1974 and has been included in almost every modern anthology of American poets. His best-known works are Howl *(1956) and* Kaddish and Other Poems *(1961).*

Kaddish

for Naomi Ginsberg 1894-1956

Strange now to think of you, gone without corsets & eyes, while I
walk on the sunny pavement of Greenwich Village,
downtown Manhattan, clear winter noon, and I've been up all night,
talking, talking, reading the Kaddish aloud, listening to Ray
Charles blues shout blind on the phonograph
the rhythm the rhythm — and your memory in my head three years
after — And read Adonais' last triumphant stanzas aloud —
wept, realizing how we suffer —

And how Death is that remedy all singers dream of, sing, remember, prophesy as in the Hebrew Anthem, or the Buddhist Book of Answers — and my own imagination of a withered leaf — at dawn —
Dreaming back thru life, Your time — and mine accelerating toward Apocalypse,
the final moment — the flower burning in the Day — and what comes after,
looking back on the mind itself that saw an American city
a flash away, and the great dream of Me or China, or you and a phantom Russia, or a crumpled bed that never existed —
like a poem in the dark — escaped back to Oblivion —
No more to say, and nothing to weep for but the Beings in the Dream, trapped in its disappearance,
sighing, screaming with it, buying and selling pieces of phantom, worshipping each other,
worshipping the God included in it all — longing or inevitability? —while it lasts, a Vision — anything more?
It leaps about me, as I go out and walk the street, look back over my shoulder, Seventh Avenue, the battlements of window office buildings shouldering each other high, under a cloud, tall as the sky an instant — and the sky above — an old blue place.
Or down the Avenue to the South, to — as I walk toward the Lower East Side — where you walked 50 years ago, little girl — from Russia, eating the first poisonous tomatoes of America — frightened on the dock —
then struggling in the crowds of Orchard Street toward what? — toward Newark —
toward candy store, first home-made sodas of the century, hand-churned ice cream in backroom on musty brownfloor boards—
Toward education marriage nervous breakdown, operation, teaching school, and learning to be mad, in a dream — what is this life?
Toward the Key in the window — and the great Key lays its head of light on top of Manhattan, and over the floor, and lays down on the sidewalk — in a single vast beam, moving, as I walk down first toward the Yiddish Theater — and the place of poverty
you knew, and I know, but without caring now — Strange to have moved thru Paterson, and the West, and Europe and here again,
with the cries of Spaniards now in the doorstoops doors and dark boys on the street, fire escapes old as you
— Tho you're not old now, that's left here with me —

Myself, anyhow, maybe as old as the universe — and I guess that dies with us — enough to cancel all that comes —
What came is gone forever every time —
That's good! That leaves it open for no regret — no fear radiators, lacklove, torture even toothache in the end —
Though while it comes it is a lion that eats the soul — and the lamb, the soul, in us, alas, offering itself in sacrifice to change's fierce hunger — hair and teeth — and the roar of bonepain, skull bare, break rib, rot-skin, braintricked Implacability.
Ai! ai! we do worse! We are in a fix! And you're out, Death let you out, Death had the Mercy, you're done with your century, done with God, done with the path thru it — Done with yourself at last — Pure — Back to the Babe dark before your Father, before us all — before the world —
There, rest. No more suffering for you. I know where you've gone, it's good.
No more flowers in the summer fields of New York, no joy now, no more fear of Louis,
and no more of his sweetness and glasses, his high school decades, debts, loves, frightened telephone calls, conception beds, relatives, hands —
No more of sister Elanor, — she gone before you — we kept it secret — you killed her — or she killed herself to bear with you — an arthritic heart — But Death's killed you both — No matter —
Nor your memory of your mother, 1915 tears in silent movies weeks and weeks — forgetting, agrieve watching Marie Dressler address humanity, Chaplin dance in youth,
or Boris Godinov, Chaliapin's at the Met, halling his voice of a weeping Czar — by standing room with Elanor & Max — watching also the Capitalists take seats in Orchestra, white furs, diamonds,
with the YPSL's hitch-hiking thru Pennsylvania, in black baggy gym skirts pants, photograph of 4 girls holding each other round the waste, and laughing eye, too coy, virginal solitude of 1920
all girls grown old, or dead, now, and that long hair in the grave — lucky to have husbands later —
You made it — I came too — Eugene my brother before (still grieving now and will grieve on to his last stiff hand, as he goes thru his cancer — or kill — later perhaps — soon he will think —)
And it's the last moment I remember, which I see them all, thru myself, now — tho not you

I didn't foresee what you felt — what more hideous gape of bad mouth came first — to you — and were you prepared?
To go where? In that Dark — that — in that God? a radiance? A Lord in the Void? Like an eye in the black cloud in a dream? Adonoi at last, with you?
Beyond my remembrance! Incapable to guess! Not merely the yellow skull in the grave, or a box of worm dust, and a stained ribbon — Deathshead with Halo? can you believe it?
Is it only the sun that shines once for the mind, only the flash of existence, than none ever was?
Nothing beyond what we have — what you had — that so pitiful — yet Triumph,
to have been here, and changed, like a tree, broken, or flower — fed to the ground — but mad, with its petals, colored, thinking Great Universe, shaken, cut in the head, leaf script, hid in an egg crate hospital, cloth wrapped, sore — freaked in the moon brain, Naughtless.
No flower like that flower, which knew itself in the garden, and fought the knife — lost
Cut down by an idiot Snowman's icy — even in the Spring — strange ghost thought — some Death — Sharp icicle in his hand — crowned with old roses — a dog for his eyes — cock of a sweatshop — heart of electric irons.
All the accumulations of life, that wear us out — clocks, bodies, consciousness, shoes, breasts — begotten sons — your Communism — 'Paranoia' into hospitals.
You once kicked Elanor in the leg, she died of heart failure later. You of stroke. Asleep? within a year, the two of you, sisters in death. Is Elanor happy?
Max grieves alive in an office on Lower Broadway, lone large mustache over midnight Accountings, not sure. His life passes — as he sees — and what does he doubt now? Still dream of making money, or that might have made money, hired nurse, had children, found even your Immortality, Naomi?
I'll see him soon. Now I've got to cut through — to talk to you — as I didn't when you had a mouth.
Forever. And we're bound for that, Forever — like Emily Dickinson's horses — headed to the End.
They know the way — These Steeds — run faster than we think — it's our own life they cross — and take with them.

Magnificent, mourned no more, marred of heart, mind behind, married dreamed, mortal changed — Ass and face done with murder.

In the world, given, flower maddened, made no Utopia, shut under pine, almed in Earth, balmed in Lone, Jehovah, accept.

Nameless, One Faced, Forever beyond me, beginningless, endless, Father in death. Tho I am not there for this Prophecy, I am unmarried, I'm hymnless, I'm Heavenless, headless in blisshood I would still adore

Thee, Heaven, after Death, only One blessed in Nothingness, not light or darkness, Dayless Eternity —

Take this, this Psalm, from me, burst from my hand in a day, some of my Time, now given to Nothing — to praise Thee — But Death

This is the end, the redemption from Wilderness, way for the Wonderer, House sought for All, black handkerchief washed clean by weeping — page beyond Psalm — Last change of mine and Naomi — to God's perfect Darkness — Death, stay thy phantoms!

Joseph Glazer

Joseph Glazer was born in Atlanta, Georgia. He was educated at Emory University and currently practices dentistry in Atlanta. His poems have appeared in a number of magazines, and he is the author of one book of poems, as yet unpublished, Memo to the Next Tenant.

A Visit Home

The platform I stood upon began to move,
My train shrieked out its *shofar*
Announcing the revival of the dead.

Streets ran from me cobbled, swollen,
Bits of grass milked through loaf-of-bread stones,
All this mapped in memory but
Real, grayer,
European light, shadowy,
And I never saw a Jew or a Hebrew letter. . . .
(The word kosher, names Levy, Cohen,
Echoes of sing-song Yiddish,
Little stores and synagogues exhaling
Incense of pain).
The town lay still
Waiting for nightfall,

A cemetery of sidewalks,
Curbstones,
Shuttered, plastered-over. . . .

Only a whirlwind of dust blazoned up
Funneling, twirling,
Knees high in ecstasy
Caftan-tails flying,
Airy figure of poignancy,
One ghostly Hasid
Out to greet me.

Albert Goldbarth

Albert Goldbarth was born in Chicago in 1948 and has since lived in Iowa, Utah, upstate New York, and currently Austin, Texas. He is the author of ten volumes of poetry, of which Jan. 31 *was nominated for a National Book Award and* Different Fleshes *is the most recent.*

Dime Call

Dead Jews, dead Jews, just points now an underground
telephone cable runs through. When I dial my
father up, *his* father, long gone, jolts in the
earth between us. —Picture an archaeologist,
unaware of that skeleton shocked to
life by my dime call. But

I believe the fathers have something
to say. And I believe
in the archaeologist, ear to ground
and eye sun-thin
through his lens, translating the many
dead tongues.

Like the phone
on the wall, black box
with its message . . . I'm going
to tie these phylacteries

till my head rings,
till they tell me.

Recipe

Greatgrandma's bending to pluck some vegetable,
squat, yellowed, like a tooth

from the hard ground, and like a tooth it yields
painfully. There she is, lashing sunlight with the roots

in my fantasized version of Poland. For the soup.
Poland's all soup, a chicken claw angled up

into air like a grapnel: the way birds really die.
The houses are just a little more coarse

than the shirts. Breathing's
brown, and fibrous, and talking's a series of nests.

The bread's a braid. The beetle's the only
limousine. I make a story: a cock eats the

stars like scattered grain. A black
I know, from Cincinnati, thinks Africa

his homeland this same way: savage,
supportive, featherstitched

dealings with God, and rainblow striped like *dashiki*.
We who were born recipients

of the myths, but not their citizens, twist
and jerryrig whatever ekes through

or leads back. Recipe: we live our days, a
clear broth—just water

that tastes of these roots.

ENGLISH

Lynn Gottlieb

Lynn Gottlieb is a storyteller and serves as a rabbi to the deaf community in the New York area. She is currently studying for rabbinic ordination.

Eve's Song in the Garden

I had no mother
to sing me through the night;
the earth was my mother
playing her flute of wind and moon
teaching me the quiet hum.

I had no father
to protect me from harshly growing things;
the sun was my father
teaching me to count the days of light and fire.

I had no sister
to share the memory of a parent's weaving on my loom;
the snake was my sister
teaching me to shed the past and live with its design upon my skin.

I had no brother
to build armies of little men
and fight off demons in secret hiding places;
the shallow stream was my brother
teaching me to walk the tumbling road of stone and flow.

I lived in a still garden
with another one like me,
but something made me eat
something made me eat
from the ripe tree of summer . . .
and life broke out of dreaming.

In those first days
we had no need to understand our dreams
we had not yet eaten
from the tree in the center of the garden
which taught us
how to know death.

Arthur Gregor

Arthur Gregor (originally Goldenberg) was born in 1923 in Vienna. He has worked as an editor and taught at several universities, including California State University, Hayward and Hofstra University. His seven books of poems include Figure in the Door, A Bed by the Sea, Selected Poems *and* The Past Now.

Spirit-like Before Light

My parents are making the journey
they had hoped-for long before
the expulsion that brought us here. Their destination
is Haifa. I went to see them off.
Their cabin was shockingly narrow.
An imposition of crude figuring.
My mother looked at first as if
this lack of regard had hurt her,
but not for long. My parents

Have crossed many seas,
have been exposed
to more than one narrowness
dangerously close,
to walls too tall
too near for human need,
to bars crisscrossing overhead,
the iron web of political ends.

At such times my parents have been accustomed
to construct in their minds the doors
that lead to stairs. To see themselves
pacing up and down on decks—
sea and sky falling away before them—
attending with their hearts
the names of their children
and of their children's children
announced and repeated behind clouds.

On this perhaps the last of their journeys
my parents are once more on the way
toward the promise
their trapped and hunted fathers

and their fathers' fathers
had never doubted.

Beyond the roofs of the rooms that are narrow
the breeze that parts sea and sky
in endless succession—
for its rules there
is at home there
in whatever it is comes after the parting—
my parents have had an instinct for.

They do not need to hear the voice
thundering forth behind clouds
to know it is there
but have heeded the ancient prediction:
of Zion, the homeland, the holy dwelling.

This it is. Not a place.
It is not a place toward where they go.

They go, my parents,
whether they would admit to it or not
their whole being turned toward that—
spirit-like before light—
which no Jew will pronounce by name.

The place given as destination
is important and significant
but only in that it is the embodiment
of elsewhere—

elsewhere
where the breeze uplifts
where narrowness drifts
thin as a thin cloud
and is gone

elsewhere
where apparitions of sea and sky merging
vanish like mists in the sun

elsewhere
where the voice that is deeply embedded
in all tones
but does not speak in the world
speaks
calls home its own

calls home its own

and the children enter.

1963

Allen Grossman

Allen Grossman presently teaches at Brandeis University. He has published three volumes of poetry, the most recent of which is And the Dew Lay All Night Upon My Branch. *He has also written a book and several essays of literary criticism.*

Lilith

I was the first made woman. I first wept
Alone in the changed light of evening in a chamber
For love.
I am in the trees when the wind visits them
With altering voices
As the year clothes and unclothes.
It is not good to be alone.

I rose with the maples on the evening of the first day
Flaming.
Of all birds I loved the Tanager for his scarlet.
I would have filled all the spaces of his song,
Enfolded him as the orange flame enfolds
The blue of its own cooling heart.
I cannot say what I could not have been:

The plenitude
Meted to his emptiness
The heat of which he dreams in the cold night
And the light
All lost.

Oh Tanager, first and last you are a slave to shadows.

Each tree sings,
The leafed tree with the fullest sound.
I am Lilith, the unmarried,
Whom three strong angels could not haul
Back to Eden.
Let Adam howl like a whipped child,
The loss was my loss.
I kneel upon the bank, and take my hair down
Weeping like a woman.
Let exiles and altarless men worship me
As night without stars.
I spread my hair over them.

Martin Grossman

Martin Grossman was born in Chicago in 1943. He currently lives in Kalamazoo, Michigan, where he edits Skywriting *and works as a free-lance writer and editor. His poems have appeared in numerous journals. He has recently published a chapbook of poems entitled* The Arable Mind.

Into the Book

A Bedouin springs from his horse
the two tables of the law
cradled in his arms
spits out a mouthful of pork
beneath the cliche of a desert moon
kneels to begin working
a medieval cape
affixing a yellow star

lifts his head to find himself
in a sweatshop
surrounded by women
their machines humming
like locusts in a swarm.

The Bread of Our Affliction

This bread is rock, not wheat.
The stone of life, not the staff.
No man can eat it daily.
Not without coughing, choking,
And flying, finally,
Through the black sky, the earth.

This bread will not rise
But sink.
We eat it now
Even as we did
in Egypt.

Anthony Hecht

Anthony Hecht was born in 1923 in New York City. He has taught at Kenyon College, New York University, Smith College and Bard College. His books of poetry include A Summoning of Stones, The Hard Hours *and* Millions of Strange Shadows.

"More Light! More Light!"

Composed in the Tower before his execution
These moving verses, and being brought at that time
Painfully to the stake, submitted, declaring thus:
"I implore my God to witness that I have made no crime."

Nor was he forsaken of courage, but the death was horrible,
The sack of gunpowder failing to ignite.
His legs were blistered sticks on which the black sap
Bubbled and burst as he howled for the Kindly Light.

And that was but one, and by no means one of the worst;
Permitted at least his pitiful dignity;
And such as were by made prayers in the name of Christ,
That shall judge all men, for his soul's tranquillity.

We move now to outside a German wood.
Three men are there commanded to dig a hole
In which the two Jews are ordered to lie down
And be buried alive by the third, who is a Pole.

Not light from the shrine at Weimar beyond the hill
Nor light from heaven appeared. But he did refuse.
A Lüger settled back deeply in its glove.
He was ordered to change places with the Jews.

Much casual death had drained away their souls.
The thick dirt mounted toward the quivering chin.
When only the head was exposed the order came
To dig him out again and to get back in.

No light, no light in the blue Polish eye.
When he finished a riding boot packed down the earth.
The Lüger hovered lightly in its glove.
He was shot in the belly and in three hours bled to death.

No prayers or incense rose up in those hours
Which grew to be years, and every day came mute
Ghosts from the ovens, sifting through crisp air,
And settled upon his eyes in a black soot.

Jack Hirschman

Jack Hirschman was born in New York in 1933 and lives in San Francisco, California. He has published many books of poetry, including, Black Alephs, *as well as poster poems and broadsides. His translations into English include French, German, Russian, Greek and Italian poetry.*

Zohara

Once more it seems   far which is   and Other   another place
you I have come down Off   what is left over   this duration

of distance   a city in your hair somewhere I am loning through
New York London Paris Rome Athens   your darkness around me
the tough occult of your having been here and left and left in
your wake all the others   the sisters and their train   the
old bustards dancing on mountains of persimmon or sleeping drunk
or stoned on the hardening wooden benches of the heart   where
there's dust and dirt and the taste of a woman insisting upon
shabby songs under the vague stare   insisting upon what hurts
and continues   the road   the only road I go with   your quietly
golden shema

I'm only an old synagogue   Snore   my fingers climb the steps
of letters I don't understand   hair always over there in the
hand of some mistake—stink of sex and war and the remains of
a humor whose sparks stick in the corner of my mouth   alive
and rotting   My friends are demons and witches   we can't stand
each other with a passionate invisible love   We send the congre-
gation of our stink into the cities   that cleanliness be damned
the apocalypse be equal to a pair of old army pants worn by a
fool who's killed himself over and over and still it goes on   You
showed me the way into and out of this rut   You came from the far
place I had grown in myself full of panthers and flowers   sexless
who drives me mad for the body   merciless who fills my eyes
ruthless who became Ruth   infinite who gave me this rich and this
sordid freedom

A hard fact lies down   next to the body of love   Thus I came
to the tall shell of myself   and see   what holds still what's
dull and what's lived through   breasts thighs bones   still holding
the splendor still keeping the faith   of the worm or the small
flying thing like a child is   Cut loose never to be cut loose   Look
at me   I'm dancing on creation's body   and she is a bookish woman
who keeps her secret in the leaves   Who is You   Her dark   Her
green outspreading

*NHR**

1
The oil came
in the form
of my sister
Shekhina.

*NHR represents the letters of the Hebrew word *nahar,* which means river.

ENGLISH

Then you are
the nature I
live with
hereafter

lost. She is
the soft swan
under the wit—
cherries of the city.

Elect
trick. And dark
eyes in her age
now they are yours.

Who came down from
the high places
to darken to satin
our bodies

Bound in this strange
fruit of a bondage
and an old knowledge
daft.

2
I woke upon my fear the garment
of the madman then
the tyrant entered into
the where of War.

I took the vows of the hap
hazards. Magic
pillow. The dance
of the Apple

scent to my nostrils from far off
home
          in my homelessness pulp
of the tree I taste

nuts of the eyes
of the three
of us together
in the garden

spading the six meridians.

3
My sister is mallow spoiled
child of a fascist teaching.
She moves your arm through
the links of mine.

The bush in my face burns
quietly. The Thou is withdrawn
deeper than I ever could have
believed.

Nahar is a river come out of
the depth of ocean. Nahar
who came for me with
the fragrance of you.

O brother I will always be
sister to the goings on
of darkness,
my sensitive travesty.

4
She is for this spell the queen

To the King, for whom the Radiance
was spoken

It is this wind I make in a wave
and upon your desolation reign

The voice of the horse on the hill
side is a dun musk and sauve

She has descended broken

Hart

In death my sister and sister again.

5
The radiant crown of her longing
Her heart is in my face
for the
          son is my reception
before the whiplash millions
in this vulva of dying stars.

6
Make room, make room, for King Messiah
is coming to the Academy of
R. Simeon. And the embryos
sing.

And the walls dance with our painted
lunacies. And the three hundred
and seventy illuminations
of the lone spark

trebling through the night be the grace
granted to the ears
of the hereafter
voluptuous.

A cycle of volt
age is finished.
I rake my hair
and feet

the silk of fetal
waters. Your child by
me and her and Thou
incredible

sentence of fire.

7
My words run to the end of
my mouth
            and cease bleeding
                    and set the seal
of silence
              upon the revolutions
of the atomic
heart
      floating everywhere in salt
water
      lighting up from within
      with the real thin
              bones of the rainbow
body.

John Hollander

John Hollander attended Columbia and Indiana Universities, and presently teaches English at Hunter College and the Graduate Center at City University of New York. In 1958 his book A Crackling of Thorns *was chosen by Auden for the Yale Series of Younger Poets. Since then he has published four books of poetry and a book of criticism, and has edited several anthologies. His selected poems,* Spectral Emanations, *was published in 1978.*

The Ziz

What is the Ziz?
                    It is not quite
Written how at the Beginning,
Along with the Behemoth of
Earth and the deep Leviathan,
A third was set forth (as if air
Could share a viceroy with fire,
A third only): This is the Ziz.

The Rabbi Aquila then asked:

Can we thrall him and his entailed
Space in our glance? And can we cast
A look wide enough to draw up

A glimpse of fluttering over
The chimney-stacks, of flashing in
Huge fir-boughs, or among high crags
Sinking at dusk? How could we have
Lime or twigs or patience enough
To snare the Ziz? The Phoenix lives
Blessedly in belts of hidden
Fire, guarding us from the hurt of
Light beyond sunlight: but where is
The Ziz? A gleaming, transparent
Class, kingdom of all the winged?
Pre-existing its instances,
It covers them, it covers us
With no shadow that we can see:
But the dark of its wings tinges
What flutters in the shadows' heart.

*Even more,
Rabbi Jonah
said:*

In their last whispered syllables
The muffled whatziz, the shrouded
Whooziz (trailing a sorrowful
Feather from beneath its cloak) tell
False tales of the Ziz: his is not
Theirs, nor he their wintry answer.
—Nor should we desire August light
Showing a permaturely full
Sight of the Ziz entire, lest we
See and see and see our eyes out:
No: Praised be the cool, textual
Hearsay by which we beware the
Unvarying stare of the Ziz
In whose gaze curiosity
Rusts, and all quests are suspended.

*At which
Ben-Tarnegol
recalled:*

One day at the end of days, the
General Grand Collation will
Feature the deliciously
Prepared Ziz, fragrant far beyond
Spiciness, dazzling far beyond
The poor, bland sweetness of our meals;
Faster than feasting, eternal
Past the range of our enoughness:

So, promised in time, the future
Repast; but now, only vastness
We are blind to, a birdhood
To cover the head of the sky.

Barry Holtz

Barry Holtz was born in Boston and was educated at Tufts and Brandeis. He is currently chairman of Publications at the Melton Research Center of the Jewish Theological Seminary. His poetry and essays have been published in many journals, including Response, Midstream, *and* The Jerusalem Post. *He has co-edited (with Arthur Green)* Your Word Is Fire: The Hasidic Masters on Contemplative Prayer.

Isaac

Now in old age, quiet in his tent,
Eyes dim, lost in reverie, he turns and
Hears the untroubled steps of his elder son
Trudging toward the open air, red body
(Color of stones the father can barely see)
Made redder still by sun and wind, pursuit of game
And calm unworried sleep on stone and desert sand—
Common pleasures of a common man—pure desire, pure response,
The uncomplicated rest of the simple.

Isaac, the sightless one, smiles—his keen ear
Discerns the heavy step of this hunter
Loaded down with the tools of his animal trade.
The taste of game in the old man's mouth,
The satisfaction with this, the chosen son (the
Inheritor by birth who walks with heavy, but
Unworried step) his mind slips back to darkness,
To peace, the calm repose of his later days.

Clatter from the next tent startles him
Sounds of cooking—at work, his wife Rebekah, perhaps
Or even the boy, the other son, the whiteskinned one,
Learning at his mother's side, the deceptive acts
Of womanhood, of stirring, ladling, boiling the brew,

ENGLISH

Fiery potions that inflame the brain
Fulfill desire with a wave of the hand,
Potions that could calm an old man's pain,
Lift an enormous rock from a well
Deceive appointed order of heaven and hell.

Unnerved, excited now, the terrible future
Before his eyes, his mind returns to an unescaped past,
Decades back to his father's home, the unforgotten journey,
The climb alone; he, the quiet son atop the silent hill,
Knife upraised in his father's hand, the cloud,
The whirling madness of divine command—
"Again? In this generation too?" he shouts,
Eyes open, the unchanging darkness before him.

Anxiously seeking a shape, a form, his mind
Grasps for Esau, Esau alone in the open air—
Unafraid, a part of it—his young, hairy body
Red, blending into stone and animal worlds—
Part of the wild, safe from all but natural
Terrors, his life defined by taste and smell,
The hunt, the thrill of simple mastery.
Isaac falls back assured. Recalling the power of his
Blessing and this the rightful inheritor, the son who
Smells of land and dew, he smiles—it is certain,
On the elder the blessing will fall. The crooked
Son, deceiving with his cookery, has stolen but
A birthright, and not the generations. The future
Lies in Esau's image, destiny on his red
Shoulders. A vow escapes those ancient lips:
"He may deceive the birthright, that sullen, quiet one,
But never the blessing, my blessing never." And calmed,
He sinks deep into innocent sleep.

David Ignatow

David Ignatow was born in Brooklyn in 1914. After several years of various jobs and free-lance writing, he is now poet-in-residence and professor of English at York College, CUNY. He has published ten books of poetry, the most recent of which is Tread the Dark.

1905

While my father walked through mud
and wore his sister's borrowed shoes,
Russia attended Coq D'Or and cheered,
and while he worked in a cellar bindery
and slept on work benches rats leapt over
at night, Dostoevsky's White Nights
and Anna Karenina were being read avidly,
amid joy, tears and protests. My father
was not heard from, he was the silent one
walking through the streets where the hot
arguments went on about guilt and poverty.
He walked, his work bundle underarm,
from cellar to monastery to bind holy books
and volumes of the Russian classics,
and when they had enough of classics
and needed blood, he fled,
for his was real to them; only he
had worked and starved. All others were
but characters in a novel or a play,
bless Chekhov, Gogol and others for their genius,
but my father was the one who had not been
immortalized and made untouchable.
Only he was real in Russia's torment.
Only he stood for life. All else was books
and that was the torment
that he with his woman's shoes
and work bundle underarm and cellar job
could exist, apart from their classical giants,
and he fled, and they turned back to their classics
and to themselves, conversely unbelievable
and unalive, to feed their rage, but to decay
as books do in the dusty air.

ENGLISH

Kaddish

Mother of my birth, for how long were we together
in your love and my adoration of your self?
For the shadow of a moment, as I breathed your pain
and you breathed my suffering, as we knew
of shadows in lit rooms that would swallow the light.

Your face beneath the oxygen tent was alive,
but your eyes were closed. Your breathing was hoarse,
but your sleep was with death. I was alone with you,
as it was when I was young but only alone now
and not with you. I was to be alone forever,
as I was learning watching you become alone.

Earth is your mother, as you were mine, my earth,
my sustenance, my comfort and my strength,
and now without you I turn to your mother
and seek from her that I may meet you again
in rock and stone. Whisper to the stone,
I love you. Whisper to the rock, I found you.
Whisper to the earth, Mother, I have found my mother
and I am safe and always have been.

Dream

I am lying face up on a raft
floating upon a lake. The waves
are small, rocking me gently;
I can't think of suffering:
I am myself, in love with ease,
my arms and legs loose; my breathing
is so low I study myself being alive.
And at last, invigorated by this ease,
I turn, cup my head in my hand
supported by an elbow against the raft
and search the woods and waters
for friend or stranger with whom to share
my self and in return to add their beauty
to mine. I'll find you
in a rocking raft or lying close
against the ground like its lover.

The Heart

My heart has an opening that discharges blood
and one that lets the blood pour in:
how eyelids in the morning lift
and let in light and close in sleep,
turning inward for relief:
how the heart cleanses the blood of arrival.
Nobody sees, as with the secret of the eyes
that open on the day, fresh and willing
from having studied the heart.

Dan Jaffe

Dan Jaffe was born in Elizabeth, New Jersey, in 1933. He was educated at Rutgers University and the University of Michigan, and currently teaches creative writing at the University of Missouri-Kansas City. In addition to poetry, Jaffe has edited anthologies, written his own jazz opera, and recently completed the play Don't Be Bashful, Survive. *He has also translated a volume of the Jewish Liturgy,* Again Light.

The Owl in the Rabbi's Barn

The owl in the rabbi's barn
Blinked balefully down
At the dangerous children
Poised in the shaft of summer.
They tilted their necks back like lids,
Pouring their attention upwards
Into the cavernous eyes.

The owl in the rabbi's barn
Nudged the air with his feathers,
Questioned the shape of the shouts below
With a huge silence
Hung like a bell from his beak.

There are blessings the pious say
Meant for mystery, for mountains
And owls, for the mouths
Of silent explorers by unnamed seas.

The owl left the leaky barn.
The rabbi inwardly wept.
Whistling Yiddish tunes
The children rocked the rafters
Where Tanta Minerva's pet
Had posed like a Christian icon.

My grandfather hunts the Torah,
Says one life's not enough
To study meanings out.
He will not probe for symbols
In the Missouri weather.

But struck in his window
By a rainbow framing the world,
A prayer pressing his tongue,
He calls out, cries "stay"
To the featherless, invisible wings
He knows are there.

*Yahrzeit**

He lists them,
all the dead
ones he loved
& those they loved.
He lists them
on brown paper
bags to hang
in the sudden snow.

Like a scribe
he fashions their names,
weeping with each,
staining the crumpled bags.

**Yahrzeit* is the yearly commemoration of a person's death.

It gives him pleasure
to think on them
shaking in April wind
like candleflames, warming
the early sprouts;
knowing his tears
will turn to dew.

Rodger Kamenetz

Rodger Kamenetz was born in Baltimore, and educated at Yale, Johns Hopkins, and Stanford. He lives and works in Baltimore, where he teaches in the Maryland Poets in the Schools program. His first book of poems, The Missing Jew, *was published in 1979.*

Why I Can't Write My Autobiography

Anyone who has ever lived
should have written a little book

The anonymous dead are unread

The next time you take a walk
shaded by enormous trees
think of the rotting leaves
you kick out of the way:

life is deciduous

What falls off
is often more brilliant
than what remains

In the Zohar it is said
"great splendor"
Every life is a spark
from the generator
every spark is an angel
who lives in eternity
only an instant—
that instant is a man's life

ENGLISH

And the great splendor
of all these lives
sparking into space
as if every color in
the aurora said,
Look at me, look at me

Just to consider an individual
even oneself, takes so much effort
at distinction, it's a wonder
we aren't blinded by the glare

as Isaac was, who lying on his back
on the heap of burning wood
forgot his father
in the presence of the Shekhina

His eyes grew so dim
he could no longer tell
Jacob from Esau

as I no longer can tell
who exactly I am
when I feel the brilliance
of those around me

because the desire to merge
with angelic voices
makes life lucid

The only way you can
see through yourself
through this thick body
these ungainly bones
is in the presence
of an awesome light

"great splendor"

*Pilpul**

Rabbi, if a child is born with two heads
which head should wear the *yarmulke*
on which head the *tefillin*?
Some say the right head and some
say the left. All quote Torah.
Some say both heads, just in case.

But if a man is born with two heads
he is always confused. He never knows
on which head to wear the yarmulke.

Two heads and only two eyes.
He walks toward himself
in the old cemetery, where the rabbis
are buried. There seems to be some
disagreement: some are saying
we are dead, others, we are alive,
some say both, all quote Torah.

Marc Kaminsky

Marc Kaminsky was born in New York City in 1943. His poems and essays have appeared in many magazines. He has published three books of poems and has been involved with poetry workshops for older people.

Erev Shabbos

for Esther Schwartzman

On Sunday, when she visits him, she must come prepared.
What will she bring?
She will come alone, with only a daughter.
There is no ceremony they know between them.

**Pilpul* is a Talmudic discussion of a fine point, such as the question proposed in the first lines of this poem.

ENGLISH

She goes to the table where for fifty-five years
they sliced an apple and drank a glass of tea
before going to bed. How can she tell her daughter
what kind of man he became when company left,
and for her alone he was a man of holidays?
There was no night when he did not take her
into his arms and play with her, for hours,
before going to sleep. And people thought
they went to bed early because they were old.

She spreads the white tablecloth
to set this evening apart.
And tonight, she sets another place at the table.
It is all prepared, as she prepared it for him
when he came home from work, after a week of
hauling egg crates and candling eggs.
He had strong arms and delicate fingers,
an excellent thing in a man.
And when he came home from work, on Friday evening,
he left whatever heaviness he had in the market.
There was no ritual, no ceremony between them.
She spread out the white tablecloth,
and that is how they lived:
a man and a woman in the traditional way,
each one knowing the hour and the season.

In Yiddish, she writes down the words
that come to her now, and these are the words
she will say to him, when she visits the grave:
Alter, I will never forget you.
I miss you in every minute, I think of you steadily.
With a broken heart,
I light the second *yahrzeit* candle. Esther.

Jascha Kessler

Jascha Kessler was born in New York City in 1929 and studied at New York University and the University of Michigan. He is presently an associate professor of English at UCLA. His stories and poems have been published in many major journals and he has won the Hopwood Award for Poetry.

Waiting for Lilith

Eve is angel, though bone of bone. She is
the wealth of women, she makes my garden
love's maze, all flesh and fruit: the sweat of bliss
is dew upon our bellies. She is the warden
of this world, and its colors speck her eyes
as riches soil her hair. Fear can't harden
her heart, silver under breasts of gold: cries
from dispossessed night burnish her sweet sleep.
Yet I hear you from Eden, where wind sighs
over the ruined metropolis, where you keep
vigil in that waste, mounting your old tower
to watch deserts of stars, count dead moons, and weep
the dust from your eyes. Even here this hour
is yours, Lilith, my demon wife before time,
like my years before the sun, my power
knotted in your long black hair. Steps that climb
to Eden lead down again. Heirs of blood
may walk in the shade with Eve, giants prime
yoking the mammoth mountains to her good
will and farming men in her big daughters.
They may stretch their dominions over the flood
of time, and crown Eve mother of waters—
but, Lilith, your song rises from the stones' curse
at night, and I turn to hear you. No laughters
of sons, no wife from my bone, can drown your voice.

Sol Lachman

Sol Lachman received his M.F.A. from Bowling Green State University. He is the publisher of Anti-Ocean Press. *His first book of poems is* We Have Been Such Birds.

Sukkot

we waited in the desert encircled
for the vessel of years to be filled
in circles of tents & hasty enclosures

ENGLISH

a brace of birds
hung in a circle by their feet
an old woman plucking feathers
by the tuft
humming a tune & swaying in a circle

we have been such birds
hung by one leg upside down
& we have sprinkled the blood
of birds on the altar

a pomegranate swelling
seeds translucent with juice
each seed is a gear
turning in the desert

we hang red fruits from the rafter
crush red seeds in our mouths
running sweet & wet

we have been such seeds
crushed in the beaks of angry birds

we shake the palm branch
& it rustles loud in each of the four corners

we have lived in corners
& feared the rustling of every branch

now we face the wind & we shout
& we shake our branch in all directions
& the wind is cedar boughs & citron
& the harvest is clear & sweet on our tongues
& even the birds are made joyful
by our shouts

Barbara F. Lefcowitz

Barbara F. Lefcowitz lives in Bethesda, Maryland, and is the author of A Risk of Green, *a first collection of poems.*

Driftwood Dybbuk

All day the driftwood
reconstructed itself
in the rock-pillowed cove,
a waterskeined face
with two perfect eyes
& shanks of kelp-hair,
roughly rounded breasts,
arms of green gnarl—
under unrelenting gullsong
I watched it clink & bang
into place, then slipped a wild iris
in its groove of a smile.

That night, when the gulls became
white looping stars
I felt a chill of wood
follow me with its iris tongue
until my skin sprouted knobs
& my hair became strings of kelp.

Do not look for me on any shore
unless you are patient enough
to wait for me piece by sea-
battered piece.

At the Western Wall

So this is it.

A *sheitled* woman sways
& wails in the swaying heat,
her face puckered like cabbage leaves.

Across the metal barrier between the sexes
a Yemenite Jew waves his arms
in a language more alien
than the squalling crows, the bearded moss
that droops between the slabs
with their mortar of tightly wadded words.

I unroll a note or two and smile, hoping
God is an easy grammarian—when
suddenly my bones become candles
in the blood orange sun. Kerchiefed,

I kiss the hot honey-
colored stone, run my fingers
along the centuries of fingerprints
inside its cratered mysteries. When I scrawl
my own tiny story on a slip of paper
fortune-cookie thin,
the wad does not stick, falls to the ground
three times before at last I make my entry

to the swarming bazaar
where ginger-bellied men ply me
with cheaply embroidered smocks & boxes
of holy sand dyed magenta & gold.

Which alley out of this maze?

When I ask a bottle-curled Hassidic boy
the way to Jaffa Gate he lowers his eyes
& does not answer.

The Mirrors of Jerusalem

1.
This is no country for hedonists.

In the Jaffa Street cafes they serve
pious carrot juice. At breakfast
the shredded beets have no blood
& the yogurt in stiff white cups
has a crabbed & meagre taste
unrelieved by the honeypot.

On the buses men brawl
about politics, politics. Tautly
tongued sabras strut in Zion Square
& everywhere the soldiers bear their rifles
deceptively casual.

There is no dancing in Jerusalem.
Only the taxi-drivers & old men
are singing their rumpled songs.
Newsmen are grim: no Brinkley pomade
or crazy widows who stash
their money in mattress ticking.
Here there is no madness
except a paranoia common as the sun,
rung by Russian tanks that hulk
between the olive trees.

But once in these Judean hills
holy craftsmen hewed pomegranates
from the stone; roses, grapes
& seashells whose lyre-shaped grooves
not Persian, Greek, or Roman,
Crusader, Turk, or tourist
have dared to rub silent.

2.
This is no country for puritans.

The Shrine of the Book hovers
above Jerusalem like an upturned breast.
In the old Jewish market off Jaffa Street
women with embroidered shawls
press the plump chicken feet
dangling from open-air stalls. Velvet
brimmed Hassidim wipe the herring juice
from their beards, spit, & dip their fingers
into vats of olives in the shout
& spice riddled air.

On the buses there is always music.
A sabra with six gold chains around her neck
hugs a soldier whose collar hangs loosely open
in a garden of flesh-colored roses.
When the drone of a jet
upsets his siesta, the rabbi shrugs; resumes
his dream about darkly-haired women
who serve him grapes & fat pomegranates
in bowls of shimmer.

Yet once in these sands
the protocols of guilt
germinated like the gray
& purple thistles
that everywhere poke from the roadside.

Harris Lenowitz

Harris Lenowitz was born in 1945. He is presently associate professor of languages, linguistics, and comparative literature at the University of Utah. He was co-editor of A Big Jewish Book *with Jerome Rothenberg. He has also translated* Sayings of Yakov Frank.

The Fringes

Shabbes Noah

Bless you God our God
king of the world
the one who has made us holy in his commands
who has commanded us
to wrap up in fringes

Where I put on the *tallis** I am usually early
the *tallis* I put on has become the same *tallis* every shabbes
a commentary on how small the praying number
a nylon *tallis* of great size
the prayer peeling off the *tallis*
there is a sailor's picture must be a Jew
must be dead
I put on wrap in
my death wrap my life up in my death
in one eternal life

*A *tallis* is a prayer shawl.

How dear your mercy   god
that Adam's sons can cover in the shadow of your wing
full in the fat of your house
the river of your pleasure   Eden   water them
for lifespring is with you
in your light   we see light
Keep your mercy coming
to those that know you
and your right
to the right-hearted

Panegyric

Golden goats with lapis eyes
Eucalyptus trees and bushes of yew
Chewing goats up on hindlegs
Green bellies green

Standing on their hindlegs
golden goats with lapis eyes
chewing at the bushes
Goats the goats of Cyprus
of Hydra
of Jerusalem outside the Goat Gate
Heads of goats and kids
tongues of bloody matted hair
eyes rolled up looking out,
behind, beneath. Dead here
holy or magic
Feet for glue or cloven feet or hooves
that split the world from knowing too much

ENGLISH

Molly Myerowitz Levine

Molly Myerowitz Levine was born in Connecticut and was educated at Radcliffe and Yale. She currently teaches courses in classics at Bar Ilan University.

Safed and I

Old enemies
ten year adversaries.
Wife of the hills
the foaming gold grasses,
bride of the mystics,
crooked pines sigh and
groan in your hair.
At your hem a lair
of cracked tombstones
where lizards play.
Everywhere, pinned crazily
with young men's death wreaths
your evil brooches, Safed.

Still they come
the black and white men
with their pale passionate faces
their black lovelocks
their black and white letters
that swarm
catching fire in your sun glow.
Your body is a shambles, Safed,
but your shameless stones
still warm.

Once I came to you
a bewildered bride of twenty
you tried to rape me,
old dyke,
to carry me off on your dybbuks, your winds
to your fetid ritual pools,
the black and white men's rules.
There was only the creaking pines,

cobblestones, your hag bones.
The deep bed had no bottom.
I was falling
falling.
The shuttered room
the red-cheeked groom
pressed pressed
till I thought I would break
with a soundless scream.

Maybe it was a dream.
I woke in the sun.
The blue waters of the Kinneret
and my nakedness laughed together.

I came to you again
at twenty-two
ponderous with a child in me.
I carried my fate like
a Sisyphean stone.
Again you had a victim.
You laughed and took me
to your hem
to death's debris
the battered stones
the thistles.

"Here is the end
in my earth, my hem
I gather them all.
Soon, quite soon, judging by the looks of you,
I'll gather you too."

The great stone moved
and I turned and fled
to the painful vortex
the bloody bed.
But I survived, Safed,
I'm back alive.

ENGLISH

Now I've come to you at thirty
a pretty woman
to laugh at you
with your effete knot of lovers.
The black and white tribe is in ruins.
In ruins the synagogues, your trysting rooms.
The bees mistook me for a meadow
my silks were so beautifully flowered
so cleverly confident.
Your jealous gusts slapped my skirts to my face
exposing white legs, the vulnerable place.
The vulgar lace made a whore of me
a mockery.
Old crone, always the bride,
always the winner.

This time I will not run away.
This time I choose to stay
with the black and white men
with their songs
their sublimations.
In a room, a slick
for stashing dreams.
I'll learn your tricks, old bitch.
I'll learn from you,
old witch,
who bewitches men
and women, too.

Philip Levine

Philip Levine was born in Detroit in 1928 and was educated at Wayne State University. He currently teaches creative writing at California State University at Fresno. He has published nine books of poetry.

Zaydee

Why does the sea burn? Why do the hills cry?
My grandfather opens a fresh box
of English Ovals, lights up, and lets the smoke
drift like clouds from his lips.

Where did my father go in my fifth autumn?
In the blind night of Detroit
on the front porch, Grandfather points up
at a constellation shaped like a cock and balls.

A tiny man, at 13 I outgrew his shirts.
I then beheld a closet of stolen suits,
a hive of elevator shoes, crisp hankies,
new bills in the cupboard, old in the wash.

I held the spotted hands that passed over
the breasts of airlines stewardesses,
that moved in the fields like a wind
stirring the long hairs of grain.

Where is the ocean? the flying fish?
the God who speaks from a cloud?
He carries a card table out under the moon
and plays gin rummy and cheats.

He took me up in arms
when I couldn't walk and carried me
into the grove where the bees sang
and the stream paused forever.

He laughs in the movies, cries in the streets,
the judges in their gowns are monkeys,
the lawyers mice, a cop is a fat hand.
He holds up a strawberry and bites it.

He sings a song of freestone peaches
all in a box,
in the street he sings out Idaho potatoes
California, California oranges.

He sings the months in prison,
sings salt pouring down the sunlight,
shovelling all night in the stove factory
he sings the oven breathing fire.

Where did he go when his autumn came?
He sat before the steering wheel
of the black Packard, he turned the key,
pressed the starter, and he went.

ENGLISH

The maples blazed golden and red
a moment and then were still,
the long streets were still and the snow
swirled where I lay down to rest.

1933

My father entered the kingdom of roots
his head as still as a stone
(Laid out in black with a white tie
he blinked
and I told no one
except myself over and over)
laid out long and gray

The hands that stroked my head
the voice in the dark asking
he drove the car all the way to the river
where the ships burned
he rang with keys and coins
he knew the animals and their names
touched the nose of the horse
and kicked the German dog away
he brought Ray Estrada from Mexico in his 16th year
scolded him like a boy, gave him beer money
and commanded him to lift and push
he answered to the name father
he left in October without his hat
who my mother later said was not much at love
who answered to the name Father

Father, the world is different in many places
the old Ford Trimotors are gone to scrap
the Terraplane turned to snow
four armies passed over your birthplace
your house is gone
all your tall sisters gone
your fathers
everyone
Roosevelt ran again
you would still be afraid

You would not know me now, I have a son taller than you
I feel the first night winds catch in the almond
the plum bend
and I go in afraid of the death you are
I climb the tree in the vacant lot
and leave the fruit untasted
I stare at the secrets, the small new breasts
the sparse muff where no one lives
I blink the cold winds in from the sea
walking with Teddy, my little one
squeezing his hand I feel his death
I find the glacier and wash my face in Arctic dust
I shit handfuls of earth
I stand in the spring river pissing at stars
I see the diamond back at the end of the path
hissing and rattling
and will not shoot

The sun is gone, the moon is a slice of hope
the stars are burned eyes that see
the wind is the breath of the ocean
the death of the fish is the allegory
you slice it open and spill the entrails
you remove the spine
the architecture of the breast
you slap it home
the oils snap and sizzle
you live in the world
you eat all the unknown deeps
the great sea oaks rise from the floor
the bears dip their paws in clear streams
they hug their great matted coats
and laugh in the voices of girls
a man drops slowly like brandy or glue

In the cities of the world
the streets darken with flies
all the dead fathers fall out of heaven
and begin again
the angel of creation is a sparrow in the roadway
a million ducks out of Ecuador with the names of cities
setting on the wires

storks rise slowly pulling the houses after them
butterflies eat away the eyes of the sun
the last ashes off the fire of the brain
the last leavening of snow
grains of dirt torn from under fingernails and eyes
you drink these

There is the last darkness burning itself to death
there are nine women come in the dawn with pitchers
there is my mother
a dark child in the schoolyard
miles from anyone
she has begun to bleed as her mother did
there is my brother, the first born, the mild one
his cold breath fogging the bombsight
there is the other in his LTD
he talks to the phone, he strokes his thighs
he dismisses me
my mother waits for the horsecart to pass
my mother prays to become fat and wise
she becomes fat and wise
the cat dies and it rains
the dog groans by the side door
the old hen flies up in a spasm of gold

My woman gets out of bed in the dark and washes her face
she goes to the kitchen before we waken
she picks up a skillet, an egg
(I dream:
a man sets out on an inner-tube to Paris
coming back from dying "the ride aint bad atall")
the kids go off to school without socks
in the rain the worms come out to live
my father opens the telegram under the moon
Cousin Philip is dead
my father stands on the porch in his last summer
he holds back his tears
he holds back my tears

Once in childhood the stars held still at night
    the moon swelled like a plum but white and silken
    the last train from Chicago howled through the ghetto
    I came downstairs
    my father sat writing in a great black book
    a pile of letters
    a pile of checks
    (he would pay his debts)
    the moon would die
    the stars jelly
    the sea freeze
    I would be a boy in worn shoes splashing through rain

After

After the fall of the tree
the ants came out to see the sun pass
to the Kingdom of Shadows

After the water bled
the toad grew a shell
and held still

After the wren pierced her eggs
after the snake went to sea
the clouds rusted
and wept in snow
no one could explain

After her husband died
she said, He's gone away
he was here in his heavy bed

The milk stayed neutral
the Turk made a round sandwich
and ate in the light
the broom lay down with the dust

After the windows were locked
and the front door
I found chips of smoke
in my little drawer of shirts

The old auntie screamed
in the shop of white stones
with her little gloved fists
she beat the wheel of our car
we left her the flowers the trees
the cold grass the afternoon of rain
that goes on and on

Again at dawn I come home
to my head on this pillow
the coverlet frozen
the fingers hidden, home
to a name written in water

Now It Can Be Told

What would it mean to lose this life
and go wandering the hallways
of that house in search of another self?
Not knowing, I wore a little amulet
to keep the evil from my heart, and yet
when the Day of Atonement came I did not
bow my head or bind myself at wrist and brow
because I knew I would atone. Silently
I would become all the small deaths
which gave me this one life.
I told this to the woman who loved
me more than life, and she wept
inconsolably, and thus I learned we
must love nothing more than life,
for when I am gone who will she
take her one loss to? Will she know
that somewhere close, perhaps in
the glow of old wood or in the frost
that glistens on the ripening orange,
is the grist and sweat of the one she loved?
Curse the sky. All it can answer
with is rain or snow. Curse
the sun, and perhaps the dead moon
will dawn tomorrow on a planet
equally dead. I am ready. I walk
the paths the children made, under

the canopy of branches and heavy leaves,
I find small tunnels where I could
find warmth and silence for a century.
In the high grasses of mountain meadows,
though it is marshy underfoot, I could
come to rest even in wind. Perhaps
a thousand years from now, a lost
boy or girl will catch the sight
of the bronze star that fortunately
saved me from nothing, and as he
stoops to untangle the blackened chain
he will have bowed his head the one time
I could not. He will raise the last
persistent portion of me and under a clear
sky wonder at its meaning, and let it
fall back to rest. Now it can be told:
I lived wisely, in the sight of everything,
and told no one how to live, and one day
after the spring rains I helped a child
find his way. If there are tears, they
should be tears of joy, for I am found
who was lost, and once more I've come back
to this earth, smudged and clouded with
a child's wonder. Warmed, close to life,
though dull and ancient, I still gleam,
like worn cloth, not like a woman's eyes.

Words

Another dawn, leaden
and cold. I am up
alone, searching
again for words
that will make
some difference
and finding none,
or rather finding these
who do not
make a difference.
I hear my son
waking for work—

ENGLISH

he is late and doesn't
have time for coffee
or *hello.* The door
closes, a motor
turns over, and once
more it's only
me and the gray day.

Lately I've been
running by day,
drinking by night,
as though first to build
a man and then destroy
him—this for
three months, and
I don't find it foolish
—a man almost 50
who still knows so
little of why he's
alive and would turn
away from answers,
turn to the blankness
that follows my nights
or the pounding of
the breath, the sweat
oiling every part
of me, running
even from my hair.

I want to rise above
nothing, not even you.
I want to love women
until the love burns
me alive. I want
to rock God's daughter
until together we
become one wave
of the sea that brought
us into being. I
want your blessing,
whoever you are who
has the power to give
me a name for

whatever I am. I want
you to lead me to
the place within me
where I am every
man and woman, the trees
floating in the cold haze
of January, the small
beasts whose names
I have forgotten, the ache
I feel to be no
longer only myself.

Here and Now

The waters of earth come and go
like the waters of this sea
broken as it is out of the dust
of other men. Don't ask me why
I came down to the water's edge—
hell, I was young, and I thought
I knew life, I thought I could
hold the darkness the way a man
holds a cup of coffee before
he wakens, the way he pulls
at a cigarette and wonders
how he came to this room, the walls
scarred with the gray brush
of years, how he traveled so long
to waken this sagging bed, and takes
up his gray socks one by one
and the heavy shoes smelling of oil,
and doesn't cry out or even sigh
for fear he will hear. So I stood
and let the waves climb up
the dark shore. The village
slept behind me, my wife,
my kids, still dreaming of home,
and I, the dog of the house,
prowled the darkened streets
which led here and to silence,
the first cold light smearing
the eastern sky and the Levant

blowing its warm salt breath
in my face. If I had commanded
the sun to stand still the day
would have come on moment
by moment climbing the white walls
of the town, if I'd cursed the air
it would've lightened before
my eyes, at last a fire
at the tip of each wave, and in
its depths the sea turning from gray
to a dense blue. So I said
nothing, but when my eyes filled
slowly with the first salted
rains of sorrow, I let them
come believing I wept for joy
at the gift of one more day.
I suppose the wind still blows
at ease across the sleeping face
of the village I fled all those years
ago, and some young man comes
down to the sea and murmurs a word,
his name, or God's, or a child's,
or maybe just the sea's. Let him
be wiser than I, let him fight back
the tears and taste only the sea's salt,
let him take what he can—
the trembling of his hands,
the silence before him, the slow
awakening of his eyes, the windows
of the town opening on first light,
the children starting suddenly
from their twisted sheets with a cry
of neither victory nor defeat,
only the surprise of having come back
to what no one promised, here and now.
Tonight my son
will come home, his
hands swollen and cracked,
his face gray with
exhaustion. He will
slump before his dinner
and eat. He will say
nothing of how much

it costs to be 18
and tear some small
living for yourself
with only your two hands.
My wife will say nothing
of the helplessness
she feels seeing her
men rocking on
their separate seas.
We are three people
bowing our heads to
all she has given us,
to bread and wine and meat.
The windows have gone
dark, but the room is
quiet in yellow light.
Nothing needs to be said.

On a Drawing by Flavio

Above my desk
the Rabbi of Auschwitz
bows his head and prays
for us all, and the earth
which long ago inhaled
his last flames turns
its face toward the light.
Outside the low trees
take the first gray shapes.
At the cost of such
death must I enter
this body again,
this body which is
itself closing on
death? Now the sun
rises above a stunning
valley, and the orchards
thrust their burning
branches into the day.
Do as you please, says
the sun without uttering
a word. But I can't.
I am this hand that

would raise itself
against the earth
and I am the earth too.
I look again and closer
at the Rabbi and at last
see he has my face
that opened its eyes
so many years ago
to death. He has these
long tapering fingers
that long ago reached
for our father's hand
long gone to dirt, these
fingers that hold
hand to forearm,
forearm to hand because
that is all that God
gave us to hold.

Stephen Levy

Stephen Levy was born in a Sephardic community in Brooklyn in 1947. He attended Queens College and the New School. He has published the chapbook Some Sephardic Poems, *and his poetry has also appeared in many journals. Levy is the co-founder of ADELANTRE!, The Judezmo Society, whose purpose is to promote interest in all facets of Sephardic culture.*

Home Alone These Last Hours of the Afternoon, Dusk Now, the Sabbath Setting In, I Sit Back, and These Words Start Welling Up in Me

    What is
eternity?
    Maybe it is
this lilt, these blue
flute notes, this
sunfilled deep
green road
of my round moist
mouth, voice
I am wandering down
thankful
    as I ask.

Friday Night After Bathing

for Ellen

I said, I like our bodies clean when we lie in bed
naked.
You said, Yes, I do too, we are smooth and smell
so good.

Freely, from a Song Sung by Jewish Women of Yemen

1
Beloved,
my parents mock me
because of you.
The more they mock me
the more I love you.

2
My beloved
has gone off.
But first
he unbuttoned my gown,
inflamed me.

A Judezmo Writer in Turkey Angry

bitter bitter
my family's
rag washing the floors for years
in school the poor one
in old clothes
on an outing once
by noon I had already eaten
the bread and cheese I always got
nothing extra nothing special
from my mother
the others ate I was hungry I wanted
to disappear

quit school go out
and work and all day my father
in the coffeehouse or with
the holy books bitter oh
bitter my husband's
fool earn the money make
the food he goes out
and screws
but even when
I was very young
I wrote I wrote
I loved to write
compositions poems
I'm still writing I don't
stop I'll get
all of it published yet
I'll get them all

Susan Litwack

Susan Litwack was born in St. Louis and presently lives in New York City, where she teaches English. Her first book of poems, Inscape, *was published in 1976. She has also published poems in several magazines.*

Inscape

for Michael Harper

When a woman cannot open her heart
she cannot breathe.
When she opens it
strange things fly in:
demons and angels
without wings
snow falling
homeless whisperings
calling
from a world
without words.

When a woman opens the heart
she is praying for her soul.

Tonight Everyone in the World Is Dreaming the Same Dream

Each person lies in their bed, restless,
calling an unknown name.
An angel comes to each and every one
and says: "Choose one hand," its own hands
shimmering behind its back.
"In the right is life, in the left
death, called emptiness." At that moment
sobs are heard all over the earth,
and in the heavenly spheres
a rain of tears.

In the dream I am weeping,
for the angel has no hands,
only wings; and each person gazes
at their own palms, purified and glowing.
One hand holds a spark, the other
a dry coal. Each person
spreads their wings.
The earth is created, and moves us
on our journey
towards remembering.

ENGLISH

*Havdolah**

Tonight the spirit of an elder
calls me out of my dream.
Together we find fragrance,
hoard candles and wooden sticks,
cut down trees, collect the fat for wax,
take down the braids of a child
unable to speak
or pray.

They say all visions have a past,
a beginning, an end,
a fire that blazes and is not consumed;
all illusions are signs, signaling
the spirit, wounds that may bleed,
may heal, or may inscribe us
with new life.

Tonight we do not kneel,
do not call upon
magicians or men
to read the messages
of fire and spice.
Words light up the night
with their sparks,
the wine reeks of old age
and spices float in the dark
climate:
We are falling from this life
into the next.

**Havdolah* is the ceremony performed to signify the end of the Sabbath.

Creation of the Child

After its guardian angel has given it a fillip upon the nose, the newborn child forgets all the infinite knowledge acquired before its birth in the celestial houses of learning. "But why," Eliezar asks, "does the child forget?" Because if it did not forget, the course of this world would drive it to madness, if it thought about it in the light of what it knew.

—Gershom Scholem
Major Trends in Jewish Mysticism

I dream of the birth of the child
who does not forget.
He is a diamond in a dark womb;
his body moves in this sea.
The walls are windows of light
through which he sees the world
in innocence;
and there is nothing he cannot believe.

His heart is like a beautiful woman,
the soul looking deep in her eyes
which are the eyes of a woman,
the eyes of Adam and Noah,
of Abraham; the eyes of God;
there is nothing he does not see.
His heart captures the fever of its beating
like the wings of a white bird,
like the arms of love;
there is nothing he cannot be.

And then, I dream he is in love
with me, his ears are two doves
whose beating wings are the music
of speech. He listens.
He is a diamond in a dark room
filled with windows,
rivers of light flow through him
into the sea.
The angles of his body open,
arms reach back to the beginning,
head extending to the near-human end;
there is nothing he does not see.

I dream of the birth of this child
and the darkness unfolds;
he falls from me like a polished seed.
His eyes are the eyes of a beautiful woman
closing her door, sparks fly
out from his face, out of the body.
Then, his soul grows wings,
it can do nothing but fly away from me;
and there is no death. . . . I awake
at the unforgettable instant
he dies.

Mordecai Marcus

Mordecai Marcus was born in 1925 in Elizabeth, New Jersey. He is professor of English at the University of Nebraska-Lincoln and the author of two collections of poems, Five Minutes to Noon *and* Return from the Desert.

Two Refugees

My father is a fugitive
from the villages of Chagall.
But he left the holy truth
of their color and song
never known
or far behind him.
He stumbled over strings of violins
as a country boy might crack his shins
on the curbs of a strange city.
When he thought of kissing girls,
his lovelocks curled around his mouth
like steel.
He said his prayers
like a man wolfing down hardtack
at a banquet table.
So it matters little
that he fled before those villages
sailed up from that palette
into the Western world.

Well beyond the edge of boyhood,
my father became a refugee
in a transplanted country
of old Vienna waltzes
where he pumped a dancing ardor
into his empty skin of youth.
My father's dreams still swing his ninety years
around the vacant ballroom of his fears.
That is why the joyful body-music
of old Vienna
puzzled me to blindness
and left him starved.

David Meltzer

David Meltzer was born in Rochester, New York, in 1937. Editor of Tree Books, Meltzer lives in Richmond Hills, California. His books include The Dark Continent, Hero/Lil, Tens: Selected Poems, *and* The Eyes, the Blood; *the last is given here in its entirety, with a newly added coda.*

Tell Them I'm Struggling to Sing with Angels

Tell them I'm struggling to sing with angels
who hint at it in black words printed on old paper gold-edged by
    time
Tell them I wrestle the mirror every morning
Tell them I sit here invisible in space
nose running, coffee cold & bitter
Tell them I tell them everything
& everything is never enough
Tell them I'm another cross-wired babbling being
songs coming out all ends to meet & flash above the disc above my
    brain
Tell them I'm a dreamer, new-born shaman
sitting cross-legged in trance-stupor
turning into the magic feather contemplated
Tell them there are moments when clay peels off my bones
& feeds a river passing faces downstream
Tell them I'm davening & voices rise up from within to startle
    children

Tell them I walk off into the woods to sing
Tell them I sing loudest next to waterfalls
Tell them the books get fewer, words go deeper
some take months to get thru
Tell them there are moments when it's all perfect
above & below, it's perfect
even moments in between where sparks in space
(terrible, beautiful sparks in space)
are merely metaphors for the void between
one pore & another

The Eyes, the Blood

1

My mother of the blue
Anglo-saxon eyes,
my father of the brown
eyed Jews, they fused
to form my exile
here on earth,
this year turning into next year
while the turn of my songs
goes out to renew source,
ancient sorrows
tomorrow become
newly-cast. The sky
swept of gray clouds
turns into a blue dome
unmarked by birds
or the gold of Monarchs.
My mother's eyes
hold the Bolinas sky
as in my father's eyes
the mud of its roads.

Her father stood 6 foot 5
& in the old photo stands between railroad ties
holding a sledge-hammer,
cap aslant, blue-eyed.
My father's father in a snapshot,

short & stocky, holds me to the Kodak,
his face shaded by the brim of a pearl-gray fedora.
I adored him more than all the rest
for what he brought of Russia & Jews.
Chain-smoking Old Golds,
bouncing me on his knees,
he saw in my eyes dark roads
3 sons came to America to travel.
He could never accept it.
Born in Moscow, an intellectual,
America he could care for less.
An exile, he knew the mark,
could read it instantly in the eyes of others.
A light like pain's spark sudden in Cain's eyes
driven deep into the dark brown.

My mother's mother ran off with a lover
& left her to her widowed mother
whose life came carved from Plymouth Rock.
Tough, orderly, a gritty Yankee,
clean & decent, everything in place.
Blue-eyed *shiksa,* my father's servant.
Aunts & uncles would whisper the curse
of Christ in her blood
mixed in the children's blood.
A contamination.
By Law we were neither here nor there.
Dispossessed, exiled at birth by blood.
They held her to blame for it all.
Dachau, Belsen, Buchenwald.
In secret rage she bleached her brown hair wheat-blonde
& ladled-out chicken soup into their bowls.

~ ~

My mother's blue-eyed brother,
6 foot 2, blond crewcut, Lieutenant, US Navy,
visited our Brooklyn flat,
battle-ribbons flashing on his dark blue chest.
Pink-cheeked, he walked into our twilight livingroom,
sat down on the piano bench
& often hit a key as he talked.
We passed around a snapshot of the submarine

he worked on in Florida's green tropic mystery
where old Jews go to spend the end of their money
in mock *Pardes* under the sun,
pseudo-Riviera where they're rocked in wicker chairs
pushed by young Puerto Ricans in white uniforms
up & down the boardwalk,
roast on sparkling beaches,
skin turning parchment-brown,
Torah scroll,
the brown my father's skin turned
sunning himself on the stoop.
Cars moving constantly over Linden Boulevard.

2
Each family to its mysteries
whispered thru the branches.
A cousin in Syracuse with dark brown eyes
died the day before her 18th birthday.
A rare blood disease.
She had a pale narrow face
framed in famous long black hair
reaching her knees.
Her mother's pride,
the hair grew as the girl grew,
braided into one huge braid the day she died,
carried into the grave, her triumph.
She looked like a Russian countess
in a photo passed around the table by
Grandmother Sarah.
It runs in the family,
in the blood, in the eyes,
the diluted tribe of Judah.

~ ~

Dark-eyed cousins.
Lonnie from Minneapolis
came to 'Frisco after high school
with his buddy Ivar.
One night they climbed Golden Gate Bridge
& sat across from each other,
each to his own tower,

kings in iron castles
swaying high above a new domain.
Sparkling Oakland, shimmering 'Frisco,
Marin's dark forests.
He showed me thick suede workgloves torn thru the palms,
edges burnt away, pulled back
like a row cut into earth for seed,
where he slipped going down,
grabbing cables on both sides to brake the slide.

Ivar told me Lonnie would climb anything. St. Paul radio tower, the highest peak there. Lonnie climbed it after sign-off time. Later someone told him the power was turned on every hour on the hour. Lonnie didn't care.
Climbed skyscrapers, telephone poles, church
steeples.
Once climbed to the top of the biggest water tank in town & tipped over the edge in triumph, nearly drowned.
Last heard of Lonnie was holed-up in a cave in the Minnesota hills.
Meditating, fasting, climbing.

3

Her tall blond blue-eyed men all came to California,
straight & proud they stood & each one remembered by my great-grandmother,
a century old & still going strong.
Broke her hip at 87 painting the outside of her home.
A Freeway now benedicts her frontyard with shadows.
Mexicans like snipers fill the run-down neighborhood splendour
3 blocks from LA County Jail.
She took me to its steps when I disobeyed her.
Until I was 13 she'd send me a yearly subscription
to the National Geographic Kodachrome world,
world she saw, world of postcards
where well-fed pink Americans all over the world
stood straight & proud beneath glossy-blue skies.
Blue the light breaking thru her blue eyes.
Radiance of new shores,
History of plains & railroads.
Marks in the land. Carved-out places
where secure & righteous her forefathers spawned

blue-eyed generations of upright men & women
forever heroic in bright postcard light.

~ ~

She keeps an orderly home.
In a glass-doored bookcase stand leather albums of officers & gentlemen who fought & perished in the Civil War; scrapbooks of family history fat with luncheon programs, photographs, Lodge meeting announcements, callingcards, clippings of concerts, meetings, social news metal-typed black on dried-out newspaper turned gold, preserved upon black scrapbook pages, photos held in place by black triangles.
She keeps all evidence she can find of her blue-eyed men
who came to make it new, renew it right,
to reduce the space extended from the shore by green
timber vistas of the New World,
hills whose verdure dipped into dark forests
edging into shapely female plains
turning into painted deserts
into primordial mesas transformed into bayous
feeding into wide rivers roaring into waterfalls
filling lakes that hold reflections of great mountain ranges
& all of it, before that moment,
unmarked or tracked by the blue-eyed presence.
No wonder Indians thought them divine.
How to deny ownership's sure white stride?
They broke the seal of America's shore
& where they wounded earth
they closed the wound with cities
that spread as root-systems thru the landscape.
White rightness wed with the pure goal of progress.
Linked by telegraph & steam engine & automatic rifles.
No questions asked. There was work to do.
Bridges, doors, connections to make new.
Soon to cramp all of it into zoos & cells
men & animals spend lifetimes breaking out of.

~ ~

Lovelace.
I saw it as cotton doilies over stiff armchairs
in my great-grandmother's livingroom.

White lace *mantillas,* white choirboy collars.
Doily dress of mandalas
worn over the dark skin of a Toltec hooker.
16 years old, her skin webbed white,
cunt hairs, beard curls,
loop & spring thru the weave.
Mid-noon *fiesta.*
Her bare feet on carpets of time-darkened flowers
break the tomb-quiet of my great-grandmother's livingroom.
I throw silver dollars at her feet,
aluminum pennies.
She does a split & juice from her slot sparkles
a snail-trail on petals of the rug's shadowy blossoms.
Tequila guzzled straight from the bottle
while *tortillas* cook on the griddle.
The old blue-eyed lady's stomach
would turn against our smells.
Love. Lace.
I saw it as a dress on the Mexican whore
who stood in a doorway whispering,
Love, love, love, I got it!
Love, love, love, I got it, *si!*
See, I got it. You want it?
Take it, have it, come
on my great-grandmother's bed.
Sheets brittle as newspaper.
Everything stinks of sachets.
Gutstring guitars outside our window,
mariachi trumpets, thump of
the *gitaron,* boogie-woogie
V-J Day thru a metal Arvin radio.
I push into her,
she milks me with a frenzy.
It is no matter she will not let go
& covets Limoges teacups on teakwood stands
in the antique cupboard.
No matter she's a dream I tangle with in sheets,
look out to see two orange trees in the backyard,
not a leaf misplaced.
Their boughs kept trim by the old lady.
Lovelace. A space
where stars burn thru black to create
a lace illusion not unlike the common household doily

covering every stiff stuffed chair
in my great-grandmother's LA livingroom.

4
Grandmother Sarah
re-married at 90 & went back to Europe on her honeymoon.
No more hotel rooms
with milk & sweet butter on the windowledge.
No more Workman's Circle
monthly ghost-quest socials
for Grandfather Benjamin,
who came to America to become a tailor
& died on my bed in Brooklyn,
cancer spreading terrible wings within his body.
Grandmother Sarah
always a good touch for music & money
playing mandolin with thick fingers
as sun set over Broadway parkbenches 13 floors below.
Minor-key schmaltz trembling Yiddish grief,
pain & pride of time & tribe
in a lacey white blouse clicking her tongue
making music for her grandson, a wolf
in the room's only chair
listening to Russia, hearing Jews in Paradise.

When the music left her hands
Grandmother Sarah told me stories
of the village she was born in,
a river ran thru
its green & golden fields.
Young men intrigued by her dark beauty
called her The Gypsy.
But now, she'd say,
the village is no more,
its young men all dead,
bombed off the map by Germans
during the last war.

∾∾

What do I know of journey, they
who came before me

no longer here to tell of it
except baggage of old papers
bound-up & found in library stacks.
The crying of history makes it all vague.
Was it myth we all came here to be?

What do I know of journey, I
who never crossed the seas into the alchemy of USA
no longer anyone's dream of home.
Their great great grandchildren jump state's ship,
drown in void *Torah* is too late to warn of.
Here *tohu* is *bohu* & form void & America
another pogrom, another concentration camp
more subtle & final
than all Hitler's chemists could imagine.
Home, *ha-makom,* no longer hope. It holds
light reaching back from eyes
watching Asians & Blacks die on TV.
We restore the shore & our dream is gone.
It mixes into shadows growing tall behind us.

What do I know of journey,
they who came before me
kept what they left but now they are gone.
Invisible shells cast off
& in flaming hair arise
orphans of collapsed Shekhina
caught between earth's end & heaven's end
& what do I know of journey,
I a child when children were murdered
waiting in lines with their mothers & fathers,
gone in gas or the flash of atomic *ain-sof*
squinted at in movie-theatres.
Ancients sit on stoops too tired to mourn,
turn inward to blood rivers mourning lost *shtetls.*
They can not take me with them
& I can not bring them back
& what do I know of journey, I
who never spoke their language.
The old ones are dead or dying
& what is left desires less & less
& what is less is what is left

& children run off screaming
Elohim Elohim!
into freeways filled with the starlight of cars.

~ ~

Coda

My father was a clown
My mother was a harpist.
We do not forget
How close to death love leads us.

I do not forget my father
Crying in the uncomfortable chair
Of a Long Island railroad car.
His first and only son unable to turn or run
From a father's public grief.

My mother crying on the kitchen floor
A carving knife
She couldn't use against her flesh.
Black metal cast away. Broken.
I do not forget.

From these parts a music once was made.
She at the piano, he at the cello.
Late afternoon. Slow
Removal of light from the livingroom.

Discomfort between father and son
As in each other was the other
Neither could forget.

The smells of her body
In nylons, undergarments, buckles.
The scar across her belly,
Dark fold of Death the Angel's touch.

I do not forget it starts in the blood
And ends in the eyes.
A Bible impossible to read,
The Rabbi I turned away from.
Kittens murdered in the garage
Hurled against the walls.
Sensual hips of my sisters.

He died in Hollywood.
Nobody to say Kaddish.
His common-law wife
A Christian Scientist
In love with astrology
Insisted no music be played.

My children will never know my father.
My mother will not see nor bless my daughters.
I do not forget
That from these parts
A music once was made.
I heard it as a child.

Susan Mernit

Susan Mernit is a graduate of Bard College. She has published three books of poems: The Angelic Alphabet, Tree Climbing, *and* Pictures of the Swan Queen.

Song of the Bride

What is there for us
that is not outside
the branched walls of the garden
shading the woman alone?

Everything stands veiled
in a garment, only behind that
some are hollow,
while others rest full.

The skin of the apple
was a good skin.

ENGLISH

The flesh of the apple
was sweet,
glistening at the core.

This story is only told
to those who have heard it
listening in their sleep
for the sleeve of the moon at their window
and for the horsemen chasing the swan
across the wheel of stars.

What they heard was muffled,
but it was this same song.

The heart pumps into hollowness,
without blood or fiber,

The cells float underwater,
dusty and veiled.

What was it but light
we had all been told to watch for?

The man said it was between the thighs.
The woman spoke of its colors.

The light was between them,
pushing through the deep grass
so there was a hole in the stone.
Saying Here, this is inside,
and Here, here I am
to show you.

They found there was a difference
in particles.
That rain fell in a shower
while roots plunged down.
That ice was a mirror that melted
while mica clouded but remained cold.

And, in this, they became transformed

Finding a way out of the garden
into what they called light
and new darkness

The whole thing only a touch of the hand.

The Scholar's Wife

for R. R.

If I stay quiet, I am always praying
inside with the blood
like our bodies are supposed to do.

Every morning before he gets up
my husband says
                the life of a woman is like sleeping.

He prays rising
                Woman be silent
        Woman   get up
the stove   the lights
        the household
Serve me.

We make the blessing
and he goes to study Torah.

My bread in his hands
is silent.
It will touch holy letters
I am forbidden.

Jerred Metz

Jerred Metz lives in St. Louis. His books include Speak Like Rain, The Temperate Voluptuary, *and* Angels in the House.

Angels in the House

Their wings beat the floor,
stirring the dust.
The hook in the fireplace
trembles and food spills
on the flames.

The dining room rings with their chewing,
their gluttonous cries, their
rumbling bellies. Plates rattle on the table;
the human guests cannot enjoy the meal.

In all the bed chambers
angels cluster about
the dead. Fiercely breathing the
thick air, they lay eggs on the turning flesh.

Books scattered about the floor,
ladders climbing the walls,
the walls themselves full of books,
golden letters stamped on each spine,
the room is filled with words.
In each corner an angel writes and
as it writes it sings of each room in turn
praising each room's name.

Speak Like Rain

or a ship's mast
or a hungry sail's belly moaning
frantic to catch every morsel of wind.

Speak like rain needful in oceans
to feed kelp for kelp wants watering
as much as wheat and corn
which bend when waves
angered by storm crash against them.

Speak like the mast the ocean's
tree whose roots remember sweet odor
and taste of soil, whose
rasping against wind is a
cry for lost forests.

The sail talks in language of mutes.
The words mimic corn which, as you know,
catches celestial wind in its sails
propelling the world through space.

Her True Body

Her true body
(not the one hinted at by marble hands
and face or even the one behind clothes)
her true body (not the one imaged in dream)
her true body (beyond flesh and bone)
were it revealed to naked eye, would seem a
chart of ocean currents, accurate, detailed,
perfect for safe navigation. Even this
touches far from her true body, for all the grace
of all the waves and kelp moving
everywhere in all directions, the intricate
growth of coral, consequential play of sea on rock,
motion of fish, motion of sea birds hovering
still above the water cannot be
marked by numbers and cursive arrows.
Yet curve of thigh and breast, hair-fall's flow,
seven dark openings, and the eye mirroring oceans,
though touching far from her true body,
make the loveliest of maps.

Divination

by
birds
bird flocks
oracular utterance Bible
ghosts crystal shadow
cloud forms birth
star meteor wind
fish animal and-
human entrails mice
their bedding or feces or
edges of books they
have chewed grain
a rooster pecked

snakes herbs fountains
red-hot iron
pool stream wand
altar smoke fire
dough meal barley
salt lead dice
arrows hatchet balance
sieve ring suspension
random dots precious
and semi-precious
stones pebbles pebble
cairns mirrors ash
writing dreams palm
nail rays finger
rings numbers passages
from books names
lettering the manner
of laughing ventriloquism
circle walking wax
hidden springs wine
and shoulder blades.

Bert Meyers

Bert Meyers was born in Los Angeles and taught English and comparative literature at Pitzer College in Claremont, California. He published four books of poems: Early Rain, The Dark Birds, Sunlight on the Wall, *and* The Wild Olive Tree. *He died in 1979.*

The Garlic

Rabbi of condiments,
whose breath is a verb,
wearing a thin beard
and a white robe;
you who are pale and small
and shaped like a fist,
a synagogue,
bless our bitterness,
transcend the kitchen
to sweeten death—
our wax in the flame
and our seed in the bread.

Now, my parents pray,
my grandfather sits,
my uncles fill
my mouth with ashes.

The Dark Birds

The dark birds came,
I didn't know their name.

They walked in Hebrew on the sand
so I'd understand.

They sang, the sea flowed,
though no one made a road.

I shivered on the shore
when the water closed its door.

Then as I felt the birds return
to me like ashes to an urn,

and sunlight warmed the stones,
fire undressed my bones.

When I Came to Israel

I saw my daughter
when I came to Israel.
She sat between its wars
by a soldier on a hill.

Stones and olive trees
and the bright air all around . . .
So many stones! like stars
painted yellow and brown.

Suddenly, my son appeared,
carrying on his back
the soft horizon
like a huge, blue knapsack.

He strode from a field
and lifted me,
the way a young cliff
lifts the grey-haired sea.

My little father, he said,
at last you're here.
The fields, the orchards,
everything seemed so clear.

Then my daughter ran
down down the hillside,
excited like a stream.
She called me; and I cried.

But my wife was a dove
in the wailing wall.
She lit the moon.
Snow began to fall.

And she laid the snow,
as if at home again,
proudly, under the lights
of Jerusalem.

Robert Mezey

Robert Mezey was born in Philadelphia in 1935. He was educated at Kenyon College and the University of Iowa. He has published nine volumes of poetry, and received an Ingram Merrill Award and Guggenheim Fellowship. He presently teaches English at Pomona College in Claremont, California. His books include White Blossoms, A Book of Dying, *and* The Door Standing Open.

New Year's Eve in Solitude

Night comes to the man who can pray
only on paper.
He disappears into paper
with his old mouth shaped to say no
and his voice is so tiny
in all these miles of silence and cold grass.

As I write
the fog has eaten away the mountains
the princely hills and the fields
everything but this house
and this hand
and the few feet of light it throws out against the dark.

I try to talk
to the drunken god who sleeps in my arms and legs
tell him god knows what
but what's the use he won't listen
or else he listens in his sleep

and the dead listen in theirs
up on the hill
up past the drifting
iron gates the dead leaves
listen and the frozen
water pipes.

And at last I know what to ask.
I know what I really want
and it hurts me.

Nothing any more against the darkness,
nothing against the night,
nothing
in which the bright child is silent and shines very dimly,
cover me with your arms,
give me your breast,
that will make me forgetful and slow
so I can join him in sleep—

Hurry down now good mother, give me
my life again
in this hand that lives but a moment and is immortal,
cover my eyes and I will see them,
those companions clothed head to foot in tiny fires
that I said goodbye to when I first opened my eyes.

Give me my robes of earth
and my black milk.

ENGLISH

The Wandering Jew

When I was a child and thought as a child, I put
The golden prayershawl tassel to my lips
As if I kissed God's hem in my child thought.
I touched the scroll with burning fingertips.

On my left temple there is a shallow dent;
Rabbi called it "the forceps of His will."
I was a boy then, and obedient;
I read the blessings and I read them well.

I strapped my arm and forehead in the faith
With the four thongs of phylacteries,
Imagining how when we were nearest death,
God brought the proud Egyptians to their knees.

The savage poems, the legends of his mercy,
Fell on these years like rain and made them green—
What simple years they were. I loved him fiercely
For loving the Jews and hating the Philistines.

Leaving for evening prayers, I felt the breath
Of the hot street on my face, I saw a door
Alive with shadow, hips and breasts and mouth,
And thought, Is she one? with a thrill for fear.

Filthy scarlet neon. A black drunk
Holding his head together with a rag.
The squad car parked across the street. A bank.
And *Fuck You* chalked on the wall of the synagogue.

One great door took me in, as in a dream.
Rich darkness falling on the congregation,
A voice in the darkness crying Elohim!
And I cried with it, drunk on sweet emotion.

2

I cannot now remember when I left
That house and its habitual old men
Swaying before the Ark. I was adrift,
And much in need of something I had seen.

At morning and at evening in my head,
A girl in clear silk over nothing on
Smiled with her eyes and all the while her hands
Played with the closing and opening of her gown.

I made the rounds then, married and unmarried,
And either way I seldom slept alone,
but always a familiar presence tarried
Behind the headboard and would not be gone.

Or so I thought. Leaving a girl one night,
I saw how my whole life had been arranged
To meet his anger in a traffic light,
And suddenly I laughed, and the light changed.

And the next night, obedient to my nature,
My head was filled with dew as I leaned to kiss.
Why should I leave this Egypt, while most creatures
Were killing each other in the wilderness?

Sucking for milk and honey at her breasts,
I strained against her till I ground on bone,
And still I heard a whispering of the past
When I awoke beside her in the dawn.

I lay unmoving in the small blue light—
What were the years then but the merest ash
Sprayed by a breath? And what half-buried thought
Fastened its pincers in my naked flesh?

Rabbis, I came, pounding with red knuckles
On the closed Ark, demanding whether a Lord
Lived in the vacuum of the Tabernacle
Or had departed, leaving only his word—

3
For years I ate the radish of affliction
Till I was sick of it, and all along
The sparks flew upward, upward. Crucifixion
Screamed at my delicacies of right and wrong.

ENGLISH

Blacks swarmed on the stone hills of the city—
Women fucked and abandoned gathered around me—
A sea of voices crying Pity! Pity!
My life's misery rose as if to drown me.

Taste your own bondage in the lives of others—
Isn't it bitter, indigestible food?
If all the wretched of the earth were brothers,
How could I find their father in my god?

I could find rest until a dream of death
Flooded the idling mechanism of my heart:
Nightly now, nomads with broken teeth
Come mumbling brokenly of a black report.

Reeking of gas, they tell what ancient fame,
What mad privation made them what they are,
The dead, the dying—I am one of them—
Dark-blooded aliens pierced with a white star,

A flock of people prey to every horror,
Shattered by thirty centuries of war,
The sport of Christian duke and Hauptsturmfuehrer—
Is this the covenant we were chosen for?

Sometimes, at noon, the dull sun seems to me
A Yahrzeit candle for the millions gone
—As if that far, indifferent fire could be
Anything to the black exploded bone!

Tempted and fallen, your Lord God is brooding
Over the ashes where Job sits in pain,
And yet his tribe is ashes, ashes bleeding
And crying out to the sun and to the rain.

I speak of those that lived by rope and spade,
Of those that dug a pit for friend and brother
And later lay down naked in its shade—
There, at last, the prisoners rest together.

I speak it in an anguish of the spirit—
What is man, I ask—what am I?
Am I but one of many to inherit
The barren mountain and the empty sky?

It is a brutal habit of the mind
To look at flesh and tear its clothes away,
It makes consoling speech a figment of wind
And rescue seems like something in a play.

The nights are darker than they used to be.
A squalid ghost has come to share my room
And every night I bring him home with me,
If one can call dissatisfaction home.

All week long I have read in the Pentateuch
Of how I have not lived, and my poor body
Wrestled with every sentence in the book.
If there is Judgment, I will not be ready.

The book I read last night will be my last;
I have come too far lacking a metaphysic.
Live says the Law—I sit here doing my best,
Relishing meat, listening to music.

White Blossoms

Take me as I drive alone
through the dark countryside.
As the strong beams clear a path,
picking out fences, weeds, late
flowering trees, everything
that streams back into the past
without sound, I smell the grass
and the rich chemical sleep
of the fields. An open moon
sails above, and a stalk
of red lights blinks, miles away.

It is at such moments I
am called, in a voice so pure
I have to close my eyes and enter
the breathing darkness just beyond
my headlights. I have come back,
I think, to something I had
almost forgotten, a mouth
that waits patiently, sighs, speaks
and falls silent. No one else
is alive. The blossoms are
white, and I am almost there.

Theresienstadt Poem

In your watercolor, Nely Sílvinová
your heart on fire
on the gray cover of a sketchbook
is a dying sun or
a flower
youngest of the summer

the sun itself
the grizzled head of a flower
throbbing
in the cold dusk of your last day
on earth

There are no thorns to be seen
but the color says
thorns

and much else that is not
visible it says also
a burning wound at the horizon
it says Poland and winter
it says painful Terezin
SILVIN VI 25 VI 1944;
and somehow
above the light body on its bed of coals
it says spring
from the crest of the street it says
you can see the fields

brown and green
and beyond them the dark blue line of woods
and beyond that smoke
is that the smoke of Prague
and it says blood
every kind of blood
blood of Jews
German blood
blood of Bohemia and Moravia
running in the gutters
blood of children
it says free at last
the mouth of the womb it says
SILVIN VI 25 VI 1944;
the penis of the commandant
the enraged color
the whip stock the gun butt
it says it says it says

Petrified god
god that gave up the ghost at Terezin
what does it say but itself
thirteen years of life
and your heart on fire
Nely Sílvinová!

I Am Here

for Naomi, later

1

I want to speak to you while I can,
in your fourth year before you can well understand,
before this river
white and remorseless carries me away.

You asked me to tell you about death.
I said nothing. I said

This is your father,
this is your father like water,
like fate,
like a feather circling down.

And I am my own daughter
swimming out,
a phosphorescence on the dark face of the surf.

A boat circling on the darkness.

2
She opens her eyes under water. The sun climbs.
She runs, she decapitates flowers.
The grass sparkles. Her little brother laughs.
She serves meals to friends no one has seen.
She races her tricycle in circles.
I come home. The sun falls.

3
You eat all day.
You want to be big. "Look how big!"
you cry,
stretching your arms to heaven,
your eyes stretched
by all the half terrified joy of being in motion.

The big move clumsily, little love,
as far as I can see.
They break everything
and then they break,
and a pool of decayed light sinks back into the earth.

Writing these words tonight,
I am coming to the end
of my 35th year. It means nothing to you,
but I rejoice and I am terrified
and I feel something I can never describe.
They are so much the same,
so much the sun blazing on the edge of a knife. . . .

We are little children
and my face has already entered the mist.

4

I hear you cry out
in the blackened theatre of night.
I go in and hold you in my arms
and rock you, watching
your lips working,
your closed eyelids bulge with the nightly vision.

5

I get lost too, Naomi,
in a forest that suddenly rises
from behind my breastbone on a night of no moon.
Stars hang in the black branches,
great, small,
glittering like insoluble crimes,
ceaselessly calling me
toward that thick darkness under the trees.
I turn, sobbing, to run,
but it is everywhere.

6

I wanted to give you something
but always give you something else.
What do you call it when it is underground
like a cold spring in the blood,
when it is a poem written out of naked fear
and love which is never enough,
when it is my face, Naomi,
my face
from which the darkness streams forth?

The petal falls,
the skin crumbles into dirt,
consciousness likewise crumbles
and this is one road the squirrel will not cross again.

I was here, Naomi,

I will never be back
but I was here,
I was here with you and your brother.

ENGLISH

Stephen Mitchell

Stephen Mitchell was born in Brooklyn in 1943 and studied at Amherst, the Sorbonne, and Yale. He has translated widely from the Hebrew. His publications include Selected Poems of T. Carmi and Dan Pagis, Dropping Ashes on the Buddha: The Teachings of the Zen Master Seung Sahn, *and* Into the Whirlwind: A Translation of the Book of Job.

Adam in Love

The earth around him: he within his life:
How simple it had been. And every evening
As light began to nestle in the grass
He had walked with God, two figures moving slowly

Beside one shadow. He had learned so many things,
He thought the days would bring him to a day
Where he could stand and see, far below him,
All he had done, and call it very good.

Then She appeared. He rubbed his eyes. And the world
Cracked into a thousand fragments, each
One a world, each one a part of that
Infinite dark body which was hers,

Then his, beyond the grasp of recognition.
Sometimes he felt as if he were falling back
Behind his eyes, into an earlier realm
Where everything had lost its name. The sky

Became her deep blue skin; a pear he found
One morning, soft and insect-chewed, smelled so
Of her most secret corridors that he could
Hardly keep his balance; and when he lay

At night inside her, breathing with her breath,
Holding the moon between his teeth for patience,
Her slightest movement dropped upon his mind
And vanished like a stone into a lake.

Where was he now? Where had all his days gone?
And all these weeds that were spreading through his garden—
The most fantastic weeds, curled and graceful,
With iridescent leaves and flowers that beckoned

Shamelessly to any passing fly.
He walked and walked, and felt the ghostly hush
Of some event about to be uncovered.
He felt it in the muttering of the beasts

(Which he no longer understood), in voices
Of wind and water, in the shadowed woods
Where summer had returned with every dawn
For as long as he could remember.

Now and then,

In the cool of the evening, always with surprise,
He would catch a glimpse of God observing him,
His hands behind his back, a tiny smile
Flickering from the distance like a glowworm.

Abraham

What had become very clear to him
That night on the fast-disappearing
Summer pavements—the air thick
With jasmine, the bony cats

Sniffing among the garbage heaps—
Was that he would be able to take along
Nothing. Precisely nothing.
Not even the memory of his face

Glimpsed some morning in a mirror
Or the name of the woman he had loved.
He would have to leave it all
Behind, here, in this world

Which had come to fit him like
His own skin. Soon enough,
In due time, perhaps in no time
At all, he would have to step out

Beyond the boundaries of his life, move
Where there is no place to move, grope
In the alien light, toward a goal
He could be sure of never reaching.

Jacob and the Angel

Her arms pinned back, impaled against the night
He held her in his desperate embrace
For minutes, hours. Until at first half-light
He looked into the shadows of her face.

Something about the eyes . . . He *knew* those eyes,
Intimately, the mouth, the child's skin,
Forgotten long ago. Beyond surprise,
He caught his breath and stared.
Recognition

Came casually, like an afterthought.
He felt her body ease, then move away
A fraction of an inch. A bird cried out.
Already what she had come there to bestow—
A wound, a name—was lucid as the sky.
The sun had risen. He could let her go.

Howard Moss

Howard Moss was born in New York City in 1922. He is the author of seven collections of poetry including his Selected Poems, *two critical books,* The Magic Lantern of Marcel Proust *and* Writing Against Time, *and several plays. He is also the poetry editor of* The New Yorker.

Elegy for My Father

Father, whom I murdered every night but one,
That one, when your death murdered me,
Your body waits within the wasting sod.
Clutching at the straw-face of your God,
Do you remember me, your morbid son,
Curled in a death, all motive unbegun,
Continuum of flesh, who never thought to be
The mourning mirror of your potency?

All you had battled for the nightmare took
Away, as dropping from your eyes, the sea-
Salt tears, with messages that none could read,
Impotent, pellucid, were the final seeds
You sowed. Above you, the white night nurse shook
His head, and moaning on the moods of luck,
We knew the double-dealing enemy:
From pain you suffered, pain had set you free.

Down from the ceiling, father, circles came:
Angels, perhaps, to bear your soul away.
But tasting the persisting salt of pain,
I think my tears created them, though in vain,
Like yours, they fell. All losses link: the same
Creature marred us both to stake his claim.
Shutting my eyelids, barring night and day,
I saw, and see, your body borne away.

Two months dead, I wrestle with your name
Whose separate letters make a paltry sum
That is not you. If still you harbor mine,
Think of the house we had in summertime,
When in the sea-light every early game
Was played with love, and if death's waters came,
You'd rescue me. How I would take you from,
Now, if I could, its whirling vacuum.

Stanley Moss

Stanley Moss was born in New York City and educated at Trinity College and Yale University. He has served as editor of New American Review *and* New Directions. *His books include* The Wrong Angel *and* Skull of Adam. *He founded and runs* Sheep Meadow Press.

God Poem

I

Especially he loves
His space and the parochial darkness.
They are his family, from them grow his kind:
Idols with many arms and suns that fathered
The earth, among his many mirrors, and some
That do not break:
Rain kept sacred by faithful summer grasses,
Fat Buddha and lean Christ, bull and ram,
Horns thrusting up his temple and cathedral;
Mirrors—but he is beyond such vanities.
Easy to outlive
The movement's death having him on your knees;
Grunting and warm he prefers wild positions:
He mouths the moon and sun, brings his body
Into insects that receive him beneath stone,
Into fish that leap as he chases,
Or silent stones that receive his silence.
Chivalrous and polite the dead take
His caress, and the sea rolling under him
Takes his fish as payment and his heaps of shells.

II

As he will,
He throws the wind arch-backed on the highway,
Lures the cat into moonlit alleys,
Mountains and fields with wild strawberries.
He is animal,
His tail drags uncomfortably, he trifles
With the suck of bees and lovers, so simple
With commonplace tongues; his eyes ripple
Melancholy iron and carefree tin,
His thighs are raw from rubbing, cruel as pine,
He can wing an eagle off a hare's spine,
Crouch with the Sphinx, push bishops down
In chilly chapels, a wafer in their mouths;
Old men cry out his passage through their bowels.

III

No words, none of these, no name, "Red Worm! Snake!"
What name makes him leave his hiding place?
Out of the null and void,

No name and no meaning: God, Yahweh, the Lord,
Not to be spoken to, he never said a word
Or took the power of death: the inconspicuous
Plunge from air into sea he gave to us,
Winds that wear away our towns . . . Who breathes
Comes to nothing: absence, a world.

Two Fishermen

My father made a synagogue of a boat.
I fish in ghettos, cast toward the lilypads,
Strike rock and roil the unworried waters;
I in my father's image: rusty and off hinge,
The fishing box between us like a covenant.
I reel in, the old lure bangs against the boat.
As the sun shines I take his word for everything.
My father snarls his line, spends half an hour
Unsnarling mine. Eel, sunfish and bullhead
Are not for me. At seven I cut my name
For bait. The worm gnawed toward the mouth of my name.
"Why are the words for temple and school
The same," I asked, "And why a school of fish?"
My father does not answer. On a bad cast
My fish strikes, breaks water, takes the line.

Into a world of good and evil, I reel
A creature languished in the flood. I tear out
The lure, hooks cold. I catch myself,
Two hooks through the hand,
Blood on the floor of the synagogue. The wound
Is purple, shows a mouth of white birds;
Hook and gut dangle like a rosary,
Another religion in my hand.
I'm ashamed of this image of crucifixion.
A Jew's image is a reading man.
My father tears out the hooks, returns to his book,
A nineteenth-century history of France.
Our war is over:
Death hooks the corner of his lips.
The wrong angel takes over the lesson.

Scroll

Long after dark
In my throat and thought
My mother wrote
A scroll of dangers:
Salt is poison,
And white bread;
If you wrong someone
Only he
Can pardon you,
—Not God. Your knee
Cut while playing
Is still infected,
So if you must,
Pray standing.

Apocrypha

You lie in my arms,
sunlight fills the abandoned quarries.

I planted five Lombard poplars,
two apple trees died of my error,
three others should be doing better,
I prepared the soil,
I painted over the diseased apple tree,
I buried the available dead around it:
thirty trout that died in the pond
when I tried to kill the algae, a run-over raccoon,
a hive of maggots in every hole.
This year the tree flowered, bears fruit.
Are my cures temporary?

I chose abortion in place of a son
because of considerations.
I look for the abandoned dead,
the victims, I shall wash them,
trim their fingernails and toenails.
I learn to say Kaddish,
to speak its Hebrew correctly,

a language I do not know,
should I be called upon.
I abandon flesh of my flesh
for a life of my choosing.

I take my life from Apocrypha.
Warning of the destruction of the city,
I send away the angel Raphael
and my son. Not knowing if I am right
or wrong, I fall asleep in the garden,
I am blinded by the droppings
of a hummingbird or crow.
Will my son wash my eyes with fish gall
restoring my sight?

You lie in my arms,
I wrestle with the angel.

Jack Myers

Jack Myers was born in Lynn, Massachusetts, in 1941. He has studied at the University of Massachusetts and the Iowa Writers' Workshop, and now teaches creative writing at Southern Methodist University in Dallas. He has published three volumes of poetry: Black Sun Abraxas, Will It Burn, *and* The Family War.

The Minyan

in memory of Sadie Myers

I took one small breath to lift her
body into death, four to lay her down.
Now I need ten men to reach the dead
through God. You must be old enough
to help me make the sun go down to her.
Stand here. This is faith in emptiness,
covering her eyes with coins, chanting
prayers over the dark ends of each day,
sleeping on half a bed, hoping the other half
isn't just earth.

Day of Atonement

On the Day of Atonement we fasted
and threw our money into the sea;
a few faces bright with guilt
went up against the wind
and fell like sinful children
without a splash.
Eventually we lugged God down there
and dumped him in.
It changed the taste of the sea.

Those cold October afternoons seemed carved
out of the light and wind that howled
through the ram's horn. Each dry blast
was a mountain in Israel. A word.
When the emptiness in us folded
its corners into a heavy silver star,
we doubled over and feasted on resentment.
Everything taught us how to win.

Did we really whisper to each cent
each sin? Now money whispers back.
The emptiness that drilled us out
has hungered, blackened, knotted into sex
until we think of hauling our belongings
down to the sea and following them in.

The waves scrub the sea from Israel
to our feet, as we sway above our lives,
ablaze, wondering how to throw the light in.

Joachim Neugroschel

Joachim Neugroschel grew up in New York and studied at Columbia University. His poetry has appeared in various journals, and he was co-editor of Extensions, *a now-defunct magazine of experimental writing. He is also a prolific translator of foreign authors, including Racine, Chekhov, and Sholem Aleichem. He has edited and translated* Yenne Velt: Great Works of Jewish Fantasy.

Eve's Advice to the Children of Israel

Tell the random pilgrims
that the whirlwind has left a road.
They'll find their way without a compass
and save their questions for later on.
If the travelers asked one another
about the land beyond the desert,
they would only lavish pointless replies.
(I often think of paradise.)

Let them return my thoughts to me,
asking directions somewhere else,
wondering whether phoenixes
sail beyond the desert.
Nothing was written on the sand,
only a promise that couldn't be kept:
be present-foolish and future-wise—
I often dream of paradise.

Doves

He, the indiscreet agent,
bruiting about the anchorite's opium,
translucent like your lethargy,
treads the margins of foster-life,
in these fickle decades of withering.

The shaken pillars of Gaza
reverberate
beyond the savannahs of separation.

And afterwards,
the field-flowers harp on the Uranian year,
and steep the talleys of desire in chitchat.

Yew, comets,
precepts of solitude,
no one renounces the neap-tide
in these ripples of eagerness.

You, who dared to bathe in the lake,
fear the foothills, the tainted north.
My brain,
unsealing the skin of moonlight,
was written in the register
long before the adversary
struck these trees from his mind by rote.

Why else this fullness of time,
this suffering of laws,
this scheme of significance?

Passive in pre-texts,
the inscription left dangling by the Norn
infuses sense,
sense,

like a fading allegory,
like doves,

like our own far-blood on forgotten altars.

Gerda Norvig

Gerda Stein Norvig, a native of New York City, was educated at the Ethical Culture Schools, Sarah Lawrence, and Bennington Colleges and received her doctorate from Brandeis University. In 1975, while teaching at Ben Gurion University in the Negev, Israel, she wrote The Equally True, *a journal of poems from which the poems in this anthology were selected. She is currently a professor at the University of Colorado, where she teaches Romantic poetry and a course in the relations between literature and the visual arts. A new book of poems,* Dark Figures in the Desired Country, *and a critical work on Blake and Bunyan are in preparation.*

Desert March

I came, a scooped out woman,
mind and womb,
and threw myself into the mold of myths
I saw in these archaic hills.
The hooded Arab matrons, faces wrapped

and mummified in black gauze
as they walked, blindly reproached me.
But the mountains lay down naked
as a nurse at night
and mothered me.
I rocked in them and rode them
with the heat of a zealot
driving over the Derech Hevron
to keep the holy Word alive
between Jerusalem
and the open
desert.

Burning, thirsting, I stayed.
Each day I was an earth sponge
drinking color from the sun,
a stone
casting it back
with a ruddy blush
on the almond blossoms
suddenly studding the terraces.

God is visible here,
for in this air
where everything is reciprocal,
the land, the light, the breath
continually convert themselves
to flesh. And I,
smoothed on my edges,
turned by the salt
of my zeal
softer and full,
am no more a columnar woman.

Yesterday I visited the Wilderness
of Zin,
and strong in my separateness
from the separateness of things
spare, stark;
equal to those bleak prospects shining
in a shining land;
grounded,
I return home.

ENGLISH

The Tree of Life Is Also a Tree of Fire

There's no Avenging Angel
and there is no flaming sword
turning in all directions
warding me off.
The garden gates are open north and south,
and in the east, the west,
the heat of day
melts guardian shades,
like parent-power,
away.

I turn in all directions
facing inward
with the flame
of self burning.

If I branch out,
I go where my feet go,
talk what my tongue talks,
feel what my heart feels.

The tree of the knowledge of good and evil
bears fruit and flower,
but trees of life light up
with their own power.

The Joining

There is a woman running
into the desert.
A fish among reeds
is not more easily lost than she
through the hills of the Negev
weaving drunkenly.
I watch her
constantly disappearing to herself,
and I am contemptuous, until she looks
at me with *my* face, *my* eyes.
We have come together for a purpose,

driven below sea level
by a prophecy
that stemmed like a divining rod
from your unyieldingness.
Then I see it:
a crater
without bottom,
and you are in it;
you are its skeletal mouth
opening
to kiss me with a word
of warning
against the void of being
voided by your being
cold, dark and untouchable
in the night
sky.

George Oppen

George Oppen was born in New Rochelle, New York, in 1908, but was educated in California. He has published seven volumes of poetry, and he won the Pulitzer Prize in 1969. He lives in San Francisco.

If It All Went Up in Smoke

that smoke
would remain

the forever
savage country poem's light borrowed

light of the landscape and one's footprints praise

from distance
in the close
crowd all

that is strange the sources

ENGLISH

the wells the poem begins

neither in word
nor meaning but the small
selves haunting

us in the stones and is less

always than that help me I am
of that people the grass

blades touch

and touch in their small

distances the poem
begins

~ ~

to make much of the world
of that passion *that light within*
and without   no need

of lamps in daylight writing year
after
year the poem

discovered

in the crystal
center of the rock   image

and image   the transparent

present tho we speak of the abyss
of the hungry we see their feet their tired

feet in the news and mountain and valley
and sea as in universal

storm the fathers said we are old
we are shrivelled

come

~ ~

to the shining
of rails in the night
the shining way the way away
from home arrow in the air
hat-brim fluttered in the air as she ran
forward and it seemed so beautiful so beautiful
the sun-lit air it was no dream all's wild
out there as we unlikely
image of love found the way
away from home

~ ~

The Poem

how shall I light
this room that measures years

and years not miracles nor were we
judged but a direction

of things in us burning burning for we are not
still nor is the place a wind
utterly outside ourselves and yet it is
unknown and all the sails full to the last

rag of the topgallant, royal,
tops'l the least rags
at the   mast-heads

to save the commonplace, save myself, Tyger
Tyger still burning   in me burning
in the night-sky burning
in us the light

ENGLISH

in the room it was all
part of the wars
of things brilliance
of things
in the appalling
seas language

lives and wakes us together
out of sleep the poem
opens its dazzling whispering hands

disasters

of wars o western
wind and storm

of politics I am sick with a poet's
vanity legislators

of the unacknowledged

world *it is* *dreary*
to descend

and be a stranger how
shall we descend

who have become strangers in this wind that

rises like a gift
in the disorder the gales

of a poet's vanity if our story shall end
untold to whom and

to what are we ancestral *we wanted to know*

if we were any good

out there   the song
changes the wind has blown the sand about
and we are alone the sea dawns
in the sunrise verse with its rough

beach-light crystal extreme

sands dazzling under the near
and not less brutal feet journey
in light

and wind
and fire and water and air *the five*

bright elements
the marvel

of the obvious and the marvel
of the hidden is there

in fact a distinction dance

of the wasp wings dance as
of the mother-tongues can they

with all their meanings

          dance?   *O*

O I see my love I see her go

over the ice alone I see

myself   Sarah   Sarah   I see the tent
in the desert my life

narrows my life
is another I see
him in the desert I watch
him he is clumsy
and alone my young
brother he is my lost
sister her small

ENGLISH

voice among the people the salt

and terrible hills whose armies

have marched and the caves
of the hidden
people.

waking who knows
the great open

doors of the tall

buildings and the grid

of the streets the seed

is a place the stone
is a place mind

will burn the world down alone
and transparent

will burn the world down tho the starlight is
part of ourselves

the tongues

of appearance
speak in the unchosen
journey immense
journey there is loss in denying
that force the moment the years
even of death lost
in denying
that force   the words
out of that whirlwind his
and not his strange
words surround him.

the natural

world that which is
born the secret
knowledge of all
who live the pressure
of emotion in those
who enter
the world the light
of each other   the glow   the light
of the world *'the fog*
coming up in the fields'   we learned those
rural words later   we thought it was ocean
ocean the flooding
light the light
of the world
it was the light
of the world help me I am

of that people the grass
blades touch

and touch the small

distances   the poem
begins

Cynthia Ozick

Cynthia Ozick was born in New York City and educated at New York University and Ohio State University. Her books include Trust, *a novel,* The Pagan Rabbi and Other Stories, *and* Bloodshed and Three Novellas. *Her poetry, short stories, and criticism have appeared in* Commentary, Esquire, The New Yorker, *and numerous other periodicals.*

ENGLISH

The Wonder-Teacher

The rabbi of Kobryn said: "We paid no attention to the miracles our teacher worked, and when sometimes a miracle did not come to pass, he gained in our eyes."

—Martin Buber, *Tales of the Hasidim*

When the morning hymn
unbound its alphabet to fall
like flies into his hand, when he would call
*Ayin** to stand upon its limb
and utter (who was mute)
voices of the living flute,
and bid lame *Lamed*‡ caper to his whim,
we thrust our watching to the wall.

Another time he made
the letters into curds
fed beggars on the foam, and feasted birds.
That day we swallowed blessings unafraid,
prayer was silken-white like cheese;
what our mouths sang, our teeth would seize.
Repast mounted on our brains and weighed
so burdensome we beat away his words.

And once we saw him levitate.
He tramped on nothing, stuttered like a wire;
hanged, he gnawed for the leash to shock him higher
in holy space, and longed to wait
in air for the unknotting of the Name.
He was a maimed man when he came
back down to us and toed our common slate.
But we hugged the floor and fled the cord of his desire.

Last night he said: "I am worn
of working wonders. Custom's stung
my magickings, my craft limps witless on your tongue.
What are my labors?—like the ram's horn:
swift to enter, the dwindling door a trap."
So saying, he laid his head within a pupil's lap

**Ayin* is, in Hebrew, an unvoiced consonant.
‡*Lamed* is the crooked letter L.

and slept like any one of us, as if to scorn
all prodigy. We huddled near the marvel of his lung.

A Riddle

I walk on two legs.
The right wears a tough boot and is steadfast.
The other is got up in a Babylonish slipper of purple laces,
and hops, hops.
All day they are lacing and unlacing the ties,
the little one in his first cap and the old one in his last shawl,
in, out,
digressing through the eyelets
as past a chain of windows the turn of one bird
grows four birds, their four bills painted
with fleet phantasmal jokes.

My dancer foot is honeyed,
and its way is where it wills.

My stronger foot is sternly shod and treads behind a hedge.
The toe is the pointer, the heel in logic follows,
and mediating is the arch exegetical,
latching the former to the latter, the rear to the forward,
and the last to the first.
Its laces rein, its print governs.
The prime one in his prime runs to keep pace.

My stepping shoe is hard,
but the way has not worn it.

I have walked time thin
to bring Messiah in.
My dancer foot can kick,
my binding step may prick,
but my slipper and my boot
shall stamp my exile out.

Know how I comment,
solve my name in a moment.

Answer: *Gemara (commentary on Bible), with its two elements: Aggada (legend, tale, and lore) and Halachah (law and code)*

Gary Pacernick

Gary Pacernick, born in 1941, teaches at Wright State University. He has published one book, Credence, *with original prints by Sidney Chafetz, and has a poetic play,* I Want to Write a Jewish Poem.

I Want to Write a Jewish Poem

It will be in the form of an old man
Praying in the Orthodox synagogue
Across the street from the gas station
And kitty-corner from the Yeshivah
Where boys with dangling ribbons of hair
And stern eyes learn the Talmud.
This old man is my grandfather Aaron.
A strong man, a farmer in White Russia
Who lifted heavy bushels of wheat on his back,
He came to America to flee the cossacks.
But my grandfather Aaron was silent in America,
Riding his horse-drawn cart through alleys,
Collecting valuables from garbage cans.
He never spoke English. He seldom spoke Yiddish.
His eyes turned inward to an earlier time
When prophets, poets invoked the words he whispers now.
Standing to the side of the Sacred Ark
Covered by his zebra-striped Tallith,
His yarmulka on his head,
He is one of a tribe of ancient worshippers
Touched by sacred garments, scrolls, words,
Men and women who lift their faces toward the burning bush,
The parting sea, Moses receiving the tablets of The Law on Mt. Sinai.
For my grandfather there is a burning light of holiness.
So let the sun go down, so let the darkness come.
Let the other, more worldly Jews,
Some of whom have become rich, leave the synagogue.
There is no place for my grandfather in America
But his synagogue where he stands
Confronting me now with his sad, intense eyes staring through his
 spectacles.
"So Gershon. You think you are a poet.
Yet you have not listened to the poetry of your Fathers.
Come and worship with me now."

Linda Pastan

Linda Pastan was born in New York City in 1932 and studied at Radcliffe and Brandeis. Her poetry has appeared widely in magazines. Her four books of poetry are A Perfect Circle of Sun, On the Way to the Zoo, Aspects of Eve, *and* The Five Stages of Grief. *She has won the Dylan Thomas Poetry Award.*

Yom Kippur

A tree beside the synagogue atones
of all its leaves. Within the ram's horn blows
and sins come tumbling down to rest among
old cigarettes and handkerchiefs. My sins
are dried and brittle now as any leaves
and barely keep me warm. I have atoned
for them before, burned clean by October,
lulled by the song of a fasting belly.
But sins come creeping back like unwed girls,
and leaves return to willing trees for spring.

After Reading Nelly Sachs

Poetry has opened all my pores,
and pain as colorless as gas
moves in. I notice now the bones
that weld my child together
under her fragile skin; the crowds
of unassuming leaves that wait
on every corner for burning;
even your careless smile—bright teeth
that surely time will cut through
like a rough knife kerneling corn.

At the Jewish Museum

("The Lower East Side:
Portal to American Life, 1887-1934")

We can endure the eyes
of these children lightly,
because they stare

from the faces of our fathers
who have grown old before us.
Their hungers have always been
our surfeit. We turn again
from the rank streets, from
marred expectancies and laundry
that hangs like a portent
over everything.
Here in a new museum
we walk past all the faces
the cameras have stolen from time.
We carry them like piecework
to finish at home,
knowing how our childrens' sins
still fall upon the old Jew
in a coal cellar, on Ludlow Street
in Nineteen hundred.

Pears

Some say
it was a pear
Eve ate.
Why else the shape
of the womb,
or of the cello
whose single song is grief
for the parent tree?
Why else the fruit itself
tawny and sweet
which your lover
over breakfast
lets go your pear-
shaped breast
to reach for?

Elsewhere

Like a Shabbos Goy
I turn the lights on and off

so that somebody else
may speak with God.
Or like a young squire
I polish the armour with steel wool
and sharpen the pure
blade of a sword
for other people's battles.
At the doorway
your kiss brushes my mouth
like the wing of a bird
whose feathers
will be used elsewhere
for arrows, for pens,
for prophecy.

Stuart Z. Perkoff

Stuart Z. Perkoff was born in St. Louis in 1930 and died in Los Angeles in 1974. He published nine volumes of poetry, including Alphabet Poems, Kowboy Pomes, *and* Vision for the Tribe.

Aleph

it is the man, himself
man
lord & master, the center
of his own
structured cosmology

it is
he is
the central point, the line
the direction taken
the road life walks thru his cells & stars

the power of the single
thrust, the pure
gesture of
self

Gimel

within the cave, it is dark. safe
tunneled deep into the mountain. safe
in the womb

traveling the long passage, moving
like song thru the throat to ultimate shaping
we see
the fire, the lite, day, the brite openness
dancing. darkness fragments. all known
patterns dissolve into shifting brilliances

now voices are raised in fear
now questions echo from the walls of the enclosure
some insist only the flickering shadows have reality
they make their prayers a worship of measurement & reflection
some try to turn back, to the black
their chants celebrate blindness

it is a natural rhythm brings forth
all, all, spewed into the lite
to take form
to sing, cry, fear, dance, love, pray, move
to be
to be flesh
to be man
within the totality
of his functioning

Hai

the divine winds upon the waters
before there was lite & dark
before there was beast, man, angel
the winds
the breath
moved

the divine breath entered the clay
entered the stolen bone

to become
life. spirit & flesh
breathing, flowing, moving
the waters &
the generations

the rhythm of our lungs echoes the movements of the waves
all air is spirit in which the souls fly free
i breathe the souls of all the dead & all the living
i breathe the poisons which man feeds the winds
i breathe the power & the death
i take it in, let it out, take it in, i am revived, i am alive
the waters move & i am alive

William Pillin

William Pillin was born in Russia in 1910 and emigrated to Chicago in 1923. He later settled in Los Angeles, where he and his wife operate a pottery studio. His poems have been published in numerous journals, including Poetry, Prairie Schooner, *and* Southwest Review. *He has produced seven volumes of poetry, and a new volume,* Poems, New and Selected, *is in preparation.*

O, Beautiful They Move

If I could hide in the woods
like a wolf tormented by violins;

but white and naked they move,
their mouths tense and red,

each bearing a rose that flames.

O, beautiful they move
in the cold lunar night—

and I am a wild bird on a cliff.
I clack, clack

into the veins of all Creation.

ENGLISH

Night Poem in an Abandoned Music Room

I lay quietly listening to some musical rabbi
expound his angelic lore
when I heard a conflicting piano
from an abandoned music room.

From this room, for ages
the silent refuge
of moths that fly into houses at night,
I heard a haunted mazurka
as if an ancient player piano
started up
after decades of silence.

I entered the vast room with its odor of moist loam.
Three women I saw whom I've loved,
still handsome but with faces tired and lined.
Four men were there whom I counted as friends
and they had a bewildered look in their hollow eyes.

The crystal chandelier was dull with insect droppings and dust.
A single candle
flickered on eroding walls.
I pushed aside the rotting curtains
hoping to see children playing on the lawn
but a thick fog
concealed and silenced the world.

Pianos lost in memory,
a tremor
in a room vast and empty.
The desire
for yet another dawn!

I wept and I cried:
"It can't happen, not now, not like this!"
and my words were a mist on the wind.

I lay silently, waiting, waiting. . .

A Poem for Anton Schmidt

A German army sergeant, executed in March 1942 for supplying the Jewish underground with forged credentials and military vehicles.

I have properly spoken
hymns for the dead, have planted
white roses in the high air.

And because my pen is a leech
to suck out blood's poison
I had a need to write

of death's clerks and doctors;
but my pen dissolved
in an inkwell of acid

and my paper, litmus of shame,
crumbled to ashes.
Anton Schmidt, I thank you

for breaking the spell that numbed
the singing mouth. I need not write
of the mad and the murderous.

That a vile camaraderie
caused streets and meadows to weep
no longer surprises us;

but a lone soldier's
shining treason
is a cause for holy attention.

Anton Schmidt, whose valor
lessened the vats of human fat
and looms of human hair

I thank you that no poison
is burning my veins
but a wine of praise

for a living man
among clockwork robots
and malevolent puppets.

Farewell to Europe

1
We, the captives of a thousand skies,
sang the airs of many peoples,
tango, waltz and leaping czardash;

but the waltz stumbles, the oboe
is poised on the brink of a scream.

We whispered madrigals of woe
in sewers and cellars.
We learned sparrow wit, hangman humor,
at the bottom of scaffolds,
at the gates of stone chimneys.

Europe, the odor of your guilt
lingers in our nostrils.
You are a perspective of walls
diminishing in cold moonlight.

Vanish from our songs!

2
Will your pianos haunt us to the end?
The stars in your snows, O steppes?
The sunlight bleeding gold
on the rim of a snow-foaming mountain?

Façade of roses and wings,
shall we cloak our memories in blue
because your gardens sang to the sun?

The kaftaned companions of the Presence
are swept from the streets of your cities.
Our migrants kiss a new wind
scented with ancient cedars.

Farewell, the Vienna woods are no longer calling,
or the grimacing spires of Cologne,
or your gleaming cupolas, Kiev.

3
Your temples are Gothic stalactites,
frozen tears of eternity;
your gardens are lavender clouds;
your streetlamps shimmering buoys
of musical boulevards.

But you were never our motherland.
We were born
not on the Rhine or the Vistula
but in Abraham's tent
on a journey from Ur to Judea.

This you never ceased to remind us;
that we are alien,
remote from you, the light of a dead star
that faintly lingers upon this planet.

4
We are leaving. We take little with us;
some music, a few poems.

It is well that we stand under new arches
bequeathing to our children
our praises, our celebrations.

Our Einstein will toughen the mental sinews
    of other continents.
Our Freud will plumb the dark soul of Asia.
Our Marx will rally the cadres of jungles
    and savannahs.

5
We are leaving. No longer will you have to cross
    yourself, people with pitchforks and cudgels,
    as our huddled remnants trudge over your
    meadows.

O mother of white nights, after a millennium on
your steppes your hostages are pleading: let
us depart!

We are leaving our ancestral tombs, our shrines,
our wealth endlessly plundered by the card-
playing nobles.

We are leaving you forever, belching Siegfried,
Vladimir red-eyed from distilled potatoes!

6
Europe, you realm of carnivorous blondes!
Your grand canals are clogged by chemical silt.
The sculptures of your saints are eroded by
pigeon droppings.
Smokestacks spew their black spittle on the
vineyards of Chateau de Rothschild.

Elegant bushmen celebrate your Requiem Mass
with tom-toms and banjos.
Even as you revel in your utopia of pig-fat,
blood sausage and Pilsen
you look nervously over your shoulder
at the lean wolves of the east.

They will strip your flesh leaving
the bare bones of cathedrals.
What the wolves will not eat—
monuments, fountains, castles—
will be shipped stone by antique stone
to the Disneylands of America.

7
Basta! Genug! Assez! Dostatochno!

Farewell, blue-eyed maiden. You need no
longer exclaim on seeing the mark of
our ancient covenant: "You cheated me!
You never told me!"

Farewell, priests whose blood mysteries at
Lent goaded the tavern heroes to wield
their axes among us.

Zbigniew, whom will your children curse?
Zoltan, astride a stallion, at whom will
you lash out galloping by?

You have no one to bludgeon but each other!

Ode on a Decision to Settle for Less

Take what is at hand
as sparrows take to doorways
when the rain and the wind
conspire against them.
Take to the mountains
to harvest rocks
when wolf-eyes gleam
in the fat valleys.

Better, though the work is beneath you,
to sell your muscles to a mason
than to ask favors from God.
Take what is at hand
to look freely
in God's blue eye.

You, riders of clouds, wake up!
One can starve waiting
for singing tomorrows.
Black bread freely eaten
makes a melodious Sabbath.
Wait no longer
for favors from heaven
but light your candles
to bless what is at hand.

Poem

To be sad in the morning
is to blaspheme
God's shy smile
breaking into leaves and lights.

In darkness and silence
I will be sad
but not in the morning
with its angelus of birds
and its covenant of blue.

Hyam Plutzik

Hyam Plutzik was born in Brooklyn in 1912 and studied at Trinity College and Yale University. His volumes of verse are Aspects of Proteus, Apples from Shinar, *and* Horatio. *Plutzik died in 1962.*

The King of Ai

They hanged the King of Ai at eventide
On a high tree at the gates of the gutted city,

And the smoke rose out of the ruck of the city
Where the fierce captains shouted at eventide.

Now on the tree the rope was heavy at eventide
Where the gods lay broken under the ash of the city.

He turned once more toward the ravished city
And the head swung slow toward the eventide.

Ah, the smell of the blossoms at eventide
From the almond trees beyond the gates of the city:

But the tightened rope on the tree at the gates of the city
And the swaying shape in the air at eventide.

God, God, for the evil done at eventide,
For the bloody knife and the torch on the doomed city.

And the girls who screamed on the sand by the gates of the city,
With the strange seed within them at eventide—

O God be merciful at eventide:
Remember him you condemned by the flaming city,

Where he lies under his cairn at the gates of the city,
And the vultures circle the sky at eventide.

The Begetting of Cain

Longing at twilight the lovesick Adam saw
The belly of Eve upon the golden straw
Of Paradise, under the limb of the Tree.
He thought that none was near, but there were three
Who were upon the mortal grass that dusk,
Under the wispy cloud, breathing the musk
Of the young world. Creature of pointed ear,
Of the cleft hoof and the tight-mouthed sneer,
The other passed, wound round within his thought.
And Adam in his mounting passion caught
The white shoulders of that woman there. . . .
All were engulfed—these two, the birds of the air,
The burrowers of the earth, by the quenchless mind
Roaming insatiate on that lowland, blind
In its lonely hunger, lusting to make all things
One with itself. Brief as the flutter of wings
Was his mastery, though ranging through world and void
To the dusk-star shining. But all, all were destroyed:
The two on the odorous earth in the garden there;
The beasts, the birds in the nest, the fireflies in the air.

On the Photograph of a Man I Never Saw

My grandfather's beard
Was blacker than God's
Just after the tablets
Were broken in half.

My grandfather's eyes
Were sterner than Moses'
Just after the worship
Of the calf.

O ghost! ghost!
You foresaw the days
Of the fallen Law
In the strange place.

Where ten together
Lament David,
Is the glance softened?
Bowed the face?

Carl Rakosi

Carl Rakosi was born in 1903 in Berlin. He came to the United States in 1910. He attended the University of Wisconsin and the University of Pennsylvania, where he received a degree in Social Work. He has practiced psychotherapy and marriage counseling, and has also taught at the University of Wisconsin and Michigan State University. His books of poetry include Selected Poems, Amulet, Ere-Voice *and* Ex Cranium, Night.

Meditation

after Moses Ibn Ezra

Men are children of this world,
yet God has set eternity in my heart.

All my life I have been in the desert
but the world is a fresh stream.

I drink from it. How potent this water is!
How deeply I crave it!

An ocean rushes into my throat
but my thirst remains unquenched.

Meditation

after Solomon Ibn Gabirol

Three things remind me of You,
the heavens
who are a witness to Your name
the earth
which expands my thought
and is the thing on which I stand
and the musing of my heart
when I look within.

A Lamentation

after Solomon Ibn Gabirol

Awake.
Your youth is passing like smoke.
In the morning you are vital,
a lily swaying,
but before the evening is over,
you will be nothing but dead grass.

Why struggle over who in your family
may have come from Abraham?
It's a waste of breath
Whether you feed on herbs
or Bashan rams

you, wretched man,
are already on your way into the earth.

Meditation

after Jehudah Halevi

How long will you remain a boy?
Dawns must end.
Behold the angels of old age.

Shake off temporal things then
the way a bird shakes off the night dew.
Dart like a swallow
from the raging ocean
of daily events
and pursue the Lord
in the intimate company
of souls flowing
into His virtue.

Till the breath becomes natural.

Rochelle Ratner

Rochelle Ratner was born in 1948 and presently lives in New York City, where she writes the poetry column for the Soho Weekly News. *She has published several volumes of poetry and a play, and co-edits the magazine* Hand Book.

The Poor Shammes of Berditchev

Because he studied texts
without understanding
but felt them in his heart
when others prayed

and because he knew their God
was his God also:
never counting them,
Praised be His name . . .

in the end
they had to cut him down,
having tied the rope himself
to the chandelier, in the synagogue

thus dividing the part which loved
from the mind not worthy.

Davening

Lost in the words

his body
sways
gradually
building the love up

clutching the book
as the drunk would grasp
a lamp post

his fingers move
across page after page
praying for the sounds
to carry

Friday dark he lies
beside his wife
as God perhaps
with the Sabbath

then lies back
himself in the silence.

there are always new words
new books he can turn to

till the breath becomes natural

Charles Reznikoff

Charles Reznikoff was born in 1894. He studied journalism and law, but decided to pursue a literary career. He was the author of many volumes of verse, prose, and drama. Black Sparrow Press is in the process of bringing out a definitive multivolume edition of his work. He was awarded the Jewish Book Council of America's Award in 1963 and the Morton Dauwen Zabel Award for Poetry in 1971. He died in 1976.

The Hebrew of Your Poets, Zion

The Hebrew of your poets, Zion,
is like oil upon a burn,
cool as oil;
after work,
the smell in the street at night
of the hedge in flower.
Like Solomon,
I have married and married the speech of strangers;
none are like you, Shulamite.

Jacob

In his dream Jacob was in a wilderness;
And in the sun the angel sang
In a voice that echoed and re-echoed.
As Jacob trod through the bushes each cried out against him.
The grains of sand took up the song, the distant cliffs.
The particles of air that build the heavens:
The wilderness sang against Jacob.

Jacob is like the stars
Which rise to their station,
Which the winds cannot blow away,
Nor clouds extinguish.
But we become names upon gravestones and upon books;
Our desire for the Law an inheritance
Among our grandsons.
It was good to labour, and after labour
It is good to rest.

Luzzato

Padua 1727

The sentences we studied are rungs upon the ladder Jacob saw;
the law itself is nothing but the road;
I have become impatient of what the rabbis said,
and try to listen to what the angels say.
I have left Padua and am in Jerusalem at last, my friend;
for, as our God was never of wood or bone,
our land is not of stones or earth.

Out of the Strong, Sweetness

Out of the strong, sweetness;
and out of the dead body of the lion of Judah,
the prophecies and psalms;
out of the slaves in Egypt,
out of the wandering tribesmen of the deserts
and the peasants of Palestine,
out of the slaves of Babylon and Rome,
out of the ghettos of Spain and Portugal, Germany and Poland
the Torah and the prophecies,
the Talmud and the sacred studies, the hymns and songs of the Jews;
and out of the Jewish dead
of Belgium and Holland, of Rumania, Hungary, and Bulgaria,
of France and Italy and Yugoslavia,
of Lithuania and Latvia, White Russia and Ukrainia,
of Czechoslovakia and Austria,
Poland and Germany,
out of the greatly wronged
a people teaching and doing justice;
out of the plundered
a generous people;
out of the wounded a people of physicians;
and out of those who met only with hate,
a people of love, a compassionate people.

Lament of the Jewish Women for Tammuz

Ezekiel 8:14

Now the white roses, wilted and yellowing fast,
hang in the leaves and briers.

Now the maple trees squander their yellow leaves;
and the brown leaves of the oak have left Ur and become wanderers.

Now they are scattered over the pavements—
the delicate skeletons of the leaves.

ENGLISH

Dew

1

Let other people come as streams
that overflow a valley
and leave dead bodies, uprooted trees and fields of sand;
we Jews are as the dew,
on every blade of grass,
trodden under foot today
and here tomorrow morning.

2

You have seen a bush beside the road
whose leaves the passing beasts pluck at
and whose twigs are sometimes broken
by a wheel, and yet it flourishes,
because the roots are sound—
such a heavy wheel is Rome;
these Romans,
all the legions of the East
from Egypt and Syria,
the islands of the sea and the rivers of Parthia,
gathered here
to trample down Jerusalem,
when they have become a legend
and Rome a fable,
that old men will tell of in the city's gate,
the tellers will be Jews and their speech Hebrew.

The Body Is Like Roots Stretching

The body is like roots stretching down into the earth—
forcing still a way over stones and under rock, through sand,
sucking nourishment in darkness,
bearing the tread of man and beast,
and of the earth forever;
but the spirit—
twigs and leaves
spreading
through sunshine
or the luminous darkness

of twilight, evening, night, and dawn,
moving
in every wind of heaven
and turning
to whatever corner of the sky is brightest,
compelled by nothing stronger than the light;
the body is like earth,
the spirit like water
without which earth is sand
and which must be free or stagnant;
or if the body is as water,
the spirit is like air
that must have doors and windows
or else is stuffy and unbreathable—
or like the fire
of which sun and stars have been compounded,
which Joshua could command but for an hour.

Raisins and Nuts

Thou shalt eat bread with salt and thou shalt drink water by measure,
and on the ground shalt thou sleep and thou shalt live a life of trouble . . .
—*Mishnah, Aboth 6:4*

Salmon and red wine
and cake fat with raisins and nuts:
no diet for a writer of verse
who must learn to fast
and drink water by measure.

Those of us without house and ground
who leave tomorrow
must keep our baggage light:
a psalm, perhaps a dialogue—
brief as Lamech's song in *Genesis,*
even Job among his friends—
but no more.

Like a tree in December
after the winds have stripped it
leaving only trunk and limbs
to ride and outlast
the winter's blast.

Te Deum

Not because of victories
I sing,
having none,
but for the common sunshine,
the breeze,
the largess of the spring.

Not for victory
but for the day's work done
as well as I was able;
not for a seat upon the dais
but at the common table.

Autobiography: Hollywood

I

I like the streets of New York City, where I was born,
better than these streets of palms.
No doubt, my father liked his village in Ukrainia
better than the streets of New York City;
and my grandfather the city and its synagogue,
where he once read aloud the holy books,
better than the village
in which he dickered in the market-place.

I do not know this fog,
this sun, this soil, this desert;
but the starling that at home
skips about the lawns
how jauntily it rides a palm leaf here!

II

I like this secret walking
in the fog;
unseen, unheard,
among the bushes
thick with drops;
the solid path invisible
a rod away—
and only the narrow present is alive.

III

I like this walk in the morning
among flowers and trees.
Only the birds are noisy.
But if they talk to me,
no matter how witty or wrong,
I do not have to answer;
and if they order me about,
I do not have to obey.

IV

These plants
which once halted the traveller
with thick thorny leaves
and clusters of spines
have become ornaments
to guard beds of flowers.

V

In the picture,
a turbaned man and a woman are seated in a garden
in which—this very tree
with large white blossoms like tulips.
It is a long way from Persia to the Pacific,
and a long time from the Middle Ages;
yet both picture and blossoming tree
have lived through time and tide.

VI

A clear morning
and another—yet another;
a meadow bright with dew;
blue hills
rising from a lake of mist;
single flowers
bright against a whitewashed wall
and scattered
in the grass;
flowers in broad beds
beside the narrow walk;
look, soldiers of Ulysses,
your spears
have begun to flower, too!

The Letter

I have heard of this destruction—
it is in our books.
I have read of these rains and floods,
but now I have only to go to the window
and see it.

I was always with Noah and the animals,
warm and comfortable in the ark,
and now—
is it possible?—
am I to drown
in the cold flood
with the wicked,
among the animals that have crawled upon the rocks and hills
in vain?

I walk slowly in the sunshine watching
the trees and flowers,
smelling a pungent weed, noting a bird's
two notes.

Martin Robbins

Martin Robbins has published three books of poems. He also edits a weekly column of Jewish poetry for the Boston Jewish Advocate. *He is a Cantor at a large suburban temple in Boston.*

A Cantor's Dream Before the High Holy Days

As summer ends and leaves fall like dust
in old synagogues's sunbeams, I dream
my prayer book's upside down, I don't know
the place—I can't even read Hebrew.

The rabbi gives a sermon that stuns
all of us strayed sheep; and I can't sing
the cantor's humbled words, "Here I stand,
unworthy, trembling, afraid to pray."

I stammer *buh, bah, beh*. I'm dizzy
from fasting. Flames that once burnt Torahs
swirl me up to that classroom two floors
above the ark where I began to learn.

I chant sobs, like old records, against
dark ages which hearts answered yearly,
flaming from the depths of a yearning
to return to words of the purest tongue.

Edouard Roditi

Edouard Roditi was born in Paris in 1910 of American parents. He studied at the University of Chicago and the University of California at Berkeley. He returned in 1946 to Europe, where he works as a free-lance multilingual interpreter. He has published several books of poetry as well as works of literary criticism and art history.

*Shekhina and the Kiddushim**

1
He who becomes his contrary
Is still himself to those who know.
Both self and partner in one being,
He simulates his birth and death
In womb or tomb, in agony,
Love and birth-pangs ever begetting
Only himself and equal only
To himself in changeless change.
He who is She must always seem
To be He or She, never both.

*Shekhina might well be, in Kabbalah, but a vestigial and hypostasized residue of a much more ancient matriarchal earth-goddess who had once been worshipped as Yahweh's partner, though both deities might then have represented but the male and female elements of an even more ancient hermaphroditic deity. The Kiddushim, sacred dancers and male Temple prostitutes, had survived under the early Kings from earlier Canaanite cults, but were massacred when the Prophets condemned them as "an abomination."

[Author's note]

ENGLISH

2
In our mind's distorting mirror
We see night or day, man or woman,
Never the whole, the union of both
In the full identity of contraries.

3
Mortals must get and beget,
Must acquire and multiply,
Must toil, trade, copulate
And die and be forgotten.

Striving to cheat death, to survive
In words still read and repeated
When my nephews are dead, I fail,
Childless and poor, to do my mortal duty.

4
The dance most pleasing to Him
Who is He and She must shock
His priests. Immodest mimickry
Of love can rouse every lust.

A woman in man's eyes, the dancer
Is man too in a woman's eyes
And his sacred dance that praises life
Leads men to lust for the dancer too.

Priests banned the dance and the dancers
Were condemned to die for pleasing man
As well as Him for whom they danced,
But the world stopped whirling when they died.

Their dance that mimicked life and love
Was found unfit for mortal eyes
And prayer must now replace the dance
To keep the world from stopping dead.

*The Paths of Prayer**

1

With the years my woes increased
And my laments grew loud
As I strove to keep afloat
On a sea of perplexities.

Night and day I pondered
My troubles and despaired,
Amazed again and again
When I felt the weight of my load.

Till I feared at last I might fall
Into madness, worse than death,
And chose, to forget my woes,
This task of telling a tale.

Let the music of my speech,
Like a minstrel's in my ears,
Revive my faith, renew
My wisdom, worn by the world

So thin, I forget to confide
In the starlike promise that guides,
With hope of its fulfilment,
Through my life's calms and storms.

2

Why repeat, from Adam's fall,
The generations of decline
That lead, from bad to worse,
To the sacrifice of six millions?

In the years that followed the knowledge
That I had been spared to die
A later, more lonely death,
No burnt offering in a camp

*The first sixteen lines of this peom are a free adaptation of the Prologue to a little-known Hebrew Arthuriain romance of the thirteenth century. The "trimming of the trees" of a garden is a Kabbalist commonplace, as a symbol of righteous living and the study of the Law. The tale of the maze planned to reproduce the Arabic name of God comes from a Sufi Moslem text which may, however, be of Kabbalist origin.

[Author's note]

On the altar of the State as God,
I wondered how I might fill
With useful tasks this respite,
But found none useful enough.

My vanity still required
Some monumental task,
Too vast for man's mere powers,
Though all are equally useful

Who serve the Law and pray
For fulfilment of the Promise,
Trimming the trees in life's garden
And treading its ordained paths.

3
In the gardens of the Alcazar
Where the Christian King resided
Who drove the Moors and Jews
From their Andalusian home,

A wondrous maze was planted
With paths that lead between
Trees clipped in a curious pattern
By an unknown Moorish gardener.

Daily the King would tread
Its pattern in peaceful thought,
Pondering the cares of state.
Each day he found there respite

From all these cares. Wise thoughts
Cleared his mind as he trod the paths
That wound around each other
To lead to the heart of the maze.

Wondering why this garden
Could always rest his mind
From all its cares, the King
Once stopped to ask the gardener.

Dark-skinned, a Moorish slave,
The gardener replied: "My Lord,
These paths, that form the Name
That none dare utter, lead

Your feet in silent prayer.
Though your mind and lips and heart
May not be praying too,
You pray with but your feet."

The King then knew that he
Who'd banished Moors and Jews
Still daily prayed their One God,
Who listened to his prayers.

4
I learn to pray with mind and lips,
With heart and hands and feet.
I hope to pray with every hair
That still grows on my head.

My prayers are nothing. May they rise.
But one man's humble offering,
And, added to a myriad others,
Bring promised peace to all who live.

Kashrut

for Paul Goodman

To destroy or deride Creation's task
And return from the eve of the Sixth
To the dawn of the First of days, confusing
The child of the mammal with its own

Mother, all these are forbidden, unclean.
The ravenous sow that devours her own
Litter, of all creatures condemns herself most.
Boiled in its own mother's milk, the kid

Provides proof of man's spite, a devilish derision.
No god, man can neither create nor destroy
With evil, though intended and accomplished
In magic that avoids the action implied.

Neither starving nor arresting Creation's task
In a world that ever creates itself,
Man accomplishes his own Creator's will
Forever through birth, copulation, death.

Those beasts of the field that man may eat
Must die no natural death. Their throats,
Slit artfully, must let their life-blood flow
Back to the earth as a sacrifice

To the task of Creation, of growth in the fields
And of the generation of all beasts,
World without end, providing man,
Favored above all creatures, with food.

A Beginning and an End

1

With the one and the two and the three
And the five and the seven and the naught
All emerging from numberless chaos
And confusion that knows no beginning

To impose on disorder and darkness
Of worlds shaped and broken, begotten
And as soon destroyed and forgotten,
New order and light, in space and time,

While teeming matter into itself
Again and again overflows,
Timeless in the birth-pangs of time,
Shapeless till space crystallizes,

What no mind has ever yet witnessed
No words can describe or now tell,
Before the emergence of mathematics,
Before the beginning, before the Word.

2
Around me all things fade in confusion
Great tides of sound ebb and flow
Tall dark forms stride across the earth
The long shadows of their legs striate the hills
A sudden gale shakes the one small tree
Everything is dim and gray
In this eclipse while a dark moon
Cancels the sun: listen to the sea.

The sea is gray and roams and moans and cannot be caressed,
Exiled beyond hand's grasp, lip's kiss,
Moonstruck and never at rest.
Listen, across the sands the swift waves hiss.

Great serpent ever coiled around our land,
Beyond it and beyond your very self,
Great weight of fate that cannot create,
Mirror reflecting in passive unrest
Greater creators of heaven and earth.

From the sea came light and the sea was called night
From night came heaven and the sea was called waters
From waters came dry land and the sea was the sea
From the sea came six days of male creation
Leaving the sea each day more female and reflective
Till on the seventh day the sea was no more than a mass
Of womanhood stretched out in the sun, softly moaning
Slyly rippling and waiting to be embraced and caressed.

Then after the seventh day the sea grew restless
Till now the sea is fickle and moody
Decked with shoals and ships like a woman with straw jewels.

3
Man in God's image and after His likeness
Male and female in the sixth day
In the seventh male and female still conjoined
Hermaphroditic in the perfect poise of seven balanced forces
Lay curved there in splendid repose

Which perfection did last until the second sixth
In which five days all things were named
And each made aware of its own identity
While man became aware of his own and of theirs.

And on the second sixth man slept and did dream.
In this dream he cast forth three feminine forces
And awoke on the seventh endowed with only three forces
Thus the seventh day of rest was broken like a fast

By the birth of the strife of sex called life
Strife of man and of woman reflected from within him
Of the body that begets and the shadow that conceives
Of the body that preys on its own feminine reflection

And the perfect poise of seven forces was broken for all time

Nor did they know it, knowing as yet no shame.

Habakkuk

He received indeed two embracings,
one from his mother, one from Elisha.
—Sefer Zohar

Habakkuk, reborn of the embrace
Of man, no son of woman, son
Of Elisha's embrace, with Elisha's breath
Still in his lungs, remembers:

Abyss and confusion between two lives
In the deaf night of death that cannot hear
The voice of the word. Seven gates
Of wisdom are closed to the fool, seven seals

Set on the book. Between death and birth,
Ignorance and wisdom, flow
Seven rivers. These he has crossed,
Then returns, remembering all:

"Having heard the report of that
Which has happened, is happening, shall
Till days end yet happen, I feared.
For the manifold work of the Word

In the midst of the years, in the midst
Of places, made manifest, was such
That I knew that my eyes could never
Behold the whole world, and therefore feared.

But a figure arose from the midst
Of the seething chaos of unshaped shapes
A shape that was no shape, a voice
But no lips, no flesh-bound sound.

Having heard the report and speech
Of the work, I feared the Worker.
Worker, revive Thy work
In the midst of the years, in the midst

Of Thy wrath, remember mercy.
Revive, with Thy light, this darkness;
Moist, with one drop of Thy blood,
The parched world of Thy work.

After the vision between two dreams,
When I saw the violence to come,
How long must I wait? Are there none to hear?
No witness to prove my vision true?

Must I live forever among those who cannot
Strengthen my faith nor destroy my doubts,
Distinguishing truth from surrounding dream
Now that life obscures the light with gradual mist?

He who has seen, between death and birth,
The violence that lies in the Shaper's hand
Can never make known the unknown, forgets
All the truth and returns to his dream."

ENGLISH

David Rosenberg

David Rosenberg is the author of Blues of the Sky, *translations of Psalms;* Job Speaks, *a translation of Job; and* Lightworks: Interpreted from the Original Hebrew Book of Isaiah, *all of which have appeared in his ongoing series of translations* A Poet's Bible. *He is also the author of* A Blazing Fountain: A Book for Hanukkah. *He has been a graduate fellow in poetry at Syracuse University and the University of Essex, in England, as well as a teacher of writing at York University, in Toronto, and the City University of New York.*

Maps to Nowhere

But when I looked further
under the sun I found
sitting in the seat of justice

beasts
and in the lap of wisdom
lizards

I heard myself thinking
the creator has made a road
from the heights of wisdom

to the conscience in every man
and each must find his way
meanwhile the court is abandoned

to the claws of influence
the school is abandoned
to the gnawing animal of despair

a season of disbelief
blows sand in the eyes
of the Lord's creatures

and I saw clearly
men are no higher than the camels
they must ride on

horse and rider
both arrive together
at the end of the journey

their skeletons come clear
like maps to nowhere
buried under ground

their bones gallop into dust
together   they both run out
of breath

a breath is all
a creature takes in
in a lifetime of action

it joins the infinite grains of sand
on the shore of the life
its blood flowed to

who knows if the man's spirit
rises
while his faithful steed's falls

who has seen this parting of ways
in the midst of his own journey
fixed in life's precious saddle

and so I came to see
man is made to be happy
taking care and keeping clear

his own vision
embracing the world
with the arms of his work

along the road
of his conscience
who or what

manner of creature or act
could bring him far enough
out of himself

out of the sun's pull
to see the unbreathing future
beyond the living present

and beyond the little picture show
of stars and galaxies
cheapened by superstition.

Translated from the original Hebrew Book of Ecclesiastes (3:16-22)

Rain Has Fallen on the History Books

They say it's better to be poor
when young—and wise
than a rich, old celebrity

a king   clamped
in the throne of his mind
unable to hear the clamoring streets . . .

the youth can walk freely
out of a king's prison
to become a king himself

while the born leader
even become a dictator
can only topple over

in his heavy mental armor
reduced to his knees
like a wordless beggar

but then I thought about that youth
rising to take his place
how the mass of people were inspired

by him   by his success
as people embrace the rags
to riches morality play

the longing masses
eager to start over
to wipe the messy history slate clean

and suddenly the man as all men
is gone   and his son
slouches in his place

rain has fallen on the history books
and the sun bleached it dry
for the new generations

which are endless in number
as were the ones preceding him
and for both alike he is unknown

the living page of his time
bled white out of memory
another page lost in the sea of the present

where even the beautiful craft
of inspired imagination
have their sails reduced to tatters

and their vain hopes discolored
like old photos
by the vague tears of sentiment

the memory of that star
like any moment of triumph or despair
is cut loose from the mooring of its time

adrift like a lifeless raft
after an explosion
after the countless explosions of moments

and the photos a living mind has made
in fits of hope or doubt
forgotten utterly as the sounds

of shutters clicking open
spoken words
a wind has blown away.

Translated from the original Hebrew Book of Ecclesiastes (4:13-16)

ENGLISH

Joel Rosenberg

Joel Rosenberg has taught Hebrew language and literature at Wesleyan University. His poetry and essays have appeared in Response, Moment, *and* National Jewish Monthly, *among other publications. He is currently completing a literary study of biblical narratives and his first book of poems.*

The First Wedding in the World

I

The eighth day was the wedding.
He awoke amid a dewy moss,
and saw two swans gliding
between the cattails. It was dawn.

His side felt sore. He felt
a yearning where before
he'd felt protected, like a dream
had stolen out of reach.

It still was early,
and the moon still gleamed,
and crickets still posed
questions to their answering chorus.

Two large lions sat nearby,
amid the mist,
placidly gazing at the tiny rabbits
nibbling lettuce in their grassy niches.

II

The man had never seen an angel.
He thought it strange
that rainbow-colored fire
took on human image.

When he met Michael
and Gabriel, who told him
they were witnesses,
he thought their garments

were cascades of golden leaves,
their eyes a burning agate,
and their wings
a wreath of northern lights.

He called some names,
and beast and fowl
perked up their ears,
and forest noises filled the air.

III

God had the woman
waiting for him near the meadow,
standing on a shell,
her hair down to her knees.

She thought it all so strange,
this garden, jabbering animals,
this stranger standing dumbfounded
and stuttering out her name in joy.

She'd never seen a wedding canopy.
The golden gauze
was spun by angels
in the middle of the night.

She thought herself
a thousand years of age,
though looking like a girl of twenty,
all the sad, expensive wisdom

of society about to waken
in her bones, the secrets
of the wind and stars,
the human arts

of strife and cultivation,
tincture of the eyelids,
epic meters, and, as well,
concealments and apologies.

She smiled at the young man's
innocence, while, lovingly,
and for forever, she held out
her hand to him.

IV
The two of them,
with honeybees weaving among
the wreaths of flowers
at their brows,

the two of them,
with hope for clothes,
and no disqualifying memories,
and nothing that was not

within them from the start,
the two of them joined hands
and stood before the shimmering light
to make their vows.

The Violin Tree

A while back, my father got some letters
from some people with our name.
Some pictures were enclosed,
and they were in a hurry.
And my father read them and he cried.
The ground would tremble when he got that way.
I asked him what was wrong:
did he want them not to come?
He threw the letters in my lap
and shouted: "Choose one!
One can live; the rest must die."

From that day on, I knew
that my father was God.
He went out in the yard,
and carved a tree into a violin.
The letters rested on the floor for weeks:
a baker and his wife, three kids, our name;

a physicist who asked to be our gardener, our name;
a smiling pair of newlyweds, our name.
Our name is carved into my father's tree.
And what a tree! It plays, at night,
a wonderful and piercing melody
from off the northern wind.
It casts a long, black shadow
at the start of Sabbath,
when my father, restless,
is out breaking the cedars of Lebanon.

Jerome Rothenberg

Jerome Rothenberg was born in New York City in 1931. He has published over thirty volumes of poetry including Poland/1931, A Seneca Journal, *and* Vienna Blood. *He has edited several major anthologies including* A Big Jewish Book.

The Alphabet Came to Me

in memory of Wallace Berman

the Alphabet came to me
in a dream
he said
"I am Alphabet
"take your light from me
& I thought
"you are numbers first before you are sound
"you are the fingers' progression & you end in the fist
"a solid mass against the world
but the Alphabet was dark
like my hand writing these words
he rose
not as light at first though issuing from light
but fear a double headed body
with the pen a blacker line at center
A began it but in Hebrew not a vowel
a choked sound it was the larynx stopped the midrash said
contained all sound

sound of Alphabet initial to all speech
as one or zero
called it WORK OF CREATION in my dream
a creature more than solid more than space or distance
& he said
"all numbers & all sounds
"converge here
but I knew it said
that I would count my way
into the vision
grooved thus with numbers & with sound
the distances to every side of us
as in a poem

A Letter to Paul Celan in Memory

of how your poems
arise in me
alive
my eye fixed on
your line
"light was salvation"
I remember
(in simpler version)
Paris
nineteen sixty seven
in cold sight of
our meeting
shivered to dumbness
you said "jew"
& I said "jew"
though neither spoke
the jew words
jew tongue
neither the mother language
loshen
the vestiges of holy speech
but you said
"pain"
under your eyebrows
I said "image"

we said "sound"
& turned around to
silence   lost
between two languages
we drank wine's words
like blood
but didn't drink toward
vision   still
we could not speak
without a scream
a guttural
the tree
out of the shadow of
the white cafe was not
"the tree"
roots of our speech
above us
in the sun
under the sewers
language of the moles
"who dig & dig
"do not grow wise
"who make no song
"no language
into the water silence
of your death
the pink pale sky of Paris
in the afternoon
that held no constellations
no knowledge of the sun
as candelabrum
tree   menorah
"light knotted into air
"with table set
"chairs empty
"in sabbath splendor
the old man stood beside
in figure of a woman
raised his arms to reach
the axis of the world
would bring the air down
solidly

& speak no sound
the way you forced
my meaning
to your poem
the words of which still press
into my tongue
"drunk
"blest
"gebentsht

Muriel Rukeyser

Muriel Rukeyser was born in 1913 in New York City. She attended Vassar College and Columbia University. She has published many books of poetry, including Theory of Flight, *which won the Yale Series of Younger Poets,* Waterlily Fire: Poems 1935-1962, *and* The Speed of Darkness. The Complete Poems of Muriel Rukeyser *was published in 1978. She died in 1980.*

*Akiba**

The Way Out

The night is covered with signs. The body and face of man,
with signs, and his journeys. Where the rock is split
and speaks to the water; the flame speaks to the cloud;
the red splatter, abstraction, on the door
speaks to the angel and the constellations.
The grains of sand on the sea-floor speak at last to the moon.
And the loud hammering of the land behind
speaks ringing up the bones of our thighs, the hoofs,
we hear the hoofs over the seethe of the sea.

*Akiba is the Jewish shepherd-scholar of the first and second century, identified with the Song of Songs and with the insurrection against Hadrian's Rome, led in A.D. 132 by Bar Cochba (Son of the Star). After this lightning war, Jerusalem captured, the Romans driven out of the south, Rome increased its military machine; by 135, the last defenses fell, Bar Cochba was killed. Akiba was tortured to death at the command of his friend, the Roman Rufus, and a harrow was drawn over the ground where Jerusalem had stood, leaving only a corner of wall. The story in my mother's family is that we are descended from Akiba—unverifiable, but a great gift to a child.

—M.R.

All night down the centuries, have heard, music of passage.

Music of one child carried into the desert;
firstborn forbidden by law of the pyramid.
Drawn through the water with the water-drawn people
led by the water-drawn man to the smoke mountain.
The voice of the world speaking, the world covered by signs,
the burning, the loving, the speaking, the opening.
Strong throat of sound from the smoking mountain.
Still flame, the spoken singing of a young child.
The meaning beginning to move, which is the song.

Music of those who have walked out of slavery.

Into that journey where all things speak to all things
refusing to accept the curse, and taking
for signs the signs of all things, the world, the body
which is part of the soul, and speaks to the world,
all creation being created in one image, creation.
This is not the past walking into the future,
the walk is painful, into the present, the dance
not visible as dance until much later.
These dancers are discoverers of God.

We knew we had all crossed over when we heard the song.

Out of a life of building lack on lack:
the slaves refusing slavery, escaping into faith:
an army who came to the ocean: the walkers
who walked through the opposites, from I to opened Thou,
city and cleave of the sea. Those at flaming Nauvoo,
the ice on the great river: the escaping Negroes,
swamp and wild city: the shivering children of Paris
and the glass black hearses; those on the Long March:
all those who together are the frontier, forehead of man.

Where the wilderness enters, the world, the song of the world.

Akiba rescued, secretly, in the clothes of death
by his disciples carried from Jerusalem
in blackness journeying to find his journey
to whatever he was loving with his life.
The wilderness journey through which we move

under the whirlwind truth into the new,
the only accurate. A cluster of lights at night:
faces before the pillar of fire. A child watching
while the sea breaks open. This night. The way in.

Barbarian music, a new song.

Acknowledging opened water, possibility:
open like a woman to this meaning.
In a time of building statues of the stars,
valuing certain partial ferocious skills
while past us the chill and immense wilderness
spreads its one-color wings until we know
rock, water, flame, cloud, or the floor of the sea,
the world is a sign, a way of speaking. To find.
What shall we find? Energies, rhythms, journey.

Ways to discover. The song of the way in.

for The Song of Songs

However the voices rise
They are the shepherd, the king,
The woman; dreams,
Holy desire.

Whether the voices
Be many the dance around
Or body led by one body
Whose bed is green,

I defend the desire
Lightning and poetry
Alone in the dark city
Or breast to breast.

Champion of light I am
The wounded holy light,
The woman in her dreams
And the man answering.

You who answer their dreams
Are the ruler of wine
Emperor of clouds
And the riches of men.

This song
Is the creation
The day of this song
The day of the birth of the world.

Whether a thousand years
Forget this woman, this king,
Whether two thousand years
Forget the shepherd of dreams.

If none remember
Who is lover, who the beloved,
Whether the poet be
Woman or man,

The desire will make
A way through the wilderness
The leopard mountains
And the lips of the sleepers.

Holy way of desire
King, lion, the mouth of the poet,
The woman who dreams
And the answerer of dreams.

In these delights
Is eternity of seed,
The verge of life,
Body of dreaming.

The Bonds

In the wine country, poverty, they drink no wine—
In the endless night of love he lies, apart from love—
In the landscape of the Word he stares, he has no word.

He hates and hungers for his immense need.

He is young. This is a shepherd who rages at learning,
Having no words. Looks past green grass and sees a woman.
She, Rachel, who is come to recognize.
In the huge wordless shepherd she finds Akiba.

To find the burning Word. To learn to speak.

The body of Rachel says, the marriage says,
The eyes of Rachel say, and water upon rock
Cutting its groove all year says All things learn.
He learns with his new son whose eyes are wine.

To sing continually, to find the word.

He comes to teaching, greater than the deed
Because it begets the deed, he comes to the stone
Of long ordeal, and suddenly knows the brook
Offering water, the citron fragrance, the light of candles.

All given, and always the giver loses nothing.

In giving, praising, we move beneath clouds of honor,
In giving, in praise, we take gifts that are given,
The spark from one to the other leaping, a bond
Of light, and we come to recognize the rock;

We are the rock acknowledging water, and water
Fire, and woman man, all brought through wilderness;
And Rachel finding in the wordless shepherd
Akiba who can now come to his power and speak:
The need to give having found the need to become:

More than the calf wants to suck, the cow wants to give suck.

Akiba Martyr

When his death confronted him, it had the face of his friend
Rufus the Roman general with his claws of pain,
His executioner. This was an old man under iron rakes
Tearing through to the bone. He made no cry.

After the failure of all missions. At ninety, going
To Hadrian in Egypt, the silver-helmed,
Named for a sea. To intercede. Do not build in the rebuilt Temple.

Your statue, do not make it a shrine to you.
Antinous smiling. Interpreters. This is an old man, pleading.
Incense of fans. The emperor does not understand.

He accepts his harvest, failures. He accepts faithlessness,
madness of friends, a failed life; and now the face of storm.

Does the old man during uprising speak for compromise?
In all but the last things. Not in the study itself.
For this religion is a system of knowledge;
Points may be one by one abandoned, but not the study.
Does he preach passion and non-violence?
Yes, and trees, crops, children honestly taught. He says;
Prepare yourselves for suffering.

Now the rule closes in, the last things are forbidden.
There is no real survival without these.
Now it is time for prison and the unknown.
The old man flowers into spiritual fire.

Streaking of agony across the sky.
Torn black. Red racing on blackness. Dawn.
Rufus looks at him over the rakes of death
Asking, "What is it?
Have you magic powers? Or do you feel no pain?"

The old man answers, "No. But there is a commandment saying
Thou shalt love the Lord thy God with all thy heart, with all thy soul
and with all thy might.
I knew that I loved him with all my heart and might.
Now I know that I love him with all my life."

The look of delight of the martyr
Among the colors of pain, at last knowing his own response
Total and unified.
To love God with all the heart, all passion,
Every desire called evil, turned toward unity,
All the opposites, all in the dialogue.
All the dark and light of the heart, of life made whole.

Surpassing the known life, day and ideas.
My hope, my life, my burst of consciousness:
To confirm my life in the time of confrontation.

The old man saying Shema.
The death of Akiba.

The Witness

Who is the witness? What voice moves across time,
Speaks for the life and death as witness voice?
Moving tonight on this city, this river, my winter street?

He saw it, the one witness. Tonight the life as legend
Goes building a meeting for me in the veins of night
Adding its scenes and its songs. Here is the man transformed,

The tall shepherd, the law, the false messiah, all;
You who come after me far from tonight finding
These lives that ask you always Who is the witness—

Take from us acts of encounter we at night
Wake to attempt, as signs, seeds of beginning,
Given from darkness and remembering darkness,

Take from our light given to you our meetings.
Time tells us men and women, tell us You
The witness, your moment covered with signs, your self.

Tell us this moment, saying You are the meeting.
You are made of signs, your eyes and your song.
Your dance the dance, the walk into the present.

All this we are and accept, being made of signs, speaking
To you, in time not yet born.
The witness is myself.
And you,
The signs, the journeys of the night, survive.

Benjamin Saltman

Benjamin Saltman began writing poetry seriously in 1965. A first collection, Blue with Blue, *appeared in 1968. This was followed by* The Leaves the People *in 1974,* Elegies of Place *in 1977,* and Deck *in 1979. A new book of poems,* Wood County Elegies, *is scheduled for publication. Saltman lives in Northridge, California, and teaches at California State University, Northridge.*

The Journey with Hands and Arms

Tefillin: phylacteries
a brief treatise on the significance of this
important *mitzvah*
the arm wrapped in leather
wrapped tight the prayer tight
held by the root
the fist also wrapped in leather
the knot of the club
the sound make by boxes con-
taining prayer
a terrifying wail
ever to remember
blessedness upon the cerebrum
application of hand and head and
heart
of the earth mixed with sand
of mulch damp at the base
of small trees with rooted knuckles

On the new moon
those who plow and those used for
plowing
allow no others
there is creaking of wood or leather
of wheels on gravel
cries
of children who smell like loaves

In many communities it is customary
for the Divine Hand to close said
Rabbi Halevi

in remembrance of the departure
clearly the stone for each finger
to manage the walls and locked
doors

To manage the explanations
to live in the pink land of the nails
the straps always to be black side
up
on the bare arm
the flesh must swell between straps
the arm must be bound
and bound again

The Fathers

I see the sparrow bones folded in their thin shoes
I hear their whistle like a toy bird
I see the clay in their foreheads
they gather and pull my house at the corners
they blockade the closets of children's clothes
I see them prepare for my journey
they ignore my wife's tears and her belly
they put their fingers in the soup
they dance in their black coats shaking the pictures
they say nothing will be forgotten
they say history is preparing a special for television
Bach and Jefferson are pressing their wigs in a leaf
in the vase on the sewing machine in the living room
they are smoke that curls out of corners
and the corners are gone and nothing is closed off
they say all are guilty no one is to blame.
I see them work faster than flight crews a blur
they fill each brick with night
they lay the feathers to each shingle carefully
they set the heart at aerial rate
and bird calls rising from the open stove
the boards are pliable as skin
when the whole house rises with wires and pipes
to soar with me forever
while my face of yellow horn plunges in the wind

Susan Fromberg Schaeffer

Susan Fromberg Schaeffer teaches at Brooklyn College in New York. She has published four volumes of poems; one, Granite Lady, *was nominated for a National Book Award. She has also published two novels including* Anya, *and her short fiction has appeared in numerous journals.*

Yahrzeit

Grandfather, we come to you now
For the coins on your eyes.
The trolleys have run into the ground
And we are in a dark town
Where the sky is purple, and the buildings are black.
Flowers are blackening before each door.

Your grave keeps announcing your name
Like a butler, but you
Stay alive in a small store of your own
And though we arrange your memories like wares
Above your narrow shelf of grass
Your fist stays closed against us, and above us
The sky is wearing its many-colored coat
And we are cold in our skins.

At eight, you sold clothes from town to town
Pushing your wheelbarrow like a belly.
The sky was your roof, full of holes.
You took the clouds with you, attached
Like balloons to your wrists and your knees.
Everyone tried to cheat you, but you grew up
Like a cactus in sand. *You were born old,*
Your daughter said. You packed up your family
Like others pack clothes, and came here to live.

You came to live among the cut-glass swans,
The palms, the rockers in shade
And the swing on the porch: the children in school,
And the children in satin, and the chopped liver duck.
Your children grew taller than trees. Then, we said,
You were not wise.
Keeping records in your black book,

Reckoning the sins and the shames,
The insults and blunders, charging us tax.
We said you could not trust.
Then night closed you in like the lids of your book.
Now you live in the weddings, bar mitzvahs,
The photograph rooms—elegant; while we
Are dressed in the tents of our innocence,
Tattered, like cloth.

Angels stand on tiptoe above these stones.
Father of us all, you were wiser than most.
You kept your many colored coat
And watched the children grow.
Abraham, grandfather, we come to you now
For the coins on your eyes
And you give us more:
You wore
Your coat of many colors under the many colored sky
And wore it well, and wore it long,
And did not die.

Delmore Schwartz

Delmore Schwartz was born in Brooklyn, New York, in 1913. He studied at the University of Wisconsin, New York University, and Harvard University and became a renowned writer, editor, and teacher. He died in 1966. His books are In Dreams Begin Responsibilities, A Season in Hell, Genesis: Book One, Vaudeville for a Princess and Other Poems, *and* Summer Knowledge: New and Selected Poems 1938-1958.

Abraham:

to J. M. Kaplan

I was a mere boy in a stone-cutter's shop
When, early one evening, my raised hand
Was halted and the soundless voice said:
"Depart from your father and your country
And the things to which you are accustomed.
Go now into a country unknown and strange

I will make of your children a great nation,
Your generations will haunt every generation of all the nations,
They will be like the stars at midnight, like the sand of the sea."
Then I looked up at the infinite sky,
Star-pointing and silent, and it was then, on that evening, that I
Became a man: that evening of my manhood's birthday.

I went then to Egypt, the greatest of nations.
There I encountered the Pharaoh who built the tombs,
Great public buildings, many theatres, and seashore villas:
And my wife's beauty was such that, fearing his power and lust,
I called her my sister, a girl neither for him nor for me.
And soon was fugitive, a nomad again.
Living alone with my sister, becoming very rich
In all but children, in herds, in possessions, the herds continually
Increased my possessions through prodigies of progeny.

From time to time, in the afternoon's revery
In the late sunlight or the cool of the evening
I called to mind the protracted vanity of that promise
Which had called me forth from my father's house unwillingly
Into the last strangeness of Egypt and the childless desert.
Then Sarah gave me her handmaid, a young girl
That I might at least at last have children by another
And later, when a great deal else had occurred,
I put away Hagar, with the utmost remorse
Because the child was the cause of so much rivalry and jealousy.

At last when all this had passed or when
The promise seemed the parts of dream,
When we were worn out and patient in all things
The stranger came, suave and elegant,
A messenger who renewed the promise, making Sarah
Burst out laughing hysterically!

But the boy was born and grew and I saw
What I had known, I knew what I had seen, for he
Possessed his mother's beauty and his father's humility,
And was not marked and marred by her sour irony and my endless
    anxiety.

Then the angel returned, asking that I surrender
My son as a lamb to show that humility
Still lived in me, and was not altered by age and prosperity.

I said nothing, shocked and passive. Then I said but to myself alone:
"This was to be expected. These promises
Are never unequivocal or unambiguous, in this
As in all things which are desired the most:
I have had great riches and great beauty.
I cannot expect the perfection of every wish
And if I deny the command, who knows what will happen?"

But his life was forgiven and given back to me:
His children and their children are an endless nation:
Dispersed on every coast. And I am not gratified
Nor astonished. It has never been otherwise:
Exiled, wandering, dumbfounded by riches,
Estranged among strangers, dismayed by the infinite sky,
An alien to myself until at last the caste of the last alienation
The angel of death comes to make the alienated and indestructible
One a part of his famous society.

Sarah

The angel said to me: "Why are you laughing?"
"Laughing! Not me. Who was laughing? I did not laugh. It was
A cough. I was coughing. Only hyenas laugh.
It was the cold I caught nine minutes after
Abraham married me: when I saw
How I was slender and beautiful, more and more
Slender and beautiful.
I was also
Clearing my throat; something inside of me
Is continually telling me something
I do not wish to hear: A joke: A big joke:
But the joke is always just on me.
He said: you will have more children than the sky's stars
And the seashore's sands, if you just wait patiently.
Wait: patiently: ninety years? You see
The joke's on me!"

Jacob

All was as it is, before the beginning began, before
We were bared to the cold air, before
Pride, fullness of bread. Abundance of idleness.
No one has ever told me what now I know:
Love is unjust, justice is loveless.

So, as it was to become, it was, in the black womb's ignorance
Coiled and bound, under the mother's heart.
There in the womb we wrestled, and writhed, hurt
Each other long before each was other and apart,
Before we breathed: who then committed greed,
Impersonation, usurpation? So, in the coming forth,
In the noose and torment of birth, Esau went first,
He was red all over. I followed him, clutching his heel,
And we were named: Esau, the one of the vivid coat,
Jacob, the one who clutches the heel of the one
Who has a vivid coat. The names were true
As the deceptive reality into which we were thrown.
For I did not know what clutching was, nor had I known
Would I have known whose heel I clutched, my brother's or my own!

So, the world we entered then and thus was one
In which the second must be second that the first may be first.
The world of precedence, order, other, under and above,
The darkness, sweetness, confusion and unity of love!
How the truth of our names became, as we grew, more true,
Growing like truth. How could it be otherwise? For truth abides
Hidden in the future, in the ambush of the marvellous,
Unknown and monstrous, at the very heart of surprise.

The gift was mind. The gift was eminence. The gift
Like every gift, was guilt. The guilt began
In the darkness and dark mystery where all begins.
The mystery of the perpetual invisible fires whence flow
The very beasts and woods where—
with what happiness!
what innocence!—
Esau my brother hunted, cantering like the horses of summer,
And sleeping, when he returned, the sleep of winter farms,
Spontaneous and blessed, like energy itself, sleeping or awake.
Until the hour when the angel struck!

ENGLISH

So it was: so:
O angel of the unspeakable,
Why must a gift be guilt and hurt the gifted one?
O angel of the unspeakable, power of powers,
Locking my reins, my arms, my heart all night
So that my body was burdened as with the load of all stones
Dost thou remember what, in the darkness, I cried,
During the desperation in which I died
The last death of hope and the little deaths of the heart
Wrestling and writhing between two rivers—on one bank,
Esau, awaiting me, like a river slept—beneath me once more.
"Hast thou not seen," I cried aloud, to the unspeakable,
"Esau my brother: his handsome hunting heart upon a horse?"
How should it seem so strange that I should win,
Since victory was my gift? Unjust, like every gift,
A something neither deserved, nor gained by toil . . .
How else could it be gift and given?
Favor: favored: favorite:
Gold hair: great strength: Esau was very tall,
Possessed by the supple grace of the sea's waves, breaking.

Now Joseph is, as I was: in Egypt's pit,
In that accustomed depth and isolated height
The solitude of eminence, the exiled intelligence,
Which separated me even as it created me:
Estranged and unloved, gifted and detested,
Denied the love of the servants and the dogs.
Joseph a stranger in Egypt may only know
What I have known: my gifts, my victory, my guilt.
For Egypt is a country like a gift.

The gift is loved but not the gifted one.
The coat of many colors is much admired
By everyone, but he who wears the coat
Is not made warm. Why should the gift be the cause of pain,
O thou unspeakable? Must the vivid coat
Of eminence select the favored favorite
As scapegoat or turncoat, exile or fugitive,
The loved of mother and God, and by all others
Shunned in fear or contempt?
I knew what it was,
When Joseph became my favorite: knew the sympathy
Of the long experience of the unasked-for gift:

Knew the nature of love: how many colors
Can a coat have? What should I desire
—Not to have loved my son, the best of sons?
Rejected the choice of love? Should I have hidden
My love of him? Or should he have concealed the self
I loved, above all others, wearing the coat
Which is customary, the coats his brothers wore?
To how many coats can a color give vividness?
How can the heart know love, and not love one the more?
Love is unjust: justice is loveless.

Howard Schwartz

Howard Schwartz was born in St. Louis, Missouri, in 1945. He attended Washington University in St. Louis, and presently teaches at the University of Missouri-St. Louis. He is the author of two books of poems, Vessels *and* Gathering the Sparks, *and of four books of fiction,* A Blessing Over Ashes, Lilith's Cave, Midrashim: Collected Jewish Parables *and* The Captive Soul of the Messiah.

Our Angels

for Yehuda Amichai

Our angels
Spend much of their time sleeping
In their dreams
They tear down the new houses by the sea
And build old ones
In their place.

No matter how long they may sleep
One hundred two hundred years
Ten centuries is not too much
The first to wake up
Takes the torch that has been handed down
Adds a drop of oil to the lamp
Blesses the eternal light
And then recalls the name
Of every other angel
And one by one as they are remembered
They wake up.

For them as for us
There is nothing more beautiful
Than memory.

Gathering the Sparks

Traces of the divine light adhered to the fragments of the broken vessels like sparks. Therefore it should be the aim of everyone to raise these sparks from where they are imprisoned in the world and to elevate them to holiness by the power of their soul.
—Israel Sarug, 1691

Long before the sun cast a shadow
Before the Word was spoken
That brought the heavens
And the earth
Into being
A flame emerged
From a single
Unseen
Point
And from the center of this flame
Sparks of light sprang forth
Concealed in shells
That set sail everywhere
Above
And below
Like a fleet of ships
Each carrying its cargo
Of light.

Somehow
No one knows why
The frail vessels broke open
Split asunder
And all the sparks were scattered
Like sand
Like seeds
Like stars.

That is why we were created—
To search for the sparks
No matter where they have been
Hidden
And as each one is revealed
To be consumed
In our own fire
And reborn
Out of our own
Ashes.

Someday
When the sparks have been gathered
The vessels will be
Restored
And the fleet will set sail
Across another ocean
Of space
And the Word
Will be spoken
Again.

Adam's Dream

And the Lord God caused a deep sleep to fall upon the man, and he slept; and He took one of his ribs, and closed up the place with flesh instead thereof. And the rib, which the Lord God had taken from the man, made He a woman, and brought her to the man.
—Genesis 2:21-22

The blossoms closed into buds
Singing only to themselves.
The sweet hand that guarded my heart
Stirred within my body.
I reached for you as you pulled away
And followed the arm's length
That linked us. I could hear
The dark pools filling, the breath you took
Rising over the waters.

I felt the life leave me
With a gasp that gave me life.
No eyes opened to ask or to answer,
Yet then I knew you were another
That I had lost,
That you would never remember
Why the wound could not heal itself
Once we had awakened.

Abraham in Egypt

And there was a famine in the land;
and Abraham went down into Egypt to
sojourn there, for the famine was sore in the land.
—Genesis 12:10

Somehow
I had come to the desert
Too soon
There nothing flourished
But the twin herbs of fear
And despair
And there was nothing
Not even a single star
To guide me
For my fire was out.

Still
I kept watch
And so I saw the white bird
Flying toward me
That dropped a single seed
At my feet—
And I cradled it
And kneaded the earth to make it ready
And planted it
While the seed was still damp
From its source.

In this way
White blossoms came to appear
And soon there was a single fruit
And when I broke it open

I found as many seeds
As stars
And when I tasted it
I drank from the spring that winds
Within
And followed it as far as I could
Knowing it would lead me
Out of Egypt.

Iscah

Rabbi Isaac observed: Iscah was Sarah,
and why was she called Iscah? Because
she foresaw the future by divine inspiration.
—Sanhedrin 69b

She is the dark sister
Standing in the shadow
Of the cave
Who peers into the bonfire
That is burning
Within.

Sometimes
She accompanies you
With her instrument
Sometimes
She lets you pray
With her voice
Or share
The sound of her breathing
Or even
Her song.

This time
She lets you read
Your lifeline
As if the words were already
Written.

If only
You would kneel by the fire
She whispers

You would understand
Why no water
Can extinguish
This flame—
Why all the logs burst into buds
And all the kinds of wood
Put forth
Fruit.

The New Year For Trees

for Shlomo and Hava Vinner

All year
They have kept a careful record
Of everything
The waters of the moon
The slow descent
Of every sun
All year
They have charted the course of every comet
Eyes drawn to the center
To the star that supports
The planet
The beam that holds up every arch
The line that continues into the future
Unbroken
Unchanged.

But tonight
As the light descends into sleep
The trees
All lift their branches to the sky
Cradling the moon
That shines through the night
Like the blossoms of the almond
That have already appeared
To announce
That all fruit that follows
Belongs to the new year
To come.

The Eve

for Laya, Zev, and Rachel

In one room of the house
My grandfather completes the prayer
That blesses the sun as it sets
In another
My father takes down a wooden box
With a candle in each corner
And a small scroll inside it
A gift he has been saving to give me
Downstairs
The bride of my brother
Brings him a prayerbook
A ribbon marking the evening's prayer
They read the book inside a chamber bedroom
And while they read
A sacred presence rises up from the page
Outside their room
We are preparing a great celebration
Tomorrow
The men will count their age in half
The women will carry everything
To the sea
And before the sun sets
There will be a great new beginning
We will take out the blond guitar
That has started to sprout
Its first flowers
And all of us will dance in a circle
And sing.

The Prayers

for Mary Ann Steiner

There is the prayer of the father
Of rain the prayer of the golden coin
Buried in a black box
All the prayers in the cracks in the Wall

Marked down one by one
Sorted out
Waiting to be heard
Then there are the prayers
Of all the sunsets never seen
Prayers closed like sleeping flowers
Prayers whose fire
Is forgotten whose darkness
Is not enough
Listen
There is also the prayer of the daughter
Who waits for the season like a tree
Her wishes silent
And the prayer of the son
Who waits for the fruit to fall
For the seeds to break open
In the earth
These are the prayers
The angels take up together
That fuse to form the prayer of the child
They receive in return
Who brings these words back
With a blessing
From the dark sun
Of their source.

Vessels

We too were created from clay
Mined from a cavern
Or the bottom of a dark pool,
Shaped by the hand of a father
And mother
And blessed
With the breath of life,
That light that shines through us
Like a small sun
Concealed in the embryo
Of an egg.

We too are vessels,
Baked in the sun by day,

Filled with the light of the moon
At night.
This moonlight
Has taken root inside us,
Has given us this bright glaze.
It is our memory of the shadow
Of many pale hands
Waiting for us to grow ripe enough
To receive.

To receive
And to transmit,
To grow transparent
In the hour of the offering,
The sacred time
Between two ceremonies
When at last
The pool can be replenished,
When you walk around me
Seven times
And I begin to glow.

A Song

A song
That seemed so brief at first
Has lasted
The fire living in your hands
Still mingles in mine
Like wood near water
I am an old poplar sprouting at the root
Whose branches would burn
In your fire
Whose seasons would find shelter
In your house of song
For the wind that blows between us
Speaks also to the spark
That clings to me like a prayer
Like a dream that shapes shadows
Into moons
That settle to the surface
Like perfect pools

Of light
That haunts my buds into blossoms
My voice
Into song.

These Two

Forty days before the formation of a child
a voice goes forth out of Heaven to announce
that this one will marry that one. And each
match is as difficult for the Holy One to
arrange as was the dividing of the Red Sea.
—Sota 2a

The question is
How to overhear
The angels
As they whisper
Among themselves:

Forty days
Before they were born
It was revealed
That these two
Whose souls are like twin stars
Shall meet
And be married
In a city that is itself
A bride.

I tell you
I have heard them
And I have heard the spirits
Of sons and daughters
Still unborn
Begging me to take care
Take care that the nest does not
Burn down.

Somehow
We must learn how to read
The letters written
In the stars that circle
Our souls.

Blessing of the Firstborn

for Tsila

Like new waters that form nightly
We embrace
The breath of the beginning
With arms
Of air
And submerge
In these waters of the moon
To receive the blessing
Of the firstborn
Whose seed
Has taken root
Inside you
Whose breath
Is drawn
Through the stars
Whose pool is replenished
In caverns of sleep
By the waters that swirl around us
Before the circle they inscribe
Becomes a full moon
At rest.

Shira

A white bird
Half human
Whose wings in flight
Echo the crystal music
Of the stars
She descends into my sleep
Blessing my voice
My name
The letters of the kingdom
Even the crown.

A white bird
Winged messenger
Whose feathers are woven
Of moon rays

Whose heart
Is a living opal
She rises to the surface
Unsung
From the cradle of the seed
Rocked in the waters
Of the womb.

A white bird
Sister of my soul
She balances between
The stars above
And the stars
Below
There
We rock in each other's arms
One of us sleeping
One always
Awake.

Psalm

Father
You are the trunk
We are the branches
When the Ark opens
We stand beside your silver tree
On this side of the earth
Reading your words
Over and over
Raking the coals.

And when we look up
And glimpse the future
Lashed to the mast of an ark
Rolling over the waters
Of a dark sea
We wrap ourselves
Once more
In your garment of light
Your prayer shawl
Woven from the fabric
Of history.

But Father
We are still waiting
For the rain that must come
On its own
And for the tree that will spring up
Out of those waters
And bear fruit.

Harvey Shapiro

Harvey Shapiro was born in Chicago in 1925 and studied at Yale and Columbia Universities. In addition to his five books of poetry including Battle Report, This World, *and* Lands & Nightsounds, *he has served on the editorial staffs of* Commentary, The New Yorker, *and* The New York Times Magazine. *He is presently editor of* The New York Times Book Review.

The Six Hundred Thousand Letters

The day like blank paper
Being pulled from my typewriter.
With the six
Hundred thousand letters of the Law
Surrounding me,
Not one of them in place.

Lines for the Ancient Scribes

The past sends images to beach
Upon our present consciousness.
The sons of light war with the sons
Of darkness still. The congregations
Of the sleek and sure rule at will.

Jerome and Origen can tell
How Greek redactions of the text
Stalled at the Tetragrammaton.
And violent in archaic script
The Name burned upon parchment—

Whence springs the ram to mind again
From whose sinews David took
Ten strings to fan upon his harp.
So that the sacrifice was song,
Though ash lay on the altar stone.

Exodus

When they escaped
They carried a pack of bones
In a mummy-coffin like an ark.
Of course they had the pillar
Of clouds by day and fire by night,
But those were like dreams
Or something painted on the sky.
God was in the bones
Because he had said,
God will remember you
If you take me hence.
This was before the miracle
By the sea or the thundering mountain,
Before the time of thrones
And cherubim. They were
Only now drawn forth
To eat the history feast
And begin the journey.
Why then should they carry history
Like an ark, and the remembering
Already begun?

Riding Westward

It's holiday night
And crazy Jews are on the road,
Finished with fasting and high on prayer.
On either side of the Long Island Expressway
The lights go spinning
Like the twin ends of my tallis.
I hope I can make it to Utopia Parkway
Where my father lies at the end of his road.
And then home to Brooklyn.
Jews, departure from the law

Is equivalent to death.
Shades, we greet each other.
Darkly, on the Long Island Expressway,
Where I say my own prayers for the dead,
Crowded in Queens, remembered in Queens,
As far away as Brooklyn. Cemeteries
Break against the City like seas,
A white froth of tombstones
Or like schools of herring, still desperate
To escape the angel of death.
Entering the City, you have to say
Memorial prayers as he slides overhead
Looking something like my father approaching
The Ark as the gates close on the Day of Atonement
Here in the car and in Queens and in Brooklyn.

For the Yiddish Singers in the Lakewood Hotels of My Childhood

I don't want to be sheltered here.
I don't want to keep crawling back
To this page, saying to myself,
This is what I have.

I never wanted to make
Sentimental music in the Brill Building.
It's not the voice of Frank Sinatra
I hear.

To be a Jew in Manhattan
Doesn't have to be this.
These lights flung like farfel.
These golden girls.

Like a Beach

Even the unlived life within us
Is worth examining.
Maybe it is all we have.
The rest is burned up

Like fuel in the furnace.
But the unlived life
Stretches within us like a beach.
There is a gull's shadow on it.
Or it is at night and the moon
Crusts the sand.
Or it is a house at night
With people talking in the next room
Over cards.
You believe
In these observations?
Doesn't the sea sweep in,
The action begin in the house
At night, the voices of the players
Loud in argument,
Their motives, their needs,
Turbulent as the sea?
Whose happiness
Even here
Is being sacrificed?

Musical Shuttle

Night, expositor of love.
Seeing the sky for the first time
That year, I watched the summer constellations
Hang in air: Scorpio with
Half of heaven in his tail.
Breath, tissue of air, cat's cradle.
I walked the shore
Where cold rocks mourned in water
Like the planets lost in air.
Ocean was a low sound.
The gate-keeper suddenly gone,
Whatever the heart cried
Voice tied to dark sound.
The shuttle went way back then,
Hooking me up to the first song
That ever chimed in my head.
Under a sky gone slick with stars,

The aria tumbling forth:
Bird and star.
However those cadences
Rocked me in the learning years,
However that soft death sang—
Of star become a bird's pulse,
Of the spanned distances
Where the bird's breath eddied forth—
I recovered the lost ground.
The bird's throat
Bare as the sand on which I walked.
Love in his season
Had moved me with that song.

Karl Shapiro

Karl Shapiro was born in Baltimore in 1913. He was educated at the University of Virginia and Johns Hopkins University, and is currently professor of English at the University of California-Davis. Shapiro won the Pulitzer Prize in 1945 for V-Letter and Other Poems *and has served as consultant in poetry for the Library of Congress. Other publications include* Essay on Rime, Poems of a Jew, *and* White-Haired Lover.

The Alphabet

The letters of the Jews as strict as flames
Or little terrible flowers lean
Stubbornly upwards through the perfect ages,
Singing through solid stone the sacred names.
The letters of the Jews are black and clean
And lie in chain-line over Christian pages.
The chosen letters bristle like barbed wire
That hedge the flesh of man,
Twisting and tightening the book that warns.
These words, this burning bush, this flickering pyre
Unsacrifices the bled son of man
Yet plaits his crown of thorns.

Where go the tipsy idols of the Romans
Past synagogues of patient time,

Where go the sisters of the Gothic rose,
where go the blue eyes of the Polish women
Past the almost natural crime,
Past the still speaking embers of ghettos,
There rise the tinder flowers of the Jews.
The letters of the Jews are dancing knives
That carve the heart of darkness seven ways.
These are the letters that all men refuse
And will refuse until the king arrives
And will refuse until the death of time
And all is rolled back in the book of days.

The 151st Psalm

Are You looking for us? We are here.
Have You been gathering flowers, Elohim?
We are Your flowers, we have always been.
When will You leave us alone?
We are in America.
We have been here three hundred years.
And what new altar will You deck us with?

Whom are You following, Pillar of Fire?
What barn do You seek shelter in?
At whose gate do You whimper
In this great Palestine?
Whose wages do You take in this New World?
But Israel shall take what it shall take,
Making us ready for Your hungry Hand!

Immigrant God, You follow me;
You go with me, You are a distant tree;
You are the beast that lows in my heart's gates;
You are the dog that follows at my heel;
You are the table on which I lean;
You are the plate from which I eat.

Shepherd of the flocks of praise,
Youth of all youth, ancient of days,
Follow us.

Jew

The name is immortal but only the name, for the rest
Is a nose that can change in the weathers of time or persist
Or die out in confusion or model itself on the best.

But the name is a language itself that is whispered and hissed
Through the houses of ages, and ever a language the same,
And ever and ever a blow on our heart like a fist.

And this last of our dream in the desert, O curse of our name,
Is immortal as Abraham's voice in our fragment of prayer
Adonai, Adonai, for our bondage of murder and shame!

And the word for the murder of God will cry out on the air
Though the race is no more and the temples are closed of our will
And the peace is made fast on the earth and the earth is made fair;

Our name is impaled in the heart of the world on a hill
Where we suffer to die by the hands of ourselves, and to kill.

David Shevin

David Shevin was born in Rochester, New York, and studied at Lewis and Clark College and Bowling Green State University. He is currently an Elliston Fellow at the University of Cincinnati. His collections of poems are Musics, The World Series, The Red Herring of Courage, Expecting Ginger Rogers, *and* The Stop Book.

Shechem

In terror the aches
give comfort. When
I move the blood threatens
to flow again,
and stones rest
in my back like children
come home
after a long journey.

There was blood
where we slept
and the earth held anger
in its hand of memory.
Now the hand
releases me to the clinch
hug of pain,

my dowry. My brothers
are wounded and shout out
when they try to stand.
Oh my brothers,
we will dwell by the altar,
our cattle and gold.

Dawn

the flames rising up
from the cautions of history
drive the night demons
from the body:

yellow herbivorous glint
where the sun plucks
the coin from its grassy cocoon:

I see a man who steps
away from his coffin
and flies away singing
into the new blossoms:

fresh water flows
from the cisterns:

if this is not the true
tomb of David, surely
that was one
of his sons.

Danny Siegel

Danny Siegel lives in New York, where he is a lecturer and teacher. He is the author of three volumes of poetry: Soulstoned, And God Braided Eve's Hair, *and* Between Dust and Dance.

Binni the Meshuggener

Binni the Madman
knew to the gram
how much protein
the Great Leviathan would yield
to the Righteous
at God's Feast.
He knew numbers and nicknames
of angels
no scholar ever heard of,
no volumes described.
He measured Eve's height,
weighed Jacob's weight,
and counted every ripple
in Samson's mammoth chest.

Binni der Meshuggener
from Lomza,
selling his books of mishigoss,
all the way
to the Nazi Gates of Hell.

Snow in the City

The roads were jammed.
Then they were closed,
and the last train from Tel Aviv
was packed with Israelis
coming to Jerusalem to see.
As we climbed the hills,
there were children of every age

rolling their hands in it
and throwing snowballs at the windows.
It was dark as we arrived,
mystical,
and we were slow and nearly knee-deep
tracking from the station to our home.
No traffic, no sound,
other than the flakes
and the buzz of the streetlamps.
In the distance, the mosques
looked like holiday yarmulkas,
and the miracle of JNF was multiplied
by millions of glistening branches—
trees from Hebrew Schools
in Texas and London and Johannesburg
standing in *kittels* of snow,
like a wedding
of Heaven and Earth.

The Crippler

I had always been told
my Zeyde cut his own finger off
to escape the 20+ years' exile in the Czar's army
but now I know the truth:
that there was this man in their community
in one-day-Poland next-day-Russia
called the Crippler
who obliged the Jews
by maiming the children
before the officers conscripted them.
And as the game developed
the Jews found
an index-finger was not sufficient—
the Czar would be a laughingstock.
So the cry arose for variety
to give appearance that everything
was from a natural accident.
And so the Crippler got new sticks and saws
and a holy sense of destiny

for it was he who said:
From this one I will take an eye
from that a leg
and those each shall be broken-backed.
Now I think that this
was how
his own Zeyde
came to be a deaf-mute tailor—
a stick in the ear,
acid in the mouth—
and he was free to stay home
bear children
and sail to America
before the last pogrom
robbed him
of his good fortune.
Here he could gesticulate his way
to old age
and pass on the tale
to his grandson
my Zeyde
who would tell me
in an Aleph-plus hotel
in Yerushalayim
how it was back then
back there
so that I might rise above
the shame
and promise my own children
that there are other ways
better ways
to be chosen.

Maxine Silverman

Maxine Silverman is a native of Sedalia, Missouri. She attended Washington University and now lives in New York City. Survival Song, *her first book of poems, was published in 1976. A second collection,* There there Now now *is forthcoming.*

Hair

Ardently down the backs of cousins
in Poland until it brushed their ribs
the silkworm cousins grew the hair
Sarah Fishoff Silverman peddled
in Missouri.
In Sedalia meager enterprising waves
swelled over coils and switches
off Polish Jews, hair grown
to drape on Sarah's forearm.
She walked the town selling hair
of those who stayed behind,
sticking her other palm out with coins,
trusting strangers to make change
for the hair that caught the fancy
of stylish Midwestern ladies,
the curls and braids that pleased the Nazis
who trimmed their lampshades with Jewish hair,
fashioned bellcords to summon butlers
from my cousins' hair that grew no more.

Myra Sklarew

Myra Sklarew is presently visiting assistant professor in the Department of Literature at American University in Washington, D.C. Her two books of poetry are In the Basket of the Blind *and* From the Background of the Diaspora.

What Is a Jewish Poem?

Does it wear a *yarmulka*
and *tallis*?
Does it live
in the *diaspora*
and yearn for homeland?

Does it wave the *lulav*
to and fro inside
a plastic *sukkah*

or recite
the seven benedictions
under the *chupah?*

I wonder,
what is a Jewish poem?
Does it only go to synagogue
one day a year
attaching the *tefillin*
like a tiny black stranger
to its left arm?

Does it open
the stiff skins
of the prayerbook
to reveal the letters
like blackened platelets
twisting within?

Little *yeshiva bocher,*
little Jewish poem
waving your sidecurls
whispering *piyyut* to me
in my sleep,
little Jewish poem
in your *shtreimel* hat,
little grandfather
sing to me,
little Jewish poem
come sing to me.

Benediction

Sometimes I see them coming
and going along the road
where they were swallowed up
carrying their empty luggage
or walking out from doorways
whose last inhabitants they were
or going to market as though
for one day's food

I took a scissors to the map
that was forming and cut away
places I hadn't named
I tore up their footsteps
their empty hands the valises
they left behind

Now they have begun to walk inside me
their feet move in a night march
the agreement has broken down
like time at the year's end
come I say to them *be still* I say
gather under the prayer shawls
of the fathers these benedictions
as under so many tents

Instructions for the Messiah

do you think
you must work signs
and miracles
or resurrect the dead

it is sufficient
that you have diligently
studied the law

we would ask of you
only the rebuilding
of the temple
and the gathering in
of the exiles

these will define you

and nothing will seem changed
night will follow day
as it always has

it was never for dominion
that we invented you
but only that we might
return to our houses

inside
we would know
the hidden things
of this world

Arlene Stone

Arlene Stone is a poet and playwright who currently lives in Saratoga, California. Her books of poetry include The Shule of Jehovah, The Image Maker, Through a Coal Cellar, Darkly, *and* The Women's House.

Germination

Out of the breath of Gehennah,
out of the void and before
the conception,
the blood-letting;
Out of the cesspool of sorrow
and moons confounded by morning,
before hope grew in a wishbone
or the artery of a fly;
Lapped by the spiral tides
and the loosening tooth of the shore—
Out of the pit of Ben-Hinnom,
and the sickly wit of pain,
from mindless cockroach eyes,
the bulls' eyes of surprise,
Jehovah House of Torment
sends forth the chosen tribe
in a Rose,
the cradle of slaughter,
saying
You shall inherit.

Jehovah conceives The Rose
from the earlobe of a stone:
Milk pores,
ash fingertips,
a Messianic stamen.

ENGLISH

She
of the seed of Aaron
shall bear two infant goats—
Saul,
the priest-Messiah,
descended from Jehovah;
and Jacob,
the goat for fattening,
to be known as Jacob the Cuckold.
And she—
Old ladies' lips are leeches
cracked like bittersweet;
their kisses are wet as graves;
their stares are frames for crucifixion.

Precise as sleet or salt,
the Sloth of Sheol
measures
dimensions for The Shule,
the temple of cubits
with the sapphire eye of a roach
Jehovah Resplendent Cemetery
saying,
I shall embrace you.

The goats shall be led through the marketplace,
the horns menorahs of cactus,
their ears aquiver with bells,
into the kiln of the Shule of Jehovah—

Cricket cantors,
Take up your arks,
the tenors of sacrifice, for the dance
of the jewels
of the tabernacle—
Kill one goat for Jehovah Yahweh.
Send one goat to Azazel.
He snores in the bonewhite wilderwild
on a buried camel spine.

Down
  from the fire,
    the coveting ore,
      the pistons of the Whoring Orator;
Down
  from the serpentine trumpets,
    blinking like hills of salt,
      each with the mask of Messiah
          (a leprous chicken lung),
into the crater of brambles
petalled with crumbling yods,
Jehovah the Master Arsonist
    saying
          I shall maintain you.

But here is the Demon, black as dung,
the Cricket Azazel Baal Zebub.
Mark his passage.
His hands are firecracker planets,
ants,
in global constellations,
ocean barques of salt.

He speaks: a barge of spiders.
He laughs: a pavilion of wings.

Below
    the jawbone of Ben-Hinnom,
the crickets sob like turtles,
the turtles, hunched, are tablets,
and cactus gropes
for marrow and for pulse.

Jehovah whips His tail.
Ashes spill from His plaster lips;
his nails are empty horns,

Jehovah the Blind Oculist
    saying
          You shall be borne.

ENGLISH

Nathaniel Tarn

Nathaniel Tarn was born in 1928. He lived for many years in England. He is now a professor of Comparative Literature at Rutgers University. His books of poetry include Lyrics for the Bride of God *and* The Beautiful Contradictions.

Where Babylon Ends

'Nec Babylonios temptaris numeros'

Where Babylon ends
no one knows now.

I'd like before the world is ripe
to make men cry for what they are
once and for all so that
they never cry again
and this old top
stops spinning—
for then we can begin

to clarify the city,
to build with bricks you know
tall cliffs of fiery letters
far, far from Babylon
to touch the thunder's lips—
but where Babylon ends
no one knows now.

I am Hebrew they say,
i.e. I do not understand
the gambler's spinning wheel,
the rules of wanton chance,
raps on the knuckles for Jupiter's triplets,
the sag in each thread of our lives:
art for art's sake.

It may be true. It may be true.
Where they preach this, in any case:
silence. With us, a generation gone,
the ache of standstill
and then quite suddenly

the recovered gasp
of the teaching breath.

Now lights will flash on
and off in quick succession.
Flat on your bellies you will be amazed
by simple things
violently lit, then occulted.
Leave labyrinths to birds and moles
who brook no obstacles

but men wish clear well-water.
In the cracks of Babylon
willows grow
where light awakes.
I rise to the holy Jerusalem of all angels
and speak to you in those provinces
she has in every nook and cranny of your countries.

Constance Urdang

Constance Urdang is a native of New York who now resides in St. Louis. She is the author of two books of poems, Charades and Celebrations *and* The Picnic in the Cemetery, *and of one novel,* Natural History.

The Invention of Zero

Without it, nothing exists.
Thinking of those ancient mathematicians
In their skin tents
Bending dark Semitic faces
In the odor of goat-turds and camel-dung
To decipher the hermetic universe,
Those venerable magi whose fastidious fingers
Dissected out this pearl
Of nothing, this naught, nil, nihil,
This iridescent bubble of wisdom, hollow at the core,
This insubstantiality, this absence,
This egg of being,
I am amazed anew
At the inexhaustible fertility of the natural world.

Birth

Before, there was one
Without a name

I killed it
It had no heart

One wrenched away
With a single cry

My body floated
Inches above the bed

Another drowned
In freshets of blood

It was warm in the bed
But a cold hand touched my heart

In the eyes of the newborn
I see an ancient woman

She thinks nothing was
Before she came.

Change of Life

Ashes of roses, forsythia bones,
tulips with blackened teeth,
let me read in you
what has become of the young girl in the legend
who so craved honey
that her entire life was changed by it.

When she lay down
roses sprang from her side
her body became a trellis
for ardent tropical blooms
with corollas so deep
you could drown in them,
disappearing in those mysterious caves.

In this way the bees found her;
in the laboratory of the hive
they are transforming her into an old woman,
drained, shrivelled, and unsexed
like a quince-blossom mutilated by the frost.
She has been rendered to her essences;
her voice comes to you through the lips of a crone.

Ruth Whitman

Ruth Whitman is a member of the faculty at Radcliffe College. She is the author of six books of poetry and translations, including Tamsen Donner: A Woman's Journey, The Marriage Wig, *and* The Passion of Lizzie Borden: New and Selected Poems. *She has also edited and translated* An Anthology of Modern Yiddish Poetry.

Translating

for Jacob Glatstein

The old man was cold.
King David, they said,
we've heaped piles of clothes
on your bed, but your feet
are still icy, night after
night. Let us find you
a girl, a young
Shulamite, intelligent,
kind, who can spread
her warm bones
over you. . . .

Abishag's
black hair lay
like a shawl on his throat,
her breasts and belly
and her rosy thighs
rode his flesh
shyly all night.

He did not enter her.

But as they lay,
slowly warming,
his voice found her ear,
and since he was sleepless,
he told her what
he was thinking:

how a slingshot had won him
a great lopsided battle
when he was a boy;
how he slew his ten thousands;
how his soul was knit
to his lover Jonathan;
how he answered Saul's
hatred with mercy;
how he danced unashamed
before the Ark
with songs and lyres
with harps and cymbals
and made his wife angry;
lusted after
married Bathsheba;
got himself children,
was betrayed
by a son, a son;
how songs still came
to him. . .

And Abishag,
after all those hours
of listening, the world
in his voice,
rose in the morning
full of spermatic words.

Dan, the Dust of Masada Is Still in My Nostrils

those roman stones
hard and strong as the muscles of young David
still press against me

you led me
out of that pasture of bones
to deserts where orange groves
lay in the arms of cypresses

where drops of anemones
blazed red on the hills of Galilee
among the pungent vines

Dan
you led me to the Wall

my hands were drawn to touch it
my head bowed forward

a force of gathered tears poured through the rock
floods ran through my fingers
filling me

with the cries of centuries

I married the Wall
I became
a vessel of history

last night you held the city
like a jewel in your hand
turning each side towards me
under the new moon

three times you led me around your treasure
(the beginning of an ancient wedding)
three times

we circled your hoard of diamonds
your city
spilled among the Judean hills.

Jerusalem.

ENGLISH

Mediterranean

1
The sun is a gold coin slipping into
an envelope of sea.

2
The sea is a mouth
that opens at the horizon.
Everything in the sky
falls into her.

3
She is hungry for the first fruit
of evening.
She draws him into her,
a round harvest.

4
She is swallowing
an orange.
She is sucking it in
slowly,
whole.

5
He slips down her throat,
a pocket of fragrance.
His orchards
burst open.

6
Tomorrow he will rise
crescent by crescent
above the dusky hills.

7
A rosy air washes his absence.

Watching the Sun Rise Over Mount Zion

Orange fish are swimming
over the roofs.

The air is tinseled
with scales of gold.

Someone is coming.

All the harps cymbals violins
drums horns cellos
sing
    one blinding note.

The tower is on fire.

It is today.

Melvin Wilk

Melvin Wilk was born in 1939 in Brooklyn, New York. He studied literature and writing at Queens College and the University of Montana, and earned a master's degree in creative writing at Boston University, a second master's degree in contemporary Jewish studies at Brandeis University, and a doctorate in English at the University of Massachusetts, Amherst. He lives in Creston, Iowa, where he teaches at Southwestern Community College. His first book of poems, In Exile, *was published in 1979.*

Blessing

My grandfather leads me through snow
to a river he says dances.

He steps into a sunlit rush of water,
and warmed by reason of ritual, he raises his eyes
and the sun becomes a suggestion only
of a warmth beyond and yet to be.

In a language I do not follow
he talks the story of our lives to me,
his voice turning in me
like the pages of a *siddur.*

In the water, his fingers swirl, songlike,
and psalms spill from his arms as he beckons.
I don't budge.
He dips to his neck in the stream
murmuring his Yiddish pleasure.
Then, before he is immersed,
he calls me by my Jewish name.

J. Rutherford Willems

J. Rutherford Willems is a native of San Francisco. He is a former editor of Isthmus Press and the author of several books of poems, including Amid America *and* The Harlequin Poems.

Hebrew Letters in the Trees

The stick was almost a staff
and only a little crooked
perhaps, like me.
Its bark peeled off
able to take my weight
when I walked
I used it to climb the hill
in winter.
The snow was like sand
I could hear my footsteps.
They sounded like the paper
of rejected poems
drifting away
into the wicker basket
to sleep.
Walking along the edge
my eyes
tearing slightly
    the cold, perhaps

I saw the wooden trunks
and branches
make black letters
on a whitening sky.
I recognized the letters
and some of the words.
And I read along the ridge
along the surface of the land
to where it met the sky.
It read like a scroll
running into the white, cold mist.
Even the twigs were letters
    points upon the solid trunks
    of the trees
And the sun was the same as yesterday.

C. K. Williams

C(harles) K(enneth) Williams was born in 1936 in Newark, New Jersey. He attended the University of Pennsylvania, and has taught at Beaver College, Drexel University, and Franklin and Marshall College. His books of poems are I Am the Bitter Name, Lies *and* With Ignorance. *He has also translated* Women of Trachis *with Gregory Dickerson.*

Spit

. . . then the son of the "superior race" began to spit into the Rabbi's mouth so that the Rabbi could continue to spit on the Torah . . .

—The Black Book

After this much time, it's still impossible. The SS man with his stiff
    hair and his uniform;
the Rabbi, probably in a torn overcoat, probably with a stained beard
    the other would be clutching;
the Torah, God's word, on the altar, the letters blurring under the
    blended phlegm;
the Rabbi's parched mouth, the SS man perfectly absorbed, obsessed
    with perfect humiliation.
So many years and what is there to say still about the soldiers
    waiting impatiently in the snow,
about the one stamping his feet, thinking, "Kill him! Get it over
    with!"

while back there the lips of the Rabbi and the other would have
brushed
and if time had stopped you would have thought they were lovers,
so lightly kissing, the sharp, luger hand under the dear chin,
the eyes furled slightly and then when it started again the eyelashes
of both of them
shyly fluttering as wonderfully as the pulse of a baby.
Maybe we don't have to speak of it at all, it's still the same,
War, that happens and stops happening but is always somehow right
there, twisting and hardening us;
then what we make of God— words, spit, degradation, murder,
shame; every conceivable torment.
All these ways to live that have something to do with how we live
and that we're almost ashamed to use as metaphors for what goes on
in us
but that we do anyway, so that love is battle and we watch ourselves
in love
become maddened with pride and incompletion, and God is what it
is when we're alone
wrestling with solitude and everything speaking in our souls turns
against us like His fury
and just facing another person, there is so much terror and hatred
that yes,
spitting in someone's mouth, trying to make him defile his own
meaning,
would signify the struggle to survive each other and what we'll enact
to accomplish it.

There's another legend.
It's about Moses, that when they first brought him as a child before
Pharaoh,
the king tested him by putting a diamond and a live coal in front of
him
and Moses picked up the red ember and popped it into his mouth?
so for the rest of his life he was tongue-tied and Aaron had to speak
for him.
What must his scarred tongue have felt like in his mouth?
It must have been like always carrying something there that weighed
too much,
something leathery and dead whose greatest gravity was to loll out
like an ox's,
and when it moved, it must have been like a thick embryo slowly
coming alive,

butting itself against the inner sides of his teeth and cheeks.
And when God burned in the bush, how could he not cleave to him?
How could he not know that all of us were on fire and that every
word we said would burn forever,
in pain, unquenchably, and that God knew it, too, and would say
nothing Himself ever again beyond this,
ever, but would only live in the flesh that we use like firewood,
in all the caves of the body, the gut cave, the speech cave:
He would slobber and howl like something just barely a man that
beats itself again and again onto the dark,
moist walls away from the light, away from whatever would be light
for this last eternity.
"Now therefore go," He said, "and I will be with thy mouth."

Linda Zisquit

Linda Zisquit was born in Buffalo, New York, in 1947. She studied at Tufts, Harvard, and the State University of New York at Buffalo. Her poems have appeared in various magazines in the United States and Israel.

Rachel's Lament

It was seven years then
I saw you walking bone-dry
the well as cool as night.
I served you water
and turned my face away.
My father took my sister into you
blinding you who knew her in my time.
I waited by your tent where she was large,
soared the maiden's dream
and did not speak.

All my faults, my imperfections
in waiting came to flower.
Words fed my womb, your altar.
Myrtle or thornbush, who
can know the difference
if only by touch by smell
when they are full-grown
I do not blame you:
man's soul is like a flying bird,
impatient with a woman's gross impurity.

I hid the idols of my father's court
that you might flee unheard. You cursed me
as you would a common thief
this curse, of sleeplessness unborn
remorseless final distance all the years.
My fragrances are woman, sustenance—
Two sons I bore you joyful to survive,
only to be muted by a cry.
What sons I bear in this painful desert now
I weep for them.
Wanderer, Spring-loss, water-fed and dried,
how I have loved you
whose eyes have twice misjudged me.
For the root of mandrake I shared you in silence,
impaled myself on the edges of your face.

I need a voice.
Out of this thick-walled distance
out of barrenness
my tomb becomes a song
that streaks the air like tears
ringing at last in ecstasy my sex
my name my naked virtue
for your tribes.

Sabbatical

Seven years I orbit around you
under the canopy veiled and namelessly
sprung from some unholy ground
haunted by ill-wishers in the crowd.
You totter between two walls—
Western prayer, words in its chink of time
and the stark white expanse of these rooms.
I have done this to you, torn you,
bound you again.
Your friend warned me before all this,
tore me vessel from voice for I was not schooled,
took me drunk and weeping, washed me down:
rehearsal of immersions I would make
endlessly to dip
to be ritually cleansed of his negative truth.

I cannot be your wife
severed from roots to grow in return through you.
The language of prayer is not learned he said.
I immerse, *baruch ata,* the fluid words
my body unclothed
my shining teeth and nails
my hair is separate, clean, I dip and dip
and dip for you again,
pass the woman's gaze,
melt in that water, return a kosher bride,
repeating the hope to erase his ominous words,
to remove the blood
that covers me everywhere.

The Circumcision

If he does not look at her face
she will suffer and if he dares
to touch her, she will fly.

Her eyes upon him who holds
the child, her cheeks are wet
from the mist of the Seraphim.
If he loves her she will hate
his earthly ways.
There must be a book she can go to
that speaks of these things.

Men recite, binding the child
to fathers, to permanence,
to the words, "Ethereal Jew,
your deaths rise up to slaughter.
A wordly view. You are the ashes
and the dust of generations.
Nothing fails to reach you,
there is no end to your limbs,
your human form."

Comely men dance, a celebration
hand in hand to the music around a mountain
rising out of God's hand
dressed in fire.

She alone stands distant, ill at ease.
Though she is covered, too.
Nameless vowels stretch across her lips,
the marriage wig, appropriate.
In this room of holy men,
who can know how his eyes undress her,
how she yields to him, immodest,
how future stars explode against her skin.

Louis Zukofsky

Louis Zukofsky was born in 1904 in New York City. He was the originator of the "Objectivist" poetry movement, whose other members included Charles Reznikoff, Carl Rakosi, and George Oppen. Zukofsky's most famous work is A, *to which he added sections over a long period of time. He died in 1978.*

From the Head

In Hebrew "In the beginning"
Means literally *from the head*
A source creating
The heaven and the earth
And every plant in the field
Before it was in the earth.
Sweet shapes from a head
Whose thought must live forever—
Be the immortelle—
Before it is thought
A prayer to the East
Before light—the sun later—
To get over even its chaos early.

A Voice Out of the Tabernacle

Sabbath, the pious carry no money
Make no purchases. They have everything
From Friday—the Eve of the Sabbath.
Rest.
A long Sabbath.

His father, my grandfather
Maishe Afroim (the Sephardim speak differently)
Faced East in the synagogue.
Ebon hair?
On the Eve of Sabbath, at the end of Sabbath
At home
So good his singing voice
"Sing bridegroom to bride"
"Sabbath has gone"
Neighbors stopped at his windows
Leaned on the sills.

A voice out of the tabernacle—
For the ark
Shittim wood—the acacia.

Expounding the Torah

Rabbi Pinhas:
From true prayers
I took as goodness gave,
The pupil is dark and
Receives every ray of light.

Bread and a coat:
Both are—considering
Our nature—enough with
Which to see the sky.
There, night, and sense sure,
Else not motion or rest.

Rabbi Leib:
What is the worth of their
Expounding the Torah:
All a man's actions
Should make him a Torah—
So to light up
Whether he moves or is still.
Given a share, the body
Comports the soul.
It sees its reflection
Only when it bends to it.

ENGLISH

It is not the same
Asking a friend,
The world is its place.
It joins mouth and heart,
The place and its presence
where each creature sings its song,
It is ruled and acts
First note to fourth,
Because of its holiness
Its song seems not holy at all,
As in the "Section of Praise"
Uniting the degrees:
As it is, created—
And—ashes and ear—
Do you hear yourself,
You must stop.
If it helps, diffract crystals and tracers.
Rabbi S said:
—You can learn from everything.
What man has made
Has also something to teach us.
His chassid jumped:
—Does a train?
—Yes, in a second
One may miss everything.
—A telegraph?
—Every word weighs.
—And the telephone teaches?
—Also. What we say
Here is heard there.

ENGLAND

A. Alvarez

A. Alvarez was born in London in 1929. He was educated at Oundle School and Corpus Christi, Oxford. He has written several books of criticism. His recent works include The Savage God: A Study of Suicide; *two novels,* Hers *and* Hunt; *and a collection of poems,* Autumn to Autumn and Selected Poems 1953-1976.

A Cemetery in New Mexico

to Alfred Alvarez, dead 1957

Softly the dead stir, call, through the afternoon.
The soil lies too light upon them and the wind
Blows through the earth as though the earth were pines.

My own blood in a heavy northern death
Sleeps with the rain and clay and dark, thick shrubs,
Where the spirit fights for movement as for breath.

But among these pines the crosses grow like ferns,
Frail sprouting wood and mottled, slender stones,
And the wind moves, through shadows moves the sun.

Delicate the light, the air, a breathing
Joins the mourners to the dead in one light sleep:
I watch as I would watch a blind man sleeping,

And remember the day the creaking ropes let slip
My grandfather's heavy body into his grave,
And the rain came down as we shovelled the earth on the lid.

The clods fell final and flat as a blow in the wind
While the mourners patiently hunched against the rain.
There were Hebrew prayers I didn't understand.

In Willesden Cemetery, honoured, wealthy, prone,
Unyielding and remote, he bides his time.
And carved above his head is my own name.

Over and over again the thing begins:
My son at night now frets us with his cries
When dark above his crib the same face leans.

And even here in this clear afternoon
The dead are moving like wind among the pines;
They touch my mouth, they curl along my spine.
They are waiting for me. Why won't they call my name?

The Fortunate Fall

Perhaps Eve in the garden knew the sun
With her whole flesh, and pruned the rose's soul—
The thing was thornless, pliable, like Eve—
And she the garden whence all flowers sprung.

But Adam knew her as the fruit he stole,
The apple, sleeping, God made him conceive.
His side and eyes were opened. They were bare,
The tree despoiled and knowledge risen whole.

Before she even fumbled with the leaves
Adam was finished. Of course, she had a flair
For fumbling that was folly to oppose,
Tricky, pleading, knowing. Why should he grieve?

So he chose for her, chose his own despair.
Her hair, like rain, closed on the thorny rose.

Dying

after the Ancient Egyptian

Death is before me today
like recovering from an illness
and going into the garden
Death
the odour of myrrh
a sail's curving shadow on a windy day
Death
like the scent of the lotus
like lingering on the shore of drunkenness

Death
a quick, cool stream
a soldier coming home
Death
like a break in the clouds
a bird's flight into the unknown
Death
like homesickness
like homecoming after captivity.

Mourning and Melancholia

His face was blue, on his fingers
flecks of green. 'This is my father,'
I thought. Stiff and unwieldy
He stared out of my sleep. The parlourmaid
Smiled from the bed with his corpse,
Her chapped lips thin and welcoming.
In the next room her albino child
Kept shouting, shouting. I had to put him down
Like a blind puppy. 'Death from strangulation
By persons known.' I keep the clipping
In my breast-pocket where it burns and burns,
Stuck to my skin like phosphorus.

I wake up struggling, silent, undersea
Light and a single thrush
Is tuning up. You sleep, the baby sleeps,
The town is dead. Foxes are out on the Heath;
They sniff the air like knives.
A hawk turns slowly over Highgate, waiting.
This is the hidden life of London. Wild.

Three years back my father's corpse was burnt,
His ashes scattered. Now I breathe him in
With the grey morning air, in and out.
In out. My heart bumps steadily
Without pleasure. The air is thick with ash.
In out. I am cold and powerless. His face
Still pushes sadly into mine. He's disappointed.
I've let him down, he says. Now I'm cold like him
Cold and untameable. Will have to be put down.

ENGLISH

Anthony Barnett

Anthony Barnett was born in London in 1941. He lived in England until 1969 and spent the following seven years in Denmark and Norway, returning to England in 1976. He has worked as a bookseller, actor, music therapist, and child-care worker. He writes about music and works, self-taught, in the field of improvised music as a percussionist and wind instrumentalist. He was a founder-member of the Association of Little Presses of Great Britain and edited the multilingual review Nothing Doing in London *and the paper* The Literary Supplement. *His books of poems are* A Marriage, *1966;* Poems for the Daughter of Charles Lievens, *1971;* Fragile & Lucid, *folio, 1973;* Poem About Music, *1974;* Blood Flow, *1975;* Titular I-VI, *1975;* Fear and Misadventure, *1977;* Mud Settles, *1977;* Blues That Must Not Try to Imitate the Sky, *1978;* Quiet Facts, *1979;* A Cowfoot, *1979;* Report to the Working Party. Asylum. Otiose., *1979.*

A Marriage

For M. P.

I had lost even my name and was as much a pauper in this as those exiled Jews who were not entitled to engage in the occupations of their forefathers because the Prophet could not find their names in Ezra's register.

—Edward Dahlberg

Semite: to find a way for myself.
—George Oppen

His
name was

come
from what

a suicide

he hadnt a
country

who loved HER
to changed his name

He became Arabic
numerals
a
count
her
unbrok
en hymen

but a
Jew
who not
lived
their
families
Koran
or Testament

meant nothing

of
Abraham common
patriarch

He could no
longer be bothered

We followed

the
cemetery

buried (a
neither here nor there)

her was beautiful

For
know
he lived

Celan

I did not know you
but I
well enough imagine
Do I?

Night behaviour
and dirt

into which You were fallen

You pushed.

Executor,
estranged, prayerless,

by a followed memory.

Cloisters

The grey friar.
Who is the grey friar?

And the black Jew.
The black-haired Jew.

Who is the black-haired Jew
alone sits

at pane of the square?

Is the Franciscan celibate?
And is the tree what it is

and what
its railings?

Does the Jew recite
at the wall?

In what language?

Where, by the way, his family.

The Book of Mysteries

Here, in the
book
of the what?

What foolishness.

How?

In rock and tree,
and, soundlessly,

what can I ask from you?

I told you,
I told you,

I formed you, the anger and the nothing that would
hold you; I, on you, hold.

Crossing

Germanic.

Irreligious.

You blaspheme. You utter your God.
You are renewed
in mountains where you were lost.
You sluice
yourself with water,
untouched. You are baptised.
You remain
with
your Jewishness.

At times
you await your dying,
your adoration and birth
of another; but you remain
with your Jewishness.

ENGLISH

Asa Benveniste

Asa Benveniste was born in 1925 in New York City, his parents having emigrated from Ismir and Salonika. He claims descent from the seventeenth-century Venetian printer Emanuel Benveniste, who, between 1644 and 1648 in Amsterdam, printed the whole of the Babylonian Talmud. He founded Trigram Press in London in 1965, to print and publish English and American poets. He has lived for long periods in France, Morocco, and England. He now lives in Yorkshire. He became a British subject in 1965. His books include Poems of the Mouth, The Atoz Formula, Count Three, A Part, Edge, *and* Dense Lens.

The Alchemical Cupboard

As much for the seatide ages of my sons
your body
with so many things
now alone
following
that ascendent line at which
I am last of all
just to be taken
as a Jew
long
past
the three stages
fledgling runner finally
out of the sky
down from the head
never to try the sun
again so far mistaking
distance for clarity

~ ~

Contains a command of all
my sexual
appointments
Bain-marie Mary
whose hands
whose moist thigh
thrown over carelessly
my language mouth

dumb with sucking
her body
hopefully
a sulphurous digression
of fire & soaring
briefly
to the top of my throat
a sign of calx
the re-entry into metal
that return to fulgid
earth
(over)
earth

~ ~

& Fludd awakens Paracelsus the skin Pythagoras to Kelly
your Dee names Lully who turns Bruno Dellaporta the axis
Ashmole of Jabir earth who Hermes smeared Philadelphus
across Zosimus my Maimonides tongue Dorn lies Avicenna
to Gerard break Abulafia argument of Aquinas city wound
Dastin in the Bonus head Wu child against Vaughan the
storming Eleazar black Benveniste birth

~ ~

on no account of green names
but of blue in many ways
crucibled
a dark mercury
as though blood
had been added in pollution
herein the only city
putting ink to paper
how they could believe
(altogether)
in transformation
in sullen gold
more than red slime
as near to
martyrdom

∾∾

It is in my poems
which process
planetary notations
a house to be born in
a movement in the eaves
some cupboards
that conceal
recognition
cover names for a prayer
of conjunctions & near misses
a certain shyness
a shading of the eyes
as sun devours lion
symbolic furnace
hermetic bed
50 yarrow stalks
thrown out of the green cup
O blind mother
two-bodied fierce
oration
tallis at my cheek
the poem stopped as it does
mid meaning

∾∾

            you have your fingers
to Ark so long
that swan bent wrist
shadows my wall
            1925
birth then pummel me back
to time silence is what I mean
when I call it
            flight
the corners of my work
clean clean pymander
shroud from the davening
            machine
raise wings and down
river womb silvergrey fish

we know by familiar
corners in the eye
            talisman
four qualities contains
out of ignorance
            we depart
before we once more fire
gold for kissing
            lunar sol
black swan its crucible
            snow descends

            horizon

∾ ∾

I told you
            once
            we are given
ten stages to go through

decade the tree numbers
            first volatization

            from primal material
the light is intense

I am asleep in blazing rooms
            the body blackened
            the dream wave overcomes
the great unmeasurable brokenness

'Hang on' you said
            which surprised me
            because
there was nothing
. . . .
in sight

∾ ∾

            but the sea
this soft anglo-saxon speak
my head iambic breaks

through the devouring water
wasting the coastline
                this land
                for so many
                years
all poems have been
dedicated to
music   contained
rot lute   transparent fingers
there is a colour of honey
which comes out of
body english
& soft winter
changes
time
high
in their
low
   scuttled
land

~ ~

So Sepher says
would none the less subsist
would be no time or place
what is here advanced
exist in ideas only
who almost was
more eminent than
but also to the nature
of dependency

The parts of space are
that cannot increase
or diminish but that
in change takes place
which can be imagined enters
and a kind of perception
since without true unities
is dominance my body
the sorcerers bowl stones
in the swaying cot
let fall

Not only to diminish
justice which marked
the figure to hear
this noise as we do
by the motion of this law
like music takes time
ending an open casement
from wardrobe to roof
to field outside
and finally to voices
in the gates
of home

Richard Burns

Richard Burns was born in London in 1943 and now teaches in Cambridge. His poetry includes The Easter Rising 1967, *1969;* The Return of Lazarus, *1971;* Double Flute, *1972;* Avebury, *1972;* Inhabitable Space, *1976;* Some Poems, Illuminated by Frances Richards, *1977;* Angels, *1978; and* Learning to Talk, *1979. He has lived in Italy and Greece. His translations include poetry by Aldo Vianello, Cesare Pavese, and Nasos Vayenas. He has edited several books. In 1975 he founded and organized the Cambridge Poetry Festival, an international biennial event.*

Mandelstam

in memory of Michael Goulston

I grow together everywhere
Song untitled in a harvest of corpses
Its poppy blazes on the fields of your breath
A stone's throw beyond my death

And I said to the presence, Leave me
Over the snows she flew like a magpie
Towards her mate where the cold slopes teem
With hidden seeds spring will redeem

Each seed uniting two worlds of shadow
Blown by the wind of years on your tongue
To root there and bind a dream through your head
Begging this day heaven's bread

No, cried the bird, half black, half white
No, my mouth called through the frozen soil
No, said the stone, still trapped under snow
Yes, laughed the song, Now go

Nestle in hollows between open lips
Under open eyelids find unborn children
Fly to the city and stand there and wait
For the beggar at the gate

Angels

We were a multitude, until the hunters,
scouting the immemorial pastures
with hewn weapons, on foot and horseback,
tracked us down where we ambled grazing
and fell upon us with poisoned javelins,
picking us off, first one by one, then
scourging by hundreds as they closed in,
burning, smoking us from the homelands,
hounds baying, snapping our heels,
till, blood-glutted, gorged on our meat,
wearing our hides, copying our calls
and rubbing our fat, death-scented,
into their flesh to charm and ensnare us,
in droves ambushed, for blood smell only,
as to wipe out a hunger for hunger
by slaughtering, to become us, to be us,
their glazed eyes deep, ice-covered pools
where our charred valleys were drained moistureless
and our own murders measured and mirrored,
and we scattered to barren tundra.
And there evolved. In full light and day ebb
and utter darkness, warily through every
season, kept watch, and by winds smelled them,
learned their shadow shapes and cunning
and when to rush through the closed circles
of their web-knit formations that hemmed us in
amid moving henges of hurlers and missiles
and, leaner, hardened, lighter-footed,
wove secret speech of our own.
But on they harried us, overtaking

infants and aged as they fell back,
hacked off limbs, and what was left
of crippled mutilated bodies
hanged for trophies on bark-stripped poles,
while we who still had strength enough
fled through the few remaining trees,
stumbled aimless over moors and heathland
into deserts to die of thirst, hid
in caves and were lost in their windings
under bleak hills, or perished in forests
beyond borders of the known world rim.
We who survived, ten, twelve, sixteen,
now wild in willpower and aware of destiny,
waking more sternly with each weary step,
came out of despair and to land edge
and plunged for refuge in deep waters
under the ice floes. And six or seven died
frozen or drowned, and there were no more
young. Lungs afire for want of air,
the rest swallowed, held on, swam deeper,
limbs attuning to water's rhythms,
building fat under newly sealed pores,
muscles till now unused growing firmer,
breath longer, blood beat slower,
the whole skin another ear drum,
eyes widening to take in darkness.
Self-delighting in a borrowed world,
slow to learn grace, we received as a rite
water's gift, laughter, that drowns weeping
and engulfs memory of all time but presence
which, itself a flood, buoyed us up
to sing across aeons, and our long calls
spanned oceans' depths and embraced the other
depths we embraced in and through one another,
till our speech took on the pitch and resonance
memory's currents had eroded in us
wound round the endless whorls of the sea.
And so multiplied, grew sleek and lazy,
vast in girth, living only for music, when
their sensors picked up our frequencies.
Then slaughter was unstinted and our cries,
churning placid waters, hammering the soft
inverted womb the seas had become, whose walls

we beat on, numbing last strengths uselessly,
jammed their tracking instruments as too late
remembering a nightmare from another
world, or other existence, again we woke
and dragged their bucking vessels leashed behind us
across the waves' vertiginous surface. Then blood
stained estuaries and caked whole coastlines
where our hauled wrecks were carved and heaped
in messes on the beaches, till the creeks stank.
Then we were few: three, perhaps, four.
To zones unhaunted, by no fish followed,
where water's weight and sheer blackness
pressed till we shrank and merged with shadows,
down we dived, deeper than terror.
Then we were two, and we sang each other
of Tipharet, of the Throne, of the Glory.
Indescribable our lamentations,
we, the uncounted, the unaccountables,
sons and daughters of the starry heavens
become a lost calling without a name
drifting among unfathomed valleys,
until I called, recalled, and heard
no answering song. Then quietly I climbed
and on a still sea trumpeted, took air
and dived for ever. And you'll not find me
nor you nor you, till the almond tree flowers
on the mountain, and there is no more sea.

Ruth Fainlight

Ruth Fainlight was born in New York City. She lives in London. Her books include eight volumes of poems, most recently Another Full Moon, *1976. Two new volumes are in preparation, including* Sibyls, *to be published in America, and* Sybils and Others, *to be published in England. She has translated poetry and drama from the Portuguese and Spanish and published several short stories, some of which were collected in the volume* Daylife and Nightlife, *1971.*

Lilith

Lilith, Adam's first companion,
Assumed her equality.
For this she was banished.

God had created her
from the same earth as Adam.
She stood her ground, amazed
By the idea of differences.

Adam and God were embarrassed,
Humiliated. It was true—
They had been formed
At the same time, the two
Halves of His reflection.

Her expectations
Should have seemed justified
But Adam needed to understand God.
A creature must now worship him,
Constrained and resentful
As he was. God encouraged him.

To guard His mystery, God
Caused Adam to swoon. There, when he awoke,
Awaited Eve, the chattel.

Eyes downcast, his phallus
The first thing she noticed.
The snake reminded her of it.
Easy to equate the two.

That nagging ache in his side
Where the rib was extracted
(In memory of which
The soldier thrust his spear)
Keeps Adam irritable.

Lilith's disgrace thus defined
Good and evil. She would be
Outside, the feared, the alien,
Hungry and dangerous.
His seed and Eve's fruit
At hazard from her rage.

Good wives make amulets
Against her, to protect themselves.
Lilith is jealous.

God's Language

Angels have no memory,
God's language no grammar.
He speaks continually,
All words variations
Of his name, the world a web
Of names, each consonant
Proclaims a further meaning;
The unacceptable
Also the true, beyond
Time's bondage. Thus angels
Forget all contradictions,
Accepting every statement
As a commentary.
Their purpose is to gaze
Upon God's works, and listen,
Until the day that he
Pronounce the name: Messiah.

The Hebrew Sibyl

I who was driven mad and cast out
from the high walls of Syrian Babylon;
I who announced the fire of God's anger;
who prophesy to those about to die
divine riddles,
am still God's oracle.

Mortals in Hellas will claim me,
name me as from another city of birth—
Erythrae—one of the shameless.
Others will say I had an unknown father,
and my mother was Circe—
brand me a crazy impostor.

But when all has taken place,
when the walls collapse and the Tower crumbles—
that coming time, when knowledge is lost
and men no longer understand each other,
no-one will call me insane—
but God's great sibyl.

Sibyl of the Waters

Noah's daughter
sibyl of the waters

first sibyl
the most ancient

with Shem Ham and Japhet
saw her father naked

already she had prophesied
the flood

and understood
it was the nakedness of God.

Arms raised in invocation
officiating at the altar

where the ark had grated
upon Ararat

she placed the burning brands
shielding her face—

ominous oracular gesture—
then crushed the dove to death

against her breast:
propitiation.

Elaine Feinstein

Elaine Feinstein was born in Lancashire in 1930. She was educated at Cambridge, and now lives there. She has worked in publishing, and as a university lecturer. She is the author of several volumes of poetry, including most recently Some Unease and Angels, Selected Poems, *1977; and several novels, most recently* The Shadow Master, *1978. She is the translator of* The Selected Poems of Marina Tsvetayeva, *1971, and her biography of the poet will be published in 1980.*

Against Winter

His kiss a bristling
beard in my ear, at 83:
'aren't you afraid of
dying?' I asked him (on his knee).
who shall excell his shrug for answer?

and yet was it long after,
senile, he lived in our front room,
once I had to
hold a potty out for him, his
penis was pink and clean as a child

and what he remembered of
Odessa and the Europe he walked through
was gone like the language I
never learned to speak, that
gave him resistance,

and his own sense of
favour: (failed
rabbi, carpenter,
farmer in
Montreal)

and now I think
how the smell of
peppermint in his yellow
handkerchieves and the
snuff marks under his nose

were another part of it:
his sloven grace
(stronger than abstinence) that
was the source of his
undisciplined stamina.

Under Stone

for Asher Korner

Who believes
he is dead?
in the ground
that lies over his head
in the rain, under leaves, in the earth
who believes he is
there?

In the tick
of our blood
in the blue
muscles under our tongue
in our skulls
where a hidden ice-pick may be waiting
we must
learn

how at last
motionless
we shall fall without
breath into place
and the pain of our questions will melt like the
wax of our flesh
into silence.

ENGLISH

Dad

Your old hat hurts me, and those black
fat raisins you liked to press into
my palm from your soft heavy hand:
I see you staggering back up the path
with sacks of potatoes from some local farm,
fresh eggs, flowers. Every day I grieve

For your great heart broken and you gone.
You loved to watch the trees. This year
you did not see their Spring.
The sky was freezing over the fen
as on that somewhere secretly appointed day
you beached: cold, white-faced, shivering.

What happened, old bull, my loyal
hoarse-voiced warrior? The hammer
blow that stopped you in your track
and brought you to a hospital monitor
could not destroy your courage
to the end you were
uncowed and unconcerned with pleasing anyone.

I think of you now as once again safely
at my mother's side, the earth as
chosen as a bed, and feel most sorrow for
all that was gentle in
my childhood buried there
already forfeit, now forever lost.

Rest in peace, Yisroel ben Menachem Mendel!

Survivors

In these miraculous Catalan streets, yellow
as falling barberry, and urine-scented, the
poorest Jews of Rome are at every orifice,

those that remain, the centuries have
left moneyless, and the new Romans
drive past them with a blank polaroid stare.

Even in the Synagogue their service
goes on separately in a cellar
because they came through Fez once, not directly

out of Spain. Whatever happened then
their latest dead sit in gold letters
with the rest. All that is puzzling to understand

is what the power could be that brings them out
on Friday night, after so many lessons
to laugh in garrulous Sabbath on this pavement?

Michael Hamburger

Michael Hamburger was born in Berlin in 1924. He emigrated to England in 1933. He studied at Oxford and has taught German at several universities in England and America. His translations from the German have received several prizes in England and Germany. His books of poetry include Ownerless Earth, New and Selected Poems 1950-72. *Critical books include* The Truth of Poetry, *England 1969, U.S.A. 1970. His many translations include several editions of Hölderlin, and his anthology* German Poetry 1910-1975, *England 1978.*

At Staufen

for Peter Huchel

1
'Too tame, too pretty', you said,
Sitting in front of your borrowed villa
Overlooking vineyards, the wide plain
That far off, when the haze lifts,
Outlines the Vosges;
Or, if you turned your head,
Closer, the mountainous fringe
Of the forest they call black.

Not black enough, for you,
Driven out of your true home,
The menaced, the menacing East?
Tamed for timber, tended,

ENGLISH

Its nature trails
Pedagogically furnished
With the names and provenance
Of representative trees;
And the foxes gone,
Gassed, for fear of rabies.

Not black enough, for you,
On their hill, the castle ruins
Pedagogically preserved
With a plaque for Faust?

2
Yet the homeless cats,
Untouchable, gone wild,
Came to you for food,
One of them dragging
A leg ripped by shot.
Above the swimming pools
Buzzards hung, cried.
High up, from a tree-top
An oriole slid
Through its small range of tones
And once, once only
Flashed in quick flight,
Making oak, ash, fir
Look blacker.

Nor would you let
Ladybirds, butterflies
Drown, or be gutted alive
By the black water beetle
That ruled the pool.

Too late I skimmed off
A golden gardener,
And returned to my book,
Old-fashioned Fabre's
'Social Life in the Insect World',
To find that very species
Observed, recorded there:
Its mass killing
Of caterpillars,

The female's nuptial feast
On the male.
I closed the book,
And kept the corpse
For the green and gold of its wings.

3

Dark the gravestones were, too
At Sulzburg, the Hebrew letters
Blacked out by centuries
Of moss on the oldest;
With no new ones to come,
With the last of a long line
Gassed, east of here, gone.

Well tended, fenced off
From the camping ground
And the forest's encroachment,
That site was black enough
Even where sunbeams lit
New leaves, white flowers.

You said nothing, looking:
Slabs of stone, lettered or blank,
Stuck into black loam.
The names that remained, German;
The later inscriptions, German;
No stone, no inscription
For the last of the line,
Who were carrion, Jewish.

4

Yes, much blacker they'll be,
Much bleaker, our landscapes, before
'Desert is our history,
Termites with their pincers
Write it
On sand.'

But with eyes that long have stared
Into the dark, seeing,
You can look still
At the vineyards, the forest's edge

Where even now
A pine-marten kills, as it must,
Wild or tame prey;

Still can feed
The homeless cats,
Can save, as you must,
From natural, from
Man-made death
Insects that, brilliant or drab,
Are skilled, fulfilled in killing
And willing, in turn, to be killed;

Can write, still, write
For the killers, the savers
While they survive.
For the termites, eaters
Of paper, while they survive.
Or the sand alone,
For the blank sand.

The Search

As commanded, I looked for my origin,
Passed through the town in which my grandfather settled
And found no street that I knew;
On through the suburbs, blind bungalows,
Lilac, laburnum, narrowly flowering
And out into mountains, woods,
Far provinces, infinities of green.
Walked, walked, by day, by night,
Always sure of the route
Though the people grew foreign, bizarre;
And the birds, a species unheard of, remembered me.
At last I came to a village
Where they told me: here you were born.
An unlikely place—no petrol pump, office block, poster?—
Yet I could not deny it, and asked them the name:
Why, Mors, need we tell you, m o r s, MORS.

Gad Hollander

Gad Hollander was born in Jerusalem in 1948. He immigrated to the United States in 1958 and lived in Israel from 1967 to 1973; since then he has been living in London, holding various jobs and studying English literature, linguistics, classical Hebrew, and mathematics. His poems have appeared in the periodicals Curtains, European Judaism, Gallery, Littack, Prospice, *and* Tangent.

Axioms

1. Sword

I, named by the tribe, am no rabbi.
I am not its disembowelled writer.

Posterity's sword is a smiling one.
What is there but to smile back.

2. Time

There was a time when leaves meant—
but even their meaning has withered.
Was it offered or taken—their falling,
their budding, their absence.

Posterity laughed in the midst of prayer.
What was there but to wrap words
in one's mouth, create one's own momentum,
while they fell or not.

3. Dance

Cohen am I without priesthood.
Tree of water, my fruit is salt.
Song with the meaning of leaves.

I lead the congregation of the dead
through the arc of a rusted blade.

They do not dance for me.
They dance for themselves.

ENGLISH

Argument Against Metaphor

God spoke in a dream:
draw three straight finite lines,
let their end-points meet.
Do not draw a triangle.

I drew three lines of verse,
their end-points met at the word God.
I saw that it was not a triangle.

~ ~

God said, go
to Nineveh; there you will learn
what you've drawn. I went,
learned it was not a triangle.

I returned an outcast, served,
waited for, on, God.

~ ~

I lived in a dream expanse.
I drew three lines a day.

In the absence of triangle
a presage appeared: three syllables
rose from the corners of my skull.

In Memoriam Paul Celan

I

Trees have been born.
Three seasons in four
their leaves have kept dumb.
What has passed over them
was christened the wind.
It too falls into a void.

Upward it falls.
Earthless, invisible,
slow as the snow,
drawing your breath in its wake.

II

You know
that tanks have no voice.
When they screamed my survival
you went deaf.

Pour milk in his ear.

My grandmother said:
go, child. my hand
forged the iron. When they
Screamed my survival.

Pour milk in his ear,
o masters of fear.

III

Lord had a soul.
Its nighness burned.
Rain-thin it rose,
smoke of my smoke.
Nocturnal,
a column of names.
It guided the poet, it washed up the dead.
Lord had a soul. It moved
on your face. Eye-deep it led
to the naked and cold.

Fugato (Coda)

I made a song and placed it far, near God,
a doublewind, a song of love;
I made it out of breath, it gasped for touch.
I made it in the empty mind, a thought
of smoke, of limb and skull, of memory;
I placed it far, a poem for the pure one.

I taught my song the algebra of praise,
it sang the praise of God, it sang in a space
confined to song, far, near God.
A doublewind, a song of love,
children pranced according to its rhythm,
and all the summers heard it, the summers of smoke.

I made it in the mind, and the empty sky
soon filled, and the far places heard it;
it gasped for God, I made it out of breath.
A song, a thought, a memory of song;
I made it once, and twice, and always.

I made a song and placed it far;
it sang the praise of God, in a space confined
to breath it sang. I made my song
in the empty mind, God claimed it as his own;
the song of love,
the doublewind.

Lotte Kramer

Lotte Kramer was born in Mainz, Germany, and emigrated to England before the war as a child. She has had various jobs and studied art and art history in evening classes. She is also a painter. Her poems have been widely published in magazines, papers, and anthologies in England and North America.

Genesis

When all has passed,
When skies have lost their last lament,
Shrunk to the bone
The full heart's ache,
And yesterday's mute cloud condemned
To final thunder,
Will there be two, strangers before,
Walking in Eden;
Will it begin:
The unfailing lightning, the core
Of good hours, days,
Of wide-eyed nights,
The short word 'us' at a table.

Francis Landy

Francis Landy was born in London in 1947. He lives in Brighton, where he is working for a doctorate on the Song of Songs. *He edited the Ancient Egyptian, Ugaritic, and Mesopotamian sections (as well as translating the Ugaritic section) in the* Anthology of Oriental Verse *(American title:* Poetry of Asia*), edited by Keith Bosley, published in England, America, and Australia in 1979. His forthcoming books include* The Tale of Aqhat, *translated from the Ugaritic;* Poems by Avraham Shlonsky, *translated from the Hebrew; and* Beauty and the Enigma: A Study of Some Related Passages in the Song of Songs. *He has also written a book of parables,* The Castle in the Kingdom, *as yet unpublished.*

The Princess Who Fled to the Castle

(From a tale of Nachman of Bratslav)

i

The trees are growing
in the forest where I lost her!
The trees are growing
on the banks of the river!
Ash and vermilion; the twilight river.
The heart drained away
Everything was lost
in the great river!
Only the trees are growing
on the banks of the river.

ii

She tore off her clothes
Like shreds of leaves
Through the autumn
To the snowflood river!

iii

I put her in my hand and in the ring of sunshine
She was like a drop of water, a piece of broken ice,
A fragment all-a-glitter, a sparkle caught for a moment,
She was like a drop of water in the sunlight,
I saw all colours through her, and through her for a moment
I saw the Castle.

ENGLISH

Lament for Azazel

They cast lots on the day of Azazel
They cast lots between blood and blood
This one for Azazel—

The demon, crouched like a warrior over the fire,
Left foot drumming, goat-foot, waiting
Which is the goat for Azazel?

The festive wool, red as dust, red as Adam,
Twisted round black horns, star-reaching,
Sews a yellow star for Azazel.

Pavement of the sun, pale marble,
Dispassionate fire, where stands the Only Kid
For Azazel.

The white stranger, weight of hands,
Echo of voices through the hands,
White hands for Azazel.

Tormenting crowds in the city of Ariel,
Voices of crevices in the earth, mosquito lust,
Cry cruelly "Bear him to Azazel."

To Azazel—where crowds pile wood for the faith,
Where Isaac is sacrificed each day,
For Azazel.

And the ashes of the Inquisition,
The ashes of Dachau, melt into the ecstatic silence,
The quartz-dust flesh, the empty fire
Of the wilderness of Azazel.

Do you see in the shadow of the rocks?
Do you see where the demon guards his fire,
The scorpion hides under the heart,
Driven out from inhabited places?
Do you see the Ineffable Name,
The High Priest crying in the fall of Jerusalem?
While the worshippers, in foxholes and in sewers,
Bless His Kingdom for ever and ever.

For God who feeds us feeds us to darkness,
He sows us in the abyss, like cries in the night.
(The terror of the child who woke in the night before Creation).

Do you see in that drift,
That expiation, that gift to the wilderness,
God Himself sent to Azazel?
They cast lots on the Day of Azazel,
They cast lots between blood and blood.
Both are for Azazel.

Midrash on Hamlet

If Hamlet would betray,
Leafy and simple, in his shaky wit
A little little scar—
Such as I bear, or Jacob when he limped;
So tiny, one would hardly notice—
His life would change that day.

He would be cold and sing,
Like Tom o' Bedlam; he would crack his throat
And singe dreams from his eyes,
And shelter on the road to Colonus.
The battlements are empty night by night,
And no birds sing.

For he could not—not look,
Not let go of the angel who blessed him,
Not escape with his life.
He's exiled to the stage, plays tit for tat:
His father sleeps, and Hamlet tries to read,
And Cain meets Abel in his book.

Selichos

(midnight penitential prayers)

Being awake still and not unhappy
I came to the breast-beating
Ranks of floodlit Hasidim

A tourist in mythic time

who watches the match
and cannot return

Nothing but trips—
to the sewers full of *piyyutim*,
medieval shards, and the sea bursting against God,
cleansing the walls, cleansing the filth
from the chambers

and I wait
for the child to wake
who died when I was born
the light is too strong for his eyes
—he can only weep—

Fallow fallow
chance it

Emanuel Litvinoff

Emanuel Litvinoff was born in Whitechapel in London's East End in 1915. He left school at fourteen and worked in various trades until the Second World War. He served in Ulster, Africa, and the Middle East, ending up as a major. He published wartime poetry in Conscripts *and* The Untried Soldier *and subsequently published* A Crown for Cain *and* Notes for a Survivor *in 1973. He is the author of several novels, including the Russian Revolution trilogy* A Death out of Season, Blood on the Snow, *and* The Face of Terror. *He also has written a book of autobiographical short stories,* Journey Through a Small Planet, *and several television plays. He edited the book* Soviet Antisemitism: The Paris Trial.

If I Forget Thee

Alone in this desert under the cold moon
spilling its thin blood of a ghost
dimly among the voices of my grief
how can I give you my life's love
alone in this desert I cannot map
where perhaps we wandered with our common father
towards Jerusalem our proud punishment?

Do not think I can forget
or my laugh be careless ever
that I shall look upon old hands
or young faces without remembering
O do not think the white face of Moses
Staring down from a mountain
invokes no resolution.

Others may bind you in the still
map of silence
blind your great eyes with discs
others may forget;
perhaps Ptolemy following his planets round
saw how you fell burning
among the incandescent demon stars
and forgot his horror
but O my children how can I forget?

One day my love will find
a road over the desert and my joy
will blossom among you like primroses
one day you will see me with my hands
filled with flowers sprung from the desert
your death made fertile and
I shall crown your innocent heads
with twelve stars of Israel.

To T. S. Eliot

Eminence becomes you. Now when the rock is struck
your young sardonic voice which broke on beauty
floats amid incense and speaks oracles
as though a god
utters from Russell Square and condescends,
high in the solemn cathedral of the air,
his holy octaves to a million radios.

I am not one accepted in your parish.
Bleistein is my relative and I share
the protozoic slime of Shylock, a page
in Stürmer, and, underneath the cities,

a billet somewhat lower than the rats.
Blood in the sewers. Pieces of our flesh
float with the ordure on the Vistula.
You had a sermon but it was not this.

It would seem, then, yours is a voice
remote, singing another river
and the gilded wreck of princes only
for Time's ruin. It is hard to kneel
when knees are stiff.

But London Semite Russian Pale, you will say
Heaven is not in our voices.
The accent, I confess, is merely human,
speaking of passion with a small letter
and, crying widow, mourning not the Church
but a woman staring the sexless sea
for no ship's return,
and no fruit singing in the orchards.

Yet walking with Cohen when the sun exploded
and darkness choked our nostrils,
and the smoke drifting over Treblinka
reeked of the smouldering ashes of children,
I thought what an angry poem
you would have made of it, given the pity.

But your eye is a telescope
scanning the circuit of stars
for Good-Good and Evil Absolute,
and, at luncheon, turns fastidiously from fleshy
noses to contemplation of the knife
twisting among the entrails of spaghetti.

So shall I say it is not eminence chills
but the snigger from behind the covers of history,
the sly words and the cold heart
and footprints made with blood upon a continent?
Let your words
tread lightly on this earth of Europe
lest my people's bones protest.

Tali Loewenthal

Tali Loewenthal was born in 1944 in Haifa. He spent his childhood and youth in England. He studied psychology, Hebrew literature, and Jewish history at University College, London. A Lubavitch Hasid, he works as a student counselor, researches and translates Hasidic philosophy, and teaches in the Lubavitch Senior Girls School in London. His publications include essays on Jewish subjects in various anthologies and contributions to the Encyclopaedia of Hasidism.

Hebrew Script

(Eight Poems)

It could only be seen
when he closed his eyes;
on each eyelid
a few Hebrew letters
had been tattooed.

∾ ∾

As one approaches,
Hebrew letters
marked on one's forehead
and hands,
beings with veiled faces
move back into
the shadows.

∾ ∾

A warrior rising
fully armed
from a river of fire,
alone in the universe,
and sinking
back.

∾ ∾

In the synagogue,
suddenly seeing myself as lost
in a dense,
dense forest.

ENGLISH

~ ~

An indeterminate region;
whether words
or the noise of animals,
I cannot tell.

~ ~

In the clear illumination of morning,
paying no heed
to one's enemies
in the shadows,
saddling a horse
and riding
forward.

~ ~

Engraved on my bones,
in a stern script,
the names of ancient
ancestors.

~ ~

A thousand arms on his left,
each bearing a bow,
raining arrows of fire
into the great darkness.

Edward Lowbury

Edward Lowbury was born in London in 1913 and educated at Oxford. He has worked for many years as a microbiologist on infection of wounds and burns for the Medical Research Council. He has published many papers and chapters and two books on these subjects. Over the same period he has written and published twelve verse collections and, in collaboration with two musicians (one of them his wife), a book on the poet-composer Thomas Campion. His most recent book of poems is The Night Watchman, *1974. His* Selected Poems *appeared in 1979. He has edited two anthologies and recorded his poems for Harvard University, as well as for the BBC. In 1974 he was elected a Fellow of the Royal Society of Literature.*

Tree of Knowledge

Made in his Maker's image?
Perhaps; but it's a poor kind
Of self-portrait—even
As first conceived; think of
A likeness that omitted
Ears, nose, eyes—
In a word, Man forbidden
To taste the fruits of knowledge;
Or (stranger still) created
With eyes that can't see
And ears that don't hear—
Anticipating his own idols;
Would He have said "Let there be
Light" merely for it to fall
On senseless retinas?

I see a different Garden,
A Tree of Life-and-Knowledge
To replace the old myth:
At the heart of Eden it stands
In leaf, alone, pulsating,
Plant-animal. In the beginning
Man swallowed the fruit,
And the fruit grew inside him,
Its seed entered his seed.

Exiled from Eden—
From eternal boredom—he rose
From animal to angel;
Made sense of matter; peered
Into the secret cell—
Until one day he found
He too could make a cell;
Then forged away, creating
A life immune to virus,
To cancer, to death,—
Only to be himself
Blown sky-high from the earth
By some resentful Cain!
And now we see again
Two Trees in Eden—
And eat, once again,
Of that forbidden fruit.

In the Old Jewish Cemetery, Prague, 1970

The headstones, like a petrified congregation,
Are huddled together, some so tightly packed,
A cat would have to squeeze its way between them.
Enormous trees cast shadow, keep the place
Quite dark at noon, though horizontal rays
Break through at sunset, throwing yellow light
On seven centuries of hard suspense.
Packed, huddled together, some leaning
Against each other, they cast longer shadows
Across the harrowed soil, faintly recalling
An ominous rumour, a whisper in the silence,
A deafening knock at midnight on the door.

Staring so long, struck dumb and strangely cold,
I seem to have joined that petrified congregation.
No chanted screed, no finger following
The luminous text in the boneyard; only a murmur
Of blown leaves and a memory of prayers
In a tongue at once foreign and, strangely, mine;

Meaningful, though incomprehensible.
I feel the branding iron; the years of terror
Come back as though it was I who once lived through them;
And the muffled last meeting with loved ones
Under the yellowing leaves, before the journey
To the camps from which no traveller returned.

Some potent magic carried them through ages
When Death was commonplace, like colds or headaches;
And even Death fought shy of one strange Rabbi
Who gave a statue life: he knew too much:
It took some greater force—a red rose
Carried by a girl—to deal the fatal blow
(Or so they say). But this moss-covered slab
Locates the Rabbi's bones; to half-shut eyes
It looks more like a man glued to the spot
Than a slab of stone; a mad illusion
That keeps me waiting for the whole assembly
To shake off stupor and resume its prayer.

They don't wake up; it's I who shake myself
Out of a stupor. Here are no tormentors,
No martyrs, ghetto walls; no muffled partings
Or fatal midnight hammerings at the door.
After long centuries of hate, a harmony.—
And yet, in every face, under the greeting,
A spark, a flicker of irony seems to throw
Light on the shadows now and then, recalling
Two human torches, one thrown to the ground
For promising new life, and one burning
To death—in tune with the sentence that confines
Gentile and Jew to the ghetto of this world.

Tom Lowenstein

Tom Lowenstein was born near London in 1941; he lived in Israel for eight months in 1960. He read English at Cambridge and taught in London from 1967 to 1971. Between 1971 and 1974 he was instructor in English at Northwestern University. Since 1975 he has been working on legends and history of an Eskimo village in northwestern Alaska. He is author of Our Afterfate, *1971;* Eskimo Poems from Canada and Greenland, *1974;* The Death of Mrs. Owl, *1977; and* Booster, *1977.*

Noah in New England

Wind picks at the clapboard,
Snow and paint break off.
Brittle as a harpsichord,
The splintery house.

Floorboards crease with footsteps,
Where the knot-holes ooze.
Creatures underneath the house
Enter by twos.

Ash from the warm city,
Rain from the great lake
Caulk the draughty shingles
With threads of rock.

Nausicaa with Some Attendants

We were sure to interrupt the traveller's siesta,
running with our sewing
by the edged auriculas.

Frayed black silk patches
(older than were many of the Rabbi's jackets):
these were whispered
to have dull authority.

Horizon Without Landscape

Dithering towards the horizon
over the potato-mines and the explosive earth,
the cone-shaped mountains could be approached
at the gun-point of both eyes looking straight.
And the mountains would not move or rebuke
the oddity of a confused gait,
or the false certainty of little hands
that felt their way into the distance.

The heart would trot directions
back and forth and back. But there were no exits
or illusions on the sand-farm.
And when the cactus raised its alphabet
with juiceless arms around the sunset,
and the *aleph beth* wrinkled its spines,
and the grey night started to explore,
the sand rolled in its sleep and swept itself away.

Caution, blinker at dreams, head sawn in two.
Slim, dented seeds depend from watermelons,
white thread grazed to needles
on the pink shavings. (The rinds of crocodile
are also inked. The green has yellow
dreams and wets the newspaper.)
What you have cut, your teeth make sore.
The Arab sews the shells up as you sleep.

And on. To something radiant, fugitive.
On to the precipice to catch the view.
To where you get it, into it, no view, in view.
And there it can be heard at distances,
sorting its myths before faring through,
and biting off its roots, it disappears.
The night was with you as you searched.
Without a hat, sawn-off binoculars.

ENGLISH

Asher Mendelssohn

Asher Mendelssohn was born in London in 1944, where his parents had fled Hitler in 1936. He broke off Oxford studies of Far Eastern languages to travel as a translator and journalist. He has been a hotel night porter, street musician, stagehand, newspaper editor, actor, mental hospital orderly, and director of a social welfare agency. After sojourns in Munich, Tangier, Paris, Amsterdam, Belfast, Ankara, and Jerusalem, he now lives in Vienna with his wife and two children, where he works as a therapist in psychodrama and psychoanalysis. His poetry, prose and journalism have appeared in various periodicals, including New Departures *and* The Jerusalem Post.

Cordoba

In Cordoba the Caliph's Gardens
    know three levels, three arcades
of fountains, and the Jew
    who walks there watches
the sun dance
            on the water's arches.

In the Mezquita he sees again
    the change in the patterns,
frozen, traced
            in light knots of stone.
The Mystery always repeated, always varied.

His mind's eye turns to the ruined synagogue,
    an empty cube, bare of everything but signs,
stone characters on the walls and stone shapes,
    that interlock and echo
                        the squares in the writing
(narrow walls that held
    Judah ha Levi, Maimonides
and dim Moses, known
    as Cordovero, the inventor
of many ageless moves
    in the magic game: who went
to Palestine and died young.)
    This place the Christians found too small to use . . .

—unlike the Mosque
    so big that its new masters (dwarfed
by a multiplicity of arches, stone arcades)
    could take only the centre for their church.

In the square the sun weaves threads of light
through cobwebs on the orange trees
The nets are real, are strands enclosing Nothing
a way of allowing space to breathe . . .

Purpose is in
the blindness of the spider
who does not see the web's wholeness
acts only its sequence
turns
always in the same position:
an attempt
to trap the Other.

And the Jew who walks in the Caliph's Gardens
casting the net of thought around fountains,
stone buildings, orange trees and images
of men long dead,
turns
with open heart and eyes
in the linked circles of history.

Jeremy Robson

Jeremy Robson, a Londoner, was born in Wales in 1939. He has worked as a journalist and is presently managing director of Robson Books, a publishing house. His publications include Thirty-three Poems, *1964; and* In Focus, *1970. He has edited several anthologies, including* The Young British Poets, *1971.*

The Departure

We spoke tonight
of the departure from Egypt
Climbing down the spiral of the years
Trailing our minds over the desert
Over the Sea of Death over the Promised Land
Over the might of Moses toppled
in the harvest of his field.
We sang tonight
chanting the ancient ageless songs
the wailing of a People
crumbling the barrier of the years.

Over the cities of the world hung our songs
Over the abyss of the centuries hung our words.

We opened our doors
for Elijah, Elijah the Prophet
but prophetically he was forewarned and frightened;
they are all frightened
Prophets
Prophets are crucified
only Hitlers are heard
shrieking damnation.

And soon our songs hung silent
over the cities of the world.
Soon the tongues stood still
And the dust settled again
On the pavements of prayer.

Isaac Rosenberg

Isaac Rosenberg was born in Bristol in Southwestern England in 1890, of Latvian Jewish immigrants. From 1897 they settled in Stepney in the East End, London's "Lower East Side." Rosenberg left school at fourteen and was apprenticed to a firm of art engravers. In the evenings he went to art school and also worked on his poetry. His friends included the painters Mark Gertler and David Bomberg, and the poet and translator Joseph Leftwich. Thanks to the munificence of three Jewish ladies, Rosenberg went to the Slade School of Fine Art in 1911. He finished in 1914 and, unemployed, ill, and penniless, went to South Africa for a year to stay with his eldest sister. His first pamphlet, Night and Day, *was published at his own expense in 1912. His second pamphlet,* Youth, *was published in 1915. His third and last,* Moses, *a play, followed in 1916. Rosenberg enlisted in 1915 and was killed on the night of March 31, 1918. There have been several editions of his poems. The definitive* Collected Poems and Other Writings *was published in 1979. In 1975 three biographies of Rosenberg were published: by Joseph Cohen, Jean Wilson, and Jean Liddiard. Jon Silkin's* Out of Battle, *1972, contains a valuable study of the poet.*

God

In his malodorous brain what slugs and mire,
Lanthorned in his oblique eyes, guttering burned!
His body lodged a rat where men nursed souls.
The world flashed grape-green eyes of a foiled cat
To him. On fragments of an old shrunk power,

On shy and maimed, on women wrung awry,
He lay, a bullying hulk, to crush them more.
But when one, fearless, turned and clawed like bronze,
Cringing was easy to blunt these stern paws,
And he would weigh the heavier on those after.

Who rests in God's mean flattery now? Your wealth
Is but his cunning to make death more hard.
Your iron sinews take more pain in breaking.
And he has made the market for your beauty
Too poor to buy, although you die to sell.
Only that he has never heard of sleep;
And when the cats come out the rats are sly.
Here we are safe till he slinks in at dawn.

But he has gnawed a fibre from strange roots
And in the morning some pale wonder ceases.
Things are not strange and strange things are forgetful.
Ah! if the day were arid, somehow lost
Out of us, but it is as hair of us,
And only in the hush no wind stirs it.
And in the light vague trouble lifts and breathes,
And restlessness still shadows the lost ways.
The fingers shut on voices that pass through,
Where blind farewells are taken easily . . .

Ah! this miasma of a rotting God!

Break of Day in the Trenches

The darkness crumbles away—
It is the same old druid Time as ever.
Only a live thing leaps at my hand—
A queer sardonic rat—
As I pull the parapet's poppy
To stick behind my ear.
Droll rat, they would shoot you if they knew
Your cosmopolitan sympathies.
Now you have touched this English hand
You will do the same to a German—
Soon, no doubt, if it be your pleasure

To cross the sleeping green between.
It seems you inwardly grin as you pass
Strong eyes, fine limbs, haughty athletes
Less chanced than you for life,
Bonds to the whims of murder,
Sprawled in the bowels of the earth,
The torn fields of France.
What do you see in our eyes
At the shrieking iron and flame
Hurled through still heavens?
What quaver—what heart aghast?
Poppies whose roots are in man's veins
Drop, and are ever dropping;
But mine in my ear is safe,
Just a little white with the dust.

Chagrin

Caught still as Absalom,
Surely the air hangs
From the swayless cloud-boughs,
Like hair of Absalom
Caught and hanging still.

From the imagined weight
Of spaces in a sky
Of mute chagrin, my thoughts
Hang like branch-clung hair
To trunks of silence swung,
With the choked soul weighing down
Into thick emptiness.
Christ! end this hanging death,
For endlessness hangs therefrom.

Invisibly—branches break
From invisible trees—
The cloud-woods where we rush,
Our eyes holding so much,
Which we must ride dim ages round
Ere the hands (we dream) can touch,

We ride, we ride, before the morning
The secret roots of the sun to tread,
And suddenly
We are lifted of all we know
And hang from implacable boughs.

Dead Man's Dump

The plunging limbers over the shattered track
Racketed with their rusty freight,
Stuck out like many crowns of thorns,
And the rusty stakes like sceptres old
To stay the flood of brutish men
Upon our brothers dear.

The wheels lurched over sprawled dead
But pained them not, though their bones crunched,
Their shut mouths made no moan.
They lie there huddled, friend and foeman,
Man born of man, and born of woman,
And shells go crying over them
From night till night and now.

Earth has waited for them,
All the time of their growth
Fretting for their decay:
Now she has them at last!
In the strength of their strength
Suspended—stopped and held.

What fierce imaginings their dark souls lit?
Earth! have they gone into you!
Somewhere they must have gone,
And flung on your hard back
Is their soul's sack
Emptied of God-ancestralled essences.
Who hurled them out? Who hurled?

None saw their spirits' shadow shake the grass,
Or stood aside for the half used life to pass
Out of those doomed nostrils and the doomed mouth,
When the swift iron burning bee
Drained the wild honey of their youth.

ENGLISH

What of us who, flung on the shrieking pyre,
Walk, our usual thoughts untouched,
Our lucky limbs as on ichor fed,
Immortal seeming ever?
Perhaps when the flames beat loud on us,
A fear may choke in our veins
And the startled blood may stop.

The air is loud with death,
The dark air spurts with fire,
The explosions ceaseless are.
Timelessly now, some minutes past,
These dead strode time with vigorous life,
Till the shrapnel called 'An end!'
But not to all. In bleeding pangs
Some borne on stretchers dreamed of home,
Dear things, war-blotted from their hearts.

Maniac Earth! howling and flying, your bowel
Seared by the jagged fire, the iron love,
The impetuous storm of savage love.
Dark Earth! dark Heavens! swinging in chemic smoke,
What dead are born when you kiss each soundless soul
With lightning and thunder from your mined heart,
Which man's self dug, and his blind fingers loosed?

A man's brains splattered on
A stretcher-bearer's face;
His shook shoulders slipped their load,
But when they bent to look again
The drowning soul was sunk too deep
For human tenderness.

They left their dead with the older dead,
Stretched at the cross roads.

Burnt black by strange decay
Their sinister faces lie,
The lid over each eye,
The grass and coloured clay
More motion have than they,
Joined to the great sunk silences.

Here is one not long dead;
His dark hearing caught our far wheels,
And the choked soul stretched weak hands
To reach the living word the far wheels said,
The blood-dazed intelligence beating for light,
Crying through the suspense of the far torturing wheels
Swift for the end to break,
Or the wheels to break,
Cried as the tide of the world broke over his sight.

Will they come? Will they ever come?
Even as the mixed hoofs of the mules,
The quivering-bellied mules,
And the rushing wheels all mixed
With his tortured upturned sight.
So we crashed round the bend,
We heard his weak scream,
We heard his very last sound,
And our wheels grazed his dead face.

Saul

Why quails my heart? God riding with
A mortal would absorb him.
He touched my hand, here is my hand the same.
Sure I am whirled in some dark fantasy—
A dizzying cloven wink, the beast, the black,
And I ride now . . . ride, ride, the way I know
That rushing terror . . . I shudder yet.
The haughty contours of a swift white horse
And on its brows a tree, a branching tree,
And on its back a golden girl bound fast.
It glittered by
And all the phantoms wailing.
Then sudden, here I ride.
His monstrous posture, why his neck's turn
Were our thews' adventures; some Amazon's son doubtless
From the dark countries. Can it be
The storm spirit, storm's pilot
With all the heaving debris of Noah's sunken days
Dragged on his loins.

What have I lived and agonised today, today.
It seems long centuries since I went to the town
For our week's victuals, I saw the beast
And rode into the town a shaken ghost,
Not Saul at all, but something that was Saul,
And saw folk wailing; and men that could not weep.
And my heart utterance was Lilith,
Whose face seemed cast in faded centuries
While the beast was rushing back towards her,
Sweeping past me, leaving me so with the years.
Mere human travail never broke my spirit
Only my throat to impatient blasphemies.
But God's unthinkable imagination
Invents new tortures for nature
Whose wisdom falters here.
No used experience can make aware
The imminent unknowable.
Sudden destruction
Till the stricken soul wails in anguish
Torn here and there.
Man could see and live never believed.
I ride. . . . I ride . . . thunder crowned
In the shelter of a glis'ning chanting giant.
What flaring chant the storm's undertones,
Full of wild yearning,
And makes me think of Lilith
And that swift beast, it went that way.
My house my blood all lean to its weird flight.
But Lilith will be sleeping . . . ah miss my Lilith.
Swifter my mules swifter
Destroy the space . . . transport me instantly
For my soul yearns and fears.

from The Unicorn

The Jew

Moses, from whose loins I sprung,
Lit by a lamp in his blood
Ten immutable rules, a moon
For mutable lampless men.

The blonde, the bronze, the ruddy,
With the same heaving blood,
Keep tide to the moon of Moses.
Then why do they sneer at me?

Returning, We Hear the Larks

Sombre the night is.
And though we have our lives, we know
What sinister threat lurks there.

Dragging these anguished limbs, we only know
This poison-blasted track opens on our camp—
On a little safe sleep.

But hark! joy—joy—strange joy.
Lo! heights of night ringing with unseen larks.
Music showering on our upturned list'ning faces.

Death could drop from the dark
As easily as song—
But song only dropped,
Like a blind man's dreams on the sand
By dangerous tides,
Like a girl's dark hair for she dreams no ruin lies there,
Or her kisses where a serpent hides.

The Destruction of Jerusalem by the Babylonian Hordes

They left their Babylon bare
Of all its tall men,
Of all its proud horses;
They made for Lebanon.

And shadowy sowers went
Before their spears to sow
The fruit whose taste is ash
For Judah's soul to know.

They who bowed to the Bull god
Whose wings roofed Babylon,
In endless hosts darkened
The bright-heavened Lebanon.

They washed their grime in pools
Where laughing girls forgot
The wiles they used for Solomon.
Sweet laughter! remembered not.

Sweet laughter charred in the flame
That clutched the cloud and earth
While Solomon's towers crashed between,
The gird of Babylon's mirth.

Anthony Rudolf

Anthony Rudolf was born in London in 1942. He studied at Cambridge. He lives in London, where he has had various jobs. He runs The Menard Press *and is advisory editor to the* Jewish Quarterly *and* Modern Poetry in Translation. *He is the former editor of* European Judaism *and guest editor of various magazines. He has contributed poems, stories, book reviews, articles, and in particular translations of poetry from French and Russian and other languages to various periodicals. His translations have also appeared in anthologies. His books include a volume of poems,* After the Dream, *1980, and translations of Yves Bonnefoy, 1968; Alexander Tvardovsky, 1974; Evgeni Vinokurov, 1976; and Eugene Heimler, 1976; and, as editor,* Poems for Shakespeare IV, *1976. Most recently his translation from Edmond Jabès' early poems was published.*

Ashkelon

J'ai vie

In the space of time
we found

a bone
with a flower
growing out of it

a decapitated
terra cotta virgin
lying between
a coffin-nail
and a column of ants

the wedding-
ring of a Philistine
by a heavy
eucalyptus tree

a tiny obol
a bit of glass
the handle of a jug
a broken plate

ruined mosaics
shattered marble columns
and a sheik's tomb

mezuzas of a sought past

two amorous lizards
embraced in the sands

It was raining
we made
a fire on
the beach the flames
survived the rain
and the meal we cooked was good
after we had eaten
we smothered the flames with sand
some charred egg-shells
and *matsoh* crumbs remained
they can't
have lasted long

Hands Up

In Yad Vashem, where all vows are renewed,
the small boy roots me to his death in no time.

The paper says that he's alive, in London,
father of four. It is a miracle

he is alive, and yet the picture stays
as unchanged as we are changed. God's word

is written in light: black fire on white fire.
Does it matter if it *isn't* him? What does

is children were suffered to be murdered.
How many *raised their hands?* Oh, say a prayer

for one only kid, son of Our Father
Avraham, who wandered like a gypsy.

Evening of the Rose

Let the exiles in-gather,
the word has come home:
a memorial prayer
to a place and a name.

As he laid his head
on Shulamith's breast
the unbecoming dead
sang him to his rest.

Dubrovnik Poem (Emilio Tolentino)

'The Jew was always treated
well, in this part of the world.
Zudioska Ulica,
this street, the Jews have lived in
always. You see the grilles?
Behind them the women sat,
entering the dark space
by way of our house next door.
My family has cared for
the synagogue from there
for rather more than three
hundred years. The little
gallery was built later.'

'Now we are seventeen,
seven men in all Dubrovnik,
not even a *minyan.* Six
hundred years it has stood,
this synagogue, on this street.
And I am old. I am ill.'

'Always the Jew was treated
well, in this part of the world.
From Venice we came, from Spain.
When we came back from Auschwitz
the archives had disappeared:
gone, like so many lives.
Hidden under floorboards
some we retrieved, some treasures.'

'Solomon Tolentino,
my ancestor, signed in Hebrew
that scrap of paper pasted
up on the wall downstairs;
dead in the sixteen-hundred-
and-sixty-seven earthquake.
The synagogue survived it.
This letter came from Moses
Montefiore with thanks
for our congratulations
sent on his hundredth birthday.'

Prayer for Kafka and Ourselves

We walk alone on our roots
in Prague, dead centre of Europe,

Golem's dream, tears of stone.
He is our child. The stone

the builders had doubts about
has become the corner-stone.

Ancient of Days

To die old
like a late night:

the aged man,
ancient of days,

is tired and tired
and none

shall make him afraid.
He walks

humbly before
God and returns

to his village
where nothing

remains but one oak
broader

than six
men in a ring.

Jon Silkin

Jon Silkin was born in London in 1930. After army service he worked for six years as a manual laborer in London. In 1958 he was awarded the Gregory Fellowship in Poetry at the University of Leeds, which he retained for two years. His book Out of Battle, *on the poets of the First World War, was published in 1972. In 1965 he moved to Newcastle-on-Tyne to continue editing the magazine* Stand, *which he had founded in London in 1952. In recent years he has visited America several times, giving poetry-reading tours. He has also held the post of visiting lecturer at Denison University, Ohio, and taught at the Writers Workshop at the University of Iowa. He read poetry and taught in Australia in 1974. He is the author of ten volumes of poetry, including most recently* The Little Timekeeper, *1977. His anthology of poets of the First World War was published in 1979.*

Death of a Son

(who died in a mental hospital aged one)

Something has ceased to come along with me.
Something like a person: something very like one.
And there was no nobility in it
Or anything like that.

Something was there like a one year
Old house, dumb as stone. While the near buildings
Sang like birds and laughed
Understanding the pact

They were to have with silence. But he
Neither sang nor laughed. He did not bless silence
Like bread, with words.
He did not forsake silence.

But rather, like a house in mourning
Kept the eye turned in to watch the silence while
The other houses like birds
Sang around him.

And the breathing silence neither
Moved nor was still.

I have seen stones: I have seen brick
But this house was made up of neither bricks nor stone
But a house of flesh and blood
With flesh of stone

And bricks for blood. A house
Of stones and blood in breathing silence with the other
Birds singing crazy on its chimneys.
But this was silence,

This was something else, this was
Hearing and speaking though he was a house drawn
Into silence, this was
Something religious in his silence,

Something shining in his quiet,
This was different this was altogether something else:
Though he never spoke, this
Was something to do with death.

And then slowly the eye stopped looking
Inward. The silence rose and became still.
The look turned to the outer place and stopped,
With the birds still shrilling around him.
And as if he could speak

He turned over on his side with his one year
Red as a wound
He turned over as if he could be sorry for this
And out of his eyes two great tears rolled, like stones, and he died.

The Coldness

Where the printing-works buttress a church
And the northern river like moss
Robes herself slowly through
The cold township of York,
More slowly than usual
For a cold, northern river,
You see the citizens
Indulging stately pleasures,
Like swans. But they seem cold.
Why have they been so punished;
In what do their sins consist now?
An assertion persistent
As a gross tumour, and the sense
Of such growth haunting
The flesh of York
Is that there has been
No synagogue since eleven ninety
When eight hundred Jews
Took each other's lives
To escape christian death
By christian hand; and the last
Took his own. The event

Has the frigid persistence of a growth
In the flesh. It is a fact
No other fact can be added to
Save that it was Easter, the time
When the dead christian God
Rose again. It is in this,
Perhaps, they are haunted; for the cold
Blood of victims is colder,
More staining, more corrosive
On the soul, than the blood of martyrs.
What consciousness is there of the cold
Heart, with its spaces?
For nothing penetrates
More than admitted absence.
The heart in warmth, even, cannot
Close its gaps. Absence of Jews
Through hatred, or indifference,
A gap they slip through, a conscience
That corrodes more deeply since it is
Forgotten—this deadens York.
Where are the stone-masons, the builders
Skilled in glass, strong first in wood;
Taut, flaxen plumbers with lengths of pipe,
Steel rules coiled in their palms;
The printers; canopy-makers—
Makers in the institution of marriage?
Their absence is endless, a socket
Where the jaw is protected neither
Through its tolerance for tooth,
Nor for blood. Either there is pain or no pain.
If they could feel; were there one
Among them with this kind
Of sensitivity that
Could touch the dignity,
Masonry of the cold
Northern face that falls
As you touch it, there might
Be some moving to
A northern expurgation.
All Europe is touched
With some of frigid York,
As York is now by Europe.

ENGLISH

A Word About Freedom and Identity in Tel Aviv

Through a square sealed-off with
a grey & ornate house,
its length bent, for one corner of that,
a road leads off, got to down steps:
wide, terraced, ample.
The road's quiet, too; but nudges as
the square did not. Walking
some below the city I heard
a pared, harsh cry, sustained
and hovering, between outrage
and despair; scraped by itself
into a wedge-shape opening on
inaccessibly demented hurt
it can't since quite come at;
imitative, harsh, genuine.
A pet-shop four feet below
pavement level; in its front yard
a blue parrot, its open beak
hooked and black, the folded wings
irregularly lifting a little;
under which, dull yellow soft plumage,
the insides of itself, heaved, slightly.
Its tail was long, stiff. Long in stiffness
that at once bends entirely
if bent too much. And as it
turned in its cage, bending the tail
against the wires, it spoke
into the claw it raised
at its hooked face, the word
'Toràh, Toràh' in the hoarse, devotional
grief religious men speak with
rendering on God the law
their love binds them with. Done,
it cried its own cry, its claws tightening
onto its beak, shaking slowly
the whole face with the cry
from side to side. This cry was placed
by one Jew inside another. Not belonging though;
an animal of no distinct race,
its cry also human, slightly;

wired in, waiting; fed on
good seed a bit casually
planted. Granulated, sifted,
dry. The Toràh is:
suffering begets suffering, that is.

It Says

Thinking on my life under
the smoked glass, I come near
its substance. As a man watching
another scraping light
off grass, dropped by the sun
across it. As if
he very carefully thought
which blades he should not
deprive. So that each time
I brood, it is not on
my own love, or another's
merely, since I touch
now, even, the fiction which
in the Talmud speaks
of how a man each night
works at the book. This is permitted.
And each night, his wife
attends him, but not just
because she does not read
the Hebrew. It does not
say if this married girl
is beautiful; each night,
the book insists, this man
brailles at the Hebrew's uncial
text. Here, the story slightly shifts:
it is another night. His wife
weeps lightly, so lightly it is
neither against him nor
upon the Talmud but
for her lacking him.
The Talmud hardly speaks
more, but, as if sun
closed up, momently,

a few scraps, a few
hesitations in grammar, adding
that for the tear she dropped
the man dies.

Jerusalem

This 'good plan, fleshed in childhood'; these fruits
raised out of the lintel. Meagre light

smoked the aperture where Rome, elbowed
in brass, illuminates the war-caves

the North's bashed out of; but not Israel,
a stone sumptuous with carved light.

Hollows fruit under the olive tree, pith
to cram the black seed. Every creature

works out from the dark: miners
cough in Solomon's emerald caves, scooped

by lust for delicate Sheba, in whose flesh
the fertile cock never sates. This good plan.

Without which no God would be adored, none to
raise earth's pillars, or the North's mild orange brick.

So much of the world is as this, fine
arousals of flesh pinioned in spirit tack

through ginnels: the soft wood-pigeon.
Sieged Jerusalem runnels on the sword:

like wind famine clings the canvas walls.
Yiddisher flesh concaves; children, mothers

in seed lie like Babylonish reeds
wailing outside the wall, whose stench

spasms Roman muscle. Our temple's
the Sabbath candle, and our prayers

disperse in rubble. This wall is a straight
piece of misery whose root like babies' teeth

is a row of tears that blench and harden, altogether
changed from grief; and the small figure, god,

undone of clothes, stares doll-like on ashes.
I can't tell you.

To think hurts. It hurts not to: still
I can't tell you. Jerusalem, olive

and white; light glutinous against
stone. Flesh sings as if spirit;

would to God it were, but then, no. All
I have to do, where clashes

of serene absence whiten blank stone
is lift you to where this illumination

overfills with space.

Resting Place

In . . . c. 1230, John le Romeyn, then subdean of York Minster, recorded the sale to the commune of the York Jews of a plot of land in Barkergate adjacent to what was already antiquum cimiterium Iudeorum. *It is therefore on that site, immediately west of the river Foss and now under the tarmac of [a] civic car park, that archaeologists will no doubt one day disturb the posthumous tranquility of Jews who can have rarely been completely tranquil while alive.*

—The Jews of Medieval York and the Massacre of March 1190,
by R.B. Dobson, 1974, p. 47

1

Where the camshaft weeps
oil, where the pained axle
contracts

over Barkergate, what there is is still in pain.

The car, the cracked plated animal,
these oils weep by degrees back from their cells.

Their crouched forms
tremble above our graves: Judah'd with oil
their iron drips into our mouths.

What is it then, is it nothing?

Earth's justice
cakes the skull with the clay's
bronze confections,

we are
oil creeping to the Foss
where a sword rests its two edges:

it is not nothing to lie anywhere
that they will let you. The sword
rusts like a child,

the Jewish child, the gentile sword, earth
sells itself to us.

Camphored in oil, I lose all memory.

2
Church minds its force and men nurse souls but through
each passage, hope, a furled lamp casts its beam.

Of that Church, John; by whose furled lamp I sold
our loam for dormitory to the Jews.
Earth hold them gently, and be gentler to
this woman than her child is, nursing her
each part of death's submissions. To mind so
the flesh is nurse to death. If more life is,
then they must each become a door of selves
each enters by in suppliant need: their own.

They never heard of this. Angel of death
made of desire and mercy raise your wings.

Daniel Weissbort

Daniel Weissbort was born in 1935 in London. He is chairman of the M.F.A. program in translation at the University of Iowa and editor of the London-based quarterly journal Modern Poetry in Translation. *He has been advisory director of Poetry International in London. Besides two volumes of his own poetry,* In an Emergency, *and* Soundings, *he has translated and edited a number of collections of poetry in translation, including most recently* The War is Over: Selected Poems of Evgeny Vinokurov, From the Night and Other Poems by Lev Mak, *and the anthology* Post-War Russian Poetry. *He is currently assembling a collection of the most significant English-language documents dealing with problems of translation and with translation theory.*

Anniversary

The original family rock is three parts restored.
It fits together—
you can almost hear it.

August—
I remember the hot times best
(when you died it was hot).
We walk stiffly, stop
before your slab.

Each year I try to shape a prayer,
to think of you.
Suddenly I want to shout, like a child.
Then that impulse too is gone.

At last she stoops, places a pebble on the slab—
we follow suit.
She turns, we turn and,
heads bowed, solemnly, leave you to yourself.

Returning to the car park,
absently we read
other inscriptions as we pass,
remark, philosophically,
how the dead are increased.

In the back seat,
she who has convened us slumps,
conserving herself.
In front, we
loosen our collars,
remove our skull caps . . .
I start the car.

The rock sunders.

Murder of a Community

Ordered to strip prior to execution,
Many of the men held their hands in front of their genitals.
The guards strolled with sub-machine guns,
And it seemed to matter less and less.
It was an end of sorts to everything—
Naked men gathered in one place,
Naked women and children in another,
Guards strolling about with machine guns,
Smoking and exchanging words.

The disease that killed them
Had nothing to do with them really—
These people about to die but not actually dying,
Gathered to bear witness to their lives,
Knowing each other:
Shlomo, the butcher,
Yankel, the shoemaker,
Zwi, the advocate—
They were idle now, as though on holiday,
Except they were naked.
They looked at each other,
But what was there to say?
All they could do was look at each other's familiar faces
And unfamiliar bodies.

Did some, perhaps, absent-mindedly begin to pick up their clothes
again,
One man to search in his jacket pocket as though for a tram ticket,
Until the guard swung his gun and shouted?

Then, maybe, they remembered where they were—
and where their women and children were—
Began to weep, to wail in Yiddish,
To recite Hebrew prayers,
Prayers made, apparently, for just such an occasion.

Some, it may well be, remembered pogroms
And wished them back,
For then you could run, hide,
You might even, God willing, pour burning fat over a drunken
muzhik . . .
Whereupon, the guards, sensing a stir,
Tightened their grips on the guns.

. . . And there were no daughters of Jerusalem to lament their shame
And no progeny to revenge their fallen manhood.

Walking Home at Night

The damp fallen leaves smell of ripe bananas.
I am the sound of footsteps.
Cats' bodies slide through the night like worms.
The small synagogue is alight, full of conspirators.
I finger the bunch of keys in my pocket.
My hand comes out with it.
I home on the lock
and my life explodes about me.

ENGLISH

CANADA

Leonard Cohen

Leonard Cohen was born in 1934 in Montreal, Quebec. He attended McGill University and currently makes his home in Montreal. He has published six books of poetry, including The Spice-Box of Earth, Parasites of Heaven, Selected Poems 1956-1968 *and* The Energy of Slaves, *as well as two novels,* The Favorite Game *and* Beautiful Losers. *He is also a well-known songwriter and singer.*

Story of Isaac

The door it opened slowly
    My father he came in
    I was nine years old
And he stood so tall above me
    blue eyes they were shining
    and his voice was very cold.
Said, "I've had a vision
    And you know I'm strong and holy
    I must do what I've been told."
So he started up the mountain
    I was running he was walking
    And his ax was made of gold.

The trees they got much smaller
    The lake a lady's mirror
    We stopped to drink some wine
Then he threw the bottle over
    Broke a minute later
    And he put his hand on mine.
Thought I saw an eagle
    But it might have been a vulture,
    I never could decide.
Then my father built an altar
    He looked once behind his shoulder
    He knew I would not hide.

You who build the altars now
    To sacrifice these children
    You must not do it any more.

A scheme is not a vision
    And you never have been tempted
    By a demon or a god.
You who stand above them now
    Your hatchets blunt and bloody,
    You were not there before.
When I lay upon a mountain
    And my father's hand was trembling
    With the beauty of the word.

And if you call me brother now
    Forgive me if I inquire
    Just according to whose plan?
When it all comes down to dust
    I will kill you if I must
    I will help you if I can.
When it all comes down to dust
    I will help you if I must
    I will kill you if I can.
And mercy on our uniform
Man of peace or man of war
    The peacock spreads his fan.

ENGLISH

Deborah Eibel

Deborah Eibel was born in Canada in 1940 and presently lives in Montreal. She has taught at several colleges and universities and has published her works in many anthologies and literary journals. Her book Kayak Sickness *was published in 1972.*

Hagar to Ishmael

Come out of the shrubs now,
My Ishmael,
Come out of the shrubs.
The road to death
Becomes again
The road to Egypt.

When we ran out of water and bread,
My Ishmael,
Out of water and bread,
I sensed suddenly
That fear of music
Had overtaken the wilderness of Beersheba—
Fear that turned to hate:
There was no echo
When I sang
A Canaanite lullaby.
The wilderness had rejected
My song, me, us.

When I sensed this,
My Ishmael,
When I sensed this,
I became a coward,
And you, therefore,
Became an orphan:
I left you in the shrubs
And would not watch you die.
But God made the wilderness
Love music again,
And He made me brave enough
To take you out of the shrubs.

So now that we are together again,
My Ishmael,
Together again,
Let us consider your future.
God warned me once in Shur,
That my son would be recalcitrant.
But if it is up to me,
My Ishmael,
Up to me,
You will have no reason
To be recalcitrant.

I shall not force you,
My Ishmael,
Not force you,
To assume unnecessary responsibilities.
We shall leave such things
To Isaac, your illustrious half-brother.
Your genius is for archery:
I know this, Ishmael.
You have always studied
The movements of beasts
And the contours of the wilderness:
You have the makings
Of a great archer.

One thing more,
My Ishmael,
Just one thing more:—
We shall walk slowly to Egypt,
More slowly than you may consider necessary.

There is a reason for walking slowly:—
Remember that God is the vessel,
Time the thing contained.
Now time often flees its vessel,
And mockingly challenges it
To a race.
In such a race as this
God deliberately lags behind.
You and I must wait for God,
My Ishmael,
Must wait for God.

ENGLISH

The Kabbalist

Because his madness had outgrown the world,
He asked the moon to magnetize his hand.
He died a fledgling, as a mystic should.
His transit levelled trees, made shadows stand.

The night he tunnelled winter-to-the-moon,
A distance saints and outlaws undertake,
Disciples wept. The scrutinist was gone:
A book would henceforth be an undragged lake.

No. Every night he came as passerby.
His mind an anchor, he transformed their minds
Into inverted boats. Moon-magnetized,
He mastered men and trees and birds and winds.

Freethinkers

Holy men
Have been known to endorse
The dancing of freethinkers.

There are freethinkers
Among the bereaved grandfathers
Of Haifa.
After the war
They gave up listening to good music—
The rhythms of grief
Are somewhere on noisy streets.
The rhythms of grief
Are the essential liturgy.

It is midnight in Haifa:
The freethinkers
Among the bereaved grandfathers
Are dancing, hand in hand,
Down a noisy street,
To the rhythms of grief.
They always stay out late.
They have become a new underworld.

Phyllis Gotlieb

Phyllis Gotlieb was born in Toronto in 1926. Her published works include four volumes of poetry, Who Knows One?, Within the Zodiac, Ordinary Moving, *and* Doctor Umlaut's Earthly Kingdom. *She has also published four novels.*

The Morning Prayers of the Hasid, Rabbi Levi Yitzhok

Levi Yitzhok:
binding *tefillin* on
arm head hand till his spirit shone:
and his forehead burned
black and white in the light
of the eastern sun:
sang
   Good morning: good morning
   dear God: little Father:
   I beg You: hear the prayer of:
   Levi Yitzhok: son of Sara
   hear the prayer of
   Levi Yitzhok
   son of Sara
   Rabbi of Berditchev, disciple of
   : Dov Baer
always blinded by the light of God Levi
Yitzhok eyes opened wide
to the countryside of Heaven
                                        Lord!
Your petitioner:
will not move from here:
from this place

son of Sara: Rabbi of
Berditchev will not move or stir
till You come to account with us!

for Your promises
are bound on the brows of Your children
and Your children
are the phylacteries of Your brow;

there are angels: made of fire and snow
who may sing Your praises more
than the one who prays before You
: Levi Yitzhok :

but do angels ask forgiveness?
and are angels beaten to dust?
are they killed by men and eaten
by pigs in the streets of Berditchev?

when my son died : I sent You in return
a spirit pure
as the one You lent me
a handful of years
: do angels cry till the tears
run through their fingers?
   I live only to magnify
   Your name and fill the world with
   Your presence
as Your worshipper :
Your petitioner :
Levi Yitzhok :
son of Sara
as a
Jew
who took Your Torah
when You hawked it in the marketplaces of the world!

till Your feet were sore and dusty
and the gold wore off the cover
and the parchments turned musty—

remember! only Moses
clasped it like a lover!

people of czar and emperor
people of king and throne
turned away the Law
we made our own!

shema Yisroel adonoy
elohenu adonoy echod
we have no king
we have no King but God!

for we wandered with Your promises
in the lightning of Your Law
by the hand from the pillar of fire
the voice from the burning
bush, the face in the cloud
    as mountains are bowed
    before the Lord
    so is Your servant
    : Levi Yitzhok
    : and a son of Yours
    : Levi Yitzhok
                        for is not my son Ephraim
my delight though I speak against him?
I will have mercy upon him, surely
and I will remember him

adonoy echod
there is no King but God

beardneedled grey & black silk caftan
: Levi Yitzhok danced and sang
angels watching from Paradise laughed and
climbed down rungs of light and the laughter
filled the rooms to rooftree pushed out
teacher disciple pupil

deafened argument agreement *pilpul*
dishes clapped hands walls clashed cymbals
samovar turned to beaten
gold and the fire rose and bowed
silver in every ember
: and a thousand miles below
: below in his red sty Satan

clasped black wings over ears closed eyes and
shivered in every member :

adonoy echod
there is no King but God

Who will bless us with his wisdom
at that Festival?

: Solomon the King will give the blessing
Moses the rabbi will teach us Torah
David the King will play the psalter
Miriam the Prophetess will dance before us
at that Festival

A. M. Klein

A. M. Klein was born in Montreal in 1909 and studies law at McGill University and the University of Montreal. His books of verse are Hath Not a Jew, Poems, The Hitleriad, *and* The Rocking Chair and Other Poems. *Most of these were included in* The Collected Poems of A. M. Klein. He died in 1972.

And in That Drowning Instant

And in that drowning instant as
the water heightened over me
it suddenly did come to pass
my preterite eternity
the image of myself intent
on several freedoms

fading to
myself in yellowed basel-print
vanishing
into ghetto Jew
a face among the faces of
the rapt disciples hearkening
the raptures of the Baalshem Tov
explaining Torah

vanishing
amidst the water's flickering green
to show me in old Amsterdam
which topples

into a new scene
Cordova where an Abraham
faces inquisitors

the face
is suddenly beneath the arch
whose Latin script the waves erase
and flashes now the backward march
of many

I among them

to
Jerusalem-gate and Temple-door!

For the third time my body rises
and finds the good, the lasting shore!

Irving Layton

Irving Layton was born in 1912 in Neamtz, Romania. He is the author of many books of poems, including The Improved Binoculars *and* A Red Carpet for the Sun. *His* Collected Poems *was published in 1965.*

Jewish Main Street

And first, the lamp-posts whose burning match-heads
Scatter the bog fires on the wet streets;
Then the lights from auto and store window
That flake cool and frothy in the mist
Like a beaten colloid.
In this ghetto's estuary
Women with offspring appraise
The solemn hypocrisies of fish
That gorp on trays of blue tin . . .
They enter the shops
And haggle for a dead cow's rump.

Old Jews with memories of pogroms
Shuffle across menacing doorways;
They go fearfully, quietly;
They do not wish to disturb
The knapsack of their sorrows.

O here each anonymous Jew
Clutches his ration book
for the minimum items of survival
Which honoured today—who knows?—
Tomorrow some angry potentate
Shall declare null and void.

Seymour Mayne

Seymour Mayne was born in Montreal in 1944 and presently teaches at the University of Ottawa. He is the author of over ten volumes of poetry, including the prize-winning book Name *(1975) which won the J. I. Segal Prize. His most recent collection,* Diasporas *(1977), includes many poems written in Israel.*

In the First Cave

In the first cave
they bent in worship
rites engraved
upon a rock's memory
were done with song
wood sound
silence's thuds

until blood moved stone
to the final haul of rubble
raised—become temple

Bow your forehead
like a headstone sinking
towards the sun and rising winds

Locusts of Silence

In the Egypt of my night
ten fingers freeze like plagues
firstborn fruits hang damaged
while in the morning
eyes, siamese Josephs
proclaim the prisms of water

The white and brilliant light
bursts to break forth
into shapes, substances—
into names
that proclaim
and ravage with a hunger
the noises and cries
of slaves, Pharaohs, lawgivers

and prophets broken by gold
turned towards the mirror
of God's infinite back

Worshippers in the rubble
of Sinai stone
buzz with prayer
in the forsaken silences

ENGLISH

Abraham Sutskever

Tired and bloodshot
your aging eyes
match your bald
pate and full moustache
memento of your girth
and Partisan strength

You speak and sing
always of some past's
indefinite future
which is not the present
ever but that frozen
waste where unpeopled
the ghosts of millions
wind into the snow
and darkening light—
northern hell
of the world, Siberia
where history
is grimly imminent

Surrounded by paintings
Vilna mementos and nameplates
here in your flat
over lightwashed Tel Aviv—
here you say
you never write
but only find yourself reflected
in the books and portraits

Hurrying you seem
always rushing and writing
poems as all poets now do
in haste, secretly,
unseen in no man's
land, invisible place,
the impossible promised land
where all the refugee words
are gathered and make shelter

Yehuda Amichai

What has aged you so
in two seasons, friend,
that leaner and unportly,
less the sanguine man
of appetite you were
you now hold a head
full of grey and eyes
tired as a devoted
chasid's staring
at the blessed page

Towards Jaffa Gate
you walk hand in hand
with your little son
and it is he
who seems to lead
you to another gate
whose key may
be yours to give
and the entrance—
but the exit
in time will be his alone

Your fatigue
is an elegy etched
for a moment
on disappearing flesh

ENGLISH

Afternoon's Angel

Dream on stone,
children,
trip each other
up with ladders
of afternoon

Who is that
arriving under noon's
shadow—
menacing arms
flexed for the embrace
of danger?

Children,
skip round
disarm him
Chant
with innocent
depthless eyes

Did he plug
oracle's pit
with debris
and bulldoze
old ramparts?

Curse
Wrestle him to the ground
where he shrinks to reptile
voracious still
for the more unsuspecting
of the feathered young

Sharon Nelson

Sharon Nelson was born in 1948 in Montreal, where she currently teaches and writes. Her books are Delta Quarterback, Six, A Broken Vessel, Sayings of My Father, Seawreck, *and* Blood Poems.

Pedlar

pedlar
schlepping books
across the cart tracks
of galicia

small mirrors
spare needles
a tinsmith to boot

all a cover
for the dissemination
of books

everything but the earlocks
it's too late for that
the bag so heavy

you carry a feather
to hold under your nose
make sure you're still alive

the herring is salted
it stinks on your back

the bread is hard it has to be
dipped in something
before you can
break it   the birds sing

dawn is coming
retribution is coming

the messiah is coming   pedlar
arise

take out your bread
face east   say prayers
make
ablutions

bless
the bread
you cannot break
the clouded water
the rotted fishes

pedlar   arise   a new day   a new day
to be
hocked
in the streets

Joseph Sherman

Joseph Sherman was born in Bridgewater, Nova Scotia, grew up in Cape Breton, and presently lives in New Brunswick, where he teaches. He has published several books of poems, the most recent of which is Chaim the Slaughterer.

Sarai

I was beautiful when we came into Egypt
where my husband called me sister
that he might live
and we might prosper—yet
                                        though I toiled with him
I was without blemish
and my beauty was extolled
to Pharaoh Amenemhet

In his great city was I praised,
my husband blessed by wealth,
and in the evening
in a garden
comely women bathed me
anointed me
                              whispered
                              Pharaoh's love pledge in my ear
                              and sang
how I was lovely above all women

My husband
when he came
kissed me as a brother
but gripped me as a bridegroom
                              wordless in his prayers
while in his eyes
there burned the same light
as burned in Amenemhet

And the women caressed me
                                    with their plumage
and I was led to his chambers
where crouched his gods
where
as he made to approach me
the blood was blown from his face
and his eyes pierced by fiery thorns

His cries were a bitter anthem,
and I was returned to my husband
who
summoned by the priests
healed the Egyptian king—
each
          knowing anger and shame
in the embers of the other's eyes

Stone touched stone
as we left the mighty city . . .
Talons brushed my cheek

We went up from Egypt into the Negeb
Into Gerar
                    whose king was Abimelech
and I was beautiful

Miriam Waddington

Miriam Waddington was born in Winnipeg. She has a professional degree in social work and an academic degree in English, which she now teaches at York University. She has published ten volumes of poetry, the most recent of which are The Price of Gold *and* Mister Never. *In addition, she has published numerous critical essays and translations from Yiddish and German.*

The Survivors

In your quiet hand I touch
the touch of your gentle mother's hand
and hold her death in mine;

and in your opened eyes I see
the bareness of your younger brother's eyes
and miss your missed farewell.

The troubled journeys that you since have made
from war to war, record the faulty pulse
of time so timeless lost between the wars,

and wake the terrible child in us all
to rage against fixed bedtime and to cry
himself to lonesome sleep inside a world

of you-can't-go-home-again or painted cities
flat as lakes and bland as German summers:
the innocent seasons of the never never

are unmarked graveyards of the spoiled time
where even your hand must mourn against mine
to mark the graveyard of that other time

with angers that your Jewish father's face
buried against your will in every act
to make your hearing deaf   your speaking dumb;

and what I touch with my uninjured hand
is your survival: immune to love   we move
to ancient Jewish law   and strict command.

The Field of Night

for Philip Surrey

Messiah will not come
and I must sing the time
that every poet knows
so ravel up the threads
the golden fleece of song,
seize armfuls of cloud
above the gilded domes
of Moscow's onion roofs
and spin the world round.

And I will read the time
from sundials in the air
where London used to sleep
and Paris frivolous
danced on teetering feet;
the hives of all New York
swarmed in the street
and neighbours did not keep
to caves and private work.

Our cowardice is known
and all the ill is done,
alone or with another
the body is our brother,
and Messiah will not come
though we may wait the time
till kings of good become
the presidents of wrong,
there's nothing left but time.

Such time as others shape
to their elected hopes
with songs that rise above
the golden concert halls
or reach of telescopes;
there my defeated choirs
sing in broken keys
of all the doors I forced
by solar acts of love.

The wind has howled them shut
and sealed them in my blood;
and all the frozen songs
that winter in the north
lie on a field of night,
they wait the touch of sun
and I am sick and dumb;
the fastness of the world;
Messiah, when will you come?

Desert Stone

From out of our
dwellings have I heard
the voices call
and from the locked
mountain have I heard
the voices and from
the burning nest
in the desert from

the driest reaches
have I carried
the seeds of fire
and placed them
in a nest of fire
and my face was
lighted by the dark
waiting waters.

In our tents
extinguished were
the nests of fire
and in our tents
blighted were
the seeds of light
and to the desert wind
ravenous
as a burning lion
we awoke.

And you said:
Miriam make dance
the desert stone;
and I answered:
blind Moses younger
brother who sailed
through seas of grass
to autumn pyramids,
I said: from the
buried heart of
Miriam you have
struck the bitter
waters.

I will bathe the feet
of salty wanderers
until they lift and dance
upon the desert stone,
and all my tears will fall
upon the desert stone,
until my tears will melt
the world of desert stone.

ISRAEL

Henry Abramovitch

Henry Abramovitz was born in Montreal and presently lives in Jerusalem. He is the author of Abraham: Psychology of a Spiritual Revolutionary and His Hebrew Chroniclers.

Psalm of the Jealous God

Who says
the Old Man
stayed his hand?
Are not his sons
still slaughtered
under the psalm
of the jealous god?

The pillars
have become markers,
the hand bears the name
of the slain,
the stone dagger glitters
in the tear light,
and the stars
still remain
uncounted.

Ruth Beker

Ruth Beker was born in Vienna but brought by her family to Seattle in 1940. She studied at the University of Washington, and has had stories and poems published in several journals. She lives in Kfar Shmaryahu, Israel.

Don't Show Me

Don't.
Don't show me any more pictures.

I don't want to know
  about children in horse carts
  about men in cattle cars
  about women being taken away
  about mass goodbyes, unearthly cries.

Let me pretend
  that my people were kings in freedom
  that the children were princes on horseback
  that the women were queens of it all.

Throw away those pictures I said.
I don't want to know.

No. My grandparents were not murdered.
No. My parents were not slaves.
No. My arm has no number.

It happened once to another tribe.
It happened once in another age.

Put away those pictures I said.
Don't show them around my house.

How can I tell my children that we were
treated worse than rubbish, for the garbage
men here wear gloves.

And pictures were taken of it all.

Don't show me anymore.
Don't tell me anymore.
Don't.

ENGLISH

Edward Codish

Edward Codish came to Israel in 1971 after teaching literature and poetry at several American universities. He lives in Be'er Sheva and teaches at Ben Gurion and Bar Ilan Universities. He is completing his thesis on modern American love poetry.

*Yetzer ha Ra**

Only snake writes, a coil sprung in my fingers.
Teeth tearing in the dark of my breast
A tail flexing and relaxing around my legs,
The scaled body around my gut
Wound in the windings.
Sometimes snake sleeps
Or sheds, in cold weather, while the rains
Wash away hunger, when the children
Play quietly and the light lies a little.
Sometimes
I wake up snake, before the peace
Settles too thickly; and my head aches,
My hand lies like red leaves, not moving,
Missing the rustle of snake.

I snicker and invite my snake;
My ears fill and empty with the hiss! of snake.

**Yetzer ha Ra* is the evil impulse in every person.

A Juggle of Myrtle Twigs

They tell of Judah b. R. Ila'i that he chose to take a myrtle twig and dance before the bride and say: 'Beautiful and graceful bride.' R. Samuel b. R. Isaac danced with three twigs.
—Kethubot 17a

To stop time, a twig spinning
Always on top, two side sprigs,
A trick of the eye, the eyes
Of the groom and bride, a wall of fire
Between Reb Samuel and the other just
Of his generation. Myrtle for its smell
To fix time in the mind, the dance
So time, stopped by illusion,
Moved with art and sensually
In the Rabbi's feet, in the close
Three bunched myrtle leaves, the three sticks
Turning and tumbling, only a rustle
Revealed their turning and tumbling.
The bride was led away by ladies
Before Reb Samuel's strength softened,
The small branches slowing
Speeded time to what, in his own end
Was a great fire; the honor comes
Only once or twice in an age.

Tonight, no juggler, unable
To offer prestidigitation
Against clocks or calendars
Or to compete with odors
Of the bride, the countryside
Here, in late March, I mix
Words for you, that won't stay still
Themselves, be more than memory,
But I know love held Reb Samuel
Out of time and moving
While he had strength, and you
Know that all that love can do.

ENGLISH

David Eller

David Eller was born in New York City in 1948 and moved to Israel as a child. He was killed while serving in the Israeli army in 1967.

To a God Unknown

To a God unknown
I write these lines:
A mirror of life
inside us, around us
between us. As alive
as breath, the God
of a sun: burning
the sands of a beach
long since scorched.
The waves, gently praying—
the white foam of a kiss
still on their lips—
to a God of love, so
infinitely distant in his
nearness. The God
whom men have called
so many names;
for lack of a proper name
for themselves,
for life.
Do you hear me, whispering
your name voicelessly,
tenderly?
Or must I shout?

Richard Flantz

Richard Flantz was born in Warsaw in 1936, but fled Poland with his parents in 1939. He studied at Tel Aviv University, where he now teaches poetry in the Department of English. His first works were published in Australia, but more recently he has published two books in Israel, The Poetry Connection *and* The Jewish Connection.

Shir Ma'alot/A Song of Degrees

Where's the meeting place for
a man watching smoke rise from
an ashtray bowl on a blue day,
and children held hostage in
a suspense drama from which
there may be release but not
catharsis, and philosophers
progressing to a better statement,
and the many more who come
to mind:

where's the place
where the philosopher's progress
will touch the man's involuntary
movement of nostalgia to
the familiar song radioing through
the smoke between the news reports,
or work a release, even without
catharsis, of hostage children
this blue day?

William Freedman

William Freedman was born in Newark, New Jersey, in 1937. He emigrated to Israel in 1969 and is presently professor of English at Haifa University. His poetry has appeared in many American journals. He has published many critical essays and is editing an anthology of English-language poetry by Israeli poets.

Benediction

Take this blessing
from the three-fingered tree,
needles of anointment
from the sky.
They promise there is pattern
not in your life
but in what takes place,
not in occurrences but things,
nor yet in things but in each thing,
a separable god.

Stay away from roads and bridges.
You are prone to accidents of purpose.
Take your blessing not from destinations
nor the meaning of the oil,
but how they touch the skin.
Concentrate on these three fingers,
how they spread against the sky
like interlocking angels on the glide.
Pieces of the puzzle of the night
that fit nowhere
and precisely where they are.

Formations

Two books a prayer shawl and one glass eye
to pack away the city brings

ten mourners strewn like crumbs
around his grave and one who sings

as though he knew overhead twenty-seven birds
in perfect formation like an angel's wings.

You had to be there, God,
it was a lovely thing.

You had to be there. God,
it was a lovely thing!

Rivka Fried

Rivka Fried was born in Tel Aviv in 1950. She was educated in the United States and Israel, and has published poems in Jerusalem and London.

Sabbath

Tonight the Sabbath dreams stalk
my faceless borrowed streets. Dimmed
images of Jewish demons and the flickerings
of mumbled rituals
dancing in the fragile candles.

I dreamt I was leaving for Jerusalem.
(Why Jerusalem? That hardened city
bruised with trampled stone.)
and the rabbis came riding down
to round up the Sabbath deserters.

Contorted and black, like Cossacks,
the Hassidim have come to claim their own.
They point their beards at me
to claim their savage piety.
I left the other children hiding

in their prayer-books and shawls.
And walked through the gates hearing
the flapping of many wings
rising upwards.

ENGLISH

Robert Friend

Robert Friend was born in Brooklyn in 1913 and settled in Israel in 1950, where he now teaches English and American Literature at the Hebrew University. He has published five books of poems, the most recent of which is Somewhere Lower Down. *He has also published numerous translations of Hebrew poets, including three volumes of selected poems by Leah Goldberg, Nathan Alterman, and Gabriel Preil.*

The Practice of Absence

"If we cannot 'practice the presence of God,' it is something to practice the absence of God."
—C. S. Lewis

In dream the waterfall
speaks Your silence

the mirror grown vacant
gives back Your face,

Your darkness
in the interstices

of stone or flesh
comforts me.

But when I wake
I am, for all

the cascades of bravura,
a spilt water only,

a mirror brimming
with my emptiness

a body falling
through the bodiless dark.

Therefore do I faithfully
practice Your absence

listening for the silence
in the water's voices

seeking a face
in the teeming mirror

reaching to touch
in the veined body

of woman or pebble
the body of the dark.

Identity

Words are written
on the Wailing Wall
I cannot read.
My name?

I have come to read my name
where even the birds are Jewish
and the cats yowl
in the holy language,

whose mystery I master,
its stubborn consonants
and its warm vowels,
but not that mystery

I shroud in English.
Robert, I say,
pronouncing who I am
in the cold syllables

of the tongue I love.

ENGLISH

Shirley Kaufman

Shirley Kaufman was born in Seattle, Washington, and presently lives in Jerusalem. Her poems have appeared in many journals and anthologies, and she is the author of four books of poetry, most recently From One Life to Another. *She has also translated the works of Amir Gilboa and Abba Kovner.*

Wonders

When it was late
the Baal Shem Tov
set a tree on fire
to warm his friends
so they could leave their wagon
in the snow
and say the evening prayers
at the right time

merely by touching it.

Night will come on
before we get to the next town.

We make a place
for silence
in the dark

and your arms reach out
to hold me

for the small time
we have
by our own
light.

Next Year, in Jerusalem

One by one, the ancient
shapes are dying.
But an old aunt leans there
from *seder* to *seder*
with her cancerous skin
flaking off the sides
of her nose.

Jerusalem waits
where it always was.
They are growing
deaf, though in different degrees.
Thin, yellow fingers twist
at their breasts
for the hearing-aid dials.
Should I repeat it
again for you? Slowly.

Turn up the sound. I am learning
their smiles. I am pleading.
Elijah's cup is untouched.
I hear myself hearing
my breathing. Loud.

Looking for Maimonides: Tiberias

Here is the place.
The flies are too fat
to rise from the dirt.
Three men in dusty caftans
come running with candles.
Their nails are the yellow
of their beards, greased
with doing the grieving.

The edge of his mind
was clean, with thirteen
signals staking out the way.
The whole of that warm ark
rocking order and light.

ENGLISH

Whoever whitewashed the tomb
this year knocked over the can;
white islands puddle the ground.

I look away from them,
and the sun eats at my eyes.

There is a smell of rotting
melons where a grey cat stares.
Some sticky coins
compose their prayers.

He is not there.

New Graveyard: Jerusalem

The earth runs furrows under my skin.
Landscapes arrange themselves
like pages turning, old brown
snapshots between my fingers,
patriarchs staining my thumbs.

I fit into their sky. I wrap their sun
around my arm. And I deceive them
looking for larger prophets.

I should make more of it, led here
by signs I always knew. Sometimes
I lick a stamp so long it doesn't stick.
Even the old extravagance of faith
forgets what it has to do.

I walk
the paths till they become huge
freeways that the dead ride on.
And I'm not sure who sleep away
their lives, what we are here for,
where they've gone.

Leah

. . . but Rachel was beautiful
—Genesis 29:17

I do what I have to
like an obedient daughter
or a dog. Not for your fingers
in my flesh. I watch you
every day as you watch her.
Since I'm the ugly one,
the one pushed into your bed
at night when you can't
see the difference.

I've got another
son inside me, and still
you watch her. She doesn't
sag as I do after each birth
until you fill me again.

Why can't you look at me
in daylight or take
my hand and press it
against your mouth?
I'm not a stone, a shell
your foot rolls over
in the sand. The life
gone out of it.
Maybe I am.
Your sons have sucked me
empty and dull.

I leave your tent at dawn
and walk to the river where I
throw my clothes off
and the water shows me
my body floating
on the surface. It shivers
when I touch the blue dome
of your unborn child.
I touch my unwanted self
where the smooth skin
stretches over my breasts,
the silver veins. I'm cold.

I enter the water
as you enter me. Quick.
Like insects doing it while
they fly. The shock of it
lifts me
and I swim raging
against the stream.

Starting Over

All day the geese fly south
in their old departures

nights when you sleep
among the dead
your hair keeps growing
out of your skin

nothing is casual
sometimes
you feel like swimming away
inside yourself
as if the time and place
already converged

if you go forward long enough
you'll come around
to the back door

the world is full of chances
to miss
even if the key fits
you mustn't go in

this is where you

begin

Loving

There is a tiny wind in our room
where the fan hums
it moves the hands of the clock
like the fine hairs on your back
in every direction
we are going nowhere

all day we swam in the sea
to learn how water
lifts us from our lives
waves that we kept repeating

wherever we are
there are things we can count on
when I wake before dawn
the room is already light

Gabriel Levin

Gabriel Levin was born in Paris in 1948 and has lived in France, the United States, and Israel. He studied at New York University and now lives in Jerusalem.

Adam's Death

Today I'll draw
A line in the dust.
This is the place
Where I hide my socks;
Here are the prints
Of my breath; here
Is the eyeglass

Through which I spied
On myself. I saw an arm
Longer than its brother.
I ate a dish and broke it
In two.

Tomorrow I'll swallow my words,
Closing my eyes on each letter.

ENGLISH

Ishmael

Call me Ishmael and listen
I don't have a playmate

Give me your color-book
I'll fill-up the pages

I won't stick to the figure
I'll mess up your colors

My hand is impatient
Hand-me-downs I'll take

And ice-cream in winter
I'm not desperate just wanting

I make my own supper
I fall asleep early

Then pigeons arrive
The size of my hands

They tap at the pane
Then at my mouth

Its seeds they want
They peck beckon and enter

Bushels they take
And spread over the streets.

Étude for Voice and Hand

The voice is Jacob's, but the hands are the hands of Esau.
—Genesis 27:22

Again observing how my hands
Come together, stepping outside,
Calling to my brother, his low voice

Answering from within; with his hands
Signaling his need, he takes me aside
Begs me, begs me, to give voice

To his wish, to give a hand
Where he is all thumbs. From inside
He extracts the thread of a voice

I can barely grasp with my hands;
I move closer to his side
Then back, feeling my own voice

Stealing away from me. Are these my hands
That carry a stranger's voice,
Or is my voice in a stranger's hands?

Marsha Pomerantz

Marsha Pomerantz was born in New York and studied at Cornell University and Hebrew University. She currently lives in Jerusalem, where she writes and edits for The Jerusalem Post.

Adam and Eve at the Garden Gate

This is a lie:
holding on to words
longer than it takes to say them,
fruiting some seeds,
burying others,
drying them for a
choker round your neck, saying
See my white skin.

ENGLISH

This is an apple:
whittled with a small knife.
Parings bit to the rhythm
of the mind turning. Eat, then watch
the core brown in your hand.

How to Reach the Moon

1
Three halves of you are elsewhere.
One crescent mine. Cradle me.

2
On a night street, follow the black shine.
Make a face like jasmine.

Breathe in, open an eye around the moon.
Swallow.

Balance it on the tip of your nose,
sucking up moonmilk.

Be bad. Bat it out of the sky
with small fists.

Shriek and burst its circle.

3
Make a play for the earth.
Lie on a hill, caress grass.
The moon will slide low in the sky,
heavy and tired.

Then run down to the sea
and climb the tide.

4
How do you carry your spores,
the stars, and will you
let them go?

Paul Raboff

Paul Raboff was born in Philadelphia in 1934 and emigrated to Israel in 1959. His poems have been published in several small magazines.

Jars

In dark sockets
Of stony mountains,
Ancient caves,
Are broken jars
Laid open
By the whip of time,
Cupped to the roof
Stiff as roaches,
Half shadowed
As desolate moons.

The dust a potter
Formed around a vacuum
Lies exhausted
And the nothing fled.

You are less, less
Than nothing . . .
Of no function,
Fit for exhumation
Among dry bones
Linen shreds eaten,
Scrolls, brass
Marked and dated.
The weird tone
One had blown in you
                    freed . . .
Scuttles round the floor
Whirls down wadis,
And on the tops
Of rocks in the desert
Is mad as a dervish.

*Reb Hanina**

In my shanks
Is the power
Of Reb Hanina
Who ate one carob
In a Shabbat,
Grew in beauty
As the desert-aged
Rock-fractured
Hills peeled away
Sand took on
The rainbow,
As moon-ciphered
Body died
And untouchables
Interred in white . . .

Do not come near;
Purity begins
By pale ash
On limbs.
Fall of Jericho
Of your character
And loneliness,
As after fire
Smoking char.

Betsy Rosenberg

Betsy Rosenberg was born in New York City and presently makes her home in Jerusalem, where she works as an editor and translator. She is a former associate editor of Ariel *magazine.*

*According to the Talmud, "Every day a heavenly voice issues forth and says: 'The whole world is nourished for the sake of my son Hanina, and my son Hanina is content with a measure of carobs from one Sabbath eve to the next' " (Ta'anith 24b-25a). *[Ed. note]*

Bird Song

I wished you awake for the bird song,
Such a sophisticated bird song at five in the morning
Like a twelve bar blues, each chorus had a variation,
What a bird, I could hardly believe it.
I wished you awake to witness,
Lying restlessly by your side.
It's true I wanted to make love,
But it's true about the bird, believe me.

Unearthing

I will found a habitation by the water

And wear a dress in the manner of the "peplos",

A warrior will marry me by the fire
With stars and with ashes,

Our runes will be indecipherable,
And you will be jealous of our tombs.

Harold Schimmel

Harold Schimmel was born in the United States, but has lived in Israel since 1962. His poems have been published in Italy and Israel in literary magazines and anthologies. He has also translated several Hebrew poets into English including Yehuda Amichai and Avot Yeshurun.

Ancestors

My walls tonight are lined with ancestors
    like the sukkah of a Ticino Jew.
Red-bearded,
he reared his sons on tinted photos
of the recent sages,
their faces shadowed by the hanging fruit:

ENGLISH

We are father killers—idol-smashers—
    no one else like it!
Abraham's hedging followed by his sons',
the good smell
of their own distinctness, like a Red flag
waved from a kitchen table.

        Albritton stumbling on the plain
    wrongness of the action,
    every man to his idol, or as a self-made
    Boston philospher put it,
        beware of mystics with fat cigars—
    Reb Shimon poking in the flower bed.

Babel was a little Jew, my mother said. But we learned, all of us, to respect his learning. He borrowed Milton from the family shelves and went through, one by one, a limited edition of the complete Montaigne. He spent his summers in an upstate dairy farm; there were mice on the front porch, but the cooking was reported good and the air extraordinary. Sometime before the fifties Babel left for Canada, and it was only through an East Side bookseller that we ever got word of him again.

    The holy family
    in his bed, dreaming his thick dreams
    of success:
        Isaac with fedora,
    his daughter in delicious white—
    Isaac with cap and horse-fragment, leaning
    from the shoulders like a jockey, the sun
    across his eyes, with that
    late-morning smile of Philip Rahv—

        Babel on a candy-striped
    settee,
    his legs folded under him,
    the gleam in his eye not so prover-
    bial as the dilating eye
    of a chicken soup,
    but getting attention importance
    and convenience such as ten poor Jewish mammas
    could not hope to give him.

Myra Glazer Schotz

Myra Glazer Schotz currently teaches literature at Ben Gurion University of the Negev in Be'er Sheva. She has written several scholarly books and articles, and has edited the anthology Burning Air and Clear Mind: Contemporary Israeli Women Poets. *Her poems and translations have appeared in numerous magazines.*

The First Love Poem

It's the way you perceive the world I love—
seeing in Sinai the backbone of God,
hauling up the sun, you

believe in the mind, have
faith in anything whose fragrance
is God. And your God

lives in the flesh, glows in the air
around you, speaks
in your eyes. With you

the universe opens & opens yet
you're hard, too, critical—
you shred our courage

to pain. I would be married to you, bring you
ground to stand on, firmly,
and to plant.

ENGLISH

Thespian in Jerusalem

I am a man of few beliefs.
Thespian, light opera baritone,
sometime playwright, amateur organist:
I have been screen-tested,
voice-tested,
measured for wigs,
and tried out.
I am tired out.
I do not like the buildings
the builders are building.
Blocked is my view of Mount Moriah,
the gold-domed mosque,
the site of sacrifice.
I have joined committees
for the preservation of Jerusalem.
I oppose the Master Plan.

I love my wife: she is overweight,
comely, warm. She brews jasmine tea
on summer evenings.
I am teaching her to sing.
At night, nestling like spoons,
my body aches with her sadness.
She is afraid,
married to a man of so few beliefs.

I have written a play.
Two people caught on a border.
They can't go back and they can't go on.
They swing on the border sign
without smiling.
Their kites are lost in the sky.
They have run out of tea.
It is my Noh play, my last play.

After the war, I gave up meat.
After living—
Ruefully.
For I love my wife.

Santa Caterina

I never learned the names
of flowers or herbs
that grew there. I woke

either slowly,
contracting my legs &
arms, having to crawl out
of dream's burrow

and all day listened for the dripping of water
behind the spring
caressed the ferns,
vanished, for a while,
when black goats came to drink

or quickly, as dawn
stroked me, and waking
would amaze—

Then I would walk till dark
in gullies and wadis
among rocks

gathering weeds &
stones shaped like
mountains
and hide them
till dreams of power
entered me again
like magma—

ENGLISH

Mark Elliott Shapiro

Mark Elliott Shapiro was born in Canada in 1949. He has been living in Israel since 1970 and is currently a student at Hebrew University. His poetry and dramas have been published in English and in Hebrew.

Dying Under a Fall of Stars

Black skull-caps
In bright sunshine
Closing
Fresh graves
Remembering stone monuments

Yellowed newspaper clippings
With greying headlines in block letters
Whirling
Endless circles
Through deserted city streets
Whirling
In the cruel wind

Cruel rain sun cloud moon tree

And every hour
On the constant radio
The news

Like a final stab of darkness.

Richard Sherwin

Richard Sherwin has been living in Herzliyah, Israel, since 1964. He teaches English and American literature at Bar Ilan University. His book of poems, A Strange Courage, *was published in Tel Aviv in 1978, collecting poems which had previously appeared in Australia, New Zealand, England, Israel, and the United States.*

Jacob's Winning

Not that God's dead. Just
that Satan never bites the dust
before he draws first blood.
His art is mixing mud
to throw the soul in.
So Saul's compassion
fell mercifully to grief,
bleeding for man's relief.
Not that God's unjust. Just
that dreaming Jacobs wrestle dust.

Call it an angel. I too once ground
dreams from dust and found
light. I climbed
no ladders. Fleshed, unrhymed,
I limped away
broken with day.
My adversary grieved
for all I still believed.
Not that God's dead. Just
that Satan never bites the dust.

Our sons shall bleed again. He
grinds the flesh eternally
against our rocky souls.
Compassion must be whole:
they wrestle
mortar and pestle
the light of Heaven and Hell
compacting Israel.
Not that God's unjust. Just
that dreaming Jacobs wrestle dust.

ENGLISH

Dennis Silk

Dennis Silk was born in London in 1928 and has lived in Jerusalem since 1955. His books of poems are Face of Stone *and* The Punished Land. *He has also written stories and plays, and has edited the book* Retrievements: A Jerusalem Anthology.

Guide to Jerusalem

1

1st Edition

Don't live in a frontier-town; it's governed by the ill-will of two countries.
—Rabbi Pinchas of Kovetz to his son

Jerusalem is a limestone cracked
by destitution, it is a beggar rattling
his tray for money or Messiah.
Here the past walks with a religious stoop at twilight,
talking to itself overmuch.
And the bawling prophets are all dead;
the pious in their conventicles
are not consumed by any rapid fire
fetched down by the former travelling angels.
No bush burns in streets narrow as doctrine.

A stranger here, poking around the town,
observes the only holy visitor,
in border-slums the five o'clock light
shining like a ghost on the washing of the poor.

II

No-Man's Land

A house stands in the sinister land,
its top floor a slanting staircase
accepted as such by aspiring weeds,
and outer walls by some personal will
of stucco and of braced stone
married as never Jerusalem.

Married but living in barrenness.
Not even a stupid hen
to lay thriftless eggs here, not
an amorous cat.
Weather is the tenant now.

III

For Shalom Cohen

'Heat in gay colours,' and Herzl* riding
from Jaffa to Jerusalem.
'These three tracts must be bought. Make a note.
These three tracts must be bought.'

But the beggarly Jews
of the Eternal and moribund City depress.
'Pond ducks when the wild ducks fly by.'
He lodges in Mamilla Street,
courted or hated, a giant
or a jumped-up Jew, observes
local holiness that needs
some interpreter to sweep away its dust.

Then Von Bülow waits, and the Kaiser,
and he dares to talk of Palestine, they consult the map
of his faith and the dry wells.
From the Kaiser's encampment he drives back
to a town of paupers and ghosts.
How tall he looks in Jerusalem
in the *hamsin* time, driving back.
Scared of his new blaze,
the town becomes a somnambulist by midday,
winces at sunlight and pulls down the blinds.

IV

Doubtless at Delphi the priests cheated
the Pythia of her words, and sold them
to Persia if it paid enough.
She should have lived among atheists.

No place so noisome with flies
as a streaming altar, and in this town
the small guard the tombs of the great.

*In 1898 Theodor Herzl visited Palestine, and had several audiences with the Kaiser, a pilgrim at the time. The quoted lines or phrases are from Herzl's diaries. —D.S.

V

Just think how this corpse rolled all the way from London to Jerusalem, along a concealed but commodious tunnel, fed at stations on his way by repentant Adam, Elijah's ravens and a mourning Shekhina. The silly thing didn't know he'd snuffed it. For three days before his death he'd mumbled: 'Not on this day be Thy judgment, O Lord, not on this day be Thy judgment, O Lord.' He rolled the entire way in this prayer-cocoon. When they told him, at Jerusalem, that he was dead, his chrysalis died of shock.

VI

A hemmed-in dependency, I find
sun, water, stone have other names
in this exile's town.
And I have no name
for the aridity or the peace of Jehovah.
A ghost looking for a body,
I enjoy a small enclave of the sun.

*Matronita**

I

The mountain is wild with men,
has her pilgrims, her blood,
where her blueflower
launches you into the valley, laughs.
Claims her lieutenant
shot under her wall,
khaki in the wadi-grass,
combs the hair of her suicide
in his crumbly half-way house.

**Matronita* (The Lady)—A Kabbalistic appellation for the Shekhina, the feminine Divine Presence of God.

II
Surface tranquillity in the stone
makes it talk so high
yet it fears
underground waters of the Lady.
She calls
Petra in Jerusalem to her.

III
The Scandinavians, the hitchhikers,
their haversacks from the sea,
taste petrified town in their mouth.
Walls of May have a hot taste.
The riverine consider a mystery.

Listen to one under stone
blond, and dark, do not hear.
She alone unfolds the town-plan,
sculling away on water.

Avner Strauss

Avner Strauss was born in Jerusalem in 1954. He studied music in the United States and now lives in Jerusalem as a singer and musician. He is the author of a book of poems, Birds of the Mind and Chameleons of the Heart. *He is a grandson of the Hebrew poet A. L. Strauss.*

The Hollow Flute

I have a dream bone
with flesh of memories
I had built a human
out of this material.

Sometimes I think that
it is a memory bone with
flesh of dream, I made
myself a brother out of this,
when I am awake he is asleep.

Dry bones make good flutes.

ENGLISH

Portrait of a Widow

Inside every widow
there is a spider that weaves its webs
in the corners of her heart.

And every one of them
that has his ears in his legs
can hear her moan.

As the shawl on her shoulders
and her sweater,
in her head—as the black scarf.

In every deserted chest,
robbed of desires, there are ladders
going up and down in the spirit-wind,

where love
is a fly in the net of
a rope ladder to the sun.

AUSTRALIA

Nancy Keesing

Nancy Keesing was born in Sydney, Australia in 1923. Her work includes poetry, short stories, radio scripts, and critical essays. In addition to collecting books of Australian folk ballads, she has published four volumes of her own poems: Imminent Summer, Three Men and Sydney, Showground Sketchbook, *and* Hails and Farewells.

Wandering Jews

Out of Palestine, out of Babylon,
out of Egypt, Persia, Arabia,
Their trees turned desert, hills to rock,
Forsaken by rain, grown desolation
From dark rain of blood . . .
Scholars? Teachers? Peasants? Artisans?
Out of arched stone synagogues, carrying
Lore in narrow heads, law on careful parchment
They wandered, furrowing the face of centuries
With shod foot, hoof beat, cart, litter, river barge . . .
And tramped again—road, camel, and caique
Into Spain. Into song, into court of Caliph. . . .

Breeding, across the face of centuries
Boys like hawks and girls like glittering
Fruit-eating birds that peck in orange groves,
And stern old turbanned men with magic,
Algebra and music, surging, casketed
Behind subtle eyes and faces like rock. . . .

And Spain, the golden, opulent, fruitful
Split like an over-ripe citron to spew them
Across grey oceans . . . Some to Holland
To peer out of paintings; where
Thin, long, beaky
Arabian faces ponder astrolabes;
Dissected animal cadavers; manuscripts;
Or lurk as foils—the fine-boned, dark-skinned
Contrast beside the portly housewife
Who plucks her ptarmigans in profusion
Of nuts, grapes, peaches, fish, and wine-skins . . . .

Beckoned by Cromwell, warts, Bible, money-bags.
Lore in their hawk heads, law on parchment
Judezmo in their mouths and into England. . . .

ENGLISH

Seven tall brothers spurned the hungry forties,
Sailed from England out to New Zealand
Clean round the Horn. They braced to sloping
Decks sleet-slippery, jutted fierce beards
At sheer green ice-cliffs depending over
Spars and masts and topsails, dwarfing
Lore and Law. While rime made brittle
Seven long, lean enduring faces
That, gratefuller than any who stumbled on Sambatyon
Turned to the Land of the Long White Cloud
And found the Maoris, locked in legend
Living by myths of the world's creation
In cool and fruitful rain-filled forests
And regions of sulphur and soil thin as skin,
A land recalling the first chapter of Torah. . . .

And found the Maoris (locked in legend
Wrapped like hawks in pride and feathers,
Stout and warrior-muscled, but breeding
Beaky, thin, fair sons for chieftains)
Strangely familiar, as if known somewhere
And dimly remembered, despite their features
Scored and cauterized into patterns
Peculiarly atavistic, allusive
Of Egyptian? Indian? Persian? Akkadian?
In Eighteen-hundred-and-forty-two. . . .

David Martin

David Martin was born in Hungary in 1915. He has lived in Germany, Israel, Spain, Scotland, India, and now Australia, where he resides with his family. He is the author of novels, children's books, and six volumes of poetry.

I Am a Jew

I am a Jew,
I walk
The streets of each city.
You see my shadow
Falling on your door
As it fell before
On Jerusalem,
On Granada.

I am a Jew,
I gave David
A sword and a harp.
I taught Mohammed
And set to the West
The heart of Columbus.

I am a Jew,
I walk
The streets of each city.
I marched with the legions
Of Alexander.

I am a Jew,
I lie entombed
In the caves of the East,
In Western trenches.
Dig deep, dig deep,
You will find my bones.

ENGLISH

Fay Zwicky

Fay Zwicky was born in Melbourne in 1933 and is currently lecturer in English the University of Western Australia. She has published poetry, stories, and literary criticism in numerous Australian anthologies and journals. She is the author of Isaac Babel's Fiddle.

The Chosen—Kalgoorlie, 1894

I The Escape

His father said: Marry her. She's had a hard life—
With you lighter it can't get. She cooks,
Breathes, a little ankle, eyes not bad . . . what
More do you want? For mother's sake . . .
Her heart won't beat for ever . . . a grandchild, a family!
And he ran away. He ran and ran from that
Abrasive calico breast, virgin ankle, awkward
Menial hands, his heart burdened with crimson sunsets.
(Grandmother-mother, hands that moulded love in me but
Passive lay in his impatient palms). Thin spectacled,
Sixteen he fled the fatherland across the Nullarbor.
His mother had her heart-attack and Yahweh,
Rhadamanthine Yahweh (blest be He!) galloped
Snorting after the little puffer, Bobtails blinked,
Smiling among grey stones to see
God go off His Head.

II Retribution Plotted

And Yahweh the Extravagant,
Prodigal Yahweh swore revenge,
Stamped in a desert way off His patch:
A Desert-Dweller all My life!
Don't they know of Me? The trumpet-tones
Shatter on flat stones; ant-hills heave,
Turn over in a dreamless sleep:
My Chosen do not stray far! My ways are wondrous,
Perilous; I am the One (no other shalt thou have)
Who does the choosing here!
Braying maniac brewing cataclysms.
Antediluvian mouths yawn
Under the unshriven sun.

III The Plague

They handed him a key:
This is your house. A sagging box,
Smoke-licked pane webbed by
Sleepy crab-spiders. He'd read
In the old country, Talmud-ridden
Fly, 'In hot climates Spiders
Are able to produce a certain amount of
Local pain.' His skin bristled with small
Spiked crowns. Pain's antidote in peeled
Tub—a pink geranium, stationmaster's ward,
Barren season's suckling.
Weekly his charge gnawed the track to the
Flat horizon, covered a hemisphere in his
Kindled sight, gabbling caterpillar.
But came the Day of the Scorpion.
Clanking, thundering scales, buckling linkages,
From its final poisoned segment issued Yahweh,
Mighty polyphemal ruby eye to sear the spider,
Flower and stripling stationmaster, belching
Plague through flaring nostrils, scattering
Dybbuks through the land.
I CHOOSE, HEIR TO ASHES! Squeaking demons,
Metal-winged, buzz and swoop, pegged within
The confines of His breath.
Ten days he lay reflected in his death, his
Bowels curled limp beside his shoes.
Next train his grieving father
Brought him home.

IV Retribution Achieved

She said: This is the station key.
Your grandfather watched trains as a young man.
I waited.

SOUTH AFRICA

Sydney Clouts

Sydney Clouts was born in Cape Town, South Africa in 1926. His book One Life *was published in 1966. He now lives in London.*

Of Thomas Traherne and the Pebble Outside

Gusts of the sun race on the approaching sea.

In the air Traherne's Contentments shine.

A jewelled Garden gazed at him.

What shall be said of Paradise?

Obscure vermilion heats the dim pebble I hold.

The long rock-sheltered surges flash with spume.

I have read firm poems of God.

Good friend, you perceived bright angels.

This heathen bit of the world lies warm in my palm.

The Portrait of Prince Henry

from the painting by Nuño Gonçalves

His hatbrim's full Copernican ellipse
of cloth of night encircles him.

The long monastic face renounces land,
at Sagres, in the tower
of his life's long nightwatch:
night of the sea routes
night of the waves of God
and of the starry spice routes
round and round the sun.

His eyes forgive the possible
its stormwind its astrolabe
its monster isolation
with humility,
gazing free and full,
and only then suggest
his shorter kingdom,
Portugal.

The Sleeper

for Marge

When you awake
gesture will waken
to decisive things.
Asleep, you have taken
motion and tenderly laid it within,
deeply within you.
Your shoulders are shining
with your own clear light.
I should be mistaken
to touch you even softly,
to disturb your bold
and entirely personal devotion
to the self that sleeps
and is your very self,
crucial as when you hasten
in the house and hasten through the street,
or sit in the deep yellow chair
and breathe sweet air.

Unaware of the stars
outside our window
that do not know they shine,
as well as of the wild sea
that can have no care,
as well as of the wind
that blows unaware
of its motion in the air,
sound be your rest

and gentle the dreaming
of your silent body
passionately asleep.
Can a cloud stay so still?
Can a bird be so lonely?
It seems you have found
great patience in your breath:
it moves with life,
it rehearses death.

Firebowl

Kalahari Bushman fires flowing
in the hollows of the desert
click all night
stick stuck upright
click
click
of starlight
bowstring
toes of the eland
thk thk the big raindrops
tk tk tk the sandgrains
drinking.

Sssskla!
sparks of honey
arrowheads
we who dance
around the circle
around the circle
spoor him
find him

my arrow clings to the thick thick
grunt of darkness
my arrow sings through fire.

we who dance we find
the
fire
of the fire.

Mannie Hirsch

Mannie Hirsch was born in Oudtshoorn, South Africa, in 1938 and presently lives in Israel. His poems have appeared in various magazines in English, Afrikaans, and Russian.

Cry for a Disused Synagogue in Booysens

This ground once was consecrated.
God lived here: and bearded men
Rocked between the benches
Like pendulums of prayer.

Bandaged in fringed shawls
They shuttled
Against the walls
And kissed their leather halos
Drinking heady Sabbaths
From a time-filled cup.

Twice a year a high-horned note
Rammed its head above the mines
And hung, joyous in the frosted air,
Announcing packs renewed again.

Instead of prayers the packing cases
Now stand stacked against the ceiling.
And broken hoardings
Have replaced the antique scripts
God has gone.
Only
The lonely
Leaded window
Still retains his fingerprints.
And his voice lies buried in the amber glass.

Allan Kolski Horvitz

Allan Kolski Horvitz was born in Vryburg, South Africa, in 1952. He studied philosophy at the University of Cape Town and has lived in Israel since 1974. He is presently a professional singer and songwriter.

King Saul

1
The middle-aged king
ginger streaks on his hands
in his beard
across the sash of a Philistine
back wound

pads from room to room
woolen tufts of his tunic
snared on spear tips
his face still flushed
with the coronating cries
inflicted on Samuel.

2
The mules bray in the courtyard
of his queen's chest.
She coughs with cold
when he campaigns.
Dreams of Amalekite teeth
bared in death.

3
Her hands rest on a messy tangerine.
Its juice drips onto her Gibeonite sandals.
Patterned, they were taken
from an enslaved elder.
(Remember the ruse they loosed
on Joshua).

Characteristically,
Saul only admires
their thick souls.

The Radiance of Extinct Stars

Why not despair of this world
and its ovens of pain

I mourn you Chana Senesh
you are my sister and my love

you are the star spoken of
in many writings

you are aflame in me
as a conflagration of beauty and courage

you are a sign for me
you are a cipher of the best in us

can it have been?
the conspiracy of your execution

I will comfort the many thousand children
and the bereaved mothers
and for the homeless build a hearth

yours has been the startling flash.

Jean Lipkin

Jean Lipkin was born in Johannesburg, South Africa, and presently lives in London. Her works have appeared in numerous journals and have been read on BBC and SABC radio. She has published one book of poems, Among Stones.

Apocalypse

At night Babylon is remembered,
Constellations of Babylons recalled.
Cold world haunt the heavens.
Those who weep, forget
What came before the water.

Afterwards trains galloped into silence.
Death fires glowed till day waned them.
On the ash, the tracks
Of chariot wheels
Disquieted the despoilers:
What should have been easy to explain
Remained mysterious, filled with omen.

In an image, grasses in flight,
Great yellow surges
Blow across the world,
Over generations of fields,
Immense cauldrons at the boil
Let loose seeds that steam
Into clouds of turmoil;
The chaff prepares the whirlwind.
And the valley is lifted to the hill
Leaving a vast still wing of darkness.

Fay Lipshitz

Fay Lipshitz was born in Cape Town, South Africa in 1941. She came to Jerusalem in 1973, where she currently works as a free-lance journalist and librarian. She has published poems and children's stories.

Encounter in Jerusalem

At that soft pale hour
When holy spirits are abroad in the City's quiet places
I met a prayer, contained so lightly
In the figure of a man,
An incandescent soul
That glowed through the eyes of fire
Such passion must consume—
And so it was.
The body but a wisp of smoke, that lightly wove
Through the shadows of the waiting City.

Judean Summer

Thistle whips spitefully across brown thigh;
Blood wells, crimson snake
Slides down cracked skin
And creeps into the dust.
Other seekers of dark—
A field of dying sunflowers,
Drooping dumbly earthwards,
Here and there, defiant,
A shout of gold.

The Aleph Bet

I fear you letters,
Square and black, uncompromising,
Not welcoming me, not letting me in.
And yet, I have seen you sometimes,
Transformed into leaves,
Far-scattered,
And into fingers of flame.
Can you be both so unyielding,
So stern and straight,
And yet burn so high,
And fly so bright?

SCOTLAND

A. C. Jacobs

A. C. Jacobs was born in Glasgow in 1937. He moved to London at the age of fourteen. He lived in Israel in the early 1960s for three years. Later he lived in Italy but returned to Scotland in 1976. He has translated widely from the Hebrew and Yiddish. His poems and translations have appeared in many periodicals. His first volume of poems, The Proper Blessing, *was published in 1976, as was his translation of David Vogel's* The Dark Gate: Selected Poems.

Poem for My Grandfather

On the Anniversary of His Death

Today, a candle in a glass
Burns slowly on the mantelpiece.
Wheesht, the dead are here.

My father, your grey-haired son,
Tastes again the salt, wax prayers
Of your sacred, dying day.

You are a name, holy in his presence,
The last solemn date
In our calendar of death.

Truly a ghost, my father sees, you.
A kind man's regret softens his face.

But for me there is no introduction:
For me you are a light on the mantelpiece,
A half shadow on the wall.

Yiddish Poet

He moved among blocked facades,
And the remains of an old life kept growing
Here and there, for its quaint satisfaction.
In everything the habit of tragedy
Had framed his saddened view.
Sometimes he could not trust himself to speak
For fear of weeping.

He loved his language
Like a woman he had grown old with,
Whose beauty shown at moments in his memory
But saw how time had stricken what was his
And pondered on the truth of his desire.

And he could not remember his own poems
Yet hoped something would live of them,
The scent perhaps, or a sudden particular cry
Made in a night he summed up suffering.

At the end he wrote always of death
As if it was his meaning all along,
And what he hoped from life was not perfection
But difficult glints of certainty.

For a man was this one intimate with sorrow,
His dreams led nowhere—yet alive he sang.

Isaac

It was my father forced him into the desert—
My father, the patriarch, fearing for my inheritance,
And my mother, jealous of the strength of a concubine's child.

And I vaguely remember the mocking, knowing boy
Who played his secret games around our tents
And crept in at night to his mother the slave woman's pillow.

He could do marvellous things: whistle wild songs,
Climb trees I couldn't, find unknown caves and streams;
His exploits were legend among our lesser household.

ENGLISH

But there was that day my father, a man perplexed,
Rejected his furtively proud, unorthodox son:
His God wanted me and my father always listened.

I hear now my brother is a chief of a tribe in the desert;
He lives by conquest and has many enemies.
His children plot and starve when he is defeated.

I hear rumours he dreams of marching against me.
To seize his inheritance. What shall I do against God and my father?
I, too, believe in the destiny of my children.

I, too, have suffered, perhaps more than he:
I have had a sacrificial knife laid at my throat.
These lands are a small exchange for that terrifying moment.

I would like to help my brother, but he is still proud.
There will be no discussion of peace between us;
And our father, the old God-fearing man, has been dead many years.

Painting

The Jew, in the painting by Chagall,
praying.
Armoured in objects of his holiness
He can speak out blessing.
In his dark surroundings
The white *tallis* enfolds him
Like the tent of his piety,
But one edge of it ends,
jaggedly,
Near the thongs of the *tefilin*
On his arm.

Under the black box on his forehead
His face burns, sombre, lucid,
But some of it retreats.

The anxiety clenched in it
Mingles with something
Almost a grin.

He sits against darkness
Curling into light.

He is a man
Who bears the weight of his own experience,

What he utters
Will touch
The depths of survival.

ENGLISH

WALES

Dannie Abse

Dannie Abse was born in Cardiff, Wales, in 1923. He qualified as a physician and served in the RAF. He was poet-in-residence at Princeton University, 1973-4. He is the author of several volumes of poetry, many plays, and other books, including the autobiography A Poet in the Family. *His volume of* Collected Poems *was published in 1977. He lives in London.*

Song for Dov Shamir

Working is another way of praying.
You plant in Israel the soul of a tree.
You plant in the desert the spirit of gardens.

Praying is another way of singing.
You plant in the tree the soul of lemons.
You plant in the gardens the spirit of roses.

Singing is another way of loving.
You plant in the lemons the spirit of your son.
You plant in the roses the soul of your daughter.

Loving is another way of living.
You plant in your daughter the spirit of Israel.
You plant in your son the soul of the desert.

Tales of Shatz

Meet Rabbi Shatz in his correct black homburg.
The *cheder* boys call him Ginger.
If taller than 5 foot you're taller than he;
also taller than his father,
grandfather, great-grandfather.

Meet Ruth Shatz, née Ruth Pinsky,
short statured too, straight backed.
In her stockinged feet
her forehead against his,
her eyes smile into his.
And again on the pillow, later.
Ah those sexy red-headed Pinskys
of Leeds and Warsaw: her mother
grandmother, great-grandmother!

Mrs. Shatz resembles Rabbi Shatz's mother.
Rabbi Shatz resembles Mrs. Shatz's father.
Strangers mistake them for brother, sister.

At University, Solly Shatz, their morning star,
suddenly secular, all 6 foot of him—
a black-haired centre-forward on Saturdays—
switches studies from Theology to Genetics.

~ ~

A certain matron of Golders Green,
fingering amber beads around her neck,
approaches Rabbi Shatz.
When I was a small child, she thrills,
once, just once, God the Holy One
came through the curtains of my bedroom.
What on earth has he been doing since?

Rabbi Shatz turns, he squints,
he stands on one leg
hoping for the inspiration of a Hillel.
The Holy One, he answers, blessed be He,
has been waiting, waiting patiently,
till you see Him again.

~ ~

ENGLISH

Consider the *mazel* of Baruch Levy
who changed his name to Barry Lee,
who moved to Esher, Surrey,
who sent his four sons—Matthew, Mark,
Luke and John—to boarding school,
who had his wife's nose fixed,
who, blinking in the Gents,
turned from the writing on the wall
and later, still blinking, joined the golf club.
With new friend, Colonel Owen,
first game out, under vexed clouds,
thunder detonated without rain,
lightning stretched without thunder,
and near the 2nd hole,
where the darker green edged
to the shaved lighter green,
both looked up terrified.
Barbed fire zagged towards them
to strike dead instantly
Mostyn Owen, Barry Lee's opponent.
What luck that Colonel Owen
(as Barry discovered later)
once was known as Moshe Cohen.

Now, continued Rabbi Shatz,
recall how even the sorrows of Job
had a happy ending.

Being a religious man Shatz adored riddles.
Who? he asked his impatient wife.

Who like all men came into this world
with little fists closed, departed
with large hands open, yet on walking
over snow and away from sunsets
followed no shadow in front of him,
left no footprint behind him?

You don't know either, opined his wife.
You and your Who? Who?
Are you an owl?
Why do you always pester me with riddles
you don't know the answer of?

Rabbi Shatz for some reason wanted to cry.
If I knew the answers, he whispered,
would my questions still be riddles?
And he tiptoed away, closed the door
so softly behind him
as if on a sleeping dormitory.

Often when listening to music
before a beautiful slow movement
recaptured him, Shatz would blank out,
hear nothing. So now, too, in his lit study
as night rain tilted outside
across dustbins in the lane
he forgot why his lips moved, his body swayed.

INDIA

Nissim Ezekiel

Nissim Ezekiel was born in Bombay, India, in 1924 and now teaches at the University of Bombay. In addition to reading tours in the United States and Australia, he has published six volumes of poetry, the most recent of which is Hymns in Darkness.

Totem

The wings of a bird
for imagination
but not the whole bird.
The hoofs of a goat
but not the whole goat.
Cat's eyes to see in the dark.
A death mask.
A phoenix egg.
And sundry decorations,
not without meaning.

Lamentation

My lips lack prophecy
My tongue speaketh no great matters
The words of the wise are wasted on me
Fugitive am I and far from home
A vagabond and every part of me is withered
The season comes and men bring forth their fruit
But I am bare beside the abounding sea
Rivers feed my roots yet I do not prosper
Day unto day no speech is spoken
And night unto night knowledge is hidden from me
The lamp commands no more with friendly light
And laws desert my bones till I am sick
Desire postponed is death to me
Pursued it rots the bowels
Give me vision and I shall be clean
Slack and slow no more to hear instruction
And let my leaf be green with love
And let me live.

How My Father Died

My father talked too much
and too loudly,
but just before he died
his voice became soft and sad,
as though whispering secrets
he had learned too late.
He called me close to him
and put his truths to me.
I only felt the breath of his love
but did not hear a word.

ENGLISH

SRI LANKA

Anne Ranasinghe

Anne Ranasinghe was born in Germany but fled to England just prior to World War II. She now lives in Colombo, Sri Lanka, with her husband and children. Her poems, stories, and radio plays have been published in Sri Lanka and abroad in journals and anthologies.

Holocaust 1944

to my mother

I do not know
In what strange far off earth
They buried you;
Nor what harsh northern winds
Blow through the stubble,
The dry hard stubble
Above your grave.

And did you think of me
That frost-blue December morning,
Snow-heavy and bitter,
As you walked naked and shivering
Under the leaden sky,
In that last moment
When you knew it was the end,
The end of nothing
And the beginning of nothing,
Did you think of me?

Oh I remember you my dearest,
Your pale hands spread
In the ancient blessing,
Your eyes bright and shining
Above the candles
Intoning the blessing
Blessed be the Lord. . . .

Auschwitz from Colombo

Colombo. March. The city white fire
That pours through vehement trees burst into flame
And only a faint but searing wind
Stirring the dust
From relics of foreign invaders, thrown
On this far littoral by chance or greed,
Their stray memorial the odd word mispronounced,
A book of laws
A pile of stones
Or maybe some vile deed.

Once there was another city; but there
It was cold—the trees leafless
And already thin ice on the lake.
It was that winter
Snow hard upon the early morning street
And frost flowers carved in hostile window panes—

It was that winter.

Yet only yesterday
Half a world away and twenty-five years later
I learn of the narrow corridor
And at the end a hole, four feet by four,
Through which they pushed them all—the children too—
Straight down a shaft of steel thirteen feet long
And dark and icy cold
Onto the concrete floor of what they called
The strangling room. Dear God, the strangling room,
Where they were stunned—the children too—
By heavy wooden mallets,
Garroted, and then impaled
On pointed iron hooks.

I am glad of the unechoing street
Burnt white in the heat of many tropical years.
For the mind, no longer sharp,
Seared by the tropical sun
Skims over the surface of things
Like the wind
That stirs but slightly the ancient dust.

IV Other Languages

Introduction to Book IV
by Edouard Roditi

1. *French and German Models*

In all the other literatures and linguistic areas that concern us here, problems of a Jewish identity can prove to be more complex than in the more limited context of Israel or of contemporary Hebrew or even Yiddish poetry. In French literature, for instance, the literary movement which is now widely accepted as "modern" began some time before 1870, in the age of Baudelaire, and reached a climax a generation later, in the age that produced Rimbaud, Lautréamont, Verlaine, Mallarmé, and a whole galaxy of other poets who are defined by literary historians as either Parnassians, Decadents, or Symbolists. By now, the writings and the theories of the poets of these three schools or groups have profoundly influenced the "modern" poetry of a great number of other languages or nations, throughout Europe, the Americas, and even Asia and Africa. If one excepts Poe and Whitman in American poetry, because they both exerted an important influence on many of these early French "modernists," French poetry thus proved to be "modern," in our contemporary sense, a few decades before the poetry of England, Germany, or any other nation which began only after 1880 to follow the example of the major French innovators of 1870 or even earlier.

Among these French pioneers of modern poetry, a few Jews happen to have played a relatively prominent part: Catulle Mendès as a popular and somewhat realist Parnassian who has long ceased to be of major interest even to discriminating French poetry lovers, Ephraïm Mikhaël as a somewhat idealistic and withdrawn Parnassian whose verse and prose poems continue to be unjustly neglected, and Gustave Kahn as a major Symbolist innovator who has indeed been credited, by several reputable literary historians, with the invention of free verse.

Were these three French modernists, however, at all specifically Jewish as poets? Can one reasonably attribute Mikhaël's exotic orientalism, for instance, to an obscure and atavistic nostalgia for Biblical scenes and ages, or is it rather of the same generally Post-Romantic nature as the orientalism of so many Gentile academic painters among his contemporaries and also of many of the poems of Leconte de Lisle among Mikhaël's immediate Gentile masters? Only Gustave Kahn, of the three gifted French poets of his generation who were Jews, has left us any poems, in fact a whole book of them, that handle specifically Jewish themes. These poems, on traditional Biblical themes, never on the so-called "Jewish experience in the modern world," were all written late in the poet's life and published long after the Dreyfus Affair, which may well have revived in Gustave Kahn's mind a latent awareness of being a Jew and thus weaned him away from the more specifically Post-Romantic orientalism of his earlier and more famous *Palais nomades* in order to publish, after 1920, this somewhat anachronistic volume of Symbolist poetry that no longer met with as much interest as any of his earlier work.

In France as elsewhere in Western and Central Europe, nineteenth-century emancipation thus appears to have exerted, on most poets who were of Jewish extraction, an influence that usually led them to eschew all overtly Jewish themes. Jewish pioneers of modernist poetry were indeed led to express their *judéité*, as the French writer Albert Memmi would now call it, only indirectly or unconsciously; if at all, in the *boulevardier* or metropolitan ironies, the realism and cynicism of Catulle Mendès, or in the orientalism of Mikhaël and of the earlier poetry of Gustave Kahn.

The outstanding example of Heinrich Heine, among the great German Romantics of the first half of the nineteenth century, seems to have encouraged a greater number of young Jews of later generations to express themselves in poetry in German-speaking countries rather than in France. But none of these German-language poets achieved any real distinction before the early years of our century, when German and Austrian Symbolism, especially in the group headed in Germany by Stefan George, began belatedly to follow the example of Baudelaire, Mallarmé, Verlaine, and other major French innovators. Among these German-language Symbolists, the Austrian poet Hugo von Hofmannsthal was one of the leaders; though of partly Jewish origin, he has left us no specifically Jewish work, either in his poetry or in his prose. Nor can one find anything specifically Jewish in the work of Alfred Mombert, a German-Jewish poet who led for many years a very withdrawn and provincial life in southwestern Germany before becoming, in his old age, a victim of Nazi persecution and then dying, an exile, in a Vichy-French internment camp. Richard Beer-Hofmann, however, was their contemporary among

Austria's few Symbolists and has revealed his awareness of being a Jew in one truly remarkable lyric, "Lullaby for Miriam," which moreover exerted many years later a powerful influence on the early poetry of Paul Celan. Franz Werfel, Friedrich Torberg, and Alma Johanna Koenig later distinguished themselves too as Jewish poets in a second generation of Austrian Symbolists.

In the immediate circle of Stefan George, two other German-Jewish poets, Rudolph Borchardt and Karl Wolfskehl, distinguished themselves as leaders in the German Symbolist movement. Borchardt's translation of Dante's *Divine Comedy* remains a remarkable achievement, indeed a monument of sheer scholarship and linguistic virtuosity. Wolfskehl, who made for many years a considerable display of being a German rather than a Jewish poet, began to be inspired by Jewish themes only late in his life, after 1930 and under the imminent threat of the Nazi persecutions that subsequently sent him into Antipodean exile in New Zealand.

The majority of Germany's and Austria's more gifted and original modern poets of Jewish origin belonged, however, to the literary generation of the Expressionists, which immediately followed that of the Symbolists. Most of the Expressionist poets who were Jews chose, moreover, to communicate in their work the same kind of ironical or skeptical moods and views of the very assimilated Jews of the big cities as Heine had once done, thus eschewing in general all more specifically Jewish themes. This is true, for instance, of the poetry of Alfred Lichtenstein and Jakov van Hoddis, two veritable pioneers of German Expressionist poetry and of the pessimistic moods which some critics have called *Menschheitsdämmerung* ("Twilight of Mankind"). Only in his two satirical and almost untranslatable poems about the absurd adventures of his fictional Lene Levy can Lichtenstein be said to have written any overtly Jewish poetry; only in his famous "End of the World" eight-line lyric can van Hoddis be said to have yielded to a curiously prophetic awareness of impending doom, though he worded it here in typically Expressionist terms of the absurd rather than in the traditionally sublime terms of Old Testament prophecy.

French-born Yvan Goll and his German-born wife Claire Goll, German-born Mynona (Salomo Friedlaender), Austrian-born Alfred Ehrenstein, and German-born Alfred Wolfenstein also achieved some eminence in Germany as Expressionist poets, without, however, handling in their work any specifically Jewish themes. Else Lasker-Schüler thus proved to be, in this respect, a remarkable exception among her Expressionist contemporaries. Long before she settled in Palestine as a refugee from Nazi Germany, she had often expressed in her poetry and her prose a hauntingly nostalgic and often almost obsessive awareness of her Jewish origin and inheritance. This awareness had moreover been strengthened, quite early in her literary career, by her curious emotional relationship with the Sabra sculptor Yusuf Abbo, a Sephardi of Syrian origin from the shores of the Sea of Galilee who settled in Berlin before the First World War. Another such exception among German Expressionist poets was Hugo Sonnenschein, once better known as Bruder Sonka, a Slovak Jew who survived internment in Auschwitz and then died in a Communist prison on his return to his native land. Among Sonnenschein's poems, which have never been reprinted in post-war Germany, one finds a couple of lyrics on Jewish themes.

When the storm clouds of Nazism began, especially after 1934, to foreshadow the impending Holocaust, then in the years of persecution and, after the war, in those that followed the Holocaust, an increasing number of German-Jewish and Austrian-Jewish poets of real talent felt urged to express in their work a more acute awareness of their being Jewish, of the Jewish fate, of "the Jewish experience in the modern world." It was then that Else Lasker-Schüler, long considered a mere eccentric by most German Jews, achieved among them the status of a modern prophetess because so many of them now began to share her passionate interest in their common Jewish past and in their possible Jewish future in Zionism. It was then too that Wolfskehl wrote and published, before emigrating to New Zealand, his few poems that express his awareness of being a Jew, and that Yvan Goll too, though now more often in French or even in English rather than in German, wrote those poems in which he reveals his awareness of his own Jewish destiny as a perpetual wanderer or exile, a *Jean sans terre* or "John Lackland" doomed to emulate in the modern world the legendary fate of the Wandering Jew.

Gertrud Kolmar and Alma Johanna Koenig, both destined to perish in Nazi concentration camps, also wrote in those years some poems that now appear to express premonitions of the doom that threatened them. Whereas Alma Johanna Koenig remained, in her poetry, faithful to the Austrian Symbolism of which Rilke's *Sonnets to Orpheus* are typical, Gertrud Kolmar achieved a peculiarly personal synthesis of Symbolist and Expressionist trends. Always leading a very withdrawn life, she never attracted much attention in Berlin's literary circles under the Weimar Republic and became deservedly famous in postwar Western Germany only after her death. Among the few German-language Jewish poets who survived the persecutions of the Nazi regime, Nelly Sachs and Paul Celan continued, after 1945, to communicate to their readers, in their poetry, an acute awareness of the significance of personal survival and of the Holocaust as a collective fate. Among German-Jewish poets who managed to emigrate to America, Ilse Blumenthal-Weiss and Hans Sahl have variously expressed in some of their poems a similar awareness, while Alfred Grünewald, an Austrian-Jewish poet who was deported as a refugee from occupied France to a Nazi death camp, revealed in some of his later poems a deeply rooted sense of impending doom.

2. *The Influence of German Poetry on that of Neighboring Countries*

The evolution of German literature had long exerted a powerful influence on that of some neighboring countries, and this is particularly true in the case of the literatures of several of the so-called "succession states" of the former Austro-Hungarian Empire and also of the Netherlands. We thus find that several Jewish poets writing in Dutch have followed by and large the example of German or Austrian poets, but often with strong French or English influences too as well as an awareness of the traditions of their own native Dutch poetry. Jakov de Haan, Judith Herzberg, and Leo Vroman display, in many of their poems, a peculiarly wry quality of irony that is both very Dutch and very Jewish.

The Jewish poets of Czechoslovakia, on the other hand, though often influenced in much the same manner by German or Austrian examples, yet display, in their choice of the language in which they express themselves, some political or cultural considerations or convictions of a very different nature. As long as these poets were still citizens of the Austro-Hungarian Empire, they tended to express themselves in German rather than in Czech, Slovak, or any other minority language, such as Ruthenian or Hungarian, of the future Czechoslovak Republic. Franz Kafka, for instance, was a Jew of Prague who wrote all of his prose, some of which can truly be said to be prose poetry, only in German. Hugo Sonnenschein, a Slovak Jew, likewise wrote all of his poetry in German, and Alma Johanna Koenig, who was born in Prague and later became Austrian by marriage, wrote all her fiction and poetry in German.

After 1920, however, a new generation of Jewish poets began, in the newborn Czechoslovak Republic, to express itself in Czech or in Slovak rather than in German, and this linguistic choice reveals a deeper involvement in the political and cultural life of Czechoslovakia, in fact in a cultural life that was now influenced by French and Russian examples as much as by those of contemporary German poetry. We thus find, in Czechoslovakia, a Surrealist movement inspired by French examples rather than by German Expressionism. At the same time, the linguistic choice of those Czechoslovak Jewish poets who no longer wrote in German reveals their more profound cultural assimilation and their increasingly explicit loss of interest in Jewish traditions that were not of a more narrowly local nature, such as the picturesque legends of the Golem of Prague.

The same kind of assimilationist trend can also be observed in the work of the very few Yugoslav-Jewish poets of Slovenia and Croatia, except that their writings in Slovene or Croat sometimes reveal Hungarian influences too. In other areas of Yugoslavia, such as Bosnia, which had never been as culturally integrated in the Austro-Hungarian Empire as Catholic Croatia and Slovenia, or as Serbia or Macedonia, where the Christian majority is of the Orthodox Church rather than Roman Catholic, those few Jewish poets who wrote in Serbian, a language closely related to Croat, or in Macedonian, which is related to both Serbian and Bulgarian, were less exposed to the various trends of contemporary German or Hungarian poetry or to the assimilationist pressures felt by most urban Jews during the last decades of the Austro-Hungarian Empire's existence. A majority of the Jews of Bosnia, Serbia, and Macedonia were, moreover, Sephardim who continued, well into the early decades of the twentieth century, to speak Judeo-Spanish, generally known as Ladino or Judezmo, at least in their homes. Although Stanislav Vinaver, a Serbian Jew who never expressed any significant awareness of being a Jew in any of his writings, distinguished himself for many years as a major Serbian poet, very few Sephardic Jews of Bosnia, Serbia, or Macedonia have emerged. Monny de Boully, who wrote poetry both in Serbian and in French, has attracted some attention in Paris and in Belgrade mainly as a dissident Surrealist of the Paris "Grand Jeu" group.

3. *The Choice of a Language*

The choice of the language in which the Jewish poet decides to express himself becomes particularly significant in those nations which have several important linguistic minorities or whose cultural life was at one time subjected to powerful alien cultural and linguistic influences. In Poland, for instance, Yiddish remained, especially in central and eastern Poland though not in some areas of western Poland, the mother tongue of the majority of Jews well into the twentieth century. According to his social or geographical origin within the area that became Poland after the First World War, a Jewish poet could thus be faced with the choice of three or more languages as idioms of self-expression. In western Poland, a writer such as Ernst Toller, who was born in Samotschin and educated in German schools, could choose to write only in German and never refer to his Jewish origin. Osip Mandelstam, on the other hand, came of a Polish-Jewish family that moved from Warsaw, when it was still a provincial Russian administrative center, to the czarist capital; Mandelstam wrote only in Russian and remains one of the very greatest Russian poets of our age. Polish-Jewish poets, such as Lesmian, Slonimsky, Tuwim, Wittlin, and Wat, who were mainly of upper-class urban extraction, wrote only in

Polish. Among Polish-Jewish poets, Yiddish thus remained the idiom preferred by those poets who wrote consciously for an exclusively Jewish and more popular public, and was also often used as a linguistic vehicle for expressing the Populist or Socialist ideas of the Bund. Hebrew, on the other hand, was chosen as an idiom of expression only by a few more learned poets or by Zionist activists.

The choice of any one of these five languages indeed implied basically an existential or a political choice which would, of course, be reflected in much of the poet's work, above all in his choice of themes. The choice of German, Russian, or Polish thus implied, in most cases, a rejection of traditional Jewish life in favor of a set of assimilationist beliefs which, in the eyes of the more orthodox, are tantamount to apostasy or at least to the abhorred aberrations of the Epikoīrosim or "disbelievers" of traditional Talmudic lore. A Polish-Jewish poet writing in German, Russian, or Polish would therefore express himself but rarely, if ever, on a specifically Jewish theme. Occasionally, however, such an assimilationist poet might also, as in the case of Tuwim or of Wittlin, be shaken out of his apparently assimilationist complacency when he found himself facing violent anti-Semitism, which might then inspire him to write on a Jewish theme.

The choice of Yiddish, on the other hand, did not always imply strict observance of Jewish orthodoxy, but more often a faith in a certain ethnic or linguistic nationalism that we often associate with populist, socialist, or even Communist ideas. Many of the Yiddish poets of Soviet Russia, for instance, remained convinced Communists until Stalin began to persecute all those Jews of Soviet Russia who expressed their faith in any form, whether religious, cultural, or linguistic, or Jewish particularism.

As for the Jewish poet from Poland or Russia who chose, like Berl Pomerantz or David Vogel, to write in Hebrew, he too might not necessarily be expressing traditional or orthodox beliefs and ideas in his poetry, nor indeed Zionist beliefs. On the contrary, he might well, like David Vogel, have chosen to write in Hebrew out of some strangely personal and quite unpolitical linguistic particularism which, at least in the Diaspora, still had much in common with the cultural ideals of the poets of many a Gentile minority of czarist or Soviet Russia, such as the Ukrainians, the Georgians, or the Armenians, who often resisted in much the same manner the pressures exerted by Russian culture on their own national language and culture.

The choice of German or of Russian can also be interpreted as implying a rejection of the more narrowly provincial scope of both Polish or Yiddish cultural life and of Zionist nationalism, within the context of a Poland that was still divided between the Russian, German, and Austrian empires, in favor of the much broader contexts of German, Austrian, or Russian cultural life. Berlin, Vienna, St. Petersburg, and Moscow indeed exerted until 1920, whether in the West or in the East, a powerful attraction on Polish intellectuals, whether Jews or Gentiles, who still refrained from choosing, like Joseph Conrad in England or the Polish-Jewish playwright Alfred Savoir in France, the paths of both political and linguistic exile.

By now it should be apparent that "the Jewish experience in the modern world" consists to a large degree in a justifiably more constant and acute awareness of the need to make choices that often have truly existential implications, as well as of the precarious nature of the whole Jewish condition. This awareness, which is not always shared by all other peoples or communities, may well be what Paul Celan refers to in his book of poems *Die Niemandsrose (No One's Rose),* when he affirmed, as a survivor of the Holocaust who had escaped into Soviet Russia after Hitler's armies invaded his native province of Bukovina in northern Romania, that "all poets are Jews," quoting the Russian poet Marina Tsvetayeva, who was not Jewish but lived and died an almost typically Jewish life and death as a victim of Stalinist persecutions of intellectuals, artists, dissidents, marginal Bohemians, and, of course, Jews. Writing in German as Jewish poets who had survived the Holocaust, Celan and Nelly Sachs, who was awarded a Nobel Prize, both display in their poetry an awareness of their exemplary status as representatives of the few who have mysteriously escaped the mass-slaughter of an ambivalently "chosen" people. They have thus introduced into their poetry a new existential element of consciously "bearing witness," thereby expanding the whole context of the possible expressions, in one's poetry, of one's awareness of being a Jew.

4. *The Jewish Experience in the Modern World and the Sephardic Tradition*

Among all modern poets who happen to be Jews, the most intrinsically Jewish poets, in terms of their *judéité* or existential Jewishness, might therefore be those who, whether consciously or unconsciously, display in their writings the most acute awareness of all these existential contradictions and who word this awareness most eloquently; in fact, somewhat paradoxically, either poets who, like Mandelstam, never expressed very overtly or recognizably Jewish beliefs, ideas, or sentiments, or else poets who, like Lazarus Aaronson in England and Max Jacob in France, became converts to Christianity in the throes of a typically Jewish spiritual crisis. Or else poets who, like Edmond Jabès in France, have expressed in their writings so all-pervasive and obsessive an interest in Jewish traditions and beliefs that they manage to invest in them a universal significance which can be valid both to Jew and Gentile, like the prophetic books of the Old Testament.

Modern Jewish writing of the kind that Jabès produces in French—especially in his seven-volume prose masterpiece *Le Livre des questions,* from which our selection is not taken, apart from one brief extract—should indeed, at least in theory, communicate to any reader as intense and convincing a faith in Judaism as a religion or as an ethical tradition as the faith of Christianity that T. S. Eliot expressed in some of his French poems. If it does not, this is because the writings of Jabès are not only "Jewish" but at the same time magnificent examples of post-modern texts (*écriture*) rooted in the poetics of Mallarmé. Jacques Derrida has alluded to this in his remark "Edmond Jabès, as everyone knows, is not a Jew." Modern poetry lends itself only in rare and exceptional cases to intensely religious experience. We find occasional examples of it, however, in the works of a few Jewish poets who wrote in German in the years of Nazi persecution and of the Holocaust: in some of the poems of Nelly Sachs, for instance, and in Friedrich Torberg's *Amalek.* Because French-speaking Jews are numerically so few when one compares their numbers with those of French-speaking Christians, Jabès appears to be an almost unexplainable, if not miraculous, literary phenomenon, especially if one considers that he originally made his appearance on the French literary scene, some four decades ago, on the periphery of the outspokenly antireligious French Surrealist movement.

But the puzzling case of Edmond Jabès becomes more understandable, however, if one examines it against his Egyptian-Jewish rather than French-Jewish social background. Among upper-class French-speaking Sephardim of Egypt and of other areas of the eastern Mediterranean, a powerful undercurrent of Kabbalist or Messianic mysticism appears to have survived ever since the days of the false Messiah Shabbetai Tzvi and in spite of all nineteenth-century attempts to smother or eradicate it by importing educational disciplines of French rationalism or positivism. A native of the Greek island of Cephalonia, the French novelist Albert Cohen thus wrote and published, between the First and the Second World War, several novels in which Messianic and Kabbalist elements are interwoven in picaresque plots that remain typically Sephardic, if not unconsciously Spanish. From Egypt, the philosopher Carlo Suares likewise developed over the years, in a series of books written in French, a profoundly original if somewhat heretical system of neo-Kabbalist thought. The work of Edmond Jabès can indeed be best interpreted in terms of this Sephardic-Jewish context of the eastern Mediterranean that has enriched French literature. From this whole area that was once part of the great

Ottoman Empire, most of the more educated Jews have faced, since the beginning of our century, a drastic linguistic choice, if they wished to be writers and to find sympathetic and appreciative readers.

No Egyptian, Lebanese, or Syrian Jews are known to have achieved, as indeed some Jews of Iraq have done, any prominence as poets in Arabic. The Arabic-Jewish poets of Iraq have moreover all emigrated to Israel, where as fine an Arabic poet as Shmuel Moreh now finds it increasingly difficult to publish his work except occasionally in Palestinian newspapers and periodicals which do not enjoy, throughout the Arabic world, the same prestige as the literary periodicals of Lebanon, Syria, Egypt, or Iraq. Only two Turkish-Jewish poets who write in Turkish, Musa Moris Farhi and Jozef Habib Gerez, have been brought to the editors' attention: their almost epigrammatical poetry is typical of the literary movement which, headed by such Turkish poets as Orhan Veli Kanik in the years that immediately followed Mustafa Kemal Ataturk's reform of the Turkish language, sought to liberate Turkish prose and poetry from the servitudes of classical Turkish, which could be understood only by a small traditionalist elite. They therefore limited the idiom of contemporary Turkish literature to the ordinary spoken Turkish of the man in the street.

From most of these areas of the eastern Mediterranean and the Near and Middle East, the few known Jewish novelists and poets of our age have generally written in French, with the exception of a few Arabic-Jewish poets from Iraq, the handful of Turkish-Jewish poets, and a couple of Greek-Jewish poets, among whom Joseph Eliyia remains the most outstanding, who have chosen to write in modern Greek. Others who are natives of these areas and have emigrated to Israel are of course now writing in Hebrew, while a very few still write poetry in the Judeo-Spanish dialect that is commonly known as Ladino or Judezmo.

5. *Poetry in the Jewish Dialects of the Diaspora*

Until the Alliance Israélite Universelle, a Paris-based French-Jewish cultural foundation, established its schools for Jewish children, in the second half of the nineteenth century and the early decades of our century, in many of the major cities of Arab North Africa, the Balkans, Egypt, and the Ottoman Empire, most of the Jews of these areas could read or write only a local vernacular of their own. In a few areas of northern Greece, this vernacular was Judeo-Greek. In most other areas of Greece, of the Balkans and the coastal regions of the Eastern Mediterranean, the vernacular of the local Jews was the Judeo-Spanish which is generally known as Ladino or Judezmo. In the coastal cities of Morocco, many of the Jews spoke a somewhat different dialect of Judeo-Spanish that was locally known in Arabic as Haketiyeh; elsewhere in the interior of Morocco, they spoke Judeo-Arabic and, farther south, a Judeo-Berber dialect. In Syria, Lebanon, Iraq, and the interior of Egypt, they spoke various other Judeo-Arabic dialects. Farther east, in the mountains of Kurdistan, many Jews still spoke Aramaic; in Iran, they spoke a Judeo-Persian dialect and, in India, Judeo-Mahrati or else Judeo-Malayalam. In some areas of the Soviet Caucasus, the Jews speak Judeo-Georgian or else Judeo-Daghestani, while the Karaitic Jews who lived in the Crimea until Stalin deported them to Siberia speak a Judeo-Tartar dialect, and the Jews of Soviet Bokhara speak a Judeo-Persian dialect of their own.

Because most of the Jewish vernaculars have never been taught to any appreciable extent in schools even at the primary level, they have generally failed to develop any literature in the modern sense. Anonymous folk poetry continues, however, to be produced in many of these dialects, but we are concerned here with poetry of the kind that the Italian philosopher Benedetto Croce once defined as *poesia d'arte* in order to distinguish it from folk poetry, which he called *poesia popolare.* Jewish folk poetry composed in all these various dialects that have still been spoken by Jews in our age might well constitute the subject of a very different anthology from the present one. It has nevertheless been decided to include, in the present anthology, a few samples of the poetry of a number of poets who have written in our age in two of these dialects, the Judeo-Spanish or Ladino or Judezmo of the Near East, and the Judeo-Romanesque dialect of the Italian Jews of the ghetto of Rome. The poets selected to represent these two vernaculars here are, moreover, not, like most folk poets, anonymous.

Isaac de Botton and Clarisse Nicoïdski thus chose to continue writing in their increasingly rare and almost obsolete Judezmo, as the modern spoken form of Ladino is known, and their poetry remains for this reason more closely allied to the traditional and anonymous Sephardic-Jewish poetry of their immediate sociocultural Judeo-Spanish background than to the more consciously modern and literary poetry now written by Jewish poets in most other languages. In this respect, these two Judeo-Spanish poets offer us here an interesting Sephardic analogue to the more popular Yiddish poetry of some Ashkenazi Jewish poets of Eastern European origin.

Jewish poets from many of these regions of the Near and Middle East who were unwilling to accept the limitations inevitably imposed on them if they continued to write in their traditional vernacular generally had to make a linguistic choice. In Iraq, some Jewish poets thus chose to write in literary Arabic; in Turkey, we have seen, a few Jewish poets chose to write in Turkish. Because in many Islamic nations such as Egypt, Syria, and Lebanon, the more educated Jews had generally attended foreign schools, those among them who became poets chose later to write in the foreign language of their education—above all, until relatively recently, in French. This was also true of most Jews of Greece who came from Salonica and the cities of Thrace which, until 1912, remained a part of the Ottoman Empire. Only after 1912 did the majority of the Jews of Greece begin to attend Greek schools, so that the poet Joseph Eliyia, a Jew who had already achieved, some decades ago, considerable prominence as a pioneer of modern Greek poetry, remains a truly exceptional figure in his age and generation.

6. *Judeo-Romanesque Dialect Poetry*

The presence, among the many poets represented in this anthology, of the Judeo-Romanesque dialect poet Crescenzo del Monte may well deserve some more ample introductory comment. The literature of Italy, like that of England, Germany, and some other linguistic areas, can boast of a number of eminent Pre-Romantic or Romantic poets who, like Robert Burns in a Lowland Scottish dialect of English or our own James Whitcomb Riley in Hoosier American, chose to express themselves in a regional dialect rather than in the traditional literary language of the Establishment. The Italian poet Carlo Porta thus chose to write in Milanese, while Gioachino Belli and Trilussa achieved eminence as poets in the dialect of Rome and others in the dialect of Naples or of Sicily. But no major poet writing in any dialect of English happened to be a Jew, and the same can be said of German dialect poets, if one excepts Yiddish as a dialect of German and, of course, Heinrich Heine on the grounds that he appears to have spoken German with the Rhineland accent of his native Düsseldorf since he occasionally rhymes words, such as *Zeiten* and *bedeuten,* which can rhyme only when pronounced with a distinctly Rhineland accent.

Satirical poetry written, often anonymously, in the dialect of Rome had long been, when the city was still ruled by the Pope as the capital of the Papal States, of considerable sociopolitical importance, especially in the last decades of the eighteenth century and during the first half of the nineteenth century, when the authority of the Pope as a temporal ruler was sometimes very precarious and his government was proving to be increasingly inefficient and corrupt. Originally attributed to Pasquino, a somewhat legendary tailor or barber in Renaissance Rome, and composed for generations anonymously and most often in a kind of dog Latin, the earlier poems of this kind came to be known as pasquinades, but began to be written more and more frequently in the Italian dialect of Rome in the eighteenth century and above all in the sonnet form which Belli later used so effectively.

The critic Emilio del Carro has ably traced the development of this tradition of Italo-Romanesque satirical poetry and stressed its political significance as an expression of local patriotism, but also of xenophobia whenever the Papal States were invaded by a foreign power, and of loyalty to the reactionary papal regime when it was restored. Del Carro points out that this kind of poetry, throughout the late eighteenth century and the first half of the nineteenth, was generally conservative in its politics and opposed, for instance, to French military or political intervention, during the years of the French Revolution and of the Napoleonic Wars, when French troops on several occasions occupied Rome. Anti-Jacobin and sometimes even violently anti-Semitic, because the French freed the Jews of the ghetto of Rome from their traditional restrictions and humiliations under Papal rule, this anonymous satirical poetry, after the fall of the short-lived Roman Republic in 1799, after the defeat of Napoleon a few years later and again after the failure of the 1848 Revolution, often adopted the Judeo-Romanesque dialect of the Jews of the Roman ghetto in order to humiliate them in their own terms, much as the Nazi journalists of Julius Streicher's infamous *Der Sturmer* later used Yiddish words to rouse the German rabble against the Jews in the early years of Hitler's campaign and of his accession to power.

In twentieth-century Rome, Crescenzo del Monte appears to have come forth, perhaps somewhat belatedly, as the poetical spokesman, in the Italo-Romanesque dialect of Rome's ghetto, for the city's Jews who claim traditionally to have been there "since the days of the Caesars." His poetry thus offers us a Jewish variant of the sonnets of an earlier generation which had used derisively, for anti-Semitic purposes, the same Judeo-Romanesque dialect as he.

7. *The Diversity of the Diaspora*

In spite of all the anti-Semitic propaganda of the Soviet regime, few contemporary literatures can boast of a more important and creative contribution of Jewish poets than that of Russia. The most famous of all modern Russian poets of Jewish origin was certainly Boris Pasternak. Pasternak refrained from publishing anything that might overtly distinguish him as a Jew among his Russian peers. It might well be argued that Osip Mandelstam likewise generally refrained from any overt expression of awareness of being a Jew in his writings, except that the very nature of his dissidence and the persecutions that he suffered under the Stalinist regime mark him as a true poet of the kind that the Russian poetess Tsvetayeva had in mind when she stated that "all poets are Jews."

The majority of the Russian-Jewish poets of the older generation who chose to write in Russian rather than in Yiddish or Hebrew were indeed cultural assimilationists and, whether they remained in Soviet

Russia like Pasternak, Mandelstam, and Ehrenburg or went into exile like Khodasievitch, seem to have refrained in general from handling specifically Jewish themes in their poetry or from expressing overtly Jewish sentiments or beliefs. Their poetry therefore tended to be extremely personal and inventive, in the same generally avant-garde manner, with all its variations of schools, esthetics, and poetics, as that of other Russian poets who were not Jews, such as Akhmatova.

It would be wrong, nevertheless, to believe that all Russian Jews who wrote and published poetry in the Leninist or the Stalinist era were persecuted. Some of them, even among those who wrote in Yiddish, managed to remain, like Ehrenburg, on good terms with the Communist regime, though often at the cost of many denials and betrayals. Only in recent years, and above all in the clandestine publications of the so-called *samizdat* or underground press, do we now discover more and more Russian poetry that is quite overtly written, though anonymously, by Jews and on Jewish themes.

Few European nations have produced a greater number and a broader variety of important and gifted modernist Jewish poets than Romania, though many of these poets wrote in other languages than Romanian. Tristan Tzara, one of the founders of Dadaism, thus wrote most of his poetry, except for some early work, in French. Paul Celan likewise wrote all his known work in German. Other Romanian-Jewish poets have written in Hungarian, Yiddish, or Hebrew. Others again, like Benjamin Fondane, Ilarie Voronca, and Marcel Blecher, have written poetry both in Romanian and in French. Though Voronca remains above all an important Romanian poet and Blecher's most significant works are those that he wrote in prose in Romanian, Fondane, who was deported by the Nazis from France and died in a concentration camp, stands out quite exceptionally as both an outstanding Romanian Expressionist poet and literary critic and an equally significant French Post-Surrealist poet and, in his French critical writings, a precursor of Sartre and the postwar French Existentialist writers.

The kind of linguistic diversity that characterizes the Jewish poets of Poland, as we have already seen, and also of Romania, where many a poet was faced with a choice between at least two languages in which to write, now appears to have been peculiar, in a more liberal era, to all those areas that spread between Germany or Austria, as defined by their present frontiers, and Russia proper in the east or, toward the south beyond the Balkans, Greece and Turkey. These areas have long been inhabited by a great number and variety of ethnic and linguistic groups with which local Jewish communities, whose own language may well have been Yiddish in Eastern Europe or Judeo-Spanish in the Balkans, have maintained through the centuries very close economic and other contacts. Throughout the more liberal nineteenth century and the early decades of the twentieth, these contacts often tended, especially in the more urban centers, to adopt an increasingly assimilationist nature, at least in terms of language and general culture, so that many talented Jewish writers could choose to express themselves in a language other than that which had long been traditional in their own community.

Only two of the three former Baltic republics, Lithuania and Latvia, had important Jewish communities, while the third, Estonia, like Finland and the three Scandinavian nations, Sweden, Norway and Denmark, have never been areas where large Jewish communities have settled. In Lithuania and Latvia, Yiddish continued, until the years of the Holocaust, to be the national language of the Jewish masses, and the idiom of expression of their poets, although a few upper-class urban Jews, especially from Lithuania, chose to express themselves as writers in Russian, Polish, or German. No outstanding Jewish poets who may have written in Lithuanian, Latvian, Estonian, or Finnish have thus been brought to the editors' attention for inclusion in the present anthology.

Although Scandinavian Jews, such as the Swedish painters Ernst Josephson and Isaac Grunewald, have achieved considerable distinction as leaders in the arts, except for Oscar Levertin, no important Jewish poets yet seem to have written in Swedish, Norwegian, or Danish.

Cultural anthropologists have long ago studied the peculiar ethnic and religious stratification that traditionally distinguished the population of Hungary and of those areas of Yugoslavia and Romania, such as Croatia, the Voivodina, the Banat, and Transylvania, which long remained under Hungarian rule. Hungarian Jews and those of neighboring Hungarian-dominated areas tended, moreover, to be divided in their linguistic loyalties, even in Budapest, where many of them were basically German-speaking, while others, even in the distant marches of Croatia and other peripheral provinces, remained staunchly Hungarian-speaking. The passionate devotion of the latter to the Hungarian language, and to the cause, especially after 1848, of liberal Hungarian nationalism, explains the remarkable number of important Hungarian-Jewish poets and the significance of the contribution of some of the best among them, such as Miklós Radnóti, to contemporary Hungarian literature.

Whereas the Jews of Hungary were very numerous before the years of the Holocaust, those of Italy have long been few and have tended to be scattered, except in Milan and the old ghetto of Rome, in a number of relatively small but ancient communities which, since the middle of the nineteenth century, have generally followed strong assimilationist trends. The number of really important Italian-Jewish poets, such as Umberto

Saba and Primo Levi, is therefore all the more surprising, though it will appear less surprising if one also considers the even more remarkable number of outstanding contemporary Italian-Jewish novelists, which includes bestselling Alberto Moravia, Carlo Levi, Giorgi Bassani, and Natalia Ginzburg as well as Italo Svevo, who ranks with Joyce, Proust, and Musil among the most important pioneers in the field of the modern psychological novel.

A Triestine Jew like Italo Svevo, Umberto Saba is already recognized as one of the few truly important Italian writers of his generation. Unlike Montale, who has often been thought to be a Jew because of the frequency of crypto-Jewish themes in his poetry, Umberto Saba has but rarely expressed in his poems any very overt awareness of his intrinsic *judéité.* Though Giorgio Bassani acquired international fame as the author of the best-selling novel *The Garden of the Finzi-Contini,* which handles with great success a very moving Jewish theme, one finds little overt awareness of Jewish themes or problems in his few poems. Primo Levi, on the other hand, is an industrial chemist who never set out to be a poet or even a writer. Deported to Auschwitz by the Fascists and their Nazi allies, he survived the Holocaust almost miraculously and then wrote two remarkable prose accounts of all that he had witnessed. In addition, he has now written and published a few poems which should be counted among the very finest examples, in any language, of the testimony of a survivor of death camps. Primo Levi's Italian poetry and prose acquire moreover an additional impact, in their original Italian text, from his great familiarity with the language and imagery of Dante's *Divine Comedy.* In the eyes of Italian readers, who are at all familiar with their great national classic, Levi's descriptions of the real-life inferno that he has witnessed acquire a special significance from their similarity with Dante's allegorical inferno.

The Spanish-language poets included in the present anthology are all Latin Americans of Eastern European Jewish origin; most of them come from families that have settled relatively recently in Latin America, where Argentina and Brazil now have the largest Jewish communities. No particularly significant Brazilian-Jewish poets appear to have yet expressed themselves in Portuguese, but Argentinian-Jewish writers are already fairly numerous. In the poetry of Isaac Goldemberg, among others, we discover a very curious synthesis of Latin American Post-Surrealism and of the sense of the absurd that distinguishes some of the finest contemporary Yiddish writing. Goldemberg's poem "The Jews in Hell" is in this respect particularly significant. In the Cuban poet José Kozer's "Cleaning Day" we find a similar, though slightly different, synthesis of these two widely divergent literary and cultural traditions.

Around the turn of the century, the Dreyfus affair revealed to the

Jews of France the real danger of the powerfully anti-Semitic forces that were still latent in some sections of the French people. It was then that the poet Gustave Kahn became more overtly conscious of his own Jewish heritage and that a group of younger poets, Henri Franck, Edmond Fleg, and André Spire, began to attract attention by handling Jewish themes more frequently in their poetry. The poetry of Edmond Fleg, which consisted to a great extent of rather free French adaptations of traditional biblical or liturgical texts, soon enjoyed a kind of official status in the eyes of the French rabbinate and of all the more conservative leaders of the French-Jewish community. Of these three poets, only André Spire obtained recognition as a major poet among non-Jewish French readers as well.

At his best, Spire proves to have been both a kind of Robert Frost of the French countryside and a Whitman of traditional French liberalism as well as of Judaism, always advocating or illustrating in his poetry a return to simpler ways of life and to less sophisticated and more reasonable habits of thought and action, in fact an abandonment of the more recondite letter of Judaism in favor of its essential spirit and ethical content. As a Frenchman, he remained uncompromisingly faithful to the democratic principles of the French Revolution, always distrustful of the power of riches and emotionally attached, with an almost Romantic and pre-Marxist socialism, to the cause of the working class. As a Jew, though himself a perfect example of apparent assimilation to French culture, he repudiated both the pretenses of middle-class assimilationism and the institutionalized self-righteousness of organized religion. In an age of intellectualism, however confused or superficial, he remained an unhesitating believer in the "simple truths" of the eighteenth century's enlightened cult of reason, freedom, and nature.

Among living French poets who are of Jewish origin, Claude Vigée and Edmond Jabès now stand out as quite exceptional examples of a profound concern, in much of their poetry, with their intrinsic identity as Jews. Their poetry nevertheless remains of a kind that is generally recognized, by discriminating Gentile readers, as having a significance that transcends the possible limitations of a more strictly Jewish context. Only Paul Celan and Nelly Sachs, as German poets, have achieved since 1945, in all of Western Europe, this kind of distinction and more general appeal.

Edouard Roditi was born in Paris in 1910. He came to the United States in 1924 and studied at the University of Chicago and the University of California at Berkeley. He returned in 1946 to Europe, where he works as a free-lance multilingual interpreter. He has published several books of poetry as well as works of literary criticism and art history.

AMHARIC

Yosef Damana ben Yeshaq

Yosef Damana ben Yeshaq is a Falasha Jew who was born in Lasta, Ayna Bugna, Ethiopia. He now lives in Jerusalem.

The Rusted Chain

My history crucified, buried under the muddy flood of time,
I, rusting in the island of sufferers,
My ancestry, my heritage to many a bookball game.
Who am I? What am I?
Speak my people of yonderland, House of Israel,
Of ruined history, of identity stolen,
Switch off your silence.

Sweet land, mother of my forefathers,
You spewed me out, you anathematized me,
From highland to lowland, from lowland to highland; So I wander,
"Falasha" . . . you disdain me, you accuse me, my cousin,
You pronounce me guilty for fashioning with my hands,
Ere, is it sinful to earn one's bread?
Speak my people of yonderland, House of Israel.

Ah, worse the deception that ends in false hopes,
To kiss the earth of your Orit, the land of your childhood dreams,
Only to be smeared with dust by the long-sought-for kin,
Grudgingly welcomed with a stinging, wet humility.
The rejected do also reject, the humiliated do humiliate,
They ask "Are you Jewish too?," tearing at my identity through my
tired ears.
When moved by compassion some do concede "Perhaps you are of
the Ten Tribes,"
Of Dan, of Asher, of Gad, of Yosef,
Or even maybe of Moses drowned or lost ones,
From the bottom of the Red Sea or the Desert.
All these speculations!
Is it my blackness or Africa's dazzling light that puzzles them?

OTHER LANGUAGES

Speak my people of yonderland, House of Israel.
Can your Orit defend you? Can your temple rebuild you?
Can your Segd raise you up? Or your Sabbaths return your joy and peace?
Can your bellows talk? Can your washing cleanse you?
Your God has become a heretic.
Wake up rusting chain, Speak people of yonderland!

Translated by Ephraim Isaac

ARABIC

Shalom Katav

Shalom Katav was born in Baghdad in 1931. He began publishing prose poetry when he was only sixteen. His first book, of prose poetry, was The Pageant of Deprivation. *He emigrated to Israel in 1950 and subsequently published three additional books of poetry in Arabic, including* Whispers of Dawn.

Pleading Voices

"This is the hand of all mankind, stretched out towards
a fate darkened by battle and warfare—and these
are its cries—reverberating, demanding its share
in life—in a calm and peaceful life—for that is
the right of every man living on the face of this earth."

Hands upon hands
Stretching, stretching,
Pushed back by a
mysterious destiny.
Where is stillness? Where is stillness?
And welcome peace
In a raging world?

Over the hovels of the destitute
Over the palace of the prince
Delirious black clouds
Flow endlessly on.
What is the end to be? What the end?
While the hand moves
Accompanying great leaders
Where is conscience? Where is conscience?
Mankind screams
From its very marrow
Cries endlessly for help.

Let the birds fly
Let compassionate mothers
Quieten the suckling child.
Let the vast universe
Live in peace.

Let us live
Let all people live
In peace . . .
Peace.

Translated by Yoffee Berkovitz

Shmuel Moreh

Shmuel Moreh was born in Baghdad in 1933. He emigrated to Israel in 1951 and completed his studies at Hebrew University in Jerusalem. In 1962 he joined the University of London. Since 1966 he has taught at Hebrew University. He has published several studies of modern Arabic poetry and has published his own Arabic-language poems in various newspapers and journals.

The Tree of Hatred

The thorn tree, pale and sharp,
In the wild blazing desert,
Sending its roots to the bottom
Of the dark deep pit,
Black water, skulls and bones,
Nourish it in the deep darkness.
All the ten plagues of Moses
Cannot uproot its stubborn cling.
The yellow tree of evil,
Each thorn is a glowing eye,
Nailing all the bare hands,
Piercing the heart of the nightingales.
Only bones and blood can nourish
The thorn tree in the desert.

The eyes of Pharaoh, glowing with hatred,
Chasing the Chosen Seed;
The eyes of the expelled Hagar,
Which glowed with revenge and despair,
Weeping in pain for the thirsty child,
Blended in a look of revenge,
In Cain thirsty eyes for blood,
Standing on the frontiers to greet his brother
With his loaded machinegun.

Upon the thorn tree,
In the blazing wild desert,
No place for a nest of olive leaves,
For the tired dove to rest.
Upon the thorn tree,
No nightingale can sing.
The blood of his heart
Will be the cost of his song,
From the thorn tree of hatred,
Rooted deep in the hearts of millions.

Translated by the author

Melody

to B. K. Zahra

Oh, my wandering melody
Shimmering in the shadows of my life,
I feel it in my blood.
In the chords of my heart.
It chants, it springs.
Why am I so tortured?
Is it because I don't know
How to write your notes?

Oh my immortal melody
And, oh, the ode of my life.
I read it in your lips.
And in the flash of your eyes,
And on your cheeks
And in the flashes of pain
I suffer.
Oh melody of my life
How can your notes be fixed?

Zahra—you are the melody of my life,
Ablaze with magic.
I hear it, a hymn to resurrection
Flowing through the deserts of my hope.
It sows life in the path
Of my desperation, my life,
It awakens memories of youth
In my spirit,
Of a past life
When we were lovers,
Memories of passion and torture

Promises of meetings, recriminations
My song is confusion
But I returned,
Not even knowing
How your notes are written.

Zahra, you are
The melody of happy youth.
Zahra, oh poem of life
I read it in your features.
Its notes are magic,
Its melodies secret,
But I don't know
How to fix
Its notes.

Oh my wandering melody,
I would wish you free,
Free of fetters,
Free of chains,
Free and soaring.
Your notes are resurrection
Ever renewed,
Perplexing song
Impossible to write.

The Return

to my father, God rest his soul

My father returned
His face shone with holiness
My father returned
And when he returned
The shadows crouching in our house dissolved
He returned and every mouth was singing
He returned and happiness once again
Inhabited our dwelling
He returned, the whole world smiled
And even the sorrow
Which for decades had lodged
In my mother's brow
Began to melt.

The prophet of the Return came back
The return they had announced
For so long
Spoken of
For so long:
"The day will come
When we will return
To our father's land
We live in the land of exile, of darkness
But soon we will return
To the Land of Light
To Jerusalem
On eagles' wings . . ."
The hope we have lived for
The living hope
Has finally reached us
Through hundreds of years
A hope stronger than death
More forceful than the oppressor's whip
Tomorrow we will return
Most surely we will return
And though each day
Has its own tomorrow
And though time drags out
Still Jerusalem is the appointed place.

But now he has returned
From the land of gold and darkness
His eyes are joy incarnate
He bears the hopes of his fathers
They have, like him, continued to dream
Of the Land of Light
And the eagles' wings.

The prophet of the Return has come back
And stands on the threshold of the house
Like a human angel
Strong, vanquishing time
Giant, conquering years
No greyness masks his temples
In spite of his fifty odd years
The darkness in our house scatters
And even the door laughs

And even the walls
Even the sorrow lodged in my mother's brow
Laughs—even our tears laugh
The place is swimming with joy
And the holiness
Radiating from his head
Like the halo of light of . . .
Samuel.

Translated by Yoffee Berkovitz

David Semah

David Semah was born in 1933 in Baghdad. He emigrated to Israel in 1951 and studied at Hebrew University, where he received a degree in Arabic literature. He presently lectures in modern Arabic literature at Haifa University. He has published two books of critical essays and one volume of poems, Till Spring Comes.

Prostration

I went out alone to gather rocks
There on the sleeping hillside,
To weave an armor round my heart
And protect it from violent temptation,
I swore to spurn that beauty
If a day went by when
I were not it, nor it me,
But each free of the other.
And when the flowers' fragrance spreads,
And my ears play with the pigeons cooing,
And a spirit of beauty envelops the universe,
Gladdening the heart and quenching thirst,
Wonder grasps me, a deep, reverberating silence
Takes possession of me,
My heart is in ecstasy at such a vision,
And beauty almost prostrates itself.

Tomb

Youthful passion seeps through my mind
At the thought of you.
I caught its flame, kindled it,
Was near to revealing all
With its clarity.
I resisted, hid it,
Yet happiness, in spite of me, begged.
I reached for it, did not taste it;
I made as if to fetch a drink;
I filled my cup and smashed it.

It is time for you, my heart, to rest,
Run away from love to a safe place,
Shake off from you this ancient dust,
Forget your passions, do not dissuade me.

I am weary of what was: the intoxication of torture,
The flame of craving,
The shimmer of a mirage.
I shall pluck my love from my chest
And bury its memory under the ground.

Translated by Yoffee Berkovitz

Anwar Shaul

Anwar Shaul was born in 1904 in Iraq. He worked as a lawyer, wrote poetry and short stories, and translated European literature from French and English into Arabic. He emigrated to Israel in 1971, where he wrote his first poems in Hebrew. His books include The First Harvest *and* The Whispers of Time.

Mother

Mother, my eyes wait on you, unfulfilled.
My mouth has not obtained a kiss from you.
My life, since you have gone, has not mellowed,
And my heart, Mother, complains of sickness
And though my eyelids, from passion, have shed tears.
Yet at night my soul groans.

Oh Mother, who will listen to me, I wonder?

You burdened me with a compassionate heart,
Trembling at the slightest breath.
You burdened me with a free soul,
Unable to endure suffering,
A large soul, longing passionately
For the heights of the Most High.
O Mother, although you conceived me thus,
Yet the days have no mercy,
They stick relentlessly to their design.

How many noble ones have suffered this fate?
How many sinners tomorrow will give thanks?
For fate is forever at war with freedom,
And the comfort of freedom has become a privilege,
As if, its secret being revealed,
It has become both deaf and blind.

Oh Mother, is there anyone to plead on our behalf?

To a Cactus Seller

The cold stings your bare cheeks and arms.
The field is desolate, there is no companion
To relieve your sadness,
Only the birds circling and gliding through the sky.
If only they could crush your hurt with beak or claws
Or protect you with their eyes.

An icy gale is your raging companion,
Not the gentle east wind.
It whips through the plains, lashes the summits of hills.
It snakes through the morning cold like an adder,
Stings like a scorpion.
Look after your beauty, young woman,
Take care lest it fade.
Be compassionate,
Young woman of chapped hands.

Your back is bowed from the burden it bore;
Your neck bent, a witness to its shackles.
How can the heart take comfort from the illusions it cherished,
Or the mind from its hopes, how can its visions give joy?
As you stand there, staring.

The thorns, not delicate or gentle, draw blood from your hands.
Tomorrow will bring light, protecting others in the night.
They will be warm, you, shivering in the frosty night.
Your misery provides comfort to the fortunate,
Your affliction is others' delight.

Is this a drop of dew on the thorns,
Or a tear from your eye?
Is it a raging grief,
Or a faint light of hope that you hide?
I see you walking swiftly towards the town.
Beware of its glitter and tinsel;
In word or deed deception abounds
Do not believe your eyes.

Prayers to Liberty

To you, morning and evening,
I recount my prayers and implorings,
Inciting memories of happiness and sorrow.

> Open your ears—my freedom.
> Listen to my sad song.
> Without you my secret
> Would have remained hidden.

From the time that God commanded Adam,
Saying: do not eat the apple
While you are in Paradise,
Reaping bliss,
Man has hated to tie up his life
In the bonds of captivity,
For captivity is death.
So he praised you instead
In every land.

Where do you dwell? Within these palaces?
In the wilderness of the land?
The haughtiness of rocks?
Where is your dwelling place?
In the ocean bed?

Where have the hands of fate hidden you,
As they have hidden the most precious of pearls?
Where is your abode?
I do not know.

OTHER LANGUAGES

How can I love you?
With copious tears?
With the throb of a broken heart?
Or my song
Strong in love?
In my thoughts
When darkness pounces
Scattering its dreams
Among the sleeping?
How can I love you,
Confused as I am?

How can I reach you?
How can I attain your purity?
Through pride? or fame? or generosity?
Through silent truth?
Or through blood?

Or through entreaty, weakness, submission?
Through the rib-grilling fires of war?
How can I reach you—for I have lost patience.

How many imposters sing of their love for you,
While in their hearts they remain
Your greatest enemy!
They substitute wine for your blood.

Alas, my freedom, for this existence
Harbors too many envious men,
Too many spiteful ones,
Too many fools
Inflicting their views on men.

If your pastures are in the Near East,
Then come, revive our hearts.
Or are your fertile pastures in the West?
If so, then search out those lands, with your fragrance
Instill the spirit with peace . . . but, alas,
They are not to be found
Neither in East nor in West.

Translated by Yoffee Berkovitz

CZECH

Ludvik Askenazy

Ludvik Askenazy was born in Czechoslovakia in 1921. He is the author of political prose, short stories, plays and poetry.

The Wall

More than 77,000 Czech and Slovak Jews died at the hands of the Nazis during World War II. Their names are inscribed on a wall in one of the oldest synagogues in the world.

In a place of worship I know, they made a strange mosaic
of letters, numbers and symbols.
It was a mosaic of first names and last names,
of Adams, Barbaras, Caris, Davids,
of Emils, Rosies, Josephs, Sues;
in short, of Jews.
They all had a single gravestone in common,
cool, smooth, scrolled with delicate veins.
Not a single name had a flower,
no little willows wept there,
no one walked the paths with a
sprinkling can—why sprinkle carved letters?
Several times, a lady came
and searched the wall for her name.
We told her,
"Lady, this must be some mistake,
you're alive.
Look, lady,
you've got turnips in your basket."
But she kept right on looking
for her name on the wall, with a tiny,
almost childish index finger.
"I must be here," she said,
"somewhere
between John and Joseph."

Translator unknown

Otakar Fischer

Otakar Fischer was born in 1883 into an assimilated Jewish family in Kolin and became professor of German literature at Prague's Czech University. He edited two literary reviews and served as director of the Prague National Theater. He translated the poet André Spire into Czech. His outstanding translation from German literature is his version of Goethe's Faust. *He also translated Heine, Kleist, Nietsche, Schiller, and many other authors. His best-known collection of poems is* Voices, *published in 1923. Fischer died in 1938.*

From the Depths

I cannot acclaim you,
You hostile stars,
Under the tent of the sorrowing heavens
Which blaze in silvery array;
Unto you, that amid the abyss of my spirit
Have hurled the torch of dreams,
Invisible I call,
I, whirling atom of dust.

Wherefore,
O wherefore after a day stifling and laden
With fugitive pondering
Did you kindle in my senses
Outcry of yearning for the endless
And terror of my very self?
I was as a thirsty acre
Which placid, meekly awaits
Moisture of coming days:
I lived, a man amid mortals,
Unaware that he moves in the universe
Towards unending change.
Now across the furrows of my acre
A fire is wafted, and my heart,
My mortal heart is enkindled,
Death am I now, and life and belief and rapture—

Now from unfathomable distances
God's shadow has fallen on me.

Translator unknown

Pavel Friedmann

Pavel Friedmann was a Czech victim of the Holocaust. His poems were written in concentration camps. He died in Auschwitz at the age of twenty-one.

The Butterfly

He was the last. Truly the last.
Such yellowness was bitter and blinding
Like the sun's tear shattered on stone.
That was his true color.
And how easily he climbed, and how high.
Certainly, climbing, he wanted
To kiss the last of my world.

I have been here seven weeks.
Ghettoized.
Who loved me have found me,
Daisies call to me,
And the branches also of the white chestnut in the yard.
But I haven't seen a butterfly here.
That last one was the last one.
There are no butterflies, here, in the ghetto.

Translated by Dennis Silk

Jiri Gold

Jiri Gold was born in Ostrava in 1936. His two volumes of poetry are Bright Green Sky *and* Minotaur.

In the Cellars

Life in the cellars
affords many discomforts

But since our fathers and
our fathers' fathers
built their homes in them
we live here too
and multiply and work

OTHER LANGUAGES

And we dream

Like our fathers and our fathers'
fathers we know that only the dream
gives meaning to our work
our multiplying our life We dream
of lofts

Of wondrous
arid wooden lofts
where the sun blinds
and we choke on the hot
quivering air

Of such lofts we sing
to our children

The story goes that one rainy summer
when the damp cellars were flooded
the fathers left their century-old homes
to set off
after their dream

When they had struck down the guards
on the marble stairs
they rushed helter-skelter up
to the lofts

They broke down the door
breathed in the musty air
and knelt

They knelt and it seemed to them—

They were in the loft

Then one toothless elder exclaimed:
Blessed be this day my brothers but surely this is only the
ante-loft of the wondrous arid lofts that our children
must win blessed be it I say but will you forsake
forever the bones of your ancestors?

With bowed heads
they descended the marble staircase down
down down
to the cellars

Because only here
is it possible to give oneself up to the dream
of wondrous
arid lofts
where the sun blinds
and we choke on the hot
quivering air

An Inhabited Emptiness

Only totems protrude
from the debris and burnt out places
Only boldly carved
blazing with colors
totems

Some corpses are rotting
in the grass but
no matter Holes
in stone are already
overgrown with moss and the fires
have long since been put out
by the rains

And anyway
something is happening all the time
and totems
jut out into the empty sky
And actually there is an emptiness here
Emptiness after something Emptiness
before something

And wooden pillars
are wooden conceptions
of a wooden world

to float through
the deluge

Translated by Jaroslav Kotan and Daniel Weissbort

František Gottlieb

František Gottlieb was born in Klatovy, Czechoslovakia in 1903. He was an early Zionist and made Jewish nationalism the basis of his first book of poems, The Way to Canaan. *He lived for a time in Palestine but returned to Prague during World War II. Gottlieb is the author of several books of poetry and short stories.*

Between Life and Death

The first star shot up
and your death
returns from night
into memory.

How many days
wore a veil of mourning?
How many nights
saw a flash of hope?

Time between us
has not reached equilibrium,
I still seek the fountain
with your wisdom's imprint.

You are silent,
only the days
count the milestones
of our meeting.

Just a While

Somewhere we should sit down and rest
like runners after victory or defeat!
We're no longer able, in our hurry, to tell
when we overtake,
when we fall behind.

Somewhere we should sit down and wait
for the pointer inside us to come to rest.
For a while sit down at the table:
window lit into darkness—
under the light of the family circle.

Translated by Ewald Osers

Dagmar Hilarová

Dagmar Hilarová was born in Czechoslovakia in 1928. Some of her poetry has been translated into Hebrew.

Questions

Where was I at the hour of sowing
I—a grief-stricken sleeper?
I missed my chance of
germinating.
Is my lethargic sleep at an end?
Was I not exterminated,
crushed,
cast to the winds?
Interrogated by my own conscience?

My mirror shows me no reflection.

Stripped of vulnerability
I cannot convince myself.
I cannot prove I am I even by waking.
Nothing of this world belongs to me
any more

Translated by Ewald Osers

OTHER LANGUAGES

DUTCH

Jakov de Haan

Jakov de Haan was born in Holland in 1881. He was raised in a strictly Orthodox family, a background he rejected as a student of law in Amsterdam. After a period as socialist and anarchist, he returned to the Orthodoxy of his youth. He was assassinated in Jerusalem in 1924 for his political activities. He was a poet, novelist, and political essayist.

Unity

When God's holy law is read out
Do you think I forget one bold lust?
And enjoying each lust with fearing,
Do you think I know not God's law?

All is God's

Man has separated lust and sorrow.
But God holds them together like day and night.
I know lust. I know intense suffering.
I praise God's one name.

God's Gifts

My most pious songs have I written
On rising from my sinful bed.
God has given me a wealth of sins,
And God alone has saved me from my sins.

Hanukah

And if you would ask me "Where do you find your songs
Celebrating with joy or sobbing with sorrow"
Then shall I answer "Not in hate, nor in longing
But in listening to the silence in your heart
And in waiting like the late winter nights,
Before the sun breaks through the dense clouds.
And in waiting like the white candles wait
On the chandelier before a lad lights them."
And this evening, as your lights were burning,
How much my heart reflected its sorrowful lot

All the ways of my joy and of my shame.
Everything: my love, my hate, my mockery,
My songs I place in God's holy hands:
"The voice of the poet is the voice of God."

Sabbath

How wonderful you were, so pious and holy,
In the flowering years of my youth,
No day gave us more pious joy,
Happy dedication, undisturbed and safe.
So shamefully I have mutilated your beauty,
Jeered at your holiness, reviled your dedication.
And yet: You return, marvel without hatred,
And heal with love my searing wounds.
They are many with whom I laughingly shared
The days and nights of my youth,
Like sparkling wine, I poured out my joys.
And now; as I gambled away youth and beauty,
Who remembers my grim fate?
Not one of the many, but you, Sabbath, alone.

Translated by David Soetendorp

Judith Herzberg

Judith Herzberg was born in Amsterdam in 1934. She has published five volumes of poetry, including Beemdgras *and* 27 Liefdesliendjes, *an adaptation of the* Song of Songs, *plays for stage and television and filmscripts.*

On the Death of Sylvia Plath

We stand naked behind the line
those in front try to hide
those in back press forward.

They're bickering over us
the frightened ones have most to fear
nobody knows what he is chosen for.

I've heard the bad news
having saved my own skin miraculously
I'm mourning now for my sister.

Mene tekel is a beast
an ant a crab and crawls with black
claws from the cinders onto the hot tracks.

OTHER LANGUAGES

Consolation for the roofless never
comes in the form of houses but
from the mouths of nomads.

For the astonished child
space does not
turn inside out.

It must find refuge with the wolves
if such motherly wolves
still exist.

Yiddish

My father sang the songs
his mother used to sing,
to me, who half understood.

I sing the words again
nostalgia flutters in my throat
nostalgia for what is mine.

Sing to my children
what I myself don't grasp
so they may later, later?

We had to throw the flowers out.
We needed the water to drink.

Sad intimate language
I'm sorry that you withered
in this head.
It no longer needs you
but it misses you.

The Voice

Translated into language it is something like this:
a voice likeable as a saxophone
that comes leaping from a great distance
over mountains, over me
just like the voice of Solomon—
making me tremble like a bell tower
when the bells ring
"when we no longer do this
what will we do?" or like
the rib cage of a frightened dog.

A voice that says with jazz, with Solomon,
that we must either be on edge
or not at all, or not at all.

Commentaries on the Song of Songs

After Rabbi Akiba, Buxtorf, Herder,
mature men who are serious but dead,
who have paged through, consulted, held meetings,
read what they wished to see,
now it's me making my way
through the old books
(reading more leather-bound books
as my own death comes closer).
And I recognize, after Chateillon (1544),
Grotius (1644), Lightfoot, Lowth,
to my amazement Solomon.

Hello love from the middle
of a body and the middle of a life,
closely heard and closely spoken
breath felt and skins smelled;
we are still sailing under the same flag.

Kinneret

The water does not lie heavy and deep
but hangs like a mist between the hills
a safety net stretched to its limits
and hooked to a few points of light
visible here and there along the coasts.
A safety net for the stars?
Not one falls, the sky is solid enough
but there is much left to wish for
by this waiting and charged water
where peace was preached more often
than anywhere else
and conquerors
strong as tornadoes, left their
faith in the form of ruins. Gods
differ so. Even tonight
rifles take aim:
for each light there is another light
wanting to stifle it.

April, 1965

Nearer

To know there are rhododendrons on the slopes of the Himalayas
is not enough. To see a green beetle crawl
on a shiny leaf see it fall off
in the shadow underneath to recognize the color of the earth
not once or twice
but year after year, not on the slopes of the Himalayas
but here with this grass, this earth
and thus to know a small part of a larger
land, so huge it might be called motherland
mother Russia, mother Europe.
And winters, when the clouds stop
in front of the window, flashes of a precise longing,
leaves, each vein in them.
Later to be able to say: this is me,
I come from this part of the country—
instead of having only the trek
for a homeland like a nomad, only gravel
along the railway, a breath of scorched
earth for the smells of childhood, as stake
for a new start only the fact
that scorched earth can still be used.

Translated by Shirley Kaufman

Hanny Michaelis

Hanny Michaelis was born in 1922. Her first book of poems, Small Prelude, *appeared in 1949. She has since published* Water from the Rock, The Rock of Gibraltar, *and* Galloping Off to a New Utopia.

We Carry Eggshells

We carry eggshells filled
to the brim with tears
carefully through time.

In the mirrors of our eyes
the world rises inhospitably.
We have been everywhere
We return nowhere.

Laden with memories
we stoop towards the earth.
Ignorant and unwise
we wither away from the light
without a trace.

Under Restless Clouds

Under restless clouds
the wind slipped by
like an animal that has no hole.

You hid your face in my neck
as if all hope were lost
to find a hiding place for our felicity
which is unruly like the clouds
and as homeless as the wind.

Listening

Listening to the music
we used to hear together,
I tug at my grief
like a dog at his chain.

Violins and flutes
weave a silver web
across the abyss
until silence locks
me in again.

Under its frosted glass bell
the soundless battle
between expectation and despair
for the no man's land
of my existence
breaks out anew.

Translated by Marjolijn de Jager

Leo Vroman

Leo Vroman was born in Gouda in 1915. By profession he is a biologist. During the German invasion he fled to England and later to the Dutch East Indies. Since 1945 he has lived in New Jersey. Though most of his poetry is written in Dutch he also writes in English; the selection here is from recent English poems. His books include 126 Gedichten *(1964) and* Poems in English *(1953).*

Old Miniatures

A bundle of orange flames
stands in the upper sky.

Two deer, gold, black, shy,
play their bashful games.

Patterns of little flowers
melt and recrystallize

and in the distance rise
belled and bannered towers.

The deer had been trotting around.
Now they stand still and begin

to breathe from skin to skin;
feeling approaches sound.

Peace is here preserved
of sadly long ago;

peace, and even so
the black deer now has swerved.

And now there is gold on its horns,
gold splashes the leaves

and a trail of gold weaves
away under weeds and thorns.

The River

The mountain tips are white and dead.
The brown sky, bulging in between,
sags under steps of claws unseen
and rustles overhead.

A river comes around the bend,
stiff and a bottleglassgreen
with fishy bubbles, where fish have
been drawn to a drooly blend.

Tinkling strings of bottleglass air
sail deep and earnestly by,
and cracks like stars or twisted hair
where the water is too dry.

Next come the people, all afloat.
Where not embedded they live:
a back like the belly of a boat,
an embrace like a torsion sieve.

Cheeksome bodies, mumbleshaded,
warp away from draining thought;
eyes from which the pupils faded
marble visiontaut.

Here float the maidens in the dusk;
between their eyelids glimmer
little junglefilms, tusk, tusk,
dimmer and dimmer.

Their gentleness, of which too much
stains under them farewell
quilts the darkness into touch
and sleep of smell.

Hail pregnant women, dressed in gold
and stars of lionslaugh red,
inside out the orchids fold
when snails rush through their bed.

OTHER LANGUAGES

Tell this story to your child
while drifting towards the rocks,
and tell of me, who rode so wild
a perch with the whiting flocks

that I broke down on Deadman's Face,
smiling a rain of air;
while you ripple away in space
towards nowhere.

Tell of the fatsoflies that crawl
over the hills of Splatt,
where the butterfrogs fly; and when they fall . . .
No, don't tell them that.

A snake appears around the bend,
all mouth without a head;
and it shall never, never end
till I am dead.

FRENCH

Charles Dobzynski

Charles Dobzynski was born in Warsaw in 1929 but was brought to France in 1930. He is currently editor-in-chief of the journal Europe. *He is an editor and translator of Yiddish poetry, including the major anthology* Le Miroir d'un peuple *(1971). Among his twenty books of poetry and prose is* Un Cantique pour Masada, *from which the first three translations were made.*

Memory Air

In the beginning was the air   A table
  of dawn   that turns on its axis
to offer to each from South to North
  the same meal   the same rest
Its unleavened bread   palimpsest
  He who eats it is born anew
    in writing
The eye without respite   paternity of blue
  Matzoh of the azure   Abyss
by the opening midpoint   And from his mouth
  all words rain down
  The view is erased by being gulped
  The word is illumined by being killed
The table is set   Supper of Stars
For each sun a plate
For each memory a crumb of sky
  The air says: You are my host   My hostage
Witness my wedding   If you sit down
    before the table of my law
You become me   Now my bright countenance
    Now the dark side of my head
You breathe me   I inscribe you
    circular memory

Zealot Without a Face

Reb of ruins   My father   Ice-
    cutter in Lublin ghetto
    Zealot without a face

Reb of sands My father Wind-
peddler in the Vilna ghetto
Zealot without a face

Reb of dreams My father Poet
of Drancy the key word buried in the mud
Zealot without a face

Reb of rats My father Rebel
in the sewers of Warsaw dawn elapsed
Zealot without a face

Reb of Sabbaths My father Log fallen
from the beheaded tree Babi-Yar
Zealot without a face

Reb of pennies My father Violinist
string torn from the grass at Auschwitz
Zealot without a face

Reb of ashes Gold-washer My father
of a book without shape or meaning
the lips' gold turned to candle grease
Zealot without a face

My father Reb of all that begins
Mute commentary Cracked
into that which never ends
but mimics itself Magnet
of which you are the Future Pole
Zealot without a face

The Never Again

And if death were only the eyelid
Of another life
Another view?
By the blue stone I have plural The why
of death copulates with the mouth of heaven
The Never Again falls once more as rain
from a suicidal sun
The Never Again of Masada Of a throw of the dice
that does not obliterate memory

Fate cheated of the father's death
By the death of the son before him
The Never again falls once more as life
veins the void
Out of the stone is born an orange
Dead sea deadly agaric
The salt that kills saturates the birth
Awakens the green eye of the olive
The herb of death is the mouth
of what is silenced by the earth
The herb of life is the book
That opens at the foot of the tree And each word
of each death holds out the palm branch
Time soars overhead
wings of ochre and ozone
Life opens out down below
The father streams within the son
Death knows nothing (nor the sea)
but to slow down the flow
Face of the waters where blue hibernates
Life learns what breathes
and its spiral climbs, dawn ivy,
up to the lips of Masada
Up to the book of air shut once more
by the Never Again of Masada.

Translated by Anita Barrows

The Fable Merchant

to Louis Aragon

I'm only a merchant of time
From heart to heart
I sell dreams then beat a retreat
With heart on my mind and hand on my heart
I know the strange tenderness of pools
I sell flowers
I sell thread to sew silence
I'm only a merchant you see my gaze
Woven of sky and geography
You see in it woods rivers stars
Mingled with sweat
Mingled with muscular labor, an industrial
Cadastre of gleams and shadows

OTHER LANGUAGES

I'm only a merchant pay me the coin
Of tales and remembrances
Pay me the coin of my broken dreams
Pay me the coin of martyred bodies
You know the rate of exchange for a sorrow
You have to pay counting with the strength of your eyes
For a heart squashed like an egg all over the sky
For a land destroyed all of life
For a people enslaved the weapon of light!

I'm only a merchant going along the days
Merchant of oblivion merchant of love
On the lofty boulevards of images
On the sidewalks of time the fog of the suburbs
And I drag along my shadow it's my only baggage
For beating the drum
For beating the call of fountains and ages!

I've nothing left to offer but hands and footsteps
And gestures mingled with the streets' movement
And I Drag my body like a plow
So as to till the morning's transparence
Give me the coin of the voices in wheat
And of turning motions windmills on the plain
For crushing human joy!

I've nothing to offer but this melody
And words in spite of myself rhythms of fire
I'm only a merchant of word-anvils
Look at both my hands where the vines cross
Space is lost in the confluence of paths
In the detour of a stone where I left my heart
I go off in the wind I go off on the roads
I'm only a merchant no one hears me
For I sell only a song
For I sell the future in a mere flower!

Translated by Charles Guenther

Edmond Fleg

Edmond Fleg was born in Geneva, Switzerland, in 1874. He fought in the First World War. Fleg was the author of many volumes of poetry, fiction, and drama. In 1954 his poems were collected in the volume Écoute, Israel. *He died in Paris in 1964.*

The Dead Cities Speak to the Living Cities

"Look at us now, destroyed.
We too had statues and corn,
Armies and ships. Like you
We wanted to storm the heavens.
Punished we are, in the grave.

"You do not give ear to our voice.
How you run! Here is a land of
Marble and honey, of orange,
of mandolins played in the sun.
Here's a land of snow and blue furs."

Translated by Anthony Rudolf

Benjamin Fondane

Benjamin Fondane (Fundoianu) was born in 1898. Uncomfortable in the literary society of Romania, he traveled to Paris and became a spokesman for Dadaism. He served in the French army but was captured and deported to Auschwitz. He died in the gas chamber in 1944. His volumes of poetry are Landscapes *(1930), and* Ulysses *(1938). He also published several books of literary criticism. He was working on "Lullaby for an Emigrant" when he was deported. Fondane wrote in both French and Romanian. The final two poems in this selection, "Hertza" and "Plain Song," were written in Romanian. They are included here so that Fondane's poems remain together.*

Lullaby for an Emigrant

The Queen declares: "The evening wears
   her pearls—see how she glows!
Pin a rose on my breast!" "Fie!" they protest:
   "To be sure, 'tis but a rose."

   The sea is stirring,
   sleep, sleep, little dear:
   when dawn comes red, all
   will disappear.

"Ah," the Queen sighs, "enchantment lies
   abroad—where are my sandals?
   Let's dance to the light of candles!
Where's Leiba? Fetch the cobbler" "The wretch
   is lying among his candles."

OTHER LANGUAGES

The shadows flicker,
sleep, dear, 'tis late:
the wheel is turning,
the wheel of fate.

"What is that scream?" the Queen says: "I dream
that blood is being shed!"
" 'Tis about the refrain as it goes down the drain
of the fountain water," they said.

A star is spinning
in a new sky,
delicate, doomed:
sleep, dear, bye-bye.

"A refrain? It isn't!" the Queen says. "Listen:
there is fighting hand to hand!"
" 'Tis only the cocks that are fighting, the knocks
as they spill their blood on the sand."

Sleep. After the storm
the rainbow, the larks:
the sea is lulling
the little sharks.

"Oh dear," the Queen babbles, "is someone in trouble?
Someone calls for relief!"
" 'Tis only a slave who dreads his grave,
but his bed brings him no grief."

The dawn stretches forth:
my child, take heed!
That is the color
flying fish bleed.

"Run, run!—for it may be a poor little baby,
its soul at its last ebb,
far from its home like a mislaid comb:
break up this spiderweb!"

'Tis the Night of the Lord,
a creaking sky:
a whole province has
a pain in its eye.

"Are they ghosts who mumble psalms as they stumble
along with torches of tallow?"
"No, Queen, we pursue the perfidious Jew*
who wears a star of yellow."

'Tis the wind, the old
white horse that weeps:
'tis the hour of the
Apocalypse.

"The Jews, those twerps?" the Queen says, and burps:
"I never was a big eater.
Oh damn, I fear for later!
Lock up the garret, bring me my parrot
that comes from beyond the Equator!"

Full fathom five
the fishes lie
who used to fly . . .

And yet they sing
in shoals, in *shuls*
and in God's hand
they place the pearls

that are each eye.
Next year in . . . where?
Fie, fie!

Translated by Keith Bosley

By the Waters of Babylon

It's to you that I speak, men of the Southern hemisphere,
Speaking to you as man to man
With the little in me that is still human
And the little of my voice that subsists in my throat.
My blood has been shed on my paths and may it, ah, may it
Cease to cry aloud for revenge!
The kill has been called, the beasts hunted down,
So let me address you with those same words
That once we could share:
So little is still intelligible!

*perfidious Jew: Until Vatican II, Catholics prayed every Good Friday *pro perfidis Judaeis.*

OTHER LANGUAGES

A day must come, I'm sure, of slaked thirst
When we'll all be beyond memory, when death
Will have accomplished all its tasks of hatred.
I'll then be only a clump of nettles beneath
Your feet, but remember then that I once had
A face like your own and a mouth that could pray
Like yours. When dust entered my eye, or a dream,
My eye wept salt like yours and when
An unfriendly thorn scratched my skin
My blood that it drew was as red as yours!
Yes, I was cruel, as cruel as you, but could still
Thirst for tenderness too, or else for power
Or for gold, pleasure or even pain.
Like you I could be evil or anxious,
Reliable in peace or drunken in victory
And haggard and stumbling when I felt frustrated.

Yes, I've been a man like all other men,
Fed on bread and dreams and despair. Ah, yes,
I've loved and wept and hated and suffered
And purchased flowers and sometimes failed too
To pay my rent. On Sundays I went
To the country, went fishing beneath God's gaze
After unreal fish, or swam in a stream
That sang among the reeds, and I ate French fries
In the evening. After that, well, after that
I went home and slept, weary, with my heart
Brimful with loneliness and self-pity
And pity for all mankind while I sought
In vain, while I sought on a woman's body
That impossible peace that we had lost
In the dim past in a great orchard blossoming
In its heart with a Tree of Life . . . .

Like you, I read all the newspapers, the paperbacks,
And failed to understand the world at all
And failed ever to understand man too,
Though I often happened to affirm
That I could.
And when death came, my death, perhaps,
I claimed I knew what it was, but in truth,
I can tell you now, in this very hour,
Death entered my wide-open staring eyes
That were surprised that they understood so little.
Have you understood it better than I?

And yet no, after all!
I was never a man like you.
You were not born as I was, on the roads.
Nobody ever cast your children into the sewers
Like kittens whose eyes are not yet open.
You have never wandered through cities pursued by police,
Have never known disaster at dawn
Or been deported in cattle cars,
Never known the bitter sobs of humiliation
When accused of a crime while the corpse was still lacking,
Never changed your name and even your face
So as no longer to bear a name that had become an insult
And a face into which all your fellow citizens
Had spat!

A day may yet come, I'm sure, when this poem
Will be found before your eyes. It demands
Nothing. Forget it, forget it. What is it?
Only a cry that can never fit into
A perfect poem: was I left enough time to polish it?
But when you tread at last on this clump of nettles
That I once was, in some later century,
Long after the forgotten century when I lived,
Remember only that I was innocent
And that, like you, men and women of the future,
I once had a face like yours that was marked
By anger and pity and joy, in fact
Simply a human face and no more!

The Wandering Jew

Buried beneath his poems, here lies
    The Wandering Jew, Isaac Laquedem.
Too often, his mind was drawn to extremes,
    This poor descendant of old Shem.

Round the whole world he had wandered
    And known all kinds of living men,
But nothing seemed to him eternal,
    Though everything caught his fickle eye.

A good guy, after all, but unstable,
    (It's a hereditary disease)
Everywhere he wrote in sand
    But in the language of Heaven.

Translated by Edouard Roditi

Hertza

The cows in Vatra Dornii lumber on the grass-wet
asphalt, with their seagaze from the past,

their lowing tied to their throats like a bell,
as in Hertza when silence snowed on my bench.

I remember the sunset collapsing as in sleep
in the small treeless town zigzagged with lizards,

with roofs draping over the windows like hoods
to make day sneak through the yard like a servant.

Who brought the herds in from the meadow?
The cows had glass eyes then, as now, and crooked necks,

but they littered streets with manure from the field
and tied a loose thread of sun in your smile.

In the evening a dark murmur swelled from the synagogue.
They were praying to heaven for a shelter

as was given to their ancestors in the past
to save them from terror of the red fields.

Suddenly, candles were lit behind the windows
and a shadow entered the shops, through locked doors,

and sat at the table. Silence as in a salt mine
froze in the house, and the night's icicle

was dripping on the sills. Grandfather, amid
the flames from the menorah, was praying:

"If I forget you, O Jerusalem, let my right arm
wither and my tongue cleave to the roof of my mouth."

The ceiling with plaster angels rose to the sky.
What a fire flashing on the iron shutters.

The ice-bright blast of the wind weakened
and the house rocking like a boat at night

cut loose from the town street and floated up.
Like a wine pourer, sleep was getting drunk

and I don't know whom grandfather talked with.
Nobody was listening to his cry from the depths

as he mingled in his grandson's stupid head
the small-house prayer and the lowing fields.

Plain Song

And an evening will come when I will leave,
with little idea where I'm going, nor whether

the time of rot or germination is to come.
The silence will spread over me like earth.

I know you will come in the evening as always
to bring the cold shadow of walnut leaves.

From the stillness you will know I am gone.
Erect by my head like the first candle,

you won't ask anyone why your ripe knees,
your earrings, your soul is superfluous.

Be still. For new landscapes, other words
are needed. Lock up your tumultuous memories.

But keep a trapped cry of I love you—
as I love a stone with Hebrew letters on it.

Autumn in the urban graveyard dispenses
honeycombs of sadness on the slabs

and hangs plant creepers in our eyes—
and I can no longer hide from death.

Translated by Matei Calinescu and Willis Barnstone

Yvan Goll

Yvan Goll was born in the Vosges in 1891. He studied at Strasbourg and Berlin, and was associated with the Expressionist and Surrealist movements. He emigrated to the United States in 1939 but returned to Paris shortly before his death in 1950. Goll was a prolific writer of prose, poetry, and drama. Although the bulk of his poems were written in French and German, the first two of the following poems were among those written in English.

Lilith

I

Bird-Woman of the ultra-world
The Algol of your eyes
Rotating at high dementia

Eagle-bred daughter of an occult womb
Royal with lice-ridden wings
Damnation of all love
Listening to the call of clouds

O Lilith Androgyne
Double-scented breath and breast
Twin-engined angel
Led by a totem pole
In a marathon contra-dance
With a finale well known to none

Wiser than famed herbs
Wiser than sleek-eyed onyx

Double-mouthed orchid
Tomb of the colibri
Berth of the thought

While matter weeps
A new sex calls from the edge of nothing

Pearl unrobed skin by skin
For the dance of the idea
In pristine nakedness

O universal solitude
Infinite desire
Pregnant with the bird of death

At last a golden feather
Plummeting to the empty sands

II
Return: o beautiful equestrian
Astride the stallion of wind
Let the hoof of your charger
Kindle stars from my heart's ecstasy

Turn the wheel of our circus again

In your long absence Lilith
Women taught me the secrets of the earth

They fed me the spirit of grain
They whirled the white chicken around my head
To redeem my crime

I learned to defile the rain with my flute
I drove the youngest of volcanos
Graze on violet lava

But now return to free the son from his mothers
Who gravely sit in the amphitheater of the past
Sad mountains
Keeping Time tied to their withered udders

Who watch the young bull in the arena of day
Exposed to both laws mortal
Sol y sombra
To the dagger of light
And the veil of shadow
In the death circle

Return O Matriarch
From your breasts: sun and moon
Churn the two principles
The milk the wine
The strength the weakness

In your fiery embrace let me find
Ever new freedom from flesh
Ever older growing God

At last remains the insect's hull
Closing the compass of its legs
In a prayer to the Absolute

Raziel

to Kurt Seligmann

I

Grace of the Word immaculate
By implacable sacrifice

Though the tithe is inhuman
And redeems no safe laughter

The Word as primal as snow
And conclusive as a raindrop

Raziel with his albatross heart
Rose to the realm of solitude

Having displayed the Eastern Mountain
And late discovered the River Sambatyon
He leaned back toward midnight

II

Insane king of the abstract
In the desert of reality

Through the alchemy of sounds
Recreating the creation

With roots of words with roots of trees
Wringing wisdom from the earth

Viaduct of sister arches
From silence to prophecy

Word: cloth of the infinite
Mantle of azure around the thought
Beyond rapture beyond death

III
Through seven thousand midnights
Writing the Book of Signs

Unaltered Raziel sat
Building the singing city

Casting alphabets and magic keys
To find the 70 names of God

Under colonnades of Shins
Under golden roofs of Daleths

Implacable sacrifice
For he bled more than those children
Iphigenia Quetzalcoatl

IV
At last he heard the name
By rivers sung by lions roared

He found it in the depths of sapphires
In the blood-count of weary rubies

In the fear of waterfalls
In the geometry of butterflies

At the udder of old glaciers
In the ram's horn by the tumbling temple

From earth arose the flaming Name
From floral whorls from spectral horns
On the high hour of death

Clandestine Work

Between dawn and the Opera
I saw hands grow old
I saw eyes fall like leaves
The whole time
Death was working

Neïla

Oh Neïla
borne away by evening
you open up
the gallery of stars
which leads
to our immense fathers.

Out of the young night
songs reddening
arise to free
shackled peoples. Together
we shall enter
the Bush and hear

God's ancient cry

Translated by Anthony Rudolf

Edmond Jabès

Edmond Jabès was born in Cairo in 1912. He has lived in Paris since 1957 after being obliged, as a Jew, to leave Egypt in the wake of the Suez crisis. In 1970 he was awarded Le Prix des Critiques. His eleven volumes of poetry have won him international recognition. His major work, The Book of Questions, *is available in English, as is a selection of his early poems.*

The Condemned

They erect gallows in the prison yard
in the songbird gardens proud girl
that the sun convicted
they erect gallows on absence

The axe with fine needles for stitching through the dead
the axe with valences of moon for the hangman's smile
Century of hangings they erect gallows for the zebra-
striped loiterers of the cat-tongue Life's no longer a secret
Only the eyes the gaze alone waiting questioning
They erect gallows on the fear of the mob
The grass insists it be heard they push it back down
The grass by which the condemned forget they are going to die
The bird tufted axe tormenting the wind
powdering the cheeks of the young windy wives
The inplacable axe with idylls of coffins of Justice
a world in decay suspended before its fall
a world with its tongue out and feet not touching the ground
anymore
the wind balancing it indifferently
I remember all the faces I took time to recognize them
as long as the last day
They erect gallows on impatience The master with his pumice stone
pommels the thin unstained fingers of the humiliated pupils
You read I read innocent words
the axe interrupts
They erect gallows every Sunday
A head tumbles into the open notebook
They erect gallows on the hangman's memory
on the memory of life and death
on the misery of love
on a cut braid
on a cut
on a broken
neck.

Translated by Jack Hirschman

Song of the Last Jewish Child

for Edith Cohen

My father was hung from a star,
my mother flows with the river,
my mother shines
my father does not shine,
in the night that denies me,
in the day that destroys me.
The stone is not heavy.
The bread is like the bird,

I watch as it flies.
Blood is on my cheeks.
My teeth
seek a less empty mouth
in the earth or in the water,
in the fire.
The world is red.
All the iron bars are spears.
Dead horsemen always gallop
in my sleep and in my eyes.
On the lost garden's ravaged body
flowers a rose, flowers a hand
of rose I shall squeeze no more.
Death's horsemen bear me away.
I am born to love them.

Song of the Trees of the Black Forest

In the black forest
where hanged men laugh on trees,
where soldiers keep guard,
a fire breaks out.
But who lit the torches?
But who set the trees on fire?
The soldiers panicking,
—some thought their task easy—
call for help with all their might,
try to flee their own weapons.
Now the forest is red
and the hanged men still laugh,
but do not burn.

A Circular Cry

A circle
and, in this circle, another
circle
and, in the new circle, a further
circle
and so on
until the final circle
becomes an all-embracing
point,

then an imperceptible point;
yet unbelievably present;
yet majestically absent.
A woman and a word.
A woman turning in a ring
around a word turning in a ring;
slowly at first, then quickly;
unbelievably quickly
until, in the space they were raised up, they are nothing
but a circle,
seeking a smaller circle,
smaller and smaller,
grotesquely small at present.
A hole, an empty eye;
a night eye;
a blinded eye.
Then what? One has a look.
One penetrates.
Is that what they call Unity?
A disintegrated circle?
A circular cry, step,
avowal?

Song

On the side of the road
there are leaves
so tired of being leaves
they have fallen.

On the side of the road
there are Jews
so tired of being Jews
they have fallen.

Sweep away the leaves.
Sweep away the Jews.

The same leaves, will they
grow again in spring?

Will there be a spring
for the downtrodden Jews?

The Pulverized Screen

I saw the dead
dying a second time
as they lay on the sea
I saw them
inventing bridges
If you were to pass
I would follow you
Always there is
between two fires
between two pyres
an empire of storm
or of flagstones
a frenzy of poison
to drink from the phial
of fishes
of swallows If you
were to pass I'd be
your steps' design
the mysterious obstinacy
of the thread and I'd take
the time I need
to fix on your face
The days are reckoned up
on the tip of silenced
voices Then all is black
I have seen the dead
breathe with our lungs
and the sea beneath
perpetuate their breath
while you constructed
for each antenna
a pulverized screen
of patience

Water

Before, there is water.
After, there is water;
during, enduring.

∾ ∾

—Water
from the lake?
—Water
from the river?
—Water
from the sea?

Never water on water.
Never water
for the sake of water;
but water
where there's no more water;
but water
in the dead memory of water.

To live
in living death
between memory and oblivion of water
entered between
thirst and thirst.

∾ ∾

Water enters
Ceremony.
Water
settles and flows.
Fertile.

OTHER LANGUAGES

Always water
for the sake of water.
Always water on water.
Plenty.

*(The desert was my land.
The desert is my journey,
my wandering.)*

Always between two horizons;
between horizon
and horizon calls.
Beyond-border.

~ ~

The sand glows like water
in unendurable thirst.

Torment night lulls.

Our steps
splash around thirst.
Absent.

—Water
from the lake?
—Water
from the river?
—Water
from the sea?

And soon the rain will come
to cleanse the soul of the dead.

~ ~

Let the burned shadows pass by,
mornings of sacrificed trees.
Smoke, smoke.

(Cries, once, in fruit,
in flower,
in leaf
and their long arms outstretched.)

To each arm, its horizon.
To each flower, to each fruit
their season.
To the leaf, its inclination.

The sky
looks up to the earth.
Writing would be
letting words flow out
and irrigate the soil.
Every sentence
is of rain
and of light.

∾ ∾

I write the desert.
So strong is the light
the rain
has faded away.

There is nothing but sand
where I go.

Translated by Anthony Rudolf

The Book Rises Out of the Fire

I do not know
if you were taught
that the earth is round
like thirst.
And that,
when lovers' shadows move
at the approach of dawn,
the poet's tongue,

OTHER LANGUAGES

the tongue of wells and centuries,
is dry,
is rough and dry.
It has done so much service
and disservice,
has been so long exposed to the air,
to the noise,
to its own words,
that it has hardened,
glazed,
and crumbled.
After the road,
and before the road,
there are stones
and ashes on scattered stones.
The book
rises out of the fire
of the prophetic rose,
from the scream of the sacrificed petals.
Smoke.
Smoke
for all who see only fire,
who smell only
dawn
and death.
But the order of summits,
the order of ruins,
is wedding gladness.

Translated by Rosmarie Waldrop

Gustave Kahn

Gustave Kahn was born in Metz in 1859. One of the early Symbolists, he founded in 1885 a magazine, La Vogue, *which was the cradle of* vers-librisme. *His first book of poems,* Les Palais nomades *(1887), was the first book in French to be composed in* vers libre. *He died in Paris in 1936.*

The Temple

A living being, the Temple was killed.
The arms of gold that raised its domes,
Drip with blossoms, now cut, instead of stones.
Scattered over the cemeteries, their pollen
Yet flourishes blue: periwinkles, pansies, violets,
Whispering in the breeze, with a low clear voice,
God's words, Who has abandoned Israel.
From the deserts of sand to the distant salt marshes
A new song of hope with a similar rhythm
Has flowered, a scattering of frail synagogues.

"The Temple's golden vine has cast its shoots
Into the world's vast ocean in which we bathe
(Exiled and pursued, the Rabbis repeat),
And the stubborn hope of rebirth is inscribed
In the sunset's clouds and the fall's golden leaves.

In the agony of life's eve tomorrow's soul
Meditates, preparing itself for prayer
While the ancient stones rise in a new wall."

The Temple is dead, but Israel still lives in the world
Though the barbarian's violent blade now trims
Only men from the branches of the Tree of Life
While everywhere new communities are born
Of the living spirit and of stubborn hope.

From the stones of Zion, a thousand temples are rebuilt.

The Word

The iron flower of the prophet's angry message
Blossoms only on the hurricane's cries, at the peak
Of his fury aroused by the people's unconcern
While it shouts and whores after ghosts of gold.

His voice, if it reaches the dark roof of branches
And twigs that the eagle's talons have wounded,
Is scattered too high in the sky's clear cavern
And only the cloud that is deaf hears its rule.

But the voice from the sky rises skyward too
And is lost in the multiple shivering of leaves
Without reaching human ears that might welcome it.
To the smiling angels it sounds heavy, uncouth.

Translated by Edouard Roditi

Joseph Milbauer

Joseph Milbauer was born in Warsaw in 1898, but lived in Brussels until 1921, when he went to Paris. After being taken as a prisoner of war he escaped to Palestine. He published several volumes of poetry and translated Sholem Aleichem, Tchernichovsky, and Agnon among others. He died in 1968.

Interior

I'm not alone.

There are lovely beings in this world.
In a blue velvet pouch my phylacteries are sleeping
And sharp creakings rise from floor boards.

The door shivers and the window panes shake
And the ashes, as they fall, let the coals crumble.
In the folds of the curtains a thousand dreams are at work.
The lamp casts circles of light on the ceiling.

Am I alone?

How about all those reflections, those lights like illusions?
These trembling witnesses of my motionless life?
And you, my shadow, my huge and dark shadow,

Seated beside me, like an obedient child?

Paris by Night

I'm thirty years old
And strolling along the Seine
Already thinking of her.

Of her, I mean of death.

Before the world was created
The spirit of God hovered too on the surface of deep waters.

My own image now hovers too on the surface of deep waters.

Deep, because of night
And because the idea of death pursues me.

Before the creation of the world
Nobody was thinking of you.
Today, you exist
And are strolling through Paris
With a poet, side by side.

Notre Dame, grave as a wise man of the East
Appears with arms uplifted to be blessing the river,
The river and all that it contains,

Including my own reflection.

Translated by Edouard Roditi

Pierre Morhange

Pierre Morhange was born in Paris in 1901, of a family of French Jews which lived uninterruptedly in Lorraine, as its name implies, for perhaps as much as a thousand years. In 1932, he was appointed professor of philosophy in Riom, and then continued to teach philosophy, except under the Vichy government, in various other French cities until his retirement in 1966. During the German occupation of France, he went underground and was active in the Resistance.

Lullaby in Auschwitz

My lovely child all clothed in blue
Now clothed so well in the velvet anguish

My lovely child all clothed in hunger
I'm the great cloud where you seek your bread

My lovely child all clothed in blood
Your mother can no longer feed you her own

My lovely child all clothed in worms
That glisten for your mother like stars

My lovely child all clothed in madness
On the hook of my heart they'll hang your rags

My lovely child all clothed in smoke
They never told me I might turn back

Jew

I saw my face
The star in a smashed mirror
I embraced my own bosom
In my arms that remain lonely
I embraced in my heart that they hate
The diamond of justice

Salomon

He taught Math at the Ecole Centrale
And liked to burp while teaching
The students in the front rows knew
When it had been coffee with cream
From the odor of the burp
And the stains on his shirt front
He lived on Rue Ordener and had blue eyes
And was married but never lost his temper
Because he was a Jew
His name was Salomon
And a gust of stars
Had stranded him in the sciences
Lost there with his genius
Very far from us
And with no knowledge of how to live

Translated by Edouard Roditi

Shlomo Reich

Shlomo Reich was born in Romania in 1937. He started writing poetry at an early age. He traveled for three years among the Gypsies in Transylvania and finally settled in Israel in 1961. He has published five volumes of poetry. Migrations: Selected Poems of Shlomo Reich, *the first volume of his poetry to appear in English translation, is forthcoming.*

The Golem

In the ghetto of my mouth
Prague wound in cere cloth of spittle and mist.
Two or three teeth shift in panic.
We are under the roofs of the street of the alchemists.
The tongue glides. Ice rink of my unutterable rays
Under a diaphanous parasol, in the depths of my palace
Rabbi Judah Loew Ben Bezalel constructs the Golem.

This Mongolian does not love me.
His slanting eyes strangle my flawed windpipe
Because once, facing a vacant country, I talked too much.
But I can't spit him out.
He lies there and he weeps.
For thirty-three winters we shall dream
Of a look that must be pierced.
For thirty-three springs we shall
Stammer the Secret Name of God: "Emeth,"
Drowned in the royal court of my ghetto.

The Windmill of Evening

In the windmill of evening
the four-armed vampires
perch under the bastard sky.
We expect the stones to recover their youth
and turn into children
telling miraculous lies.
The rays recede
before a lagging ghost
and darkness devours
the painful moment.
How do we know
that the wind sometimes
betrays its own maliciousness
and dresses like an absent-minded page
forgetting that one can turn
time about
without returning the earth
to the lovers
of spheres with lead
under their wings.

The Vigil

My lips murmur
only one promise to the earth
to survive together
with my brothers in distress

What can be more calm
than a sun between two hemispheres
in search of a hearth?

Like Moses
when the sea solaced his destiny
he is there
who has never known any commandment
except the vigil on the horizon

Close to the sky
the mercenaries still live
and their only weapon
is their stare

The clouds of hope
come to rest only in countries
where the calendar
has been abolished

A Tribe Searching

With these missing pieces
we make camels and crutches
or a prayerbook cover

There are wars without prisoners
but no maimed soldiers
without the stones' pity

Between these hips conceived for children
a tribe is still searching
for revolt from the yoke
word from the earth

When this fiber goes astray
in the debris of the night
its hands reach across the sky
to shake the harmonious ghosts

To dance with a stone wall
would be easy
only listen

Translated by Mira Reich

Ryvel

Ryvel (Raphael Levy) was born in Tunis in 1898 and died in France in 1972. After graduating from the teachers college of the Alliance Israélite in Paris, he made a career in the teaching profession in Jewish schools in Tunisia and Morocco. At the time of his retirement in 1955, he was director-general and inspector of all Alliance Israélite Schools in Tunisia. He published eight books of poems and stories in French, all on Tunisian-Jewish themes. His play Tsedaka *was recently translated into Hebrew.*

The Pilgrimage to Testour

Like a tower above the tortuous
Meandering road now rises
The village of Testour.

I'm soon attacked by a swarm
Of flies and small dark-skinned guides.

At the top of the steep village
On a sunbaked expanse
The tomb of the Rab stands among others:
Rabbi Fragi, the Master, surrounded by disciples.
The stone is simple, time worn,
But scarred here and there by votive candles.

From Beja a human flood arrives
And buses are bringing from everywhere
A gray tide of pilgrims
Laden with provisions.
They bring too their superstitions
And their barbarous music.

Around the tomb
The hysterical crowd
Howls, drinks and guzzles
In a wild orgy until dawn.

Where are you, simple and pure faith of yore?

Translated by Edouard Roditi

David Scheinert

David Scheinert was born in 1916 in Czestochowa, Poland, of a family of merchants and glassblowers. In 1924 the family emigrated to Belgium. After abandoning medical studies, he began in 1936 to write for the French leftwing press. A year later, he fled with his family from German-occupied Belgium to France. In 1943, his parents and his brother were arrested in France and deported by the Germans to a death camp, from which they never returned. He managed to remain in hiding. Since 1945, Scheinert, who now lives in Brussels, has published eight novels, one volume of short stories on Jewish themes, three plays, eight volumes of poems, and a number of critical works. These have won him several literary prizes.

The Drunken Stones of Prague

And the stones in the Prague cemetery were so bored that they got drunk and the Jews were then floating between sky and earth like long silken threads.

And a tree was tormenting itself beneath the clouds that were teeming with snow and the leaves fell on the tombs like lost prospectuses.

And Kafka was walking towards a lyre-shaped door and his cheeks were hollow and eyes shone bright and he held the hand of a stooping Rabbi.

A few steps away thousands of names were crawling on the walls, pathetically lonely insects that only time respected.

As for me, I came and went between all these pasts with their darkened stains and in my heart the yellow badges became suns and the stifled words were again as roses.

And is it still winter, after all, with its black and white weapons and the slow falling of its silences, or else the leafy willow tree bending over summer?

In an instant I found again the rustling plain of Lidice and this partly crumbling wall and all these huge daisies that nibbled the sky and the song of thrushes above the reclining figures carved on tombs.

And between my arms that were wide open to greet a new season, all the dead of Prague and Lidice came forward in an indistinguishable crowd towards the quick, who greeted them with open hands that had been changed into flowers.

The Stone and the Blade of Grass in the Warsaw Ghetto

And the stranger at last stood before the monument of lava and anger, and took off his hat, and bowed his head.
He had traveled many days, had encountered frontier guards of every kind and greeted people in all languages.
Before the trees that summoned the clouds and the flowers that sang in the window boxes, he remained lost in the night of a dream.
Above Warsaw the sun was creeping like a hedgehog of gold, and the swallows were circling round the sun,
And the stranger stared at the volcanic monument of death and storm, but the gigantic stone never uttered a sound.
Then the stranger looked up towards the sun and ordered it to speak,
And the sun understood his question and answered humbly: On that day, stranger, I had fled the city, abandoning it to the jackals of the clouds.
Then the stranger summoned a swallow, which spiraled down from the sky and settled on his shoulder.
And the swallow sang with great compassion: On that day, stranger, there were no birds above the burning city.
Then the stranger turned towards an old man who was trembling at the foot of the monument and asked him to speak.
And the old man raised his arm and revealed that his tongue had been torn out.
The stranger then lowered his gaze and saw a blade of grass, and ordered it to speak,
And the blade of grass, swaying in the wind, replied: I'm the child of spilled blood, how could I bear witness?
Then the stranger cast himself on the ground and begged the blade of grass to reveal what had happened,
And the ground caressed the stranger's brow and murmured that it was a young bride and the mother of the future.
Then the stranger lay on the ground and closed his eyes, lost in a dream of dust,
And heard a muffled and harsh voice close by,

And turned around and saw that a broken stone was speaking to him.
And the stone said to him: Listen, stranger, and when you return to your own country, repeat to your brothers all that I've told you.
I'm the tear of a child, turned to stone by hatred, and a sling aimed me at the Nazi's brow,
For the sun had fled that day and the birds had abandoned the city, and the tongues of old men had been torn from their roots, and even the stones had buried themselves in hiding, but the tears of children then turned into stones for slings and bullets for rifles, and from the blood of the dead, at the foot of the monument, a blade of grass was then born, an immortal springtime!

Translated by Edouard Roditi

André Spire

André Spire was born in Nancy, France, in 1868. He worked as a civil servant until his retirement in 1926. Like many Jews he rediscovered his origins in the wake of the Dreyfus affair and became a staunch Zionist. His main collection was Poèmes d'hier et d'aujourd'hui *(1944). He died in 1966.*

Hear, O Israel!

Hear, O Israel!
Will you never tire of repeating in your prayers:
"Praised be the Eternal, who avengeth my injuries,
Who protecteth my rights, who supporteth me in need,
Who crusheth my foes, who killeth my oppressors,
Praised be the Eternal, who girdeth my loins for battle!"

Hear, O Israel!
Have you seen your enemies blush, felled before you?
Have your eyes lowered to mock them in their ruin?
Did your God splinter the bones of their jaws?
And did He break the teeth of the wicked?
Did your ears hear in gladness the loss
Of those who joined themselves against you?
And has the Eternal made your old age resplendent
As that of an olive-tree in blossom?

Hear, O Israel!
You have engraved His Law on your heart:
You unroll it from your left arm morning and evening;
You bind it as a frontlet between your eyes;
You set it upon the doorposts of your gates
—And you! You are the contempt of all nations,
They spit on you as on an impure woman!

Hear, O Israel!
Will you put your hope forever in your strong God?
Will you never dare one day to scratch at his image?
Just look at His hand trailing beneath the clouds:
Is it a hand for action?
Is it a worker's hand?
Is it a hand for justice?
Without blisters, wrinkles, calluses, or bruises?

Hear, O Israel!
Torrents still are rolling down small rounded pebbles
For the slings of the Davids to come!
Quarries are full of the fine rock to make grindstones
For resharpening the points of your old swords;
And you will find furnaces, sledges, and anvils
For reforging the shares of your wornout ploughs
Into elegant, sure-firing guns . . .

Hear, O Israel:
To arms!

Pogroms

Thus the old men lamented:
Do you want our sons to die?
Have you forgotten their bony arms,
Their gasping lungs, their hunched backs?
And how they crawl through the dark streets of our sad towns?

You—you want them to take up arms and to kill!
But they will only be slaughtered . . .
Oh, must our leaders make us still more miserable!
Each time that one of us held up his head
The Stranger branded our doorposts,
Took our firstborn, and murdered our women!

Oh! go from us! Death is the sole injustice.
The forced smile on our submissive lips
Our humble looks, and our impassive souls
Protect us more than your sword!

The Ancient Law

She appeared before me that night: the vanquished one,
her eyes bandaged, her neck bent forward, her head
hanging in defeat.
She appeared before me that night looking like the one I had
seen standing on the pillars of the cathedral, leaning her
hand of rose sandstone on the broken staff of her standard;
she, the cursed one, with her thrown-down book and her
young body covered beneath straight lines of her tunic.
She appeared before me that night, the desolate one:

"You will strive in vain," she said. "You will never really love
their theatres, their palaces, their museums, their playthings:
Your forehead leaned too early toward grief and sorrow.
Beauty will seem a luxury to you, and luxury an abomination;
and your diversions a theft.
You will think that you love your neighbors and friends. . .
But open your eyes to yourself! When does your heart quiver?
Only when you hear hoarse voices, when you see nervous
hands and close-set eyes;
When the mouth of one begging your aid cries: *You owe it to me!*
For such a one only is your brother, he has a soul like yours;
and he claims you as an equal.

You will want to make songs of daring and power.
But you will love only the dreamers unarmed against life.
You will try to listen to the merry songs of peasants, to the
brutal footsteps of soldiers, to the pretty roundelays of little
girls . . .
—Your ears are made only to hear lamentations that rise from
the four corners of the earth."

Nudities

Hair is a nudity.
—Talmud

You said to me:
I would become your comrade:
I would visit your house without fear of troubling you.
We shall spend evenings in talk together,
Talking and thinking of our murdered brothers;
Together we shall wander the earth to find
A country to quiet their heads at last.
But do not let me see your eyeballs glitter
Or the burning veins of your forehead bulge!
I am your equal, not a prey.
Look at me: my clothes are chaste, almost poor!
You cannot even see the curve of my throat!

I looked and I answered:
Woman, you are naked:
Your downy neck is a goblet of well-water,
Your locks are wanton as a troop of mountain goats,
Your round, soft chignon quivers like a breast—
Woman, cut off your hair!

You are naked: your hands now lie unfurled,
Open in nakedness across the printed page,
Your fingers, the subtle tips of your body,
Ringless fingers—that will touch mine any moment—
Woman, cut off your hands!

You are naked: your voice flows up from your bosom,
Your song, your breath, and now the heat of your flesh—
It is spreading round my body to enter my flesh—
Woman, tear out your voice!

Translated by Stanley Burnshaw

Poetics

People spoiled by too many masters,
People too rich in memories,
People of songs and of dances,
Once you knew how to invent your images,
Each one of your kisses then invented a new word.
Now you recite.
What have you done to your senses?

Listen to them.
Murmur, sing what they dictate to you.
All the rest, forget it.
When the wind caresses your hand,
Is it a god that grips you?
A water-nymph, when you dive into a pond?

Oh, read no more!
Oh, no longer learn by rote!
Watch, listen, scent, taste, eat!
Strip off your clothes, let the sky, the sea,
The sun and air, the rich odors of foods,
Possess your young body . . .
And your lips, by themselves, will then
Begin to sing young songs.

Translated by Edouard Roditi

Tristan Tzara

Tristan Tzara was born in Romania in 1895. He left there for Switzerland in 1915 and settled in Zurich, where he founded the Dada movement. Between the wars he lived in Paris and he fought in the French Resistance during World War II. He died in 1964. His books include The First Poems of Tzara *(1934) and Collected Poems (1965). Although he wrote in both French and Romanian, the following poems are translated from French.*

Evening

fishermen return with waterstars
they share bread with the poor
they string necklaces for the blind
emperors go out into parks at this hour
that is like the bitterness of engravings
servants wash down the hunting dogs
the light puts on gloves windows lock up therefore
light gets out of the room like an apricot pit
or a priest from his church

good god: soften wool for plaintive lovers
paint small birds in ink and renew the image on the moon—
let's catch scarabs
and lock them in a box—
let's go to the brook
and make terra cotta jars—
let's kiss at the fountain—
let's go to the public park
till the cock crows
and the town is scandalized
or go up into the attic
hay stings you can hear the cows moo
then they remember their calves
let's go

Mothers

my friends are on vacation
there where vowels and medicines grow
the light eats colors
you are reunited plantations and sauerkrauts

deep in you the electric buzzer sprouts
there where stones burn
000 000 those toaddds those toaddds
the telegraphist at the station turns transparent then opaque
send me the sounds tzaca tzaca tzaca tzac
the rainbows of the hanged
the lights
they are sucked in by lightning rods
gmatouco matrapolzlacar
he lost his personality
streetlamp reflector flector flector
flector flector
notebook violin goat thinks
blue explosion and chaldea in the coffee
ants circulate in the fog rash
they turn and croak over our harvests

Translated by Willis Barnstone and Matei Calinescu

Claude Vigée

Claude Vigée was born in Alsace in 1921. He was active in the French-Jewish underground movement in World War II, escaped to Spain in 1942, and reached the United States in 1943. In 1960 he went to Israel and presently serves as professor of literature at Hebrew University. Vigée is the author of many volumes of poetry and essays, and has translated Rilke, Goll, and Eliot. His poems have been collected under the title Le Soleil Sous la Mer *(1972).*

The Tree of Death

for Henry Braun

From the immense hemicycle, from the blue fire of the earth,
the eyes of the dead are turned
towards the solar arena where glow the faces
and the lands they loved in their day on earth.

Because the dead continue to drink its light,
they are forever changing in their own lives:
according to the depth of their mortal gaze
they look into their own hearts for the only real world.

OTHER LANGUAGES

We are blinded in our underground night
by the shining day of our human quest.
The big Tree of Death is planted in blood:
it flowers forever, nourished by the present.

Life is the sun of your season of death.
Like the seed at the heart of a fruit no longer living,
it shines and grows in its winter stone.
So, at your death, a poem
already makes your future meteor shine.

While passing through the teeth of flint and sand,
the language of silence flames;
the poet in the desert, haunted by the Divine Presence,
gives an indefensible emptiness to the world.

But the desired bodies, the words that erase them,
were they not at first unknown, invisible?
They must remain simply in their tracks,
rendering the dream opaque to the transparent night,
as one inverts the hourglass when the sand has run through.

The time of the poem is an explosion of the universe.
It does not reflect the unexplainable: it is
your death flowering for an eternity,
The highest symbol is in the reality.

Translated by J. R. Le Master and Kenneth L. Beaudoin

The Struggle with the Angel

. . . Sauntering in the orchard we bit the fruit:
At the feet of the celestial voyager the angel's sword
Wheeled like a peacock before the Tree of Life,
And we were racked upon the thunder's rim.
Strangers thrust forth upon the barges of the sun,
Dragged toward pyres the road's own lightning lit,
And on the mountain kneeling on the snow
Where like a cock, splintered by stars the heartwood bleeds,
We shall be always exiled,
Torn upon the tree of time.
Reopening the scar at the navel of silence
The blinded meteor falls into the sea.

Tree, we will praise you for the gift of death,
The fountains and the fawns upon your cindered earth,
From our irreparable and ardent fable of man
Blows the dark rose of butchery.
"And Jacob went forth limping of his hip";
Eden's a fire of algae in the briars of sleep,
A rose of steel that blossoms in the night
Through birds downbeaten in the rains of spring.
The future dances like a cedar in flames,
The world becomes a giant forest fire
Where none remember the lost Paradise.
The heads of sailors rising once again,
In vain they sound the conches of forgetfulness,
Their breath has dried the belly of the sea,
The weeds of exile lash against their brows,
They breathe the wind of other nebulas . . .

Translated by Elizabeth Savage

House of the Living

After the deluge
I have rebuilt my house upon the fallow earth
My house sleeps in the winter moonlight
Its hewn walls shine under the star-filled birches
(The flayed fox in the underbrush of night
Bleeds until April upon the rotted leaves)

Against forgetfulness
I have raised my castle of cards and photographs
Against absence
I have hurled at the sky the laughing arrow of a new childhood
For loneliness my sister
I have set out the dark bed of carnal tenderness
For silence
Your tongue is the flaming poisonflower of love.

Over the moor of perpetual winter and separation
My house spreads warmth and nearness
Push the door that is ajar and you will see
The stake of my wounded core spring from the hearth,
The living death which burns in the center of life
And lifts a wood of seed ashes from the tree.

Vineyard netted in flame,
The dust of the twigs nourishes my roots;
A horse's ears sway over the field of wheat
Like a buoy glimpsed above the waves
When the wind brushes the sea at break of day.

Suddenly his great chest emerges from the fog
He whinnies galloping in all the directions of space,
Centaur in ripples of underwater stars,
He ravishes the night of the terrible future:
Soon a single horse escaped out of the foam
Shall fill with fire all the ways of the world.

Translated by Henry Braun

Light of Judea

In the harbor of Askalon
Naked shepherds wash
Their sheep in the sea:

Girls with dusky feet
Make their sandals clatter
On each white flagstone.

Within the cupola of air
The eye of the sun raises
To the crest of the universe

Jerusalem of the future
Which the glare
Of the summer snow unveils.

Translator unknown

The Phoenix of Mozart

Arisen from what childhood
the bird of origins? In the blackest of hells
he sings with the worshipful mouth of an angel.

And this voice alone can save us from silence,
though we wanted to follow it and shall die with it,

and can only hear our cries in the night,
when the rings of the wind on our upturned wrists
revolve their strange fires.

Every Land Is Exile

Every land is exile,
Every language foreign.
After so many turnings, after so much useless wandering,
And rich only with oblivion, Oh my bitter childhood,
There you are, returned to the poisoned river
Where you drank ruin with the troubled water of births.
Lean over its mirror: face of the absent one,
Every word is flight and rootless leaf,
Every bird, sky's prey and bereft of origins.

Destiny of the Poet

It is always someone else,
The silent You speaking to himself in me.
Sometimes I tear myself away from the listening that is prayer

And I sing in his name in the language borrowed
From the mouths of the dead. For him in me, for him
Who is already translating me
Into other men's throats.

Song of Occident

Song of occident:
Death grinding its grain.
Till the last moment
Re-sifting its refrain
The cracked disc goes round
With a creaking sound.

The Wanderer

Thin feet are caught
In the gray stones,
Walk here and there,
Anywhere, nowhere,
Stumbling under autumnal stars.

The heart is in the middle,
It does not fix in rocks, in words,
It is not lost on this side of the world
In the somber silence of the void.
Beneath this humid garden
Abandoned at night
Among the dark rose trees,
The earth itself, abandoned, shines.

Indeed it's worth the trouble
Of returning to the world,
Bearing its fruit,
With tears and hard work,
With no hope but the shadow,
Without watching for daylight.

Poetry

What then is poetry?
A camp fire, abandoned,
smoldering on
the deserted mountain
throughout the night
in summer.

Translated by Anthony Rudolf

Ilarie Voronca

Ilarie Voronca was born in Romania in 1903. He went to France before World War II and died there in 1945. Voronca, who published seven volumes of poetry, was greatly influenced by Futurism, Dadaism and Surrealism. Voronca wrote in both French and Romanian. "The Seven-League Boots" was written in Romanian and is included here so that his poems remain together.

The Quick and the Dead

All around me, the city was falling asleep,
Drowned in night. There were sad, poor homes
With windows that open only onto airless courtyards,
Lightless too. And that teeming crowd of the dead and the quick

In the midst of which I walked without losing my way.
"What are you doing here?" Some had long been dead
But none paid any attention to them. A brightness, as of snow,
Very tender, pervaded the streets and the walls.

Oh, I was no longer but a memory, a vague suggestion
In the midst of this crowd. I was like a ship
That has weighed anchor, ready to sail
With all its sorrows, its barrels of despair in the depths of its holds.

"Is there none among you to recognize me? Even our course
Has become blind." It can no longer lead me
To the open sea that still should somewhere
Be close to the city, like a kindly spirit.

A call or a sign from a friend would have been
Welcome. I stood hesitant, on the threshold of an ancient
Inn, close to the tumbrils of hay, among keys that creaked
In rusty locks, voices heard in sleep and ghost horses.

O life, tears and joys, what have you become, and you too, silence,
And you, pain that grows like a more piercing look in my iris?
And all of you, quick and dead, gathered here, all strangers to each
other,
Among whom I go like a secret word threading through my poem?

Translated by Edouard Roditi

The Seven-League Boots

But I knew it: a verse is a magic helmet
which makes me invisible among people
all through the night like an unraveled sun.
No one tells you, poet, what you are like.

And poems are the seven-league boots, taking
me from the polar circle to the tropics.
In a verse as in a botanist's bag, you find
herbs from remotest places bunched together.

Who said the word is a rope of slow changes
and letters are captive birds in a room?
With a line you can slip through four seasons
and the pace in a poem arcs over a continent.

OTHER LANGUAGES

Through oily light of equatorial lands, I go
into the cold rooms of the north, or blue
hesitation of the wave, among sloops, snakes
of the south, by harps unstrung in the wind's hair.

I'm with the plowman furiously pushing iron horns
or near wheels whining like giant dogs,
among highways like fanbelts turning a city,
or the savages in the virgin forest.

So the poem precedes the day or overtakes
it like the scaffolding of dawn; the poem is
the coffer in which heavenly coins clink
along with the falling stars of fate.

Vowel, like a vacation prolonged in sleep,
you see yourself in seeds, the scales of autumn,
and in the bells flaming with water of dusk,
in sparrows vibrating the tree like a violin.

You are a poet, therefore eternal Ahasuerus,
shadeless, and you seek the keys of the fountain.
Love in you resounds like a clock. You sang
and the shadow was terrified, gone like a bird.

Translated by Matei Calinescu and Willis Barnstone

Jean Wahl

Jean Wahl was born in Marseilles in 1888 and died in Paris in 1974. Primarily known for his existentialist philosophy, he taught Jean-Paul Sartre. He also wrote terse, powerful poems during his time in a concentration camp in World War II. These poems have appeared in English translation as Voices in the Dark.

Decayed Time

These days in prison seem a decayed time where
There slowly whirl the smells of something stale,
All is destroyed, discolored, half-dead, pale;
An old hope shivers far in the cold air.

A Lean Day in a Convict's Suit

A lean day in a convict's suit, a smell,
Heavy turn of keys that close the lock,
The conqueror's brutal steps, his shouts and insults—
Grinding my teeth with force I bore those sufferings.
The step out in the corridor was a warning
And the key closed upon a deaf despair.
I lie down, but I've only the right to sit.
I smile; the jailer then forbids that smile.
Is my hair white now? I am feverish.
I cannot count or see myself, but must
Keep a few memories, a will, a faith
And too, some images of hair and lips.

Prayer of Little Hope

My god you shall not thus forsake me, you
The nonexisting, whom I feel and who
(Mute giant hidden in the world's multitude,
Whose power is in the fire, the flood and the sling)
Are master to whom go insults and prayers;
I never needed more your help to come
And you were never more deaf and more dumb.

Evening in the Walls

You are with me this evening, all my friends.
I hear your voices in the dark, I see your faces.
My power is made of all your little powers.
And as I think of you I gather strength.

Translated by Charles Guenther

OTHER LANGUAGES

GERMAN

Rose Ausländer

Rose Ausländer was born in 1918 in Bukovina—at that time still part of the Austro-Hungarian empire. She now lives in Germany. Selected Poems, *a volume in English translation, was published in 1977.*

My Nightingale

My mother once was a doe.
Her golden-brown eyes
her grace
remain from that time.

Here she was
half angel half human—
the center was mother.
When I asked her what she'd have liked to be
she said: A nightingale.

Now she is a nightingale.
Night after night I hear her
in the garden of my sleepless dream.
She sings of her ancestors' Zion
she sings of the old Austria
she sings of the hills and the beech woods
of Bukovina.
Cradle songs
sung to me night after night
by my nightingale
in the garden of my sleepless dream.

Father

At the court of the miracle-working Rabbi of Sadagora
father learned the intricate secrets.
His earlocks rang legends,
his hands held the Hebrew forest.

Trees of sacred letters extending their roots
from Sadagora to Czernowitz.
The Jordan then ran into the Pruth—
magic melodies in the waters.
Father sang them learnt them and sang the
ancestral legacy growing one with
forest and waters.

Behind the willows by the mill
stood the dreamed ladder
leaning against the sky.
Jacob took on the struggle with the angels;
always his will prevailed.

From Sadagora to Czernowitz and
back to the Sacred Court traveled the miracles
nesting in the blood.
The boy learned the heaven knew the
dimensions of angels their distance and numbers
was expert in the Kabbala's maze.

One day at seventeen he wanted
to see the other side
went into the temporal city
fell in love with it
and clung there.

OTHER LANGUAGES

Jerusalem

When I hang up my blue-and-white scarf
eastward
Jerusalem swings over to me
with Temple and Song of Songs

I am five thousand years young

My scarf
is a swing

When I close my eyes
eastward
Jerusalem on the hill
five thousand years young
swings over to me
in an aroma of oranges

Coevals
we have a game
in the air

Passover

The map
takes me back

In the kitchen
shining the moons
of the mythical bread

From my dead mother's sleeve
I fetch the harp
a wind from the eastern pastoral valley
touches the strings

Plagues and miracles
sand snakes

The lamb the lamb

Hasidic Jew from Sadagora

Old man of eighty.
His beard praying white
on his chest.

On his caftan
angels found rest
after the strain of worldly flights.
His sabbath crown
the *stramel**
his only ornament.

Lids downcast
his gaze hung about by veils
dwelled in the prayer-house.

Monday and Thursday fasting:
let the body be light
his nourishment: praises
rocking in the rhythm of
biblical prayers and other
holy words.

Few words—
the world of appearances deserves neither
words nor touching with obese interest.
Appearances are shadows
the Lord (not uttered His Name!)
should be served by your mind.

In the twin-scroll Torah
lie light and song
speaks the people's history.
Behold your bride:
in gold-embroidered velvet gown and
coroneted headdress
your lips may kiss her
your arms may embrace her
as you dance with her
to the glory of the Lord.

So danced the Sadagora Hasid
with the other Hasidim.

**stramel*—fur-trimmed hat worn by Hasidic Jews.

Phoenix

Phoenix
my people
the flame-devoured

Risen
under cypresses and
oranges

Honey
of bitter bees

Song of Solomon
the ancient landscape
hill-winged
in the echo
Jerusalem-new

Beyond the wall of tears
the phoenix period
in flames

In Chagall's Village

Crooked gables
hanging on
the skyline.

The well is dozing
under the light of
cats' eyes.

The farmer's wife is
milking the goat
in the dream shed.

Blue
the cherry-tree on the roof
where the bearded old man is
fiddling.

The bride
gazing into the flower's eye
floats on her veil
over the night steppe.

In Chagall's village
the cow is grazing
on the moon pasture
golden wolves are
guarding the lambs.

*The Lamed-Vov**

36 just men
hold the earth
in equilibrium
the earth holding us
in ceaseless
revolution

On their shoulders
the
36 just men
bear the recalcitrant
earth

Standing in the shadow of
their modesty
faces averted
the
36 just men
lift the recalcitrant earth
to the light

We do not know them
we never recognize the
36 just men

Translated by Ewald Osers

*The *Lamed-Vov* are the thirty-six righteous men in every generation, according to the Jewish legend. [Ed.]

Richard Beer-Hofmann

Richard Beer-Hofmann was born in Vienna in 1866. He studied law at the University of Vienna, but pursued a literary career from an early age. In 1938 the Nazis overran Vienna and Beer-Hofmann was forced to flee to New York. He died there in 1945. Beer-Hofmann, Arthur Schnitzler, and Hugo von Hofmannsthal formed the triad of Young Vienna which set the tone for poetry, drama, and narrative art of the period. His book Verse *contains all the poems he wanted preserved.*

Lullaby for Miriam

Sleep, my child—sleep, it is late!
See how the Sun there is going to bed,
Back of the mountains it's dying in red.
You—you know nothing of Sun and Death,
You bend your eyes to the glow and the light—
Sleep, there are so many suns for you still,
Sleep my child—my child, sleep well!

Sleep my child—the evening wind sighs.
Do we know where it is from, where it goes?
Dark are the tracks here, they lie concealed
From you, from me too, from us all, my child!
Blindly we go, and go on by ourselves,
No one can give to anyone help—
Sleep, my child—my child, sleep well!

Sleep, my child, don't listen to me!
For me it has meaning, to you it's a noise.
Noise merely, like water-gurgles, wind-sighs,
Words are—a life's whole earnings, maybe!
All I have earned, in my grave they will heap,
Here there's no leaving for any to keep—
Sleep, my child—my child, go to sleep!

Sleeping, Miriam?—Miriam, my child,
Banks we are, merely, and deep in us glides
Blood of the past ones, to coming ones rolled,
Blood of our fathers, their unrest and pride.
In us are all men. Who feels he's alone?
You are their life now, and their life's your own—
Life of me, Miriam, my child—sleep on!

Translated by Jonathan Griffin

Ilse Blumenthal-Weiss

Ilse Blumenthal-Weiss was born in Berlin in 1899. Her first book of poems was destroyed in the Nazi burning of the books. She currently lives in New York City and has since published two more books of poems.

A Jewish Child Prays to Jesus

I do not see you,
Jesus, on the cross,
I just see me:
Pierced by your nails,
Stained by your blood,
Crowned with your thorns,
Crushed by your pain.

You go with me through time.
You give me tears and sorrow.
You want to seek and find me,
You want to fetter and bind me
To your grief and pain.
Oh King of the Jews, the death
You once so meekly bore
Has nailed us suffering Jews
Onto the cross once more.

Translated by Erna Baber Rosenfeld

Martin Buber

Martin Buber was born in Vienna in 1878. He studied at the universities of Vienna, Leipzig, Zurich, and Berlin, where he studied philosophy and theology. During the early phases of the Nazi period, Buber traveled throughout Germany lecturing and teaching his people. In 1938 he settled in Palestine; he taught at Hebrew University until he died in 1965. He has been recognized throughout the world as one of the spiritual leaders of the age, influencing Christian as well as Jewish thinkers. His most famous book is I and Thou.

I Consider the Tree

I consider the tree:
a rigid pillar in a flood of light,
or splashes of green
traversed by the gentleness
of the blue silver ground.

OTHER LANGUAGES

I can feel it as movement:
the flowering veins around the sturdy core,
the sucking of the roots,
the breathing of the leaves,
the infinite commerce
of earth and air—
and the growing itself
in its darkness.

I can assign it to a species,
observe it as an instance
with an eye
to its construction.

Or I can recognize it
only as an expression of law;
I can dissolve it into a number,
into a pure relation
between numbers,
and make it
eternal.

Adapted by Howard Schwartz from I and Thou

The Fiddler

Martin Buber's last poem

Here on the earth's brink
I have for a time
miraculously settled my life.

Behind me in its round
without bound, the All
is hushed—only that Fiddler fiddles

obscurely. Already I stand
with you in a pack
willingly out of your tones to trace

how I came guilty without
the peculiar knowledge of it.
May I perceive, may you lay bare
to this sound soul every wound
I struck unsoundly and maintained
by pretence. Before then, Holy Player,

do not break off!

Translated by Jawaid Awan

Paul Celan

Paul Celan (Anczel) was born in Romanian Bukovina in 1920. The Nazis sent his parents to an extermination camp and Celan to a labor camp. After short stays in Vienna and Bucharest, he settled in Paris in 1948. He committed suicide in 1970. Six volumes of poems were published during his lifetime and three more were published posthumously. He also translated poetry from French and other languages. Speech-Grille, *a selection of his poems in English, was published in 1975 in America.* Selected Poems *appeared in England in 1972.*

Psalm

No one kneads us again of earth and clay,
no one incants our dust.
No one.

Blessed art thou, No-one.
For thy sake we
will bloom.
Towards
thee.

We were, we are, we shall remain
a Nothing,
blooming:
the Nothing-, the
No-one's-Rose.

With
the style soul-bright,
the filament heaven-void,
the corolla red
from the purple word that we sang
over, oh over
the thorn.

In Prague

Half of death,
suckled along with our life,
lay about us as true as an ash-image—

we too
still drank, soul-crossed, two swords,
sewn to sky-stones, born in word-blood
in the night-bed,

bigger and bigger
we grew in (con-) fusion, there was
no name anymore for
what drove us (one of the thirty-
what?
was my living shadow,
that climbed the chimerical stairway up to you),

a tower,
the half built itself into the where,
a Hradčany
all of alchemist-no,

bone-Hebrew,
ground into sperm,
ran through the sand-glass,
in which we swam, two dreams now, tolling
against time, on the squares.

Death Fugue

Black milk of dawn we drink it at dusk
we drink it at noon and at daybreak we drink it at night
we drink it and drink it
we are digging a grave in the air there's room for us all
A man lives in the house he plays with the serpents he writes
he writes when it darkens to Germany your golden hair Margarete
he writes it and steps outside and the stars all aglisten he whistles
for his hounds
he whistles for his Jews he has them dig a grave in the earth
he commands us to play for the dance

Black milk of dawn we drink you at night
we drink you at daybreak and noon we drink you at dusk
we drink and we drink
A man lives in the house he plays with the serpents he writes
he writes when it darkens to Germany your golden hair Margarete
Your ashen hair Shulamite we are digging a grave in the air there's
room for us all

He shouts cut deeper in the earth to some the rest of you sing and
play
he reaches for the iron in his belt he heaves it his eyes are blue
make your spades cut deeper the rest of you play for the dance

Black milk of dawn we drink you at night
we drink you at noon and at daybreak we drink you at dusk
we drink and we drink
a man lives in the house your golden hair Margarete
your ashen hair Shulamite he plays with the serpents

He shouts play death more sweetly death is a master from Germany
he shouts play the violins darker you'll rise as smoke in the air
then you'll have a grave in the clouds there's room for you all

Black milk of dawn we drink you at night
we drink you at noon death is a master from Germany
we drink you at dusk and at daybreak we drink and we drink you
death is a master from Germany his eye is blue
he shoots you with bullets of lead his aim is true
a man lives in the house your golden hair Margarete
he sets his hounds on us he gives us a grave in the air
he plays with the serpents and dreams death is a master from
    Germany

your golden hair Margarete
your ashen hair Shulamite

Ash-Glory

Ash-glory behind
your shaken-knotted
hands on the three-forked road.

Pontic once-upon: here,
a drop
on
the drowned oar-blade,
deep
in the petrified vow,
it roars up.

(On the perpendicular
breath-rope, at that time,
higher than above,
between two pain-knots, while
the shiny
Tartar moon climbed up to us,
I burrowed into you and into you.)

Ash-
glory behind
your three-forked
hands.

The thing diced before you
from the East, dreadful.

No one
bears witness for the
witness.

Cello Entry

Cello entry
from behind the hurt:

the powers, in echelons
toward anti-skies,
roll the inexplicable in front of
flying-lane and entrance,

the
climbed evening
is filled with lung-branchings,

two
fire-clouds of breath
dig in the book
that the temple-noise opened,

something turns true,

the yonder pierced by arrows
glows twelve times,

the black-
blossomed female drinks
the seed of the black-blossomed male,

all is less than
it is,
all is more.

In Egypt

Thou shalt say to the eye of the strange woman: Be the water.
Thou shalt seek in the eye of the strange woman those whom you
know to be in the water.
Thou shalt call them forth from the water: Ruth! Naomi! Miriam!
Thou shalt adorn them when you lie with the strange woman.
Thou shalt adorn them with the cloud-hair of the strange woman.
Thou shalt say to Ruth and Miriam and Naomi:
Behold, I sleep with her!
Thou shalt adorn most beautifully the strange woman next to you.
Thou shalt adorn her with the grief for Ruth, for Miriam and
Naomi.
Thou shalt say to the strange woman:
Behold, I slept with them!

Tenebrae

We are near, Lord,
near and tangible.

Clutched already, Lord,
clawed into one another, as
though each of our bodies were
your body, Lord.

Pray, Lord,
pray to us,
we are near.

Warped, we went there,
went there, to bend over
trough and crater.

We went to the watering-place, Lord.

It was blood, it was
what you had shed, Lord.

It shone.

It cast your image in our eyes, Lord.
Eyes and mouth are so open and blank, Lord.

We have drunk, Lord.
The blood and the image in the blood, Lord.

Pray, Lord.
We are near.

Zürich, zum Storchen

for Nelly Sachs

The talk was of too much, too
little. Of thou
and thou again, of
the dimming through light, of
Jewishness, of
your God.

Of
that.
On the day of an ascension, the
cathedral stood on the other side, it passed
over the water with some gold.

The talk was of your God, I spoke
against Him, I
let the heart that I had,
hope:
for His highest, His deathrattled, His
angry word—

Your eye looked at me, looked away,
your mouth
spoke to your eye, I heard:

We
simply do not know, you know,
we
simply do not know
what
counts.

Corona

The fall eats its leaf from my hand: we are friends.
We now shuck time from the nuts and teach it to walk:
time returns to the shell.

In the mirror it's Sunday,
in the dream there is sleeping,
the mouth speaks truth.

My eye descends to the sex of the beloved:
we gaze at one another,
we speak dark things,
we love one another like poppy and memory,
we sleep like wine in the conches,
like the sea in the blood-beam of moon.

We stand entwined at the window, they look at us from the street:
it is time people knew!
It is time that the stone condescended to bloom,
that a heart beat for unrest.
It is time it were time.

It is time.

Hut Window

The eye, dark:
as a hut-window. It gathers
what was world, is world: the migrant
east, the
gliding ones, the
humans-and-Jews,
the cloud-folk, magnetically
drawing, with heart-fingers,
you, earth:
you come, you come,
we will dwell, dwell, something

(a breath? a name?)

drifts about in the Orphaned,
balletic, lumbering,
the angel's
wing weighted with invisibility, on the
raw-barked foot, top-
heavily trimmed
by the black hail that
fell there too, in Vitebsk,

(and they who sowed it, they
wrote it away
with a mimetic anti-tank claw!)

drifts, drifts about,
seeks,
seeks below,
seeks up there, far away, seeks
with the eye, brings
Alpha Centauri down, Arcturus, brings
the ray along, from the graves,
goes to the Ghetto, to Eden, culls
the constellation that he,
Man, needs to dwell in, here,
among men,
paces
off the letters and their mortal-
immortal soul,
goes to Aleph and Yud and goes on,
builds it, the shield of David, lets it
flare up, once,
lets it go out—standing there,
invisible, standing
with Alpha and Aleph, with Yud,
with the others, with
you: in
you,

Bet—this is
the house where the table stands with

the light and the light.

Just Think

Just think:
the peatbog soldier of Masada
teaches himself homeland,
indelibly,
against
all thorn in wire.

Just think:
the eyeless ones without form
lead you free through the turmoil, you
strengthen and
strengthen.

Just think: your
own hand
once held
this piece
of inhabitable earth
that was
agonied back
up into life.

Just think:
this came towards me,
name-alert, hand-alert
forever,
from the unburiable.

A Speck of Sand

Stone from which I carved you
when the night laid waste its woods:
I carved you as a tree
and cloaked you in the brown of my softest words
as in bark—

A bird,
hatched from the roundest tear,
stirs above you like leaves:

You can wait
until among all the eyes a sand-grain glows for you,
a speck of sand
that helped me to dream
when I submerged to find you—

You take root towards the grain,
a root that makes you full-fledged
when the ground is aglow with death,
you stretch up,
and I glide ahead as a leaf
that knows where the gates will open.

Turn Blind

Turn blind this very day:
eternity too is full of eyes—
in it
what helped the images over
the road they followed, drowns;
in it
what removed you too from language
with a gesture, fades,
a gesture you allowed like
the dance of two words that are all
autumn and silk and nothingness.

Over Three Nipple-Stones

Over three nipple-
stones numbered
with brown-algae blood
in sea-
drunken sleep

turn your
sky tearing loose
from the last
string of rain.

And let
your sweetwater shell
that came riding here with you

sip all this
up before
you hold it to
a clock-shadow's ear
at dusk.

Translated by Joachim Neugroschel

Hilde Domin

Hilde Domin was born in Cologne in 1912 and studied in Heidelberg, Berlin, and Rome. From 1939 to 1954 she lived abroad in England, Italy, South America, and the United States. Since 1961 she has lived in Heidelberg. She has published four volumes of poetry, a novel, critical essays, and translations of Ungaretti and Neruda. She has been awarded the Literature Prize of the Heinrich Heine Society.

Catalogue

The heart a snail
with a house
draws in its horns.

The heart a hedgehog.

The heart an owl
in light
fluttering its eyelids.

Bird of passage, climate-changer heart.

The heart a ball
pushed
rolling one centimeter.

Sand-grain heart.

The heart the great
thrower
of every ball.

Cologne

The submerged city
for me
alone
submerged.

I swim
in the streets.
Others walk.

The old houses
have big new doors
of glass.

The dead and I
we swim
through the new doors
of our old houses.

Dreamwater

Dreamwater
full of drowned days.

Dreamwater
rising in the streets.

Dreamwater
bears me away.

Translated by Tudor Morris

Alfred Grünewald

Alfred Grünewald was born in Vienna in 1884. When the Germans occupied Austria he tried to commit suicide but survived and was imprisoned in a concentration camp. Several years later he was deported from Nice and killed in an extermination camp. Before the Holocaust he published nineteen books of poems, aphorisms, and plays.

The Lamp Now Flickers

The lamp now flickers in your hand
And they'll forget you all too soon.
For all too fast the wick burns down
And they'll forget you in the dark.
You ask yourself, how well have I
Now done my duty before I die?
Though many a man has called you friend
They'll now forget you all too soon,
For you proved lacking, regretted it,
Then lost yourself, confused, and loosed
So many ties that bound you once,
That they'll forget you now too soon.
Slowly your locks have turned to gray
Though you have known the joys of love,
But even better all its pains.
Now they'll forget you very soon,
For what you were must fade away
Since time wears out the stoutest rock.
You wander on the lone seashore
And know that they'll forget you soon
When no more lips pronounce your name.
See how you wrote it once in sand
And soon no trace of it remains.

Translated by Edouard Roditi

Jakov van Hoddis

Jakov van Hoddis (Hans Davidsohn) was born in 1887 in Berlin. In 1911 he began to publish poetry and prose, at first in the leading Expressionist periodicals. His poem "Weltende," included here in translation, is widely credited with initiating the whole Expressionist movement in German poetry. He was baptized and practiced Catholicism for a while. After 1915, he spent most of his life in private clinics and psychiatric hospitals, no longer writing at all, as far as is known. In 1942, he was deported to a Nazi death camp.

End of the World

From off his pointed head flies Herr Schmidt's hat
And as with howls the vaulted skies resound.
Off roofs repairmen crash and fall apart.
The coasts report that tidal waves abound.

The tempest's here, the roaring seas cavort
Across the land, crash through the stoutest dams.
Most people think it's flu that they have caught
And from the bridges dangle trains and trams.

Translated by Edouard Roditi

The Air Vision

Lamp, don't moan.
A lady's slender arm rose from the wall.
It was pale and blue-veined.
The fingers were daubed with precious stones.
As I kissed the hand I was afraid:
It was warm and alive.
It clawed at my face;
I took a kitchen knife and cut its veins.
A great cat gracefully lapped the blood on the floor;
While a shaggy-haired man
Climbed up after a broomstick leaning against the wall.

Tohub

Three little fellows sing to the wind
the terrible song:
Do you have bugs, lice, fleas—
your time won't be so long.

You always have to munch
a scanty this or that.
You can seize and crunch,
Lord be praised.

Why think your time is long
when you decay so nobly.
Your minutes become places,
you only see time and complain.

You hear inside your skull
your hair thrusting you from the grass.
Your jaw becomes a rattle,
moaning tediously through the years,
endlessly opening and closing.

Three little fellows sing to the wind
the terrible song:
Do you have bugs, lice, fleas—
your time won't be so long.

They climbed into the dawn
and sang day and night
and upset breakfasts and dinners
and earth and air were shattered.

Translated by Charles Guenther

Alfred Kittner

Alfred Kittner was born in Bukovina in 1906 and studied in Vienna. He was held in a concentration camp during World War II. His first poems were published as early as 1923. Since then he has gained a reputation as a poet and translator of Romanian poets into German. He lives in Bucharest.

Old Jewish Cemetery in Worms

February 1974

My steps are wet from the cold death
you received in your warm beds;
that of your children was *hot:*
smoke columns signified their end.
Not you, but I, was witness to this.
In the forest of death where you rest
time wears away rhymed phrases
stating regret at being severed
from life in the country you loved
and thought to be your own.
Grandsons of assassins act as guides,
emphasizing what has survived the Reich.
There's no one here to take the blame;
only the innocent returned:
the guilty either died or fled.
Stones placed on graves by the faithful
a century ago, now crack and crumble:
a silent reproach, a stifled scream—
the questions will remain unanswered,
and no new graves will be dug here.

Epilogue
In April, 1974, the old Jewish cemetery in Worms was devastated. Gravestones were pulled out of the ground and smashed. Those left were desecrated with the swastika.

Blue Owl Song

Do you hear the blue owl shriek?

A song in the morning,
a call at noon,
a shriek in the evening.

But at night,
at night—this silence
when blue changes to gray
and gray to silver,
the silver of the moon
to the silver of silence
that draws us
into games with shadows,
into games with worms.

My blue owl
with eyes gazing at the sky,
with beak tilted toward the grave,
holds in its claws
a ball once called noon
and now cold as ice.
It hears the blue owl shriek,
drawing out the red
that was my blood.

The ball gets tangled in thorns
and bleeds.
And the owl's eyes
pierce the dark
through a darkened window
in emptiness and madness.
Behind the owl who imitates you,
the blue, the gray
covered with silver,
eyes gazing at the sky,
beak tilted toward the grave.
Its song,
its call,
its shriek.

And it knows you're coming,
hopping, limping and hobbling
for games with shadows,
for games with worms
in the silver of night
that lies behind night
and draws you into its silence.

Translated by Herbert Kuhner

Alma Johanna Koenig

Alma Johanna Koenig was born in Prague in 1887. In addition to writing lyrical poetry of a mainly autobiographical nature, she distinguished herself as an author of fine historical novels and autobiographical fiction. In May 1942 she was deported to a death camp somewhere in Eastern Europe. Her finest poems, a series of twenty-two Sonnets for Jan, *were published only posthumously after the war.*

Intimations

My childhood was like a dark passage
Along which, pursued, I escaped.
Between crumbling walls I fled
And I wept and called as I went.

My youth was a cavernous pit
Where daylight sank like a stone.
I wandered through streets ablaze at night
In the echo of songs that rang from afar.

My womanhood now is a grinding of mills
That groan as they crush their meager grain,
Yet I needed to see your smile but once
And this was reward and more for all.

Translated by Edouard Roditi

Gertrud Kolmar

Gertrud Kolmar was born in Berlin in 1894. She lived a secluded life with her family until she was arrested in 1943 and killed in a concentration camp. Most of her poetry appeared posthumously; it has been published in various collections. A translation of a selection of poems, Dark Soliloquy, *was published in the United States.*

The Woman Poet

You hold me now completely in your hands.

My heart beats like a frightened little bird's
Against your palm. Take heed! You do not think
A person lives within the page you thumb.
To you this book is paper, cloth, and ink,

Some binding thread and glue, and thus is dumb,
And cannot touch you (though the gaze be great
That seeks you from the printed marks inside),
And is an object with an object's fate.

And yet it has been veiled like a bride,
Adorned with gems, made ready to be loved,
Who asks you bashfully to change your mind,
To wake yourself, and feel, and to be moved.

But still she trembles, whispering to the wind:
"This shall not be." And smiles as if she knew.
Yet she must hope. A woman always tries,
her very life is but a single "You . . ."

With her black flowers and her painted eyes,
With silver chains and silks of spangled blue.
She knew more beauty when a child and free,
But now forgets the better words she knew.

A man is so much cleverer than us,
Conversing with himself of truth and lie,
Of death and spring and iron-work and time.
But I say "you" and always "you and I."

This book is but a girl's dress in rhyme,
Which can be rich and red, or poor and pale,
Which may be wrinkled, but with gentle hands,
And only may be torn by loving nails.

So then, to tell my story, here I stand.
The dress's tint, though bleached in bitter lye,
Has not all washed away. It still is real.
I call then with a thin, ethereal cry.

You hear me speak. But do you hear me feel?

The Jewish Woman

I am a stranger.

Since no one dares approach me
I would be girded with towers
That wear their steep and stone-gray caps
Aloft in clouds.

The brazen key you will not find
That locks the musty stair. It spirals skyward
As a serpent lifts its scaly head
Into the light.

Oh these walls decay like cliffs
That streams have washed a thousand years;
And birds with raw and wrinkled craws
Lie burrowed deep in caves.

Inside the halls of sifting sand
Crouch lizards hiding speckled breasts—
An expedition I would mount
Into my ancient land.

Perhaps somewhere I can unearth
The buried Ur of the Chaldeans,
The idol Dagon, Hebrew tents,
Or the horn of Jericho.

What once blew down the haughty walls
Now lies in twisted ruin underground;
And yet I once drew breath
To sound its note.

Eternal worlds will echo back my call.
And when I bend my neck
The shaking earth will wreck
Its cities: I am greatest. I am all.

Sea-Monster

When I conceived the child with star-green eyes,
Conceived your child, this frail and wondrous thing,
We heard salt water in the cisterns sigh,
Saw Elmo's fire in lanterns against the sky,
And midnight wore its coral ring.

And from your breasts a seaweed mane was flowing,
So green, so green, with silent melody.
And quiet ripples splashed from gentle rowing,
From black dream-rushes songs of swans were blowing,
And no one else could hear but we.

At midnight you had risen from the sea,
Your body dripping cool and icy smooth.
The ocean spoke a hushed soliloquy
Of how you lay so gently next to me
And how your arms embraced and soothed.

Sea-virgins came and swam mysterious dances;
Dark music from wild harps resounded free.
The moon poured out its light in silvery lances
On pearly scales and submarine romances;
And all my sheets smelled of the sea.

And once again the shepherds watched their flocks,
And, as before, there shone an unnamed star.
And ships that lay at anchor by strange rocks
Tossed in their sleep and dreamed of distant docks,
The ports of home, now small and far.

And fans of flower-beasts broke open wide,
Spread out across my body by your hand,
While manta-rays swam round me with the tide
And olive-snails and periwinkles plied
Across my dune-white hip of sand.

The glances of your pale beryl eyes
Chased hooded vipers home to caves in flight,
While shining salmon leapt toward the skies.
Bright beads of spray on wave-tops crystallized,
Blue as the raven hair of night.

Oh you! Your body sank into my sea;
I wooed and sang and swept you like a shoal.
And all the winds blew kisses and caressed me.
And all the forests toppled down within me.
And all the rivers ran into my soul.

Translated by Henry A. Smith

Else Lasker-Schüler

Else Lasker-Schüler was born in Elberfeld in 1869. She was prominent in the Berlin bohemia of 1910-1930 and was a leader of Expressionism. She first emigrated to Switzerland in 1933 and then to Jerusalem, where she died in 1945. She wrote plays, prose fantasies, and poems.

Abraham and Isaac

Abraham in the land of Eden
Built himself a town of earth and leaves
And practiced talking to God.

The angels liked to rest by his pious hut
And Abraham knew each one;
Their winged steps left heavenly signs.

Until once in their fearful dreams
They heard the tortured rams bleating,
Isaac was playing with sacrifices behind the licorice trees.

And God exhorted: Abraham!
He broke shells off the comb of the sea, and sponge,
To adorn the altar high on the boulders.

And bore his only son bound to his back,
To do justice to his great Master—
But He did love His servant.

Hagar and Ishmael

Abraham's little sons played with seashells
And sailed the boats of mother-of-pearl;
Then Isaac anxiously leaned against Ishmael

And sadly they sang, the two black swans,
Such gloomy notes about their gaudy world,
And Hagar, expelled, quickly kidnapped her son.

Shed her great tears in his small tears,
And their hearts rushed like the holy source,
And even outstripped the ostriches.

But the sun burnt harshly on the desert,
And Hagar and her boy-child sank into the yellow hide,
And bit their white teeth in the hot sand.

Homesickness

I don't know the language
Of this cool country,
I can't keep its pace.

Nor can I divine
The passing clouds.

The night is a step-queen.

I always have to think of Pharaoh's woods
And I kiss the clusters of my stars.

My lips are already aglow
And speak far things,

And I am a gaudy picture-book
On your lap.

But your face is spinning
A veil of weeping.

My iridescent birds
Have had their corals poked out,
Their soft nests are turning into stone
On the hedges of the gardens.

Who shall anoint my dead palaces—
They once wore the crowns of my fathers,
Their prayers sank in the holy river.

Abel

Cain's eyes are not gracious to God,
Abel's face is a golden garden,
Abel's eyes are nightingales.

His singing is always so clear
For the strings of his soul,
But the ditches of town go through Cain's body.

And he will slay his brother—
Abel, Abel, your blood colors heaven deep.

Where is Cain, for I wish to storm him:
Have you slain the sweet birds
In your brother's face?

Jacob

Jacob was the buffalo of his herd.
Whenever he stamped his hooves
The earth flashed sparks beneath him.

Bellowing he left his dappled brothers.
Dashed through the ancient forest to the rivers,
And stilled the blood of the monkeybites.

The weary pains in his ankles
Brought him low to fever beneath the sky,
And his ox-face fashioned the smile.

Moses and Joshua

When Moses was as old as God,
He took Joshua, the wild Jew,
And anointed him king of his host.

A soft yearning passed through Israel—
For Joshua's heart refreshed like a well.
His altar was the Jewish body of the Bible nation.

The maidens liked their kingly brother—
His heart burnt sweet like a holy bush of thorns;
His smile would greet the longed-for star of homeland,

That rose to Moses' ancient, dying eye,
When his soul, a weary lion, cried to God.

Pharaoh and Joseph

Pharaoh rejects his blossoming wives,
Sweetly they smell of the gardens of Amon.

His royal head rests on my shoulder,
Which gives off the odor of rye.

Pharaoh is golden.
His eyes go and come
Like iridescent waves of the Nile.

But his heart lies in my blood;
Ten wolves came to be watered.

Pharaoh always thinks
Of my brothers,
Who threw me in the pit.

In his sleep his arms become columns
And threaten!

But his dreamer's heart
Soughs at my depth.

Thus my lips indite
Great sweetnesses
In the wheat of our morning.

Saul

The great *melech** lies waking over Judah.
A stony camel carries its roof.
Shy cats are prowling round the cracking columns.

And night sinks lightless in its grave,
Saul's full eye waned into an orb.
The keening of the women rose to howling.

But at his gates the Canaanites are standing.
—Now he subdues the first intruder, Death—
And with five hundred thousand men he swings the clubs.

Translated by Joachim Neugroschel

Lord, Listen

Night draws itself as tight
As a ring around my eyes.
My pulse has changed my blood
To fire, but all is gray

And cold around me. Lord, and in
The living day I dream of death,
Drink it with water, eat it in bread:
On Thy scales all weights fail for my grief.

**Melech*—king in Hebrew

Lord, listen: in Thy beloved blue
I sang the song of Thy heaven's roof
And in Thy eternal breath did not wake the day.
Before Thee my heart feels shame for its dumb scar.

Where must I end? Lord, in the stars
I looked, and in the moon and the valleys of Thy fruit.
The red wine is already tasteless in the grape
And everywhere, in every core, there's bitterness.

Translated by Edouard Roditi

Alfred Lichtenstein

Alfred Lichtenstein was born in Berlin in 1889. He was killed in action in World War I in September 1914. He had published a small book of verse a year before his death. Two volumes of his poems and stories were collected posthumously.

The Journey to the Insane Asylum

A little girl crouches with her little brother
beside a tumbled water cask.
In rags, a human wreck lies
like a cigarette stub in the yellow sun.

Two thin goats stand in wide, green spaces,
bound to a peg. The rope tightens at times.
Invisible behind enormous trees,
in an incredible calm,
approaches the great horror.

Repose

An ailing fish moves in tired circles
in a pool that lies upon the grass.
A tree leans near the sky—burnt and crooked.

See . . . the family sits around the big table
and picks with forks from plates.
Slowly one gets sleepy, heavy, dumb.

The sun licks the ground with a hot and poisoned mouth
like a dog—a wild fiend.
Hobos drop suddenly without a trace.

A coachman looks with worry at a horse
that, torn apart, cries in the gutter.
Three children stand around in silence.

Translated by Mary Zilzer

Conny Hannes Meyer

Conny Hannes Meyer was born in 1931 in Vienna. He has published several volumes of poetry and plays, and is director of the Komödianten Repertory Theater in the Kunstlerhaus in Vienna.

Of the Beloved Caravan

in the book of the iron angels there is nothing
of forbidden carnations and stars weren't mentioned

thus those who bore the flaming mark
came forth from the right hand of God

they wore the desert sand in their hair
and sand was their bitter nourishment

they silently ate it and it was their crown
and morning and evening it was their time

they dug for deep stones at night
but a bush never burned for them

no sanctified staff of maple
indicated the way to Gomorrah

they went alone

they followed shrouds of melancholy
their blood in golden jars
their tears in jars of clay

day after day they walked on bare feet
they walked to Gomorrah through the night
just as mutely as those who had gone before them

they were accompanied by serpents that danced
and showed them the way to Gomorrah which was far
and the serpents showed them the way silently

they were joined by vultures
that silently circled the desert sky above

and silently circled and circled
at evening at morning in darkness and light

the tent of a tree
seldom arose out of the endless dunes

and if it did it was as black as a juniper
and they looked up
but the beating of wings in the branches
came from vultures and not messengers

they bore the mark
they were chosen
they bore the grave in their hair
Gomorrah was lost to them.

The Beast That Rode the Unicorn

let go of the unicorn's reins
and step from the bloodied stirrups into a sea of tears
and wash feet and hands

then put the rings
on the bone joints
the darkest grenade of the dead Jewess

thus you make a feast of Treblinka

they hoist your flag
the white symbol
they are already singing the magic fire-song
soon the fresh smoke will crown your blond hair
death glitters steelblue at your hip

strange lights illuminate your dance
you dance lightly and proudly to the beat
of whips
along the great trenches of Treblinka

you're thinking of Erika
the little flower that blooms on the heath
and kisses the dog-pack

yours is the land where ashes lay
where the holy tablets were broken

it is the time of the golden teeth
which you give to your son to use as dice
he throws them over coffin and pennon
counting nine at each throw

and includes you
and then goes to sleep

his dream of beautiful death descends to him
you beckon to him
he offers you his hands

and he gently sways with you over Treblinka
the dead heath with the white grass
where meadows will never grow again
where the unicorn devoured all buds and traces.

Translated by Herbert Kuhner

Alfred Mombert

Alfred Mombert was born in Karlsruhe in 1872. After practicing law for several years he devoted himself to writing poetry. He was arrested by the Gestapo in 1940 and died shortly after release from a concentration camp in 1942. Mombert wrote a dramatic trilogy in free verse entitled Aeon *which was published in 1907-1911.*

The Chimera

A monster rests upon my roof,
its dragon eyes gleam murder in the stormy night.
It rests upon the marble roof,
deep in the park, its head in a flurry of crimson leaves,
its tail coiled around its monster form—
proud and sensual, it breathes a monster's breath.

Deep in the palace below
I lie in my darkened room. I cannot sleep.
I hear, I hear that constant breathing.
When will a noble warrior come to rescue me,
to free me from this wild one—when will I sleep?
A thousand archers, eyes aglow, lie hidden
in the park of bloody autumn,
taking aim:
not one will hit his mark, not one.

Down in my room I cannot sleep,
my blood begins to boil,
my thoughts are wild and closing in on me—
one thought alone is sovereign, terrible, glorious:
that I will sleep, sleep high above,
on the proud bosom, in the lover's clutches
of the terrible chimera with the murderous eyes.

Translated by Erna Baber Rosenfeld

Joseph Roth

Joseph Roth was born in East Galicia in 1894. He began a career in journalism in Germany until Hitler came to power in 1933. He died in Paris in 1939. Besides his articles, short stories and poems, Roth wrote fourteen novels, of which several have been translated into English.

Ahasuerus

Go and lose your way one night,
Peer in through the window panes,
Notice how they sit together,
How the youngest of them laughs,
Listen how the lamp is singing,
How they eat and how they chatter,
How they linger, how they tarry
When it's time to go to bed.

Out of doors you have to freeze
And shudder, wandering through the night,
And that star above you twinkles,
And you rage inside to hear it
Laughing at you, full of scorn . . .
Wandering is in your blood,
Driven by ancestral strains,
Having neither rights nor money,
Neither worldly goods nor love.
They can beat you without mercy,
And the heartless nights of winter
Will be sure to tell you, jeering
What it means to yearn for home.

Translated by Erna Baber Rosenfeld

Nelly Sachs

Nelly Sachs was born in Berlin in 1891. She lived in seclusion and fear during the Nazi regime until her escape to Stockholm in 1940. In addition to several volumes of poetry she composed a series of plays called Scenic Poetry. *Nelly Sachs received the Nobel Prize for Literature in 1966. Translations of her work into English include* O the Chimneys. *She died in Stockholm in 1970.*

Burning Sand of Sinai

But who tipped the sand out of your shoes
When you had to get up to die?
The sand Israel brought home,
The sand of his wandering?
Burning sand of Sinai
Mixed with the throats of nightingales
Mixed with the wings of the butterfly
Mixed with the longing dust of snakes
Mixed with all that fell away from the wisdom of Solomon
Mixed with the bitters from the secret of wormwood—

O fingers
Tipping the sand out of the shoes of the dead
Tomorrow you will be dust
In the shoes of those coming!

Hasidim Dance

Night flutters
with death-snatched flags

Black hats
God's lightning conductors
stir up the sea

rock it
rock it out

throw it on to the beach
there where the light
has cut out the black wounds.

On the tongue
the world is tasted
chanted
breathing with the lung of the beyond.

On the menorah
the Pleiades pray—

O the Chimneys

And when this my skin has been destroyed, without my flesh I shall see God.
*—Job 19:26**

O the chimneys
On the cleverly devised abodes of death,
As Israel's body drew, dissolved in smoke,
Through the air—
As a chimney-sweep a star received it
Turning black
Or was it a sunbeam?

O the chimneys!
Roads to freedom for Jeremiah's and Job's dust—
Who devised you and stone upon stone built
The road for refugees from smoke?

O the abodes of death
Invitingly arranged
For the host of the house who was once a guest—
O fingers
Laying the threshold
Like a knife between life and death—

O chimneys,
O fingers,
And Israel's body in the smoke through the air!

*The Hebrew reads literally "from my flesh," apparently meaning "released from . . ." Christian interpreters have generally taken the phrase to mean "looking out from . . ."—the exact opposite. The translation given above is from the German version quoted by the poet.—*Trans.*

O Night of the Crying Children

O night of the crying children!
Night of the children consigned to death!
There is no way into sleep any more.
Frightful women attendants
Have taken over from mothers,
Have stretched false death in the muscles of their hands,
They sow it in the walls and the beams—
Everywhere these brood in the nest of horror.
The little ones suck fear instead of their mothers' milk.

Mother only yesterday
Drew sleep on like a white moon,
The doll with its rouge kissed away
Came on one arm,
The stuffed animal, already
Brought to life in love,
Came on the other arm—
Now the wind of dying blows,
Shirts billow out over hair
No one will comb any more.

What Secret Desires of the Blood

What secret desires of the blood,
What dreams of delusion, what soil
Murdered a thousand times
Have let the frightful puppeteer emerge?

He who foaming at the mouth
Dreadfully blew down
The round, encircling scaffold of his deed
With the skyline of fear looming ash-gray!

O the hills of dust which as though from an angry moon
The murderers played:

Arms up and down,
Legs up and down
And the sinking sun of the people of Sinai
As the red carpet underfoot.

Arms up and down,
Legs up and down
And on the looming ash-gray skyline of fear
Colossal the star of death
Standing like the clock of the times.

To You Building the New House

There are stones like souls
—Rabbi Nachman

When you put up your walls afresh—
Your hearth, bedstead, table and chair—
Don't hang your tears around those who are gone,
Who will no longer live with you
By stone
Not by wood—
Or else it will weep into your sleep,
Fitful, still needful.

Don't sigh when you put your shroud to bed,
Or else your dreams will mingle
With the sweat of the dead.

Oh, the walls and the tools are
Sensitive as aeolian harps
And as a field where your sorrow grows,
And they track down what in you is akin to dust.

Build when the clock of the hours trickles
But don't weep the minutes away
Along with the dust
That cloaks the light.

One Chord

One chord is played by ebb and flow,
By hunter and hunted.
Many hands
Try to seize and secure,
Blood is the thread.

Fingers point to displays,
Parts of the body are put
Into dying designs.

Strategy,
Smell of suffering—

Limbs bound for the dust
And the foam of longing
Over the waters.

Translated by Keith Bosley

Chorus of the Rescued

We, the rescued,
Out of whose hollow bones Death was already carving its flutes,
Across whose sinews Death was already moving its bow—
The mourning of our bodies still resounds
With their maimed music.
We, the rescued,
Still see the nooses twisted for our necks
Hanging in the blue air.
The hour glasses are still filling with our dripping blood.
We, the rescued,
Are still gnawed at by the worms of fear.
Our stars are buried in the dust.
We, the rescued,
Beg of you:
Show us our sun slowly,
Lead us from star to star step by step.
Gently let us learn to live again.
Otherwise, the song of a bird,
The filling of a pail at the well
Could tear open again badly sealed pain
And flush us away.
We beg of you:

Do not show us a barking dog as yet.
It could be, it just could be
That we shall disintegrate into dust,
Turn into dust before your eyes.
For what keeps our substance together?
We have become devoid of breath
Since our souls fled to Him in the dark of night,
Long before they rescued our bodies.
We, the rescued,
Press your hands,
Recognize your eyes—
But what keeps us together is only the parting;
The parting in the dust
Is what connects us with you.

Translated by Harry Zohn

Hans Sahl

Hans Sahl was born in 1902 in Dresden, Germany. He studied art history, literature, and philosophy at various universities. When Hitler came to power he escaped to Prague and from there to Zurich and Paris, where he was interned at the outbreak of World War II. Escaping from a French prison camp to Marseilles, he joined the underground and finally reached New York in 1941. He has published two books of poetry, a novel, and a radio play. He currently lives in New York City.

Memo

A man whom many held for wise
Declared once that after Auschwitz
Poetry would no longer be possible.
This wise man now seems
To have held no high opinion
Of poetry and poems,
Indeed as if they were only
A sop for the souls of soulful accountants
Or perhaps colored glass panes
Through which one can see the world.
But we believe that poems
Have only now become again
Possible, since certainly in poems
Alone can one say
What otherwise
Defies all other powers of description.

Translated by Edourd Roditi

OTHER LANGUAGES

Greeting from a Distance

I see you with my inner eye—
all you who sit as if in leaden chambers,
eating leavened bread
at half-set tables
and drinking the wine of forgetting.
Remembering me, a furtive tear joins in
the already salty meal.
But life goes on, you say.

You see me with your inner eyes—
I who have been lost over night.
Since I'm so lovable
I eluded a chemical death
by flight, depriving you
thereby of the epitaph
you hoped to write of me,
reserved for better times,
but it never came to that;
and this I ask you to forgive.
For life goes on, I say.

To show you that I'm still around
I'll send on to you, from time to time,
sundry new-world things for print,
prose scrubbed clean (as you seldom
find it any more today) but usable still
because it teaches and is not without a
critical point of view, I'll send you
crumbs from the table of language, crumbs that I
knead together in my memory
and make available once more
to human pleasure.
For life goes on, I say

Translated by Erna Baber Rosenfeld

Gershom Scholem

Gershom Scholem was born in Berlin in 1897 and studied at the universities of Berlin, Jena, Berne, and Munich. For many years he was professor of Jewish mysticism and Kabbalah at Hebrew University. He was awarded the Israel Prize for Jewish Studies. His studies in Kaballah include Major Trends in Jewish Mysticism, On the Kaballah and Its Symbolism, *and* Kabalah.

The Trial

sent in a letter to Walter Benjamin on or near the 10th of July, 1934, with a copy of Kafka's The Trial

Are we quite cut off from Thee?
Is there, God, in such a dusk
No breath of Thy serenity,
Thy message, Thy design for us?

Can Thy word have died away,
Lost in Zion's emptiness?
Has it not forced at all its way
Into this magic world, pretence?

Completed sheer up to the roof
Is the great fraud of the world.
Then, God, let him awake through whom
Thy Nothing chiseled.

Only this way Revelation
Strikes into time, which refused Thee.
Thy Nothing is the one sensation
Time is allowed to taste of Thee.

Only this way there enters memory
Perception which breaks through pretence:
This is the most certain legacy
From the hidden Judgment Bench.

OTHER LANGUAGES

Our condition was measured, to
A hair's breadth, upon Job's scale;
We are being known, through and through,
Ruthlessly as on the Last Day.

What we are is being reflected
In appeals without end.
No one knows the way completely,
Every stretch can strike us blind.

Enjoy redemption? No one may—
Much too high it stands, that star:
Even if you'd come so far,
Yourself would still stand in your way.

Abandoned to such Powers as
Entreaty cannot now enslave,
No life can unfold, unless
One that sinks into itself.

True, from the center of destruction
At times a shaft of light breaks out,
Yet none of us knows the direction
Which for us the law has set.

Ever since this hopeless truth
Stood before us, unassailable.
There has been a torn-in-two
Veil before, God, Thy majesty.

Thy hearing has begun on Earth,
Will it end before Thy throne?
Thou canst not be defended,
Here no illusion carries worth.

Who here is the accused?
Thou? or the creature? But should I
Or any of us ask Thee that question,
Thou wouldst merely sink into silence.

Does such a question even arise?
Is not the answer obvious?
Ah, we still have to live our lives
Till Thy tribunal turns to us.

Translated by Jonathan Griffin

Thomas Sessler

Thomas Sessler was born in Berlin in 1915. After pursuing publishing interests in Prague, Zurich, and Vienna, he settled in Munich and established his own publishing house.

When the Day

When the day,
the day
of deathly silence
comes,
bells will be muffled,
buds and flowers
will wither,
the stars will be
extinguished,
the tides
will stop flowing,
the atmosphere
will hang heavy
and our hands will touch
once more
before the undertow
of decomposition
grinds up
flaming graves
and gives birth
to ashes.

You Move Forward

You move forward
in a tangled knot
of humanity,
stripped of dignity
and tortured
by the black claws
of assassins,
a victim
who's been selected
to take his last steps.

Fear has left you
as you walk
the sacrificial path,
unbowed
among brothers and sisters,
knowing that you'll be
one more torch
burning
in the unatonable guilt
of the executioner.

Burnt Debris

Burnt debris
covers
the charred earth
where fields once were.
The smoke has been
blown away
and forgotten.
The shadows
in the ruins
are remnants of death.
In their numbness
they will never
procreate again.
No God or Messiah
will descend
to engender a new race.
The echo of thunder
in eternity
cancels out
the last human sigh.

Translated by Herbert Kuhner

Hugo Sonnenschein

Hugo Sonnenschein was born in Czechoslovakia in 1889. Like many Czech Jews, he wrote in German. He was one of the founders of the Czech Communist Party, from which he was later expelled. Having also been driven out of Austria, he settled in Prague until his arrest by the Gestapo in 1943. He survived a two-year imprisonment in Auschwitz, but was again imprisoned in Czechoslovakia and died there in 1953. Only a small posthumous volume of his poetry has survived.

In the Open Fields

The wind's bride seized me
With her gruesome fingers
All over my body
Groping me
And clutching me in her arms,
Kneading my flesh
And licking me all over,
Till she reached the soles of my feet
And found warmth in my flesh
That grew cold from her touch.
But I walked ahead on the open road
Into the day that was breaking.

In the Ghetto

They are the slums of great cities, with narrow streets
And poor men, very poor, bowed down and small,
In Jews' quarters that, for a long, long while,
Not a single ray of sunshine has penetrated.
Oh, the men who live there
Have no knowledge of light, of sweet-smelling breezes
In these dark quarters of the whores and the Jews
Where no birds sing, no lilac blossoms.
Sometimes, but only on days blessed by God,
Perhaps only once every hundred years,
The spring breezes bring fresh air to these people
And the sun reveals itself, shy and weak.
But the sunbeam will then find
Some youth into whose heart it will fall
So as to become a homesickness of the kind
That must bring to the world the Messiah!

Translated by Edouard Roditi

Friedrich Torberg

Friedrich Torberg was born in Vienna in 1908. In 1938 he fled to Switzerland and then settled in the United States in 1940. He has published two volumes of poetry, several novels, and a novella.

Seder, 1944

Lord, I am not one of the just.
Don't ask me, Lord, for I could not answer.
I do not know, you see, why for your servants here
this night is so different
from all the others. Why?

The youngest child was happy once
to learn the answer at the table feast:
Because we were slaves in Egypt,
in bondage to wicked Pharaoh
thousands of years ago.

And because, O Lord, you led us forth
with an outstretched arm
and delivered us from oppression and grief
and treacheries numbering a thousand,
we sit, reclining, and break into crumbling pieces
our fathers' bread of affliction.

Because we could safely hide, O Lord,
beyond the parting waters, from Pharaoh's men
who perished by your breath,
because of this we eat today the bitter herbs
dipped in the salty water.

And so we give thee thanks, O Lord,
for saving us from harm,
as we gather believing
today, and here, and in every land,
and "next year in Jerusalem."

The youngest child who heard all this
has long since lost his faith.
The answer of old no longer holds,
for "next year" never came, O Lord,
and the night weighs down heavy and dark.

We still have not wandered across the sands,
we still have not seen the Promised Land,
we still have not eaten the bread of the free,
we still have not done with the bitter herbs.

For time and again in our weary wanderings
Pharaoh has set upon our trail,
behind us he comes with his bloody henchmen—
the carts, O Lord, do you hear their clatter—
O Lord, where have you led us to!

You sent us on without a star,
we stand at the shore and stare on high,
O Lord, the flood has not returned,
O Lord, the night is not yet past,
"Why is this night so different from . . ."

Amalek

Deuteronomy 25:17-18

Thus spoke the Lord to Israel:
Because you are my chosen people,
you shall not hate the ones I did not choose,
nor shall you fall into the sin of pride.

Reserve your rancor if they do you harm,
do not turn bitter if they show their scorn,
neither Babylon nor Edom shall you hate,
not the Assyrian nor the Edomite.

And even he who boasted with a hardened heart
that he would snuff you out of life and breath,
he who paid the price with man and horse—
even the Egyptian you shall forgive.

But he who slew you from behind,
once you escaped from Pharaoh's ruthless men
and made your way towards the Promised Land,
open to every hope and all deceit,

He who struck your old and weak,
who would not let you go your way—
Amalek, the enemy of Israel—
him, said the Lord, him you shall hate.

Translated by Erna Baber Rosenfeld

Alfred Wolfenstein

Alfred Wolfenstein was born in 1888 in Halle an der Saale. He lived as a free-lance writer in Berlin and Munich until the Nazis came to power. He wandered around France under an assumed name until the liberation, but committed suicide shortly thereafter in 1945. Wolfenstein published three volumes of poems, several dramas, and a collection of short stories.

Exodus 1940

Thrown suddenly into a corner of the world,
given the boot by sinister conquest,
thrown to the edges of world at war,
with millions and alone,

Fleeing with the flight of an entire people,
up to the banks of the Loire—exploded bridges
driven through bridgeless madness,
the fire before us, above us, behind,

Stumbling over city and village in ruins,
stumbling on through June-land;
crushed into dust, the command in our ears: "Here you must die!"
yet holding one wish: "But to love!"

Here, where love gets trampled and crushed,
where a tank called History races by,
where mobs worship a new god,
I look past the pilots toward the sky—

Sun, my journey halts its errant straying,
but you will shine as well when peace returns,
you do not wander from your given course,
your light will shine when other battles burn.

Foreign sun—the only friend here I can claim—
let me speak on, for nothing else
will break this brutal silence,
the foe alone speaks in his mother tongue.

And yet a breathing fills the air from far away—
is it the breath of loved ones drawing near?
Oh how the deluge of these many years
has driven us apart.

Translated by Erna Baber Rosenfeld

Karl Wolfskehl

Karl Wolfskehl was born in Darmstadt, Germany, in 1869. After his studies he became an important member of the literary George Circle. He lived in Italy and Switzerland from 1934 through 1938, when he finally left his homeland for New Zealand, where he died in 1948. His collected works have been published in two volumes.

Shekhina

Somewhere in the world
a little grain lies buried.
Hope in it
and you will thrive.

Not even gentle hands
may dig it up,
and so its gifts
remain unknown.

More precious is the grain
than gold and diamonds;
it left God's treasure chest one day
and fell into a heart.

OTHER LANGUAGES

It lay there well protected
though tempest and storm raged round.
It hoped in a tomorrow,
tomorrow never came.

And when it left its cradle
it seemed the little grain
could fly, in search
of different goals.

A thousand years and more
it roamed from heart to heart,
cradles turned to coffins,
the little grain sought rest.

The time is up—no more delay—
the time is ripe, there's thunder in the air,
dreams drunk with sleep have faded on—
Hail, lightning of the East!

Little grain, it's time to stir
after so long a rest,
put forth your leaves, begin to sprout
from every portal of your heart.

But you may only start to bloom
when everyone will need such Spring,
when pain is gone and gone as well
all of man's suffering.

Then, little grain, you will mature,
calyx by calyx, in praise of God.
Then the eternal Now will dawn,
and sweet will be your fading off in God.
Then, flower of every heart,
act and repose shall be one.

From Mount Nebo

Gentle sounds rise up to me,
the air is fragrant with the promise
of our land, the one I led you to,
the one I will not reach.
How far I see! A view blessing your crops,
your fertile lowlands and greening pastures.
How I would have longed to see my brothers' fires
burning on their native soil,
their daily labors blessed—and yet I recognize
the hidden paths you led me on
toward the final peak,
to have one final view; the world of wandering
wanes and new laws seek new masters.
I see the distant land reflecting distant destinies—
and neither can I hope to know.
Well satisfied and ready, then,
I ask you, mountain, be my final resting place.

Translated by Erna Baber Rosenfeld

We Go

Do not ask: where?
We go.
We have been told to go
From the days of our fathers' fathers.
Abraham went, Jacob went,
They all had to go,
Go to a land, go from a land,
All of them bent
Over the path of the farer,
Of those who never spared themselves,
All of them went, staff in the road-hard hand,
Promise in their hearts, eyes filled with Him,
Our God who bade us go on and on,
Turned to the one and only goal.

OTHER LANGUAGES

A hounded rest when he called a halt,
Strange farings from Nile to Rhine,
Long farings in dread
Until wells brim,
Meager wells
For wavering, restless rest—
My roots reached down before those rooted
Who hunt me now, but I was a guest
In the land of others—always a guest.
Unthinkably long I rested there,
But never knew a rest that gives repose.
Our rest was drowned in tears and sweat and blood,
A sudden lightning and it cracked
In a cry:
Gone by, gone by!
In the full flare of sun—
We go.
Again He drives us,
Again He dooms us
To His eternal law;
To go on,
To go on!

Translated by Carol North Valope and Ernest Morwitz

GREEK

Joseph Eliyia

Joseph Eliyia was born in Janina, Greece in 1901. He was conscripted into the Greek army in 1920, discharged in 1921. In addition to writing poetry, he translated several books of the Old Testament and a number of Hebrew and Yiddish poets into modern Greek. He died in 1931.

Rebecca

How you dazzle my mind, panarchaic grandeur,
Resplendence, visions in biblical magic!

The servant was resting at the edge of the well,
And his laden camels were kneeling before him.
The evening was magic, the evening was sweet,
And slender Rebecca appeared with jug in hand.
The golden gates of Paradise opened wide,
Before her shy passing, the sweetness of her eyes.
"Daughter, pride of the house, tilt thy jug,
Tilt it and give me a drop of water to drink."
And the daughter replied, "Stranger, may God be with thee,
Drink and I will water thy camels."

And the evening was magic, the evening was sweet,
But sweeter yet was all-shy Rebecca of Bethel,
But sweeter yet, the sun-beauteous wife of Isaac.

Dream

When the morning star bleeds and silver-cry the Pleiades,
And the dense trees lament for what time has buried,
Soul, slumbering in flowers, in roses and violets,
Leaving your fine grave, I sense you veiled in vapor;
You come to my embrace as I moulder desolate and alone,
And you tell me softly: I am not dead!

Rebecca, eternal virgin, Muse, rhythm of the world,
You are not dead. As long as you flourish within me, I feel
Like the amaranthine flowers and the branches of myrtle!
Thus I speak and as I deeply gaze at you and rejoice,
I extend my two hands to receive your divine body
But . . . It is my shadow that I kiss, my shadow I embrace.

Slender Maid

Slender Maid,
Azure-eyed,
Nereid famed,
How your voice
From afar
Whispers to me.

Musical,
Bacchic,
In the silence of dusk,
One Sunday,
Like a wish,
I met you, chaste friend.

And I, before you,
With outspread
Wings of desire,
Saw flashing pure,
And from afar,
A hope in my path.

But now, alas,
I drag to earth,
The wearied body,
Hope forlorn.
I search for a cliff,
To hurl a corpse.

Slender maid,
Azure-eyed,
Whisper to me,
And from the edge
Come pull me away.

Your Passing, Fleet Passing

Your passing, fleet passing, stays in my soul,
Like an angel kiss and a bitter poison.
Your airy fluttering in the deserted lane,
Was like a caress and a thunderbolt.

I know not if you guessed as I softly spoke
So feelingly, my martyric, psychic agony,
But I, I gathered pain ecstatic and silent,
Before the merry light of your eyes, O misty Madonna.

The sorry smile of autumn scattered
A chill all around, starting some storm,
But your silvery chat, how sweetly it hummed,
Beehives in the bewitching land of spring.

But while the flower of your youth with the jasmine,
Both bloom in the bower of joy,
Some soul, poor soul, in its mute weeping,
Drags the specter of pain to asphodel prairies.

Epilogue

I too was a little child once,
And I was a pet of the Muse,
I too was a little bird once,
And I sang.

For the kiss of a blue-eyed maid,
For the grace of a moon-faced girl,
My heart became a violin,
And my desire a bow.

Snowy lilies here, jasmine there,
And citron-lemon trees around me,
And I caroling, caroling,
My love.

In the sunny childlike fete,
One golden dawn I saw you appear,
Rebecca, you, exotic flower,
Palpitating by me.

And I said, "Glory to Thee Creator,
For the flower Thou lettest me pluck,
For me what other boon remains,
To ask of Thee, Jehovah?"

But one day it blew . . .
Sirocca from the heart of the East,
And the flower fell and withered,
And my poor violin cracked.

And so, forlorn and forgot in the corner,
Again the Muse forsook me one eve;
But I do not mourn, nor do I weep; I only stare
Steadfastly at pain and I am silent.

Translated by Rae Dalven

HUNGARIAN

Milan Fuest

Milan Fuest was born in Budapest in 1888. His novels and poetry reflect his search for fundamental human virtue and a yearning for a purer world. He died in 1967.

Moses' Account

After I came down from the mountain, my Lord,
Where in the stillness I spoke with You, All-Good,
They feasted in the valleys. I cannot tell you what was going on
there.
The people built themselves castles of falsehood,
Even the cloth of their shirt they wove from cunning.
I did not trust a thing there—not even a child just begotten.
(And how the women stared at me, an old man lugging tablets of
stone,
An ancient too feeble even for anger, as I was then.)
And all the rest that lived there, swarmed or sprouted on the broad
plain
Were berating with a fearful strength born of hatred.
And so a new world arose against your world while my eyes were
absent
And stands unshakable, like night itself, before me.
I should have smashed it, thus it was written . . . but I was weary.
With my shoulders I should have shoved this mighty world from its
four corners, as once before, of old,
And groaned as the wind or howled through the night,
And for this task I was too old, my Lord—
And so it was your poor tablets of stone that I broke
And I shall never see your Promised Land.

Translated by André Ungar

Agnes Gergely

Agnes Gergely, born in 1933, studied Hungarian and English at the University of Budapest and has had a varied career as a secondary-school teacher, positions with Hungarian Radio and with a literary weekly; at present she is employed by a publishing house in Budapest. She spent a term at the University of Iowa, with the International Writing Program, in 1973. Her books of poetry include the volume of poems and translations My Selected Loves *(1973) and, most recently,* Cobalt Realm *(1977).*

OTHER LANGUAGES

Birth of a Country

To be an innkeeper.
(That's all poetry is.)
—Christopher Okigbo

The terra-cotta house in the moonlight
had barely reached the ground.
Peach blossoms flew on its edges,
tufts of grass were led on a leash,
and on the picket fence, like a tent canvas,
evening opened. On the sorrel-flavored
lawn the insects' last
circle of fire revolved, the belfry
swallowed the rope, the wind towed
the bell-tolling into the graveyard. . . .
"Say, Joska," said my grandfather to his
neighbor, "I married wrong: my two
brothers-in-law lost thirty-two hectares of
Kondoros land at cards." Silver dust stuck
to my fingers. "Can you hear?" Livia chattered,
"Someone talking downstairs!" On the brick walk
we took each other's hand. "Of course," I whispered,
"that's a country down there."
"Country," Livia nodded. When she was afraid
she still lisped. "Does it also have a king?"
"An old king. A whole royal family." But I
didn't go on, for on the threshold,
arms akimbo, appeared my grandmother,
in her bun hairpins like thorns,
and a spider had webbed in the pantry's corner.
At the stroke of the clock Livia fell over,
out of the knots in the walnut branch, monkeys
shot forth. "What will the king's name be?"
Slowly, over the pillow, my fingers
waltzed with the rose petals:
"The king's name. . . . The king's name. . . .
I'll dream of it tonight."

Desert

Hold suffering on a tight leash.
Never write: "let's say."
Don't close a sentence with: "ergo."
Allow everything to fill
its own husk, as birth
fills the seed. You just
hold your hand there. For
this too is power. It's not good to
get drunk on this, either. Unless you crave the
nightmare-lights of a poster-mausoleum.
And that they respect you like a
senile umbrella. No, this you
couldn't want, if you ever
dreamed of a desert and under the moon
you were the dust grain. If you ever
knew what it means to drop out.
Get a handhold on yourself, stay in
your place, on the footstool which
they assigned you at birth, and which can be
set up anywhere, just as
formulas can. That place is a
formula-sized place in the world. Even
the roving Indian found it room enough, till
they rangered his harmless
hunting. Then he hugged close his dog, his
blanket, his cacti-roots,
and as a sign of his respect
said to the Great Shade: "same thing."

Conjuration

With twilight I gather you here:
above the couch flies the paper;
above the ashtray,
the cigarette, held by its ember.

Through my dictionaries
a glance worms its way.
Nowhere a word. The eye: nowhere.
I saw as it waved.

In it I see all things.
And in reverse: on him every article, all
angle, concavity, energy,
all refraction of light reflects.
In baroque delight an unfilled
outline of a man unites
with the genius of objects.

Music slams on me. With its aggressive
waves it lifts me, tosses me on,
covers me over, the crepuscular sea.
You start with the suction-effect
of a few square centimeters
and wind up at the Oh, no! of infinity.

Shall I scream? that wouldn't help, either.
Shall I dig into my palm? or wave?
The man they crucified fared no better
than the one who said: get him nailed.

All who have gone to death
have scattered their earthly luck.
You were dearer to me than life.
But with this I haven't said much.

Translated by Emery George.

Anna Hajnal

Anna Hajnal was born in western Hungary in 1907. She studied English in Vienna and later co-edited a major literary journal in Budapest. She has published thirteen volumes of poetry and translated Shakespeare, Edward Lear, and Walt Whitman.

Dead Girl

Soft she was, young
moon in the water,
moon floating beneath waters
a form dreamed, desired—
she was—and gone, burning in water,
dreamed there, in the mirror—
the wandering one, sinking, rising
a moon drifting, light, alive.

Tree to Flute

You, my branch, my lopped limb!—
don't you cry, it's over, for you—
you were cut away, you've recovered—
for us it's being honed, the waiting axe,
and if it falls on us,
will we become a flute, desire weeping,
a sobbing, a quavering violin?
or lie silently, merely mute, lying?
the struggle's finished for you,
lucky flute: what more could you wish?

Translated by Jascha Kessler

Eugene Heimler

*Eugene Heimler was born in Hungary in 1922. After his release from Auschwitz in 1945, he emigrated to England, where he completed his studies at the London School of Economics and Manchester University. Heimler has published three volumes of poetry in Hungary, a verse play in English translation (*The Storm, *1976), two volumes of autobiography, and books and articles on mental health, social work, and the theoretical and practical synthesis he made in these areas, called Human Social Functioning. He is now professor of Human Social Functioning at the University of Calgary in Canada but still lives part of the year in England.*

Psalm

Oh Lord, I have been staring into a mirror
of solitude for forty days and nights,
I saw the roaring whirlpool of my lust,
dark tentacles chaining me to earth,
and nameless monsters. Life had no meaning.
I drifted pleasantly in the waters
like a leaf that has not yet been
washed clean of its original colors.
I was not fertile from your light.
Denying you—I denied myself.
I fall now, pierced by a thousand terrors,
before you, my God. Orgies of memory
clamor in my brain and dimly forms
the thought that you alone are the beginning
and the destiny of everything; dimly forms
the thought that I have hidden you beneath
a layer of fear, because you lived in me
like life in the coldness of stones.

OTHER LANGUAGES

My Lord, my Lord, how strange is the taste
upon my tongue now. How strange is the light
in my eyes and strange the hues of my mind.
Damp arms of fear reach out for me
to embrace, and these words echo strangely
over the dead and cursed emptiness.
Oh God I, the man, cry to you.
Allow me to come to you, allow me
to see you. I implore you, let me see
life's real colors with my blind eyes.
Let me fall into your eternal time.
Allow my soul to be blessed in your time.
For you know too well the ways of insignificant man,
you are beyond his words and gestures
and you see deeply that we are not
what we make ourselves out to be.
My Lord, terrorized with giddiness,
I spin towards you. My words dry up.
My tongue is parched. In my innermost brain
lights flash. Speak to me, my God.

I once watched the slaves, and their masters.
My heart was full of pity
because slaveowners themselves are slaves
and in the heart of slaves burns freedom.
There is no certainty anywhere,
Storms are playing, as far as the eye can see,
with the dust of human beings. Everywhere
are empty crevices. And the soul cries out
for nourishment in the enormous desert.
Only you can be that certainty, my God.
There is no anchor in the outside world.
You are the cause, the reason, the sense
of every living thing. Speak to me, my Lord.

My mind is whirling in two dimensions.
I am different here on Sinai
than I really am. And at Masada's dawn
I shall turn into a different man,
a dead man. Who am I, oh God,
and in what time have you placed your servant?

Translated by Anthony Rudolf

After an Eclipse of the Sun

For me the night still soughs,
but over the Danube the sun is already waking.
How I listened, rapt, to you,
how I gazed at you!—
then, like a wind along devastated roads,
the blood staggered on its way. . .

The Danube seemed already to be waking,
at first still sweeping bones and wreckage to its banks,
but then the light mastered its face,
my pale face was reflected in its eyes,
and I was drawn, like a mouth maddened by fire,
towards a woman's arms, all painful mystery. . .
And the Danube's gullet wailed:
"After an eclipse of the sun the night still soughs."

Upon your veined transparent skin I felt
for the lost pulse of hours long past.
In your eyes I looked into the eyes of Eve,
in your hair I contemplated my mother's hair,
then I listened to the soughing stillness. . .
You know: in Germania the ovens were burning. . .

Summer lived then, and death lived.
Tongues of flame felt for the black sky,
the ashes of fathers and families blew
above the wires of the electric hedges,
and life sank evermore blind, down into night.
The sun's primeval furnaces grew cold,
and on the eyes of proud nations, broken, bowed,
lay the burnt dream of destiny. . .

You know, there were times I thought: it's all over . . .
and dying musics echoed from long ago,
my mother's mouth was sobbing in the night
and the shadows revealed her forgotten gesture,
church bells boomed in the dusks
above black, dead fields,
and people crazed by the sun's eclipse
could not break free of the past.

It is good now to tell how in the night
a seam began to split in the sun's blinded eye,
how over the devastation
my bitter tears and dying blood went on their way,
how your eyes' hundred dead colors revealed
the passing of the evil night,
and your eyes' hundred living colors revealed
the sign of light awaking.

Now I sleep soft, the depths no longer heave
and the warm breeze is drying out the past.
I look still at the Danube's inviting waters,
but what drew me has now gone far away,
new strengths awake in my numbed body,
my muscles flex in the sun,

and slowly now, their strength renewed, the words
set off along the road, renewed.

Translated by Peter Sherwood and Keith Bosley

Jozsef Kiss

Jozsef Kiss was born in Hungary in 1834. He held a number of jobs between 1862 and 1875, when he began to receive recognition as a poet. The first professing Jew to achieve fame as a Hungarian writer, Kiss wrote numerous volumes of poetry and published a successful literary journal. He died in Budapest in 1921.

The New Ahasuerus

My flesh is racked by plague,
My soul is sicker still,
I yearn to rest—in vain.

Mad tempest drives me on,
Throws thistles in my hair,
The brand of shame burns hot.

The curse of ages gnaws.
My path's unblessed by God.
How long yet must I roam?

I halt. I shall not go.
I shall defy you, Fate!
I'll build a hut, a home.

I'll shed my sweat and blood,
Atone for all my sins;
I'll bring a sacrifice.

My fathers' grim bequest.
The bitter hate of foes
My bitter tears will melt.

I'll tear out of my soul
The guilt, affliction, pain
That none has yet avenged.

My kin strewn far abroad
I shall deny . . . I'll be
Cruel, cold—but yours!

Yours, my sweet homeland
As secret joy entwines
I'll stand and spin my dreams.

A tree sends down its roots—
Why not I? A home
A hearth at peace I'll own.

Neighbors will not jeer
Or grudge or condescend,
We'll share and share alike.

My glory will be his,
The common good of all. . . .
—Stop, dream! Don't fly away!

From rooftops howl the hate.
I'd struggle but I'm weak.
The mocking laughter warns:

Perhaps you'll build a hut,
Of treasures hoard a heap:
You will not have a home.

Translated by André Ungar

Emil Makai

Emil Makai was born in Mako, Hungary, in 1870 and entered the rabbinical seminary in 1884. He left the seminary in 1893 to pursue his writing interests. Makai was a prolific poet and playwright and translated over one hundred operettas. He died in 1901.

The Comet

Cast out, amid so many companions
I race headlong to nothingness,
The fire flares in my dead heart,
When I tire, I start again
This demented rush.

Purple flames lick me with kisses,
The mighty sky quakes with desire,
Flighty mist turns incandescent;
My cradle is the endless cosmos,
My grave eternal emptiness.

Into the shapeless, feverish night
A restless instinct drives me on,
And like a slave of fearsome fate
I come, with burning torch in hand,
My trail sweeps wide across the sky.

O sleeping flower, slumbering nature,
How enviable is your calm!
Your soul has died out long ago
While I defy you, Destiny,
And triumph over the ages' spirit.

I have been, since the idea
That created me exists;
I do not change, I am the same
Throughout a million million years
And while the world turns, I shall be.

I shall be, and have companions
Who will wander on with me,
Sleepless in the barren night,
Whom the cruel whim of fortune
Made into fellow travelers.

Such a host of restless souls
Who roam the universe with me,
Who run this race at speed of madness
And nobody is left behind
And there is no goal to reach.

Translated by André Ungar

Otto Orban

Otto Orban was born in 1936. He lost his father during World War II and was brought up in an orphanage; for several years he attended the University of Budapest, but left without finishing his studies, and since 1958 has been supporting himself from his writing. His travels include Western Europe, the USSR, and India, the last-named commemorated in his volume of travel notes, Window to Earth *(1973).* Golden Fleece, *a volume of selected translations, appeared in 1972. Orban is the author of seven books of poems, including the collected volume* To Be Poor *(1974) and* Perspective on History *(1976). For his first five books he was awarded the Attila Jozsef Prize in 1973.*

Hymn

Some sort of fire leaped out of the dirty and poor and merciless city. The light, the comet stuck to earth, swept fire-maned corner to corner, and the shoving and the indifference, the give-my-regards-to-your-wife and the stick-'em-up, in other words concrete's and mud's every delight fit to vomit, all the killing pace and stone-age idiocy living here at each other's throats like insane lovers—all this suddenly started burning like oil from tankers on the water. What sort of magic goes setting fires here? muttered Orpheus manqué at the lookout tower, in his miserable rebelliousness. To be one of the jostling, to speak their language, to listen to their snorting and to the universal ruckus as it fills the world—all this is but the beginning of evil. Later on hate and its object come to resemble each other as do man and wife after a marriage of many years. And some peculiar love goes stealing the marrow out of our bones. Oh you blockheads! you shout at the beginning, only to murmur later: brothers, sisters. And your wildness, your pride, your New World expression—cubic time buries them all. And from then on you are one with them in your blushing for shame: just look, jackal-face, at the fool, how he kicks and screams here, how he spits his golden spittle into the stars: he shivers, terrified, as he has molted the skin of his immortality. Fling that earth-discus wherever you will, Myron's simpleton athlete, youth: your shoulders are snow-covered from cosmic birddirt. And this heap of a city is our prison and landed estate. This pathetic and ludicrous noise—yes, it's our speech. And our crown of glory and exile shall be this wheel of light forged of dust and wind above the chimneys, as long as eternal earth rolls, spokes groaning, from cell to cell.

Computer

This unheated star is not the kind to take in pious babble
MY COUNTRY OR DEATH
its genre is the concrete poetry of organization
pathos and tears are out
its sons seek their own profits and find them too
Pascal on top of the pornography
and hunger's Assyrian statue in poverty's shrine
separated by transparent walls from air conditioning and airports
in an exotic world where science goes for its summer vacation
to examine the characteristic symptoms of malnutrition
as facts worthy of special attention
data toward the case history of a continent
time is not such a fool as to give up all objectivity
so that it may stand frightened before the black riddle of hate
and tremble in a lit-up rainforest before blood's ghosts
it isn't Renaissance ideas this leafy hatchery gives birth to
it's out of the eggs of numbers that future contingency is born
downy little monsters in their mouths spigots and conduits
on their wings articles news clippings engineering photographs of
the nude
it isn't in classical garb misfortune travels around the globe
so that on an imaginary notepad it may tick off all the Gothic towers
and local aromas
he's neither scythe nor skull
he leaves his bags behind in the hotel and picking his teeth with the
stem of his sunglasses
makes a down payment on some wild vision at a burning-bush
cashier's window
on an ocean voyage on the waves of perspiration
on this ocean stammering with poverty and love

Ray

Rustle among bones. Only wind, the bodiless angel. Emptiness.
Something even so. Out of glass silence, some noise. Song or
swarming.
It's as if something were resurrected and sat down at the table,
stirred the coffee.
Someone else in our clothes, with our frowns and gestures,
characteristic accents and assumed intentions,
so that out of nothing we may fish birds and birdsong;
sits down right here, facing us; out of his empty eyes glimmers the
sun.
Some sudden ray stabs our being:
we're arrows in summer's wounds, wounds in air's flesh,
a draft among light's bones, rising in plunging.
Statues in a museum where no one comes to visit.

Translated by Emery George

Gyorgy Raba

Gyorgy Raba has published five volumes of poetry and translated into Hungarian many French, Italian, and English poets.

Message

Knock here's where I live
emperor sans empire
sans subjects

Rattle pound
sear my saga in greasy flames
decipher my legend
here's where I live
beneath a tear-laden sky
in this unmusical bone-box
tomorrow passes me by
comes back unfamiliar
but you can make it out
here's where I live
number 1 number 1

Conversation

On this piece of earth I seize a knife
no sunset in its land
nameless flagless
life cannot take on its rude rock
On this piece of earth I seize a knife
its features split into my own face
one breath, and already kicking off its seeming death
through the soils of decades of summers
the hot fountain jets up like misery
spouting balls of barren tufa
and the acids of recent strata
The shadow of charred wingbeats
flits across our sky and crashes in the outskirts
a Pleistocene beast clattering it's broken free
and its name must be uttered by no one
and tidal waves
we live in a windowless skyline
the supersaturated monsoon bursts over us
Before my eyes the coming geological age lives
my frontiers fall away from tomorrow's blank vision
seasons freeze boil each minute
my world settles in gullies
and you, straddling chairs at the door
your pupils dilate terrified
as I spin off beyond the front gardens
like a fresh galaxy in outer space

Translated by Jascha Kessler

Miklós Radnóti

Miklós Radnóti was born in 1909. His collected translations from the classics and from major European traditions appeared in 1943 under the title In Orpheus' Footsteps: Translations from Poets of Two Thousand Years. *During his brief lifetime he published six volumes of his own verse, including* Walk on, Condemned! *(1936), which in 1938 earned him the Baumgarten Prize in Poetry. Soon after that the authorities of the Horthy regime began drafting him for stints of duty on forced-labor brigades; on a third and final callup in the spring of 1944 he was taken to a camp in Bor, Yugoslavia. In late fall of that year, in the course of the general Axis retreat from Hungary, Radnóti and twenty-one of his companions were taken north on a forced march, shot, and buried in a mass grave. On exhumation there was found in his field-jacket pocket a small camp notebook containing seven poems, some of which are included here.*

Song

Whipped by sorrow now
each day I walk
exiled in my own country

and it barely matters how long or where.
I come, go, sit,
and even the distant stars
come down and attack me.

Even the distant stars
hide behind clouds.
I stumble through the night
to the shores where reeds grow.

Where reeds grow
nobody walks with me now
and I haven't really wanted
to dance for a long time.

For a long time the deer
with the chilly nose hasn't followed me.
I wade through a swamp,
mist curls up from its surface,

mist curls up from its surface
and I sink, and sink.
Above me, a pair of
hawks hang like wet rags.

OTHER LANGUAGES

I Hid You

I hid you for a long time
the way a branch hides its
slowly ripening fruit among leaves,
and like a flower of sane ice
on a window
you open in my mind.
Now I know what it means
when your hand swoops up to your hair.
In my heart I keep
the small tilt of your ankle too
and I'm amazed by the delicate curve
of your ribs, coldly
like someone who has lived
such breathing miracles.
Still, in my dreams
I often have a hundred arms
and like God in a dream
I hold you in those arms.

Root

Power glides in the root,
drinking rain, living in the earth,
and its dream is white snow.

From underneath it rises and breaks through
the soil and crawls along secretly.
Its arm is like rope.

On the root's arm a worm sleeps
and a worm sticks to its leg.
The world is rotten with worms.

But the root goes on living below.
It is the branch, heavy with leaves,
that it lives for, not the world.

This is what it feeds and loves,
sending delicate tastes up to it,
sweet tastes out of the sky.

I am a root myself now,
living among worms.
This poem is written down there.

I was a flower. I became a root.
There is heavy black earth above me.
The workers on my life are done.
A saw wails over my head.

Metaphors

You are like a whispering branch
when you bend over me,
or like the secret taste
of a poppy—

and like ripples continually forming in time
you excite me,
and quiet me
like stone on top of a grave.

You are like a friend I grew up with,
and even today I don't really know
the smell
of your thick hair.

Sometimes when you look sad, I'm afraid
you'll leave me, like
coiled drifting smoke, and sometimes when
you're the color of lightning, I'm afraid of you—

like the exploding sky, when the sun
burns it dark gold.
And when you're angry, you
are like the letter "u,"

deep-voiced, vibrating again and again,
dark. At times like these
I take smiles
and draw bright nooses around you.

In Your Arms

I sleep in your arms,
it's quiet.
You sleep in my arms,
it's quiet.
I'm a child in your arms
who is silent.
You're a child in my arms.
I listen.
You hold me in your arms
when I'm afraid.
I hold you in my arms.
I'm not afraid.
In your arms even the great silence
of death can't
scare me.
In your arms I'll
survive death.
It's a dream.

Fragment

I lived on this earth in an age
when man fell so low
he killed willingly, for pleasure, without orders.
Mad obsessions threaded his life,
he believed in false gods. Deluded, he foamed at the mouth.

I lived on this earth in an age
when it was an honor to betray and murder,
the traitor and the thief were heroes—
those who were silent, unwilling to rejoice,
were hated as if they had the plague.

I lived on this earth in an age
when if a man spoke out, he had to go into hiding
and could only chew his fists in shame—
drunk on blood and scum, the nation went mad
and grinned at its horrible fate.

I live on this earth in an age
when a curse was the mother of a child,
when women were happy if they miscarried,
a glass of thick poison foamed on the table,
and the living envied the rotting silence of the dead.

I lived on this earth in an age
when the poets too were silent
and waited for Isaiah, the scholar
of terrifying words, to speak again—
since only he could utter the right curse.

Translated by Steven Polgar, Stephen Berg, and S. J. Marks

Letter to My Wife

Lager Heidenau, above Žagubica in the mountains, August-September 1944

Down in the deep, dumb worlds are waiting, silent;
I shout; the silence in my ears is strident,
but none can send it reply from far
Serbia, fallen into a swoon of war,
and you are far. Your voice braids my dream;
by day I find it in my heart again;
knowing this I keep still, while, standing proudly,
rustling, cool to the touch, many great ferns surround me.

When might I see you? I hardly know any longer,
you, who were solid, were weighty as the psalter,
beautiful as a shadow and beautiful as light,
to whom I would find my way, whether deafmute or blind;
now hiding in the landscape, from within
my eye, you flash—the mind projects its film.
You were what is real, returned to dream in essence,
and I, relapsed into the well of adolescence,

jealously question you: whether you love me,
whether, on my youth's summit, you will yet be
my wife—I am now hoping once again,
and, back on life's alert road, where I have fallen,
I know you are all this. My wife, my friend and peer—
only, far! Beyond three wild frontiers.
It is turning fall. Will fall forget me here?
The memory of our kisses is all the clearer.

OTHER LANGUAGES

I had faith in miracles, forgot their days;
above me I see a bomber squadron cruise.
I was just admiring, up there, your eyes' blue sheen,
when it clouded over, and up in that machine
the bombs were aching to dive. Despite them, I am alive,
a prisoner; and all I had hoped for, I have
sized up, in breadth. I will find my way to you;
for you I have walked the spirit's full length as it grew,

and highways of the land. If need be, I will render
myself, a conjurer, past cardinal embers,
amid nose-diving flames, but I will come back,
if I must be, I shall be resilient as the bark
on trees. I am soothed by the peace of savage men
living in trouble; worth the whole wild regimen
of arms and power; and, as from a cooling wave of the sea,
the light of *2 x 2* is raining down on me.

Seventh Eclogue

Lager Heidenau, above Žagubica in the mountains, July 1944

Look how evening comes and around us the barbed-wire-hemmed,
wild
oaken fence and the barracks are weightless, as evening absorbs
them.
Slowly your glance lets go of the frame of our captive condition,
only the mind, it alone is alive to the tautness of wire.
See, Love: fantasy has one way to attain to its freedom,
namely, through dream, that comely redeemer who liberates broken
bodies—it's time, and the men in the camp all leave for their homes
now.

Ragged, with shaven heads, these prisoners, snoring aloud, fly,
leaving Serbia's blind peak, back to their fugitive homesteads.
Fugitive homesteads—right. . . . Dear one, is our house still standing?
still untouched by bombs? as it stood, back when we reported?
And will the men who now groan on my right, lie left, make it home
yet?
Is there a home, where people can savor hexameter language?

No diacritics. Just one line under another line: groping,
barely, as I am alive, I write my poem in half-dark,
blindly, in earthworm-rhythm, I'm inching along on the paper.
Flashlights, books: the guards of the *Lager* took everything from us,
nor does the mail ever come. Only fog settles over the barracks.

Here among rumors and worms all live, be they Frenchmen or
Polish,
loud-voiced Italian, partisan Serb, sad Jew, in the mountains,
bodies hacked and in fever; yet all live a life held in common:
waiting for good news, a loving, womanly word, for a fate free,
human; awaiting the end plumbing dusk, or a miracle—maybe.

Worm-riddled, captive beast: that is just how I lie on the plank
boards.
Fleas will renew their siege; the battalion of flies is asleep now.
Evening is here; once again our serfdom has grown a day shorter,
so have our lives. The camp is asleep. On mountain and valley
bright moon shines; in its light once more all the wires pull tighter,
and through the window you see how the shadows of camp's armed,
pacing
sentries are thrown on the wall in the midst of the night's lone
voices.

Camp is asleep, dear one: can you see us? The dreams come rustling;
Starting, one will snort on his narrow bunk, turn over;
sleeping again, his face shines. Lonely the vigil I'm keeping;
in my mouth I taste that half-smoked cigarette, not your
kisses, and dreams won't come, no sleep will come to relieve me,
since I can face neither death nor a life any longer without you.

Forced March

Bor, 15 September 1944

The man who, having collapsed,   rises, takes steps, is insane;
he'll move an ankle, a knee   a pilgrim to his pain,
and take to the road again   as if wings were to lift him high;
the ditch calls him in vain: he simply dare not stay;
and should you ask, why not?   perhaps he'll turn and answer:
his wife is waiting back home,   and a death, one beautiful, wiser.
The wretch is a fool, that's a cinch,   for over the homes, that world,
long since nothing but singed   winds have been known to whirl;
his house wall lies supine;   your plum tree, broken clear,
and all the nights back home   horripilate with fear.
O if I could believe   that I haven't merely saved
what is worthwhile, in my heart;   that home can still receive;
tell me it's all still there: the cool verandah, bees
buzzing in peaceful silence   (while some of that plum jam cools!);
end-of-the-summer quiet   sunbathing, sleepy, bent
over gardens; leaves and fruit,   naked and redolent;
that, blonde, my Fanni is waiting   before the redwood fence,
where the morning slowly traces   its shadowed reticence—
But all that *could* return—   just look at tonight's full moon!
Don't go past me, my friend—   shout! and I'll rise again.

*Picture Postcards**

30 August 1944. In the mountains.

1

From Bulgaria thick, wild cannon pounding rolls.
It strikes the mountain ridge, then hesitates and falls.
A traffic jam of thoughts, animals, carts, and men;
whinnying the road rears up; the sky runs with its mane.
In this chaos of movement you're in me, permanent,
deep in my conscious you shine, motion forever spent
and mute, like an angel awed by death's great carnival,
or an insect in rotted tree pith, staging its funeral.

Cservenka, 6 October 1944

2

Nine kilometers from here the haystacks and
houses are burning;
sitting on the fields' edges, some scared and speechless
poor folk are smoking.
Here a little shepherdess, stepping onto the lake,
ruffles the water;
the ruffled sheep flock at the water drinks from
clouds, bending over.

Mohács, 24 October 1944

3

Bloody saliva hangs on the mouths of the oxen.
Blood shows in every man's urine.
The company stands in wild knots, stinking.
Death blows overhead, revolting.

Szentkirályszabadja, 31 October 1944

4

I fell beside him; his body turned over,
already taut as a string about to snap.
Shot in the back of the neck. That's how you too will end,
I whispered to myself; just lie quietly.
Patience now flowers into death.
Der springt noch auf, a voice said above me.
Blood mixed with mud was drying on my ear.

Translated by Emery George

*These poems were found in the pocket of Radnoti's coat in the mass grave in which he was buried.—Ed.

Judit Tóth

Judit Tóth was born in 1936. She lost both parents in a concentration camp and was brought up by relatives; at present she lives in Paris. In 1959 she received her certification for teaching in France; in 1957 she won first prize in an international translation competition sponsored by the Hungarian literary monthly Wide World, *and has been a contributing editor of that magazine since. Tóth has published three volumes of her poems:* Firewalls *(1963),* Two Cities *(1972), and* Revocation of Space *(1975).*

Remembering

Pieces of memory stick together,
mixed in with the soil of the present tense.
Images darkly looming are lost
in their environments.

Tar-tufts, plankboard-slivers,
stones on the noon sand.
Water covers them repeatedly,
then once again they surface
as the sea withdraws,
but now inseparably from the sand.

The city, the river, moon-splendor of bridges,
narrow sidestreets, arcades, alleyways,
steps go clomping, here new, here old.
Algae get tangled with the sand.
In the seemingly accidental light
now this, now that housewall incandesces.
But the touch, the gaze cannot go astray
in the coincidence of scenes and of time

The onion's peel separates,
out of the vapor steps a June noon,
and my knife-grasping hand and the onion,
and an old tubful of water, the dusty leek
and a figure on the hot stairs—
It's to one system the onion
and time curving in the onion's peel belong.

The Southeast Ramparts of the Seine

This is the southeast section of town now.
The Pont-Tolbiac. Beneath it
the freight railyard will not come to an end.
An end of the world fenced in by
power lines, tracks.
The darkest moon landscape of the Seine.

Here it's industrial moorings, coal yards.
And the ashen outlines of warehouses holding
building materials: mounds of gravel, stone, sand.
And the gigantic tin tank: Béton de Paris.

On the banks, utilities' ambiguous
poetry. The empty barracks,
corrugated-metal roofs: a plant hastily
abandoned. It's silent as at the end of a village
now inside a war zone.

These gray houseblocks, cisterns, walls,
boarded-up wooden plank dwellings,
plants of the Morillon Corvol Works
are like the multistoried boxes
of a horror film. Improbable.

The hovels and the barracks. Barrel-mounds of the
wine wholesale stores. On a tower's wall: First Aid
for the Drowned. This is the route I take
each time I walk home.

Wildfire

France. Cradle and abstraction.

More strangely for years
than Portuguese barracks-dwellers,
farther out even than the
city of tanks.

Learning moderation, conception
only in the spaciousness of love.
And at the bottom of
rapture—agony, and above the pain,
renewed transport.
Love so gathers in layers:
clay, stones, gold,
as the seasons wash it,
just like the mountain's entrails.

Wildfire of increasing distance—
it denudes, all but collapses you.

Where there was a city, your birthplace,
there in your eyes is its crater,
in your memories its walls,
in your consciousness its provocation.

Wildfire. Self-knowledge.
By this flame you can decipher
the scrawl of youth:
already the sense
of the stone's inscription is final.

Translated by Emery George

István Vas

István Vas was born in 1910. He attended business school in Vienna, but returned to Hungary in 1929, and has since been publishing his poems in the liberal weeklies and magazines, chief among them West. *He is a dramatist, novelist, and essayist as well as a poet. Especially in the 1920s and 1930s, Vas was an active translator of drama (Shakespeare, Racine, Schiller, O'Neill) and of prose fiction (Defoe, Thackeray, Maeterlinck, Steinbeck). His later translations of poets are collected in the volume* Song of the Seven Seas *(1955). Between 1932 and 1976 Vas published more than twenty collections of his own verse, including the collected volumes* What Does This Man Want? *(1970). A three-volume collected edition of his poems appeared in 1977.*

What Is Left?

Jeu de Paume

And what is left for the others,
The objects, seas, the gardens,
Enormous magic of light—Monet!
The moment found, new sesame, the great fever,
Melting into flames, Rouen Cathedral,
As transformed by dawn, by night, and by day.

Then the races, circuses, cabarets,
Regattas, nightclubs, that mix of modern ways
Their strong eyes braided into a worldly halo;
But he didn't live among feasts, no, the light
Of glory he found was not of our sight,
Around things ancient: Vincent, the holy fool.

The chairs, the sunflowers, Auvers' wild temple,
The fibrous laying-on, the rough texture,
Soon—you feel—strong, attacking vegetation,
Trunks, leaves, clods, grains of sand,
The host of plant life roused to dance,
Will swallow the whole composition.

He himself: just like an insane sunflower.
Do you recall the self-portrait next door—
Old Tintoretto, bidding us farewell?
White beard, intelligent, tear-ready eyes;
But he'll not mourn what couldn't be; he bewails
Only what's his, and what he stands to forfeit still.

But Van Gogh suffers, vibrates here on the canvas,
And the blue eyes stare at you defenseless,
Thickly the blue and yellow brush strokes swirl;
Tormented, frightened sadness gone astray,
Out of his beard martyr-bright roses spray,
From his auburn hair too you see madness unfurl.

And brave of the brave, the greatest, oh I love you:
Lautrec, lord, beggar, priest, and merry-andrew,
Cruel sufferer, brother of Baudelaire!
You who feared no demons of flesh, of absinthe,
On your canvases we see the whinnying dance
Of Paris's happy ghost, his skeletal stare.

And magician of movement, Degas, who observed
The defenseless body, distorted and sad,
Though in the footlights and through veils of tulle;
You, who illumined poor little monkey-faces
Of ballerinas in motion, their faerie-graces
Gleaming in a milk-white, goblin-blue circle.

And the great flight! Primal dreams, craving-racked,
Tahiti! Many-colored faith, that once turned fact.
Epidemic spreads, a learned superstition's hold.
Animal angels, Eden far-off, naked;
In the picture's corner some writing, opiated,
And their bodies' gold . . . their bodies' gold. . . .

Catacombs

Today a silver coffin guards St. Agnes'
Ashes; above it stands a statue of bronze.
But what a narrow bed, in other ages,
Poor cellar-soil, held her in their bonds.

Clumsy drawings, bones, a deepening—
The crucifix just barely has its place.
Was then this desolation everything?
It's the birth of all that shall be greatest.

And now the Age of Constantine, right soon. . . .
Later the pyres, bells booming with lust;
The gold-benumbed frown of Byzantium
Answered the martyrs fallen here to dust.

To embrace the stone blocks of dank cellars
While, outside, authority's storm howls—
Those who survived themselves turned killers,
Received their share of eternal power.

Wearisome circus! Iron by-law! Away!
Ancient aqueduct to where I'm reborn.
All catacombs answer my martyred brain—
Grotesque experience, embittered form.

Translated by Emery George

Tambour

Whence, hardworn drum
winging past death
natural, unnatural
through siege and shelter

wan goatskin face
stained with coalcellar dust
raised again with the sweat
of palms beating out the dance

fingers dancing, and sticks
of glossy wood, bloodclot-brown
flat palm flicking
counterpoint, tapping soft
syncopated commands staccato
on the smooth parchment

Drum, resurrection drum
out of its opened mouth
swarm the lifted knee
taut rounded buttocks
tight legs
leaping burning soles
the hair floating in flight

Sounding box, drumming
its wan death's skin—
victorious, true portrait
its blackened face
making its accusation
with the searching, skeptical hand
the fugue erupting, shaking
its captive soul, the dance.

OTHER LANGUAGES

Just This

Their auburn or black hair, curly hair
or straight, their eyes, dark, brown, gold
or green eyes, their noses, straight, hooked,
long or pert, retroussé, noses, their mouths,
thick, rippling, thin or hardset mouths, their hands,
white, childlike or whittled bones, active hands,
stained by paint, sun, nicotine,
their magical fingers, their breasts, just barely rounded,
small hills or divine, muscular breasts,
their feet, tender and small, or strong, sleek feet,
their shin-thews, ankle-power, their yellowed, stamping,
pink, earth-strolling soles, long thighs, the flexing arches
of buttocks we'd have mentioned, had we been brave
enough, though for that matter Attila Joszef discussed
a girl's stomach, the slag revitalized in the gut
tunnels and hot kidney pumps—but one thing
we've never said before, not even its name,
except in execration, the name of our one joy,
and of the shells', the calyxes', of wings, altars,
winged altars, of the incendiary, maddening,
silken vehicle of flavor, spice—this four-letter word
we've never mentioned, never this name
we'll know longest of all.
A splendid death I'd have,
beyond pain, consciousness, beyond the edges
of the uttered word, if I said no more from
these compressed lips of mine, no more than this,
nothing but this, and only this.

Translated by Jascha Kessler

ITALIAN

Edith Bruck

Edith Bruck was born into a family of Hungarian Jews in 1932 and spent part of her childhood in a concentration camp. She lived for a time in Israel but has made her home in Italy for some time. Her most recent novel is Transit. *Her latest book of poems is* Il Tatuaggio, *from which the following selection is taken.*

Childhood

Your milk was already poisoned
by an ominous sign
your weary arms
offered no protection
your eyes were consumed with weeping
your heart beat with fear
your mouth opened only to pray
or to curse me the last born who sought refuge
from human shapes who fired in the dark
from dogs enraged against sulky sorrowful masters
from the spit of children nursed on ignorance
from idiots left free
from shames and from family ties
to let off steam with the Jews
by the synagogue door.

Let's Talk, Mother

Let's talk, Mother, your mouth gone to ashes
won't tell me either truths or lies.
I'm left alone; outside my window
clothes hung like your rags flutter
against the fence of rotting reeds
where behind a patched sheet
I bared my belly as a child
not to play Mommy and Daddy
but to melt your curses in the sun.
I didn't go to the woods in the evening
to play with the Aryan enemies, but to pick flowers
in exchange for something that resembled
your smile, or to lie down among leaves
in the icy mud hoping to get sick
and force you to nurse me with tender rage.
I didn't run off with the gypsies for fun,
but to end up in your punishing arms,
I didn't disobey out of wickedness
but to hear my name
repeated in your screams.
At my age you begin to add things up.
Pain has no refuge in the imagination
of a 40-year-old kid curled up
in the sterile arms of a frail
man tired of giving or receiving
with his eyes consumed over books
his mind illumined, inimical, understanding
of my measureless love
from which he has fled for a brief
or definitive leave
of absence turning me into an adult, making me
pregnant with a cemented ring
by his cold generous words
before going off closing the door
and carrying with him all the people
I loved beside him; and pain
doesn't find any comfort
doesn't take flight anymore
on wings of innocence.

Equality, Father!

Equality, Father! It's your dream come true
I catch a glimpse of you I see you again you're walking
beside Roth the shopowner who denied us
a dab of ricotta for the holidays,
Klein the shoemaker who wouldn't resole
your one pair of shoes on credit, Goldberg the butcher
with his clipped goatee who dragged us
to court when you were selling meat without a license,
Stein the teacher who taught us Hebrew
expecting divine compensation, hounded us
like a mad conductor,
breaking dozens of pointers over our heads,
your children illiterate in Hebrew destined for Hell.
And you, the poorest among them, the most recognizable
with that skinny ass! The most agile, the easiest
to exploit in forced labor.
Avanti, Father! You're prepared to meet all comers,
armed with experience,
you know the front line, the rifles, the trenches,
the daily struggle in years of plenty.
You know the prison, the hard bed in the dark cell
where you picked your lice, licked your wounds,
unrolled your cigarette butts.
You know the taste of blood in your mouth
from a rotten tooth
a cop's fist
a bullet fired
while you were defending the fatherland, stubbornly believing it
yours.
You know death lying in wait
the pettiness of men
the game of the powerful
the owners' power to exploit.
You know the whole scale of humiliation
the dark streets with ominous shadows
with starving wolves skittish horses
in sleepless nights on your solitary journeys
in the illusion of ruinous
business deals

promises unkept
except for the wrath of Jehovah!
Avanti, Father! You know decay
ice hunger! Chin up!
You don't have to hide anymore from the creditors,
they're all there, naked!
Ah, are you turning? Don't you know me?
I've grown up, I have firm breasts,
pure tender down like Mamma had
when they carried her
in the bridal chair. Father, take me!
I'll give you pleasure, not children,
love not duties,
love not reproaches,
love you never knew existed,
love I imagined—Run!
It's time for the Apocalypse!
Let us commit a mortal sin
so we can deserve our death.

Sister Zahava

Sister Zahava in the language of the Bible
your name means gold
gold like your adolescent heart
in a volcanic body
with two eyes ripe with black flame
with your mouth of fire
that spit words of love
for your little sister
in the enemies' face,
with your arms of rock
that shot up in my defense from a sea
of molten lead to thrust me toward survival,
rich with our renewed hope
with the stubbornness of the mad
for the struggle of an existence
whose tissues were already moribund
and the threads that the hook of memory
fished up were always more corroded
and unraveled in the memory
of a childhood full of humiliations

of insults at school of abuse in the street
misery at home beneath a straw roof
the rain leaked through, and Uncle stank of wine
with his fat hands joined in prayer
between my pure legs,
in a life spent
up against walls
abandoned even by dogs
instructed to pee on
Jews living or murdered
behind barbed wire
where the one living thing was death.
Then . . . Liberation:
And then it starts over, it seems
that the cloth holds,
the thin thread transforms itself
into rope for a definitive mooring.
I was ready at last
for the burst of gratitude,
for the reciprocal salvation
when the rope snapped
and here I am far from you, alone
on the shore of nothingness that received me
beyond the limit
of suffering.
Today is suspended
and asks nothing now,
desires neither life nor death.
And the light of your heart of gold
offered from beyond the sea
has extinguished itself in my darkness.

Go, Then

Go then sweet friend
a room awaits you
honed out of a shed
the desert awaits you
rot shelter ambush
your father awaits you
feeding you on hate,
on redress, in his mind
the number of his dead is growing hazy.
Go then, your mother awaits you
smiling only at your awakening
and at the chickens frightened by eyes
like yours sweet friend
lover brother son.
Go then with the sound of the siren
and the *shofar* in your ears
with the nightmare of a companion
who fired without hearing your voice
in the dark and when he stopped firing
while you fled convinced he was after you
he slowly burned out.
Go then sweet friend
and think that the enemy boy
in any case like you is afraid
and like you not guilty.
Think of this and you'll understand,
sweet friend.

Why Would I Have Survived?

Why would I have survived
if not to symbolize
guilt, especially in the eyes
of those who are close to me?
Of all their guilts
one, the greatest, would be
repentance
for having hurt
me, who endured so much.
I, who am different
from the rest and carry within me
six million dead
who speak my language,
who ask man to remember,
man, whose memory is so short.
Why would I have survived
if not to bear witness
with my life
with my every gesture
with my every word
with my every look.
And when will this mission be
accomplished?
I'm tired of my
accusing presence,
the past
is a double-edged
weapon
and I'm bleeding to death.
When my hour comes
I'll leave behind
perhaps an echo
for man, who forgets
and remembers and starts again. . . .

Translated by Anita Barrows

Aldo Camerino

Aldo Camerino was born in Venice, Italy, in 1901. He left his university studies to devote himself to the study of literature, showing special interest in French, Spanish, and English writers. He translated such writers as Shakespeare, Milton, Cocteau, Valéry, and Lopez. He published several volumes of poetry and was an established literary critic. He died in 1966. The following poems are from his collection Poesie.

Night

At every hour I wake.
And the sky that glittered
with stars now is shining
and then light. The night
seems long to me. I live
in a different time.

Endless, the sweetness
of this time of mine.
It has no bounds. The hours
are as a vague
instinct wishes them, which
during sleep apportions the flow
of hours that leads
to lovely lasting.

Night fluid like a smooth sea.

Calm

If this divine quiet
is just an illusion
and later the world will again be
dusty, overcast,
sharp, out of joint—
I ask and don't care to answer.
I reap and I don't think of next
year's harvest.

Fear

Then we descended, as into a labyrinth,
to the dark pit of the soul; and there were
swellings and interrupted flashes
and flames and sorrows stirred.
Fear is the color of darkness;
stirred by a vicious wind,
it unites with what is saddest in us.
We felt it. Life went
dry. We were whole and then suddenly
we were ashamed of life, if life
was what it was, deceitful, quick to reduce us
to ignoble wretches, unworthy of those whom
we'd known and had been: men.
It was a sin, ours and others'.
Now he who pardons the past
and doesn't judge and only remembers
knows how he grieves; how he grieves
over a past which, expired, humiliates.
He who has bid himself goodbye, who has believed
in the end of the most precious time—
even in his smile there's cutting bitterness.
And in this, how many desolate comrades.
Courage is the gift of God.
To fear is a poverty which, unvanquished,
wears out the soul and tastes of death.
This shame of so many was mine;
humble, it's my lot to remember.

For a Voice That Is Singing

How it responds with its heart
to these young, how he who listens
is renewed. And the quivering persists
through the hours of the lonely night.

The flocks of birds fled
in formation, and a gay laugh
stirred within: most deeply consoling
prelude to so vague and artificial
a peace, the charm raved on,
reaching almost in a whisper toward serene plains.

Sky color. But a definite flavor
of good fruit, ripe apricot,
very chastely invaded the heart,
leading it to blest places of light.
Then the spirit, made more human,
smiled its vehement desire.
A childish drowsiness
overcame, sure shelter, in ancient
light, overcome. And bore
where harmony, clear joy,
is enough, and nothing more is asked.

Mother

Thieving hands poke around where
your housewifely mercy
stirred lightly; and the sacred
sweetness of domestic tasks
and love of husband and children
preserved in objects, permeated
with you, who caressed them for a lifetime,
bear the filth, the infuriating smell
of a vile touch, a hateful, vulgar
wickedness that rummages and disturbs.
Troubled by the least disorder,
loving, your very breath industrious,
a busy goodness attentive to things,
now you're a spirit who, troubled,
wanders about the ruined house.
No more are those words on your lips that were
there once, to bless your loved ones;
nor does the smile of dark tender eyes
inhabit your face, grown old.
Severe, you scrutinize and can't protect
him who remained of you; you keep
him company, sorrowful company.
So we are here, united, and not against
these others; but united to cultivate
maternal love, filial love
in the old place, desecrated by barbarians.

Recluse

The first spasm became the continuous
fearful certainty of a long
wait, underlain by peace.
Each morning it seems that the eyes
search in the distance for the door
that has to open on the yellow light
of spring, stubborn in a cool
breezy dampness; and that's really how it was.
In the uncertain mind flames tossed
and offered dangerous abstractions
to the soul, strained and liquefied.
And with it, a wretched stuffiness
made for a gnawing annoyance
heavy as winter heat
when the stove makes the room too close.
But it was cold. And the imperious frost
was succeeded by the season of fervor,
and then winter returned, exhausted,
and everything was time lost.
I walked down the slippery stairs
each day, toward a pool of evil.
I wore myself out, so as not to find myself anymore
to be him perhaps worthy of love, whom perhaps I loved,
until I pitied myself, and that was the worst.
The freedom that came unexpected
found me languid and impoverished.
Then in the world again:
here I am; and I can't find myself anymore.
I'm not beginning my life over,
but waving to it from a distance.

Translated by Anita Barrows

Franco Fortini

Franco Fortini was born in Florence in 1917 and lives in Milan, and teaches at the University of Siena. He has written several books of poetry, essays, and narratives and has translated such authors as Flaubert, Eluárd, Proust, and Brecht. A selection of his poems in English translation was published in 1978.

For Our Soldiers Who Fell in Russia

They asked for bread,
and were handed a stone,
a tin Madonna, and betrayal.

"Far away
we all have homes
and mothers who light fires
of hope and expectation"
they were told, to make them pray.

Blessed are those who did not pray.

The Gutter

From the window I can see the corner of a gutter
on an old house, built of wood that's rotting
and giving way under layers of tiles. Swallows light there
sometimes. Here and there, on the roof, in joints
and along the pipes, streaks of tar, mortar
from shoddy repairs. But wind and snow,
though they may weaken the lead spouts, still
don't shatter the rotten beam.

I take much joy in thinking
how one day (no matter
that I shan't be there), all it will take is for one swallow
to light there for an instant and everything will crash down
irreparably as the bird flies off.

In Memoriam I

You used to ask me once what was wrong;
I didn't answer you.
But it has become so difficult
to speak of final things, mother.

In the last hours
you lay with your eyes wide open,
terrified of not being able
to go on speaking—
not even deep inside yourself—
of the only thing.
Now the noise is so violent
the shock of all reality so furious
the tremor must reach
all the way down
as it did in air-raid shelters.
I won't be in time to finish the reckoning,
there's no time left.
This then is what
I still did not know.
Now you know it too
we both know it
while we wait to be reborn.

In Memoriam II

I do not understand
what it could want
among these Jewish tombstones
my father's name
that is my name
name of the fathers
cry of the tribe
that turned its back
to the grave so that
a disheveled spirit
Dog God
God of Abraham
and of Job might seize
the bundle of intestines
wrapped in white linen

and leave us in peace.

Translated by Ruth Feldman

Primo Levi

Primo Levi was born in Turin (where he lives now) in 1919. He was deported to Auschwitz by the Nazis in 1944, but survived to write about the experience several years later. He has published several narratives and books of short stories. His collected poems have been translated into English under the title Shema *(1976). His most recent book is* La Chiave a Stella *(1978).*

Lilith

Lilith our second kinswoman
Created by God with the same clay
That served for Adam.
Lilith lives in the middle of the undertow,
But emerges at the new moon
And flies restless through the snowy nights
Irresolute between earth and sky.
She spins in circles,
Rustles unexpected against the windows
Where newborn babies sleep.
She seeks them out and tries to make them die:
Therefore you will hang over their beds
The medallion with the three words.
But everything she does is useless: all her desires.
She coupled with Adam, after the sin,
But the only things born of her
Are spirits without bodies or peace.
It is written in the great book
That she is a beautiful woman down to the waist;
The rest is will o' the wisp and pale light.

Shema

You who live secure
In your warm houses,
Who, returning at evening, find
Hot food and friendly faces:
    Consider whether this is a man,
    Who labors in the mud
    Who knows no peace
    Who fights for a crust of bread
    Who dies at a yes or a no.
    Consider whether this is a woman,
    Without hair or name
    With no more strength to remember
    Eyes empty and womb cold
    As a frog in winter.
Consider that this has been:
I commend these words to you.
Engrave them on your hearts
When you are in your house, when you walk on your way
When you go to bed, when you rise:
Repeat them to your children.
    Or may your house crumble,
    Disease render you powerless,
    Your offspring avert their faces from you.

For Adolf Eichmann

The wind runs free acrosss our plains,
The live sea beats forever at our beaches.
Man makes earth fecund, earth gives him flowers and fruits:
He lives in toil and joy, he hopes, fears, begets sweet offspring.

And you have come, our precious enemy,
forsaken creature, man ringed by death.
What will you say now, before our assembly?
Will you swear by a god? What god?
Will you leap happily into the grave?
Or will you at the end, like the industrious man
Whose life was too brief for his long art,
Lament your sorry work unfinished,
The thirteen million still alive?

Oh son of death, we do not wish you death.
May you live longer than anyone ever lived:
May you live sleepless five million nights,
And may you be visited each night by the suffering of everyone who saw
Shutting behind him, the door that blocked the way back,
Saw it grow dark around him, the air fill with death.

Translated by Ruth Feldman and Brian Swann

Rossana Ombres

Rossana Ombres was born in Turin and presently lives in Rome. She has published four volumes of poetry and a novel. She is literary critic for the newspaper La Stampa.

Bella and the Golem

Whoever has a yod in his name
has the sound of future galaxies:
and he was the prophet of a coming world
above all because of that minuscule yod.

He knew the names of the basilisks
that will inhabit the changing hour of transformation
and of the tortuous leviathan
and of the darting leviathan
that will emerge from the trumpets of the deluge of dust
and of all the saurians
evoked by the great crucible
on which will ride the army
of celestial disinfection.

Even the griffins that will swallow grapes of fire
under the pergola, turned red-hot,
he knew how to address with their proper names:
names with which Shemuel will call them
the angel that has a hundred eyes for a hundred different deaths.

Of Metatron too, the most impervious of angels,
he knew all nine names and the variations in sound
according to the light of day
and the darkness of night
the flowing of tides and the direction of winds.

The day he finished
building the Golem
he felt a sharp pain in his right shoulder.
He didn't notice
the angry touch of Ariel
envious prince of inventions
and sorcery,
he didn't see that, flashing, his beard
had acquired the white incandescence
of the supreme mastery of alchemy.

So it came to pass that
a terrifying Golem
rose and scoured the panic-stricken streets:
he chose twilight, which more than any hour
resembles falsehood and confusion.
His deformities were those
of an interrupted star left to rot
in the viscic wounds of neglect:
a grim sidereal water corroded him.

The Golem carried
in his burrow-maker's hands
golden jewel cases and boxes tied with silk ribbons
so the innocent victims
would not see the instrument of torture;
from a window he took a reverential drape
embroidered with silver pine cones
and used it as a scarf to conceal
his shoulders' monstrous springe.

"The Golem! The Golem!" and the spider kicking
with his weedlike legs
broke his web in the center
and jumped in the dark attached to his thread
"The Golem! The Golem!" and the sea pulled back
the pirate ship stumbled on the sand
and on the stage of its fallen sails
the silver of mullets and barbels
put on a show of sepulchral gymnastics.
"The Golem! The Golem!" the wild animals
roaming in a painting without perspective
withdrew to the bazels of rings
and the more aggressive ones to the sides of noble portals:

the scaly body of the siren crumbled
revealing that it was
only a prop for museum balconies.
"The Golem! The Golem!" and the fields poured forth
their crickets and lizards;
a large green seething edema was seen;
the dung beetle, frightened,
clung to the round coral
of a wet-nurse's necklace.
"The Golem! The Golem!"

Raziel, who every day encouraged Bella,
who was weaving a cape of nettles
locked in the bell tower
(the clock gushed forth its hours
and strokes: so, she, was in no hurry)
took Bella and carried her to where a cave opened
the first in the world
a den still encrusted
with shrimps and original sin.
Bella who has entered the grotto
knows how to read the formula with the right sound
paying attention to the cadence of letters
without making mistakes:
she has a thousand lexical cherubs
inches away from her head,
like an aureole for saints they go round and round her:
another hundred go from the Name to her eyes
and their every move makes a forest grow.
"The Golem! The Golem!" shouted a street
that used to sing: and the pigeons, escaping,
composed an indented page. . .
And a storm came
and frogs rained and embers and black stones.

When Bella reads the Name
the Golem will be a little pumice ball
but Bella must read it just right
stressing every letter in the appropriate prayer.

The Golem is using church domes as shoes!
As gloves he wears twin public buildings!
With his piss he's burned the gardens at the river's edge!
And he doesn't speak!
There: he's near the neighborhood of the merry-go-rounds:
he's turned over the carts of ten sherbert vendors!

When Bella completes her reading
the Name will fall from the Golem.
The Golem will explode, leaving only a gray marble
no larger than a juniper berry.
Already, like a soprano, Shemuel is trilling
the frightful song of shattering.

There he is! He collapses! Now he shrinks
and rolls: he ends up in a basin
where pilgrims wash their feet!

Bella has gone back to her cape of nettles.

Translated by Edgar Pauk

Umberto Saba

Umberto Saba was born in 1883 in Trieste, where he led a secluded life until he was forced to flee Florence during World War II. After the war, he returned to Trieste and died there in 1957. His highly autobiographical poems were collected into one volume in 1945.

Sleepless on a Summer Night

I have settled down
under the stars
on such a night
as makes dreary sleeplessness
a religious delight.
My pillow is a stone.

OTHER LANGUAGES

Two paces off a dog is sitting,
sitting motionless and staring
all the time at a point, far away.
It looks almost as though it is thinking,
as though it is worthy of a rite,
as though the silences of the infinite
are passing into its body.

Under such a deep blue sky,
on such a starry night,
Jacob dreamed of the angels
climbing between heaven and his pillow,
which was a stone.
In numberless stars the lad
counted his offspring to come;
in that land where he fled the wrath
of the stronger Esau,
an unshakable dominion in the flower
of wealth for his children;
and the incubus in the dream was the Lord
wrestling with him.

Translated by Keith Bosley

The Goat

I have spoken to a goat.
Alone in the meadow, a chain at her throat.
Bloated with grass, soaked
in the rain, she was bleating.

That even bleating was brother
to my grief. And I answered, first
as a joke, then because grief is eternal,
has one voice, unchanging.
This was the voice I heard
groan in a lonely goat.

In a goat with a Semitic face
I heard the lament of all other pain,
all other life.

Three Streets

There's a street in Trieste where I see my reflection
on long days of hidden sorrow:
its name is Via Lazzaretto Vecchio.
Among old identical houses like hospices
it has one note, one only, of gladness:
the sea at the end of its even rows.
Fragrant with spices and with tar
from the desolate warehouses opposite,
it trades in nets, in rope for ships.
One shop has a flag instead of a signboard,
and inside—their backs to the passerby
who rarely concedes them even a glance—
women with downcast faces the color
of every nation submit to the punishment
life doles out: innocent prisoners,
they sullenly stitch the bright-colored flags.

In Trieste where there are many sorrows
and beauties of sky and boulevard,
there's a slope whose name is Via del Monte.
A synagogue is at its foot
and a cloister at its summit; midway up
is a chapel, and a meadow from where you can see
all the dark fury of life revealed,
and the sea with its ships, and the promontory,
and the crowd and the tents of the marketplace.

By the side of the hill there's even an
abandoned graveyard, where no funeral
procession ever comes—they don't
bury anyone there anymore, as far
as I can remember: the old Jewish cemetery
so close to my heart, when I think about
my own ancestors lying there
after so much striving and dickering,
their souls and their faces all alike.

OTHER LANGUAGES

Via del Monte is the street of holy affections,
but the street of love and joy is still
Via Domenico Rossetti.
This green boulevard at the city's edge,
which each day loses some of its color,
growing ever more city, ever less country,
preserves the charm of its better years,
of its first beautiful scattered villas
and its thin rows of small young trees.
A man who strolls here on these last
summer evenings, when all the windows
are open, and each has its terrace
where someone waits, reading or sewing,
thinks that here, perhaps, his beloved
might awaken again to the old delight
of living, of loving him alone;
and his little son to rosier health.

Translated by Anita Barrows

JUDEO-ROMANESQUE

Crescenzo del Monte

Crescenzo del Monte was born in the Jewish ghetto in Rome in 1868. His poetry combined the ghetto visions of the Roman Jew and a unique poetic style to reflect the language of the community. He published three books of sonnets in the Judeo-Romanesque dialect and translated cantos of Dante's Inferno *and a novella from the* Decameron *into Judeo-Romanesque. He died in 1935.*

A Roman Roman

I'm a Roman Jew and I've been Roman
since the time of "the Times of the Ancients"
when they were eating their figs*
and no one yet spoke Monticiano.‡

I speak as they spoke then. The strange thing is
that people mock me as if to say:
Look at them—what kind of ancient Romans are you,
hook noses, going about with your rags and bones?

I've seen Julius Caesar and Pompey.
I've been in trouble with Vespasian,
and it was then that I began my cry Aio-oh!**

But with these Aio-oh's I've been able to see
many houses crumbling, step by step,
while I, thank God, am still on my feet.

*From a popular saying indicating a primitive golden age.

‡From Monti, a district in Rome where before 1870 (i.e. before the unity of Italy) a dialect purer than in other districts was spoken. Here it stands for modern Romanesque.

**Roman dialect: *Aio,* derived from *Ah! Eh! Oh!,* once the cry of Jewish rag and bone merchants. Romans made one word—noun and adjective—out of three interjections to mean a worn and tattered thing, worthy of selling only to a Jew.

Those Zionists

on the capture of Jerusalem

But they're crazy, I'm telling you.
Now that Jerusalem has been taken
—by Christians!—now that the Gentiles have invaded,
those lunatics have got it into their heads

that when it comes to bargaining
it has to be given not to those who struggled for it,
but to Israel! And why? Because they were born there!
Crazy, I tell you. Raving lunatics.

After all the thousands of years that we've been out
do you think the Christian is going to say
Let's give it back to these Israelites!?

But suppose they do turn it over. All right—
what next? When we do get there, when
that comes about, who shall we do business with?

One Thing to Take, Another to Keep

It's no use, the Christian thinks of himself first.
He knows only about squandering and having a good time.
That's the difference from the Hebrew
who thinks of others—and then of himself.

The Jew, as soon as he's earned two bits and a nickel
eats the nickel and puts two bits away
because he's not going to make his family suffer
if two bits go out, and a nickel comes in.

They say: isn't he good at money-making! Sure.
But even the uncircumcised can make it all right.
Only, as soon as he makes it he lets it get away.

But knowing how to hold on to it—
that's no skill; that's an art. An art, I tell you,
by no means given to just anyone.

Translated by Barbara Garvin

JUDEZMO

Isaac de Botton

Isaac de Botton was born in 1897 in Salonika, Greece. He was orphaned at the age of three. During World War I he founded a Salonikan Judezmo weekly; afterward, in Xanthi, Greece, he founded a Zionist weekly in Judezmo. He was also involved in Zionist groups, and he emigrated to Palestine in 1930, where he made his living as a dentist. His two books of Judezmo poems were published in Tel Aviv. He died in 1967.

Desire

In spring when everything
is shining, I long
to walk through green woods, among
green plants, to feel
the mysterious natural world
like a child—
to gaze
at gorgeous flowers
spreading their odors,
to listen to the charming
songs of small birds singing
in their nests, because
tomorrow I will be sleeping
in the grave, I will not hear
small birds singing, and my eyes,
shut, will not see
gorgeous flowers any more.

Translated by Stephen Levy

Rachael Castelete

Rachael Castelete was born in Salonika, Greece, in approximately 1884. She was the daughter of the extraordinary Yacob Abraham Yona, who, most notably, collected, published, and sang Judezmo folksongs in Salonika around the turn of the century. Rachael Castelete moved to London in 1913 and was married that year. In 1959 she brought out a chapbook of Judezmo poems entitled Esta Gimka es el Tresoro de Rachael

Casteleta Ija de Jacov Yona, *in which the Judezmo original of "When I Came to London" appears. She died in 1966.*

When I Came to London

When I came to London
I was a girl on a vacation.
I met this young man
And married him.

I had bad luck:
He left me in my old age.
And I, a fool,
Had never relished my youth.
I had brought him a good dowry,
Along with lots of Turkish liras.
I changed them into English money
And got nothing of it.

I came to this city
And have had to wage my own wars.
I thank my God
My children are all right.

If I had stayed in Salanik,
Hitler would have killed me
Just as he killed
All of my people.
Still, today in this city
I find myself
Miserable;
Today I find myself here,
And I cannot even buy a little bottle
of wine or raki.

Translated by Stephen Levy

Clarisse Nicoïdski

Clarisse Nicoïdski was born in Lyons, France, in 1938 to Sephardic parents. She writes in both of her mother tongues, French and Judezmo. She is the author of six novels written in French and numerous poems written in Judezmo. She lives in Paris.

Eyes

and how will I forget
your lost eyes
and how will I forget
the nights
when mine closed
and yours
stayed
open
when, from fright,
those of the dead opened
to give us this light
that never has gone out,
tell me,
how will I forget?

~ ~

if you gave me your eyes
I could make
with one a boat
from the other the sail

if you gave me your eyes
I could take the paths of the sea
through the sea
that is weeping
all around the earth
because of not having eyes
because of not seeing
because it only is weeping

~ ~

eyes will be torn open
in order to see
the red veil
that blinds us

OTHER LANGUAGES

eyes will be torn open
like cloth
that covers over
the truth

eyes were torn open

~ ~

tell me the story
that moves across your eyes
when you open them
the morning
when
the sun inserts its needle of light
into your dreams

~ ~

open
two doors
two windows
a sea with two islands
without anybody on them
without anybody looking
a body
falls down
into these bottomless wells
where my soul drowns

~ ~

to drink in your eyes
wine
coffee
to sing like a drunk

to drink in your eyes
and to feel the cold
of not being able to speak
of not being able to say
anything any more

the wall
is looking at me
the candle
is looking at me
also
the lamp, chair, table
with the single
eye
of things
the eye walking
around you
me

Mouth

a cry left your mouth
like a fish
that wants to fling itself out of the river into the sea

a cry left your mouth
like a knife
that wants to fling itself
out of the hand
into the body

out of your mouth came a cry
to kill

OTHER LANGUAGES

and between your lips
it died

~ ~

I have glass in my mouth
which is why it is open
which is why I laugh
which is why I speak

and when the glass down further
I seem to hear
a broken jar
piping out
a song of forgotten joy

~ ~

open like a well
I could throw myself down

shut
like a door
when they used to kill in the street

the lying mouth waits for me
knowing that sooner
or later
it will tear me apart

~ ~

written
a line of the first writing
a word from a lost language

I try to understand you
when your eyes face forehead sleep

when you are nothing more than a ship
at the end
of its voyage
nothing more than writing
which is silent

Breaking Off from Waiting

breaking off from waiting
the leaf falls
like water like
rain
long held back
the stars go out
and none of us knows what can stop
the blood

Open Earth

open earth
drinking water from
clouds
dry earth
everywhere opening up your ancient hands
torn earth
like the stomach of a woman who just gave birth
each stone on your roads speaks to us of the beating of
your heart

Remembering

remembering
your face moves goes
around
my eyes
leaves the written line
of your kisses
the breath of a mouth
or
the road of life
around
my memories

Translated by Stephen Levy

POLISH

Henryk Grynberg

Henryk Grynberg was born in Poland in 1936. He is the author of poems, stories, and a novella. He has also been an actor with the Warsaw State Jewish Theater. His works include The Crew of the Antigone, Child of the Shadows, *and* Catcher on the Roads.

Anti-Nostalgia

Here a wandering seaweed
calls forth a smile on the face
of the great southern giant
and the sun stabs through the blue and blinding deep
so I don't know
if I'm still sailing the seas
or sailing the sky

there isn't anybody here after all
only a deathless plain
like the Lord God
it doesn't end or begin anywhere
here I am and am not
I am halfways
I sail
and I don't wait for anything
here I would like to remain forever
forgotten
even if the peace showing on the surface
is a sham
while underneath in the belly of the ocean
life gasps being chased and devoured
I would like to remain forgotten
on the great plain of nothing
onto which I have finally managed to sail

OTHER LANGUAGES

I won't manage
I cannot remain forgotten
because even if I were not
they would invent me
and remember me
I won't manage for I myself cannot
forget the faces of all the anti-people
who are sometimes called anti-semites
maybe I should be grateful to them because
thanks to them I find it so easy to avoid nostalgia
thanks to them even the voice of a seagull
sounds like the squeak of a razor

because my Proustian fragrances are the burning smell
of a swastika-singed childhood
and nobody had to tell me children's tales
for I participated in those *personally*
Another possibility: I was a *living* participant
I still remember the dead voice through the megaphone
the same I hear again today
the voice of Kiczko calling from my Ukraine
and Walichnowski calling from my Lithuania

(also Mr. Drabarek from the Polish Courier
and anonymous "lon" from the banner of youth
Alexander Tarnowski from the radio
Zenon Wilczewski and Klaudiusz Hrabyk
Zdzistaw Andruszkiewicz and Alina Reutt
from the youth magazine and even
Ignacy Krasicki from the tv screen)*

it seems we haven't traveled far enough
let's sail sail on. . . .

*The names appearing in the last part of the poem are those of personalities in the Polish mass media well known for their anti-Semitic views. [Tr. note]

Poplars

They stand in a row like chimneys,
sooty Italian poplars
signposts to heaven
tall
like the local silence
they grew here all the time
in spite of
and above all
and they're still growing

while the air here is thick
with absence
clouds of absence in the air
and an emptiness called forgetting
ascends to heaven like a cloud

trodden by feet in the millions
the great Auschwitz field
        the Auschwitz field of Maidanek
        the Auschwitz field of Treblinka
        the Auschwitz field of All This

on which we stand
moves with us
wherever we try to go
so one can't get anyplace from here
nor leave here

I halted in the row of poplars
and try to grow along with them
and like them to gaze
upwards
with green eyes
I don't try to understand anything
nor say anything
what else can one
have to say here

I come here to add my own
to the growing silence

The Dead Sea

Here in veins of metal and glass
and other materials
flows bromide
inside red-hot entrails
re-creates itself
in a process of damnation and salvation
the creative fire of hells

while the gods of the old testament grown young again
pale with bloodshot eyes
peer at the eyes of the clocks
decipher the dials of their thoughts
and obey the wishes

of a shackled cyclops who drinks up a sea
which was dead
but will start childbearing again
through potash and bromide

Listening to Confucius

Current freed for a while
boastful of its voltage and potential
will sink again into the ground for a while
like greatness like pain
like seed
into this wonderful planet
which is never older than a year

But a wrinkled brain
like cauliflower
projects wrinkles on your face
like evil thoughts broadcast by radio waves
and it's curious that you worry
even when hunger does not nag at you
and death is not so eager
to come and spell you at your task

The earth you walk on is the living body
of a woman
and likes the caress of your feet
you may walk on it and listen to Confucius
one should not worry nor deceive
one must not exert himself more than is needful
because you will not gain will not buy a thing
beyond what she herself can offer you

Translated by Isaac Komem

Mieczyslaw Jastrun

Mieczyslaw Jastrun was born in Poland in 1903. He survived the years of Nazi occupation and began publishing his poetry in Resistance journals. After the war he dedicated himself to writing books on the history of Polish literature.

The Jews

Here, too, like in Jerusalem,
Stands a grim Wailing Wall.
Those who faced it
Will not see it again.
An empty night, an empty home and house.
Whence they were dragged away.
Leaving behind darkness—and fear.
And interiors—the bosom of death.

Houses in a stony procession
Under an unpitying sky—
Like thousands of families
Following a funeral procession.

Nobody cast good earth
On this mass grave,
You were sent off in silence,
Free of the treachery of words!

OTHER LANGUAGES

Christians, thrown to the lions,
Knew what they were dying for,
And you? Your vacant home
Occupied by fire, a blind landlord.

On this side of the wall
A cross spreads its arms.
Under it pickets—
To complete the chant for the dead.

Translated by Isaac Komem

Ewa Lipska

Ewa Lipska was born in Poland in 1945. She is a graduate of the Krakow Academy of Fine Arts and is presently editor of the poetry department at the Literatura Publishing House in Krakow. Her poetry has been published in Poems *(1967),* The Second Choice of Poems *(1970),* The Third Choice of Poems *(1972), and* The Fourth Choice of Poems *(1974).*

If God Exists

If God exists
—I'll be his guest for dinner.
Instead of light: red hawthorn.
An angel will stop by to pick me up.
Pigeons of fat clouds
will flutter on the folding table.
From empty jugs we'll drink
holy water and free will.

Even if God is shortsighted
he can see eternity coming.
If God is a polyglot
he can translate holy poems
for an anthology even more holy
than that holiest first drop
which first grew into a river.

Then I'll take a bicycle ride with God
in a cherry tree. Through the landscape of Paradise.
In the vases earthly bulrushes.
Beasts of prey lie fallow.

Finally God will get off his bike and say
that actually he
is God.
He'll take out his binoculars. He'll tell me
to watch the earth. He'll explain
how it came to this.
And how many years he has been in this business
and infallibly goes wrong over the world
launching toy planes of ideas into hot air.
If God believes
then he prays to himself for eternal hope.

The sun sits on the horns of an ox
on its legs the folding table rocks
God will give me medicine from his stocks
and I'll recover
straight after death.

Wedding

A wedding cortège
with the white veiled head of the bride.

Her forehead
cold as Spitzbergen.

A bouquet of lilies
crosses the intersection of her hands.

The young couple take the elevator
to their honeymoon.

They're stopped between floors
of domestic bliss.

Relatives under pressure of 500 atmospheres
switch on all the lights.

A whirlwind plays Mendelssohn's march
lifting the newlyweds.

The world rocks
like a carriage with a baby in it.

The Cock

There came two gentlemen
to inspect my brain.
The walked over my head
for hours.
They shined their flashlights
like stars in my eyes.
They were photographing the idea
that had come to my mind
five thousand years ago.
They were taking
imprints of my thoughts.
Finally they carried them out on a stretcher.
They carried out the memory of youth
and a stack of letters
notifying my friends
of the misfortune I'd had.

But in the wilderness of my brain
the cock of the future crows.

The Flood

The flood didn't save me
though already I was lying at the bottom.

The conflagration didn't save me
though I'd been on fire many years.

The crashes didn't save me
though I was run over by trains and cars.

The airplanes didn't save me
though they blew up in the air with me.

The walls of great cities toppled on me.

The poisonous mushrooms didn't save me
nor the accurate shots of firing squads.

The end of the world didn't save me
because it didn't have time.

Nothing has saved me.

I live.

Translated by Peter Jay and Geri Lipschultz

Antoni Slonimski

Antoni Slonimski was born in Warsaw in 1895. He escaped the German invasion by emigrating to England but returned to Poland in 1950 and became one of the most eloquent spokesmen of the intellectuals against totalitarian controls. He is also the author of plays and parables. He died in 1976.

Elegy

in honor of the Warsaw Ghetto uprising, April 19, 1943

No more, no more Jewish townships in Poland,
In Hrubieszcrow, Karczew, Brody, Falenica.
Vainly would you look for lighted candles in windows,
And listen for chanting from a wooden synagogue.

The last scourings, the Jewish rags have vanished,
They sprinkled sand over the blood, swept away the footprints
And whitewashed the walls with bluish lime,
Like after a plague or for a great feast day.

One moon shines here, cool, pale, alien,
Nowadays my kinsmen, the bardic Jewish boys,
Will not find outside the town, on the highway, when the night lights
up
The two gold moons of Chagall.

Those moons are now orbiting another planet,
They have flown away, frightened by the grim silence.
They are no more, these townships where the cobbler was a poet,
The watchmaker a philosopher, the barber a troubadour.

No longer does the wind weave the old Hebraic theme
with Polish airs and Slavonic pain:
those villages and orchards
where old Jews still mourned Holy Jerusalem.

They are no more, these townships, they passed like a shadow
And this shadow shall lie across our words,
Till they embrace like brothers and join anew,
Two nations which supped full of the same suffering.

Conrad

In London at Bessborough Gardens
He said abruptly:
"Waitress, please take the things away."
(An empty teacup,
A plate with bacon rind,
A little jam and toast.)
On the empty table
He smoothed a page
After long hesitations,
While thinking both
In French and in Polish,
He drafted the first word:
THE.
Having written those
Three letters
He skirted the thicket
Of the mother-speech sounds,
Skirted the flat shore
Of a shallow river
And set sail on the broad ocean
Of English speech,
Where they loom,
Those three letters:
THE.

Through milky fogs
Seeps a faint glimmer
Outlining Barclays Bank
And a cop's helmet.

In the fireplace the logs crack.
Dickens, Mark Twain.
A pipe. Big Ben strikes.
Peaceful slumbers.
While over there was Wologda,
Zytomierz and Chernihow,
And a mother weeping quietly
Under the eye of a Russian guard.
But neither calm nor fog, but only storms
Could lighten that pain and burden
Smothering the heart.
There is an English saying:
To travel is to conquer
To conquer is to redeem.

So he set out on the enormous sea
Freed of fetters,
And never came home again,
For his house in Kent
Was not a home.
On the deck, when perennial pilgrims
Cocooned in silks,
Dusky, with patches of pink heels,
Dreaming of distant Meccas
Sailed the black, starry night,
I too heard, like Lord Jim,
A voice which tempted: "Jump!"

Conversation with a Countryman

An old Jew asked me by the Jaffa Gate:
—Are the Saxon Gardens still there? Have they changed?

What about the fountain? By the Czysta Street gate
The confectioners kept a shop where you could get sodawater.

—Everything is the same: the fountain and the newspaper stands.
Prince Poniatowski* is still mounted there.

*A well-known statue in Warsaw.

—Poniatowski! The Polish army, as we used to say . . .
I don't know how things are now, it used to be good there.

I don't feel too good. When I get better,
I am going; I want to live in Warsaw.

I even have a buyer; when everything is sold off
Perhaps I'll have enough . . . Only my son won't let me.

He's well educated; his name is also Levi,
When I talk about Poland, he knows nothing about it.

I talk to him, explain myself the best I can:
"But listen, Warsaw is there!" So he doesn't understand.

Jerusalem

Behold the Mount of Olives and the Greek cloister
A minaret and spreading domes,
Squares of yellow houses like honeycomb.
Everything is sharp and small, clear-cut and clean.

The valley of Jehoshaphat, a white arid field—
And there in the rift, the place of quiet and azure,
Motionless and deep at the very bottom lies
The Dead Sea and stifling, golden Jericho.

The tree you see is the tree of Judah.
And these great stones are from Roman times,
And there, where the rusty desert juniper grows by the roadside
Jesus revealed himself to Mary Magdalene.

Do you see the line of buses, cars, carriages?
Pious tourists traveling in the dust along the white
Road where from afar among the palm leaves
Sleeps the tiny town of Nazareth, made of clay.

And here in the wild garden—this place is best of all,
I sit often here and leave with regret:
The grasses smell good at noon, when eyes close in slumber
As in a Polish countryside, the flies drone in Jerusalem.

Translated by Isaac Komem

Julian Tuwim

Julian Tuwim was born in Lodz in 1894. During the Nazi era he lived in France, South America, and the United States. After his return to Poland in 1946, he devoted himself to literature and the training of young poets until his death in 1953. A great innovator in Polish literature, Tuwim was the author of poems, satires, anthologies, and children's books, and did many translations.

The Gypsy Bible

What, do you think, is the gypsy bible?
The unwritten, wandering, prophetic one.
Whispered to women by the silver night,
Illuminated by a Witches' Sabbath.

It wafts the fragrance of grated myrtle,
The forest's rustle and starry lore,
Shadow of the grave, the Tarot deck of cards,
A graveyard beggar and pale shapes of night.

Who found this book? We, the men of learning,
Hunting through the attics of memory
Driven to the spoor, struck by foreknowledge,
Gazing spellbound at the roots of sense and senses.

In the valleys of hidden knowledge
Twisting legend runs through like a river:
Skirting life, touching death, betwixt, between them,
Against both it complains and mutters.

In the night, burning candles of mourning
Spot this book with their tears of tallow.
With will o' the wisp intuitions turn
The dreams in this book as its pages.

The verses vibrate like a mirage,
You won't grasp their hidden meaning,
It could be: the poet as martyr . . .
. . . that something needs saving . . .
And the book dissolves.

Mother

I
In the cemetery of Lodz
In the Jewish cemetery
There is the Polish grave of my mother,
My Jewish mother.

The grave of my Mother the Polishwoman,
of my Mother the Jewess,
I brought her from the Vistula's shores
To the riverbank of industrial Lodz.

A gravestone sealed the grave
And on its pale surface
Are strewn some laurel leaves
Shed by a nearby linden.

And when the sunny breeze
Plays with those leaves
They arrange themselves in patterns
Of medals won for valor in battle.

II
A Nazi shot and killed her,
When she was thinking about me.
A Nazi shot and killed her,
When she was longing for me.

He loaded—killed the longing,
He put in a fresh clip,
So that . . . —but afterwards
There was nothing left to kill.

He shot down the world of mother:
The two caressing syllables,
He threw the corpse through the window
On the holy Otwock pavement.

Remember, O daughter!
Remind us, future grandson!
The saying has come true:
"The ideal has achieved the pavement."*

I took her from the field of glory,
I gave her to mother earth . . .
But the corpse of my name
Lies there till this very day.

Jewboy

He sings in the courtyard, snuggling in his tatters
A young poor fellow, a crazy Jewboy.

People drove him out, God addled his wits
Time and exile have confused his speech.

He scratches and dances, wails and complains
That he is lost, and has to beg for bread.

The mister from above regards the madman
Look, my poor brother, at a mournful brother.

What have we come to? Where did we go astray,
Alien and disliked by the whole wide world?

Mister from the first floor, your raving brother
Dances through the cosmos with his burning head.

The mister from the first floor is become a poet:
He'll wrap up his heart in paper, like a coin:—

And cast it from the window, let it shatter,
Stomp on it, let it cease to be.

*This line comes from a poem about the premature death of Chopin, written by the nineteenth-century Polish poet Cyprian Norwid. In that poem Norwid describes how Russian soldiers, looting the apartment of Chopin during an uprising in Warsaw, threw the piano of the dead composer out of the window and smashed it on the pavement. [Tr. note]

Then each of us will go his way
On our sad and frantic wanderings

We shall never find peace and harbor
We singing Jews, we Jews possessed . . .

Lodgers

Terrible lodgings. In the frightful lodgings
Terribly lodge all the awful burghers.
While wintry horrors and nighttime dyings
Crawl up the walls in soot and mold.

Babble reigns here. They babble, grumble;
It rains, inflation, this and that, they complain.
They get up, take a walk, and then sit down again,
But all this is a dream. And all this is a phantom.

They look at a watch, count the change in their pockets,
Straighten the tie, smooth down a wrinkle
And issue forth from their apartments—
To walk the familiar, solid, round earth.

Here they come, all buttoned up,
They look to the left, they look to the right.
But looking, they see everything as distinct:
A horse . . . a tree . . . the boy Stasiek . . . a house . . .

They grasp newspapers in their fingers like cake
And chew them into a doughy pulp,
Until their heads swell, round and fat,
Stuffed and tight with the paper yeast.

Again they talk, about Ford . . . the movies . . .
About God . . . and Russia . . . sports . . . war . . . disasters . . .
Layer upon layer grows a monstrous delusion
And they sail like ghosts through the jungle of events.

Their bursting head grows heavier towards evening
As it nods down blindly to the floor.
Nosing for burglars under the four-poster
They clink heads with a cool chamber pot.

Again they check bills, receipts and wallets,
Trousers mended lovingly by spouses,
Holy property, saintly acquisitions,
Their own, unique and so well-deserved.

Afterwards, prayer . . . "from death deliver . . .
From war . . . from famine . . . our daily bread"
And so to bed, resting face on breast,
Terrible burghers in terrible lodgings.

Translated by Isaac Komem

Aleksander Wat

Aleksander Wat was born in 1900. His sarcastic tales of anticipation, The Unemployed Lucifer, *foreshadowed his later poetry. In 1939, fleeing the Nazis, he found himself in the area taken over by Soviet troops, was arrested, and spent some six years as a prisoner and a deportee in Russia. His poems, published in 1956 after a long compulsory silence, were greeted by the young generation as an important event in Polish letters. Since 1959, when he went to the South of France because of his health, Wat has been living abroad.*

Willows in Alma-Ata

Willows are willows everywhere.

You're beautiful in frost and brightness, willow of Alma-Ata.
But if I forget thee, oh sapless willow on Rozbrat Street,
may my right hand dry up.

Mountains are mountains everywhere.

Before my eyes Tian Shan sailing in violet tints
a foam of light, a boulder of colors, it pales and turns to nothing.
But if I forget thee, distant peak in the Tatra range,
the Biala stream where I launched colorful boats with my son
sent off by the quiet smile of our patroness
let me become a stone in the Tian Shan!

If I forget you all
If I forget thee native city

the Warsaw night, the rain and the doorway, where
the old beggar holds out his hand in the doorway
the wicked dog has torn his shirt and run away.
Sleep, little Piotr . . .

I spread my hands, like a Polish weeping willow.

If I forget you,
the gas street lamps of Zurawa, the stations in the Via Dolorosa of
my love—
the lighted hearts sunk in the dark shyness of leaves
and whispers and rustles and rain, the clatter of a hansom cab in the
street,
and the gold-feathered dawn of pigeons.

If I forget thee, embattled Warsaw
blood-foaming Warsaw

if I forget Thee
if I forget You

There Is No Place

There is no place where
the flying arrow
has the right to say:
Here I am.
Here.

Achilles is unable to overtake the tortoise.

Nevertheless:
Achilles always overtakes the tortoise.
The arrow states: "Here was the start of my flight.
And here is my finishing line!" . . .

Await
you will be overtaken
You too will say:
here—here—here is my finishing line.

Translated by Isaac Komem

Adam Wazyk

Adam Wazyk was born in Poland in 1905. He was one of the founders of the Second Vanguard of Polish Poetry, which led to a clear and simple standard of verse.

Ars Poetica

The phrase which was to be the axis of my poem's crystallization
I carried through cities and forest ways
through winters and women
through rescues known to me
through rescues unknown to me
through changes of underclothes putting on my hat
the phrase self-rejected
which found no fitting neighbors
for forty years my God
the phrase about which I may say many bad things
but also many good things
one thing is certain there are no stars nor birds in it
nor goblets nor rings nor wells nor mirrors
nor any beasts from the ark of symbols
nor any archetypes
and if there is it isn't in a catalogue
and it is not learned poetry
and these are not words divorced from meaning
opaque signs
and it is not is not
I know what it is not but I don't know what it is

Hotel

Wake me up at five-thirty please
I'm leaving on the morning train
The window is ajar the room is overheated
They should switch off the heat but there's no key
I remember three turnings before I reached my room
An old woman in a dressing gown crooked a finger at me
Mister have you ever been in Czorsztyn
You remind me of a man I knew there

And who has been dead for ages
There is no key to the words of the old lady
There is no key to the heating unit
In the dark I see anonymous eyes
Perhaps these are my eyes yes they must be mine
I turn over to my right side
I turn over to my left side
I turn over to my third side

*Nike**

Soldiers are marching over the pontoon bridge,
underneath flows the genuine, yellowish Vistula.‡
Beyond the bridge stand the first graves of those
who came from the shores of the river Oka,** the pauper earth
has wrapped them in a spread of sand and silence,
the artilleryman reminisces about them by means of shells in the
night.

Rivers flow behind us, history floats by,
we've watered our hopes in distant rivers,
we have pushed impatiently in summer floods
the wheels of guns, alien clay holds the prints of our feet—
each river grows more beautiful in memory.

In a hut by the candle my submachine gun slumbers
and my watchful shadow would like to return inside me.
Do not go back before the coming of rosy Dawn,
sleep sweetly on my bed, oh armless statue,
I've thrown a soldier's blanket over your woman's breast,
over your folded wings, which will soar tomorrow.

Translated by Isaac Komem

*Nike—the winged goddess of victory.

‡In 1944, the Soviet armies were sweeping across Poland in their victorious advance towards Berlin. Many Jews, who had fled the Nazis from Poland into Russia, were returning to their native land as soldiers in those armies.

**Oka—a river in Russia. [Tr. note]

Jozef Wittlin

Jozef Wittlin was born in Dmytrow in 1896. He is a poet, novelist, and translator who presently lives in New York.

To the Jews in Poland

I am blood of your ancient blood, bone of your fragile bone,
oh my brothers in the ghettos, I lack words for my great sorrow.
Your martyred blood coagulates on the cobblestones of Poland,
My song can barely bear the burden of your martyred blood.
Your shattered bones whiten on the Polish fields,
The hungry dogs don't touch them; these bones exhale a curse.
Your guts are harried by hunger and rent by a hangman's bullet,
You await a miracle in vain, death wraps you in paper.
In paper, the dirty wings of the new Angel of Death,
Rustles the song of my pain—in the insomniac nights.

Where are you, heavenly manna, on this world's new desert?
Where are you, miracle-working staff of Moses?
Where are you, fount of Grace, which washes clear the sins of mortal
life?
Where are you, new light of day, which drives away the darkness?

A fountain of milk is spouting from the cobblestones of Newolipie,
Purest flour is pouring from the brick walls of slavery.
Leszno is growing vines like the slopes of Mount Carmel.
My friend, you intoxicate your innocent soul with daydreams.
You await help from America as once people awaited a Messiah,
Your Jewish doctor exorcises in vain the demons of plague.
A brotherly Christian has brought you secretly some potatoes,
Your head of the ghetto, Adam Czerniakow,* has taken poison.
Mayor Starzyaski‡ welcomed him in the townhall of eternity.
I shake your hand, brother!—he said and did not ask for details.

*The head of the Judenrat in the Warsaw ghetto who committed suicide in 1942 when the full extent of the Nazi plans for the extermination of the Jews of Warsaw became known to him.

‡The mayor of Warsaw in 1939, who led the inhabitants of the city in a heroic defense against the Wehrmacht at the beginning of World War II.

Blood of your ancient blood, bone of your fragile bone,
Oh brothers, I send you a sad song from a distant free land.
Your guts are harried by hunger, pierced by a hangman's bullet,
You await a miracle in vain, death wraps you in paper.
Paper in the dirty wings of the new Angel of Death
Rustles the song of my pain—in the insomniac nights.

St. Francis of Assisi and the Miserable Jews

They call your name in vain,
The rich, the proud, the virtuous and well-fed ones.

But you, if you lived,
Would surely not overlook us, who are beaten.

We poor, tattered Jews,
We the lepers of the soul,
Walking with a yellow badge.

You would not feel disgusted,
You would, you saintly goyish patriarch,
Call the most wretched of us: my brother,
My brother-abscess!

On the Jewish Day of Judgment in the Year 1942 (5703)

We have been on trial for our life for so many years,
Our age-long execution grinds on without your verdict.
Call the witnesses for the defense and let us end this bloody
Parody of the Day of Judgment.

In our cradles we are given shrouds instead of swaddling clothes.
Our palms are cramped from beating our breasts.
O, Jehovah! Appear at the Trial and discover the error in the
 proceedings.
Come down from your throne in heaven and defend us against
 Yourself!

The first stars appear in Your sky,
The old men blow the holy horns, their beards have burst into
flame...
We have sinned, just like the others in this vale of tears—
Exiles, sons of Eve, the accursed seed of Cain.

A Hymn About a Spoonful of Soup

I want to give you a spoonful of hot soup,
You brother, freezing in a foreign land,
Who has plodded through three long winters
Has wandered through three hot summers
Through the miles of trackless fields—
And marched and marched
And laid your head on a wet clod
And rotted in railway cattle cars
And eaten moldy bread in a ditch
And chewed tobacco made of cow dung
And drunk water from stinking marshes
And marched, and marched—
While eaten by reddish lice
And stung by lead bullets
Until desirous death drank you up.

Oh, she drank you to the very dregs,
You, who shriveled thrice with the heat of July
Until you dried up, like this wondrous pool
Full of dark at the setting of the sun.

I want to give you a spoonful of hot soup!
Perhaps you will shake off this deathly stillness,
You, who froze in the dugout
But nobody spelled you at your watch!

Brother, what did you fight for, over there,
Why were you eaten by reddish lice,
Why did you plod and plod and plod so,
And ate weeds,
And drank from cow-byres—
Neither you nor I know about that,
Perhaps some other time God will tell you.

But I know only one thing,
That when death walked up to you,
Walking in ice-armored battle harness,
Walking on tiptoe, quietly—on dainty tiptoe,
You did not call for your mother,
Nor father nor your wife,
But only called from your aching breast,
Calling with spasm of legs and hands,
And with eyes staring into night,
And you called with blood cooling in your veins:
—A spoonful of soup!—A spoonful of hot soup,
Which I want to give you on this day in vain.

Translated by Isaac Komem

Stanislaw Wygodski

Stanislaw Wygodski was born in Bedzin, Poland, in 1907. During World War II he was deported to Auschwitz, where he managed to survive until the Liberation. He then returned to Poland and resumed his literary career. He has published many volumes of poetry and prose, which have been translated into many languages. He emigrated to Israel in 1968.

Voyage

And what shall I bring back from such a voyage,
and what still awaits me on my travels?
Each river shall be exile-like
and every hillock alien.

Perhaps I'll keep for the distant future
a brick, black like a phantom,
a talkative flock of worried birds,
a white building by a rail crossing,

pages blackened with tallow,
read in an unheated house,
a single, leafy, slanting poplar
burning with silver and carefree,

a stolen, sidelong look,
a white ribbon in a girl's hair
and a damp, abandoned book
in the city morgue.

Winter Journey

On the 26th of October, in the evening,
the first rains came,
one doesn't see the drops,
one hears each, how it places its wet foot
on the leaf,
which inclines,
straightens and then again—

On that night in Givataym
the bushes smelt like those in Poland—
the wet grass, the plank over the ditch.
Come, rains,
come,
come again
and again.

Those Betrayed at Dawn

Those betrayed at dawn,
were already dead by noon,
the men betrayed at noon,
were already dead by night.
Those awaiting betrayal, alert
till dawn,
till noon,
till night,
were killed year by year.

Going to the North

"I'm going to the North on my left side
and approaching the shores of the South
on my right"
—Andrzej Strumillo

I'm going to the North on the left rail,
and approaching the shores of the South on the right one,
on one side a skiff is awaiting me,
on the other side a silent well,
on the left side I see a deep gully
on the right an empty desert space
on one side—the quiet of deepest night
on the other—the wind and autumn drizzle.
I'm going to the North and the shadow lengthens,
and in the South a
black,
dead
corridor.

Translated by Isaac Komem

ROMANIAN

Maria Banus

Maria Banus, born in Bucharest in 1924, studied law and philology. Her first poem appeared when she was fourteen. She translated from German, Russian, Spanish, Turkish, and French, including poems by Goethe, Pushkin, Neruda, Hikmet, and Rimbaud. In addition to her poems, she has written plays and many articles. After the war she was one of the official poets. Later, disenchanted, she embarked on a defiantly individual course, producing poems reminiscent of her best early work. Her volumes are The Girl's Country *(1937),* Joy *(1947),* I am Speaking to You, America! *(1955),* Metamorphosis *(1963), and* Anyone and Something *(1972).*

Eighteen

Wet streets. It has rained drops big as silver coins,
gold in the sun.
My mind charges the world like a bull.
Today I am eighteen.

The good rain batters me with crazy thoughts.
Look. Drops are warm and slow
as when I was in a carriage, pinned tight
in diapers, drenched and unchanged for an hour.

Yes, it rained as tomorrow, in the past, always.
The heart scrapes through time, is one heart.
My temples beat stronger than temples of time.

Like a common bum I think of drinking life,
but I am burnt, even by the hot stream of its juices.
I am eighteen.

Gift Hour

From moonwater, from mirror mist, a slender porcelain body
emerged.
A vase pale and heavy. Ponderous with raspberries of blood.
How can you stand this sadness, my lover, my love?

Don't be late. Give me your ankle and forehead. Not tomorrow.
Today my bedroom walls are fresh,
tender and concealed like the inside of bread.

Look, they still flash white and delicious at night:
my knees. Take them. They're yours. You don't see them,
shivering and full like two cups of milk.

Translated by Matei Calinescu and Willis Barnstone

Nina Cassian

Nina Cassian was born in Galati in 1924. She studied at the University of Bucharest and the Conservatory of Music; she is a composer and musician as well as a translator and poet. She has won prizes for her many books, including children's books. Her translations from the French and German include works by Molière, Heine, Becher, and Brecht. A former social realist, Cassian has become one of the most distinctive and intelligent voices in contemporary Romanian poetry. Her works include On the Scale of One to One *(1947),* Outdoor Performance—A Monograph of Love *(1954),* Everyday Holidays *(1961), and* Outdoor Performance—Another Monograph of Love *(1974).*

Blood

O, how I remember the pain of it.
My surprised soul jerked
like a decapitated hen.
Everything was sprayed with blood,
the street, the table in the bar
and especially your unknowing hands.
My spread hair swept between the glasses
like a monster, brushing against them
like a mildewed breath, then dancing
stood up hissing to fall at your feet,
crumpled there like one condemned.
I remember how cruelly I laughed,
and how I transposed myself
in order to be more like myself.
And that I screamed just once,
long afterwards when I was alone
as the lights went out and the traces
of blood had been wiped from the tables.

Cripples

When cripples throw their crutches into the air
they land on the heads of those of us who are whole,
and we're the ones who catch the cripples
just before they fall to the ground,
and we stand there holding them in our arms
while they do something vile and despicable to us:
they empty their bladders on our clothes
and whisper obscenities in our ears,
but we still continue to support them
so that they don't collapse,
although if we hadn't grabbed them at the start
we'd have seen them beaming and cackling
and hopping on one leg, rushing and flying up
to retrieve the crutches which are essential to them
since they need them to beat us with.

Self-Portrait

I've been given this triangular face to wear,
a visage fit for the prow of a pirate ship
with a weather vane that's off to one side
and topped with lanky, moon-colored hair.
This invitation for aggression and mockery
is recognized wherever I go from dawn to dusk.
Wherever my image happens to be projected,
it's sure to offend the retina that catches it.
To whom do I belong? My parents and forefathers
deny me. No race claims me. Not in the least.
Neither white nor black, nor red nor yellow.
Even my sex disavows me whenever it can.
Only when I've been hurt and I cry out
and dare complain, when I am cold and lonely
and time has wounded me, then I'm allowed
to be accepted as human—and even beautiful.

All Night Long

The window was open all night long.
The forest came in and leaned against the wall.
A squirrel hung itself on the lamp.
Snow covered my easy chair.

At morning death entered
to see if his order had been carried out.
I had slept too deeply
to enjoy that beautiful scene.

Translated by Herbert Kuhmer

Like Gulliver

Like Gulliver pulling a hundred ships,
I draw you, my lovers, to the shore,
clumsy, in all colors, cunning with your
tiny swords and shooting from the hips.

Like Gulliver I spare you, even though
you hit my skull cruelly and hope it breaks.
I laugh at you through strings and snakes
of blood, my furious lovers with your tiny bows.

Translated by Matei Calinescu and Willis Barnstone

Veronica Porumbacu

Veronica Porumbacu was born in Bucharest in 1921 and educated at the University of Bucharest. She translated extensively, mainly poetry by women, and edited an anthology of world women poets. After practicing "committed" poetry in the 1950s, she found her true voice—a mixture of childlike naiveté and subtle allegories. She was killed in the March 1977 earthquake when the apartment house in which she was living collapsed. Her volumes include Dreams of Old Dokia *(1947),* Poems, Retrospective Selection *(1962), and* Circle *(1971).*

Of Autumn

In the night there was a murder in the street.
Summer was killed.
At the window you could hear the wind yelling
In the garden.

The trees stopped talking.
Blood drips from the ivy on the walls.
King Herod of the Autumn massacred hundreds
Of leaves with his words.

Translated by Matei Calinescu and Willis Barnstone

OTHER LANGUAGES

RUSSIAN

Margarita Aliger

Margarita Aliger was born in Odessa in 1918. Her father had musical and linguistic talent; her first husband, Constantin Mazakov-Rakitin, was a composer. They had two children before he was killed in World War II. This was the period in which Aliger won fame as a poet and was closest to Fadaeev (Secretary of the Writer's Union from 1939 to 1953). Aliger was among the writers concerned with the publication of Tsvetayeva's work in the Soviet Union after years of neglect.

To a Portrait of Lermontov

My twenty-six-year-old ensign,
please forgive me, please forgive
the twice as many years I've lived
in this bright world, where I still am.
Forgive me, please forgive me, for
every feast and every day, it's
been my fortune to have more,
twice as many more than you!
And yet if I've had twice your days
there has been room in them for twice
as many fears and injuries.
Who knows which century it was
easier to bear? Between us
who was luckier? What weighs more,
heavy blows the living feel, or
grass that's growing overhead?

You don't answer, since you're dead
and I won't answer . . . I'm alive.

Two

Once again they've quarreled on a tram
    shamelessly indifferent to strangers.
I can't hide how much I envy them.
    I can't take my eyes off their behavior.

They don't even know their good fortune,
  and not knowing is a part of their luck. . . .
Think of it. They are together. Alive.
  And have the time to sort things out and make up.

House in Meudon

Gray and dingy house in Meudon.
dull and gray old house in Meudon,
flat as board   four stories high
uncolored brick, unlit, unchosen
there by someone else's garage, like
a burnt-out candle, dripping wax:
there it was you lived, Marina.

Gray and dingy house in Meudon.
Nothing grows on the verandah.
There's no smile behind the window,
just a dead house, stiff with cold, with
no dogs, no cats and alone
deserted like a bivouac.

How long since the Russian language
was used there? To cry or laugh or
hide your misery from children,
suffer in,   or breathe, or be
written in notebooks until morning.
Now this upright narrow house
has fallen into French silence
with its gates closed at the bend.
It conjures up by day and night
all your memories in my heart.

From now on, to move or not, will
alter nothing. Magic cannot
change the bends that wait for you,
hollows ahead, and more mirages—
houses by other people's garages.

OTHER LANGUAGES

Now I have it on my palm,
in my own hand: the dingy house.
Look, how bare it is, how lonely,
always facing down the road
three hundred meters. To the station.

—I must pack my bundle now.
—What's the hurry? Off to Paris?
What's the fever, what's the panic?
You've seen Berlin once already.
Do you want to go to Prague?
—No. I'd rather die. I'll go to
no more foreign cities. Ever.

I must go to Trekhprudny,
to Granatny, Plyushikha, the Arbat. . . .
Yes, let's be going. Soon, as soon
as can be. Fast. At a run.
Still the dingy house in Meudon—
Stubbornly, its black stare follows.
While you find your last dark river
Kama, rocks, insects, and that
small town reaching down the hill.

To the Kama, then, from Meudon.
To be without a home or foothold.
Not to prison. Not to freedom.
With a great stone in your throat.
Two years. No address. No shelter.
Without word. Without a word.
Without daughter. Without husband.
Only horror, hard frost, sirens,
and the war shriek overhead.

Still your son was with you, in that
wooden hut above the river.
Who was guilty then? Of what?
In that dark house, on that rough road.
All around you, Russia, Russia
danced in golden rings barefoot
in the small woods
on the steep banks,
Russia who had brought you up

a daughter once—then let you go.
So, did you displease her? How?
Because you went away from home
and lost yourself in foreign lands?
That she forgave you long ago.
Russia had no time, not then,
to understand you, all her women
wept in all the villages,
wagons always on the move,
steppes on fire, and all her people
running away. How could she then
remember you? Or bother with you?
There you were. Behind the fence.
Yelabuga. The edge of war.
For no fault of yours forgotten.
Mother Russia. Mother Rus'.
This cold. Bleak. I am afraid.

What comes next, Lord? Every August
is the end of summer. So
what happens? Every year
rains come and the hardest clay
erodes, and crumbles, winter comes.
Marina. How will you live through it?
The Kama will not move. No way
to cross. By foot or horse. No path
Or road. Only the snow. Blizzard.
No friend. Not even an enemy.
Only snow and snow and snow
like your landlady's featherbed!
You won't be able to leave the yard.
Marina. How will you live through it?
Even you can't handle this.
You've gone too far.
—Yes. This is it.
  And your last trick?
  A hempen rope.

Translated by Elaine Feinstein

Joseph Brodsky

Joseph Brodsky was born in Leningrad in 1940. In 1964 he was sentenced to five years of hard labor for "social parasitism" but did not serve out his term. In 1972 he became an involuntary exile and settled in the United States after brief stays in Vienna and London. Only four of his poems have been printed in Russia, but a book of his poems is available in the United States, and translations continue to appear in periodicals.

A Jewish Cemetery Near Leningrad

A Jewish cemetery near Leningrad.
A crooked fence of rotten plywood.
Behind the crooked fence lie side by side
Lawyers, merchants, musicians, revolutionaries.
For themselves they sang.
For themselves they saved.
For others they died.
But first they paid the taxes
respected the law
and in this unavoidably material world
pored over the Talmud
idealists to the end.

Perhaps they saw further.
Perhaps they believed blindly.
But they taught their sons to be patient
and to endure.
They sowed no grain.
They never sowed grain.
They just laid themselves down in the cold earth
like seeds.
And fell asleep for ever.
Then they were covered over with earth
candles lit
and on the Day of Remembrance
hungry old men with shrill voices
choking with cold
shouted about peace.

And they got it.
In the form of material decay.
Remembering nothing.
Forgetting nothing.
Behind a crooked fence of wet plywood.
A couple of miles from the tram terminus.

Pilgrims

For then my thoughts, from far where I abide,
Intend a zealous pilgrimage to thee.
—Shakespeare

Past arenas, sanctuaries
past smart cemeteries
past churches and bars
past big bazaars
past calm and gloom
past Mecca and Rome
in the sun's blue glow
across the earth
the pilgrims go.

They are lame, hunchbacked
hungry, ill clad.
Their eyes are full of sunset
their hearts are full of dawn.
Behind them deserts sing
lightnings flare
stars rise above them

and birds hoarsely screech to them
that the world will stay as it was.
Yes. Will stay as it was
snowy enough to blind
and dubiously refined.
The world will stay false.
The world will stay eternal

maybe within reach of the mind
but still without end.
Meaning that faith in self and God
will be in vain.
Meaning that the illusion and the road
are all that remain.
And there shall be sunsets over the earth.
And there shall be dawns over the earth. . . .

With soldiers for dung.
With poets for a song.

OTHER LANGUAGES

Verses on Accepting the World

All this was, was.
All this burned us.
All this rained on us
struck us, shook us
took our strength
dragged us to the grave
set us on a plinth
then cast us down
then forgot us
then summoned us
to seek other truths
that we might be lost
in the scrub of ambitions
in the thicket of prostrations
associations, conceptions
and among mere emotions.

But we learned to fight.
But we learned to take heat
from the hidden sun
and to steer earthward
without pilot or chart
but, above all
not to repeat ourselves.

We like routine.
We like the dimple
on our momma's neck
and we like our flat
which is a bit small
for a temple dweller.
We like to let our hair down.
We like to nod in the wind.
We like the swish of cotton
and the roar of sunspots
and generally our planet
is like a recruit
sweating on a march.

Étude

I embrace these shoulders and I look
at what looms up beyond the back
I see the proffered chair grow pale
against the iridescent wall.
The light bulb with its keener glare
shows up the shabby furniture
and makes the corner couch aglow
its brown leather appearing yellow.
The table is empty, the floor flickers
the stove is dark, a landscape has
frozen in its dusty frame: it seems
only the dresser lives and dreams.
A moth flutters about the room
and jogs my gaze out of its gloom.
If here a ghost has ever been
then it has left this house and gone.

Monument to Pushkin

And Pushkin falls
onto the bluish
piercing snow
—Eduard Bagritsky

. . . and silence
And not another word
and an echo.
And weariness as well.
. . . He concluded
his poems with blood.
They plopped
earthward.
Then they gazed long
and tenderly.
They felt odd, cold
strange.
Over them gray doctors and seconds
leaned without hope.
Over them twitching stars
sang
over them winds
stopped . . .

. . . The empty boulevard.
And the snowstorm singing
The empty boulevard.
And a poet's monument.

The empty boulevard.
And the snowstorm singing
and the head
drooping wearily.

. . . On such a night
tossing in bed
is more comfortable
than standing
on pedestals.

Translated by Dimitry Pospielovsky and Keith Bosley

To a Tyrant

He used to come here till he donned gold braid
a good topcoat on, self-controlled, stoop-shouldered.
Arresting these café habitués—
he started snuffing out world culture somewhat later—
seemed sweet revenge (on Time, that is, not them)
for all the lack of cash, the sneers and insults,
the lousy coffee, boredom and the battles
at twenty-one he lost time and again.

And Time has had to stomach that revenge.
The place is now quite crowded, bursts of laughter,
records boom out. But just before you sit
you seem to feel an urge to turn your head round.
Plastic and chrome are everywhere—not right;
the pastries have an aftertaste of bromide.
Now and again before close-down, he enters
straight from a theater, anonymous, no fuss.

When he comes in, the lot of them stand up.
Some out of duty, the rest in unfeigned joy.
Limp-wristed, with a languid sweep of palm
he gives the evening back its cozy feel.
He drinks his coffee—better nowadays,
and bites a roll, while perching on his chair,
so tasty that the very dead would cry
"Oh yes!" if only they could rise and be there.

Soho

Reflected in a venetian mirror, heavy-framed,
the composed profile of a beautiful woman, her speaking mouth
a gaping wound. Her partner contemplates the walls,
where the pattern has altered over the eight years to "Scenes
at Epsom Races"—flags. A jockey in scarlet cap
drives towards the winning post on a two-year-old
colt. All merged into one great blur, the wind rising in his ears.
In the stands they're going mad. . .—"didn't reply
to my second letter, so I decided. . ." The voice is
as it were , a struggle between the verb and the
absent tense. A hand, young, thin,
adjusts her hair, flowing, falling
nowhere, like the waters of many
rivers. Saddling the wooden quadrupeds
around the table with its half-drunk glasses, those who
died a hero's death go bucking and prancing on alien
sheets by candelabra-light, as far as the turning
into—ton Lane, powdered with snow.—The flags
droop down. The wind dies; and drops of moisture
suddenly stand out on rivals' chins.
And the stands are lost to view. . . —At the turning
a yellow lamp is burning, lightly gilding the snowdrifts,
like the crumbling crust on Viennese pastry. No matter
who got here first, the bell in the lane
doesn't ring. And the hooves of the gray or the bay
in the present past, even reaching the post,
leave no trace on the snow.

Translated by Alan Myers

Eva Brudne

Eva Brudne studied at the Moscow Gnesin School of Music and the Institute of Foreign Languages in Moscow University, and also studied comparative literature at the University of Texas at Austin. She was a member of a literary workshop in Moscow and belonged to the avant-garde movement. After emigration from Russia in 1974 she lived in Rome, where some of her works were translated into Italian. She came to New York City in 1975. Her poems, essays, and translations have been published in Russian and English in the United States.

Memento Vivendi

Dedicated to Vil Mirimanov

Those who loved me,
Let them come to the valley where the wind
Scatters my ashes, to the purple
Mirages of heather which look like the rock
Tassilin-Adjer frescoes in Africa,
Having the dimness of watercolors in a dream.
They look like paintings by hippies who flocked
From the 1960s up into the purgatory
Where Earth prepares
Its changes. Let them
Come to that land,
Come purged of quarrels,
Purged of vanity, pettiness, argument,
No more jealousy or debts or violence,
No more hypocrite friends. Let them come to the land
Where poppies grow from fire and return to fire
Scattering black seeds of dream over the Earth,
To the land where scent and sound has color,
Where dark blue light
Cloaks with night the hills, and other hills, and hills
Behind those hills, the Kabbalistic open sky beyond them . . .
The sky that gives
Stars to the whole Earth, but speaks
With stars only where the poppies grow . . .
Those who loved me
With the love of a thousand years.
Those who sailed with me from the shores
Where I knew happiness and wisdom,
Those who loved me boring and mad,
Torpid, or blind with tears of happiness,
Screaming with fear or passion,
Enslaved and at last free
For life and death, those
Who went through love for me, let them
Come to the valley where my ashes are blown by the wind
And laid to rest.

A Farewell Ballad of Poppies

There is in me the sadness that King David
Gave as a kingly gift to a thousand years.
—Anna Akhmatova

The whole field of poppies billowed, my beloved!
Grasses were pallid, half dead, half alive—
And forests, ravine, the slopes, and the eyes,
Yellow eyes through the branches, pathways deserted
And sky, in the thicket the madness of nightingales,
All this was ours, it was ours, my beloved.

No longer the moon-made magic over the forest,
No more rain rustling all over the forest,
Or leaves underfoot,
Mysterious lime trees shedding their flowers,
When June covered earth with a fleece for us,
A skylark of stars was July, and August
The fruit we had waited for, fires in September
Blazed, October was hills and sea—
Upon the piano a tea rose, a hell, paradise
And a shroud of mountains,
Violet, dark, in place since creation began,
And your smile as you said goodbye . . .

And now only the poppies remain:
Poppies—the dreams at night, and kisses
Of poppy, humiliation, pain,
Poppy-death, poppy Ascension, the poppies
Blushed above your door, a nest of them
Over the window, dead in the North sun,
But they flame all the more in the valley
Where runs the river of my tenacious ancestors,
Jordan, its waters illumined reflect
Stars in their configurations, and secret signs,
Signs that are strange to those not versed in them,
Strange, keening; and in the North—unplaceable . . .
Door, yours . . . and the key—lost in the waters,
Waters of sacred lunar Jordan. Always
Burning the poppies, putting the sleep in them.
Poppies the last I shall see as they close
Over my sinful earth.

Translated by the author

Sasha Chorny

Sasha Chorny was born in 1880 and died in 1932. His books of poetry are Satires and Lyrics, Thirst, *and* Poetry.

A Vilna Puzzle

O, Rachel, your very gait
Wakes an echo in my heart . . .
Like the gentle dove is your voice,
 Like the hillside poplar, your form.
And olivelike are your eyes,
So guileless and so deep,
Like . . . (I've sounded all the notes—
 No similes are left!)

Your bridegroom, though . . . Good god!
You and he—just think, my dear:
Pure dandelion and frog,
 Gentle moth and vampire bat.
Such gestures and such smiles,
Such braces and such pants,
Sticky as glue to the core,
 This cheapjack and parvenu.

But the strangest thing of all,
Child, that to cap this marriage deal,
To an idiot like this,
 You present three hundred thousand . . .
O, Rachel, queen of Vilna,
Reason must give up the ghost—
This crazy puzzle, even
 Spinoza could not solve.

Translated by Daniel Weissbort

Dovid Knut

Dovid Knut was born in 1900 and emigrated to Paris from Russia at an early age. He began to publish his poetry in the mid-1920s and attracted a great deal of attention with his first book, Of My Centuries. *Knut fought in the French Resistance during the Second*

World War; his wife was also involved in the movement and was killed by Germans. After the war Knut emigrated to Israel and is said to have begun writing in Hebrew. His books, which have appeared in small editions in the West, have never been published in the U.S.S.R. They include Of My Centuries, Parisian Nights, Daily Love, *and* Selected Poems. *He died in Israel in 1955.*

Walking Along the Sea of Galilee

I was walking along the Sea of Galilee,
And in a divinely morose joy
(as if my heart were glad and yet not glad)
I wandered among the Stones of Capernaum
Where once . . . Listen, ponder
In the shade, in the dust of this olive garden.

In the bar of the universe
The same unsleeping voice
Howled with sexual desire,
And from the walls of the eternal city
Leered cinematic shouts.
For everyone! Cheap!! Incessant!!!

What can I tell you of Palestine?
I remember deserted Sedzhera,
The orange cloud of the Khamsin,
The dignified voice of an Astrakhan Ger,
The narrow insulted back
Of a murdered Shomer boy,

A haughty camel at the watering trough,
The *peyas* of mute Tzaddiks from Safed,
The dry sky of a hungry eternity
Hovering over the world's doomed childhood,
The smooth endless tombstones
Of the Josephate's insane dead,
And a girl named Judith
Who for a long time
Waved a tanned hand after me.

A Woman from the Book of Genesis

I remember a dim evening in Kishinyov:
We'd just walked past Inzov Hill
Where a short, curly-haired official—Pushkin—
Used to live. He had hot negroid eyes
Set in a plain but lively face
And they say he was quite a dandy.

I could see a dead Jew being carried on stretchers
Down dusty, frowning, dead Asia Street
Past the hard walls of the orphanage.
Under the rumpled shroud
You could see the bony outlines
Of a man gnawed away by life,
Gnawed so far away
That the skinny worms of the Jewish cemetery
Had little to look forward to.

Behind the old men carrying the stretchers
Was a small group of wide-eyed Jews.
Their moldy old-fashioned coats
Reeked of holyness and fate.
It was a Jewish smell—of poverty and sweat,
Of pickled herring and moth-eaten fabric,
Of fried onions, holy books, the synagogue.
And especially—of herring.

Their hearts sang with a great grief,
And their step was silent, measured, resigned—
As if they had followed that corpse for years,
As if their march had no beginning,
No end . . . These wise men of Zion, of Moldavia.
Between them and their black burden of grief
Walked a woman, and in the dusty twilight
We couldn't see her face.

But how beautiful was her high voice!

To the slap of the steps and faint rustle
Of falling leaves and coughs
There poured forth an unknown song.
In it flowed tears of sweet resignation

And devotion to God's eternal will
And ecstasy of obedience and fear . . .

Oh, how beautiful was her high voice!

It sang not of a thin Jew
Bouncing on stretchers. It sang—of me,
Of us, of everyone, of futility and dust,
Of old age and grief, of fear and pity,
And the eyes of dying children . . .

The Jewess walked smoothly,
But each time the stretcher-bearers
Stumbled on some cruel stone
She would scream and rush to the corpse.
Her voice would wax strong,
Ringing with threats to God,
Rejoicing in raging curses.

And the woman waved her fists at Him
Who floated in a greenish sky
Above the dusty trees, above the corpse,
Above the roof of the orphanage,
Above the hard, crusty earth.
But then she grew afraid
And beat her breast
And begged forgiveness in a husky wail
And screamed insanely of faith and resignation.
She pressed herself to the ground,
Unable to endure the heavy burden
Of severe, grieving eyes staring down from heaven.

What actually was there?
A quiet evening, a fence, a star,
A dusty wind . . . My poem in "The Courier,"
A trusting high-school girl, Olga,
The simple ritual of a Jewish funeral
And a woman from the book of Genesis.

But I can never tell in words
What it was that hung over Asia Street.
Above the street lights on the outskirts of town,
Above the laughter hiding in the doorways,

Above the boldness of some unknown guitar
Rumbling over the barks of anguished dogs.

. . . A peculiar Jewish-Russian air . . .
Blessed be he who has breathed it.

Translated by John Glad

Haifa

1

Amidst fruitless activity and fat idleness,
In the snowy wilderness, where beasts do not live,
Again, like an oasis: a monk's cell to the rescue,
Geometrical manly comfort.

And again, the vast sheet of virgin paper
Selflessly awaits life-giving ink,
The last spare tears, the blessed moisture,
Which men keep by for a dark hour.

The country is working—pen, shovel, spade—
And soul's sweat is salty, like the sweat of the brow.
But where farmers sowed, spring the flowers of Ecclesiastes,
Your sagacious garden, mad Solomon.

2

O, poor Carmel! The grave-cubes stand
Guard over a hygienic resting:
Radiophone—and gold teeth,
Through which brazen souls vomit.

Fire and sulphur of European lava,
Cinematograph, factory hooter . . .
But over it all, through it all, like poison,
The penetrating Biblical cold.

Safed

Mounds of humped rust-colored hills,
Camels sprawled over the slopes.
The faded color of barrenness, where rarely is
The thirsty gaze consoled by any spot of green.

Autumnal caravan of sullen hills,
Weary of aimless wanderings,
Of the motley sameness of many lands
Of the tedium of clouds, and sands, and disasters.

Too long it has born poor humankind's
Wretched goods and chattels: its homes, its graves,
The millennial burden and the senselessness
Of an impotent faith, unconsummated anger . . .

The mysterious cubes of the houses,
Clustering blue in terraces.
Herds of rocks, of camels and donkeys,
Donkeys' braying, tedious and coarse.

And then again—an all-dissolving peace
Over the enchanted Biblical eternity.
And through the glassy stationary heat,
I can hear God, leaning over Safed.

Rosh Pina

The stars shine down
From the blue nonbeing
On the houses, the square, the synagogue.
The wind returns
To its rounds
And sighs in the eucalyptus grove.

The wind returns
To its rounds,
Picks up a eucalyptus leaf.
Here, through these
Inscrutable regions,
Went the groaning slaves, out of Egypt.

The wind returns for the hundred-thousandth time,
Worrying the slopes of Canaan.
Like witnesses of truth, O, Ecclesiastes,
Are Hermon's inexorable crags.

Returning from the sea, from the high peaks,
The wind blows, like a moist eternity.
Cypresses sway decorously in the quiet,
Like witnesses of sorrow and death.

Life returns: Rebecca with the pail of water
On her shoulder . . . So it was, so it will be.
Death returns. But, under the same star,
It's not slaves who die, but people.

Translated by Daniel Weissbort

Naum Korzhavin

Naum Korzhavin was born in Kiev in 1925. He began publishing in 1941 but was exiled to Siberia for anti-Stalinist verse. He now lives in the United States. His book Years *was published in the Soviet Union in 1963.*

Children of Auschwitz

Men tortured children.
Cleverly. Deliberately. Efficiently.
It was a routine job for them.
They worked hard, they tortured the children.

And every day it began again.
Swearing, curses for no reason.
But the children couldn't understand
What the men wanted of them.

Why were they abused, beaten, starved,
Snarled at by dogs?
And the children thought at first
It was because they were naughty.

They couldn't imagine how
It was possible they might be killed;
Children reason traditionally,
They look to grown-ups for protection.

But the days kept on coming, terrible as death,
And the children became "good" children.
They were still beaten, though. Just the same.
And the guilt was not lifted from them.

They clutched at people. They begged them.
And they went on loving.
But the men had "ideas" in their heads.
The men tortured children.

(And when the orders came, at the precise time,
Having worn them out finally, they killed them.
And summing it all up, they deposited
The little shoes in the stores.)

I live. I breathe. I love people.
But I lose my taste for life
When I remember that this thing happened!
Men tortured children!

Translated by Daniel Weissbort

Aleksandr Kushner

Aleksandr Kushner was born in Leningrad in 1936. During the years when Leningrad was under siege and blockaded, he was evacuated to the south of Russia. He graduated from Leningrad's Herzen Pedagogical Institute. He has taught Russian literature and, in addition to poetry and translation, he writes criticism.

To Boris Pasternak

Photographed at midday
You are already gray.
A terrace, a verandah
A doorway are behind you.

Is it the gloom of going—
Autumn through forests blowing?
You stand, your big hands held
Low in a simple fold.

OTHER LANGUAGES

Or, in your Sunday best
Do you await a guest?
You stand, day out day in
Behind the times, alone.

Now sifted rain, now snow
Now skies are all aglow.
You stand, in black and white
Blinking into the light.

You do not skimp or scare
Or choose your words with care
And nothing do you crave
Of all that earth could give:

Nor cloud, nor blade of grass
Nor tears, nor nothingness
Nor do you need to study
Photographs, as (look) I do.

Brushing hair from your eyes
Lips tightening, you gaze
Into an unseen crack
Where only you can look.

Out there is light—so much
You almost overreach
Yourself: on that account
You must remain silent.

Translated by Dimitry Pospielovsky and Keith Bosley

Lev Mak

Lev Mak was born in 1939 in Odessa, where he studied engineering. In 1970 most of his life's work—400 poems, several plays, filmscripts, and a novel—was confiscated. He was expelled from Russia in 1974 and emigrated to Israel and later settled in the United States. He has had poems published in several journals in the United States.

Eden

1

. . . You enter the garden and do not recognize it.
Inhale its rustle and its breath:
Sweet-smelling, the tree sings.
Full of reverence, the wind abates.

Do not forget, Temptation has its price,
And the fruit on the apple tree is from the Serpent:
On the graftings of knowledge and retribution,
Newton-apples hang from the Tree of Evil.

Try to bite through their skin:
In an instant, feathers fall;
And, swelling with unbelief and sin,
Through the wings—the whiteness of hands.

You view a new dwelling place.
You jump up and down, you wave . . .
You shed tears.

2

The snow falls to the ground, and now
Enters the garden, faint, smelling of blood:
A mighty, coercive sameness,
A nation smothered with featherbeds.

The garden, sugar-coated, crusting over,
Sends crows soaring above the empty treetops—
How the bony cries trill along
The bony shoulders of the ancient willows!

And how their nests stand out among the branches!
What have they done with your peoples, garden,
My homeland, where have they been hidden?
Where are their lives . . .
                    Snow. Crows' droppings
Stand out in the whiteness. And the high branches
Click like billiard balls.
                    Soap patch of the moon
On the thin crust of ice.
Destruction. Mob law.
And always: man and branch.

Translated by Daniel Weissbort

The Flood

The Old Testament, a bygone age,
Seventeen minutes until the flood. . .

Winegrowers dance in their vats;
Potters fire jugs,
There is the crying of children, the snoring of old women in
  hammocks,
The creaking of the well sweep. . .

Parasites on the pier stare at the black ark.
The respected old man takes away the menagerie—
Miaowing, roaring, barking.
His son Shem, drunk as a lord, started an uproar—
Listen! . . . There is his wife crying in the cabin! . . .

The preparations are complete, the holds are filled.
Low clouds, thunder.
Noah gasps for breath: he was nearly left behind,
He guffaws and minces about,
He carries the nearly forgotten rats in his sack.

THE ARK SETS OUT
    THE LAST SIGNAL,
        GOODBYE!!!

The first drops of the flood moisten the handkerchiefs.
Those who have come to see them off put on the jackets they've
  thrown over their arms.

Keeping their dignity,
They climb the stairs to the city.

Translated by Neil Muhlberger and Marvin Misemer

Prayer

From your high bridge wave & wail,
Russia. For my death nears. And let
No one, I implore you, forget
My shaking deck & my drenched sail.

From your unkissed lips I wait an answer.
But they stay tightly sealed. Instead:
Blood & dirt stain your forehead.
And your jailors' sneers acknowledge my prayer.

But, Darling, stay still. Though I'm bereft
Paradise pulls me. Nothing can alter it.
I have one hope: A direct hit
Of global truth on my fragile raft.

Now will I hear your exalted opinion
When into your outstretched palms,
Up from the depths of separation,
Float the splinters of my poems.

Translated by Dan Jaffe

Osip Mandelstam

Osip Mandelstam was born in Warsaw in 1891 and grew up in St. Petersburg. His persecution for his literary nonconformism began in the early 1930s, and he was arrested in 1934. After being exiled for several years, he was rearrested in 1938 and died shortly thereafter, probably en route to a concentration camp. Three volumes of his poems were published during his lifetime. Several volumes of his poems in translation are now available.

This Night

This night cannot be remade
And there is still light in your house.
At the gates of Jerusalem
A dark sun rose.

A terrible yellow sun—
Hushaby, hushaby—
In the bright temple the Jews
Were burying my mother.

Owning no paradise,
Bereft of priesthood,
In the bright temple the Jews
Performed the rites of the dead.

And over my mother's remains
The voices of Israel rang out.
I awoke in my cradle
In the dark sun's light.

Like a Young Levite

Like a young Levite among the priests,
He remained long on the morning watch.
The Judaic night thickened over him
And somberly the ruined temple was created.

He spoke: the alarming yellow of the skies!
Over the Euphrates it is already night, priests, take flight!
But the elders thought: We are not to blame for this;
The dark yellow light, the joy of Israel.

He was with us when, on the banks of the stream,
We swathed the Sabbath in precious flax
And with the heavy seven-branched candelabrum
Lit up the night of Jerusalem and the smoke of nonexistence.

Translated by Daniel Weissbort

Concert at the Station

You can't breathe, the hard earth wriggles with worms,
and not one star says a word,
but God watches, there's music up above,
the station shakes with the singing of the Aonians,
and once more, after the screeching of the locomotive
the torn violin-like air comes pouring together.

An enormous park. The glass ball of the station.
The ordinary world, somehow bewitched.
To a loud-voiced feast in a fogbound Elysium,
my festive rail car is being drawn.
The screech of the peacock and the bang of the pianoforte—
I'm behind time, I'm frightened. It's a dream.

As I enter the crystal forest of the waiting room,
the order of the violins is in confusion and tears.
The night choir begins wildly.
There's the smell of roses in a greenhouse
where under the sky of glass are sleeping
many beloved shadows crowding together in the dark.

And I imagine that everything is music and singing
and the iron world so shakes like a beggar
that I rest against the entrance hall of glass.
Where are you off to? The funeral feast of a shadow—
for the last time, we seem to be hearing the music.

Twilight of Freedom

We preside, brothers, over the twilight of freedom,
in a massive, gloom-gathering year.
Down boiling nocturnal water
we drop like a fishnet of forest.
You have come to the deaf years,
of People, our sunshine, our judge.

We commemorate a fatal era,
even the Leader of the People assumes it in tears.
We signalize the power of a darkening time,
with its unimaginable yoke,
whoever has heart will feel this moment
like a ship that is going to the bottom.

We've lashed all our swallows
to the backs of our fighting legions—and now we
can't see the sun! the whole creation
chirrs, vibrates, alive
as through a net—turgid and dim,
the sun is not to be seen and the earth swims.

But still let's try. Enormous and awkward,
squeaking, revolves the wheel.
The earth swims. Courage, friends!
Moving like a plow, dividing the ocean,
we'll try to remember, even at the freezing of Lethe,
this earth we possess has cost us ten heavens.

Translated by Andrew Glaze

Bitter Bread

Bitter bread, and blazing arid air.
Wounds impossible to bind.
Joseph, sold into Egypt, could not have pined
With more despair.

Bedouin under the starry sky,
Eyes shut, on horses,
Improvise
Out of the troubles of the day gone by.

Images lie close at hand:
He traded horses;
I lost my quiver in the sand.
Haze of happenings disperses.

If genuinely sung,
Wholeheartedly—at last
Nothing is left
But space, and stars, and song.

A Reed

I grew out of a vicious, viscous swamp,
Rustling like a reed,
And, with rapture, languor, caresses
Inhale a prohibited life.

In my cold and marshy refuge
No one noticed me,
And I was welcomed by the whisper
Of intimate autumn minutes.

This brutal insult made me happy.
And, in a dream-like life,
Secretly I am envious of everyone,
And with everyone secretly in love.

Translated by James Greene

Samuel Marshak

Samuel Marshak was born in Russia in 1887 and studied in St. Petersburg and London. He won numerous awards for his poems, children's stories, and translations of Shakespeare, Burns, and others. He died in 1964 in Moscow.

The Little House in Lithuania

In Lithuania, on the Neman,
An izba stands in the tall grass,
In its window seven children,
All of them gazing at the street.
Fairer than flax the children's heads,
Yet one is darker than the rest.

One of these seven children is
So utterly unlike the others.
The other day a Jewish woman
Brought him to this distant village,
Secretly, by stealth, at dusk,
Under a dark, wool shawl she brought him.
The mother fed the child, undressed him,
Put him down to sleep, and stood,
But before she went into the darkness,
She spoke these words to him:

"My child, from this day forth
You'll grow without me towards manhood.
Play with the children, be obedient,
And your own tongue forget!"

OTHER LANGUAGES

The child began to sob, he said:
"I won't stay here! I won't!
I do not want to play with them.
Please take me home! Please take me home!"

The mother took him in her arms
And for a long time paced the room,
Walked about this strange izba,
While in the chimney howled the wind.

At dead of night, the strange woman
Left the hut, went from the village,
And the drowsy baying of the dogs
Accompanied her into the dark.

Far from any town, in Lithuania,
In the tall grass stands a little house.
Below it, barely ruffled by the wind,
Flows the blue Neman.

In Egypt too there is a river,
A river long and broad,
And it is called the River Nile.
Once down the Nile there floated,
In a wicker basket made of twigs,
Moses, a Jewish child.

And gazing down upon the waters,
A woman said: "Farewell, my son!"

Translated by Daniel Weissbort

Yunna Moritz

Yunna Moritz was born in Kiev in 1937. She now lives in Moscow and is highly regarded as a poet, although for many years she published very little. She has translated Yiddish poetry. A new book of her poems was brought out in 1977.

In Memory of François Rabelais

To lie at the edge of the forest
with your face in the earth is miraculous
for idleness is tender, and
can be possessed entirely
in vegetable joy just as
bees sing into clover.

Feel the space under the planet.
Hold on to grass and beetles.
Gulp down the smell of the zoo
on your own skin. We live among
fair booths, where time is short,
packed in together densely.

In Paradise no more idols!
People do what they like
joyfully, bathing and lazing,
without any thought of manners.
The healthy spirit of Rabelais
rules the whole population there.

No better world to wait for!
laughter rises easily,
And stories—Pierrot can
dance on his drum as naked
as if he were in a bath-house.
The show is for everyone.

When laughter beats in your ears,
your soul knows it is immortal.
The freedom is like a mouthful
of wine a breathing space
a forgetting of this life's brevity.
The saddest truth can be funny.

OTHER LANGUAGES

Now go back to your anthill,
put coffee on the stove there.
Chew at your greens for supper.
Enjoy the simplest flavor,
and as you do so savor
the strangeness of carrying on!

Once you can shout and laugh
like a monkey at death and fate
and how men and women act—
the pause is wholly blessed.
A laugh   is the outrageous sign
that your soul remains alive.

Unhealthy fevers shake us
in this stern world. Tormented,
by chasing after success,
we may lose all we possess.
Even our souls may leak away
then, and only return to us
with Hell and horned beasts!

Whiteness

Whiteness   the whiteness of these skies
heavily clamping down over our bodies;
when the time comes our souls will pass through you
only too easily. So here I am, Lord,
blocking my mother's entrance to paradise
ready to curse the light blue roof of it
however you harass me into the cracks
like a snake I won't give her up to you yet
gnawing stones and howling where I sit.
And I refuse to let my mother past.

Snow-Girl

Misfortune is as huge
    and heavy as this cold.
I'm half-dead. Without home.
    Without a roof or wing

Alone under bare skies.
  A stump of birchwood chair
my table drowned by rain
  abandoned, covered in snow.

My pages rustled through
by icy winds. Mother!
Twig. Small bird.
Snow-girl. Don't touch the fire!
The bonfire. Lie quite still.
Like a water drop on sand
Like a red tear on my cheek.
Don't touch! Lie quite still.
Don't touch the fire. Lie there.
Perhaps death will hold back.
And Spring will come. Spring!
with peas and beans returning
A star will fall in the well
Or a single drop of dew.
Spring birds where are you flying?
A frail old woman can so easily
dwindle away to nothing
before you return. It's hard not to!

I wait in the hospital courtyard
and sitting, here make up my prayer.
Trees. Trees. Lake. Lake.
While there is time to spare
before my mother's small body is bruised
yellow and blue. Please. Give me
a small piece of Spring, whose
time will come anyway, spring always comes:
beans appear, peas come up,
and small prickly cucumbers.
I won't believe it, I won't believe it. No.
It is impossible mother should go
for ever before the first strawberries.
And yet the stars are bright over the fields.
There is snow in the wind over the poplars.
Against the wall a snowdrift. Like a breast.
And we are children. Grant us a little Spring!

Translated by Elaine Feinstein

Lev Ozerov

Lev Ozerov (Goldberg) was born in Russia in 1914. He has published several volumes of poetry and numerous translations.

Babi Yar

I

I have come to you, Babi Yar.
If grief can be said to have age,
Then I am immeasurably old.
In centuries not to be counted.

I stand on this ground and I pray:
If I do not go out of my mind,
Earth, I shall listen to you—
Speak.

What a murmuring comes from your breast!
I cannot make out what it is—
Either water under the ground,
Or the souls that are buried there.

I ask the maples: Answer me!
You are witnesses. . . . Tell what you saw.
Silence,
Only wind-
Whispering leaves.

I ask the sky: Tell your tale!
You, so indifferent it hurts.
Life was and life will be.
Yet your face betrays not a thing.

Perhaps, then, the rocks will answer me—
No.

It is quiet.
August in the rock-hard dirt.
An old nag grazes the scanty grass,
Chews on a red rag.

—Will you, perhaps, answer me?

But the nag glanced sidelong at me,
The white of its eye flashing blue,
And at once,
My heart filled with the silence,
And I felt the dusk enter my mind,
And death's newness, old as the world. . .

II

It is hazy today. People will walk about Lvov.
They'll walk a long time, a long way, pressing close to each other,
Down the road,
Over the red maple leaves,
Over my heart they'll walk.

Streams empty into the river.
German and Polizei
Stand by each house, by each fence.
Just try turning back,
Or stepping aside—it can't be done,
German submachine gunners have the whole road in their sights.

And the autumn day is saturated with sunlight,
The crowds flow . . . dark against light.
And the last candles of the poplars smoke into the sky,
And in the clear air:
—Where are they taking us!

—Where are they taking us? Where are they taking us today?
—Where? ask the eyes in one final entreaty.
And the long, inconsolable procession
Moves on to its own funeral.

Beyond Miller Street are hillocks, fences and waste ground.
And the low red wall of the Jewish cemetery. Stop!
Here death has set the tombstones sensibly close together.
And the way out to Babi Yar
Is plain as death.

OTHER LANGUAGES

Thus do the people come to this their last home in the world.
They stand on its threshold. They wait . . .
Death too has its changing rooms.
And the businesslike Germans
Relieve the new arrivals of their clothes and place them in piles.

And suddenly
A still greater reality
Is substituted for reality.
Thousands of intent
Eyes, absorbing life,
The evening air,
And the sky,
And the earth,
Staring through things,
See all we may ever in a lifetime see—
Just once!

And then, the shots . . .
Shots.
Stars of shocking light.
And brother embraces sister for a last time . . .
If there is a God and this God saw and heard it all,
Why did he not lie down and die alongside them!

And people come up and fall into the ravine—like stones.
Children onto women, old men on top of children.
And, like flame, with arms stretching to heaven,
They catch at the air
And, growing weak, they croak curses.

In the pit, a girl calls: Don't cover my eyes with dirt!
And a boy: Must I take my socks off too?
Then he was still,
In a last embrace with his mother.

And just next to him, a little girl or boy maybe:
—Please leave me alone, uncle . . . I'll sing you a song!
And suddenly, bouncing up like a ball,
Falling back into the pit onto the still stirring heap.

And then a man started covering over the living in that pit.
But suddenly out of the earth an arm rose up.
And the back of a head with gray locks . . .

The German struck it persistently with his shovel.
The earth grew damp,
Was leveled out, hardened over.

III
I have come to you, Babi Yar.
If I can hold onto my senses,
I'll surely acquire the gift
To summon the dead as I rage.

Still do their bones lie here,
Skulls yellowing in the dust.
There where my brothers lay down,
The lichen grows white.

Here, the grass does not want to grow,
And the sand is white, like a corpse.
And faintly whispers the wind—
It's my brother gasping for breath.

Into Babi Yar, how easy to fall . . .
I have only to step on the sand,
And the earth half-opens its maw,
My old grandfather asks for a drink.

My nephew wants to stand up,
To rouse his sister and mother.
They want to work an arm free,
To ask just a moment of life.

And the earth is soft underfoot:
Now arching, now twisting itself.
In the temple-silence, I hear
A child's voice:
—Give me bread!

OTHER LANGUAGES

Where are you, little one?
I've grown deaf with the dull pain of it.
Drop by drop I'll give you back life—
I too might have been here with you!

We might have embraced at the end,
Fallen into the pit together.
Till I die, it will torment me
That I did not share your death!

For a moment I closed my eyes
And listened hard, and then
I heard the voices cry:
—Where were you going? Where!

An angry hand tugged at a beard,
And from the empty ravine there came:
—Where?—Then, go! But why
Are you standing here? Why?
Wait, then!

—You've a life to look forward to.
You must live for us as well.
You who bear no grudges, don't go!
You who forget, you must not!

And the child said: Don't forget!
And the mother said: Do not forgive!
And the earth closed its gates again,
And I found myself on the road.

This road leads to retribution,
Along which I now must go.
Don't forget!
Do not forgive!
(1945)

Translated by Daniel Weissbort

Ilya Rubin

Ilya Rubin was born in Moscow in 1941. He got into serious trouble when he became the editor of an underground journal, and nearly all his works were destroyed in searches. In 1976 he emigrated to Israel and pursued his literary career by writing poetry and editing journals. He died suddenly in 1977.

Poem from "The Revolution"

I leaf through the flat plains.
I sit in distant rooms filled with
half-witted rabbis
like the prologue to a riot.

In town squares and synagogues
they nurtured me
as they caressed the blue-eyed women
with hands of future time.

My sacred failure, Russia.
I weep and I am silent.
Your slap in the face like change
jingles in my pocket.

With my thin narrow shoulders,
with my eyes full of moon
I love you, I love you sadly
like hunchbacks love women.

So I measure your breadth and your distance
with the scrupulous pace of an ant.
So your tenderness is in me
and only the spite is not yours.

Only slow tears, and the shadow
of eyelashes on the ceiling. . . .
My tragedy a speck
in your radiant hand!

No Sense Grieving

No sense grieving about that tenderness.
I will enter the waiting room with its rude secretaries.
I will give my face and my lips to an official
not daring to call the mirror by its name.

I have changed. Master, hurry up.
Lash out your orders to me.
This blind flesh is ripe for movement
within the burnt-out carcass of my soul.

It is hard to flip the beads of the abacus
when He is bustling around behind your back,
when the Master wants to gain favors,
when everything around is bare and light.

I have changed. The Master is still crying,
still fussing about me. But it does not
become me even to think of Him.
I am nothing but a weight on His scales.

Escape

I ran until lips tripped over
remembering the skill of horses.
Flutes whistled. Trumpets blared.
I ran until I wasn't anymore.

Like a gray smoke I vanished in the dark.
I spun like the ghost of a wheel
remembering the skill of dogs
sniffing at someone's voice.

Flutes whistled. Trumpets blared.
On the edge of a knifewound
I ran until corpses rose
remembering the skill of the living.

Don't let me die in dust, God.
Bless my lonely run.
I ran until gallows tripped over
remembering the skill of love.

Slow Oxen

With the heavy steps of slow oxen
my last evening craves a watering.
And I begin to crave the quiet
to crave lips and flowers and domes.

I begin to crave a slow-moving God
to crave the blood on His hands
as the cold and clumsy ashes
are drawn home on slow oxen
treading sluggish and stern.

It has come, the blissful time
when the earth is a description of a tree
on the point of a quill.

When the earth is a description of God
and the oxen's heavy bodies
draw His sad deeds,
and the road wails, stumbling.

Handful of Ashes

to N. Rubinstein

Blessed is he who has found the break-weed,
who has forgotten our burnt-out Moscow
as after Rastopchin's papers
it soared in yellow flames . . .

But you and I will never forget
the Sisters of Exile, rivers of Babylon,
for us God has saved
a warm handful of alien ashes.

The sky above us like a blue hump.
The memory behind us like a pillar of salt.
Sodom enveloped in human flames,
our unloved, our native home . . .

Translated by Linda Zisquit

Boris Slutsky

Boris Slutsky was born in the Ukraine in 1919. He served in the Red Army between 1941 and 1945, an experience which has influenced much of his poetry. His first book, Memory, *was published in 1957. Several collections of his poems have appeared since then.*

God

We were all under God
And in his steps we trod.
No *deus absconditus*—
He often appeared to us.
Alive. Making a speech.
There was nothing you could teach
This God: he had it over
The one they call Jehovah
Whom he hurled from His place
Burned to cinders, ignored,
Then yanked from the abyss
And gave him bed and board.
We were all under God
And in his steps we trod.
Once as I took the air
God in five cars went by.
His mousegray escort were
Hunchbacked in terror: I
Could see their trembling fear.
It was both late and early.
Dawn glimmered in the skies.
He peered out, cruel, wise
With his all-seeing eyes
All-penetrating gaze.
We were all under God.
Ours were the steps he trod.

Translated by Dimitry Pospielovsky and Keith Bosley

How They Killed My Grandmother

How did they kill my grandmother?
This is how they killed my grandmother:
In the morning a tank
Rolled up to the city bank.

One hundred fifty Jews of the town,
Weightless
from a whole year's starvation,
Pale,
with the pangs of death upon them,
Came there, carrying bundles.
Polizei and young German soldiers
Cheerfully herded the old men and old women,
And led them, clanking with pots and pans,
Led them
far out of town.

But my diminutive grandmother, Lilliputian,
My seventy-year-old grandmother,
Swore at the Germans,
Cursed like a trooper,

Yelled at them where I was.
She cried: "My grandson's at the front.
Just you dare
Lay hands on me.
Those are our guns
that you hear, Boche!"

Grandmother wept and shouted
And walked.
And then started
Shouting again.
From every window rose a din.
Ivanovs and Andreyevnas leant down,
Sidorovnas and Petrovnas wept:

"Keep it up, Polina Matveyevna!
You just show them. Give it them straight!"
They clamored:
"What's there to be so scared
About this German enemy!"
And so they decided to kill my grandmother,
While they were still passing through the town.

A bullet kicked up her hair.
A gray lock floated down,
And my grandmother fell to the ground.
That's how they did it to her.

Dreams of Auschwitz

I often dream of Auschwitz now:
the road from the station to the camp.
I shuffle along with the crowd, like some poor Lazarus,
and my suitcase bangs against my back.

I must have suspected something
and taken a convenient, light case with me.
I walk, light, like some holiday-maker,
walk and survey my surroundings.

But people have brought with them
cases and bundles,
                                        coffers and trunks,
tall like mountain villages.
And these trunks weigh heavy on them.

In the dream the road's much longer
than it really was, and more painful, more drawn out.
It's not as if you're walking, rather swimming,
and each stroke's quieter and slower.

I walk like the others, both hurrying and not,
and my heart has forgotten to beat.
It's long, long since the frozen spirit
could warm itself on this highway.

The simple industry there smokes,
in greeting,
                        with a foul, sweet smoke,
and with its slow, swanlike
                                                flight,
wears down what's left of people.

Burnt

Burdened with family feelings, I went
To my aunt's place,
                                        to see my uncle,

To press my girl cousins to my breast,
Who were so carried away,
as it happened,
By music and the other arts!

I found neither uncle nor aunt,
I did not see my cousins either,
But I remember,
remember
to this day,
How their neighbors,
looking down at the ground,
Said to me quietly: They were burnt.

Everything's gone up in flames: the vices with the virtues,
And children with their aged parents.
And there am I, standing before these hushed witnesses,
And quietly repeating:
burnt.

Translated by Daniel Weissbort

Anatoly Steiger

Anatoly Steiger was born in 1908. He began publishing in the mid-1920s and is often referred to as a member of the "younger generation" of emigré poets in the period between the wars. Steiger died in 1943. In the West, four volumes of poetry have been published in Russian, one of them posthumously: This Day, This Life, Ingratitude, *and* 2 X 2 = 4.

An Ancient Custom

It is an ancient custom
That certain people lie
And others help them
to lie
(Even though they see through everything),
And all this together is called love.

Words from the Window of a Railway Car

We believe books and music,
We believe verse and dreams,
We believe words . . . (Even when
They're said to us in consolation
From the window of a railroad car) . . .

Translated by John Glad

SERBO-CROAT

Monny de Boully

Monny de Boully, born in 1904, was an outstanding but tragic member of the progressive group of Belgrade Surrealists. In 1932 he made his home in Paris where he associated with Breton, Aragon, Eluard, Adamov, and other famous writers and artists. He wrote in Serbo-Croat and French, and hanging between the two languages he never found full expression in either. He wrote and published very little, mainly in the short-lived Surrealist "little magazines" of Belgrade and Paris. Between the world wars his works were collected in two books, Winged Gold *(1926) and* Death's Antenna, *(1928). But it was not until 1968, the year he died, that modern Yugoslav readers became aware of his achievement, when his collection of poems and memoirs* Gold Bugs *was published.*

Beyond Memory

for Paulette

Those gathered by heartache in alien lands,
Treacherous lovers of love, faithful mistresses of their eternal
 blood,
Gathered by half-forgotten tongues,
By even more fully forgotten customs,
By their desperate clinging to hope,
They alone make me breathlessly break their silence.
A poem of words picked in a dream, what vanity!
What utter folly the wish to name the promised land!
But there's no more time to waste on excuses and babble,
The voices of others shall speak through us
Or else we must be silent!
Don't you hear the swarms of yearnings on the edge of my lips,
Don't you see the honey of suffering in the depth of my eyes?
These are the yearnings and sufferings
Of those who have walked the endless circle
With death on all sides,
Thousands of innocent human beehives aflame!
Are my hands wrapped in fire and pain?
Is this what made my breath burn, my heart smudged, singed,
 calcined?
Each time I am honored by living another springtime

In the safe rounds of day-to-day labor,
Along the banks of the Seine, carved to lodge peace and sweetness,
Along the bars where I lean staring at life unashamed
Facing the slow intermittent flow of passers-by,
Along the creepers of my plans for the future,
Along the ripening harvest of memories,
Along the laughter and chatting with the ones I love
As much as myself, I say to my bees:
"Thank you for living inside me! Unto the last hour
May the Lord let you stay by me!
No one but you knows my infinite pain
Beyond words and lamentations,
Beyond memory itself!
Why should I cry out in my calamity?
Vain are prayers over the beehives' ashes:
The sentence without appeal, the sentence without appeal remains a
dead letter!

Translated by Aleksandar Nejgebauer

Stanislav Vinaver

Stanislav Vinaver was born in Sabac, Yugoslavia in 1891. He witnessed the Revolution in Russia and survived a prison camp in World War II. He published four books of poetry as well as books of criticism, translations, and essays. He died in Belgrade in 1955.

The European Night

Wooden shoes resounded and died down
In the narrow corridor when a rush light twinkles
A rush light so quiet and humble.

The camp is asleep, the barracks are in slumber
A hundred thousand European camps sleep.
The cities are darkened and murky
The rivers are turbid and muffled
Without the old incandescent wave
Without the ancient cheerful decoration—
(The light is our lost gem
The old-fashioned charming jewelry
Taken off the night.)

The night lies naked, immeasurable, pregnant
Larger and more gigantic than ever
It breathes hard and intermittently
In labor pains.
It holds on to the bridges with its tired dark hands.
O, they have robbed, knocked unconscious the great enchanting
  wanton night.

It used to glitter in a jetty light,
A coquette,
Wherever someone's seething nerve vibrated

Wherever a sheaf of thought sparkled,
Wherever a joining of senses appeared, even if as a tinsel,
The night swayed in splendor
It swung radiantly and then refracted.

They have darkened Europe like a pine forest,
Like a mountain village at the damp foot of the hills,
Like a drunken brothel of sailors
In the moldy ditch of the sea ports.

They have put us away in herds in millions,
For our testimony to remain scantier
About who does what, with whom and where . . .
So that the ulcers of our eyes ooze out from our skulls
Gazing at the unfathomed spiderwebs of relationships.

Our rebellious thought
Rises from the bed of a convict
And with its meager, subdued flashing
It would like to light up expanses
And to chase away apparitions.

An Inscription

Over the sheer rocks over the gorges
Spirits circle
Unconcerned about passing ecstasies.

They watch that murkiness does not leave the world
That rivers do not wake up in the clumsy beds
And that clouds don't take refuge in the old treachery.

For it would be terrible (they say)
Like once, at the beginning of centuries,
If the world became sleepless and buoyant—

If the sky lost its ornaments,
If birds flapped their transparent wings against cheerfulness
If the blue sonority murmured poisonously

And a frightening clarity set in.

A Cathedral

In a small wheelbarrow
I hauled a heavy stone
From the mountain into the valley.

Numberless dark people
Dragged the stone from which
A singing church would rise.

In the middle of their silent work
Those desperate men stopped
And prayed to their saint.

Sins have accumulated
Like a murky teeming swarm
Pecking at the heart like a raven.

The sins are enormous
Because of them they left
The warm nest of their home.

The sins overtake them in sudden ambushes,
Full of raging darkness
And primordial monstrosities.

Each looks horrible to itself
And miserable in its wickedness
Beyond salvation.

The men will repent for their sins
Through pious walks, humble fear,
Tame thoughts, and gentle deeds.

I don't know the place of that mountain,
I don't know the fall of that valley,
I don't know the age of that antiquity.

I don't know the name of that temple,
Nor of the saint for whom it is built
Nor of the people building it.

I pulled with all of my soul.—
For a forgiving prayer
There was no strength left.

And generations will again
Surround the church with a ringing halo
For angels to dwell in it.

And some other speech
Will ring out on the lips
And blossom forth in the hearts.

And different prayers
Will disperse the world's darkness
With a more excited murmur.

Alone, lonely and without a friend
I will drag the stone forever
For all new places of worship,

For brighter and clearer ones,
More glittering and passionate,
More babbling and louder.

Whenever anxiety whispers in sin
Wherever a desperate doubt crawls
Where a thought fears itself:

—Until the entire earth
Is transformed from stones
Into a prayer of flames.

Translated by Vasa D. Mihailovich

SLOVAK

Susannah Fried

Susannah Fried was born in Zhilina, Slovakia, in 1944. She studied in Prague before leaving for England in 1964. She has lived in Canada but has now settled in England. Her poems have appeared in magazines in Czechoslovakia, Canada, and England.

Winter Day

Beneath the snow the broad sad wastelands
stretch the black of my eye to the point of pain,
beneath the wild scene's dead brilliance
involuntary small pines stand motionless.
Here, there, again, a nameless wanderer's
footprints are seen. A lost seagull is heard
shrieking in fear against the sharp contours
of stumps that withstood the fire. Bewildering
new forests have been replaced by the uneven
line of twisted half-built shacks resting
beneath the weight of winter and the unending
electric cable. Oh, my little town,
your winter gnaws at my bones with the strength
of your unceasing melancholy . . .

To My Father

Father, the visit
was so unexpected
even you had to feign
surprise when we met.
Father, I must
admit to a fear
as I passed through the gates
guarded by dogs,
by iron and spear,
by that face peering out
behind rusty bars:

"closed for repairs."
Being your daughter,
father, I persisted,
pushed my way through:
but the horror grew
inside me: I heard
the screams of my childhood,
the sound of endless
sirens, the sweaty
hands pressing my mouth,
choking, persistent.
I thought to turn back.
Father, the road
was long, strewn with leaves,
shriveled old tombstones,
brambles and weeds.
I searched through the maze,
thought of you and of me,
your world, calm, severe,
unpretentious; my world
hypocritical, calamitous.
That's why I found you
surrounded (of all things)
by a sea of wild strawberries,
and you found me burst open
with memories, rotten memories.

Scraps

Those scraps of paper
yellow and tattered
waiting for me
to pick them up
and warm them after
a life of dark . . .

Those nameless scribbles:
"allowed to pick up
three paintings," unreal
behind the locked door

OTHER LANGUAGES

of Mr. X, Mrs. Y,
those twisted shreds:
five hundred for his life,
cheap . . . considering . . .

Mined fields, the horror
of dark woods, the dogs
howling in the distance,
explanations and pleas,
the images of death,
the hopes trampled down,
the thought of empty
cartridges and dampness,
grief on parade . . .

Another note penned
by an official
keen to please:
"declared dispossessed
and poor and
approved as such."

Old papers: the key
to memory, the need
for a human's touch,
but what's remembered
is distant and cold:
dried scraps crumble
under the impact
of the touch, crumble
like an old leaf
on a path, in winter.

Translated by Anthony Rudolf

SLOVENE

Tomaž Salamun

Tomaž Salamun was born in 1941. A student of art history in Ljubljana and a member of the International Writing Program in Iowa City for two years, he was involved in Conceptualism in his early work, as a member of the OHO Group in Ljubljana. His numerous books of poems, translated into sixteen languages, include Turbines, Snow, The Druids, *and* The Stars.

Air

Your body is a pipeline
conveying wheat, oil and food,
a bridge for galloping horsemen.
Your arms are a window,
your words are a window,
your body is a window.
Whatever you touch
or caress in your thoughts
burns with terrible flames and smells,
in each movement,
in each breath you guide me,
And I bend down,
and I bend down,
and I rise,
and I rise and go.
You tell me not to use any more
swelling shrewd weapons,
hungry dry weapons of the air,
and to take care.
You tell me to be kind and I am kind.
You tell me to be rich and I am rich.
Sky-blue,
sky-high are my fortresses
and I can swish through the souls of kings
traveling from Babylon to Nineveh,
from Nineveh to Babylon.
You have named me:

I am fair and puffed up, for I am mighty and moist.
Your body is a pipeline
conveying wheat, oil and food,
a bridge for galloping horsemen.
Your arms are a window,
your words are a window,
your body is a window.
Whatever you touch
or caress in your thoughts
burns with terrible flames and smells.

Translated by Aleksandar Nejgebauer

Eclipse

I

I will take nails,
long nails
and hammer them into my body.
Very very gently,
very very slowly,
so it will last longer.
I will draw up a precise plan.
I will upholster myself every day
say two square inches for instance.

Then I will set fire to everything.
It will burn for a long time,
it will burn for seven days.
Only the nails will remain,
all welded together and rusty.
So I will remain.
So I will survive everything.

II

Chuck chuck chuck my dear little pigeon,
come a little closer, come
step from the shell of your childhood
step from those innocent chambers.

And now I've got you by the neck
my love.
Little by little I'll let your blood,
into your body I'll stab precious stones.

With the thin knives of the past
I will cut you up into seven little pieces.
Every piece I will put into a different drawer.
Every drawer I will paint a different color.

Translated by Michael Scammell and Veno Taufer

OTHER LANGUAGES

SPANISH

Juan Gelman

Juan Gelman was born in Buenos Aires in 1930 and is a leading member of the "new wave" Argentine poets.

Customs

We make a home so as not to stay at home
we love so as not to stay in love
and we do not die in order to die
we are thirsty and
have the patience of animals.

The Knife

My hand on your breasts the kitchen
resting at that hour the coffee
that boiled the talking in low tones
not to disturb the sweetness of our bodies
that were trembling and glowing
with a kind of light like the knife that you used
while it was in your hand.

The Stranger

My father would walk about for hours with a lit cigarette
in the darkness of the dining room and the patio plants
his wife would say to him "stop this walking around, José"
but he didn't want to eat or sleep or stop
his feet ran out on him one afternoon
he turned over and closed his eyes like a little bird.

Translated by Yishai Tobin

Isaac Goldemberg

Isaac Goldemberg was born in Peru in 1945. After a year in Israel, he came, in 1963, to New York, where he teaches Spanish and Latin American literature at New York University. Goldemberg has published a book of poems and a novel. His poetry has been published in the United States, Spain, and Latin America.

Bar Mitzvah

My father comes to see me on Friday night.
He scrubs my ears,
brushes my smelly suit,
and drops two vitamins down my mouth.
On Saturday he shows up with sleepless eyes,
makes breakfast
and polishes my shoes.
He takes my best shirt out of the closet
and gently dresses me like a divorced mother.
He takes my hand,
and we quickly pass by a church door.
Hunched over, almost touching the ground, we walk back and
forth down endless streets,
chasing off flies as they land on our faces.
Three old men, a tray of sardines and tomatoes, wine,
a loaf of white bread wait for us at the Brena Synagogue.
The rabbi makes me climb up to the *bimah*
the old men smile at me,
praying through their beards.
The rabbi nods for me to start the prayers,
instead I kneel down,
ashamed, my father blushes,
an old man points to a few words in the Bible,
I begin to stammer,
I look at my father out of the corners of my eyes,
my old, gray father celebrating this rite curled up like a fetus.

The Jews in Hell

As the story goes,
the Jews bought for themselves
a private spot in hell.

OTHER LANGUAGES

In the first circle,
Karl Marx sits on a wooden bench
using his hand as a fan.
The prophet Jeremiah
fights off the heat by singing psalms.

In the second circle,
Solomon carefully studies
the stones from His Temple.
On some yellowing rolls of paper,
Moses draws hieroglyphics.

Christ dreams of Pontius Pilate
in the third circle.
Freud's clinical eye
follows every move he makes.

In the fourth circle,
Spinoza edits
a history of the Marranos.

In the fifth circle,
Jacob wrestles with a devil.
Cain and Abel
treat each other like brothers.

In the sixth circle,
Noah rides drunk on a zebra.
Einstein searches for atoms
in the space between rocks.

In the final circle,
Kafka tilts his telescope
and bursts out laughing.

Translated by David Unger

José Isaacson

José Isaacson is an Argentine poet whose works have received numerous awards. In addition to his six volumes of poetry, he has published critical anthologies and essays.

Pre-positions

I stand in front of the tree,
before the tree.

Those green pulses
come to me from the tree
measure me.

A beat among beats
I establish a relationship
The wavering of my pencil
is its measure.

All of its space
reduced to between.

Every measure
and every excess
hurt me.

Naked,
like a wave
that insists on flying,
it is useless
to invent a shell,
stiff shields,
plans that cannot be distorted.

History
consumes all
and it is useless to imagine
a time without time,
eternal
like a dead heart.

Only the beat
and the between
have left us.

The wavering of my pencil
designs
the limits and defeats.

I know
that I cannot leave you.
You are my witness
and my testimony
and I dedicate these words to you
because one March afternoon
you gave me
a between
a beat.

Translated by Yishai Tobin

Noé Jitrik

Noé Jitrik was born in Buenos Aires in 1928. He has published two volumes of poems and numerous essays. Since 1960 he has been a professor of Argentine literature in Cordoba.

Addio a la Mamma

The nights here are usually clear and the shadows
are like the noise, that is, that burns
the tremulous subjectivity and raises an ambiguous fear,
the confused fear that harasses childhood.

I will be asked from where I come, what I am pursuing:
I should have said it a long time ago,
when things could still be said,
without great sufferings but with desire instead,
when I could speak.

My ingratitude was reproached and I stood up,
and I ran through an intense street with closed eyes,
I walked about the night places,

I spoke with residents of the night,
and everywhere they insinuated sadness to me,
and among everyone someone would always suggest love to me.

No one can know it, no one can find this direction
if the separation was not sunk between his shoulders,
if he didn't share, even lightly, this calamity.

What misfortune the ones called without an answer,
to walk through padded places for hate and feeling,
and, broken, with doubt inserted in the heart
and crumbs of past glories in the pockets;
What misfortune to see the women, eating other meals,
breathing as if without air other atmospheres,
and no longer being the usual child,
no longer being the submissive lamb,
the soft child that death would respect.

How can these things be told, who would believe them?
One howls explanations and always begins again,
goes out of the way with a phrase, with the ability,
handles an intelligent drink
but sooner or later they will put their finger on his shoulder
and say, discovered! with a thick voice,
to which very little can be added.

It is clear that one can travel
and beautify the memories for new publics,
spending sleepless nights awaiting the miracles of tomorrow,
or one can grow old, but grow old, what a story!
it never occurs to you that this could happen.

Definitively one accepts, pale from terror,
that it is the same to die anywhere
and by any death.
All of us recognize this save for the police,
everyone receives caresses everywhere even if it isn't the same,
we all look for freedom, and are about to know what it consists of,
but we pursue each other and then look for consolation,
silence, audience, a promise
in the women that call from life
assuredly because they give it.

One way or another, someone announces death,
someone is in charge of telling mother that she'll never see us again.

Translated by Yishai Tobin

Ruben Kanalenstein

Ruben Kanalenstein was born in Uruguay and emigrated to Israel in 1965. He is the author of one book of prose, Abraham in Ur, *and one book of poetry. He currently edits a Spanish-language newspaper in Jerusalem.*

Jerusalem

Two Jerusalems rise up
before my eyes
one
of the poor
without God
and the souls
of abandoned youth
and corrupt politicians
sold to any god
        (it's all the same)
and the other
the streets where
talisman vendors
do not walk
stairways to the greatest heights
and underground
        (they're the same).

Kafka is a dentist
on Ben Yehuda de Kuds street
and Marcuse
a plumber
the neighbor of a crazy old woman
who never tires of asking
like any Jewish child
when Shabbat is.

My hand remembers them all,
I write with my hand,

with this same hand that touches the rock.
with this same hand that caresses the circle.
With this same hand
I shake the hand
of the Yemenite
of Ein Karem
of the mysterious Armenian
of the Old City
where the Wall is,
where the Tomb is,
where the Amulet is,
where the Market is.

And the wind is spirit
—the windmill of Al Kuds—
the wind is the Other
the one who keeps silent
the one who respects my solitude
and yours.
The wind is the Other
—the one who no longer forgets,
the one who no longer compares,
the one who covers the mirrors,
the one who knows a fear
and that *Ein Sof**
and Atman
are written in the same language.
Jerusalem is also mountains
and houses
and peoples
and stairways
and dangerous vegetation
and the rock full of myths
and the history
and the shrewdness
and the filth
that is the depth of all history
and words in Judezmo and Arabic
and sighs in Hebrew

**Ein Sof* ("Infinite") is the Kabbalistic term for the unknowable aspect of the Divinity.

and fatherless silences
without direction
with balls, nevertheless
the same irresolution.

Jerusalem is also students
passing from geometry
to the Talmud
and from the Talmud
to war.

I laugh at everything
and, nevertheless,
those forgotten words
in an immense room
referring to the Temple
(to the One and Only)
and one hundred years of liberation
have not been able to prepare
the base
the landscape
the scene
for a new temple
in the debris of That One.
"We have arrived too late
for the gods
and too early for the being"
but religion is not
what one makes with his solitude
but what one makes
with his people
and all the rest is commentary . . .

The Temple
(where the Menorah
and the Candelabra
will no longer be a metaphor
nor the sea
a parable)
my hand will seek out
yours there,
the other will wink at us
we will be one.

Peace will not be
an agreement
but the harmonious
memory
of the presence,
the prophets
without remorse
will be farmers
and we will fall again
in the beginning.
For this is what we look for
in Jerusalem,
the beginning,
the reason of the beginning
and the beginning of reason,
the inauguration of hope.

Translated by Yishai Tobin

José Kozer

José Kozer was born in Cuba in 1940 and presently resides in New York City where he teaches at Queens College. He has had two books of poems published, the most recent entitled This Jew of Numbers and Letters. *His poems and short stories have appeared in literary magazines in Spain, Latin America, the United States, and Canada.*

Cleaning Day

All the awnings at home had to be pulled down,
all the windows in the neighborhood had to be shut,
before it felt safe on Thursday
to throw the front door wide open.
and then the disinfectants, the mothballs, Abraham's footsteps
wiped out my grandfather's guilt-ridden body,
they all announced mother's slippers shuffling through the rooms,
polishing the seven arms of the candelabra,
sorting out the silverware for the dairy and meat,
pressing down the potato pancakes of the Exodus, of abundance,
while the street outside was an uproar of dark women full of fire,
the street burst into the wild triple beat of a Cuban bongo,
and three pretty girls danced, stirred the quivering ass of a song
while my mother doggedly straightened the mirrors.

The Store in Havana

The store in Havana has turned to dust,
dust covers the imported Irish linen,
and my father, dust-coated Jew,
comes home each day with a rye loaf under his arm.
He comes home day after day, always looking the same,
his eyes crossed from measuring bolts of fabric,
he's not a sea captain rolling his eyes,
he comes back home, a rugged but carefree volcano.
Father arrives and we lunch with our eyes on the ceiling,
I've never seen water seep in, I don't see any fish or potted plants,
my mother polishes the carved edges of the furniture again,
she changes the sheets from last Thursday,
we haven't seen a flower in any of our bedrooms.
All the stores in Havana have been shut,
the workers, all fired up, have started marching;
again, the old dust-coated Jew, my father,
carries the Ark of the Covenant on his way out of Cuba.

Translated by David Unger

My Father, Who's Still Alive

My father, who's still alive
—I haven't seen him but I know he's shrunk—
has a family of brothers dead in the ovens in Poland.
He never saw them, learned of his mother's death
by wire, inherited nothing from his father,
not even a button. Who knows if he inherited
his father's ways.
My father, who was a tailor and a communist,
my father, who wouldn't talk, sat by the terrace
to no longer believe in God,
to have nothing to do again with men.
He resented Hitler, resented Stalin.
my father, who once a year had a shot of whiskey,
my father, sitting under the neighbor's apple tree
eating the neighbor's fruit
the day the Reds entered the village
and made my grandfather dance like a bear on the Sabbath
light up a cigarette and smoke it on the Sabbath.

And my father left the village for good.
He left swearing forever against the October Revolution
insisting forever that Trotsky was a dreamer
and Beria a criminal,
shunning books forever, he sat a small man on the terrace
and told me that the dreams of man are
but a phony literature,
that history books can lie because paper
can hold anything, my father
who was a tailor and a communist.

Translated by Jorge Guitart

Alejandra Pizarnik

Alejandra Pizarnik was born in Buenos Aires in 1939 and died by her own hand in 1972. In 1954 she returned to the Faculty of Philosophy and Letters in Buenos Aires to pursue a career in philosophy, which she later forsook to study painting. She published eight books of poems and numerous critical works, stories, and plays which have been published in America and Europe.

The Mask and the Poem

The splendid paper palace
of childhood pilgrimage.
At sunset the tightrope walker
will be placed in a cage
she will be taken to a temple in ruins
she will be left
alone.

Dawn

Naked
I have lain in beastly days.
The wind and the rain erased me
like a fire, like a poem
written on a wall.

Who Will Stop His Hand from Giving Warmth

for Aurora and Julio Cortazar

Who will stop his hand from giving warmth to the small lost child? Cold will pay. Wind will pay. Rain and thunder will pay.

She had opened her eyes she alone
for a moment of brief life
for a moment of seeing
in her brain small flowers
dancing like words in the mouth of a mute.

She undresses in the paradise
of her memory
unknowing of destiny's fury.
She is afraid of not being able to name
what does not exist.

With her dress on fire
she leaps from star to star
from shadow to shadow.
She dies of a distant death
she who loves the wind.

Translated by Alina Rivero

The Tree of Diana

1
I've jumped from myself to dawn.
I've left my body near the light
and I've sung the sadness of what is born.

2
only thirst
the silence
no meeting

watch out for me my love
watch out for the silent one in the desert
the traveler with the empty glass
the shadow of your shadow

3
for a minute of brief life
the only one of open eyes
for a minute to see
little flowers in the brain
dancing like words in the mouth of a mute

4
she undresses in the paradise
of her memory
unaware of the vicious destiny
of her visions
afraid of not knowing how to name
that which doesn't exist.

5
jumps with a flaming shirt
from star to star,
from shadow to shadow
dies from a distant death
she who loves the wind.

6
These bones shining in the night,
these words like precious stones
in the living throat of a petrified bird,
this beloved green,
this warm lilac,
this heart only mysterious.

7
no more the sweet metamorphosis of a child of silk
sleepwalking now in the cornice of fog
her awakening from a breathing hand
of a flower that opens to the wind

8
to explain with words of this world
a ship carrying me came out of me

9
you have built your house
you have feathered your birds

OTHER LANGUAGES

you have hit the wind
with your own bones

you have finished alone
what no one has started

10
like a poem buried
of the silence of things
you speak so as not to see me

11
when I see the eyes
that I have in mine tattooed

12
I have been born so much
and suffered twice over
in the memory of here and there

13
in the fabulous winter
the dirge of the wings in the rain
in memory of the water fingers of fog

14
Zones of plagues where the sleeping one eats slowly
her heart of midnight.

15
sometimes
                sometimes perhaps
I will leave without staying
        I will leave like someone who goes away

16
in the cage of time
the sleeping one sees her eyes alone

the wind brings her
the soft response of the leaves

17
further away from any forbidden zone
there is a mirror for our transparent sadness

Privilege

I
The name they gave me is lost
its face wanders all over me
like the sound of water in the night,
of water falling on water.
And its smile is the last survivor,
not my memory.

II
The most beautiful one
in the night of those who leave,
oh, desired one,
your not returning is endless,
you a shadow until the day of days.

Apart from Oneself

Autumn is the blue of the wall: being sheltered by little deaths.
Each night, in the duration of a scream, a new shadow comes.
Alone
the mysterious autumn dances. I share its fear of
a very young animal on the
first night of the hunt.
The woman traveler not yet born, how does she cross
the river of death?
I tear myself down from my double meaning.

Vertigos or Contemplation of Something That Is Over

This lilac loses its leaves
Falls from itself
hides its ancient shadow
I'd die from these things.

Translated by Yishai Tobin

Jorge Plescoff

Jorge Plescoff was born in Santiago, Chile in 1940 and has been living in Jerusalem since 1969. He edits several literary magazines and has published five volumes of poetry. A selection of his poems has been translated into Hebrew.

The Ladder Has No Steps

My knee against the ground
        the left one
in order to recite dead prayers
        our age
over a bed of rock
        a veil
the tenuous veil of anxious reason.

The ladder has no steps
        nor dreams
Jacob only wanted to play.
In front of my house a smiling slide
        and the children
their knees on the ground.

Whoever prays creates mist
        without incense
without churches there are no prologues
        nor zeros
a process is misplaced in the equation
the sun repeating
    its tender warmth

Tongues of Fire

Tongues of fire, I say.
I say white moon, waiting.
I call out wheat,
a rocky projection of wit,
a foreign reef of the cry.
I look at the sky weeping
in the damp eyes of the stream.

The painted desert, I live
painting whole shadow, I live,
frames from dyed carob wood,
a background of indigo, almost blind.

I say moon, I see white,
a foam of sea of sky
over fire, consumed.

Violins in Repose

Life
anthology of bewilderments
something definitive?
almost dramatic
          in death
lightly imposed
reversible perhaps.

I renounce her, the earth
                    like a finale
I don't want her near
neither mine
nor me
she compressed.

Don't sell me water
by the weight of its color
nor the harmonic contortions
                                        of wings
I prefer violins in repose
to some undefined yearning.

Ourobouros

How many skies does the earth hold?
One.
The spheres hide their feelings.
Men are a wonder
like a pit in a funeral.

OTHER LANGUAGES

Does the arrow fly straight?
It depends on the thought.
In an empty space
wheels put silence into gear.

Is emptiness a body?
The measure of time.
Two centimeters a point
and the secret is enclosed there.

Of the spheres?
No, of knowledge.

What is the value of knowing
if it is the anathema of heaven?
If we cut down all the trees
the serpent will fall to the ground.
Let Eve cut off his head!
Only then will the return
begin.

Translated by Yishai Tobin

David Rosenmann-Taub

David Rosenmann-Taub was born in Santiago, Chile in 1927. He studied harmony, piano, and composition at the School of Musical Art and Sciences; and style, aesthetics, and Spanish literature at the university of his native land. In 1948 he received the prize of the Chilean writers' guild; and in 1951, the prize in poetry conferred by the University of Concepción. In 1975 half of his unpublished work was stolen—more than five thousand manuscript pages; and the poet's mother, on being informed of what had happened, died. The poet then abandoned all activity alien to his creative work. In 1976 he published the first section The Spoils of the Sun *in Buenos Aires. In 1977 he toured Europe and returned to Argentina on the occasion of having his poem* The Sky in the Fountain *published, a poem composed over a period of twenty-five years. He is now residing in his Santiago, dedicating his time to the completion of a poem begun in 1947,* Country Beyond.

Sabbath

With her eyes closed
before the candlesticks flickering
with Saturday, my mother. The half-light
flatters her lines. The hour

between the lighted vigils fades away.
The dead shake loose: like carnival
crowds, merciless as candlesticks,
mirrors wander. Since Friday

agony has been greedy. In the glass
and muddled with noise, the sun,
a phylactery of farewell, believes it dreams.

The house is a sob. The horizon
cuts across the house: the face of dusk
wanders between the never and the never.

To a Young Girl

Nectar, puff of sails, lily,
sprout hidden under the dress,
indescribable cloud.

Decoy pigeon, golden day,
sprout hidden under the dress,
indescribable mist.

Sunflower, swan, sandhill,
sprout hidden under the dress,
indescribable grave.

Prelude

Afterwards, afterwards the wind between two mountains,
and brother scorpion rising on his legs,
and red tides swelling over the day.
Ravenous volcano, halo without dominion.
The vulture will die: easy punishment.
Afterwards, afterwards the hymn between two snakes.
Afterwards the night we do not know
and a lone body lying in gentleness
silent as light. Afterwards the wind.

Reconciliation

The house dawned:
they worked miracles—brooms, brushes,
buckets—
with cabinets and provisions
and mosaics and groins and loft:
soap water
attacked
floors, walls,
ceilings.

Among the white groves
I brandished the baptism, joined the blood.
What a synagogue
prevailed
in the rough!
Adornment
of new-fallen snow in the teasing
shirt, in the tight pants,
in the foreskin fury of the sheets,
in the sharply pressed solid-gold slacks,
in the demanding heretic limbos,
in the hostile
trap of the splendid
festival shoes.

And I left.

Ages passed.

⁂

I come back,
tumultuous, a thief, with the first fruits
of breathless silence.
I reveal myself,
a reef, naked,
completely on an equal footing,
newborn
on newborn: tepid cold.

Oh quiet tongue
of the friendly tableware,
of the waterlily bowls! (Do they still
leave stains?) Oh
library: lintels!
Oh bedroom! Who's
in the rectangular mirror of the vestibule,
in the oval mirror of the dining room,
in the infinite
mirror of the breast?

Elegy and Kaddish

You happen to get well
I'll greet you
and I'll not show it. Shovelings . . .
Loads of them . . .
of which sod, heaven is made.

I compensating you there.
I might try another madness, perhaps
the way of secrets:
draw yourself out
in a prayer of vinelike light.

⁂

Happy yoke, you swallow
praises
of footstools,
you'll drain away the years.
Alas,
you exist for me,
cervix,
or settle my disputes.
Foolish, foolish tale!

Stop me from saying it—for goodness' sake—
for your blood.

If you go around in the square: you went:
nefarious with careful untidiness,
joy of removing the honey,
for you aren't among the circles of the tombs:
because that easy, brotherly Saturday
delayed a Sunday to eternity.
And my poem will have no meaning.

Moral Ode

Will God, always cold, have a temperature?
Cosmictear:
you break me apart and crush me,
a cohabitation of salts,
without shedding your allelujah.
Will God, always cruel, tire on the way?
Cosmictear:
how you puncture bloods
and fingernails.

Translated by Charles Guenther

Mario Satz

Mario Satz was born in 1944 in Buenos Aires, where he lived until 1966. After several years in Europe, he settled in Jerusalem in 1970 where he completed the writing of Sol, *the first volume of* Planetarium. *He is continuing with* Luna, *his second novel.*

Fish

From the center of the room to the center
    of the ceramic teapot with its leather grip,
in which tea is boiling in the spring equinox,
    dried out, wrapping a lightbulb heir of the sun
    and its positive flux,
the fragile screen and its layer of fishbones,
    the moonfish, no hills or crates: what is up is down,
in Japan or Egypt, for Thoth or Basho, dragging
over the lonely sand like a poem, what is up is down.
A legend of white horns drops from the sky and dives
    underwater
    and inner light is born in a pearl, sponge or the star
of the marine bulb.
    From the floor to ceiling, in the House of the Universe,
the moonfish, quiet, lighting the darkness of the tea.

Coconut

The soul of a coconut can't live
    without the outer bitterness of its body;
and above, among the palm tree leaves, the earth
    is still its bark.
And primordial water swims in its interior,
    hidden, fresh and darkly gestated by the sun;
a water or milk or blood under the green bark,
    which peeled is like the peeled earth: hard,
arid, impenetrable.
    But the earth cannot live without water
nor can the coconut's snow abandon its mountain,
    and its soul is only its body inside out.
So all death is nothing but rupture and separation;
    so all life is nothing but unity, a seal
that lips can reveal sealing again; water
    or milk or semen under a testicle, one is rhythm
and identical, one is height and one is vision;
    for the heart looms toward the eye's center,
moving its wheel through the mouth of the iris.
    And there the palm tree grows in its mirror, high
in the sky's center.

Lemon

And the lemon is tall. The sun is tall, and descends
with light, the lemon descends toward us, and
through it
we rise, going above in its fragrance, in
the violent
aspiration of air spreading our lips,
in the light
and grave pressure from which the earth emanates to
leave us spellbound,
to bewitch us.
A lemon is a proof of faith, of faith in the sun;
and that aroma shot out with a burst of wind,
a burst of seabreeze, a burst of muttering between hills,
is the lemon's voice talking to us.
We ought to dance under the lemon tree's icy
perfume;
like those huge yellow and black butterflies
coupling in the leaves, wiping dust from their wings
on blossoms.
We ought to dance with our heart turned outward like the
lemon's navel, with its pores open during the day,
closed at night; and we ought to see ourselves dancing!
So that truth be the fruit man eats,
the sun he drinks and shadow witnessing the great
presence of its body,
the broad tension of its hidden throat.

Reciprocity, tall wisdom of life!

And silence is not enough: let the word seize
and impel us to a star seeking its sun, the eternal
axis of its life.
A lemon is a proof of faith, of faith in the sun.

Translated by Willis Barnstone

Cesar Tiempo

Cesar Tiempo (pseudonym of Israel Zeitlin) was born in Russia in 1906, but was raised in Argentina. In addition to his poetry, he has written novels, plays, essays, articles, and literary criticism.

The Jewish Cemetery

Deaf to the bustle of the street, soporifically
happy and free from upsetting changes,
they repose facing the world with hooked noses
these terminated souls of the Jewish line.

Their ships definitely sunk now, bridges burned
after the voyage through streets without turnings
they made these beds and this prostrate city
to spend their final sleep in perfect relaxation.

The moans of old women loud with pain
do not perturb this satisfied, supine world
where the burning beat of the moaning "moles"
is sung for a fixed price including breast beating.

The days dance lazily here,
renascent flowers add their grace
and the "schnorrer," now a landlord too,
is in the ground next to aristocracy.

While the night displays its medals
above the heavy calm of this dwarf city,
the semite congregation sleeps free of vain ambition
confident that life will not begin tomorrow. . . .

Translated by Angela McEvan-Alvarado

SWEDISH

Oscar Levertin

Oscar Levertin was born in 1862 in Gryt, Sweden. His best known book of poems, Legends and Songs, *which contains a number of poems on Jewish themes, was published in 1891. Two other collections were* New Poems *(1894) and* Poems *(1901). Levertin was a literary critic as well as a poet, and was the first Jew to gain eminence in Swedish literature. He also published a number of novels and novellas. His collected works appear in twenty-four volumes. Levertin died in 1906.*

At the Jewish Cemetery in Prague

Do not place frill or border or bouquet
Around the monuments that hide their bones.
Life sent no wreath to ease them on their way
But stone. On these heap only stones!

Ancestors in exile, who were driven
From land to land with mockery and jibe,
In the ghetto's age-long darkness given
No view of dawn for their defeated tribe.

Here at last is sleep for persecuted
Wanderers footsore from the thistle path,
And numbness for the homesick hearted confuted
By its own tears and others' scorn or wrath.

Here do not taunt with summer's promise
The deathly stillness they have made their own.
Do not bring flowers here as homage
Of love, nor twigs of green! Bring stone!

Solomon and Morolph, Their Last Encounter

But nearer night than you, my younger
And light-blessed brother, was I born.
My being is ablaze with hunger
For dark before the world's first dawn.

My heart, a furnace for its fire,
My head, its hearth, my coal black hair
And eyes that feed my heart's desire
Still testify I am night's heir;
My soul, a prey to devastation
Of fires across the wilderness;
My wisdom, orient's creation,
Sad potion brewed in bitterness,
Is ancient ore culled from the womb
And flesh, by generations' need
Which each new era must assume
Again, in mating egg and seed.
Its root is an eternal thirst
For unforgotten paradise
From where the Law, still, as at first,
Flails out its chastisement of vice;
For sweat, sin, labor are the load
Borne on the shoulders of mankind.
No inn greets us along death's road;
The covenant our fathers signed
Is that atonement, conciliation
Be paid in sacrifice and pain,
That lust and thirst must meet damnation
And all joy bear the mark of Cain.
Our maker wrote this heavy law
With raised hand, on the world's first morning,
A stern commandment to ensure
Mankind and nature heed His warning.
This does not haunt you, younger brother,
Is not borne burning in your breast.
Its sombre lullaby our mother
Sang you, has never marred your zest.
For you are happy: in your hands
No buds wither, nor fragrant flowers.
I leave you to command your lands
Where joy illuminates the hours.
Dark waters call me, fiery streams,
Back to my wisdom's lone domain,
To sit with night through storm-torn dreams.
Who am the first-born of night's pain.

Translated by Richard Burns and Göran Printz-Påhlson

OTHER LANGUAGES

TURKISH

Musa Moris Farhi

Musa Moris Farhi was born in Ankara in 1935. He studied in Istanbul and London, and settled in England in 1957. Formerly an actor, Farhi has written scripts for television and films, a stageplay, and a book of poetry. He is presently completing a second novel.

Smile at Me

Luck is not smiling upon us
they say
Fortune has gone to visit Mehmet
in the next village
and Reason's on a pilgrimage
they say

who cares

come
smile at me
with your breasts

Paths to God

many paths lead
to God

mine is through
the flesh

Who Says

Who says
death is better than sex

the dead
but who hears them

God and Nature

God and Nature
are married
they say

Will He ever forgive
my adultery
as I kiss her womb
on a beach
by the tideless Aegean

Thirst

drink me
you said
offering me your lower lips
soft
creamy
perfectly shaven

drink me
you said
from my true lips
and it will make you young

drink me
you said
where I am really a woman
and you will be a man

drink me
you said
where I cascade in waterfalls
and you will find God

drink me
you said
right there between my legs
drink me
my love
my love
drink me
where I am a fountainhead
and you will be redeemed

and I drank
and I am young
and I am a man
and I found God
and I am redeemed

but the thirst
dear love
the thirst

you did not tell me about the thirst
which follows
and possesses

you did not tell me
that one can never drink enough

Translated by the author

Jozef Habib Gerez

Jozef Habib Gerez was born in Istanbul in 1928. A poet and painter, Gerez is the author of several volumes of poetry, including Narrow Angels *and* In Search.

We Are Acrobats

We are acrobats
dangling between
life and death,
With myriad skills
we have learnt to live
maybe for years.

We boasted
smiled, made others smile
saying
we have achieved things
saying
we have snatched
so-and-so's
hat from him.

But why did we
understand later
that all
our achievements
were hollow;
together
with the rest of the world
we fooled ourselves
with our false smiles.

We Fooled Ourselves

We fooled ourselves
saying
we are living
pulling air in
year after year
we lived . . .

Perhaps
we did live
for so many years
trampled, shrinking
for so many years
we lived
a few moments
a few minutes
only
for the sake of living

Call from the Afterworld

Come my friends come
I am in the other world
the afterworld.
Leave all
cast all aside
come, I am waiting.
Here
all of man's burden
lightens,
the world goes
"out of sight, out of mind."

I have not yet felt
the weight of black earth
I have forgotten
cold, hunger, everything.
Come my friends come
I am waiting for you.

Translated by Musa Moris Farhi and Anthony Rudolf

ACKNOWLEDGMENTS Continued

YEHUDA AMICHAI: "Of Three or Four in a Room," "Not Like a Cypress," "God Has Pity on Kindergarten Children" used by permission of Stephen Mitchell. Translations ©1979 Stephen Mitchell. "On the Day of Atonement," "Shadow of the Old City," "Jerusalem, Port City," "Sodom's Sister City" used by permission of Shirley Kaufman. Translations ©1979 Shirley Kaufman. "I Am Sitting Here," "I Think of Oblivion," "Advice" used by permission of Ruth Nevo. Translations ©1979 Ruth Nevo. "Lament," "I Am a Leaf," "Since Then" used by permission of Shlomo Vinner and Howard Schwartz. Translations ©1979 Shlomo Vinner and Howard Schwartz. "In the Old City," "On the Wide Stairs" used by permission of Howard Schwartz and Laya Firestone. Translations ©1979 Laya Firestone and Howard Schwartz. "The Town I Was Born In" used by permission of A. C. Jacobs. Translation ©1979 A. C. Jacobs. "Lay Your Head on My Shoulder" used by permission of Robert Friend. Translation ©1979 Robert Friend. All Amichai poems ©Yehuda Amichai.

AHARON AMIR: "Nothingness" used by permission of Aharon Amir. "Nothingness" ©1979 Aharon Amir.

EDNA APHEK: "Sarah," "The Story of Abraham and Hagar" used by permission of Yishai Tobin. Translations ©1979 Yishai Tobin. All Aphek poems ©Edna Aphek.

ELI BACHAR: "Room Poems," "A Dawn of Jaffa Pigeons," "Houses, Past and Present" used by permission of Jeremy Garber. Translations ©1979 Jeremy Garber. All Eli Bachar poems ©1979 Eli Bachar.

YOCHEVED BAT-MIRIAM: "The Monasteries Lift Gold Domes" used by permission of the Institute for the Translation of Hebrew Literature. Translation ©by the Institute for the Translation of Hebrew Literature. "Distance Spills Itself" used by permission of Robert Mezey. Translation ©1976 Robert Mezey. All Bat-Miriam poems ©Yocheved Bat-Miriam.

HAYIM BE'ER: "Tabernacle of Peace," "The Sequence of Generations," "Love Song" used by permission of Stephen Mitchell. Translations ©1979 Stephen Mitchell. All Be'er poems ©Hayim Be'er.

ANATH BENTAL: "Jerusalem in the Snow," "The Angel Michael" used by permission of Howard Schwartz. Translations ©1979 Howard Schwartz.

AVRAHAM BEN-YITZHAK: "Blessed Are Those Who Sow and Do Not Reap," "I Didn't Know My Soul" from *Anthology of Modern Hebrew Poetry,* ed. S. Y. Penueli and A. Ukhmani, Israel Universities Press, Jerusalem, 1966, used by permission of the Institute for the Translation of Hebrew Literature. Translations ©the Institute for the Translation of Hebrew Literature. "Psalm" used by permission of A. C. Jacobs. Translation ©1974 A. C. Jacobs.

HAYIM NACHMAN BIALIK: "When the Days Grow Long" used by permission of A. C. Jacobs. Translation ©1979 A. C. Jacobs. "After My Death" from *Anthology of Modern Hebrew Poetry,* ed. S. Y. Penueli and A. Ukhmani, Israel Universities Press, Jerusalem, 1966, used by permission of the Institute for the Translation of Hebrew Literature. Translation ©by the Institute for the Translation of Hebrew Literature. "Summer Night" used by permission of Robert Friend. Translation ©1978 Robert Friend. "I Didn't Find Light by Accident," "Footsteps of Spring," "My Song" used by permission of Ruth Nevo. Translations ©1979 Ruth Nevo. "I Scattered My Sighs to the Wind" used by permission of Naomi Nir. Translation ©1979 Naomi Nir. "The Sea of Silence Exhales Secrets," "Place Me Under Your Wing" used by permission of Gabriel Levin. Translations ©1979 Gabriel Levin. All Bialik poems ©Hayim Nachman Bialik Estate.

EREZ BITON: "Beginnings," "A Bird's Nest," "Buying a Shop on Dizengoff" used by permission of Judith Katz. Translations ©1979 Judith Katz. All Erez Biton poems used by permission of Erez Biton.

T. CARMI: "The Condition" used by permission of Peter Everwine. Translation ©1976 Peter Everwine. "The Author's Apology" used by permission of Marcia Falk. Translation ©1978 Marcia Falk. All Carmi poems ©T. Carmi.

VOICES WITHIN THE ARK

ABRAHAM CHALFI: "My Father," "The One Who Is Missing" used by permission of Shlomo Vinner and Howard Schwartz. Translations ©1979 Shlomo Vinner and Howard Schwartz. All Chalfi poems ©Abraham Chalfi.

RAQUEL CHALFI: "Like a Field Waiting," "A Childless Witch," "A Witch Going Down to Egypt" from the anthology *Burning Air and a Clear Mind: An Anthology of Contemporary Israeli Women Poets,* ed. Myra Glazer Schotz. Translations ©1979 Myra Glazer Shotz. Used by permission of Myra Glazer Schotz. All Raquel Chalfi poems ©Raquel Chalfi.

SHLOMIT COHEN: "The Same Dream," "An Unraveled Thought," "Wife of Kohelet" from the anthology *Burning Air and a Clear Mind: An Anthology of Contemporary Israeli Women Poets,* ed. Myra Glazer Schotz. Translations →1979 Myra Glazer Schotz. Used by permission of Myra Glazer Schotz. All Shlomit Cohen poems →Shlomit Cohen.

MOSHE DOR: "The Dwelling," "Small Bones Ache," "Among the Pine Trees," "Nightingales Are Not Singing" from *Maps of Time* by Moshe Dor, The Menard Press, London, 1978. Used by permission of The Menard Press. Translations ©1978 The Menard Press. All Moshe Dor poems ©Moshe Dor.

ANADAD ELDAN: "Words That Speak of Death" used by permission of Anthony Rudolf. Translation ©1978 Anthony Rudolf and Natan Zach. "Who Will Give Cover?" "Samson Rends His Clothes" used by permission of Ruth Nevo. Translation ©1977 Ruth Nevo. All Eldan poems ©Anadad Eldan.

JAKOV FICHMAN: "Eve," "Abishag" from *Anthology of Modern Hebrew Poetry,* ed. S. Y. Penueli and A. Ukhmani, Israel Universities Press, Jerusalem, 1966, used by permission of the Institute for the Translation of Hebrew Literature. Translations ©the Institute for the Translation of Hebrew Literature. All Fichman poems ©Jakov Fichman Estate.

AMIR GILBOA: "Isaac" used by permission of Howard Schwartz. Translation ©1979 Howard Schwartz. "Moses," "Samson," "Seeds of Lead," "Birth" used by permission of Stephen Mitchell. Translations ©1979 Stephen Mitchell. "Joshua's Face," "Saul" used by permission of Shirley Kaufman. Translations ©1979 Shirley Kaufman. "My Brother Was Silent" used by permission of the Institute for the Translation of Hebrew Literature. Translation ©1977 the Institute for the Translation of Hebrew Literature. Translation ©A. C. Jacobs. All Gilboa poems ©Amir Gilboa.

ZERUBAVEL GILEAD: "Pomegranate Tree in Jerusalem," "Absalom," "Flying Letters" used by permission of Dorothea Krook. Translations ©1979 Dorothea Krook. All Gilead poems ©Zerubavel Gilead.

LEAH GOLDBERG: "Heavenly Jerusalem, Jerusalem of the Earth," "A God Once Commanded Us," "From My Mother's Home," "Toward Myself," "Answer" from *Selected Poems of Leah Goldberg,* The Menard Press, London, 1977. Used by permission of The Menard Press and Robert Friend. Translations ©1977 Robert Friend. All Goldberg poems ©Leah Goldberg Estate.

URI ZVI GREENBERG: "With My God, the Smith," "Like a Woman," "The Great Sad One," "How It is," "The Valley of Men," "There Is a Box," "The Hour," "On the Pole" used by permission of Robert Mezey. Translations ©1976 Robert Mezey. "Song at the Skirts of Heaven" used by permission of Zvi Jagendorf. Translation ©1978 Zvi Jagendorf. All Uri Zvi Greenberg poems ©Uri Zvi Greenberg.

ZALI GUREVITCH: "Short Eulogy," "Not Going with It" used by permission of Gabriel Levin. Translations ©1979 Gabriel Levin. All Gurevitch poems ©Zali Gurevitch.

HAIM GURI: "Isaac," used by permission of Howard Schwartz. Translation ©1979 Howard Schwartz. "Anath" used by permission of Naomi Nir and Howard Schwartz. Translation ©1979 Naomi Nir and Howard Schwartz. "My Samsons," "Nine Men Out of a Minyan," "And on My Return," "Rain," and "A Latter Purification" used by permission of Mark Elliott Shapiro. Translations ©1979 Mark Elliott Shapiro. All Haim Guri poems ©Haim Guri.

Acknowledgments

SHIMON HALKIN: "Do Not Accompany Me" used by permission of Ruth Nevo. Translation ©1979 Ruth Nevo. All Shimon Halkin poems ©Shimon Halkin.

HEDVA HARKAVI: "Talk to Me, Talk to Me," "It Was Gentle," "Whenever the Snakes Come" from *Burning Air and a Clear Mind: An Anthology of Contemporary Israeli Women Poets,* ed. by Myra Glazer Schotz. Used by permission of Myra Glazer Schotz. Translations ©1979 Myra Glazer Schotz.

AVRAHAM HUSS: "A Green Refrain," "Time," "Nocturnal Thoughts," "A Classic Idyll" used by permission of Mark Elliott Shapiro. Translations ©1979 Mark Elliott Shapiro. All Avraham Huss poems ©1979 Avraham Huss.

YEHUDA KARNI: "The Four of Them," "Chambers of Jerusalem" used by permission of Jeremy Garber. Translations ©Jeremy Garber. All Karni poems ©Yehuda Karni Estate.

RAV ABRAHAM ISAAC KOOK: "The First One Drew Me," "Radiant Is the World Soul," "When I Want to Speak" from *Abraham Isaac Kook—The Lights of Penitence, The Moral Principles, Lights of Holiness, Essays, Letters, and Poems.* Translations ©1979 Ben Zion Bokser. Used by permission of the Paulist Press.

ABBA KOVNER: "Near," "Observation at Dawn," "I Don't Know if Mount Zion" used by permission of Shirley Kaufman. Translations ©1977 Shirley Kaufman. All Abba Kovner poems ©Abba Kovner.

YITZHAK LAMDAN: Excerpt from "Massada" used by permission of the Institute for the Translation of Hebrew Literature. →1979 the Institute for the Translation of Hebrew Literature.

JIRI MORDECAI LANGER: "On the Margins of a Poem," "Riddle of Night" used by permission of Gabriel Preil and Howard Schwartz. Translations ©1979 Gabriel Preil and Howard Schwartz.

RENA LEE: "An Old Story" used by permission of Rena Lee. Translation ©1979 Rena Lee.

HAYIM LENSKI: "Purity," "Language of Ancients" used by permission of Pearl Grodzenski. Translations ©1979 Pearl Grodzenski. "Upon the Lake" from *Anthology of Modern Hebrew Poetry,* ed. S. Y. Penueli and A. Ukhmani, Israel Universities Press, Jerusalem, 1966, used by permission of the Institute for the Translation of Hebrew Literature. Translation ©1979 the Institute for the Translation of Hebrew Literature.

MATTI MEGGED: "The Phoenix," "White Bird," "The Akedah" used by permission of Howard Schwartz. Translations ©1979 Howard Schwartz. All Matti Megged poems ©1979 Matti Megged.

HAYIM NAGGID: "A Snow in Jerusalem," "After the War," "Like a Pearl" used by permission of Shlomo Vinner and Howard Schwartz. Translations ©1979 Shlomo Vinner and Howard Schwartz. "My Mother" used by permission of Rose Drachler. Translation ©1979 Rose Drachler. All Hayim Naggid poems ©Hayim Naggid.

DAN PAGIS: "The Last Ones," "The Tower," "Instructions for Crossing the Border," "Draft of a Reparations Agreement" from *Selected Poems* by Dan Pagis, Carcanet Press (and later The Menard Press), London, 1972. Used by permission of Stephen Mitchell and The Menard Press. Translations ©1972 Stephen Mithell. "Scrawled in Pencil in a Sealed Railway Car" used by permission of Anthony Rudolf. Translation ©1979 Anthony Rudolf. "Brothers" used by permission of Shirley Kaufman. Translation ©1977 Shirley Kaufman. "Autobiography," "The Grand Duke of New York" used by permission of Robert Friend. Translations ©1977, 1978 Robert Friend. All Dan Pagis poems ©Dan Pagis.

ISRAEL PINCAS: "Mediterranean" used by permission of Arthur Jacobs. Translation ©1979 Arthur Jacobs. Original-language poem ©Israel Pincas

BERL POMERANTZ: "End of Summer," "Young Virgins Plucked Suddenly" reprinted from

VOICES WITHIN THE ARK

Fourteen Israeli Poets, ed. Dennis Silk, and André Deutsch, London, 1976. Used by permission of the Institute for the Translation of Hebrew Literature. Translations ©1976 the Institute for the Translation of Hebrew Literature.

GABRIEL PREIL: "Words of Oblivion and Peace," "Rains on the Island" from *Anthology of Modern Hebrew Poetry*, ed. S. Y. Penueli and A. Ukhmani, Israel Universities Press, Jerusalem, 1966, used by permission of the Institute for the Translation of Hebrew Literature. Translations ©1966 the Institute for the Translation of Hebrew Literature. "From Jerusalem: A First Poem," "Arriving" used by permission of Robert Friend. Translations ©1977, 1979 Robert Friend. "Autumn Music," "A Lesson in Translation," "Letter Out of the Gray," "Biographical Note" used by permission of Howard Schwartz. Translations ©1979 Howard Schwartz. "Like David," "Parting" used by permission of Laya Firestone. Translations ©1979 Laya Firestone. "Memory of Another Climate," "A Summing Up" used by permission of Jeremy Garber. Translations ©1979 Jeremy Garber. "Giving Up on the Shore," "A Late Manuscript at the Schocken Institute" used by permission of Gabriel Levin. Translations ©1979 Gabriel Levin. "Fishermen" used by permission of Betsy Rosenberg. Translations ©1979 Betsy Rosenberg. All Gabriel Preil poems ©Gabriel Preil.

ESTHER RAAB: "Folk Tune," "A Serenade for Two Poplars" used by permission of Robert Friend. Translations ©1977, 1979, Robert Friend.

RACHEL: "Rachel," "My White Book of Poems" used by permission of Naomi Nir. Translations ©1979 Naomi Nir. "Revolt" from *Anthology of Modern Hebrew Poetry*, ed. by S. Y. Penueli and A. Ukhmani, Israel Universities Press, Jerusalem, 1966, used by permission of the Institute for the Translation of Hebrew Literature. Translation ©1966 the Institute for the Translation of Hebrew Literature. "Perhaps" from *Anthology of Modern Hebrew Poetry*, used by permission of the Institute for the Translation of Hebrew Literature. Translation ©1966 the Institute for the Translation of Hebrew Literature. "My Dead" used by permission of Robert Mezey. Translation ©1976 Robert Mezey. All Rachel poems ©Rachel Estate.

YONATHAN RATOSH: "Lament" used by permission of Howard Schwartz. Translation © 1979 Howard Schwartz. All Yonathan Ratosh poems © Yonathan Ratosh.

DAHLIA RAVIKOVITCH: "A Dress of Fire," "Surely You Remember," "Requiem After Seventeen Years" from *Selected Poems of Dahlia Ravikovitch*, The Menard Press, London, 1977. Translations used by permission of The Menard Press and Chana Bloch. Translations © 1977 Chana Bloch.

ABRAHAM REGELSON: "Moses on Mount Nebo" used by permission of Richard Flantz and Abraham Regelson. Translation © 1979 Richard Flantz.

I. Z. RIMON: "I Am a King" used by permission of Shlomo Vinner and Howard Schwartz. Translation used by permission of Shlomo Vinner and Howard Schwartz. Original-language poem © I. Z. Rimon Estate.

DAVID ROKEAH: "Beginning," "I Am Like a Book" used by permission of David Rokeah. Translations © 1979 David Rokeah.

HEMDA ROTH: "A Young Deer/Dust," "Treason of Sand," "The Song" from *Burning Air and a Clear Mind: An Anthology of Contemporary Israeli Women Poets*, ed. Myra Glazer Schotz. Translations © 1979 Myra Glazer Schotz. Used by permission of Myra Glazer Schotz. All Hemda Roth poems © Hemda Roth.

TUVIA RUEBNER: "Among Iron Fragments" used by permission of Robert Friend. Translation © 1979 Robert Friend. "First Days" used by permission of E. A. Levenston. Translation © 1979 E. A. Levenston. "I Left" used by permission of Betsy Rosenberg. Translation © Betsy Rosenberg. "Document" used by permission of the Institute for the Translation of Hebrew Literature. Translation © 1979 the Institute for the Translation of Hebrew Literature.

PINHAS SADEH: "In the Forest," "In the Garden of the Turkish Consulate" used by permission of Harris Lenowitz. Translations © 1979 Harris Lenowitz. "Raya Brenner," "Elegy" used by permission of Gabriel Preil and Howard Schwartz. Translations © 1979 Gabriel Preil and Howard Schwartz.

SHIN SHALOM: "Splendor" used by permission of Abraham Birman. Translation © 1979 Abraham Birman.

ALIZA SHENHAR: "Trembling," "Expectation," "Resurrection of the Dead," "The Drunkenness of Pain," "Sea-Games," "The Akedah," "Song of the Closing Service" used by permission of Linda Zisquit. Translations © 1979 Linda Zisquit.

AVRAHAM SHLONSKY: "Prayer," "The Stars on Shabbat," "Pledge," "A New Genesis" used by permission of Francis Landy. Translations © 1979 Francis Landy. "Dress Me, Dear Mother" used by permission of Robert Mezey. Translation © 1979 Robert Mezey.

DAVID SHULMAN: "A Diary of the Sailors of the North" used by permission of David Shulman. Translation © 1979 David Shulman.

EISIG SILBERSCHLAG: "Abraham," "Proust on Noah" used by permission of Eisig Silberschlag. Translations © 1979 Eisig Silberschlag.

ARYE SIVAN: "Children's Song," "In Jerusalem Are Women" used by permission of David Shevin. Translations © 1979 David Shevin. "Forty Years Peace," "To Xanadu, Which Is Beth Shaul" used by permission of Anthony Rudolf. Translations © 1979 Anthony Rudolf.

JAKOV STEINBERG: "With a Book at Twilight," "The World Is Not a Fenced-Off Garden," "A Donkey Will Carry You" used by permission of Mark Elliott Shapiro. Translations © 1979 Mark Elliott Shapiro.

NOAH STERN: "His Mother's Love," "Grave at Cassino" reprinted from *Fourteen Israeli Poets*, ed. Dennis Silk, André Deutsch, London, 1976. Translations © 1976 the Institute for the Translation of Hebrew Literature. Used by permission of the Institute for the Translation of Hebrew Literature.

A. L. STRAUSS: "Lament for the European Exile," "In the Discreet Splendor," "On the Path," "Voice in the Dark" used by permission of the Institute for the Translation of Hebrew Literature. Translations © 1979 the Institute for the Translation of Hebrew Literature.

JOSHUA TAN PAI: "Trees Once Walked and Stood," "My Soul Hovers Over Me," "The Life of Hard Times" used by permission of Yishai Tobin. Translations © 1979 Yishai Tobin. All Tan Pai poems © Joshua Tan Pai.

SHAUL TCHERNICHOVSKY: "Man is Nothing But," "The Grave" used by permission of Robert Mezey. Translations © 1979 Robert Mezey. "Saul's Song of Love" used by permission of the Institute for the Translation of Hebrew Literature. Translation © 1979 the Institute for the Translation of Hebrew Literature. "The Death of Tammuz" used by permission of Mark Elliott Shapiro. Translation © 1979 Mark Elliott Shapiro.

MORDECAI TEMKIN: "Seal of Fire," "Hidden Bow," "Foul Water," "Your Presence" used by permission of Jeremy Garber. Translations © 1979 Jeremy Garber.

AVNER TREININ: "The Cage," "Deserted Shrine" used by permission of E. A. Levenston. "Salmon Cycle" used by permission of Robert Friend. Translation © 1979 Robert Friend. All Avner Treinin poems © Avner Treinin.

SHLOMO VINNER: "Jerusalem," "In the Cabinet," "Training on the Shore," "Midnight and Ten Minutes," "The Need to Love," "Parting," "Lullaby" used by permission of Howard Schwartz. Translations © 1979 Howard Schwartz. All Shlomo Vinner poems © Shlomo Vinner.

DAVID VOGEL: "Days Were Great as Lakes," "Our Childhood Spilled into Our Hearts," "How Can I See You, Love," "Black Flags Are Fluttering," "Plain, Humble Letters," "When I Was Growing Up," "In Fine, Transparent Words," "Now I Have Forgotten All" reprinted from *Selected Poems* by David Vogel, translated by A. C. Jacobs, The Menard Press, London, 1976. Used by permission of A. C. Jacobs. Translations © 1976 A. C. Jacobs.

YONA WALLACH: "Cradle Song," "When the Angels Are Exhausted" used by permission of Lenore Gordon. Translations © 1979 Lenore Gordon. "Death; She Was Always Here" reprinted from *New Writing in Israel,* ed. by Ezra Spicehandler, Schocken, New York, 1977. Translation © 1977, 1979 the Institute for the Translation of Hebrew Literature. Used by permission of the Institute for the Translation of Hebrew Literature. All Yona Wallach poems © Yona Wallach.

MANFRED WINKLER: "One Goes With Me Along the Shore," "Somewhere You Exist," "If My Hands Were Mute," "I Love What is Not," "She" used by permission of Mary Zilzer. Translations © 1979 Mary Zilzer. All Manfred Winkler poems © Manfred Winkler.

AVOT YESHURUN: "The Poem on the Jews," "The Poem on the Guilt," "The Poem on Our Mother, Our Mother Rachel" reprinted from the manuscript *The Collection, Poems 1964-1976* by Avot Yeshurun. Translations © 1977 the Institute for the Translation of Hebrew Literature. All Avot Yeshurun poems © Avot Yeshurun.

NATHAN YONATHAN: "Another Poem on Absalom," "South Wind," "And the Silver Turns into Night" used by permission of Nathan Yonathan and Richard Flantz. Translations © 1979 Richard Flantz. All Nathan Yonathan poems © Nathan Yonathan.

NATAN ZACH: "When God First Said," "The Quiet Light of Flies," "To Be a Master in Your House," "When the Last Riders," "In This Deep Darkness," "A Short Winter Tale," "Perhaps It's Only Music," "A Peaceful Song" used by permission of Peter Everwine. Translations © 1979 Peter Everwine. "As Sand," "Against Parting" reprinted from *Against Parting,* Northern House, translated by Jon Silkin. Used by permission of Jon Silkin. Translations © 1979 by Jon Silkin. "No," "Listening to Her," "A Foreign Country" used by permission of Laya Firestone. Translations © 1979 Laya Firestone. All Natan Zach poems © Natan Zach.

ZELDA: "I Stood in Jerusalem," "The Moon Is Teaching Bible," "In the Dry Riverbed," "With My Grandfather," "Light a Candle" used by permission of Marcia Falk. Translations © 1979 Marcia Falk. All poems by Zelda © Zelda.

EZRA ZUSSMAN: "At Dante's Grave," "The Last" used by permission of Leah Zussman. Translations © 1979 Leah Zussman.

II. Yiddish

B. ALQUIT: "The Light of the World," "Wandering Chorus" used by permission of Howard Schwartz. Translations © 1979 Howard Schwartz.

ASYA: "The Deer," "Celan," "Pause a Moment," "My True Memory," "My Strawlike Hair," "A Grain of Moonlight" used by permission of Gabriel Preil and Howard Schwartz. Translations © 1979 Gabriel Preil and Howard Schwartz.

EPHRAIM AUERBACH: "Seismograph" used by permission of Howard Schwartz. Translations © 1979 Howard Schwartz.

RACHEL BOIMWALL: "Diaspora Jews" used by permission of Gabriel Preil. Translation © 1979 Gabriel Preil. "Lifelong," "Round," "At Night" used by permission of Gabriel Preil and Howard Schwartz. Translations © 1979 Gabriel Preil and Howard Schwartz.

NAHUM BOMZE: "Pshytik," "City of Light" used by permission of Gabriel Preil and Howard Schwartz. Translations © 1979 Gabriel Preil and Howard Schwartz.

CELIA DROPKIN: "A Circus Dancer" used by permission of Howard Schwartz. Translation © 1979 Howard Schwartz.

LAZER EICHENRAND: "The Mute City," "Prologue," "From Life" used by permission of Gabriel Preil and Howard Schwartz. Translations © 1979 Gabriel Preil and Howard Schwartz.

VOICES WITHIN THE ARK

MALKA LOCKER: "Clocks," "Drunken Streets" used by permission of Jeremy Garber. Translations © 1979 Jeremy Garber.

ITZIK MANGER: "Rachel Goes to the Well for Water," "Abishag Writes a Letter Home," "Alone," "Autumn" reprinted from *An Anthology of Modern Yiddish Poetry,* ed. Ruth Whitman, October House, New York, 1966. Used by permission of Ruth Whitman. Translations © 1966 Ruth Whitman. "Dying Thief," "Fairy Tales," "Abraham and Sarah," "On the Road There Stands a Tree," "The Strange Guest" used by permission of Stephen Garrin. Translations © 1979 Stephen Garrin. "Evening," "Under the Ruins of Poland" used by permission of Miriam Waddington. Translations © 1979 Miriam Waddington. "A Dark Hand" used by permission of David G. Roskies. Translation © 1979 David G. Roskies.

ANNA MARGOLIN: "Ancient Murderess Night," "Years" reprinted from *An Anthology of Modern Yiddish Poetry,* ed. Ruth Whitman, October House, New York, 1966. Used by permission of Ruth Whitman. Translations © 1966 Ruth Whitman. "My Kin Talk," "Homecoming," "Mother Earth" used by permission of Keith Bosley. Translations © 1979 Keith Bosley.

PERETZ MARKISH: "In the Last Flicker of the Sinking Sun," "Your Burnt-Out Body" used by permission of Keith Bosley. Translations © 1979 Keith Bosley.

KADYA MOLODOVSKY: "In Life's Stable," "Night Visitors" reprinted from *An Anthology of Modern Yiddish Poetry,* ed. Ruth Whitman, October House, New York, 1966. Used by permission of Ruth Whitman. Translations © 1966 Ruth Whitman. "And Yet" used by permission of Seymour Levitan. Translation © 1979 Seymour Levitan.

MENDEL NAIGRESHEL: "What Will Remain After Me?" "Nation" used by permission of Joachim Neugroschel. Translations © 1979 Joachim Neugroschel.

LEIB NEIDUS: "In an Alien Place," "I Often Want to Let My Lines Go" reprinted from *An Anthology of Modern Yiddish Poetry,* ed. Ruth Whitman, October House, New York, 1966. Used by permission of Ruth Whitman. Translations © 1966 Ruth Whitman. "I Love the Woods" used by permission of Keith Bosley. Translation © 1979 Keith Bosley.

MELECH RAVITCH: "Twelve Lines About the Burning Bush," "A Poem—Good or Bad—A Thing—With One Attribute—Flat" reprinted from *An Anthology of Modern Yiddish Poetry,* ed. Ruth Whitman, October House, New York, 1966. Used by permission of Ruth Whitman. Translations © 1966 Ruth Whitman. "Twilight Thoughts in Israel" used by permission of Seymour Levitan. Translation © 1979 Seymour Levitan. "Let Us Learn," "Verses Written on Sand" used by permission of Seymour Mayne. Translations © 1979 Seymour Mayne. "Conscience" used by permission of Keith Bosley. Translation © 1979 Keith Bosley.

ABRAHAM REISEN: "The Family of Eight" used by permission of Marcia Falk. Translation © 1979 Marcia Falk. "What is the Case in Point?" used by permission of Richard J. Fein. Translation © 1979 Richard J. Fein. "Newcomers," "An Endless Chain," "Girls from Home" used by permission of Keith Bosley. Translations © 1979 Keith Bosley.

JOSEPH ROLNIK: "In Disguise," "I'm Not Rich," "At God's Command" used by permission of Keith Bosley. Translations © 1979 Keith Bosley.

LEAH RUDNITSKY: "Birds Are Drowsing on the Branches" reprinted from *Night Words: A Midrash on the Holocaust,* compiled by David G. Roskies. Translated by the editor. © 1971 by B'nai B'rith Hillel Foundation, Inc. Used by permission of B'nai B'rith Hillel Foundation, Inc.

BEYLE SCHAECHTER-GOTTESMAN: "Meditation" used by permission of Beyle Schaechter-Gottesman and Gabriel Preil. Translation © 1979 Gabriel Preil.

JACOB ISAAC SEGAL: "Candle," "Rest" used by permission of Seymour Mayne. Translations © 1979 Seymour Mayne.

ZVI SHARGEL: "Pictures on the Wall," "I Will Go Away" used by permission of Gabriel Preil and Howard Schwartz. Translations © 1979 Gabriel Preil and Howard Schwartz. "Let Us Laugh" used by permission of Gabriel Preil. Translation © 1979 Gabriel Preil.

ELIEZER STEINBARG: "Where is Justice?" "*Shatnes* or Uncleanliness" used by permission of Seth L. Wolitz. Translations © 1979 Seth L. Wolitz. "The Umbrella, the Cane, and the Broom," "The Horse and the Whip," "The Bayonet and the Needle" used by permission of Curt Leviant. Translations © 1979 Curt Leviant.

MOISHE STEINGART: "The Last Fire," "Generations" used by permission of Moishe Steingart and Gabriel Preil. Translation © 1979 Gabriel Preil.

A. N. STENCL: "Ezekiel" used by permission of Joseph Leftwich. Copyright © 1979 Joseph Leftwich.

ABO STOLTZENBERG: "In Vistas of Stone" used by permission of Howard Schwartz. Translation © 1979 Howard Schwartz. "What Am I?" "The French Mood" used by permission of Gabriel Preil and Howard Schwartz. Translations © 1979 Gabriel Preil and Howard Schwartz.

ABRAHAM SUTSKEVER: "On My Wandering Flute," "Song for a Dance," "Landscape," "Songs to a Lady Moonwalker," "The Banks of a River," "How," "Song of Praise for an Ox," "Poetry," "Under the Earth" reprinted from *An Anthology of Modern Yiddish Poetry*, ed. Ruth Whitman, October House, New York, 1966. Used by permission of Ruth Whitman. Translations © 1966 Ruth Whitman. "Yiddish," "Toys" used by permission of Seymour Levitan. Translations © Abraham Sutskever and Seymour Levitan. "A Cartload of Shoes," "To My Child" reprinted from *Night Words: A Midrash on the Holocaust*, compiled by David G. Roskies. Translated by the editor. © 1971 by B'nai B'rith Hillel Foundation, Inc. Used by permission of B'nai B'rith Hillel Foundation, Inc.

J. L. TELLER: "Lines to a Tree," "Minor Key," "To the Divine Neighbor" used by permission of Gabriel Preil and Howard Schwartz. Translations © 1979 Gabriel Preil and Howard Schwartz.

MALKA HEIFETZ TUSSMAN: "Thou Shalt Not," "Water Without Sound," "At the Well," "I Say," "Love the Ruins," "Songs of the Priestess" used by permission of Marcia Falk. Translations © 1979 Marcia Falk.

MIRIAM ULINOVER: "Havdolah Wine," "In the Courtyard" used by permission of Seth L. Wolitz. Translations © 1979 Seth L. Wolitz.

MOSHE YUNGMAN: "The Sacrifice," "Don't Say" used by permission of Marcia Falk. Translations © 1979 Marcia Falk. "The Messiah" used by permission of David G. Roskies. Translation © 1979 David G. Roskies. "Encounters in Safed," "Melons" used by permission of Gabriel Preil and Howard Schwartz. Translations © 1979 Gabriel Preil and Howard Schwartz.

AARON ZEITLIN: "A Dream About an Aged Humorist," "Text," "The Empty Apartment" reprinted from *An Anthology of Modern Yiddish Poetry*, ed. Ruth Whitman, October House, New York, 1966. Used by permission of Ruth Whitman. Translations © 1966 Ruth Whitman. "Ode to Freedom" used by permission of Keith Bosley. Translation © 1979 Keith Bosley.

RAYZEL ZYCHLINSKA: "Remembering Lutsky," "The Clothes," "My Mother's Shoes" used by permission of Marc Kaminsky. Translations © 1979 Marc Kaminsky.

III. English

United States

PAUL AUSTER: "Scribe," "Hieroglyph," "Song of Degrees," "Covenant" used by permission of Paul Auster. Poems © 1979 Paul Auster.

WILLIS BARNSTONE: "The Good Beasts," "The Worm," "Grandfather," "Gas Lamp," "Miklos Radnoti," "Paradise" used by permission of Willis Barnstone. Poems © 1979 Willis Barnstone.

VOICES WITHIN THE ARK

ANITA BARROWS: "Avenue Y," "The Ancestors" used by permission of Anita Barrows. Poems © 1979 Anita Barrows.

MARVIN BELL: "Getting Lost in Nazi Germany," from *Escape Into You* by Marvin Bell. © 1971 by Marvin Bell. This poem appeared originally in *Poetry*. "The Extermination of the Jews" and "The Israeli Navy" are from *A Probable Volume of Dreams* by Marvin Bell. © 1966, 1968, 1969 by Marvin Bell. "The Extermination of the Jews" appeared originally in *Poetry*.

STEPHEN BERG: "Desnos Reading the Palms of Men on Their Way to the Gas Chambers" from *The Daughters* by Stephen Berg © 1971 by The Bobbs-Merrill Company, Inc., reprinted by permission of the author and publisher.

SUZANNE BERNHARDT: "In a Dream Ship's Hold," "The Unveiling" used by permission of Suzanne Bernhardt. Poems © 1979 Suzanne Bernhardt.

CHANA BLOCH: "Paradise," "Noah," "The Sacrifice," "Yom Kippur" used by permission of Chana Bloch. Poems © 1979 Chana Bloch.

EMILY BORENSTEIN: "Life of the Letters" used by permission of Emily Borenstein. Poem © 1979 Emily Borenstein.

STANLEY BURNSHAW: "Isaac," "House in St. Petersburg," "Talmudist" used by permission of Stanley Burnshaw. Poems © 1979 Stanley Burnshaw.

MICHAEL CASTRO: "Grandfathers," "Percolating Highway" used by permission of Michael Castro. Poems © 1979 Michael Castro.

ERIC CHAET: "Yom Kippur," "A Letter Catches Up with Me" used by permission of Eric Chaet. Poems © 1979 Eric Chaet.

KIM CHERNIN: "Eve's Birth" used by permission of Kim Chernin. Poem © 1979 Kim Chernin.

ELAINE DALLMAN: "From the Dust" used by permission of Elaine Dallman. Poem © 1979 Elaine Dallman.

LUCILLE DAY: "Labor," "Yom Kippur" used by permission of Lucille Day. Poems © 1979 Lucille Day.

ROSE DRACHLER: "Isaac and Esau," "The Dark Scent of Prayer," "Under the Shawl," "Zippora Returns to Moses at Rephidim," "As I Am My Father's," "The Letters of the Book" used by permission of Rose Drachler. Poems © 1979 Rose Drachler.

LARRY EIGNER: "The Closed System," "Remember Sabbath Days" used by permission of Larry Eigner. Poems © 1979 Larry Eigner.

MARCIA FALK: "Shulamit in Her Dreams," "Modern Kabbalist," "Woman Through the Window" used by permission of Marcia Falk. Poems © 1979 Marcia Falk.

IRVING FELDMAN: "The Pripet Marshes" from *New and Selected Poems* by Irving Feldman, © 1964. All rights reserved. Reprinted by permission of Viking Penguin, Inc.

RUTH FELDMAN: "Lilith" used by permission of Ruth Feldman. Poem © 1979 Ruth Feldman.

DONALD FINKEL: "Genealogy," "Lilith," "Cain's Song," "Lame Angel," "Finders Keepers," "Feeding the Fire" from *A Mote in Heaven's Eye* by Donald Finkel. © 1975 by Donald Finkel. Reprinted by permission of Atheneum Publishers. "How Things Fall" used by permission of Donald Finkel. Poem © 1979 Donald Finkel.

LAYA FIRESTONE: "Listen to the Bird," "Thoughts for My Grandmother," "Crow, Straight Flier, But Dark," "For Gabriel" used by permission of Laya Firestone. Poems © 1979 Laya Firestone.

ALLEN GINSBERG: "Kaddish, Part I" from *Kaddish and Other Poems* by Allen Ginsberg © 1961. Used by permission of City Lights Books.

Acknowledgments

JOSEPH GLAZER: "A Visit Home" used by permission of Joseph Glazer. Poem © 1979 Joseph Glazer.

ALBERT GOLDBARTH: "Dime Call," "Recipe" used by permission of Albert Goldbarth. Poems © 1979 Albert Goldbarth.

LYNN GOTTLIEB: "Eve's Song in the Garden" used by permission of Lynn Gottlieb. Poem © 1979 Lynn Gottlieb.

ARTHUR GREGOR: "Spirit-like Before Light" reprinted from *Selected Poems* by Arthur Gregor, published by Doubleday © Co. 1971. © 1971 by Arthur Gregor. Used by permission of Arthur Gregor.

ALLEN GROSSMAN: "Lilith" used by permission of Allen Grossman. Poem © 1979 Allen Grossman.

MARTIN GROSSMAN: "Into the Book," "The Bread of Our Affliction" used by permission of Martin Grossman. Poems © 1979 Martin Grossman.

ANTHONY HECHT: "More Light! More Light!" from *The Hard Hours* by Anthony Hecht. Copyright 1948, 1949, 1950, 1951, 1952, 1953, 1954, © 1955, 1956, 1957, 1958, 1959, 1960, 1961, 1962, 1963, 1964, 1965, 1966, 1967 by Anthony E. Hecht. Used by permission of Atheneum Publishers.

JACK HIRSCHMAN: "Zohara," "NHR" used by permission of Jack Hirschman. Poems © 1979 Jack Hirschman.

JOHN HOLLANDER: "The Ziz" from *Spectral Emanations* by John Hollander. © 1975, 1978 by John Hollander. Reprinted with permission of Atheneum Publishers. "The Ziz" appeared originally in *Harpers.*

BARRY HOLTZ: "Isaac" used by permission of Barry Holtz. Poem © 1979 Barry Holtz.

DAVID IGNATOW: "1905," "Kaddish," "Dream," "The Heart" used by permission of David Ignatow. Poems © 1979 David Ignatow.

DAN JAFFE: "The Owl in the Rabbi's Barn," "Yahrzeit" used by permission of Dan Jaffe. Poems © 1979 Dan Jaffe.

RODGER KAMENETZ: "Why I Can't Write My Autobiography," "Pilpul" used by permission of Rodger Kamenetz. Poems © 1979 Rodger Kamenetz.

MARC KAMINSKY: "Erev Shabbos" used by permission of Marc Kaminsky. Poem © 1979 Mark Kaminsky.

JASCHA KESSLER: "Waiting for Lilith" used by permission of Jascha Kessler. Poem © 1979 Jascha Kessler.

SOL LACHMAN: "Sukkot" used by permission of Sol Lachman. Poem © 1979 Sol Lachman.

BARBARA F. LEFCOWITZ: "Driftwood Dybbuk" from *A Risk of Green.* Poem © 1978 Barbara F. Lefcowitz and Gallimaufry Press. "At the Western Wall," "The Mirrors of Jerusalem" © 1979 Barbara F. Lefcowitz. All poems used by permission of Barbara F. Lefcowitz.

HARRIS LENOWITZ: "The Fringes," "Panegyric" used by permission of Harris Lenowitz. Poems © 1979 Harris Lenowitz.

MOLLY MYEROWITZ LEVINE: "Safed and I" used by permission of Molly Myerowitz Levine. Poem © 1979 Molly Myerowitz Levine.

PHILIP LEVINE: "Zaydee," "1933," "After" from the book *1933* by Philip Levine. © 1972, 1973, 1974 by Philip Levine. Reprinted by permission of Atheneum Publishers. "Now It Can Be Told," "Words;" "Here and Now," "On a Drawing by Flavio" used by permission of Philip Levine. Poems © 1979 Philip Levine.

STEPHEN LEVY: "Home Alone . . ." "Friday Night After Bathing," "Freely, from a Song

Sung by Jewish Women of Yemen," "A Judezmo Writer in Turkey Angry" used by permission of Stephen Levy. Poems © 1979 Stephen Levy.

SUSAN LITWACK: "Inscape," "Tonight Everyone in the World is Dreaming the Same Dream," "Havdolah," "Creation of the Child" used by permission of Susan Litwack. Poems © 1979 Susan Litwack.

MORDECAI MARCUS: "Two Refugees" used by permission of Mordecai Marcus. Poem © 1979 Mordecai Marcus.

DAVID MELTZER: "Tell Them I'm Struggling to Sing with Angels," "The Eyes, the Blood" used by permission of David Meltzer. Poems © 1979 David Meltzer.

SUSAN MERNIT: "Song of the Bride" and "The Scholar's Wife" used by permission of Susan Mernit. Poems © 1979 Susan Mernit.

JERRED METZ: "Angels in the House," "Speak Like Rain," "Her True Body," "Divination" used by permission of Jerred Metz. Poems © 1979 Jerred Metz.

BERT MEYERS: "The Garlic," "The Dark Birds," "When I Came to Israel" used by permission of Odette Meyers. Poems © 1980 Odette Meyers.

ROBERT MEZEY: "The Wandering Jew," "New Year's Eve in Solitude," "White Blossoms," "Theresienstadt Poem" "I Am Here" used by permission of Robert Mezey. Poems © 1979 Robert Mezey.

STEPHEN MITCHELL: "Adam in Love," "Abraham," "Jacob and the Angel" used by permission of Stephen Mitchell. Poems © 1979 Stephen Mitchell.

HOWARD MOSS: "Elegy for My Father" by Howard Moss from *Selected Poems* is reprinted by permission of Atheneum Publishers. Copyright 1946, 1947, 1948, 1949, 1950, 1951, 1952, 1953, 1954 by Howard Moss.

STANLEY MOSS: "God Poem," "Two Fishermen," "Scroll," "Apocrypha" used by permission of Stanley Moss. Poems © 1979 Stanley Moss.

JACK MYERS: "The Minyan," "Day of Atonement" used by permission of Jack Myers. Poems © 1979 Jack Myers.

JOACHIM NEUGROSCHEL: "Eve's Advice to the Children of Israel," "Doves" used by permission of Joachim Neugroschel. Poems © 1979 Joachim Neugroschel.

GERDA NORVIG: "Desert March," "The Tree of Life Is Also a Tree of Fire," "The Joining" used by permission of Gerda Norvig. Poems © 1979 Gerda Norvig.

GEORGE OPPEN: "If It All Went Up in Smoke" used by permission of George Oppen. Poem © 1979 George Oppen.

CYNTHIA OZICK: "The Wonder-Teacher," "A Riddle" used by permission of Cynthia Ozick. Poems © 1979 Cynthia Ozick.

GARY PACERNICK: "I Want to Write a Jewish Poem" used by permission of Gary Pacernick. Poems © 1980 Gary Pacernick.

LINDA PASTAN: "Yom Kippur," "After Reading Nelly Sachs," "At the Jewish Museum," "Pears," "Elsewhere" used by permission of Linda Pastan. Poems © 1979 Linda Pastan.

STUART Z. PERKOFF: "Aleph," "Gimel," "Hai" from *Alphabet* by Stuart Z. Perkoff. Used by permission of Ann Perkoff. Poems © 1979 Ann Perkoff.

WILLIAM PILLIN: "O, Beautiful They Move," "Night Poem in an Abandoned Music Room," "A Poem for Anton Schmidt," "Farewell to Europe," "Ode on a Decision to Settle for Less," "Poem" used by permission of William Pillin and George Hitchcock. Poems © 1979 William Pillin.

Acknowledgments

HYAM PLUTZIK: "The King of Ai," "The Begetting of Cain," "On the Photograph of a Man I Never Saw" used by permission of Tanya Plutzik. Poems © 1979 Tanya Plutzik.

CARL RAKOSI: "Meditation," "Meditation," "A Lamentation," and "Meditation" used by permission of Carl Rakosi. Poems © 1980 Carl Rakosi.

ROCHELLE RATNER: "The Poor *Shammes* of Berditchev," "Davening" used by permission of Rochelle Ratner. Poems © 1979 Rochelle Ratner.

CHARLES REZNIKOFF: "The Hebrew of Your Poets, Zion," "Jacob," "Luzzato," "Out of the Strong, Sweetness," "Lament of the Jewish Women for Tammuz," "Dew," "The Body is Like Roots Stretching," "Raisins and Nuts," "Te Deum," "Autobiography: Hollywood," "The Letter" used by permission of Marie Syrkin. Poems © 1979 Marie Syrkin.

MARTIN ROBBINS: "A Cantor's Dream Before the High Holy Days" used by permission of Martin Robbins. Poem © 1979 Martin Robbins.

EDOUARD RODITI: "Shekhina and the Kiddushim," "The Paths of Prayer," "Kashrut," "A Beginning and an End," "Habakkuk" used by permission of Edouard Roditi. Poems © 1979 Edouard Roditi. "The Paths of Prayer" is reprinted from *The Jewish Quarterly.*

DAVID ROSENBERG: "Maps to Nowhere," "Rain Has Fallen on the History Books" used by permission of David Rosenberg. Poems © 1979 David Rosenberg.

JOEL ROSENBERG: "The First Wedding in the World," "The Violin Tree" used by permission of Joel Rosenberg. Poems © 1979 Joel Rosenberg.

JEROME ROTHENBERG: "The Alphabet Came to Me," "A Letter to Paul Celan in Memory" used by permission of Jerome Rothenberg. Poems © 1979 Jerome Rothenberg.

MURIEL RUKEYSER: "Akiba" from *The Collected Poems of Muriel Rukeyser.* © Reprinted with permission of Monica McCure, International Creative Management. © 1968 Muriel Rukeyser.

BENJAMIN SALTMAN: "The Journey with Hands and Arms," "The Fathers" used by permission of Benjamin Saltman. Poems © 1979 Benjamin Saltman.

SUSAN FROMBERG SCHAEFFER: "Yahrzeit" used by permission of Susan Fromberg Schaeffer. Poem © 1979 Susan Fromberg Schaeffer.

DELMORE SCHWARTZ: "Abraham," "Sarah" © 1959 by Delmore Schwartz, and "Jacob" © 1958 by Delmore Schwartz from the book *Summer Knowledge* by Delmore Schwartz. Reprinted by permission of Doubleday © Company, Inc.

HOWARD SCHWARTZ: "Our Angels," "Adam's Dream," "The Eve," "The Prayers," "Vessels," "A Song," "Gathering the Sparks," "Blessing of the Firstborn," "Psalm," "Shira," "Abraham in Egypt," "Iscah," "The New Year for Trees," "These Two" from *Gathering the Sparks: Poems 1965-1979* by Howard Schwartz. Used by permission of Howard Schwartz. Poems © 1977, 1979 Howard Schwartz.

HARVEY SHAPIRO: "The Six Hundred Thousand Letters," "Lines for the Ancient Scribes," "Exodus" from *Battle Report* by Harvey Shapiro. Reprinted by permission of Wesleyan University Press. © 1961 Harvey Shapiro. "Riding Westward," "For the Yiddish Singers in the Lakewood Hotels of My Childhood," "Like a Beach" and "Musical Shuttle" from *Lauds & Nightsounds* by Harvey Shapiro, published by Sun Press. © 1980 by Harvey Shapiro. Reprinted by permission of Harvey Shapiro.

KARL SHAPIRO: "The Alphabet," "The 151st Psalm" "Jew" from *Poems of a Jew* by Karl Shapiro. Reprinted by permission of Random House. Poems © 1979 Karl Shapiro.

DAVID SHEVIN: "Shechem," "Dawn" used by permission of David Shevin. Poems © 1979 David Shevin.

DANNY SIEGEL: "Binni the Meshuggener," "Snow in the City," "The Crippler" used by permission of Danny Siegel. Poems © 1979 Danny Siegel.

MAXINE SILVERMAN: "Hair" used by permission of Maxine Silverman. Poem © 1980 Maxine Silverman.

MYRA SKLAREW: "What Is a Jewish Poem?" "Benediction," "Instructions for the Messiah" used by permission of Myra Sklarew. Poems © 1979 Myra Sklarew.

ARLENE STONE: "Germination" used by permission of Arlene Stone. Poem © 1979 Arlene Stone.

NATHANIEL TARN: "Where Babylon Ends" used by permission of Nathaniel Tarn. Poem © 1979 Nathaniel Tarn.

CONSTANCE URDANG: "The Invention of Zero," "Birth," "Change of Life" used by permission of Constance Urdang. Poems © 1979 Constance Urdang.

RUTH WHITMAN: "Translating," "Dan, the Dust of Masada Is Still in My Nostrils," "Mediterranean," "Watching the Sun Rise Over Mount Zion" used by permission of Ruth Whitman. Poems © 1979 Ruth Whitman.

MELVIN WILK: "Blessing" used by permission of Melvin Wilk. Poem © 1979 Melvin Wilk.

J. RUTHERFORD WILLEMS: "Hebrew Letters in the Trees" used by permission of J. Rutherford Willems. Poem © 1979 J. Rutherford Willems.

C. K. WILLIAMS: "Spit" from *With Ignorance* by C. K. Williams. Reprinted by Permission of Houghton Mifflin Company. © 1972, 1974, 1975, 1977 by C. K. Williams.

LINDA ZISQUIT: "Rachel's Lament," "Sabbatical," "The Circumcision" used by permission of Linda Zisquit. Poems © 1979 Linda Zisquit.

LOUIS ZUKOFSKY: "From the Head," "A Voice Out of the Tabernacle," "Expounding the Torah" from *A 1-12.* Used by permission of Jonathan Cape. Poems © 1979 Louis Zukofsky Estate.

England

A. ALVAREZ: "A Cemetery in New Mexico," "The Fortunate Fall," "Dying," "Mourning and Melancholia" from *Autumn to Autumn and Selected Poems 1953-1976,* Macmillan, London, 1978. Used by permission of A. Alvarez. Poems © 1979 A. Alvarez.

ANTHONY BARNETT: "A Marriage" from *A Marriage,* Nothing Doing in London, London, 1968. Used by permission of Anthony Barnett. The book includes a diagram, an expanded dedication, notes, and an acknowledgment of a literary source in the poem "In memoria" by Giuseppe Ungaretti from *Vita d'un uomo,* Mondadori, Milan, 1969. "Celan," "Cloisters," "The Book of Mysteries," "Crossing" from *Blood Flow,* The Literary Supplement/Nothing Doing (formerly in London), London and Oslo, 1975. Used by permission of Anthony Barnett. Poems © 1979 Anthony Barnett.

ASA BENVENISTE: "The Alchemical Cupboard" from *Tree 1,* 1967. Used by permission of Asa Benveniste. Poem © 1979 Asa Benveniste.

RICHARD BURNS: "Angels," from *Angels,* Los, Cambridge, 1978, and Enitharmon. Used by permission of Richard Burns. "Mandelstam" Enitharmon. Used by permission of Richard Burns. Poems © 1979 Richard Burns.

RUTH FAINLIGHT: "Lilith," "God's Language," from *The Region's Violence,* Hutchinson of London, 1973. Used by permission of Ruth Fainlight. "The Hebrew Sibyl," "Sibyl of the Waters," Gehenna Press and Hutchinson, 1980. Used by permission of Ruth Fainlight. Poems © 1979 Ruth Fainlight.

ELAINE FEINSTEIN: "Against Winter," "Under Stone," "Dad," "Survivors" from *Some*

Unease and Angels, Selected Poems, Hutchinson of London, 1977. Used by permission of Elaine Feinstein. Poems © 1979 Elaine Feinstein.

MICHAEL HAMBURGER: "At Staufen" from *Real Estate,* Carcanet Press, 1977. Used by permission of Michael Hamburger. "The Search" from *Ownerless Earth,* Carcanet Press, 1973, and E. P. Dutton, 1973. Used by permission of Michael Hamburger. Poems © 1979 Michael Hamburger.

GAD HOLLANDER: "Axioms," "In Memoriam Paul Celan" from *European Judaism 1' 1977* and *1' 1978,* used by permission of Gad Hollander. "Argument Against Metaphor" from *The Wolly of Swot.* Used by permission of Gad Hollander. "Fugato" is previously unpublished. Used by permission of Gad Hollander. Poems © 1979 Gad Hollander.

LOTTE KRAMER: "Genesis" from *The Village Review,* Summer 1972. Used by permission of Lotte Kramer. Poem © 1979 Lotte Kramer.

FRANCIS LANDY: "The Princess Who Fled to the Castle," "Lament for Azazel," "Midrash on Hamlet," "Selichos" used by permission of Francis Landy. Poems © 1979 Francis Landy.

EMANUEL LITVINOFF: "If I Forget Thee" and "To T.S. Eliot" from *Notes for a Survivor,* Northern House, Newcastle, 1973. Used by permission of Emanuel Litvinoff. Poems © 1979 Emanuel Litvinoff.

TALI LOEWENTHAL: "Hebrew Script (Eight Poems)" from *Words,* North West London Chavura, 1972. Used by permission of Tali Loewenthal. Poems © 1979 Tali Loewenthal.

EDWARD LOWBURY: "Tree of Knowledge," "In the Old Jewish Cemetery, Prague, 1970" from *The Nightwatchman,* Chatto © Windus, London, 1974. Used by permission of Edward Lowbury. Poems © 1979 Edward Lowbury.

TOM LOWENSTEIN: "Noah in New England," "Nausicaa with Some Attendants," "Horizon Without Landscape" from *The Death of Mrs. Owl,* Anvil Press, London, 1977. Used by permission of Tom Lowenstein. Poems © 1979 Tom Lowenstein.

ASHER MENDELSSOHN: "Cordoba" used by permission of Asher Mendelssohn. Poem © 1979 Asher Mendelssohn.

JEREMY ROBSON: "The Departure" from *Thirty-three Poems,* Sidgwick and Jackson, 1964. Used by permission of Jeremy Robson. Poem © 1979 Jeremy Robson.

ISAAC ROSENBERG. All the poems included here are out of copyright. Acknowledgments are due to the publishers of Rosenberg: Chatto and Windus and Schocken Books.

ANTHONY RUDOLF: "Ashkelon," from *The Manifold Circle,* Carcanet Press, 1971. Used by permission of Anthony Rudolf. "Evening of the Rose," "Hands Up," "Prayer for Kafka and Ourselves," "Ancient of Days" are used by permission of Anthony Rudolf. "Dubrovnik Poem" from *The Same River Twice,* Carcanet Press, 1976. All poems from *After the Dream,* Cauldron Press, 1980. Used by permission of Anthony Rudolf. Poems © 1979 Anthony Rudolf.

JON SILKIN: "Death of a Son" from *The Peaceable Kingdom,* Chatto and Windus, 1954, and Heron Press, 1975. Used by permission of Jon Silkin. "The Coldness" from *The Re-ordering of the Stones,* Chatto and Windus, 1961. Used by permission of Jon Silkin. "A Word About Freedom and Identity in Tel Aviv" from *Amana Grass,* Chatto and Windus, 1971. Used by permission of Jon Silkin. "It Says" from *The Principle of Water,* Carcanet Press and Wild and Wooley, 1974. Used by permission of Jon Silkin. "Jerusalem" from *Poetry Review,* 1978, and Sceptre Press, 1977. Used by permission of Jon Silkin. "Resting Place" from *Sunday Times,* Jan. 15, 1978. Used by permission of Jon Silkin. Poems © 1979 Jon Silkin.

DANIEL WEISSBORT: "Murder of a Community" from *The Leaseholder,* Carcanet, 1971. Used by permission of Daniel Weissbort. "Walking Home at Night" from *In An Emergency,* Carcanet, 1972. Poems © 1979 Daniel Weissbort. Used by permission of Daniel Weissbort. "Anniversary" used by permission of Daniel Weissbort. Poem © 1979 Daniel Weissbort.

VOICES WITHIN THE ARK

Canada

LEONARD COHEN: "Story of Isaac" used by permission of Leonard Cohen. Poem © 1980 Leonard Cohen.

DEBORAH EIBEL: "Hagar to Ishmael," "The Kabbalist," "Freethinkers" used by permission of Deborah Eibel. Poems © 1979 Deborah Eibel.

PHYLLIS GOTLIEB: "The Morning Prayers of the Hasid, Rabbi Levi Yitzhok" used by permission of Phyllis Gotlieb. Poem © 1979 Phyllis Gotlieb.

A.M. KLEIN: "And in That Drowning Instant" from *The Collected Poems of A.M. Klein,* compiled by Miriam Waddington. Copyright © McGraw-Hill Ryerson, 1974. Used by permission.

IRVING LAYTON: "Jewish Main Street" used by permission of McClellend and Stewart, Ltd. Poem © 1979 Irving Layton.

SEYMOUR MAYNE: "In the First Cave," "Locusts of Silence," "Abraham Sutskever," "Yehuda Amichai," "Afternoon's Angel" used by permission of Seymour Mayne. Poems © 1979 Seymour Mayne.

SHARON NELSON: "Pedlar" used by permission of Sharon Nelson. Poem © 1979 Sharon Nelson.

JOSEPH SHERMAN: "Sarai" used by permission of Joseph Sherman. Poem © 1979 Joseph Sherman.

MIRIAM WADDINGTON: "The Survivors" from *The Glass Trumpet* used by permission of Miriam Waddington. "The Field of Night," "Desert Stone" from *Driving Home* by Miriam Waddington. Used by permission of Oxford University Press, Canada. Poems © 1979 by Miriam Waddington.

Israel

HENRY ABRAMOVITCH: "Psalm of the Jealous God" used by permission of Henry Abramovitch. Poem © 1979 Henry Abramovitch.

RUTH BEKER: "Don't Show Me" used by permission of Ruth Beker. Poem © 1979 Ruth Beker.

EDWARD CODISH: "Yetzer ha Ra," "A Juggle of Myrtle Twigs" used by permission of Edward Codish. Poems © 1979 Edward Codish.

DAVID ELLER: "To a God Unknown" used by permission of Ra'anan Eller. Poem © 1979 Ra'anan Eller.

RICHARD FLANTZ: "Shir Ma'alot/A Song of Degrees" used by permission of Richard Flantz. Poem © 1979 Richard Flantz.

WILLIAM FREEDMAN: "Benediction," "Formations" used by permission of William Freedman. Poems © 1979 William Freedman.

RIVKA FRIED: "Sabbath" used by permission of Rivka Fried. Poem © 1979 Rivka Fried.

ROBERT FRIEND: "The Practice of Absence," "Identity" used by permission of Robert Friend. Poems © 1979 Robert Friend.

SHIRLEY KAUFMAN: "Wonders" reprinted from *Gold Country* by Shirley Kaufman by permission of the University of Pittsburgh Press. © 1973 Shirley Kaufman. "Next Year, in Jerusalem," "Looking for Maimonides: Tiberias," "New Graveyard: Jerusalem" reprinted from *The Floor Keeps Turning* by Shirley Kaufman by permission of the University of Pittsburgh Press. © 1970 by the University of Pittsburgh Press. "Leah," "Starting Over," "Loving" used by permission of Shirley Kaufman. Poems © 1979 Shirley Kaufman.

GABRIEL LEVIN: "Adam's Death," "Ishmael," "Etude for Voice and Hand" used by permission of Gabriel Levin. Poems © 1979 Gabriel Levin.

MARSHA POMERANTZ: "Adam and Eve at the Garden Gate," "How to Reach the Moon" used by permission of Marsha Pomerantz. Poems © 1979 Marsha Pomerantz.

PAUL RABOFF: "Jars," "Reb Hanina" used by permission of Paul Raboff. Poems © 1979 Paul Raboff.

BETSY ROSENBERG: "Bird Song," "Unearthing" used by permission of Betsy Rosenberg. Poems © 1979 Betsy Rosenberg.

HAROLD SCHIMMEL: "Ancestors" used by permission of Harold Schimmel. Poem © 1979 Harold Schimmel.

MYRA GLAZER SCHOTZ: "The First Love Poem," "Thespian in Jerusalem," "Santa Caterina" used by permission of Myra Glazer Schotz. Poems © 1979 Myra Glazer Schotz.

MARK ELLIOTT SHAPIRO: "Dying Under a Fall of Stars" used by permission of Mark Elliott Shapiro. Poem © 1979 Mark Elliott Shapiro.

RICHARD SHERWIN: "Jacob's Winning" used by permission of Richard Sherwin. Poem © 1979 Richard Sherwin.

DENNIS SILK: "Guide to Jerusalem," "Matronita" used by permission of Dennis Silk. Poems © 1979 Dennis Silk.

AVNER STRAUSS: "The Hollow Flute," "Portrait of a Widow" used by permission of Avner Strauss. Poems © 1979 Avner Strauss.

Australia

NANCY KEESING: "Wandering Jews" used by permission of Nancy Keesing. Poem © 1979 Nancy Keesing.

DAVID MARTIN: "I Am a Jew" used by permission of David Martin. Poem © 1979 David Martin.

FAY ZWICKY: "The Chosen—Kalgoorlie, 1894" used by permission of Fay Zwicky. Poem © 1979 Fay Zwicky.

South Africa

SYDNEY CLOUTS: "Of Thomas Traherne and the Pebble Outside," "The Portrait of Prince Henry," "The Sleeper," "Firebowl" used by permission of Sydney Clouts. Poems © 1979 Sydney Clouts.

MANNIE HIRSCH: "Cry for a Disused Synagogue in Booysens" used by permission of Mannie Hirsch. Poem © 1979 Mannie Hirsch.

ALLAN KOLSKI HORVITZ: "King Saul," "The Radiance of Extinct Stars" used by permission of Allan Kolski Horvitz. Poems © 1979 Allan Kolski Horvitz.

JEAN LIPKIN: "Apocalypse" used by permission of Jean Lipkin. Poem © 1979 Jean Lipkin.

FAY LIPSHITZ: "Encounter in Jerusalem," "Judean Summer," "The Aleph Bet" used by permission of Fay Lipshitz. Poems © 1979 Fay Lipshitz.

Scotland

A. C. JACOBS: "Poem for My Grandfather," "Yiddish Poet," "Isaac," "Painting" from *The Proper Blessing*, The Menard Press, London, 1976. Used by permission of A. C. Jacobs. Poems © 1976 A. C. Jacobs.

Wales

DANNIE ABSE: "Song for Dov Shamir," "Tales of Shatz" from *Collected Poems 1948-1976,* Hutchinson of London, used by permission of Dannie Abse and Anthony Sheil Associates, Ltd. Poems © 1979 Dannie Abse.

India

NISSIM EZEKIEL: "Totem," "Lamentation," "How My Father Died" used by permission of Nissim Ezekiel. Poems © 1979 Nissim Ezekiel.

Sri Lanka

ANNE RANASINGHE: "Holocaust 1944," "Auschwitz from Colombo" used by permission of Anne Ranasinghe. Poems © 1979 Anne Ranasinghe.

IV. Other Languages

Amharic

YOSEF DAMANA BEN YESHAQ: "The Rusted Chain" used by permission of Ephraim Isaac. Translation © 1979 Ephraim Isaac.

Arabic

SHALOM KATAV: "Pleading Voices" used by permission of Yoffee Berkovitz. Translation © 1979 Yoffee Berkovitz.

SHMUEL MOREH: "The Tree of Hatred" used by permission of Shmuel Moreh. Translation © 1979 Shmuel Moreh. "Melody," "The Return" used by permission of Yoffee Berkovitz. Translations © 1979 Yoffee Berkovitz.

DAVID SEMAH: "Prostration," "Tomb" used by permission of Yoffee Berkovitz. Translations © 1979 Yoffee Berkovitz.

ANWAR SHAUL: "Mother," "To a Cactus Seller," "Prayers to Liberty" used by permission of Yoffee Berkovitz. Translations © 1979 Yoffee Berkovitz.

Czech

PAVEL FRIEDMANN: "The Butterfly" used by permission of Dennis Silk. Translation © 1979 Dennis Silk.

JIRI GOLD: "In the Cellars," "An Inhabited Emptiness" used by permission of Daniel Weissbort. Translations © 1979 Daniel Weissbort.

FRANTISEK GOTTLIEB: "Between Life and Death," "Just a While" used by permission of Ewald Osers. Translations © 1979 Ewald Osers.

DAGMAR HILAROVÁ: "Questions" used by permission of Ewald Osers. Translation © 1979 Ewald Osers.

Dutch

JAKOV DE HAAN: "Unity," "All is God's," "God's Gifts," "Hanukah," "Sabbath" used by permission of David Soetendorp. Translations © 1979 David Soetendorp.

JUDITH HERZBERG: "On the Death of Sylvia Plath," "Yiddish," "The Voice," "Commentaries on the Song of Songs," "Kinneret," "Nearer" used by permission of Judith Herzberg. Translations © 1979 Judith Herzberg and Shirley Kaufman.

LEO VROMAN: "Old Miniatures," "The River" used by permission of Leo Vroman. Poems © 1979 Leo Vroman.

French

CHARLES DOBZYNSKI: "Memory Air," "Zealot Without a Face," "The Never Again" used by permission of Anita Barrows. Translations © 1979 Anita Barrows. "The Fable Merchant" used by permission of Charles Guenther. Translation © 1979 Charles Guenther.

EDMOND FLEG: "The Dead Cities Speak to the Living Cities" used by permission of Anthony Rudolf. Translation © 1979 Anthony Rudolf.

BENJAMIN FONDANE: "Lullaby for an Emigrant," used with permission of Keith Bosley. Translations © 1979 Keith Bosley. "Hertza," "Plain Song" used with permission of Willis Barnstone. Translations © 1979 Willis Barnstone. "By the Waters of Babylon," "The Wandering Jew" used with permission of Edouard Roditi.

YVAN GOLL: "Clandestine Work," "Neïla" used by permission of Anthony Rudolf. Translations © 1979 Anthony Rudolf.

EDMOND JABÈS: "The Condemned" used by permission of Jack Hirschman. Translation © 1979 Jack Hirschman. "Song of the Last Jewish Child," "Song of the Trees of the Black Forest," "A Circular Cry," "Song," "The Pulverized Screen," "Water" used by permission of Anthony Rudolf. Translations © 1979 Anthony Rudolf. "The Book Rises Out of the Fire" from *The Book of Questions,* translated by Rosmarie Waldrop, Wesleyan University Press. Used by permission of Rosmarie Waldrop. Translation © 1976 Rosmarie Waldrop.

GUSTAVE KAHN: "The Temple," "The Word" used by permission of Edouard Roditi. Translations © 1979 Edouard Roditi.

JOSEPH MILBAUER: "Interior," "Paris by Night" used by permission of Edouard Roditi. Translations © 1979 Edouard Roditi.

PIERRE MORHANGE: "Lullaby in Auschwitz," "Jew," "Salomon" used by permission of Edouard Roditi. Translations © 1979 Edouard Roditi.

SHLOMO REICH: "The Golem," "The Windmill of Evening," "The Vigil," "A Tribe Searching" used by permission of Shlomo Reich. Translations © 1979 Shlomo Reich.

RYVEL: "The Pilgrimage to Testour" used by permission of Edouard Roditi. Translation © 1979 Edouard Roditi.

DAVID SCHEINERT: "The Drunken Stones of Prague," "The Stone and the Blade of Grass in the Warsaw Ghetto" used by permission of Edouard Roditi. Translations © 1979 Edouard Roditi.

ANDRÉ SPIRE: "Hear, O Israel!" "The Ancient Law," "Pogroms" reprinted by permission of Stanley Burnshaw from *Andre Spire and His Poetry,* Phila., 1933. "Nudities" reprinted by permission of Stanley Burnshaw from *In The Terrified Radiance,* Braziller, 1972. Translations © 1933 and 1972 Stanley Burnshaw. "Poetics" used by permission of Edouard Roditi. Translation © 1979 Edouard Roditi.

TRISTAN TZARA: "Evening," "Mothers" used by permission of Willis Barnstone. Translations © 1979 Willis Barnstone.

CLAUDE VIGÉE: "The Tree of Death," "The Struggle with the Angel," "House of the Living," "Light of Judea" used by permission of Claude Vigée. Translations © 1979 Claude Vigée. "The Phoenix of Mozart," "Every Land Is Exile," "Destiny of the Poet," "Song of Occident," "The Wanderer," "Poetry" used by permission of Anthony Rudolf. Translations © 1979 Anthony Rudolf. "The Wanderer" and "Song of Occident" reprinted from *The Jewish Quarterly.*

ILARIE VORONCA: "The Quick and the Dead," "The Seven-League Boots" used by permission of Willis Barnstone. Translations © 1979 Willis Barnstone.

JEAN WAHL: "Decayed Time," "A Lean Day in a Convict's Suit," "Prayer of Little Hope," "Evening in the Walls" used by permission of Charles Guenther. Translations © 1979 Charles Guenther.

German

ROSE AUSLÄNDER: "My Nightingale," "Father," "Jerusalem," "Passover," "Hasidic Jew from Sadagora," "Phoenix," "In Chagall's Village," "The Lamed-Vov" used by permission of Ewald Osers. Translations © 1979 Ewald Osers.

RICHARD BEER-HOFMANN: "Lullaby for Miriam" used by permission of Jonathan Griffin. Translation © 1979 Jonathan Griffin.

ILSE BLUMENTHAL-WEISS: "A Jewish Child Prays to Jesus" used by permission of Erna Baber Rosenfeld. Translation © 1979 Erna Baber Rosenfeld.

MARTIN BUBER: "I Consider the Tree" used by permission of Howard Schwartz. Translation © 1979 Howard Schwartz. "The Fiddler" used by permission of Henry Abramovitch. Translation © 1979 Henry Abramovitch.

PAUL CELAN: "Psalm," "In Prague," "Death Fugue," "Ash-Glory," "Cello Entry," "In Egypt," "Tenebrae," "Zürich, zum Storchen" reprinted from *Speech Grille,* Dutton, 1970 by permission of Joachim Neugroschel. Translations © 1970 Joachim Neugroschel. "Hut Window," "Just Think," "A Speck of Sand," "Turn Blind," "Over Three Nipple-Stones," "Corona" used by permission of Joachim Neugroschel. Translations © 1979 Joachim Neugroschel.

HILDE DOMIN: "Catalogue," "Cologne," "Dreamwater" used by permission of Tudor Morris. Translations © 1979 Tudor Morris.

ALFRED GRÜNEWALD: "The Lamp Now Flickers" used by permission of Edouard Roditi. Translation © 1979 Edouard Roditi.

JAKOV VAN HODDIS: "End of the World" used by permission of Edouard Roditi. Translation © 1979 Edouard Roditi. "The Air Vision," "Tohub" used by permission of Charles Guenther. Translations © 1979 Charles Guenther.

ALFRED KITTNER: "Old Jewish Cemetery in Worms," "Blue Owl Song" used by permission of Herbert Kuhner. Translations © 1979 Herbert Kuhner.

ALMA JOHANNA KOENIG: "Intimations" used by permission of Edouard Roditi. Translation © 1979 Edouard Roditi.

GERTRUD KOLMAR: "The Woman Poet," "The Jewish Woman," "Sea-Monster" reprinted from *Dark Soliloquy: The Selected Poems of Gertrud Kolmar,* translated by Henry A. Smith, © 1977 The Seabury Press, New York. Used by permission.

ELSE LASKER-SCHÜLER: "Abraham and Isaac," "Hagar and Ishmael," "Homesickness," "Abel," "Moses and Joshua," "Pharaoh and Joseph," "Jacob," "Saul" used by permission of Joachim Neugroschel. Translations © 1979 Joachim Neugroschel. "Lord, Listen" used by permission of Edouard Roditi. Translation © 1979 Edouard Roditi.

ALFRED LICHTENSTEIN: "The Journey to the Insane Asylum," "Repose" used by permission of Mary Zilzer. Translations © 1979 Mary Zilzer.

CONNY HANNES MEYER: "Of the Beloved Caravan," "The Beast That Rode the Unicorn" used by permission of Herbert Kuhner. Translations © 1979 Herbert Kuhner.

ALFRED MOMBERT: "The Chimera" used by permission of Erna Baber Rosenfeld. Translation © 1978 Erna Baber Rosenfeld.

JOSEPH ROTH: "Ahasuerus" used by permission of Erna Baber Rosenfeld. Translation © 1979 Erna Baber Rosenfeld.

NELLY SACHS: "Burning Sand of Sinai," "Hasidim Dance," "O the Chimneys," "O Night of the Crying Children," "What Secret Desires of the Blood," "To You Building the New House," "One Chord" used by permission of Keith Bosley. Translations © 1979 Keith Bosley. "Chorus of the Rescued" used by permission of Harry Zohn. Translation © 1979 Harry Zohn.

HANS SAHL: "Memo" used by permission of Edouard Roditi. Translation © 1979 Edouard Roditi. "Greeting from a Distance" used by permission of Erna Baber Rosenfeld. Translation © 1979 Erna Baber Rosenfeld.

GERSHOM SCHOLEM: "The Trial" used by permission of Jonathan Griffin. Translation © 1979 Jonathan Griffin.

THOMAS SESSLER: "When the Day," "You Move Forward," "Burnt Debris" used by permission of Herbert Kuhner. Translations © 1979 Herbert Kuhner.

HUGO SONNENSCHEIN: "In the Open Fields," "In the Ghetto" used by permission of Edouard Roditi. Translations © 1979 Edouard Roditi.

FRIEDRICH TORBERG: "Seder, 1944," "Amalek" used by permission of Erna Baber Rosenfeld. Translations © 1979 Erna Baber Rosenfeld.

ALFRED WOLFENSTEIN: "Exodus, 1940" used by permission of Erna Baber Rosenfeld. Translation © 1979 Erna Baber Rosenfeld.

KARL WOLFSKEHL: "Shekhina," "From Mount Nebo" used by permission of Erna Baber Rosenfeld. Translations © 1979 Erna Baber Rosenfeld. "We Go" used by permission of Harry Zohn. Translation © 1979 Harry Zohn.

Greek

JOSEPH ELIYIA: "Rebecca," "Dream," "Slender Maid," "Your Passing, Fleet Passing," "Epilogue" used by permission of Rae Dalven. Translations © 1979 Rae Dalven.

Hungarian

MILAN FUEST: "Moses' Account" used by permission of André Ungar. Translation © 1979 André Ungar.

AGNES GERGELY: "Birth of a Country," "Desert," "Conjuration" used by permission of Emery George. Translations © 1979 Emery George.

ANNA HAJNAL: "Dead Girl," "Tree to Flute" used by permission of Jascha Kessler. Translations © 1979 Jascha Kessler.

EUGENE HEIMLER: "Psalm" reprinted from *The Storm* by Eugene Heimler, The Menard Press, 1976, by permission of Eugene Heimler. Translation © 1976 Eugene Heimler and Anthony Rudolf. "After an Eclipse of the Sun" used by permission of Keith Bosley and Peter Sherwood. Translation © 1979 Keith Bosley and Peter Sherwood.

JOZSEF KISS: "The New Ahasuerus" used by permission of André Ungar. Translation © 1979 André Ungar.

EMIL MAKAI: "The Comet" used by permission of André Ungar. Translation © 1979 André Ungar.

OTTO ORBAN: "Hymn," "Computer," "Ray" used by permission of Emery George. Translations © 1979 Emery George.

GYORGY RABA: "Message," "Conversation" used by permission of Jascha Kessler. Translations © 1979 Jascha Kessler.

MIKLÓS RADNÓTI: "Seventh Eclogue," "Letter to My Wife," "Forced March," "Picture

Postcards" reprinted from Miklós Radnóti, *Subway Stops: Fifty Poems*, trs. and ed. by Emery George. Used by permission of Ardis Publishers. Translations © 1977 Ardis Publishers. "Song," "I Hid You," "Root," "Metaphors," "In Your Arms," "Fragment" from *Clouded Sky*. Used by permission of Stephen Berg. Translations © 1979 Steven Polgar, Stephen Berg and S. J. Marks. First published by Harper and Row.

JUDIT TÓTH: "Remembering," "The Southeast Ramparts of the Seine," "Wildfire" used by permission of Emery George. Translations © 1979 Emery George.

ISTVAN VÁS: "What Is Left?" "Catacombs," "Tambour," "Just This" used by permission of Emery George. Translations © 1979 Emery George.

Italian

EDITH BRUCK: "Childhood," "Let's Talk, Mother," "Equality, Father!" "Sister Zahava," "Go, Then," "Why Would I Have Survived?" used by permission of Anita Barrows. Translations © 1979 Anita Barrows.

ALDO CAMERINO: "Night," "Calm," "Fear," "Recluse," "For a Voice That is Singing," "Mother" used by permission of Anita Barrows. Translations © 1979 Anita Barrows.

FRANCO FORTINI: "For Our Soldiers Who Fell in Russia," "The Gutter," "In Memoriam I," "In Memoriam II" used by permission of Ruth Feldman. Translations © 1979 Ruth Feldman.

PRIMO LEVI: "Lilith," "Shema," "For Adolf Eichmann" reprinted from *Shema* by Primo Levi, translated by Ruth Feldman and Brian Swann, The Menard Press, London, 1976. Used by permission of Ruth Feldman and Brian Swann. Translations © 1976 Ruth Feldman and Brian Swann.

ROSSANA OMBRES: "Bella and the Golem" used by permission of Edgar Pauk. Translation © 1979 Edgar Pauk.

UMBERTO SABA: "Sleepless on a Summer Night" used by permission of Keith Bosley. Translation © 1979 Keith Bosley. "The Goat," "Three Streets" used by permission of Anita Barrows. Translations © 1979 Anita Barrows.

Judeo-Romanesque

CRESCENZO DEL MONTE: "A Roman Roman," "Those Zionists," "One Thing to Take, Another to Keep" used by permission of Barbara Garvin. Translations © 1979 Barbara Garvin.

Judezmo

ISAAC DE BOTTON: "Desire" used by permission of Stephen Levy. Translation © 1979 Stephen Levy.

RACHAEL CASTELETE: "When I Came to London" used by permission of Stephen Levy. Translation © 1979 Stephen Levy.

CLARISSE NICOÏDSKI: "Eyes," "Mouth," "Breaking Off from Waiting," "Open Earth," "Remembering" used by permission of Stephen Levy. Translations © 1979 Stephen Levy.

Polish

HENRYK GRYNBERG: "Anti-Nostalgia," "Poplars," "The Dead Sea," "Listening to Confucius" used by permission of Isaac Komem. Translations © 1979 Isaac Komem.

MIECZYSLAW JASTRUN: "The Jews" used by permission of Isaac Komem. Translation © 1979 Isaac Komem.

EWA LIPSKA: "If God Exists," "Wedding," "The Cock," "The Flood" used by permission of Peter Jay. Translations © 1979 Peter Jay and Geri Lipschultz.

ANTONI SLONIMSKI: "Elegy," "Conrad," "Conversation with a Countryman," "Jerusalem" used by permission of Isaac Komem. Translations © 1979 Isaac Komem.

JULIAN TUWIM: "The Gypsy Bible," "Mother," "Jewboy," "Lodgers" used by permission of Isaac Komem. Translations © 1979 Isaac Komem.

ALEKSANDER WAT: "Willows in Alma-Ata," "There Is No Place" used by permission of Isaac Komem. Translations © 1979 Isaac Komem.

ADAM WAZYK: "Ars Poetica," "Hotel," "Nike" used by permission of Isaac Komem. Translations © 1979 Isaac Komem.

JOZEF WITTLIN: "To the Jews in Poland," "St. Francis of Assisi and the Miserable Jews," "On the Jewish Day of Judgment in the Year 1942 (5703)," "A Hymn About a Spoonful of Soup" used by permission of Isaac Komem. Translations © 1979 Isaac Komem.

STANISLAW WYGODSKI: "Voyage," "Winter Journey," "Those Betrayed at Dawn," "Going to the North" used by permission of Isaac Komem. Translations © 1979 Isaac Komem.

Romanian

MARIA BANUS: "Eighteen," "Gift Hour" used by permission of Willis Barnstone. Translations © 1979 Willis Barnstone.

NINA CASSIAN: "Blood," "Cripples," "Self-Portrait," "All Night Long" used by permission of Herbert Kuhner. Translations © 1979 Herbert Kuhner. "Like Gulliver" used by permission of Willis Barnstone. Translation © 1979 Willis Barnstone.

VERONICA PORUMBACU: "Of Autumn" used by permission of Willis Barnstone. Translation © 1979 Willis Barnstone.

Russian

MARGARITA ALIGER: "To a Portrait of Lermontov," "Two" "House in Meudon" used by permission of Elaine Feinstein. Translations © 1979 Elaine Feinstein.

JOSEPH BRODSKY: "A Jewish Cemetery Near Leningrad," "Pilgrims," "Verses on Accepting the World," "Etude," "Monument to Pushkin" used by permission of Keith Bosley. Translations © 1979 Keith Bosley. "To a Tyrant," "Soho" used by permission of Alan Meyers. Translations © 1979 Alan Meyers.

EVA BRUDNE: "Memento Vivendi," "A Farewell Ballad of Poppies" used by permission of Eva Brudne. Translation © 1979 Eva Brudne.

SASHA CHORNY: "A Vilna Puzzle" used by permission of Daniel Weissbort. Translations © 1979 Daniel Weissbort.

DOVID KNUT: "Walking Along the Sea of Galilee," "A Woman from the Book of Genesis" used by permission of John Glad. Translations © 1979 John Glad. "Haifa, "Safed," "Rosh Pina" used by permission of Daniel Weissbort. Translations © 1979 Daniel Weissbort.

NAUM KORZHAVIN: "Children of Auschwitz" used by permission of Daniel Weissbort. Translation © 1979 Daniel Weissbort.

ALEKSANDR KUSHNER: "To Boris Pasternak" used by permission of Keith Bosley. Translation © 1979 Keith Bosley.

LEV MAK: "Eden," "The Flood" used by permission of Daniel Weissbort. Translations © 1979 Daniel Weissbort. "Prayer" used by permission of Dan Jaffe. Translation © 1979 Dan Jaffe.

VOICES WITHIN THE ARK

OSIP MANDELSTAM: "This Night," "Like a Young Levite" used by permission of Daniel Weissbort. Translations © 1979 Daniel Weissbort. "Concert at the Station," "Twilight of Freedom" used by permission of Andrew Glaze. Translations © 1979 Andrew Glaze. "Bitter Bread," "A Reed" reprinted from *Osip Mandelstam*, poems chosen and translated by James Greene (Paul Elek, 1977). Used by permission of James Greene. Translation © 1977 James Greene.

SAMUEL MARSHAK: "The Little House in Lithuania" used by permission of Daniel Weissbort. Translation © 1979 Daniel Weissbort.

YUNNA MORITZ: "In Memory of Francois Rabelais," "Whiteness," "Snow-Girl" used by permission of Elaine Feinstein. Translations © 1979 Elaine Feinstein.

LEV OZEROV: "Babi Yar" used by permission of Daniel Weissbort. Translation © 1979 Daniel Weissbort.

ILYA RUBIN: "Poem from The Revolution," "No Sense Grieving," "Escape," "Slow Oxen," "Handful of Ashes" used by permission of Linda Zisquit. Translations © 1979 Linda Zisquit.

BORIS SLUTSKY: "God," "How They Killed My Grandmother," "Dreams of Auschwitz," "Burnt" used by permission of Daniel Weissbort. Translations © 1979 Daniel Weissbort.

ANATOLY STEIGER: "An Ancient Custom," "Words from the Window of a Railway Car" used by permission of John Glad. Translations © 1979 John Glad.

Serbo-Croat

MONNY DE BOULLY: "Beyond Memory" used by permission of Aleksander Nejgebauer. Translation © 1979 Aleksander Nejgebauer.

STANISLAV VINAVER: "The European Light," "An Inscription," "A Cathedral" used by permission of Vasa D. Mihailovich. Translations © 1979 Vasa D. Mihailovich.

Slovak

SUSANNAH FRIED: "Winter Day," "To My Father," "Scraps" used by permission of Anthony Rudolf. Translations © 1979 Anthony Rudolf.

Slovene

TOMAŽ SALAMUN: "Air," "Eclipse" used by permission of Aleksander Nejgebauer. Translations © 1979 Aleksander Nejgebauer.

Spanish

JUAN GELMAN: "Customs," "The Knife," "The Stranger" used by permission of Yishai Tobin. Translations © 1979 Yishai Tobin.

ISAAC GOLDEMBERG: "Bar Mitzvah," "The Jews in Hell" used by permission of David Unger. Translations © 1979 David Unger.

JOSÉ ISAACSON: "Pre-positions" used by permission of Yishai Tobin. Translation © 1979 Yishai Tobin.

NOÉ JITRIK: "Addio a la Mamma" used by permission of Yishai Tobin. Translation © 1979 Yishai Tobin.

RUBEN KANALENSTEIN: "Jerusalem" used by permission of Ruben Kanalenstein and Yishai Tobin. Translation © 1979 Yishai Tobin.

JOSÉ KOZER: "Cleaning Day," "The Store in Havana" used by permission of David Unger.

Translations © 1979 David Unger. "My Father, Who's Still Alive" used by permission of Jorge Guitart. Translation © 1979 Jorge Guitart.

ALEJANDRA PIZARNIK: "The Tree of Diana," "Privilege," "Apart from Oneself," "Vertigos or Contemplation of Something That Is Over" used by permission of Yishai Tobin. Translations © 1979 Yishai Tobin. "The Mask and the Poem," "Dawn," "Who Will Stop His Hand from Giving Warmth" used by permission of Alina Rivero. Translations © 1979 Alina Rivero.

JORGE PLESCOFF: "The Ladder Has No Steps," "Tongues of Fire," "Violins in Repose," "Ourobouros" used by permission of Jorge Plescoff and Yishai Tobin. Translations © 1979 Yishai Tobin.

DAVID ROSENMANN-TAUB: "Sabbath," "To a Young Girl," "Prelude," "Reconciliation," "Elegy and Kaddish," "Moral Ode" used by permission of David Rosenmann-Taub and Charles Guenther. Translations © 1979 Charles Guenther.

MARIO SATZ: "Fish," "Coconut," "Lemon" used by permission of Willis Barnstone and Mario Satz. Translations © 1979 Willis Barnstone.

CESAR TIEMPO: "The Jewish Cemetery" used by permission of Angela McEwan-Alvarado. Translation © 1979 Angela McEwan-Alvarado.

Swedish

OSCAR LEVERTIN: "At the Jewish Cemetery in Prague" and "Solomon and Morolph, Their Last Encounter" used by permission of Richard Burns. Translations © 1980 Richard Burns.

Turkish

MUSA MORIS FARHI: "Smile at Me," "Paths to God," "Who Says," "God and Nature," "Thirst" used by permission of Moris Farhi. Translations © 1979 Moris Farhi.

JOSEF HABIB GEREZ: "We Are Acrobats," "We Fooled Ourselves," "Call from the Afterworld" used by permission of Anthony Rudolf and Moris Farhi. Translations © 1979 Anthony Rudolf and Moris Farhi.

Index of Poets

Aaronson, Lazarus, 839
Abramovitch, Henry, 772
Abse, Dannie, 397, 398, 822-825
Akhmatova, 845
Aleichem, Sholem, 237
Aliger, Margarita, 1084-1087
Alquit, B., 241, 243-244
Alterman, Nathan, 9-10, 13, 21-27
Alvarez, A., 398, 681-683
Amichai, Yehuda, 10*n*, 12, 13-14, 27-37, 397
Amir, Aharon, 37
Aphek, Edna, 38-39
Askenazy, Ludvik, 861
Asya, 244-247
Auden, W. H., 15
Auerbach, Ephraim, 247-248
Ausländer, Rose, 926-931
Auster, Paul, 388, 401-404

Bachar, Eli, 40-42
Banus, Maria, 1079-1080
Barnett, Anthony, 400, 684-687
Barnstone, Willis, 388-389, 405-407
Barrows, Anita, 390, 408-412
Bassani, Giorgio, 847
Bat-Miriam, Yocheved, 9, 42-43
Bavli, Hillel, 6
Be'er, Hayim, 18, 43-46
Beer-Hofmann, Richard, 833-834, 932
Beker, Ruth, 772-773
Bell, Marvin, 383, 384, 413-414
Belli, Gioachino, 843
Bental, Anath, 47-48
Benveniste, Asa, 397, 688-693
ben Yeshaq, Yosef Damana, 849-850
Ben-Yitzhak, Avraham, 8-9, 10, 48-51
Berg, Stephen, 384, 385, 415-421
Bernhardt, Suzanne, 388, 421-423
Bialik, Hayim Nachman, 3-4, 5, 11, 13, 51-60
Biton, Erez, 19, 61-62
Blecher, Marcel, 845
Bloch, Chana, 390, 423-426
Bloom, Harold, 382
Blumenthal-Weiss, Ilse, 835-836, 933
Bluwstein, Rachel. *See* Rachel
Boimwall, Rachel, 248-250
Bokher, Eliohu, 236
Bomze, Nahum, 250-251
Boraisho, Menahem, 241
Borchardt, Rudolph, 834
Borenstein, Emily, 390, 427
Botton, Isaac de, 842, 1045
Brodsky, Joseph, 1087-1093
Brody, Alter, 378, 381-382, 427-433
Bruck, Edith, 1021-1027
Brudne, Eva, 1093-1095
Buber, Martin, 933-935
Burns, Richard, 400, 693-696
Burnshaw, Stanley, 382, 433-436

Cahan, Yakov, 6
Camerino, Aldo, 1028-1031
Carmi, T., 16, 63-68
Cassian, Nina, 1080-1082
Castelete, Rachael, 1045-1046
Castro, Michael, 386, 436-441
Celan, Paul, 19, 388, 390, 400, 834, 839, 845, 848, 935-946
Chaet, Eric, 441-442
Chalfi,Abraham, 68-69
Chalfi, Raquel, 69-71
Chernin, Kim, 390, 443
Chorny, Sasha, 1096
Clouts, Sydney, 393, 810-812
Codish, Edward, 774-775
Cohen, Leonard, 391, 750-751
Cohen, Shalom, 3
Cohen, Shlomit, 72-73
Creeley, Robert, 381

Dallman, Elaine, 390, 443-444
Day, Lucille, 390, 444-446
de Boully, Monny, 837, 1129-1130
del Monte, Crescenzo, 843, 844, 1043-1044
Desnos, Robert, 385
Dobzynski, Charles, 877-880
Domin, Hilde, 946-947
Dor, Moshe, 17, 73-76
Drachler, Rose, 382-383, 446-452

Dropkin, Celia, 252
Duncan, Robert, 381

Efros, Israel, 6
Ehrenstein, Alfred, 834
Eibel, Deborah, 391, 752-754
Eichenrand, Lazer, 252-254
Eigner, Larry, 388, 452-453
Eldan, Anadad, 12, 17, 77-78
Eliot, T. S., 15, 382, 397, 840
Eliyia, Joseph, 841, 843, 987-990
Eller, David, 776
Ettinger, Shloyme, 237
Ezekiel, Nissim, 393, 826-827
Ezra, Ibn, 14

Fainlight, Ruth, 398, 697-700
Falk, Marcia, 380, 389, 390, 454-456
Farhi, Musa Moris, 841, 1168-1170
Feinstein, Elaine, 398, 700-703
Feinstein, M., 6
Feldman, Irving, 382, 456-458
Feldman, Ruth, 387, 459
Fichman, Jakov, 5, 78-80
Finkel, Donald, 383, 384, 387, 460-467
Firestone, Laya, 390, 467-469
Fischer, Otakar, 862
Fishman, Rachel, 242, 254-256
Flantz, Richard, 777
Fleg, Edmond, 848, 880-881
Fondane, Benjamin, 845, 881-887
Fortini, Franco, 1032-1033
Franck, Henri, 848
Freedman, William, 778-779
Fried, Rivka, 779
Fried, Susannah, 1134-1136
Friedlaender, Salomo. *See* Mynona
Friedmann, Pavel, 863
Friend, Robert, 780-781
Frug, Sh., 237
Fuest, Milan, 991

Gabirol, Ibn, 14
Gebirtig, Mordecai, 237
Gelman, Juan, 1139-1140
George, Stefan, 833, 834
Gerez, Jozef Habib, 841, 1170-1172
Gergely, Agnes, 991-994
Gilboa, Amir, 11-12, 18*n*, 80-85
Gilead, Zerubavel, 18, 86-88
Ginsberg, Allen, 385-386, 469-473
Glanz-Leyeles, Abraham, 241, 256-258
Glatstein, Jacob, 16, 241, 258-267
Glazer, Joseph, 473-474
Gold, Jiri, 863-865
Goldbarth, Albert, 474-475
Goldberg, Leah, 9, 10, 89-92
Goldemberg, Isaac, 847, 1141-1142
Goll, Claire, 834
Goll, Yvan, 834, 835, 888-892
Gordon, Judah Leib, 3
Gotlieb, Phyllis, 391, 755-758
Gottlieb, Frantisek, 866
Gottlieb, Lynn, 476
Graves, Robert, 387
Greenberg, Uri Zvi, 10-11, 92-96, 396
Gregor, Arthur, 382, 477-479
Gross, Naftali, 270
Grossman, Allen, 387, 479-480
Grossman, Martin, 390, 480-481
Grünewald, Alfred, 836, 948
Grynberg, Henryk, 1053-1057
Gurevitch, Zali, 96-97
Guri, Haim, 12-13, 18*n*, 98-103

Haan, Jakov de, 836, 868-869
HaCohen, Adam, 3
Hajnal, Anna, 994-995
Halevi, Yehda, 14
Halkin, Shimon, 6, 16-17, 104-105
Halpern, Moishe Leib, 238, 270-277
Hamburger, Michael, 397, 398, 703-706
Hameiri, Avigdor, 6
Hanagid, Shmuel, 14
Harkavi, Hedva, 18, 106-107
Hecht, Anthony, 382, 481-482
Heimler, Eugene, 995-998
Heine, Heinrich, 833, 834, 843
Herbert, Zbigniew, 383
Herzberg, Judith, 836, 869-872
Hilarová, Dagmar, 867
Hirsch, Mannie, 392, 813
Hirschman, Jack, 386, 387, 388, 482-487
Hoddis, Jakov van, 834, 949-950
Hofmannsthal, Hugo von, 833
Hofstein, David, 240
Hollander, Gad, 400, 707-710
Hollander, John, 382, 487-489
Holtz, Barry, 389, 489-490
Horvitz, Allan Kolski, 392, 814-815
Husid, Mordechai, 278-279
Huss, Avraham, 12, 108-110

Ignatow, David, 382, 491-493
Isaacson, José, 1143-1144
Jabès, Edmond, 388, 839-840, 848, 892-900
Jacob, Max, 839
Jacobs, A. C., 398-399, 818-821
Jaffe, Dan, 390, 493-495

Jastrun, Mieczyslaw, 1057-1058
Jitrik, Noé, 1144-1146

Kafka, Franz, 836
Kahn, Gustave, 832, 833, 848, 901-901
Kamenetz, Rodger, 386, 495-497
Kaminsky, Marc, 390, 497-498
Kanalenstein, Ruben, 1146-1149
Kanik, Orhan Veli, 841
Karni, Yehuda, 5-6, 13, 111-112
Katav, Shalom, 851-852
Kaufman, Shirley, 392, 782-787
Keesing, Nancy, 393, 804-806
Kessler, Jascha, 387, 498-499
Khodasievitch, 845
Kiss, Jozsef, 998-999
Kittner, Alfred, 951-953
Klein, A. M., 391, 758-759
Knut, Dovid, 1096-1102
Koenig, Alma Johanna, 834, 835, 836, 953
Kolmar, Gertrud, 835, 954-957
Kook, Rav Abraham Isaac, 6, 113-114
Korn, Rachel, 239-240, 279-286, 391
Korzhavin, Naum, 1102-1103
Kovner, Abba, 11, 12, 114-117
Kozer, José, 847, 1149-1151
Kramer, Lotte, 398, 710
Kulbak, Moishe, 239, 240, 286-290
Kushner, Aleksandr, 1103-1104
Kwitko, Leib, 291-292

Lachman, Sol, 390, 499-500
Lamdan, Yitzhak, 8, 118-119
Landau, Zishe, 238, 292-295
Landy, Francis, 400, 711-714
Langer, Jiri Mordecai, 119-120
Lasker-Schüler, Else, 834-835, 957-962
Layton, Irving, 391, 560
Lebenson, Adam H., 3
Lebenson, Micha J., 3
Lee, Rena, 121
Lefcowitz, Barbara F., 385, 500-504
Leib, Mani, 238, 240, 295-298
Leivick, H., 238, 241, 299-301
Lenowitz, Harris, 386, 504-505
Lenski, Hayim, 6, 13, 122-123
Lesmian, 837
Letteris, Meir, 3
Levertin, Oscar, 1166-1167
Levi, Primo, 387, 847, 1034-1036
Levin, Gabriel, 392, 787-789
Levine, Molly Myerowitz, 390, 506-508
Levine, Philip, 383-384, 508-520
Levinson, Shlomo, 3
Levy, Stephen, 389, 520-522
Lichtenstein, Alfred, 834, 962-963
Lipkin, Jean, 815-816
Lipshitz, Fay, 816-817
Lipska, Ewa, 1058-1061
Lisle, Leconte de, 833
Lissitsky, Ephraim, 6
Litvinoff, Emanuel, 397, 714-716
Litwack, Susan, 390, 522-526
Locker, Malka, 301-302
Loewenthal, Tali, 400, 717-718
Lowbury, Edward, 397, 398, 719-721
Lowenstein, Tom, 400, 722-723
Luzzato, Efraim, 3

Mak, Lev, 1105-1107
Makai, Emil, 1000-1001
Mandelstam, Osip, 400, 837, 839, 844, 845, 1107-1111
Manger-Itzik, 241, 302-312
Marcus, Mordecai, 526-527
Margolin, Anna, 312-315
Markish, Peretz, 239, 240, 241, 316
Marshak, Samuel, 1111-1112
Martin, David, 393, 807
Mayne, Seymour, 391, 760-764
Megged, Matti, 18-19, 123-126
Meltzer, David, 386, 387-388, 527-537
Mendelssohn, Asher, 400, 724-725
Mendès, Catulle, 832, 833
Mernit, Susan, 537-539
Metz, Jerred, 390, 539-542
Meyer, Conny Hannes, 963-965
Meyers, Bert, 383, 384, 542-544
Mezey, Robert, 383, 384, 544-553
Michaelis, Hanny, 872-873
Mikhaël, Ephraim, 832, 833
Milbauer, Joseph, 902-903
Mitchell, Stephen, 380, 389, 554-556
Molodovsky, Kadya, 240, 317-319
Mombert, Alfred, 833, 966
Montale, 847
Moreh, Shmuel, 841, 852-856
Morhange, Pierre, 904-905
Moritz, Yunna, 1113-1115
Moss, Howard, 382, 556-557
Moss, Stanley, 557-561
Myers, Jack, 380, 561-562
Mynona, 834

Naggid, Hayim, 18, 19, 126-128
Naigreshel, Mendel, 320-321
Neidus, Leib, 321-322
Nelson, Sharon, 391, 765-766
Neruda, Pablo, 383

Neugroschel, Joachim, 390, 562-564
Nicoïdski, Clarisse, 842, 1046-1052
Norvig, Gerda, 380, 390, 564-567

Olson, Charles, 368
Ombres, Rossana, 1036-1039
Oppen, George, 381, 398, 567-573
Orban, Otto, 1001-1003
Ozerov, Lev, 1116-1120
Ozick, Cynthia, 389, 573-575

Pacernick, Gary, 380, 576
Pagis, Dan, 11, 12, 13, 17, 128-133
Pastan, Linda, 384, 385, 577-579
Pasternak, Boris, 844, 845
Peretz, I.L., 237
Perkoff, Stuart A., 386, 579-581
Pillen, William, 382, 383, 581-588
Pincas, Israel, 134
Pizarnik, Alejandra, 1151-1155
Plescoff, Jorge, 1156, 1158
Plutzik, Hyam, 588-590
Pomerantz, Berl, 6, 135-136, 838
Pomerantz, Marsha, 789-790
Porta, Carlo, 843
Porumbacu, Veronica, 1082-1083
Pound, Ezra, 380-381
Preil, Gabriel, 6, 15-16, 137-145

Raab, Esther, 9, 145-146
Raba, Gyorgy, 1003-1004
Raboff, Paul, 392, 791-792
Rachel, 8, 10*n*, 147-148
Radnóti, Miklós, 846, 1005-1013
Rakosi, Carl, 381, 590-592
Ranasinghe, Anne, 393, 828-829
Ratner, Rochelle, 592-593
Ratosh, Yonathan, 149-150
Ravikovitch, Dahlia, 13, 16, 150-153, 390
Ravitch, Melech, 239, 322-328
Regelson, Abraham, 6, 153-154
Reich, Shlomo, 905-907
Reisen, Abraham, 237, 329-333
Reznikoff, Charles, 378, 380, 381, 396, 593-600
Rilke, 8
Rimon, I.Z., 6, 155
Robbins, Martin, 390, 600-601
Robson, Jeremy, 399, 725-726
Roditi, Edouard, 386, 601-609
Rokeah, David, 156
Rolnik, Joseph, 333-334
Rosenberg, Betsy, 392, 702-793
Rosenberg, David, 389, 610-613
Rosenberg, Isaac, 394, 395-396, 397, 399, 726-734
Rosenberg, Joel, 380, 389, 614-617
Rosenmann-Taub, David, 1158-1162
Roth, Hemda, 157-159
Roth, Joseph, 967
Rothenberg, Jerome, 386, 388, 617-620
Rubin, Ilya, 1121-1123
Rudnitsky, Leah, 334-335
Rudolf, Anthony, 400, 734-738
Ruebner, Tuvia, 12, 13, 160-162
Rukeyser, Muriel, 382, 620-626
Ryvel, 908

Saba, Umberto, 846-847, 1039-1042
Sachs, Nelly, 839, 840, 848, 968-973
Sadeh, Pinhas, 17-18, 162-165
Sahl, Hans, 835-836, 973-974
Salamun, Tomaz, 1137-1138
Saltman, Benjamin, 385, 627-628
Sandburg, Carl, 16
Satz, Mario, 1162-1164
Schaechter-Gottesman, Beyle, 335
Schaeffer, Susan Fromberg, 389, 629-630
Scheinert, David, 909-911
Schimmel, Harold, 392, 793-794
Scholem, Gershom, 975-976
Schotz, Myra Glazer, 392, 795-797
Schwartz, Delmore, 378-379, 630-635
Schwartz, Howard, 635-647
Schwartz, I.I., 241
Segal, Jacob Isaac, 336-337, 391
Semah, David, 856-857
Sessler, Thomas, 977-978
Sforim, Mendele Mocher, 237
Shalom, Shin, 9, 165-169
Shapiro, Harvey, 383, 384, 647-651
Shapiro, Karl, 378, 382, 651-653
Shapiro, Mark Elliott, 798
Shargel, Zvi, 337-339
Shaul, Anwar, 857-860
Shenhar, Aliza, 18, 19, 170-173
Sherman, Joseph, 391, 766-767
Sherwin, Richard, 799
Shevin, David, 390, 653-654
Shimoni, David, 6
Shlonsky, Avraham, 9, 13, 173-176
Shneur, Zalman, 6
Shtern, Yisroel, 240
Shulman, David, 176-178
Silberschlag, Eisig, 6, 178-179
Siegel, Danny, 389, 655-657
Silk, Dennis, 392, 800-803
Silkin, Jon, 399-400, 738-746

Silkiner, N.B., 6
Silverman, Maxine, 390, 657-658
Sivan, Arye, 180-182
Sklarew, Myra, 385, 658-661
Slonimski, Antoni, 837, 1061-1064
Slutsky, Boris, 1124-1127
Sonka, Bruder. *See* Sonnenschein, Hugo
Sonnenschein, Hugo, 835, 836, 979
Spire, André, 848, 911-915
Steiger, Anatoly, 1127-1128
Steinbarg, Eliezer, 241, 339-344
Steinberg, Jakov, 6, 182-183
Steingart, Moishe, 344-345
Stencl, A.N., 346-347, 397
Stern, Noah, 6, 184-185
Stevens, Wallace, 15, 16
Stoltzenberg, Abo, 347-348
Stone, Arlene, 390, 661-663
Strauss, A.L., 11, 186-188
Strauss, Avner, 803-804
Sutskever, Abraham, 241, 242, 348-358

Tan Pai, Joshua, 188-189
Tarn, Nathaniel, 389, 400, 664-665
Tchernichovsky, Shaul, 315, 190-195
Teller, J.L., 358-359
Temkin, Mordecai, 9, 196-197
Tiempo, Cesar, 1165
Toller, Ernst, 837
Torberg, Friedrich, 834, 840, 980-982
Tóth, Judit, 1014-1016
Trakl, Georg, 390
Treinin, Avner, 12, 17, 198-200
Trilussa, 843
Tsvetayeva, Marina, 838, 844
Tussman, Malka Heifetz, 360-365, 390
Tuwim, Julian, 837, 838, 1065-1069
Tzara, Tristan, 845, 916-917

Ulinover, Miriam, 366-367
Urdang, Constance, 385, 665-667

Valéry, 8
Vas, István, 1016-1020
Vigée, Claude, 848, 917-922
Vinaver, Stanislav, 837, 1130-1133
Vinner, Shlomo, 18, 200-206
Vogel, David, 6, 7, 13, 16, 206-211, 838
Vogler, Elkhonen, 241
Volf, Lazar, 241
Voronica, Ilarie, 845, 922-924
Vroman, Leo, 836, 874-876

Waddington, Miriam, 391, 768-771
Wahl, Jean, 924-925
Wallach, Yona, 17, 211-212
Wat, Aleksander, 837-838, 1069-1070
Wazyk, Adam, 1071-1072
Weissbort, Daniel, 399, 747-749
Werfel, Franz, 834
Wessely, Naftali Herz, 3
Whitman, Ruth, 389, 667-671
Whitman, Walt, 16
Wilk, Melvin, 390, 671-672
Willems, J. Rutherford, 386, 672-673
Williams, C.K., 673-675
Winkler, Manfred, 18, 19, 213-216
Wittlin, Jozef, 837, 838, 1073-1076
Wolfenstein, Alfred, 834, 982-983
Wolfskehl, Karl, 834, 835, 983-986
Wygodski, Stanislaw, 1076-1078

Yeshurun, Avot, 17, 216-218
Yonathan, Nathan, 10*n*, 218-220
Yungman, Moshe, 242, 367-369

Zach, Natan, 9-10, 13, 14-15, 221-227
Zeitlin, Aaron, 241, 370-373
Zelda, 15, 228-231, 390
Zisquit, Linda, 390, 675-678
Zukofsky, Louis, 381, 678-680
Zussman, Ezra, 9, 231-233
Zwicky, Fay, 393, 808-809
Zychlinska, Rayzel, 374-376

Index of Translators

AUGENFELD, Rivka and MAYNE, Seymour: Mordechai Husid, 278-279; Rachel Korn, 284-286; Melech Ravitch, 327-328

AWAN, Jawaid: Martin Buber, 934-935

BARNSTONE, Willis and CALINESCU, Matei: Maria Banus, 1079-1080; Nina Cassian, 1082; Benjamin Fondane, 886-887; Veronica Porumbacu, 1082-1083; Tristan Tzara, 916-917; Ilaria Voronca, 923-924

BARROWS, Anita: Edith Bruck, 1021-1027; Aldo Camerino, 1028-1031; Charles Dobzynski, 877-880; Umberto Saba, 1040-1042

BEAUDOIN, Kenneth L. and Le MASTER, J.R.: Claude Vigée, 917-918

BERG, Stephen, MARKS, S.J. and POLGAR, Steven: Miklos Radnóti, 1005-1009

BERKOVITS, Yoffee: Shalom Katav, 851-851; Shmuel Moreh, 853-856; David Semah, 856-857; Anwa Shaul, 857-860

BIRMAN, Abraham: Shin Shalom, 165-169

BLOCH, CHANA: Dahlia Ravikovitch, 150-153

BOKSER, Ben Zion: Rav Abraham Isaac Kook, 113-114

BOSLEY, Keith: Benhamin Fondane, 881-887; A. Ganz-Leyeles, 256-258; Leib Kwitko, 291-292; Mani Leib, 295-296; Anna Margolin, 314-315; Peretz Markish, 316; Leib Neidus, 322; Melech Ravitch, 328; Abraham Reisen, 330-333; Joseph Rolnik, 333-334; Umberto Saba, 1039-1040; Nelly Sachs, 968-972; Aaron Zeitlin, 372-373

BOSLEY, Keith and POSPIELOVSKY, Dimitry: Joseph Brodsky, 1088-1092; Aleksandr Kushner, 1103-1104; Boris Slutsky, 1124

BOSLEY, Keith and SHERWOOD, Peter: Eugene Heimler, 997-998

BRAUN, Henry: Claude Vigée, 919-920

BRUDNE, Eva: Eva Brudne, 1094-1095

BURNS, Richard and PRINTZ-PÄHLSON, Göran: Oscar Levertin, 1166-1167

BURNSHAW, Stanley: André Spire, 911-915

CALINESCU, Matei and BARNSTONE, Willis: Maria Banus, 1079-1080; Nina Cassian, 1082; Benjamin Fondane, 886-887; Veronica Porumbacu, 1082-1083; Tristan Tzara, 916-917; Ilaria Voronca, 923-924

DALVEN, Rae: Joseph Eliya, 987-990

DRACHLER, Rose: Hayim Naggid, 128

EVERWINE, Peter and STARKMAN, Shula: T. Carmi, 63; Natan Zach, 221-224

FAINLIGHT, RUTH: Moshe Dor, 75

FALK, Marcia: T. Carmi, 63-68; Abraham Reisen, 329; Malka Heiftez Tussman, 360-365; Moshe Yungman, 367-368; Zelda, 228-231

FARHI, Musa Moris: Musa Moris Farhi, 1168-1170

FARHI, Musa Moris and RUDOLF, Anthony: Jozef Habib Gerez, 1170-1172

FEIN, Richard J.: Moishe Leib Halpern, 272-274; Abraham Reisen, 329-330

FEINSTEIN, Elaine: Margarita Aliger, 1084-1087; Moshe Dor, 75; Yunna Moritz, 1113-1115

FELDMAN, Ruth: Franco Fortini, 1032-1033

FELDMAN, Ruth and SWANN, Brian: Primo Levi, 1034-1036

FIRESTONE, Laya: Gabriel Preil, 140-141; Shlomo Vinner, 206; Natan Zach, 226-227

FIRESTONE, Laya and SCHWARTZ, Howard: Yehuda Amichai, 35; Shlomo Vinner, 200-206

FLANTZ, Richard: Abraham Regelson, 153-154; Nathan Yonathan, 218-220

FRIEND, Robert: Nathan Alterman, 21-22; Yehuda Amichai, 36-37; Yocheved Bat-Miriam, 42; Hayim Nachman Bialik, 54-55; Jakov Fichman, 78-80; Leah Goldberg, 89-92; Hayim Lenski, 123; Dan Pagis, 132-133; Gabriel Preil, 137-139; Rachel, 148; Tuvia Ruebner, 160; A.L. Strauss, 187-188; Saul Tchernichovsky, 193; Avner Treinin, 199

FRIEND, Robert and SANDBANK, Shimon: Jakov Fichman, 78-80; Esther Raab, 145-146

GARBER, Jeremy: Eli Bachar, 40-42; Naftali Gross, 270; Yehuda Karni, 111-112; Malka Locker, 301-302; Gabriel Preil, 141-142; Mordecai Temkin, 196-197

GARRIN, Stephen: Itzik Manger, 306-309

GARVIN, Barbara: Crescenzo del Monte, 1043-1044

GEORGE, Emery: Agnes Gergely, 990-994; Otto Orban, 1001-1003; Miklos Radnóti, 1009-1013; Judit Tóth, 1015-1016; István Vas, 1017-1018

GLAD, John: Dovid Knut, 1097-1100; Anatoly Steiger, 1127-1128

GLAZE, Andrew: Osip Mandelstam, 1108-1110

GLAZER, Myra. *See* SCHOTZ, Myra Glazer

GOLD, Ben Zion and MEZEY, Robert; Uri Zvi Greenberg, 92-95

GORDON, Leonore: Yona Wallach, 211-212

GREENE, James: Osip Mandelstam, 1110-1111

GRIFFIN, Jonathan: Richard Beer-Hofmann, 932; Gershom Scholem, 975-976

GRODZENSKY, Pearl: Hayim Lenski, 122-123

GUENTHER, Charles: Charles Dobzynski, 879-880; Jakov van Hoddis, 949-950; David Rosenmann-Taub, 1159-1162; Jean Wahl, 924-925

GUITART, Jorge: José Kozer, 1150-1151

HELLERSTEIN, Kathryn: Moishe Leib Halpern, 274-276

HIRSCHMAN, Jack: Edmond Jabès, 892-900

ISAAC, Ephraim: Yosef Damana ben Yeshaq, 849-850

JACOBS, A.C.: Yehuda Amichai, 36; Avraham Ben-Yitzhak, 48-51; Hayim Nachman Bialik, 51-54; Amir Gilboa, 83; Yitzhak Lamdan, 118-119; Israel Pincas, 134; Rachel, 148; A.L. Strauss, 186-187; David Vogel, 206-211.

JAFFE, Dan: Lek Mav, 1107

JAGENDORF, Zvi: Uri Zvi Greenberg, 96

JAGER, Marjolijn de: Hanny Michaelis, 872-873

JAY, Peter and LIPSCHULTZ, Geri: Ewa Lipska, 1058-1061

JOHNSON, Dennis: Moshe Dor, 74, 76

KAMINSKY, Marc: Rayzel Zychlinska, 374-375

KATZ, Judith: Erez Biton, 61-62

KAUFMAN, Shirley: Yehuda Amichai, 29-31; Amir Gilboa, 82-83; Judith Herzberg, 869-872; Abba Kovner, 115-117; Dan Pagis, 131

KAUFMAN, Shirley and SCHWARTZ, Howard: Gabriel Preil, 144

KESSLER, Jascha: Anna Hajnal, 994-995; Gyorgy Raba, 1003-1004; István Vas, 1019-1020

KOMEM, Isaac: Henryk Grynberg, 1053-1057; Mieczyslaw Jastrun, 1057-1058; Antoni Slonimski, 1061-1064; Julian Tuwim, 1065-1069; Aleksander Wat, 1069-1070; Adam Wazyk, 1071-1072; Jozef Wittlin, 1073-1076; Stanislaw Wygodzki, 1076-1078

KOTAN, Jeroslav and WEISSBORT, Daniel: Jiri Gold, 863-865

KROOK, Dorothea: Zerubavel Gilead, 86-88

KUHNER, Herbert: Alfred Kittner, 951-953; Conny Hannes Meyer, 963-965; Thomas Sessler, 977-978; Nina Cassian, 1080-1082

LANDY, Francis: Avraham Shlonsky, 173-175

LE MASTER, J.R. and BEAUDOIN, Kenneth L.: Claude Vigée, 917-918

LEE, Rena: Rena Lee, 121

LEFTWICH, Joseph: A.N. Stenci, 346-347

LENOWITZ, Harris: Pinhas Sadeh, 163

LEVENSTON, E.A.: Tuvia Ruebner, 160; Avner Treinin, 198, 200

LEVIANT, Curt: Eliezer Steinbarg, 342-344

LEVIN, Gabriel: Hayim Nachman Bialik, 59-60; Rachel Fishman, 255; Zali Gurevitch, 97; Gabriel Preil, 142-143

LEVITAN, Seymour: Kadya Molodovsky, 319; Melech Ravitch, 324-326; Abraham Stuskever, 354-355

LEVY, Stephen: Isaac de Botton, 1045; Clarisse Nicoïdski, 1047-1052; Rachel Castelete, 1046

LIPSCHULTZ, Geri and JAY, Peter: Ewa Lipska, 1058-1061

McEVAN-ALVARADO, Angela: Cesar Tiempo, 1165

MARKS, S.J., BERG, Stephen and POLGAR, Steven: Miklos Radnóti, 1005-1009

MAYNE, Seymour: Jacob Isaac Segal, 336-337

MAYNE, Seymour and AUGENFELD, Rivka: Mordechai Husid, 278-279; Rachel Korn, 284-286; Melich Ravitch, 327-328

MEIRI, Alexandra and GLAZER SCHOTZ, Myra: Raquel Chalfi, 70-71

MEZEY, Robert: Rachel, 148; David Rokeah, 156; Avraham Shlonsky, 176

MEZEY, Robert and GOLD, Ben Zion: Uri Zvi Greenberg, 92-95

MEZEY, Robert and STARKMAN, Shula: Yocheved Bat-Miriam, 43; Saul Tchernichovsky, 190-193

MIHAILOVICH, Vasa D.: Stanislav Vinaver, 1130-1133

MISEMER, Marvin and MUHLBERGER, Neil: Lev Mak, 1106-1107

MITCHELL, Stephen: Yehuda Amichai, 27-29; Hayim Be'er, 43-46; Amir Gilboa, 8l, 84-85; Dan Pagis, 129-130

MOREH, Shmuel: Shmuel Moreh, 852-853

MORRIS, Tudor: Hilde Domin, 946-947

MUHLBERGER, Neil and MISEMER, Marvin: Lev Mak, 1106-1107

MYERS, Alan: Joseph Brodsky, 1092-1093

NEJGEBAUER, Aleksander: Monny de Boully, 1129-1130; Tomaz Salamun, 1137-1138

NEUGROSCHEL, Joachim: Paul Celan, 935-946; Moishe Kulbak, 288-290; Else Lasker-Schüler, 957-961; Mendel Naigreshel, 320-321

NEVO, Ruth: Nathan Alterman, 22-27; Yehuda Amichai, 31-32; Hayim Nachman Bialik, 55-59; Anadad Eldan, 77-78; Shimon Halkin, 104-105

N(IR), N(aomi): Hayim Nachman Bialik, 59; Rachel, 147

N(IR), N(aomi) and SCHWARTZ, Howard: Haim Guri, 99

OSERS, Ewald: Rose Auslander, 926-931; Frantisek Gottlieb, 866; Dagmar Hilarová, 867

PAUK, Edgar: Rossana Ombres, 1036-1039

POLGAR, Steven, BERG, Stephen, and MARKS, S.J.: Miklos Radnóti, 1005-1009

POSPIELOVSKY, Dimitry and BOSLEY, Keith: Joseph Brodsky, 1088-1092; Aleksandr Kushner, 1103-1104; Boris Slutsky, 1124

POTASMAN, Mariana: Raqual Chalfi, 71; Hemda Roth, 158-159

PREIL, Gabriel: Rachel Boimwall, 248; Nahum Bomze, 250-251; Beyle Schaechter-Gottesman, 335; Zvi Shargel, 339; Moishe Steingart, 334-345

PREIL, Gabriel and SCHWARTZ, Howard: Asya, 244-247; Rachel Boimwall, 248-250; Nahum Bomze, 251; Lazer Eichenrand, 253-254; Rachel Fishman, 255-256; Jiri Mordecai Langer, 119-120; Pinhas Sadeh, 164-165; Avi Shargel, 337-339; Abo Stolzenberg, 347-348; J.L. Teller, 358-359; Moshe Yungman, 368-369

PRINTZ-PAHLSON, Göran and BURNS, Richard: Oscar Levertin, 1166-1167

REICH, Mira: Shlomo Reich, 905-907

RIVERO, Alina: Alejandra Pizarnik, 1151-1152

RODITI, Edouard: Benjamin Fondane, 883-885; Alfred Grünewald, 948; Jakov van Hoddis, 949; Gustave Kahn, 901-902; Alma Johanna Koenig, 953; Else Lasker-

Schüler, 961-962; Joseph Milbauer, 902-903; Pierre Morhange, 904-905; Ryvel, 908; Hans Sahl, 973; David Scheinert, 909-911; Hugo Sonnenschein, 979; André Spire, 915; Ilaria Voronca, 922-923

ROSENBERG, Betsy: Gabriel Preil, 143; Tuvia Ruebner, 161

ROSENFELD, Erna Baber: Ilse Blumental-Weiss, 933; Alfred Mombert, 966; Joseph Roth, 967; Hans Sahl, 974; Friedrich Torberg, 980-982; Alfred Wolfenstein, 982-983; Karl Wolfskhel, 983-985

ROSKIES, David G.: H. Leivick, 300-301; Leah Rudnitsky, 334-335; Avraham Sutskever, 356-357

ROSKIES, David G. and SCHWARTZ, Hillel: Jacob Glatstein, 267; Moshe Leib Halpern, 276-277; Mani Leib, 297-298; Itzik Manger, 311-312; Abraham Sutskever, 356-357

RUDOLF, Anthony: Edmond Fleg, 881; Susannah Fried, 1134-1135; Yvan Goll, 888-892; Eugene Heimler, 995-996; Edmond Jabès, 892-900; Dan Pagis, 130; Claude Vigée, 920-922

RUDOLF, Anthony and FARHI, Musa Moris: Jozef Habib Gerez, 1170-1172

RUDOLF, Anthony and ZACH, Natan: Anadad Eldan, 77; Arye Sivan, 181-182

SANDBANK, Shimon and FRIEND, Robert: Jakov Fichman, 78-80; Esther Raab, 145-146

SAVAGE, Elizabeth: Claude Vigée, 918-919

SCAMMELL, Michael and TAUFER, Veno: Tomaz Salamun, 1137-1138

SCHIMMEL, Harold: Berl Pomerantz, 135-136; Tuvia Ruebner, 162; Noah Stern, 184-185; Avot Yeshurun, 216-218

SCHOTZ, Myra Glazer: Raquel Chalfi, 69-70; Shlomit Cohen, 72; Hemda Roth, 157-158

SCHOTZ, Myra Glazer and MEIRI, Alexandra: Raquel Chalfi, 70-71

SCHWARTZ, Hillel and ROSKIES, David G.: Jacob Glatstein, 267; Moishe Leib Halpern, 276-277; Mani Leib, 297-298; Itzik Manger, 311-312; Abraham Sutskever, 356-357

SCHWARTZ, Howard: B. Alquit, 243-244; Ephraim Auerbach, 247-248; Anath Bental, 47-48; Martin Buber, 933-934; Celia Dropkin, 252; Amir Gilboa, 80-81; Rachel Korn, 283-284; Matti Megged, 123-126; Gabriel Preil, 140, 144, 145; Yonathan Ratosh, 149-150

SCHWARTZ, Howard and KAUFMAN, Shirley: Gabriel Preil, 144

SCHWARTZ, Howard and N(IR), N(aomi): Haim Guri, 99

SCHWARTZ, Howard and PREIL, Gabriel: Asya, 244-247; Rachel Boimwall, 248-250; Nahum Bomze, 251; Lazar Eichenrand, 253-254; Rachel Fishman, 255-256; Jiri Mordecai Langer, 119-120; Pinhas Sadeh, 164-165; Zvi Shargel, 337-339; Abo Stolzenberg, 347-348; J. L. Teller, 358-359; Moshe Yungman, 368-369

SCHWARTZ, Howard and TAUBER, Naomi: Haim Guri, 99

SCHWARTZ, Howard and VINNER, Shlomo: Yehuda Amichai, 31-34; Abraham Chalfi, 68-69; Hayim Naggid, 126-128; I. Z. Rimon, 155

SHAPIRO, Mark Elliot: Haim Guri, 100-103; Avraham Huss, 108-110; Jakov Steinberg, 182-183; Saul Tchernichovsky, 194-195

SHERWOOD, Peter and BOSLEY, Keith: Eugene Heimler, 997-998

SHEVIN, David: Arye Sivan, 180-181

SHNAYORSON, D.: Ezra Zussman, 231-233

SHULMAN, David: David Shulman, 177-178

SILBERSCHLAG, Eisig: Eisig Silberschlag, 178-179

SILK, Dennis: Pavel Friedmann, 863

SILKIN, Jon: Natan Zach, 225-226

SMITH, Henry A.: Gertrud Kolmar, 954-957

SOETENDORP, David: Jakov de Haan, 868-869

STARKMAN, Shula and EVERWINE, Peter: T. Carmi, 63; Natan Zach, 221-224

STARKMAN, Shula and MEZEY, Robert: Yocheved Bat-Miriam, 43; Saul Tchernichovsky, 190-193

SWANN, Brian and FELDMAN, Ruth: Primo Levi, 1034-1036

TAUBER, Naomi and SCHWARTZ, Howard: Haim Guri, 99

TAUFER, Veno and SCAMMELL, Michael: Tomaz, Salamun, 1137-1138

TOBIN, Yishai: Edna Aphek, 38-39; Shlomit Cohen, 73; Juan Gelman, 1139-1140; José Isaacson, 1143-1144; Noé Jitrik, 1144-1146; Ruben Kanalenstein, 1146-1149; Alejandra Pizarnik, 1152-1155; Jorge Plescoff, 998-999; Joshua Tan Pai, 188-189

UNGAR, Andre: Milan Fuest, 991; Jozsef Kiss, 998-999; Emil Makai, 1000-1001

UNGER, David: Isaac Goldemberg, 1141-1142; José Kozer, 1149-1150

VALOPE, Carol North and MORWITZ, Ernest: Karl Wolfskhet, 985-986

VINNER, Shlomo and SCHWARTZ, Howard: Yehuda Amichai, 31-34; Abraham Chalfi, 68-69; Hayim Naggid, 126-128; I. Z. Rimon, 155

WADDINGTON, Miriam: Itzik Manger, 310-311

WALDROP, Rosmarie: Edmond Jabès, 899-900

WEISSBORT, Daniel: Sasha Chorny, 1096; Dovid Kunt, 1100-1102; Naum Korzhavin, 1102-1103; Lev Mak, 1105-1106; Osip Mandelstam, 1107-1108; Samuel Marshak, 1111-1112; Lev Ozerov, 1116-1120; Boris Slutsky, 1124-1127

WEISSBORT, Daniel and KOTAN, Jaroslav: Jiri Gold, 863-865

WEIZMAN, Tova: Hedva Harkavi, 106-107

WHITMAN, Ruth: Jacob Glatstein, 258-266; Moishe Leib Halpern, 271-272; Rachel Korn, 279-283; Moishe Kulbak, 286-288; Zishe Landau, 292-295; H. Leivick, 299-300; Itzik Manger, 370-372; Anna Margolin, 302-306; Kadya Molodovsky, 317-318; Leib Neidus, 321-322; Melech Ravitch, 323-324; Abraham Sutskever, 349-354; Aaron Zeitlin, 370-372

WOLITZ, Seth L.: Eliezer Steinbarg, 340-341; Miriam Ulinover, 366-367

ZACH, Natan and RUDOLF, Anthony: Anadad Eldan, 77; Arye Sivan, 181-182

ZILZER, Mary: Alfred Lichtenstein, 962-963; Manfred Winkler, 213-216

ZISQUIT, Linda: Ilya Rubin, 121-123; Aliza Shenhar, 170-173

ZOHN, Harry: Nelly Sachs, 972-973; Karl Wolfskhel, 985-986